Copyright © 2024

All rights reserved. No part of this publication may be transmitted in any form or by any means, including photocopying, recording, or other electronic or mechanical methods, without the prior written permission of the publisher, except in the case of brief quotations embodied in critical reviews and certain other noncommercial uses permitted by copyright law.

Disclosure: This study guide is intended for educational purposes only and does not guarantee success on any examination. The content provided is based on general information available at the time of creation and may not reflect the most current exam format, content, or requirements.
Users of this study guide acknowledge that:

Exam formats, content, and requirements may change without notice.
This guide is not a substitute for official exam materials or courses provided by authorized examination bodies.
The creators and distributors of this guide are not responsible for any errors, omissions, or outdated information.
Success on any examination depends on multiple factors, including individual preparation, understanding of the subject matter, and test-taking skills.
This guide does not replace professional advice or guidance from qualified instructors or institutions.

By using this study guide, you agree that the creators and distributors shall not be held liable for any damages or losses resulting from its use. Users are encouraged to verify information with official sources and seek additional resources as needed.
All rights reserved. No part of this study guide may be reproduced, distributed, or transmitted in any form without prior written permission from the copyright holder.

Table of Contents

INTRO...4

Security and Privacy Governance, Risk Management, and Compliance Program..8

Scope of the System...32

Selection and Approval of Framework, Security, and Privacy Controls..57

Implementation of Security and Privacy Controls........................81

Assessment/Audit of Security and Privacy Controls...................111

System Compliance..138

Compliance Maintenance..159

Practice Section...190

INTRO:

The alarm blared through the office at 2 AM, jolting Sarah from her focused trance. As the lead Governance, Risk, and Compliance analyst, she knew this wasn't a drill. The company's intrusion detection system had flagged a potential breach, one that could expose millions of customer records and derail the upcoming product launch.

Sarah's team sprang into action, their months of preparation and risk scenario planning paying off. While IT worked to isolate the affected systems, Sarah coordinated with legal to assess regulatory implications and drafted initial disclosure statements. Her foresight in implementing robust incident response procedures meant that within hours, the attack was contained, data secured, and stakeholders informed.

As dawn broke, the CEO personally thanked Sarah for averting a crisis that could have cost the company millions in damages and irreparable reputational harm. This was the world of GRC professionals – where vigilance, expertise, and strategic thinking form the last line of defense against an ever-evolving landscape of threats and regulatory challenges.

You're holding this guide because you aspire to join these ranks of elite professionals who safeguard organizations from the shadows. Mastering the Certified in Governance, Risk, and Compliance (CGRC) exam is your passport to this high-stakes, high-reward career. Imagine yourself confidently presenting to boards of directors, shaping corporate strategy to navigate complex regulatory waters, and leading teams that protect critical assets from emerging cyber threats.

This isn't just about passing an exam; it's about equipping yourself with the knowledge and skills to thrive in a field where your decisions can make or break an organization's future. Whether you're aiming to climb the corporate ladder, transition into a new industry, or solidify your expertise, the CGRC certification opens doors to roles where you'll be respected, challenged, and vital to organizational success.

This guide is your roadmap to conquering the CGRC exam and launching your career to new heights. We'll break down complex concepts into digestible chunks, provide real-world scenarios that bring the material to life, and equip you with proven strategies to tackle even the toughest exam questions. From dissecting the latest regulatory frameworks to mastering risk assessment methodologies, you'll build a comprehensive toolkit that will serve you well beyond exam day.

Get ready to embark on a journey that will transform you into a GRC expert, capable of steering organizations through the stormy seas of compliance and risk. The path ahead is challenging, but with dedication and the insights in this guide, you'll emerge prepared not just to pass the CGRC exam, but to excel in a career that makes a tangible difference in the business world. Let's begin.

The Certified in Governance, Risk, and Compliance (CGRC) exam is a prestigious certification developed by ISC2, a globally recognized leader in information security certifications. This credential validates a professional's expertise in advocating for security risk management to support an organization's mission while ensuring compliance with legal and regulatory requirements.

Purpose and Significance: The CGRC certification aims to establish a professional's competence in managing information system authorization processes within the complex landscape of governance, risk, and compliance. It's designed for information security practitioners who play a crucial role in aligning security practices with organizational objectives and regulatory mandates.

Exam Structure and Content: The CGRC exam covers seven key domains:
1. Security and Privacy Governance, Risk Management, and Compliance Program (16%)
2. Scope of the System (10%)
3. Selection and Approval of Framework, Security, and Privacy Controls (14%)
4. Implementation of Security and Privacy Controls (17%)
5. Assessment/Audit of Security and Privacy Controls (16%)

6. System Compliance (14%)
7. Compliance Maintenance (13%)

Each domain encompasses critical areas such as risk management frameworks, system development lifecycle, information lifecycle management, control implementation, audit processes, and ongoing compliance activities.

Exam Format: The CGRC examination consists of 125 multiple-choice questions to be completed within a 3-hour time frame. The exam is scored on a scale of 0-1000, with a passing score of 700 required to achieve certification.

Eligibility Requirements: Candidates must have a minimum of two years of cumulative work experience in one or more of the seven domains of the CGRC Common Body of Knowledge (CBK). For those lacking the required experience, there's an option to become an Associate of ISC2 by passing the exam, with three years to gain the necessary experience.

Difficulty Level: While specific pass rates are not provided, the CGRC exam is known for its comprehensive coverage of complex topics, requiring a deep understanding of GRC principles and practices. The exam's accreditation by ANSI/ISO/IEC Standard 17024 underscores its rigorous nature and industry recognition.

Benefits of Certification: Obtaining the CGRC certification offers numerous advantages:

1. Industry Recognition: CGRC is a globally respected credential in the information security field.
2. Career Advancement: It opens doors to senior roles in risk management, compliance, and governance.
3. Knowledge Validation: Demonstrates a professional's commitment to staying current with evolving GRC practices.
4. Networking Opportunities: Provides access to a community of GRC professionals through ISC2 membership.

While specific salary data for CGRC holders isn't provided, ISC2 certifications are generally associated with above-average compensation in the information security field.

Recertification: To maintain the CGRC credential, certified professionals must adhere to the ISC2 continuing education program. This typically involves earning continuing professional education (CPE) credits and paying an annual maintenance fee, though specific details for CGRC are not provided in the given information.

The CGRC certification represents a significant achievement in the GRC field, equipping professionals with the knowledge and recognition needed to excel in roles critical to organizational security and compliance. As the cybersecurity landscape continues to evolve, CGRC-certified professionals are well-positioned to lead in navigating complex regulatory environments and managing information security risks.

Preparing for the CGRC Exam:

Create a structured study plan spanning 3-4 months. Allocate specific time blocks for each domain, focusing more on high-weighted areas like Implementation of Security and Privacy Controls (17%) and Security and Privacy Governance (16%).

Form study groups with colleagues or online communities. Explain concepts to others to solidify your understanding and gain new insights from peer discussions.

Develop a deep understanding of key frameworks like NIST, COBIT, and ISO/IEC standards. These form the backbone of many exam questions.

Exam Day Strategies:

Arrive at the testing center early to complete check-in procedures without rushing. Bring required identification and familiarize yourself with the center's policies.

Before starting, take deep breaths and remind yourself of your thorough preparation. Visualize success to calm nerves and boost confidence.

Read each question carefully, identifying key words and phrases. For scenario-based questions, analyze the given information before considering answer choices.

Time Management:

With 125 questions in 180 minutes, allocate roughly 1.4 minutes per question. Use the on-screen timer to track progress.

Answer easier questions first, flagging challenging ones for review. This ensures you maximize points on questions you're confident about.

If struggling with a question, mark it and move on. Return to it if time permits at the end.

Approaching Different Question Types:

Multiple-choice: Eliminate obviously incorrect answers first. This increases your odds if you need to make an educated guess.

Scenario-based: Identify the core issue or risk in the scenario. Align your answer with GRC best practices and relevant regulatory requirements.

Case study: Break down complex scenarios into key components. Consider governance, risk, and compliance implications separately before synthesizing an answer.

Making Educated Guesses:

If unsure, eliminate answers that contradict GRC principles or common industry practices.

Look for qualifier words like "always," "never," or "must" in answer choices. These are often (but not always) incorrect in complex GRC scenarios.

Trust your instincts. Your subconscious may recognize correct answers based on your study efforts, even if you can't explicitly recall why.

Interpreting Complex Questions:

Break down lengthy questions into smaller parts. Identify the core ask and any conditional statements.

Pay attention to words like "EXCEPT," "NOT," or "LEAST," which can completely change a question's meaning.

If a question seems ambiguous, consider it from multiple GRC perspectives (e.g., governance view, risk management view, compliance view) to determine the most appropriate answer.

Day Before the Exam:

Review summary notes or flash cards, focusing on key concepts and definitions.

Avoid intensive studying. Instead, relax and engage in light review to maintain confidence without inducing stress.

Prepare your exam kit (ID, directions to the test center, allowed items) to avoid morning stress.

Get a full night's sleep to ensure mental alertness.

Morning of the Exam:

Eat a balanced breakfast to maintain energy levels throughout the test.

Arrive at the test center early, allowing time to settle and focus.

Do light reviews of challenging topics if it helps boost confidence, but avoid cramming new information.

Post-Exam Steps:

You'll receive your score immediately after completing the exam at the test center.

If you pass (score of 700 or above), celebrate your achievement! You'll receive official certification details from ISC2 within a few weeks.

If you don't pass, don't be discouraged. Review the score report to identify weak areas and create a focused study plan for your next attempt.

Remember, the CGRC exam tests your ability to apply GRC principles in real-world scenarios. Focus on understanding concepts deeply rather than memorizing facts. With thorough preparation and strategic test-taking, you'll be well-positioned to succeed and join the ranks of certified GRC professionals.

Security and Privacy Governance, Risk Management, and Compliance Program

Governance, risk management, and compliance (GRC) form the backbone of an organization's strategic framework, ensuring that it operates efficiently, adheres to regulations, and mitigates risks. These three elements are deeply interconnected, supporting each other to create a robust and resilient organizational structure.

Governance

Governance involves the processes, policies, and laws that govern an organization's operations. It establishes the framework within which objectives are set and performance is monitored. Effective governance ensures accountability, transparency, and ethical conduct, providing the structure through which the organization's goals are achieved.

Example: A company implements a governance policy requiring quarterly board meetings to review and approve strategic initiatives. This ensures that decisions are made transparently and align with the company's long-term goals.

Risk Management

Risk management is the process of identifying, assessing, and controlling threats to an organization's capital and earnings. These risks could stem from various sources, including financial uncertainties, legal liabilities, strategic management errors, accidents, and natural disasters. The goal of risk management is to minimize the impact of these risks on the organization.

Example: A financial institution conducts regular risk assessments to identify potential threats to its information systems. By implementing advanced cybersecurity measures, it mitigates the risk of data breaches, thus protecting sensitive customer information.

Compliance

Compliance ensures that an organization adheres to external laws, regulations, and internal policies. It involves staying up-to-date with regulatory requirements and implementing procedures to meet these standards. Compliance helps organizations avoid legal penalties and maintain their reputation.

Example: A healthcare provider adheres to the Health Insurance Portability and Accountability Act (HIPAA) by implementing strict data protection protocols, ensuring patient information is kept confidential and secure.

Interconnection and Support

The interconnection between governance, risk management, and compliance is vital for creating a cohesive and resilient organizational framework.

1. **Governance and Risk Management**: Governance provides the structure for risk management by defining roles, responsibilities, and procedures for identifying and mitigating risks. Good governance ensures that risk management is integrated into the organization's strategic planning and decision-making processes.

Example: A company's board of directors establishes a risk management committee responsible for overseeing risk assessment and mitigation strategies. This ensures that risk management is a key component of the organization's governance framework.

2. **Governance and Compliance**: Governance frameworks establish the standards and policies for compliance. Effective governance ensures that the organization adheres to legal and regulatory requirements, maintaining operational integrity and ethical standards.

Example: A multinational corporation adopts a governance policy that includes regular compliance audits. This ensures that all international operations adhere to local laws and regulations, reducing the risk of legal issues.

3. **Risk Management and Compliance**: Risk management identifies potential compliance risks and implements controls to mitigate them. By aligning risk management with compliance, organizations can proactively address regulatory changes and reduce the likelihood of non-compliance.

Example: An IT company identifies potential risks related to data privacy regulations such as the General Data Protection Regulation (GDPR). By implementing comprehensive data protection measures, it ensures compliance and minimizes the risk of regulatory penalties.

Contribution to Organizational Resilience and Effectiveness

1. **Governance**: Establishes a clear framework for decision-making, ensuring that the organization's strategies align with its objectives and values. This clarity helps organizations navigate challenges and seize opportunities effectively.

Example: Clear governance policies enable a company to quickly adapt to market changes, ensuring strategic initiatives remain aligned with overall business goals.

2. **Risk Management**: Protects the organization from potential threats, minimizing losses and ensuring continuity. It enables organizations to anticipate and prepare for uncertainties, enhancing their ability to withstand adverse events.

Example: A comprehensive risk management plan allows a manufacturing company to maintain operations during a supply chain disruption by having contingency plans in place.

3. **Compliance**: Ensures that the organization operates within legal and ethical boundaries, maintaining its reputation and avoiding legal penalties. Compliance fosters trust among stakeholders, including customers, investors, and regulatory bodies.

Example: Adherence to environmental regulations allows an energy company to avoid fines and gain the trust of eco-conscious consumers, enhancing its market position.

Governance, risk management, and compliance are integral to creating a robust organizational framework. They interconnect to support organizational resilience and effectiveness by providing structure, mitigating risks, and ensuring adherence to regulations. This synergy enables organizations to achieve their objectives while maintaining ethical standards and preparing for future challenges.

The NIST Cybersecurity Framework (CSF) is a comprehensive guide designed to help organizations manage and reduce cybersecurity risk. It encompasses five core functions: Identify, Protect, Detect, Respond, and Recover. Each function plays a critical role in establishing a robust cybersecurity strategy.

Identify

The Identify function involves understanding the business context, resources that support critical functions, and related cybersecurity risks. This foundational step ensures that organizations can focus their efforts effectively.

Components:
- **Asset Management**: Cataloging hardware, software, data, and systems.
- **Business Environment**: Understanding the organization's role in the supply chain.
- **Governance**: Establishing policies, procedures, and processes.
- **Risk Assessment**: Identifying and evaluating risks.
- **Risk Management Strategy**: Prioritizing risk management activities.

Examples:
- Conducting regular inventory of IT assets to maintain an updated list.
- Mapping data flow within the organization to understand critical data points and vulnerabilities.
- Developing a risk assessment matrix to categorize and prioritize potential threats.

Protect

The Protect function focuses on implementing safeguards to ensure the delivery of critical infrastructure services. This function aims to limit or contain the impact of a potential cybersecurity event.

Components:
- **Access Control**: Limiting access to systems and data.
- **Awareness and Training**: Educating employees on security policies.
- **Data Security**: Implementing measures to protect data.
- **Information Protection Processes and Procedures**: Establishing and maintaining security policies.
- **Maintenance**: Ensuring security of systems and assets.
- **Protective Technology**: Deploying security technologies and tools.

Examples:
- Implementing multi-factor authentication (MFA) for all critical systems.
- Conducting regular security training sessions and phishing simulations for employees.
- Encrypting sensitive data both in transit and at rest.

Detect
The Detect function involves developing and implementing appropriate activities to identify the occurrence of a cybersecurity event. Early detection is crucial for effective response.

Components:
- **Anomalies and Events**: Identifying and investigating irregular activity.
- **Security Continuous Monitoring**: Continuously monitoring systems for security breaches.
- **Detection Processes**: Ensuring timely discovery of incidents.

Examples:
- Utilizing intrusion detection systems (IDS) and security information and event management (SIEM) tools to monitor network traffic.
- Setting up alerts for unusual login attempts or access patterns.
- Regularly reviewing and updating detection protocols to address emerging threats.

Respond
The Respond function focuses on developing and implementing activities to take action regarding a detected cybersecurity event. Effective response activities are essential to contain and mitigate the impact of incidents.

Components:
- **Response Planning**: Developing and maintaining an incident response plan.
- **Communications**: Coordinating response activities with internal and external stakeholders.
- **Analysis**: Analyzing the incident to understand its impact and root cause.
- **Mitigation**: Implementing actions to prevent the spread of the incident.
- **Improvements**: Learning from incidents to improve response capabilities.

Examples:
- Establishing an incident response team (IRT) with clear roles and responsibilities.
- Creating communication templates for notifying stakeholders during an incident.
- Conducting post-incident reviews to identify lessons learned and update response plans.

Recover
The Recover function involves developing and implementing activities to maintain plans for resilience and restore any capabilities or services that were impaired due to a cybersecurity event. Recovery planning supports timely restoration of normal operations.

Components:
- **Recovery Planning**: Developing and implementing recovery plans.
- **Improvements**: Incorporating lessons learned into recovery strategies.
- **Communications**: Ensuring effective communication during and after recovery.

Examples:
- Establishing data backup and restoration procedures to ensure critical data can be quickly recovered.
- Testing disaster recovery plans regularly through simulations and drills.
- Creating a business continuity plan (BCP) that includes detailed steps for restoring operations after an incident.

Implementation in Cybersecurity Strategy
Organizations can implement the NIST CSF functions through a combination of policies, procedures, and technologies. For example:
- **Identify**: Perform regular risk assessments and update asset inventories.
- **Protect**: Use firewalls, encryption, and regular security training to safeguard assets.
- **Detect**: Deploy SIEM systems to monitor and analyze security events continuously.
- **Respond**: Develop and regularly update an incident response plan, ensuring all staff are trained on their roles during an incident.
- **Recover**: Maintain and test backup systems and recovery plans to ensure swift restoration of services.

Implementing the NIST Cybersecurity Framework helps organizations create a structured approach to managing and mitigating cybersecurity risks, enhancing their overall security posture.

COBIT (Control Objectives for Information and Related Technology) and ISO/IEC 27001 are two prominent frameworks in the field of information security and IT governance. Both frameworks have distinct strengths and focus areas that, when combined, can provide a comprehensive approach to managing and securing information assets within an organization.

COBIT Framework

Overview

- Developed by ISACA, COBIT is a framework for developing, implementing, monitoring, and improving IT governance and management practices.
- It focuses on aligning IT goals with business objectives, ensuring value delivery from IT investments, and managing IT risks effectively.

Strengths and Focus Areas

1. **IT Governance and Management**:
    - COBIT provides a comprehensive framework that covers all aspects of IT governance and management, including strategic alignment, resource management, risk management, and performance measurement.
    - It emphasizes the importance of aligning IT initiatives with overall business goals, ensuring that IT investments deliver value.
2. **Detailed Control Objectives**:
    - COBIT offers detailed control objectives and practices, which help organizations manage and govern their IT processes effectively.
    - The framework provides specific guidelines and best practices for various IT domains, including security, risk management, and compliance.
3. **Performance Measurement**:
    - COBIT includes a robust performance measurement system that helps organizations evaluate the effectiveness and efficiency of their IT governance practices.
    - It uses metrics and maturity models to assess the current state of IT processes and identify areas for improvement.

ISO/IEC 27001 Standard

Overview

- ISO/IEC 27001 is an international standard for information security management systems (ISMS), published by the International Organization for Standardization (ISO) and the International Electrotechnical Commission (IEC).
- It provides a systematic approach to managing sensitive company information, ensuring its confidentiality, integrity, and availability.

Strengths and Focus Areas

1. **Information Security Management System (ISMS)**:
    - ISO/IEC 27001 focuses on establishing, implementing, maintaining, and continually improving an ISMS.
    - It provides a structured methodology for identifying information security risks and implementing appropriate controls to mitigate them.
2. **Risk Management**:
    - The standard emphasizes a risk-based approach to information security, requiring organizations to conduct regular risk assessments and apply controls based on the identified risks.
    - This focus on risk management ensures that security measures are aligned with the specific needs and context of the organization.
3. **Certification and Compliance**:
    - ISO/IEC 27001 certification is globally recognized and can demonstrate an organization's commitment to information security to customers, partners, and regulators.
    - Achieving certification involves an external audit process, which provides assurance that the organization meets international standards for information security.

Leveraging Both Frameworks
Creating a Comprehensive Information Security Management System
Organizations can leverage the strengths of both COBIT and ISO/IEC 27001 to create a robust and comprehensive information security management system. Here's how:
1. **Integrated Governance and Security Management**:
    - Use COBIT to establish a strong IT governance framework that aligns IT goals with business objectives, ensuring that IT investments are managed effectively and deliver value.
    - Implement ISO/IEC 27001 to build and maintain a comprehensive ISMS that focuses on protecting information assets through risk management and the application of security controls.
2. **Holistic Risk Management**:
    - COBIT's detailed control objectives can be used to enhance ISO/IEC 27001's risk management processes, providing specific guidance on managing IT-related risks.
    - Combining COBIT's performance measurement tools with ISO/IEC 27001's risk assessment methodologies can create a more thorough and effective approach to managing information security risks.
3. **Continuous Improvement and Compliance**:
    - ISO/IEC 27001's requirement for continual improvement aligns with COBIT's emphasis on performance measurement and process maturity.
    - Organizations can use COBIT to monitor and evaluate the effectiveness of their ISMS, ensuring ongoing compliance with ISO/IEC 27001 and driving continuous improvement in their information security practices.

Specific Examples:
- **Policy Development**: Use COBIT to develop comprehensive IT governance policies that include information security, while ISO/IEC 27001 provides specific guidelines for creating security policies and procedures.
- **Audit and Assurance**: Leverage COBIT's audit and assurance guidelines to conduct internal audits of the ISMS established under ISO/IEC 27001, ensuring compliance and identifying areas for improvement.
- **Training and Awareness**: COBIT's focus on resource management can be used to develop training programs that align with ISO/IEC 27001's requirements for information security awareness and training.

By integrating COBIT's broad IT governance and management framework with ISO/IEC 27001's focused approach to information security management, organizations can develop a comprehensive strategy that ensures both effective IT governance and robust information security. This integrated approach not only helps in aligning IT and business goals but also enhances the organization's resilience against information security threats.

The System Development Life Cycle (SDLC) is a structured process used to develop information systems with a focus on improving quality and reducing development time. Integrating security considerations throughout the SDLC is crucial to ensure that systems are not only functional but also secure. Below is a detailed look at each stage of the SDLC, emphasizing the evolving security requirements and specific controls.

1. Requirements Gathering and Analysis
During the requirements gathering and analysis phase, the foundation for security is established. This stage involves understanding the business needs and defining security requirements.
Security Considerations:
- Identify security requirements based on business needs, regulatory requirements, and threat models.
- Conduct a preliminary risk assessment to identify potential security threats and vulnerabilities.

Specific Security Controls:
- **Data Classification**: Identify and classify data according to sensitivity and criticality.
- **Access Controls**: Define access requirements and user roles.
- **Compliance Requirements**: Ensure that regulatory and legal security requirements are identified and documented.

2. System Design
In the system design phase, detailed specifications for the system are developed, including the architecture, components, and interfaces.

Security Considerations:
- Design security architecture that includes protective measures to guard against identified risks.
- Ensure security principles such as least privilege, defense in depth, and secure by design are incorporated into the system architecture.

Specific Security Controls:
- **Secure Architecture Design**: Use architectural patterns that enhance security (e.g., network segmentation, secure API design).
- **Encryption**: Plan for the use of encryption for data at rest and in transit.
- **Authentication and Authorization**: Design robust authentication and authorization mechanisms.

3. Development
The development phase involves the actual coding and building of the system. Security must be integrated into the development process to prevent vulnerabilities.

Security Considerations:
- Implement secure coding practices to mitigate common vulnerabilities (e.g., SQL injection, cross-site scripting).
- Use automated tools to scan code for security issues.

Specific Security Controls:
- **Static Application Security Testing (SAST)**: Use SAST tools to analyze source code for vulnerabilities.
- **Code Reviews**: Conduct peer reviews focused on security aspects of the code.
- **Secure Coding Standards**: Adhere to standards such as OWASP Secure Coding Guidelines.

4. Testing
During the testing phase, the system is evaluated to ensure it meets all requirements, including security.

Security Considerations:
- Conduct security testing to identify vulnerabilities before the system goes live.
- Perform both functional and non-functional security testing.

Specific Security Controls:
- **Dynamic Application Security Testing (DAST)**: Use DAST tools to test running applications for security vulnerabilities.
- **Penetration Testing**: Conduct simulated attacks to identify and fix security weaknesses.
- **Vulnerability Scanning**: Regularly scan the system for known vulnerabilities.

5. Implementation
In the implementation phase, the system is deployed in a live environment. Ensuring a secure transition from development to production is critical.

Security Considerations:
- Harden the environment before deployment by disabling unnecessary services and applying security patches.
- Ensure secure configuration of all system components.

Specific Security Controls:
- **Configuration Management**: Use configuration management tools to enforce security settings.
- **Environment Hardening**: Implement measures like disabling unused ports and services, and changing default passwords.
- **Secure Deployment Procedures**: Follow procedures that ensure secure transfer and installation of the system.

6. Operations and Maintenance
The operations and maintenance phase involves the day-to-day functioning of the system and includes monitoring, updates, and patch management.

Security Considerations:
- Continuously monitor the system for security incidents and vulnerabilities.
- Apply patches and updates promptly to mitigate new threats.

Specific Security Controls:
- **Security Information and Event Management (SIEM)**: Use SIEM tools to monitor and analyze security events.
- **Patch Management**: Regularly update and patch system components to fix security vulnerabilities.
- **Access Reviews**: Conduct periodic reviews of access controls and permissions to ensure they are appropriate.

7. Disposal
The disposal phase involves decommissioning the system and securely disposing of data and hardware.

Security Considerations:
- Ensure that all sensitive data is completely removed or destroyed before disposal.
- Follow secure disposal procedures for hardware to prevent data leakage.

Specific Security Controls:
- **Data Sanitization**: Use tools and procedures to securely erase data from storage devices.
- **Hardware Disposal**: Follow best practices for the physical destruction or recycling of hardware.
- **Compliance Checks**: Ensure that disposal processes comply with relevant regulations and standards.

Evolution of Security Requirements
Security requirements evolve throughout the SDLC as follows:
- **Requirements Gathering**: Focus on identifying security needs and regulatory requirements.
- **Design**: Translate security requirements into system architecture and design.
- **Development**: Implement security controls and follow secure coding practices.
- **Testing**: Validate the effectiveness of security controls through rigorous testing.
- **Implementation**: Ensure secure deployment and configuration of the system.
- **Operations and Maintenance**: Continuously monitor, update, and manage security controls.
- **Disposal**: Securely decommission the system and dispose of data and hardware.

By integrating security considerations at each stage of the SDLC, organizations can build robust systems that are resilient to threats and compliant with security standards and regulations.

Data classification is a critical component of information lifecycle management (ILM), which involves categorizing data based on its sensitivity, value, and regulatory requirements. Proper data classification ensures that data is handled, stored, and disposed of in a manner that protects its confidentiality, integrity, and availability.

Common Classification Levels
Most organizations use a tiered classification system that typically includes the following levels:

1. **Public**:
   - **Description**: Information that is intended for public disclosure and poses no risk if accessed by anyone.
   - **Handling**: Minimal security measures; can be freely shared.
   - **Storage**: Can be stored on public servers and websites.
   - **Disposal**: Simple deletion is sufficient.

   Example: Marketing materials, publicly released financial reports.

2. **Internal/Private**:
   - **Description**: Information meant for internal use within the organization, not intended for public release.
   - **Handling**: Moderate security measures; restricted to internal personnel.
   - **Storage**: Stored on internal servers with controlled access.
   - **Disposal**: Requires proper deletion methods to ensure data is not recoverable.

   Example: Internal memos, internal process documents.

3. **Confidential**:
   - **Description**: Sensitive information that could cause harm to the organization or individuals if disclosed.
   - **Handling**: Strict security measures; access limited to authorized personnel.

- **Storage**: Encrypted storage with strict access controls.
- **Disposal**: Secure deletion methods, such as shredding for paper documents and secure wipe for digital data.

Example: Employee records, proprietary business information.

4. **Restricted/Highly Confidential**:
     - **Description**: Information of the highest sensitivity, where unauthorized disclosure could cause significant harm.
     - **Handling**: Highest security measures; access extremely limited.
     - **Storage**: Highest level of encryption and access control.
     - **Disposal**: Must be destroyed in a manner that ensures total irrecoverability, such as incineration for paper documents and degaussing for digital data.

Example: Legal documents, intellectual property, classified government information.

Impact on Data Handling, Storage, and Disposal

Handling:
- Different classification levels dictate who can access the data and under what conditions. For example, public data may be accessible by anyone, whereas restricted data requires strict authentication and authorization processes.

Storage:
- Data must be stored in accordance with its classification level. Public data can be stored on less secure platforms, while restricted data requires encrypted storage solutions and might also need to comply with specific regulatory storage requirements.

Disposal:
- Proper disposal methods are crucial to prevent unauthorized recovery of data. Public data may be deleted through standard means, but confidential and restricted data require more secure destruction methods, such as shredding, incineration, or digital wiping tools.

Examples of Misclassification Consequences

Security Breaches:
- Misclassifying confidential data as internal can lead to inadequate protection. For instance, if employee records containing personal identifiable information (PII) are stored without encryption due to being classified as internal rather than confidential, it can result in data breaches.

Compliance Violations:
- Regulatory frameworks like GDPR and HIPAA have strict requirements for data handling and protection. Misclassifying data can lead to non-compliance and severe penalties. For example, misclassifying patient health records as internal instead of restricted under HIPAA can lead to unauthorized access and hefty fines.

Example Scenarios:
1. **Financial Sector**:
     - A financial institution misclassifies transaction data as internal instead of confidential. Hackers breach the internal network and access sensitive transaction data, leading to financial fraud and significant reputational damage.
2. **Healthcare**:
     - A hospital misclassifies patient records as internal rather than restricted. Inadequate access controls result in unauthorized personnel accessing and leaking patient information, violating HIPAA regulations and resulting in legal and financial consequences.
3. **Government**:
     - A government agency misclassifies defense-related documents as confidential instead of restricted. An internal employee accesses the documents without proper clearance and unintentionally leaks the information, causing a national security breach.

Best Practices for Effective Data Classification

1. **Regular Training**:
     - Educate employees on data classification policies and the importance of correctly classifying data to prevent errors.

2. **Automated Tools**:
    - Utilize automated data classification tools that can tag data based on predefined criteria to reduce the likelihood of human error.
3. **Regular Audits**:
    - Conduct periodic audits to ensure data is correctly classified and that handling, storage, and disposal procedures align with classification levels.
4. **Policy Updates**:
    - Keep data classification policies up-to-date with changing regulations and business needs to ensure ongoing compliance and protection.

By implementing a robust data classification system, organizations can effectively manage data throughout its lifecycle, mitigating risks and ensuring compliance with relevant regulations.

The principle of least privilege (PoLP) is a fundamental concept in access control that ensures users and systems are granted the minimum levels of access – or permissions – necessary to perform their job functions. By limiting access rights, PoLP reduces the risk of accidental or intentional misuse of privileges, thereby supporting the core security concepts of confidentiality, integrity, and availability.

How Least Privilege Supports Core Security Concepts
Confidentiality:
- **Definition**: Ensuring that sensitive information is accessible only to those authorized to view it.
- **Support**: By restricting access to sensitive data to only those who need it, PoLP minimizes the risk of unauthorized access and data breaches. For example, a marketing employee shouldn't have access to the company's financial records, thus maintaining confidentiality.

Integrity:
- **Definition**: Ensuring that data is accurate and unaltered by unauthorized users.
- **Support**: PoLP reduces the number of individuals who can modify critical data, decreasing the likelihood of accidental or malicious data alterations. For instance, limiting write permissions on a financial database to only a few key accountants ensures the integrity of the financial data.

Availability:
- **Definition**: Ensuring that information and resources are accessible to authorized users when needed.
- **Support**: PoLP helps protect against attacks that could affect system availability by limiting the number of potential entry points for attackers. For example, restricting administrative access on critical servers reduces the risk of these systems being taken offline through misuse or attacks.

Implementing Least Privilege in Various IT Environments
1. User Accounts and Permissions:
- **Role-Based Access Control (RBAC)**: Assign permissions based on the user's role within the organization. For example, HR personnel get access to employee records, while IT staff can access system configurations.
- **Access Reviews**: Conduct regular audits of user permissions to ensure they are still appropriate for their current role.
- **Separation of Duties (SoD)**: Divide tasks among multiple users to prevent any single user from having excessive privileges. For instance, the person who approves expenditures should not be the same person who processes payments.

2. Application Development and Deployment:
- **Development Environments**: Ensure that development, testing, and production environments are separate, and restrict developer access to production systems.
- **Code Repositories**: Use version control systems with role-based permissions to control who can commit, merge, or deploy code.
- **Application Permissions**: Design applications to require the least amount of privilege needed for functionality. For example, a web application should use a database user with limited privileges, restricting it to only read and write operations necessary for its functions.

3. Network and Infrastructure:

- **Network Segmentation**: Divide the network into segments and apply access controls to limit movement between them. For example, isolate sensitive financial systems from general user access networks.
- **Firewalls and Access Control Lists (ACLs)**: Use firewalls to restrict traffic based on the principle of least privilege, allowing only necessary communications between network segments.
- **Privileged Access Management (PAM)**: Implement PAM solutions to manage and audit the use of administrative and root accounts, ensuring they are used only when necessary and for a limited time.

4. Cloud Environments:
   - **Cloud IAM (Identity and Access Management)**: Use cloud provider IAM features to enforce least privilege on cloud resources. For example, create IAM roles with specific permissions for different services and assign them to users or applications.
   - **Resource Policies**: Apply resource-specific policies to restrict access. For instance, an S3 bucket policy can limit access to only certain users or IP addresses.
   - **Audit and Monitoring**: Regularly review and monitor cloud permissions and access logs to detect and respond to potential over-privileged access.

5. Endpoint Security:
   - **Local Administrative Rights**: Restrict local administrative rights on endpoints (desktops, laptops) to reduce the risk of malware or unauthorized changes.
   - **Application Whitelisting**: Use whitelisting to allow only approved applications to run, limiting the potential for malicious software to execute.

Real-World Examples of Least Privilege Implementation
- **Healthcare**: In a hospital, nurses might have access to patient records for their unit, but only doctors can modify treatment plans. Administrative staff may have access to billing information but not to detailed medical records.
- **Financial Institutions**: Bank tellers can view and process transactions but cannot access the underlying code of transaction processing systems. Only IT administrators, under strict oversight, can modify these systems.
- **Government Agencies**: Military personnel might have access to information relevant to their missions but not to broader intelligence databases unless explicitly authorized.

By meticulously applying the principle of least privilege, organizations can significantly enhance their security posture, protecting sensitive information and critical systems from unauthorized access, misuse, and potential threats. This proactive approach ensures that security is an integral part of the organizational culture and operational procedures.

Non-repudiation is a critical aspect of digital transactions and communications, ensuring that a party in a transaction cannot deny the authenticity of their signature on a document or the sending of a message. This concept is vital for maintaining trust and accountability in digital interactions.

Role of Non-Repudiation in Digital Transactions and Communications
Non-repudiation provides proof of the integrity and origin of data, guaranteeing that the sender cannot deny having sent the message or transaction. This assurance is crucial for legal and business transactions, preventing disputes and fraud.

Digital Signatures and Non-Repudiation
Digital Signatures:
- Digital signatures use cryptographic techniques to provide a high level of security and integrity.
- A digital signature is created using the sender's private key, which encrypts the data associated with the signature. The recipient can use the sender's public key to decrypt and verify the signature, ensuring the sender's identity and that the message has not been altered.

How Digital Signatures Ensure Non-Repudiation:
1. **Authentication**: Confirms the sender's identity, as only the sender's private key could have created the signature.
2. **Integrity**: Ensures the message has not been tampered with, as any alteration would invalidate the signature.

3. **Legal Validity**: In many jurisdictions, digital signatures are legally recognized and enforceable, providing a strong non-repudiation mechanism.

Example: In financial transactions, digital signatures ensure that instructions for wire transfers are genuine and unaltered, providing a secure and traceable record.

Blockchain Technology and Non-Repudiation

Blockchain:
- Blockchain is a decentralized ledger technology that records transactions in a secure, immutable, and transparent manner.
- Each block contains a list of transactions, a timestamp, and a cryptographic hash of the previous block, linking them together in a chain.

How Blockchain Ensures Non-Repudiation:
1. **Immutability**: Once a transaction is recorded on the blockchain, it cannot be altered or deleted. This permanent record ensures that parties cannot deny the transaction's occurrence.
2. **Transparency**: Blockchain provides a transparent record of all transactions, accessible to all participants in the network.
3. **Distributed Consensus**: Transactions are validated through a consensus mechanism, ensuring that all participants agree on the transaction's validity.

Example: In supply chain management, blockchain technology ensures that all transactions (e.g., shipping records) are accurately recorded and cannot be disputed by any party involved.

Challenges and Limitations of Current Non-Repudiation Methods

1. Private Key Security:
- The security of digital signatures relies on the protection of private keys. If a private key is compromised, an attacker can forge signatures, undermining non-repudiation.
- **Solution**: Implement strong key management practices, including the use of hardware security modules (HSMs) and multi-factor authentication (MFA).

2. Revocation of Digital Certificates:
- Digital certificates used in digital signatures can be revoked if compromised, but ensuring that all parties are aware of the revocation can be challenging.
- **Solution**: Utilize robust certificate revocation lists (CRLs) or Online Certificate Status Protocol (OCSP) to check the validity of certificates in real-time.

3. Scalability of Blockchain:
- Blockchain networks can face scalability issues, with transaction processing times and costs increasing as the network grows.
- **Solution**: Develop and implement scalable blockchain solutions, such as sharding or layer 2 protocols like the Lightning Network for Bitcoin.

4. Legal and Regulatory Issues:
- Different jurisdictions have varying legal recognition and requirements for digital signatures and blockchain records, which can complicate cross-border transactions.
- **Solution**: Harmonize legal frameworks and standards across jurisdictions to ensure the universal acceptance and enforceability of digital signatures and blockchain transactions.

5. Quantum Computing Threats:
- Advances in quantum computing could potentially break current cryptographic algorithms used in digital signatures and blockchain.
- **Solution**: Research and develop quantum-resistant cryptographic algorithms to safeguard against future quantum computing threats.

Non-repudiation is a foundational element of secure digital transactions and communications, enabled by technologies such as digital signatures and blockchain. While these technologies offer robust mechanisms for ensuring non-repudiation, challenges like private key security, certificate revocation, scalability, legal issues, and quantum threats need to be addressed. By continuously evolving security practices and technologies, organizations can maintain trust and accountability in their digital interactions.

The concept of privacy by design (PbD) is a proactive approach to ensuring privacy and data protection throughout the entire lifecycle of a system or process. Introduced by Ann Cavoukian in the 1990s, PbD shifts the focus from reactive measures, often applied after data breaches or privacy violations, to integrating privacy into the design and operation of IT systems, networked infrastructure, and business practices from the outset.

Differences Between Privacy by Design and Traditional Privacy Protection Methods

Traditional Privacy Protection:

- **Reactive**: Privacy measures are often implemented after a system has been designed and deployed, typically in response to regulatory requirements or data breaches.
- **Add-On**: Privacy is treated as an additional feature, bolted onto existing systems and processes rather than integrated into the core design.
- **Compliance-Focused**: Emphasis is placed on meeting the minimum legal requirements for data protection, often resulting in a checklist approach.

Privacy by Design:

- **Proactive**: Privacy is integrated into the system development process from the very beginning, anticipating and preventing privacy issues before they occur.
- **Embedded**: Privacy is built into the architecture and functionality of systems and processes, making it an integral part of the organization's operations.
- **Holistic**: PbD goes beyond mere compliance, aiming to protect privacy comprehensively by embedding privacy-enhancing technologies and practices into the organizational culture.

Privacy by Design Principles

1. **Proactive not Reactive; Preventative not Remedial**: Anticipate and prevent privacy-invasive events before they happen.
2. **Privacy as the Default Setting**: Ensure personal data is automatically protected in any IT system or business practice.
3. **Privacy Embedded into Design**: Embed privacy into the design and architecture of IT systems and business practices.
4. **Full Functionality – Positive-Sum, not Zero-Sum**: Avoid trade-offs; ensure all legitimate objectives are met without compromising privacy.
5. **End-to-End Security – Full Lifecycle Protection**: Ensure data is securely managed from collection to deletion.
6. **Visibility and Transparency – Keep it Open**: Ensure that business practices and technologies operate according to stated promises and objectives.
7. **Respect for User Privacy – Keep it User-Centric**: Maintain a user-centric approach, offering strong privacy defaults, appropriate notice, and empowering user-friendly options.

Incorporating Privacy by Design into System Development and Organizational Processes

System Development:

- **Requirements Gathering**: Include privacy requirements from the start. For example, specify that personal data must be anonymized wherever possible.
- **Design**: Integrate privacy controls into the system architecture. Use data minimization techniques to collect only the data necessary for a specific purpose. For example, design systems to anonymize or pseudonymize personal data to reduce risk.
- **Development**: Implement strong encryption methods for data at rest and in transit. Use secure coding practices to prevent vulnerabilities that could compromise privacy.
- **Testing**: Conduct privacy impact assessments (PIAs) to identify and mitigate potential privacy risks. Include privacy-related test cases in the quality assurance process.
- **Deployment**: Ensure that privacy settings are enabled by default. For instance, a new application should not share user data with third parties unless the user explicitly consents.
- **Maintenance**: Regularly review and update privacy controls as new threats and regulatory requirements emerge. Implement automated monitoring to detect and respond to privacy incidents quickly.

Organizational Processes:
- **Data Governance**: Establish a data governance framework that includes policies for data classification, access control, and data retention. Ensure that all employees are trained on these policies.
- **Employee Training**: Conduct regular training sessions on privacy best practices and the importance of privacy by design. Make sure all staff members understand their role in protecting user data.
- **Vendor Management**: Ensure that third-party vendors comply with privacy by design principles. Include privacy requirements in contracts and conduct regular audits to verify compliance.
- **Incident Response**: Develop a robust incident response plan that includes procedures for managing data breaches and privacy violations. Regularly test and update the plan.
- **Transparency and Communication**: Maintain clear communication channels to inform users about how their data is being used and their privacy rights. For example, provide easily accessible privacy policies and allow users to control their data settings.

Examples of Privacy by Design in Practice
- **Health Applications**: A health app can implement PbD by ensuring all patient data is encrypted, both in transit and at rest. The app should require minimal personal information, with default settings that prioritize data protection and anonymization features that strip personal identifiers from data used for analytics.
- **Social Media Platforms**: Platforms can design privacy settings that are enabled by default, such as limiting data sharing with third parties and providing users with clear options to control their privacy. Features like end-to-end encrypted messaging can further protect user data.
- **Smart Devices**: Manufacturers of IoT devices can embed privacy into their products by ensuring data collected by devices is minimized, anonymized, and securely stored. Default settings should limit data sharing and provide users with clear, easy-to-use privacy controls.

By adopting privacy by design, organizations can create more secure, trustworthy systems and processes that not only comply with regulations but also earn the confidence of users by safeguarding their personal information from the outset.

Conducting a comprehensive system asset inventory is a crucial step in managing and securing an organization's IT environment. This process involves identifying and documenting all hardware, software, and data assets to understand their role, value, and vulnerabilities within the system. Here's a detailed look at how to conduct this inventory, the tools and methodologies involved, and how it supports boundary management and security control implementation.

Process of Conducting a Comprehensive System Asset Inventory

1. **Define Scope and Objectives**
   - Determine the boundaries of the inventory process: which systems, departments, and types of assets will be included.
   - Set clear objectives, such as improving security posture, ensuring compliance, or optimizing asset utilization.
2. **Gather Initial Data**
   - Collect existing documentation, network diagrams, and asset lists.
   - Review procurement records, software licenses, and maintenance agreements.
3. **Identify Assets**
   - **Hardware**: Servers, desktops, laptops, mobile devices, network equipment, IoT devices.
   - **Software**: Operating systems, applications, databases, middleware.
   - **Data**: Databases, files, emails, transaction records.
4. **Classify Assets**
   - Categorize assets based on criticality, sensitivity, and value.
   - Use classification levels such as public, internal, confidential, and restricted.
5. **Document Asset Details**
   - For each asset, record detailed information including:
     - Manufacturer and model

- Serial number or unique identifier
- Location
- Configuration details
- Owner or custodian
- Maintenance schedule

6. **Validate and Verify Inventory**
    - Cross-check the inventory against physical inspections and automated discovery tools.
    - Conduct interviews with staff to confirm asset information and usage.
7. **Maintain and Update Inventory**
    - Implement a process for regularly updating the inventory to reflect changes such as new acquisitions, disposals, or configuration modifications.
    - Schedule periodic audits to ensure ongoing accuracy.

Tools and Methodologies for Accurate Identification and Classification

1. **Automated Discovery Tools**
    - Use network scanning tools (e.g., Nmap, Nessus) to identify connected devices and software.
    - Implement agent-based tools (e.g., SCCM, Lansweeper) for continuous monitoring and inventory updates.
2. **Configuration Management Databases (CMDB)**
    - Utilize CMDB systems (e.g., ServiceNow, BMC Remedy) to manage and store detailed asset information.
    - CMDBs provide a centralized repository for tracking asset relationships and dependencies.
3. **Tagging and Labeling**
    - Physically tag hardware assets with barcodes or RFID for easy identification and tracking.
    - Implement digital tagging for software and data assets to facilitate classification and searchability.
4. **Data Classification Tools**
    - Use tools (e.g., Varonis, Titus) that can automatically classify and label data based on content and context.
    - These tools help in maintaining consistent classification policies across the organization.
5. **Manual Methods**
    - Conduct physical audits and inspections to complement automated tools.
    - Use spreadsheets or databases for initial data collection and validation.

Contribution to Boundary Management and Security Control Implementation

1. Effective Boundary Management

- **Defining Boundaries**: A detailed asset inventory helps define the boundaries of the IT environment, identifying all components that need protection.
- **Network Segmentation**: By knowing all assets, organizations can effectively segment networks, isolating critical systems from less secure ones.
- **Access Controls**: Implementing precise access controls based on asset classification ensures that only authorized personnel can access sensitive information.

2. Security Control Implementation

- **Risk Assessment**: An accurate inventory enables thorough risk assessments by highlighting vulnerable or high-value assets.
- **Control Deployment**: Knowing the specifics of each asset allows for tailored security controls, such as antivirus, encryption, and intrusion detection systems.
- **Compliance**: Helps ensure compliance with regulatory requirements by providing clear documentation of assets and their security measures.
- **Incident Response**: An up-to-date asset inventory facilitates quick identification and isolation of compromised assets during security incidents.

Examples:

- **Financial Institution**: A bank uses automated discovery tools and a CMDB to track all hardware and software assets. This enables precise network segmentation, isolating customer data servers from general office networks, enhancing data protection and compliance with regulations like GDPR.
- **Healthcare Provider**: A hospital implements data classification tools to label patient records as restricted. This ensures that these records are stored in encrypted databases and access is limited to authorized medical staff, complying with HIPAA regulations.

Conducting a comprehensive system asset inventory is foundational for maintaining robust IT security. Utilizing a combination of automated tools, CMDBs, tagging, and manual verification ensures an accurate and up-to-date inventory. This inventory is critical for effective boundary management, precise implementation of security controls, and maintaining compliance, ultimately strengthening the organization's overall security posture.

The role of the Chief Information Security Officer (CISO) is crucial in establishing and maintaining a robust compliance program within an organization. The CISO is responsible for ensuring that the organization's information assets and technologies are adequately protected against security threats, while also ensuring compliance with regulatory requirements and industry standards. This multifaceted role involves strategic planning, risk management, policy development, and continuous interaction with other C-suite executives to align security objectives with business goals.

Key Responsibilities of the CISO in a Compliance Program

1. Strategic Planning and Governance:
- **Policy Development**: The CISO develops, implements, and enforces security policies and procedures that ensure compliance with relevant regulations and standards (e.g., GDPR, HIPAA, ISO/IEC 27001).
- **Risk Management**: Identifying, assessing, and mitigating information security risks is a core responsibility. This includes conducting regular risk assessments and implementing risk management frameworks.
- **Security Strategy**: The CISO devises a comprehensive security strategy that aligns with the organization's overall business strategy. This involves setting objectives, defining security measures, and establishing a roadmap for achieving compliance.

2. Operational Oversight:
- **Incident Response**: The CISO oversees the development and implementation of incident response plans to quickly and effectively manage security breaches and mitigate their impact.
- **Security Operations**: Managing the security operations center (SOC) and ensuring continuous monitoring of the organization's IT environment to detect and respond to threats.
- **Compliance Monitoring**: Continuously monitoring compliance with security policies, procedures, and regulatory requirements, and conducting internal audits to ensure adherence.

3. Communication and Training:
- **Awareness Programs**: Developing and delivering security awareness training programs to educate employees about security policies, best practices, and compliance requirements.
- **Reporting**: Regularly reporting on the status of the compliance program to the board of directors, audit committee, and other stakeholders. This includes metrics on security incidents, compliance status, and risk levels.

4. Vendor and Third-Party Management:
- **Vendor Assessments**: Evaluating the security practices of third-party vendors and ensuring they comply with the organization's security and compliance requirements.
- **Contract Management**: Including security and compliance clauses in vendor contracts and conducting regular assessments of their compliance.

Decision-Making Processes Under the CISO's Purview

1. Risk Management Decisions:
- **Risk Tolerance**: Determining the organization's risk tolerance and making decisions on risk acceptance, mitigation, transfer, or avoidance.
- **Prioritization**: Prioritizing security initiatives based on risk assessments, potential impact on the organization, and resource availability.

2. Security Investment Decisions:
- **Budget Allocation**: Allocating budget for security tools, technologies, and initiatives that support the compliance program and overall security posture.
- **Technology Adoption**: Deciding on the adoption of new security technologies and ensuring they integrate seamlessly with existing systems.

3. Incident Response and Recovery Decisions:
- **Response Strategy**: Determining the appropriate response to security incidents, including communication with stakeholders, containment measures, and remediation actions.
- **Post-Incident Analysis**: Conducting post-incident reviews to identify root causes, evaluate the effectiveness of the response, and implement improvements.

Interaction with Other C-Suite Executives

The CISO must work closely with other C-suite executives to ensure that security objectives are aligned with business goals. This collaboration involves several key interactions:

1. Chief Executive Officer (CEO):
- **Strategic Alignment**: Ensuring that the security strategy supports the organization's overall mission and strategic objectives.
- **Risk Communication**: Communicating security risks and the potential business impact of security incidents to the CEO to facilitate informed decision-making.

2. Chief Financial Officer (CFO):
- **Budgeting and Funding**: Collaborating on budget planning to secure necessary funding for security initiatives and demonstrating the return on investment (ROI) of security spending.
- **Financial Risk Management**: Aligning on financial risk management strategies and integrating them with the broader risk management framework.

3. Chief Operating Officer (COO):
- **Operational Integration**: Ensuring that security measures do not impede business operations and are seamlessly integrated into daily activities.
- **Business Continuity**: Coordinating on business continuity and disaster recovery plans to ensure operational resilience.

4. Chief Technology Officer (CTO) / Chief Information Officer (CIO):
- **Technical Collaboration**: Working together to implement security technologies and integrate security into the IT infrastructure.
- **Innovation and Security**: Balancing the need for technological innovation with the requirement to maintain a secure environment.

5. Chief Compliance Officer (CCO):
- **Regulatory Alignment**: Ensuring that the security and compliance programs are aligned and mutually reinforcing, addressing both regulatory requirements and internal policies.
- **Audit and Reporting**: Collaborating on internal and external audits, compliance reporting, and remediation of identified issues.

6. Legal Counsel:
- **Legal Compliance**: Ensuring that the organization's security policies and practices comply with applicable laws and regulations.
- **Incident Response**: Working together during incident response to address legal implications and manage communication with regulatory bodies.

Examples of CISO-Led Initiatives

Data Protection Program: Implementing a comprehensive data protection program that includes data encryption, access controls, and regular audits to ensure compliance with GDPR.

Security Awareness Campaign: Launching a security awareness campaign that includes phishing simulations, online training modules, and regular communication to keep employees informed about the latest threats and best practices.

Third-Party Risk Management: Establishing a third-party risk management program that involves conducting thorough security assessments of vendors, incorporating security requirements into contracts, and monitoring vendor compliance continuously.

Incident Response Tabletop Exercises: Conducting regular tabletop exercises with the incident response team and other stakeholders to practice and improve the organization's response to various types of security incidents.

The CISO plays a pivotal role in establishing and maintaining a robust compliance program by integrating security into every aspect of the organization, from strategic planning to daily operations. Through collaboration with other C-suite executives, the CISO ensures that security objectives are aligned with business goals, thereby enhancing the overall security posture and resilience of the organization.

FedRAMP (Federal Risk and Authorization Management Program), PCI-DSS (Payment Card Industry Data Security Standard), and CMMC (Cybersecurity Maturity Model Certification) are three prominent compliance frameworks that address various aspects of information security. Each framework has distinct requirements and focuses on different aspects of security based on their target industries and purposes.

FedRAMP

Overview:
- FedRAMP is a U.S. government program that standardizes the security assessment, authorization, and continuous monitoring of cloud services.
- It aims to ensure that cloud service providers (CSPs) meet rigorous security requirements to protect federal information.

Key Requirements:
1. **Security Controls**: Based on NIST SP 800-53, with controls tailored for cloud environments.
2. **Assessment**: CSPs undergo an assessment by a FedRAMP-approved Third Party Assessment Organization (3PAO).
3. **Authorization**: CSPs must obtain an Authority to Operate (ATO) from a federal agency or the Joint Authorization Board (JAB).
4. **Continuous Monitoring**: Regular security monitoring and reporting to ensure ongoing compliance.

Focus Areas:
- Protecting federal data in cloud environments.
- Ensuring rigorous security through standardized controls and assessments.

PCI-DSS

Overview:
- PCI-DSS is a set of security standards designed to ensure that all companies that process, store, or transmit credit card information maintain a secure environment.
- It is governed by the Payment Card Industry Security Standards Council (PCI SSC).

Key Requirements:
1. **Build and Maintain a Secure Network**: Installation of firewalls, secure configurations for system components.
2. **Protect Cardholder Data**: Encryption of data transmissions and storage.
3. **Maintain a Vulnerability Management Program**: Use of antivirus software, development, and maintenance of secure systems.
4. **Implement Strong Access Control Measures**: Restriction of access to cardholder data by business need to know.
5. **Regularly Monitor and Test Networks**: Tracking and monitoring all access to network resources and cardholder data.
6. **Maintain an Information Security Policy**: Policies that address information security for employees and contractors.

Focus Areas:
- Protecting credit card information from breaches and fraud.
- Ensuring secure processing, storage, and transmission of cardholder data.

CMMC

Overview:
- The Cybersecurity Maturity Model Certification (CMMC) is a unified standard for implementing cybersecurity across the defense industrial base (DIB).
- Managed by the Department of Defense (DoD), it aims to protect sensitive information, including Controlled Unclassified Information (CUI).

Key Requirements:
1. **Maturity Levels**: Five levels ranging from basic cyber hygiene (Level 1) to advanced/progressive (Level 5).
2. **Security Practices**: Implementation of practices based on NIST SP 800-171 and other relevant standards.
3. **Processes**: Integration of cybersecurity processes at various maturity levels to ensure resilience and capability improvement.
4. **Assessment and Certification**: Conducted by CMMC Third Party Assessment Organizations (C3PAOs).

Focus Areas:
- Protecting CUI within the defense supply chain.
- Enhancing the overall cybersecurity posture through a tiered maturity model.

Comparison of Requirements

Security Controls:
- **FedRAMP**: Focuses on NIST SP 800-53 controls tailored for cloud environments.
- **PCI-DSS**: Specifies 12 requirements across six control objectives focusing on credit card data protection.
- **CMMC**: Integrates practices from NIST SP 800-171 and additional standards, with varying levels of maturity.

Assessment and Authorization:
- **FedRAMP**: Requires assessment by a 3PAO and authorization from a federal agency or JAB.
- **PCI-DSS**: Annual assessment by a Qualified Security Assessor (QSA) or self-assessment for smaller entities.
- **CMMC**: Certification by C3PAOs, with different maturity levels dictating the extent of assessment.

Continuous Monitoring:
- **FedRAMP**: Emphasizes ongoing monitoring and periodic reporting.
- **PCI-DSS**: Regular monitoring, testing, and logging requirements.
- **CMMC**: Continuous improvement and process integration at higher maturity levels.

Industries and Scenarios for Simultaneous Implementation

Cloud Service Providers:
- A CSP providing services to federal agencies must comply with FedRAMP. If the CSP also handles payment processing for e-commerce clients, it must adhere to PCI-DSS. If this CSP deals with DoD contracts, it must comply with CMMC. Thus, it needs to simultaneously implement FedRAMP, PCI-DSS, and CMMC.

Defense Contractors:
- A defense contractor handling CUI for DoD projects must comply with CMMC. If this contractor also processes payment transactions (e.g., for subcontractor payments), PCI-DSS compliance is necessary. If they utilize cloud services to store or process federal data, they need FedRAMP authorization.

Financial Institutions:
- A bank providing cloud-based financial services to federal agencies needs FedRAMP compliance. It must also ensure PCI-DSS compliance for handling credit card transactions and CMMC compliance if involved in defense-related financial services.

Examples
1. **E-commerce Platform**:
    - An e-commerce platform storing customer data on a FedRAMP-authorized cloud service, processing payments, and dealing with defense-related products must comply with all three frameworks.
2. **Managed Service Providers (MSPs)**:
    - An MSP serving clients across various sectors, including federal agencies, financial services, and defense contractors, would need to implement FedRAMP, PCI-DSS, and CMMC compliance measures to meet the diverse regulatory requirements.

By understanding and aligning the requirements of these frameworks, organizations can effectively manage and secure their information assets, ensuring compliance across multiple regulatory landscapes and enhancing their overall security posture.

The General Data Protection Regulation (GDPR) has significant extraterritorial implications, affecting organizations outside the European Union (EU) that process the personal data of EU residents. This regulation aims to provide robust protection for personal data and grant individuals greater control over their information, regardless of where the data processing occurs. Here, we examine the extraterritorial reach of GDPR, its impact on global organizations, key compliance challenges, and the potential consequences of non-compliance.

Extraterritorial Reach of GDPR

GDPR applies to any organization, regardless of its location, that processes personal data of individuals residing in the EU. This includes:

1. **Offering Goods or Services**: Non-EU businesses that offer goods or services (whether paid or free) to EU residents are subject to GDPR.
2. **Monitoring Behavior**: Non-EU organizations that monitor the behavior of EU residents (e.g., through website tracking) must comply with GDPR.

The broad scope of GDPR means that businesses worldwide must evaluate their data processing activities to determine if they fall under the regulation's jurisdiction.

Impact on Organizations Outside the EU

1. Data Protection Policies: Organizations must revise their data protection policies to align with GDPR requirements. This includes:

- Ensuring transparent data processing.
- Implementing data minimization and purpose limitation principles.
- Providing individuals with rights such as access, rectification, erasure, and data portability.

2. Data Transfer Mechanisms: Non-EU organizations must ensure that personal data transferred from the EU complies with GDPR standards. This involves:

- Using Standard Contractual Clauses (SCCs).
- Implementing Binding Corporate Rules (BCRs).
- Relying on adequacy decisions or other legal mechanisms for data transfer.

3. Appointment of Representatives: Organizations outside the EU that process data of EU residents must appoint an EU-based representative to act as a point of contact for data subjects and supervisory authorities.

4. Data Breach Notifications: Non-EU entities must establish procedures for detecting, reporting, and investigating data breaches, notifying EU data subjects and authorities within 72 hours of becoming aware of a breach.

Key Compliance Challenges

1. Understanding and Applying GDPR Principles: Non-EU organizations may struggle with understanding and correctly implementing GDPR principles due to differences in data protection laws and practices in their home countries.

2. Resource Allocation: Compliance requires significant investment in terms of time, money, and personnel. Smaller organizations may find it challenging to allocate resources for GDPR compliance activities.

3. Data Mapping and Inventory: Identifying all data processing activities involving EU residents can be complex, especially for large organizations with vast and dispersed data systems.

4. Cross-Border Data Transfers: Ensuring legal mechanisms for international data transfers can be cumbersome and may require renegotiation of contracts and additional safeguards.

5. Legal and Cultural Differences: Organizations may face difficulties in reconciling GDPR requirements with local laws and cultural attitudes towards data privacy.

Potential Consequences of Non-Compliance

1. Financial Penalties: GDPR imposes substantial fines for non-compliance. Penalties can reach up to €20 million or 4% of the organization's global annual turnover, whichever is higher.

2. Reputational Damage: Non-compliance can lead to significant reputational damage, eroding customer trust and impacting the organization's market position.

3. Legal Actions: Non-compliance can result in legal actions from data subjects or consumer protection groups, leading to further financial and legal repercussions.
4. Operational Disruptions: Investigations and enforcement actions by data protection authorities can disrupt business operations and lead to increased scrutiny of the organization's practices.
5. Data Transfer Restrictions: Inadequate data protection measures can lead to restrictions or bans on data transfers from the EU, affecting business operations reliant on cross-border data flows.

Practical Steps for Compliance
1. Conduct a Data Protection Impact Assessment (DPIA): Evaluate data processing activities to identify risks and implement measures to mitigate them.
2. Implement Robust Data Governance: Establish comprehensive data protection policies and practices that align with GDPR requirements.
3. Train Employees: Provide ongoing training to employees on GDPR principles and data protection best practices.
4. Enhance Security Measures: Implement technical and organizational measures to protect personal data, including encryption, access controls, and regular security audits.
5. Engage Legal Expertise: Consult with legal experts specializing in GDPR to ensure compliance and navigate complex regulatory requirements.

Real-World Examples

- **US-Based E-Commerce Business**: A US-based e-commerce company offering products to EU customers must comply with GDPR. This includes updating its privacy policy, obtaining explicit consent for data collection, and ensuring secure data transfers to its US servers.
- **Multinational Corporation**: A multinational corporation with offices in the EU and other regions must harmonize its data protection practices globally. This involves implementing GDPR-compliant policies, conducting regular compliance audits, and appointing a data protection officer (DPO) to oversee compliance efforts.
- **Digital Marketing Agency**: A digital marketing agency using tracking technologies to monitor the behavior of EU residents must ensure transparency in data collection practices, obtain consent, and provide opt-out mechanisms.

GDPR's extraterritorial reach requires organizations outside the EU to adopt comprehensive data protection measures to comply with its stringent requirements. By proactively addressing compliance challenges and aligning security objectives with GDPR principles, global businesses can safeguard personal data, avoid substantial penalties, and maintain the trust of their customers and stakeholders.

Risk appetite is a fundamental concept in enterprise risk management (ERM) that defines the amount and type of risk an organization is willing to accept in pursuit of its objectives. Understanding and managing risk appetite is crucial for aligning risk-taking with strategic goals and ensuring that risk management efforts support business priorities.

Determining Risk Appetite
1. Strategic Alignment: Organizations should start by aligning their risk appetite with their overall business strategy and objectives. This involves considering the organization's mission, vision, and long-term goals. For instance, a startup in a rapidly evolving tech industry may have a higher risk appetite compared to a well-established bank with a focus on stability and regulatory compliance.
2. Stakeholder Input: Engaging key stakeholders, including the board of directors, senior management, and business unit leaders, is essential to understand their perspectives on risk tolerance. Regular discussions and workshops can help in identifying the levels of risk that are acceptable across different areas of the organization.
3. Risk Assessment: Conduct comprehensive risk assessments to identify and evaluate potential risks. This process helps in understanding the likelihood and impact of various risks, providing a basis for setting risk appetite levels. Quantitative methods like value-at-risk (VaR) or stress testing, along with qualitative assessments, can be used to gauge risk exposures.
4. Financial Capacity: Assess the organization's financial capacity to absorb losses. This includes evaluating capital reserves, liquidity, and access to funding. A robust financial position may allow for a higher risk appetite, whereas limited financial resources may necessitate a more conservative approach.

5. Regulatory and Compliance Requirements: Consider the regulatory landscape and compliance obligations. Industries with stringent regulations, such as healthcare and finance, often have lower risk appetites due to the high cost of non-compliance and potential legal repercussions.

Communicating Risk Appetite

1. Risk Appetite Statement: Develop a clear and concise risk appetite statement that outlines the types and levels of risk the organization is willing to accept. This statement should be approved by the board and communicated across the organization to ensure consistency in risk-taking behaviors.

2. Policies and Procedures: Integrate the risk appetite into organizational policies and procedures. This includes establishing risk limits, thresholds, and escalation protocols that align with the defined risk appetite. For example, setting credit risk limits in financial institutions or defining acceptable project risks in a construction company.

3. Training and Awareness: Conduct training sessions and awareness programs to ensure that all employees understand the risk appetite and how it applies to their roles. Regular updates and reinforcement through internal communications can help maintain awareness and adherence.

4. Reporting and Monitoring: Implement robust reporting and monitoring mechanisms to track risk exposures against the defined risk appetite. Dashboards, risk registers, and regular risk reports can provide visibility into whether the organization is operating within its risk tolerance levels.

Influence on Decision-Making

1. Strategic Decisions: At the strategic level, risk appetite influences decisions related to mergers and acquisitions, new market entries, and product development. For instance, a company with a high risk appetite may pursue aggressive expansion into emerging markets, while a more risk-averse organization might focus on consolidating its position in established markets.

2. Operational Decisions: Operationally, risk appetite guides day-to-day decisions such as project approvals, vendor selections, and process improvements. A manufacturing firm with a low risk appetite for operational disruptions might invest heavily in preventive maintenance and supply chain redundancy.

3. Financial Decisions: In finance, risk appetite affects investment strategies, capital allocation, and credit risk management. A bank with a moderate risk appetite might balance its portfolio between high-risk, high-reward investments and safer, lower-yield assets.

4. Compliance and Risk Management: For compliance and risk management functions, risk appetite shapes the approach to regulatory compliance, internal controls, and audit activities. An organization with a low risk appetite for compliance risks will invest significantly in robust compliance programs and internal audits to mitigate potential regulatory breaches.

Examples:

- **Tech Startup**: A tech startup with a high risk appetite might decide to allocate a significant portion of its budget to research and development, despite the inherent uncertainties and potential for financial loss. This decision supports its strategy of innovation and rapid growth.
- **Healthcare Provider**: A healthcare provider with a low risk appetite for patient safety risks might implement stringent safety protocols, even if it means higher operational costs. This decision aligns with its mission to provide high-quality care and maintain regulatory compliance.

Effectively determining and communicating risk appetite ensures that risk management efforts are aligned with strategic objectives and that decision-making at all levels is consistent with the organization's risk tolerance. By embedding risk appetite into policies, procedures, and culture, organizations can navigate uncertainties more effectively and achieve their goals with greater confidence.

Security metrics play a crucial role in a compliance program by providing measurable insights into the effectiveness of security controls, the level of risk, and areas needing improvement. They help organizations ensure that they meet regulatory requirements, protect sensitive information, and enhance their overall security posture.

Importance of Security Metrics in a Compliance Program

Security metrics enable organizations to:

- **Quantify Security Posture**: Provide a tangible measure of how well security controls are working, helping to identify strengths and weaknesses.

- **Monitor Compliance**: Track adherence to regulatory requirements and internal policies, ensuring that the organization stays compliant.
- **Support Decision-Making**: Offer data-driven insights that inform strategic decisions about resource allocation, risk management, and security investments.
- **Enhance Accountability**: Assign clear metrics to teams and individuals, promoting accountability and transparency in security efforts.
- **Drive Continuous Improvement**: Identify trends and patterns over time, facilitating the continuous enhancement of security measures and processes.

Key Performance Indicators (KPIs) and Key Risk Indicators (KRIs)

Key Performance Indicators (KPIs) are metrics that reflect the effectiveness of security processes and controls. They help measure the success of security initiatives and compliance efforts.

Key Risk Indicators (KRIs) are metrics that signal potential risks to the organization's security. They help identify emerging threats and vulnerabilities that could impact the organization.

Examples of KPIs and KRIs

KPIs:
- **Incident Response Time**: Measures the time taken to detect, respond to, and mitigate security incidents. Shorter response times indicate effective incident management.
- **Patch Management Effectiveness**: Tracks the percentage of systems patched within a specified time frame. High patch compliance rates suggest robust vulnerability management.
- **User Training Participation**: Measures the participation rate in security awareness training programs. High participation rates indicate better-informed employees.

KRIs:
- **Number of Vulnerabilities**: Tracks the number of discovered vulnerabilities over time. An increasing number of vulnerabilities may indicate a higher risk level.
- **Unusual Network Activity**: Monitors deviations from normal network traffic patterns. Spikes in unusual activity could signal potential security incidents.
- **Failed Login Attempts**: Counts the number of failed login attempts over a period. A high number of failed attempts could indicate attempted unauthorized access.

Using Metrics to Demonstrate Compliance

Security metrics are instrumental in demonstrating compliance by:
- **Providing Evidence**: Metrics offer quantifiable evidence of compliance with regulatory requirements, which can be presented to auditors and regulatory bodies.
- **Highlighting Gaps**: Metrics identify areas where the organization may be falling short of compliance, allowing for targeted remediation efforts.
- **Benchmarking Performance**: Comparing metrics against industry standards or historical data helps assess the organization's compliance status and progress.

Driving Continuous Improvement in Security Posture

Metrics facilitate continuous improvement by:
- **Identifying Trends**: Regularly tracking and analyzing metrics reveal trends and patterns, enabling proactive adjustments to security measures.
- **Informing Strategy**: Data-driven insights from metrics support strategic planning and prioritization of security initiatives.
- **Fostering a Culture of Security**: Sharing metric results with employees and stakeholders raises awareness and promotes a culture of continuous security improvement.

Incorporating security metrics into a compliance program is essential for maintaining regulatory compliance, enhancing security controls, and fostering an environment of continuous improvement. By leveraging KPIs and KRIs, organizations can gain valuable insights into their security posture, make informed decisions, and drive meaningful enhancements in their overall security strategy.

Third-party risk management (TPRM) is a critical component of a comprehensive security and compliance program. As organizations increasingly rely on vendors and service providers for various functions, managing the risks associated with these third parties becomes essential to protect sensitive data, ensure compliance with regulations, and maintain overall security.

Role of Third-Party Risk Management

1. Protecting Sensitive Data: Third parties often have access to sensitive data, making it crucial to ensure they handle and protect this information according to the organization's security standards.

2. Ensuring Compliance: Regulatory frameworks like GDPR, HIPAA, and PCI-DSS require organizations to manage third-party risks to comply with data protection and privacy requirements.

3. Maintaining Business Continuity: Disruptions or breaches at a third-party provider can directly impact an organization's operations. Effective TPRM helps mitigate these risks and ensures business continuity.

Strategies for Assessing, Monitoring, and Mitigating Third-Party Risks

1. Conduct Thorough Due Diligence: Before engaging with a vendor, conduct comprehensive due diligence to assess their security posture and compliance with relevant standards.

- **Risk Assessments**: Evaluate the third party's security policies, controls, and practices. This may include reviewing their security certifications, such as ISO/IEC 27001 or SOC 2 reports.
- **Questionnaires and Audits**: Use detailed security questionnaires and conduct on-site audits to gather information about the third party's security measures.

2. Define Clear Contractual Obligations: Ensure that contracts with third parties include specific clauses related to security and compliance requirements.

- **Security Requirements**: Specify the security controls and standards the vendor must adhere to.
- **Incident Response**: Include clauses that outline the vendor's responsibilities in the event of a data breach or security incident.
- **Right to Audit**: Incorporate the right to perform regular security audits and assessments.

3. Implement Ongoing Monitoring: Continuous monitoring of third-party activities and security practices is essential to manage risks effectively.

- **Performance Metrics**: Establish key performance indicators (KPIs) and service level agreements (SLAs) to monitor the vendor's performance.
- **Continuous Monitoring Tools**: Use automated tools to continuously monitor third-party networks and systems for vulnerabilities and threats.
- **Regular Reviews**: Conduct regular reviews and reassessments of the vendor's security posture to ensure ongoing compliance with security standards.

4. Foster Strong Vendor Relationships: Build collaborative relationships with third parties to ensure they understand and align with your security and compliance expectations.

- **Training and Awareness**: Provide training sessions and resources to help vendors understand your security requirements and how to meet them.
- **Communication Channels**: Establish clear and open lines of communication for reporting security incidents and discussing risk management practices.

5. Establish a Risk Management Framework: Develop a structured TPRM framework that integrates with your overall risk management strategy.

- **Risk Categorization**: Categorize third parties based on the level of risk they pose to the organization. High-risk vendors may require more stringent controls and frequent assessments.
- **Risk Mitigation Plans**: Develop and implement risk mitigation plans tailored to each vendor's risk profile.

Examples of Effective Third-Party Risk Management Practices

1. Financial Services: A financial institution works with numerous third-party vendors for services such as payment processing and customer data management. To manage third-party risks, the institution conducts rigorous initial due diligence, including security assessments and audits. Contracts include stringent security requirements and the right to perform regular audits. Continuous monitoring tools track vendor compliance with security policies, and regular reviews are conducted to assess ongoing risks.

2. Healthcare Provider: A healthcare provider partners with third-party IT service providers to manage electronic health records (EHRs). The provider ensures compliance with HIPAA by including specific data protection and breach notification requirements in contracts. They use automated monitoring tools to detect any unauthorized access to patient data and conduct quarterly security audits to verify the vendor's adherence to security protocols.

3. Retail Industry: A large retailer uses multiple third-party logistics and supply chain vendors. To manage supply chain risks, the retailer implements a TPRM framework that includes thorough risk assessments, regular security audits, and performance monitoring. Contracts with suppliers mandate compliance with industry standards such as PCI-DSS for payment processing and include penalties for non-compliance.

4. Technology Company: A technology company outsources software development to third-party developers. The company uses secure coding guidelines and conducts code reviews and penetration testing before integrating third-party code into its products. Contracts stipulate security training for developers and regular security assessments to ensure that third-party code meets the company's security standards.

Third-party risk management is essential for safeguarding sensitive data, ensuring regulatory compliance, and maintaining business continuity. By employing strategies such as thorough due diligence, clear contractual obligations, ongoing monitoring, strong vendor relationships, and a structured risk management framework, organizations can effectively manage and mitigate risks associated with third-party vendors and service providers. These practices not only enhance security but also build trust and resilience in the organization's operations.

Scope of the System

Accurately documenting a system's name and scope is crucial in information security as it forms the foundation for effective risk management and compliance efforts. Precise documentation ensures that all stakeholders have a clear understanding of the system's boundaries, functionalities, and interdependencies, which is essential for identifying and mitigating risks, as well as ensuring compliance with regulatory requirements.

Importance of Accurate Documentation

1. Clarity and Consistency: Accurate documentation of a system's name and scope provides clarity and consistency, ensuring all stakeholders have a common understanding of what the system encompasses. This includes understanding the system's purpose, functionalities, components, and interactions with other systems.

2. Risk Identification and Assessment: A well-documented system scope helps in identifying all potential risks associated with the system. It ensures that all elements, including hardware, software, data, and network interfaces, are considered during risk assessments. This comprehensive view is critical for identifying vulnerabilities and threats accurately.

3. Security Controls Implementation: Clear documentation facilitates the implementation of appropriate security controls tailored to the system's specific needs. By understanding the full scope, security professionals can apply controls effectively to protect all components and interfaces, reducing the risk of breaches.

4. Compliance and Audit Readiness: Accurate system documentation is often required for regulatory compliance and audit purposes. Regulations like GDPR, HIPAA, and PCI-DSS mandate detailed documentation to ensure that organizations are adhering to prescribed security standards. Proper documentation makes it easier to demonstrate compliance during audits and reduces the risk of penalties.

Contributions to Effective Risk Management and Compliance

1. Comprehensive Risk Management: With a well-defined system scope, organizations can conduct thorough risk assessments that cover all aspects of the system. This includes identifying data flows, access points, and potential vulnerabilities. Comprehensive risk management plans can then be developed to address these risks effectively.

2. Tailored Security Measures: Understanding the specific details and boundaries of a system allows for the implementation of security measures that are specifically tailored to protect the system's assets. This targeted approach ensures that security resources are used efficiently and effectively.

3. Enhanced Incident Response: In the event of a security incident, accurate documentation helps in quickly identifying affected components and understanding the system's interdependencies. This accelerates incident response efforts, enabling quicker containment and remediation.

4. Simplified Compliance Processes: For compliance purposes, clear documentation simplifies the process of demonstrating adherence to security standards and regulatory requirements. It provides a clear map of the system's architecture and controls, making it easier to prove that all necessary measures are in place.

Examples of Consequences When System Scope is Poorly Defined

1. Incomplete Risk Assessments: If the system scope is poorly defined, risk assessments may overlook critical components or interfaces. For example, if an organization fails to document that a specific server handles sensitive customer data, this server might not receive the necessary security controls, leaving it vulnerable to attacks.

2. Ineffective Security Controls: Misunderstood system boundaries can lead to the implementation of ineffective security measures. For instance, if network connections between two systems are not documented, security controls might not be applied to those connections, creating potential attack vectors.

3. Non-Compliance and Legal Penalties: Poor documentation can result in non-compliance with regulatory requirements. For example, if a healthcare provider does not accurately document the scope of systems containing patient health information, it might fail to implement necessary HIPAA-compliant controls, leading to potential legal penalties and reputational damage.

4. Delayed Incident Response: In the case of a security breach, an unclear system scope can delay incident response efforts. If responders do not have a complete understanding of the system's components and interconnections, identifying the source and impact of the breach becomes more challenging, prolonging recovery efforts.

5. Increased Costs: Undefined system scopes can lead to increased costs due to redundant security measures or the need for extensive post-incident corrections. For example, if a system's scope is not clearly defined, organizations might either over-invest in unnecessary security controls or under-invest and face higher costs from breaches and compliance fines.

Example Scenario: A financial institution operates a customer management system that interacts with various other systems, including payment processing and fraud detection systems. If the scope of the customer management system is not accurately documented, risk assessments might miss the critical data flows between these systems. As a result, security measures might not be applied to protect these data flows, increasing the risk of data breaches. Additionally, during a compliance audit, the institution might struggle to demonstrate that all regulatory requirements for data protection have been met, leading to potential fines and increased scrutiny from regulators. Accurate documentation of a system's name and scope is essential for effective risk management and compliance. It ensures that all potential risks are identified and mitigated, appropriate security controls are implemented, and compliance with regulatory requirements is maintained. Poorly defined system scopes can lead to significant security vulnerabilities, compliance issues, and increased operational costs, underscoring the importance of thorough and precise documentation.

Defining a system's purpose and functionality is a critical step in the system development life cycle (SDLC), as it establishes the foundation for designing, implementing, and securing the system. These definitions significantly impact the selection of security controls and compliance requirements by aligning the system's goals with appropriate protective measures and regulatory standards.

Defining a System's Purpose and Functionality
The process involves:
- **Identifying Business Objectives**: Understanding the primary goals the system aims to achieve, such as improving operational efficiency, enhancing customer service, or supporting business processes.
- **Documenting Functional Requirements**: Detailing the specific tasks the system must perform, including input, processing, output, and user interactions.
- **Understanding Data Flow**: Mapping out how data will be collected, processed, stored, and transmitted within the system.

Impact on Selection of Security Controls
1. **Aligning with Business Objectives**:
   - Systems designed for handling sensitive information, such as financial data or personal health records, require robust security controls like encryption, access controls, and audit logging.
   - A system's purpose of facilitating customer interactions may prioritize controls that protect user privacy and data integrity.

2. **Tailoring to Functional Requirements**:
   - Real-time processing systems may require controls that ensure data availability and integrity, such as redundancy and fault tolerance mechanisms.
   - Systems with extensive data storage needs might emphasize data encryption at rest and regular data integrity checks.

Impact on Compliance Requirements
1. **Regulatory Alignment**:
   - Systems processing personal data may need to comply with regulations like GDPR or CCPA, necessitating specific controls for data protection and user rights management.
   - Healthcare systems must align with HIPAA requirements, implementing controls to safeguard patient information.

2. **Industry Standards**:
   - Financial systems might need to adhere to PCI-DSS standards, ensuring secure handling of payment information through encryption and stringent access controls.
   - Government systems may follow FISMA guidelines, focusing on comprehensive risk management and continuous monitoring.

Role of Stakeholder Input
Stakeholder input is crucial in defining the system's purpose and functionality as it ensures that the system meets the needs and expectations of all parties involved. Key stakeholders include business leaders, IT staff, end-users, and regulatory bodies.

1. **Gathering Requirements**:
   - Engaging stakeholders in workshops, interviews, and surveys to gather detailed requirements and expectations.
   - Balancing business needs with technical feasibility and security considerations.
2. **Addressing Conflicts**:
   - Conflicts may arise when different stakeholders have competing needs. For example, business leaders may prioritize functionality and time-to-market, while security teams emphasize robust security measures that could slow development.
   - Addressing these conflicts involves:
     - **Prioritization**: Assessing and prioritizing requirements based on business impact, risk, and regulatory necessity.
     - **Compromise**: Finding middle-ground solutions that meet critical needs without compromising essential security.
     - **Communication**: Maintaining open and transparent communication to ensure all stakeholders understand the trade-offs and rationale behind decisions.

Examples of Conflicting Stakeholder Needs
1. **Example 1: Business Leaders vs. Security Teams**
   - **Business Need**: A rapid deployment of a new customer-facing application to capture market opportunities.
   - **Security Concern**: Ensuring the application meets security standards to protect customer data.
   - **Resolution**: Implementing a phased deployment approach, where core functionality is released first with essential security controls, followed by additional features and enhanced security measures in subsequent updates.
2. **Example 2: User Experience vs. Data Protection**
   - **User Need**: Simplified login processes for a better user experience.
   - **Security Concern**: Implementing multi-factor authentication (MFA) to enhance security.
   - **Resolution**: Using adaptive authentication methods that balance user convenience and security, such as risk-based MFA that prompts for additional verification only under suspicious conditions.
3. **Example 3: Regulatory Compliance vs. Operational Efficiency**
   - **Compliance Requirement**: Strict data retention policies to comply with legal requirements.
   - **Operational Need**: Efficient data management practices to reduce storage costs and improve system performance.
   - **Resolution**: Implementing data archiving solutions that meet regulatory retention requirements while optimizing active data storage for performance and cost-efficiency.

Defining a system's purpose and functionality involves a comprehensive understanding of business objectives, functional requirements, and stakeholder needs. This foundational process directly influences the selection of security controls and compliance measures, ensuring that the system is not only effective and efficient but also secure and compliant. Engaging stakeholders and addressing conflicts through prioritization, compromise, and clear communication are essential to achieving a balanced and successful outcome.

A comprehensive system boundary definition is essential for effective security control implementation and risk assessment. It involves clearly identifying and documenting the limits of a system, including all components, interactions, and dependencies. Here are the key components and their importance in security and risk management, along with common challenges faced, especially in cloud-based or hybrid environments.

Key Components of a Comprehensive System Boundary Definition
1. **Physical Boundaries**:
   - **Hardware Components**: Servers, workstations, network devices, and other physical hardware involved in the system.
   - **Physical Locations**: Data centers, offices, and other locations where hardware components are housed.
2. **Logical Boundaries**:

- **Software Components**: Operating systems, applications, databases, middleware, and other software elements.
- **Data Flows**: Paths data takes between different components, including input, processing, storage, and output.

3. **Network Boundaries**:
   - **Network Segments**: Segmentation of the network into zones, such as internal, DMZ, and external networks.
   - **Interconnections**: Connections between different network segments, including firewalls, routers, and VPNs.

4. **Access Boundaries**:
   - **User Access**: Roles, permissions, and authentication mechanisms defining who can access the system and how.
   - **Service Accounts**: Access controls for automated processes and service accounts.

5. **Organizational Boundaries**:
   - **Internal Departments**: Different departments and their roles in managing and using the system.
   - **Third-Party Interactions**: Vendors, partners, and other third parties who interact with the system.

6. **Temporal Boundaries**:
   - **Lifecycle Phases**: System development lifecycle phases, including development, testing, production, and decommissioning.
   - **Time-Based Controls**: Temporal aspects of access and processing, such as scheduled tasks and time-limited access.

Contribution to Effective Security Control Implementation and Risk Assessment

1. **Clear Identification of Assets and Interfaces**:
   - Proper boundary definition allows for a detailed inventory of all system components and their interfaces. This clarity is essential for identifying and implementing appropriate security controls tailored to each component and interface.

2. **Accurate Risk Assessment**:
   - Understanding the system boundaries helps in identifying potential attack vectors and vulnerabilities. It ensures that risk assessments consider all components and their interactions, leading to comprehensive risk mitigation strategies.

3. **Targeted Security Measures**:
   - With well-defined boundaries, security controls can be precisely applied where they are most needed. For example, critical data flows can be encrypted, and sensitive components can be isolated within secure network segments.

4. **Compliance and Audit Readiness**:
   - Clear documentation of system boundaries simplifies compliance with regulatory requirements by providing a clear map of the system architecture and controls. It facilitates easier audits and demonstrates adherence to security standards.

5. **Efficient Incident Response**:
   - In the event of a security incident, knowing the exact system boundaries helps in quickly identifying affected components and understanding the potential impact. This accelerates incident containment and remediation efforts.

Common Challenges in Defining System Boundaries

1. **Cloud-Based Environments**:
   - **Dynamic Nature**: Cloud environments are highly dynamic, with resources being frequently added, removed, or modified. This fluidity makes it challenging to maintain an accurate definition of system boundaries.
   - **Shared Responsibility Model**: In cloud environments, security responsibilities are shared between the cloud service provider and the customer. Defining boundaries requires a clear understanding of which components and security controls are managed by each party.
   - **Visibility and Control**: Limited visibility into the cloud provider's infrastructure can hinder the precise definition of boundaries and the implementation of security controls.

2. Hybrid Environments:
- **Integration Complexity**: Hybrid environments involve integrating on-premises systems with cloud services. Ensuring a seamless definition of boundaries across both environments can be complex due to differences in infrastructure and security models.
- **Data Flow Management**: Managing data flows between on-premises and cloud components requires careful attention to ensure secure transmission and adherence to regulatory requirements.
- **Consistent Security Policies**: Applying consistent security policies across hybrid environments can be challenging due to varying capabilities and configurations of on-premises and cloud components.

Examples of Challenges:
1. **Dynamic Scaling**: In cloud environments, resources such as virtual machines and containers can scale up or down automatically based on demand. This dynamic scaling can make it difficult to maintain an up-to-date system boundary definition and apply consistent security controls.
2. **Third-Party Services**: Utilizing third-party services within a cloud environment, such as managed databases or external APIs, can complicate boundary definitions. Each third-party service may have its own security policies and controls that need to be integrated and aligned with the organization's security framework.
3. **Data Residency and Compliance**: In hybrid environments, data may reside in multiple locations, each with different regulatory requirements. Defining boundaries that account for data residency and ensuring compliance with various regulations can be a significant challenge.

Examples of Effective Boundary Management

1. Financial Services:
- A bank uses a combination of on-premises and cloud-based systems. To manage system boundaries, it employs automated tools to continuously monitor and update the inventory of cloud resources. It also establishes clear contracts with cloud providers that delineate security responsibilities and ensure compliance with financial regulations.

2. Healthcare Provider:
- A healthcare organization integrates its electronic health record (EHR) system with a cloud-based analytics platform. It defines system boundaries by documenting all interfaces between the on-premises EHR and the cloud platform, implementing strong encryption for data in transit, and ensuring that both environments comply with HIPAA requirements.

Properly defining system boundaries is essential for effective security control implementation and risk assessment. It ensures that all components are accounted for, vulnerabilities are identified, and appropriate security measures are applied. However, challenges such as the dynamic nature of cloud environments and the complexity of hybrid integrations must be addressed through continuous monitoring, clear contractual agreements, and consistent security policies.

The concept of information types in the context of system security involves categorizing and prioritizing data based on its sensitivity, importance, and the potential impact of its compromise. Understanding and correctly classifying information types are crucial steps in selecting appropriate security controls to protect data from unauthorized access, disclosure, alteration, and destruction.

Categorizing and Prioritizing Information Types

1. Identification of Information Types:
- **Business Information**: Data related to the organization's operations, strategies, and financial performance.
- **Personal Information**: Data that can identify an individual, such as names, addresses, Social Security numbers, and health records.
- **Operational Information**: Data used in day-to-day operations, including system logs, transaction records, and inventory lists.
- **Intellectual Property**: Proprietary information, such as patents, trade secrets, and proprietary software.
- **Regulated Information**: Data subject to specific legal or regulatory requirements, such as credit card information (PCI-DSS) and health records (HIPAA).

2. Sensitivity and Impact Assessment:

- **Confidentiality**: The need to protect information from unauthorized access. For example, personal health records require high confidentiality.
- **Integrity**: The need to ensure information is accurate and unaltered. Financial transaction data must maintain high integrity.
- **Availability**: The need to ensure information is accessible when needed. Operational data for a critical system must be highly available.

3. **Categorization Based on Sensitivity**:
   - **Public Information**: Data intended for public dissemination, with minimal risk if disclosed.
   - **Internal Information**: Data restricted to internal use, with moderate impact if exposed.
   - **Confidential Information**: Sensitive data with significant risk if disclosed, such as employee records.
   - **Highly Confidential Information**: Data with severe consequences if compromised, such as trade secrets and classified government information.

Relationship Between Information Types and Security Controls

The categorization of information types directly informs the selection of security controls. Controls are chosen based on the level of sensitivity and the specific requirements for confidentiality, integrity, and availability.

1. **Confidentiality Controls**:
   - **Encryption**: Encrypting sensitive data, such as personal health records, both at rest and in transit to prevent unauthorized access.
   - **Access Control**: Implementing strict access controls and authentication mechanisms to ensure that only authorized personnel can access confidential information.
   - **Data Masking**: Obscuring specific data elements within databases to protect sensitive information from being exposed.

2. **Integrity Controls**:
   - **Hashing**: Using cryptographic hashes to ensure data integrity and detect any unauthorized modifications. For example, hashing financial transaction records to ensure they are not tampered with.
   - **Digital Signatures**: Applying digital signatures to documents and messages to verify their origin and integrity.
   - **Audit Logs**: Maintaining detailed audit logs to track changes and access to critical data, enabling the detection and investigation of integrity breaches.

3. **Availability Controls**:
   - **Redundancy**: Implementing redundant systems and data backups to ensure availability in case of hardware failures or other disruptions.
   - **Disaster Recovery Planning**: Developing and testing disaster recovery plans to ensure quick restoration of operations following an incident.
   - **High-Availability Systems**: Using high-availability architectures, such as load balancing and failover mechanisms, to maintain continuous access to critical operational data.

Specific Examples for High-Sensitivity Information Types

1. **Personal Health Information (PHI)**:
   - **Confidentiality**: Encrypting PHI both at rest and in transit using strong encryption standards (e.g., AES-256). Implementing role-based access control (RBAC) to limit access to authorized healthcare providers.
   - **Integrity**: Utilizing digital signatures to ensure the integrity of electronic health records (EHRs) and maintaining audit trails to track any modifications to PHI.
   - **Availability**: Ensuring high availability of health information systems through redundant infrastructure and robust disaster recovery plans to maintain access during emergencies.

2. **Financial Data**:
   - **Confidentiality**: Protecting sensitive financial information, such as credit card numbers, with encryption and tokenization to prevent data breaches. Using multifactor authentication (MFA) for access to financial systems.

- **Integrity**: Implementing transaction logging and monitoring to detect and prevent fraudulent activities. Using hashing to verify the integrity of financial records.
- **Availability**: Ensuring financial systems are highly available with redundant servers and real-time data replication to prevent downtime and data loss.

3. **Intellectual Property (IP)**:
    - **Confidentiality**: Securing IP, such as trade secrets and proprietary algorithms, with stringent access controls, encryption, and data loss prevention (DLP) solutions to prevent unauthorized disclosure.
    - **Integrity**: Using version control systems and digital signatures to protect the integrity of IP documentation and software code.
    - **Availability**: Implementing robust backup and recovery procedures to ensure that IP is not lost and can be restored quickly in case of system failures.

Categorizing and prioritizing information types based on their sensitivity and impact is essential for selecting appropriate security controls. By aligning these controls with the specific confidentiality, integrity, and availability requirements of each information type, organizations can effectively protect their data and comply with relevant regulations. Involving stakeholders in this process ensures that all perspectives are considered, and potential conflicts are addressed, leading to a balanced and secure system design.

Determining security objectives for different information types is a critical process in information security management. This involves assessing the requirements for confidentiality, integrity, and availability (CIA) based on the sensitivity, value, and regulatory requirements of the information. The CIA triad serves as the foundation for establishing security objectives that align with organizational goals and risk management strategies.

Process of Determining Security Objectives

1. **Identify Information Types**:
    - Catalog all types of information within the system, such as personal data, financial records, intellectual property, and operational data.
    - Understand the context and usage of each information type.

2. **Assess Sensitivity and Value**:
    - Evaluate the sensitivity of each information type based on its potential impact on the organization if compromised.
    - Consider the value of the information to the organization and its stakeholders.

3. **Regulatory and Compliance Requirements**:
    - Identify any legal, regulatory, or contractual obligations related to the information.
    - Ensure compliance with standards such as GDPR, HIPAA, or PCI-DSS.

4. **Apply the CIA Triad**:
    - Determine the appropriate level of confidentiality, integrity, and availability for each information type.

Concepts of Confidentiality, Integrity, and Availability

Confidentiality:
- Protecting information from unauthorized access and disclosure.
- Ensuring that only authorized individuals can access sensitive information.

Integrity:
- Maintaining the accuracy and completeness of information.
- Ensuring that information is not altered or tampered with by unauthorized parties.

Availability:
- Ensuring that information is accessible to authorized users when needed.
- Minimizing downtime and ensuring timely access to critical information.

Examples of Security Objectives for Different Information Types

1. **Personal Identifiable Information (PII)**:
    - **Confidentiality**: High. PII must be protected to prevent identity theft and comply with privacy regulations (e.g., GDPR).

- **Integrity**: High. Ensuring the accuracy of PII is crucial to maintaining trust and compliance.
- **Availability**: Moderate. While accessibility is important, it is not as critical as confidentiality and integrity.

2. **Financial Records**:
   - **Confidentiality**: High. Financial records contain sensitive information that could be exploited for fraud.
   - **Integrity**: High. Accurate financial records are essential for financial reporting and decision-making.
   - **Availability**: High. Financial records must be accessible for audits, reporting, and operational needs.

3. **Intellectual Property (IP)**:
   - **Confidentiality**: High. Protecting IP is critical to maintaining competitive advantage.
   - **Integrity**: High. Ensuring the accuracy and originality of IP is essential for its value and legal protection.
   - **Availability**: Moderate. While access is important for innovation and development, it is secondary to confidentiality and integrity.

4. **Operational Data**:
   - **Confidentiality**: Moderate. Some operational data may be sensitive, but not all require high confidentiality.
   - **Integrity**: High. Accurate operational data is crucial for effective business operations and decision-making.
   - **Availability**: High. Operational data must be readily accessible to support continuous business processes.

5. **Customer Orders and Transactions**:
   - **Confidentiality**: High. Protecting customer transaction details is essential for privacy and trust.
   - **Integrity**: High. Accurate transaction data is critical for financial accuracy and customer satisfaction.
   - **Availability**: High. Ensuring that transaction data is accessible at all times supports seamless customer service and operations.

How Security Objectives Differ for Various Information Types

Within the same system, security objectives can vary significantly based on the nature of the information:

Example 1: E-commerce Platform
- **Customer Data**: Requires high confidentiality to protect personal and payment information. Integrity is critical to ensure customer data is accurate. Availability is also high to support continuous transactions.
- **Product Information**: Confidentiality may be moderate, but integrity and availability are crucial to ensure customers can always access up-to-date product details and make purchases.
- **Sales Reports**: High confidentiality to protect business insights from competitors. Integrity is crucial for accurate financial reporting. Availability can be moderate as it's typically accessed periodically.

Example 2: Healthcare System
- **Patient Records**: High confidentiality to comply with HIPAA and protect patient privacy. Integrity is essential for accurate diagnosis and treatment. Availability is critical for timely medical care.
- **Administrative Data**: Moderate confidentiality, but high integrity and availability to ensure smooth hospital operations and accurate billing.
- **Research Data**: High confidentiality to protect intellectual property and patient data. Integrity is vital for the validity of research findings. Availability is moderate, primarily needed for ongoing research activities.

Determining security objectives for different information types involves a careful assessment of the sensitivity, value, and regulatory requirements of the data. Applying the principles of confidentiality, integrity, and availability ensures that each information type is adequately protected based on its specific needs. By tailoring security objectives to the unique requirements of each information type, organizations can effectively manage risks and ensure the security and reliability of their information systems. This nuanced approach helps balance the need for protection with operational efficiency, supporting both security and business goals.

Conducting a risk impact level assessment is a critical component of risk management in information security. This methodology involves evaluating the potential consequences of security breaches on an organization's operations, assets, individuals, and reputation. By determining the impact levels, organizations can prioritize risks and implement appropriate security controls to mitigate those risks effectively.

Methodology for Conducting a Risk Impact Level Assessment

1. **Identify Assets and Information Types**:

- Catalog all assets, including hardware, software, data, and personnel.
- Classify information types based on their sensitivity and importance to the organization.

2. Determine Potential Threats and Vulnerabilities:
- Identify potential threats (e.g., cyberattacks, insider threats, natural disasters).
- Assess vulnerabilities in systems, processes, and controls that could be exploited by these threats.

3. Evaluate Potential Impacts:
- Consider the consequences of successful exploitation of vulnerabilities by threats.
- Analyze the potential impacts on confidentiality, integrity, and availability of information and systems.

4. Assess Impact Levels:
- Use qualitative or quantitative methods to evaluate the severity of potential impacts.
- Assign impact levels (e.g., low, moderate, high) based on the analysis.

Factors Considered in Determining Potential Impact

1. Confidentiality:
- **Data Sensitivity**: The sensitivity of the data involved, such as personal information, financial data, or proprietary information.
- **Regulatory Requirements**: Compliance with regulations that mandate protection of specific data types (e.g., GDPR, HIPAA).

2. Integrity:
- **Data Accuracy**: The importance of data accuracy and the potential consequences of data corruption or tampering.
- **Business Processes**: The reliance of critical business processes on the integrity of data and systems.

3. Availability:
- **Service Continuity**: The necessity of system and data availability for continuous business operations.
- **Operational Impact**: The potential disruption to operations and services if systems become unavailable.

4. Reputation and Legal:
- **Reputational Damage**: The potential impact on the organization's reputation due to a security breach.
- **Legal and Financial Penalties**: The likelihood of legal actions and financial penalties resulting from non-compliance or data breaches.

Impact Levels and Security Controls

1. Low Impact Systems:
- **Impact Level**: Limited adverse effect on organizational operations, assets, or individuals.
- **Examples**: Publicly available information, non-critical applications.
- **Security Controls**: Basic security measures, such as regular software updates, antivirus software, and standard access controls.
    - **Example**: A public-facing informational website might use standard HTTPS encryption and regular backups to protect data integrity and availability.

2. Moderate Impact Systems:
- **Impact Level**: Serious adverse effect on organizational operations, assets, or individuals.
- **Examples**: Internal business processes, employee records, customer information.
- **Security Controls**: Enhanced security measures, including strong access controls, encryption, regular security audits, and incident response planning.
    - **Example**: An internal HR system containing employee records might use multi-factor authentication (MFA), encryption of data at rest and in transit, and periodic security assessments.

3. High Impact Systems:
- **Impact Level**: Severe or catastrophic adverse effect on organizational operations, assets, or individuals.
- **Examples**: Financial systems, health records, critical infrastructure.
- **Security Controls**: Robust security measures, such as advanced encryption, continuous monitoring, comprehensive incident response plans, and redundancy.

- **Example**: A financial transaction processing system might implement end-to-end encryption, real-time monitoring and alerting, secure coding practices, and disaster recovery plans to ensure high availability and data integrity.

Influence of Impact Levels on Security Controls
Low Impact:
- Basic security controls are often sufficient.
- Focus on maintaining general security hygiene.
- Controls are cost-effective and easy to implement.

Moderate Impact:
- Requires stronger security measures.
- Balances cost with the need for increased protection.
- More frequent security reviews and audits.

High Impact:
- Demands the highest level of security.
- Significant investment in advanced security technologies and processes.
- Continuous monitoring and rapid response capabilities are critical.

Conducting a risk impact level assessment involves identifying assets and information types, evaluating potential threats and vulnerabilities, and determining the consequences of security breaches. The resulting impact levels (low, moderate, high) guide the selection and implementation of security controls. By aligning security measures with the assessed impact levels, organizations can effectively mitigate risks and protect their most critical assets and information.

Data flow diagrams (DFDs) are crucial tools in understanding system scope and security requirements. They visually represent the flow of information within a system, illustrating how data moves between processes, data stores, and external entities. By mapping out these interactions, DFDs help identify potential vulnerabilities and determine appropriate security controls.

Role of Data Flow Diagrams in Understanding System Scope
1. **Visualization of Data Movement**:
   - DFDs provide a clear and concise way to visualize how data travels through a system. This helps in understanding the entire system's scope, including all processes, data stores, and external entities involved.
2. **Identification of Data Entry and Exit Points**:
   - By mapping out data entry and exit points, DFDs help identify where data enters the system, how it is processed, and where it exits. This is critical for defining system boundaries and understanding how data interacts with different components.
3. **Documentation of Data Processing**:
   - DFDs document each step of data processing, showing how data is transformed at various stages. This aids in ensuring that all data processing activities are accounted for and understood.

Contribution to Identifying Potential Vulnerabilities
1. **Highlighting Data Flow Paths**:
   - DFDs expose all data flow paths, which can be scrutinized for security weaknesses. By examining these paths, potential points of vulnerability, such as unencrypted data transmission or unsecured data storage, can be identified.
2. **Revealing Data Dependencies and Interactions**:
   - The diagrams show how different parts of the system interact with each other and how they depend on data from other components. This helps in identifying weak points where a compromise in one component could affect others.
3. **Detection of Redundant or Unnecessary Data Flows**:
   - DFDs can reveal redundant or unnecessary data flows that might introduce security risks without adding value. Eliminating these can reduce the attack surface.
4. **Assessment of Data Handling Procedures**:

- They enable a detailed assessment of how data is handled at each step, helping to ensure that data is processed securely and consistently.

Determining Appropriate Security Controls
1. **Mapping Security Controls to Data Flows**:
    - DFDs help map appropriate security controls to each data flow. For instance, data in transit can be secured with encryption, while data at rest can be protected with access controls and encryption.
2. **Prioritizing Security Measures**:
    - By highlighting critical data flows and points of vulnerability, DFDs assist in prioritizing security measures. Resources can be focused on securing the most critical or vulnerable parts of the system.
3. **Integration of Compliance Requirements**:
    - DFDs help integrate compliance requirements into the system design by showing where controls need to be applied to meet regulatory standards.

Example of DFD Revealing Previously Overlooked Security Considerations

Scenario: Consider a healthcare system that manages patient records, processes insurance claims, and interacts with external labs for test results.

DFD Insight:
- **External Entity Interactions**: The DFD shows that patient data is sent to external labs for testing. Upon reviewing the data flows, it is noticed that the data sent to the labs is not encrypted. This poses a significant risk of data interception during transmission.
- **Internal Data Stores**: The DFD highlights that patient records are stored in a centralized database accessible by multiple internal departments. It reveals that access controls are not adequately segmented, meaning all departments have broad access to the patient data, including sensitive information.
- **Data Processing**: The diagram shows that insurance claims processing involves multiple steps and intermediaries, each handling sensitive financial and personal data. However, the DFD reveals that intermediate processing steps lack proper logging and monitoring, making it difficult to detect unauthorized data access or modifications.

Security Considerations Revealed:
1. **Encryption for Data in Transit**: The need to implement encryption for data transmitted to external labs to protect patient confidentiality.
2. **Access Control Segmentation**: The requirement to segment access controls in the centralized database, ensuring that only authorized personnel can access sensitive patient information.
3. **Logging and Monitoring**: The necessity to establish comprehensive logging and monitoring for all intermediate processing steps in the insurance claims process to detect and respond to unauthorized access or data manipulation.

Data flow diagrams are invaluable for understanding system scope and identifying security requirements. By providing a clear visualization of data movements and interactions, they help uncover potential vulnerabilities and inform the implementation of appropriate security controls. The example of the healthcare system demonstrates how DFDs can reveal overlooked security considerations, guiding organizations in strengthening their overall security posture and ensuring the protection of sensitive data.

System interconnections refer to the direct connection or linking of information systems for the purpose of sharing data and resources. These interconnections can significantly impact the system scope and security compliance requirements by expanding the boundaries within which security measures must be implemented and managed.

Impact on System Scope and Security Compliance Requirements

1. Expanded Scope:
- **Broader Attack Surface**: System interconnections increase the overall attack surface, making it essential to consider security measures not just for individual systems but for the interconnected environment as a whole.
- **Shared Responsibilities**: When systems are interconnected, multiple stakeholders may be involved, requiring clear delineation of security responsibilities and collaboration between parties.

2. **Increased Complexity in Compliance**:
- **Diverse Regulations**: Different systems might be subject to various regulatory requirements. Interconnections necessitate ensuring compliance across all relevant frameworks, such as GDPR, HIPAA, or PCI-DSS.
- **Consistency in Controls**: Ensuring consistent application of security controls across interconnected systems is vital to maintaining compliance. This includes standardizing policies, procedures, and technical measures.

Impact on Risk Posture

1. Propagation of Vulnerabilities:
- **Cascading Risks**: A vulnerability in one system can propagate to connected systems, increasing the risk of widespread security breaches. For example, a compromised system could be used as a launchpad for attacks on interconnected systems.
- **Trust Relationships**: Interconnections often imply a level of trust between systems. If one system is compromised, the trust relationship can be exploited, allowing attackers to gain access to other systems.

2. Data Integrity and Confidentiality Risks:
- **Data Flow Control**: Interconnected systems require robust controls to manage and monitor data flows, ensuring that data integrity and confidentiality are maintained.
- **Access Control Challenges**: Ensuring that only authorized users can access interconnected systems and data can be more challenging, requiring more sophisticated access control mechanisms.

3. Compliance and Audit Challenges:
- **Audit Trails**: Maintaining comprehensive audit trails becomes more complex with interconnected systems, as it is essential to track and correlate events across multiple systems.
- **Unified Security Policies**: Developing and enforcing unified security policies across interconnected systems is critical to ensure a consistent security posture and compliance.

Examples of Security Controls for System Interconnections

1. Network Segmentation:
- **Purpose**: Isolates different systems and limits the impact of a potential breach by preventing lateral movement within the network.
- **Implementation**: Use firewalls, virtual local area networks (VLANs), and subnets to segment network traffic.
- **Example**: An organization might segment its internal network into separate VLANs for different departments, ensuring that a breach in one department does not easily spread to others.

2. Encryption:
- **Purpose**: Protects data in transit between interconnected systems to maintain confidentiality and integrity.
- **Implementation**: Utilize strong encryption protocols such as TLS for data transmitted over networks.
- **Example**: Implementing end-to-end encryption for data exchanges between an online banking system and its backend servers.

3. Access Controls and Authentication:
- **Purpose**: Ensures that only authorized users and systems can access interconnected systems and data.
- **Implementation**: Deploy multi-factor authentication (MFA), single sign-on (SSO), and role-based access control (RBAC).
- **Example**: Requiring MFA for administrators accessing interconnected systems and implementing SSO to streamline and secure user authentication across systems.

4. Monitoring and Logging:
- **Purpose**: Enables the detection and response to security incidents by providing visibility into activities across interconnected systems.
- **Implementation**: Use security information and event management (SIEM) systems to aggregate and analyze logs from multiple sources.
- **Example**: A SIEM solution that correlates logs from a web application, database, and network devices to detect suspicious activities indicative of an attack.

5. Intrusion Detection and Prevention Systems (IDPS):

- **Purpose**: Identifies and mitigates threats by monitoring network traffic and system activities for malicious behavior.
- **Implementation**: Deploy IDPS solutions to monitor traffic between interconnected systems and alert on or block suspicious activities.
- **Example**: Using an IDPS to monitor traffic between a public-facing web application and its backend database to detect and prevent SQL injection attacks.

6. Data Loss Prevention (DLP):
- **Purpose**: Protects sensitive data from being exfiltrated or misused, especially in interconnected environments where data sharing is common.
- **Implementation**: Employ DLP tools to monitor, detect, and block unauthorized data transfers.
- **Example**: A DLP solution that monitors email communications and file transfers between departments to prevent the leakage of sensitive customer data.

System interconnections significantly affect the risk posture and compliance requirements of organizations by expanding the scope of security measures and introducing additional complexities. By implementing appropriate security controls such as network segmentation, encryption, access controls, monitoring, and IDPS, organizations can mitigate the risks associated with interconnected systems and maintain a robust security posture. Addressing these challenges requires a comprehensive approach that considers the specific risks and requirements of each interconnected system, ensuring that security and compliance are consistently enforced across the entire environment.

Conducting a Privacy Impact Assessment (PIA) is a critical process in determining system scope and security requirements, especially when handling personal or sensitive data. A PIA helps organizations identify potential privacy risks and implement appropriate controls to mitigate them. Here's an in-depth look at the PIA process, its contributions to identifying necessary privacy controls, and its relationship with other system documentation efforts.

Process of Conducting a Privacy Impact Assessment (PIA)

1. Preparation and Planning
   - **Define Scope and Objectives**: Establish the scope of the PIA, identifying the specific system, project, or process being assessed. Clarify the objectives, such as ensuring compliance with privacy regulations or identifying privacy risks.
   - **Assemble the Team**: Gather a multidisciplinary team including privacy officers, legal experts, IT professionals, and business stakeholders.

2. Data Collection
   - **Identify Information Types**: Catalog all types of personal data being collected, processed, stored, or shared by the system. This includes PII, PHI, financial data, etc.
   - **Map Data Flows**: Create data flow diagrams to visualize how personal data moves through the system. This helps in understanding data collection points, processing activities, and data storage locations.
   - **Review Legal and Regulatory Requirements**: Identify relevant privacy laws and regulations (e.g., GDPR, CCPA, HIPAA) that apply to the data being handled.

3. Risk Assessment
   - **Identify Privacy Risks**: Evaluate potential risks to personal data, such as unauthorized access, data breaches, or non-compliance with regulations.
   - **Assess Impact and Likelihood**: Determine the potential impact of each risk on individuals and the organization, as well as the likelihood of occurrence. Use risk matrices or similar tools to prioritize risks.

4. Privacy Controls Identification
   - **Determine Existing Controls**: Identify any existing privacy controls and assess their effectiveness.
   - **Recommend Additional Controls**: Based on the risk assessment, recommend additional controls to mitigate identified risks. This may include technical measures (encryption, access controls), administrative measures (policies, training), and physical measures (secure facilities).

5. Documentation and Reporting

- **Document Findings**: Compile a detailed report that includes the data flow diagrams, risk assessment results, and recommended privacy controls.
- **Develop Action Plans**: Create action plans for implementing recommended controls, specifying responsible parties and timelines.
- **Review and Approval**: Obtain approval from senior management or relevant authorities to ensure commitment to implementing the controls.

6. Implementation and Monitoring
    - **Implement Controls**: Execute the action plans and integrate the privacy controls into the system's operations.
    - **Monitor and Review**: Continuously monitor the effectiveness of the implemented controls and review the PIA periodically to ensure ongoing compliance and risk management.

Contributions of a PIA to Identifying Necessary Privacy Controls
1. **Risk-Based Approach**: A PIA provides a structured, risk-based approach to identify and address privacy risks. By assessing the potential impact and likelihood of privacy breaches, organizations can prioritize the implementation of controls that address the most significant risks.
2. **Regulatory Compliance**: PIAs help ensure that privacy controls are aligned with relevant laws and regulations. This alignment minimizes the risk of legal penalties and enhances trust with stakeholders.
3. **Enhanced Transparency**: The PIA process involves documenting data flows and privacy practices, which promotes transparency and accountability within the organization. This transparency helps in building trust with customers and regulatory bodies.
4. **Comprehensive Control Identification**: By mapping data flows and identifying all points of personal data handling, a PIA ensures that privacy controls are comprehensive and address all areas where personal data is processed.

Relationship Between PIAs and Other System Documentation Efforts
1. **System Inventory and Asset Management**:
    - PIAs complement system inventories by providing detailed insights into personal data handled by each system component. This integration ensures that privacy considerations are included in overall asset management and risk assessments.
2. **Data Flow Diagrams (DFDs)**:
    - The data flow diagrams created during a PIA are integral to understanding system scope. These diagrams should be integrated into broader system architecture documentation to ensure a unified view of data flows and system interactions.
3. **Security Risk Assessments**:
    - While PIAs focus on privacy risks, they often overlap with security risk assessments. Integrating PIAs with security risk assessments provides a holistic view of both privacy and security risks, ensuring that controls address both aspects comprehensively.
4. **Compliance Audits**:
    - PIAs support compliance audit efforts by providing documented evidence of privacy risk assessments and control implementations. This documentation is critical for demonstrating compliance during audits and for ongoing regulatory reporting.
5. **Policy and Procedure Documentation**:
    - The findings and recommendations from PIAs inform the development and updating of organizational policies and procedures related to data protection and privacy. Ensuring that PIAs feed into policy documentation helps maintain alignment between assessed risks and organizational practices.

Example of PIA Revealing Overlooked Security Considerations
Scenario: An online retail company is developing a new customer loyalty program that collects and analyzes customer purchase histories and preferences.
PIA Insight:

- During the PIA, data flow diagrams reveal that customer purchase histories are being transmitted unencrypted between the web application and the backend database. Additionally, it is discovered that access to this data is not adequately restricted to authorized personnel only.
- The risk assessment identifies the potential for unauthorized access and data breaches, which could result in significant harm to customer privacy and regulatory penalties under GDPR.

Security Considerations Revealed:
1. **Encryption for Data in Transit**: The need to implement encryption to protect customer data as it is transmitted between the web application and the backend database.
2. **Access Controls**: The requirement to implement strict access controls to ensure that only authorized personnel can access customer purchase histories.
3. **Audit Logging**: The necessity to establish audit logging to monitor access and modifications to customer data, enhancing accountability and incident response capabilities.

Conducting a Privacy Impact Assessment (PIA) is essential for understanding system scope and determining security requirements, particularly concerning personal data. PIAs identify privacy risks and recommend appropriate controls, ensuring compliance with legal and regulatory requirements. Integrating PIAs with other system documentation efforts, such as data flow diagrams and security risk assessments, provides a comprehensive view of both privacy and security risks, leading to more effective risk management and control implementation. This holistic approach helps organizations protect personal data, build stakeholder trust, and maintain regulatory compliance.

The Federal Information Processing Standard (FIPS) 199 categorization process is a critical framework used by federal agencies to classify information and information systems according to the potential impact on the organization should a breach of security occur. This categorization is foundational for determining the appropriate security controls necessary to protect federal information systems.

Concept of FIPS 199 Categorization Process

1. Purpose:
- FIPS 199 establishes security categorization standards for federal information and information systems. The primary objective is to provide a standardized approach to assess the impact of security breaches on confidentiality, integrity, and availability.

2. Categorization Criteria:
- **Confidentiality**: Protecting information from unauthorized access and disclosure.
- **Integrity**: Ensuring the accuracy and reliability of information by preventing unauthorized modifications.
- **Availability**: Ensuring timely and reliable access to and use of information and systems.

Steps in the FIPS 199 Categorization Process

1. Identify Information Types:
- Determine the specific types of information processed, stored, and transmitted by the system. Information types are derived from the organization's mission and business processes.

2. Assess Impact Levels:
- Evaluate the potential impact of a security breach on each of the three security objectives: confidentiality, integrity, and availability.
- The impact levels are defined as:
  - **Low**: Limited adverse effect.
  - **Moderate**: Serious adverse effect.
  - **High**: Severe or catastrophic adverse effect.

3. Determine Overall Impact Level:
- Assign the highest impact level identified for any of the three security objectives to the information system. This determines the overall security categorization of the system.

4. Document and Review:
- Document the categorization decision and rationale. Regularly review and update the categorization to reflect changes in the system or the environment.

Contribution to Determining Appropriate Security Controls

The FIPS 199 categorization process directly influences the selection and implementation of security controls by providing a clear understanding of the system's risk posture. Once an information system is categorized, agencies use NIST Special Publication 800-53, "Security and Privacy Controls for Federal Information Systems and Organizations," to select appropriate security controls that align with the system's categorization.

1. Baseline Controls:
- The categorization dictates the baseline set of security controls. Systems with a higher impact level require more stringent and comprehensive controls.

2. Tailoring Controls:
- Agencies can tailor baseline controls to meet specific operational needs and risk environments, ensuring that controls are appropriate for the system's impact level.

3. Continuous Monitoring:
- High-impact systems necessitate robust continuous monitoring to quickly detect and respond to security incidents.

Examples of FIPS 199 Categorization for Various Government Systems

1. Public Website:
- **Confidentiality**: Low (publicly accessible content).
- **Integrity**: Moderate (inaccurate information could mislead the public).
- **Availability**: Moderate (downtime affects public access to information).
- **Overall Impact**: Moderate.

2. Healthcare System:
- **Confidentiality**: High (sensitive personal health information).
- **Integrity**: High (inaccurate data could impact patient care).
- **Availability**: High (system downtime could disrupt critical healthcare services).
- **Overall Impact**: High.

3. Financial Management System:
- **Confidentiality**: Moderate (financial information and transaction data).
- **Integrity**: High (errors could result in financial losses).
- **Availability**: Moderate (system downtime could delay financial operations).
- **Overall Impact**: High.

4. Email System:
- **Confidentiality**: Moderate (sensitive but not classified information).
- **Integrity**: Moderate (altered communications could lead to misunderstandings).
- **Availability**: High (essential for daily operations and communication).
- **Overall Impact**: High.

5. Research Database:
- **Confidentiality**: Low (publicly funded research data).
- **Integrity**: High (data accuracy is crucial for research validity).
- **Availability**: Moderate (availability impacts ongoing research but not critical operations).
- **Overall Impact**: Moderate.

The FIPS 199 categorization process is essential for federal agencies to systematically assess and classify information systems based on potential impacts to security objectives. This structured approach ensures that appropriate and proportional security controls are selected and implemented, thereby enhancing the overall security posture of federal information systems.

An asset inventory plays a crucial role in defining system scope and determining security requirements. It involves identifying, cataloging, and maintaining detailed records of all hardware, software, data, and network components within an organization. A comprehensive asset inventory ensures that all system components are accounted for, facilitating effective risk management and security control implementation.

Role of Asset Inventory in Defining System Scope and Determining Security Requirements

1. **Comprehensive Understanding of System Components**:
    - An accurate asset inventory provides a complete view of all system components, including hardware, software, data, and network elements. This understanding is essential for defining the scope of the system and identifying all assets that need protection.
2. **Identification of Critical Assets**:
    - By cataloging assets, organizations can identify critical assets that are vital to business operations. These assets often require more stringent security controls to ensure their confidentiality, integrity, and availability.
3. **Risk Assessment and Management**:
    - An asset inventory helps in conducting thorough risk assessments by providing detailed information about each asset's function, location, and security posture. This information is crucial for identifying vulnerabilities, assessing potential threats, and implementing appropriate risk mitigation strategies.
4. **Compliance and Regulatory Requirements**:
    - Many regulatory frameworks and standards require organizations to maintain an up-to-date asset inventory. This documentation ensures that organizations can demonstrate compliance with regulations such as GDPR, HIPAA, and PCI-DSS.
5. **Incident Response and Recovery**:
    - In the event of a security incident, an accurate asset inventory allows for quick identification and isolation of affected assets. This facilitates efficient incident response and recovery efforts, minimizing downtime and damage.

Techniques and Tools for Maintaining an Accurate Asset Inventory

1. **Automated Discovery Tools**:
    - **Network Scanning Tools**: Tools like Nmap, Nessus, and SolarWinds can scan the network to discover connected devices, software, and services.
    - **Agent-Based Solutions**: Tools like SCCM (System Center Configuration Manager) and Lansweeper deploy agents on devices to collect detailed hardware and software information.
2. **Configuration Management Databases (CMDBs)**:
    - **ServiceNow** and **BMC Remedy**: CMDBs provide a centralized repository for storing and managing asset information, relationships, and dependencies.
3. **Regular Audits and Physical Inspections**:
    - Conducting periodic physical inspections and audits helps verify the accuracy of the asset inventory and identify any discrepancies.
4. **Asset Tagging and Labeling**:
    - Using barcodes, RFID tags, or QR codes to label physical assets ensures easy identification and tracking.
5. **Integration with IT Service Management (ITSM) Tools**:
    - Integrating asset inventory with ITSM tools like **Jira** or **Cherwell** allows for real-time updates and tracking of asset changes, maintenance, and incidents.
6. **Data Classification Tools**:
    - Tools like **Varonis** and **Titus** help classify data assets based on sensitivity, ensuring that data inventory is comprehensive and aligned with security requirements.

Examples of How an Incomplete or Inaccurate Asset Inventory Might Lead to Security Vulnerabilities

1. **Unprotected Legacy Systems**:
    - **Scenario**: An organization fails to include an old server in its asset inventory. This server runs outdated software with known vulnerabilities.
    - **Consequence**: Attackers exploit these vulnerabilities to gain unauthorized access to the network, leading to a data breach.
2. **Unaccounted Shadow IT**:
    - **Scenario**: Employees use unauthorized cloud services (shadow IT) for storing sensitive data, which are not documented in the asset inventory.

- **Consequence**: These services lack proper security controls, resulting in data leaks and non-compliance with regulatory requirements.

3. **Inadequate Patch Management**:
    - **Scenario**: Due to an incomplete software inventory, an organization fails to apply critical security patches to several applications.
    - **Consequence**: Unpatched software becomes an easy target for cyber-attacks, leading to potential system compromises and data loss.
4. **Overlooked Data Storage Locations**:
    - **Scenario**: An organization does not include all data storage locations, such as external hard drives or USB devices, in its asset inventory.
    - **Consequence**: Sensitive data stored on these devices remains unencrypted and unmonitored, increasing the risk of data theft or loss.
5. **Insufficient Network Segmentation**:
    - **Scenario**: Network devices like switches and routers are not properly documented in the asset inventory.
    - **Consequence**: Without complete visibility, network segmentation policies are poorly implemented, allowing attackers to move laterally within the network and escalate privileges.
6. **Non-Compliant Software**:
    - **Scenario**: An organization uses software that is not listed in the asset inventory, and this software does not comply with industry regulations.
    - **Consequence**: The use of non-compliant software results in regulatory violations, leading to fines and legal consequences.

Example of Effective Asset Inventory Usage:
- A financial institution maintains a detailed asset inventory using automated discovery tools and a CMDB. Regular audits ensure that all assets, including endpoints, servers, and software, are accounted for. When a new regulation requires encryption of customer data, the institution quickly identifies all relevant data storage locations and applies the necessary controls, ensuring compliance and enhancing data protection.

Maintaining an accurate and up-to-date asset inventory is critical for defining system scope and determining security requirements. Techniques such as automated discovery, regular audits, and integration with ITSM tools help ensure the inventory remains comprehensive. Incomplete or inaccurate asset inventories can lead to significant security vulnerabilities, highlighting the importance of diligent asset management in securing organizational assets.

The concept of a "system of systems" (SoS) refers to a collection of independent, self-contained systems that work together to achieve a common objective or provide enhanced functionality. Each constituent system within an SoS maintains its own management, goals, and capabilities but is interlinked with others to provide comprehensive, integrated solutions.

Impact on System Scope

1. Expanded Boundaries:
- The scope of a system of systems is broader and more complex than individual systems because it encompasses the interactions and dependencies between multiple systems. This expanded scope requires a comprehensive approach to security and compliance that considers all constituent systems and their interconnections.

2. Increased Complexity:
- Managing security for a SoS involves addressing the complexities of integrating diverse systems, each with its own security policies, protocols, and requirements. Ensuring consistent security across all systems while accommodating their unique characteristics is challenging.

3. Holistic Risk Management:
- In an SoS, risk management must account for the cumulative and interconnected risks posed by each constituent system. A vulnerability in one system can impact the entire SoS, necessitating a coordinated approach to risk assessment and mitigation.

Determination of Security Compliance Requirements

- **1. Unified Compliance Framework**:
  - A SoS requires a unified compliance framework that harmonizes the security requirements of all constituent systems. This involves mapping out regulatory requirements and ensuring that each system within the SoS adheres to applicable standards.
- **2. Interoperability Standards**:
  - Compliance must address interoperability standards to ensure secure communication and data exchange between systems. Protocols and interfaces must be evaluated for compliance with security and privacy regulations.
- **3. Data Protection and Privacy**:
  - Data shared across systems must be protected according to the highest applicable standards. Compliance efforts must consider data privacy regulations (e.g., GDPR, HIPAA) and implement controls to protect data throughout its lifecycle within the SoS.

Examples of Security Controls in a System of Systems Environment

- **1. Access Control and Identity Management**:
  - **Challenge**: Ensuring consistent access control across multiple systems with different user bases and authentication mechanisms.
  - **Adaptation**: Implement federated identity management systems and single sign-on (SSO) solutions to provide unified access control. For example, using OAuth or SAML to enable secure, seamless authentication across constituent systems.
- **2. Data Encryption and Integrity**:
  - **Challenge**: Maintaining data confidentiality and integrity during inter-system communication and storage.
  - **Adaptation**: Employ end-to-end encryption protocols (e.g., TLS) for data in transit and advanced encryption standards (e.g., AES-256) for data at rest. Implement cryptographic hashing to ensure data integrity across systems.
- **3. Monitoring and Incident Response**:
  - **Challenge**: Coordinating security monitoring and incident response across multiple, autonomous systems.
  - **Adaptation**: Integrate Security Information and Event Management (SIEM) systems to collect and analyze logs from all constituent systems. Develop a centralized incident response plan that defines roles, responsibilities, and procedures for coordinated actions.
- **4. Inter-System Communication Security**:
  - **Challenge**: Securing communication channels between disparate systems.
  - **Adaptation**: Utilize Virtual Private Networks (VPNs) and secure API gateways to protect data exchanged between systems. Implement mutual authentication mechanisms to verify the identity of communicating systems.
- **5. Vulnerability Management**:
  - **Challenge**: Identifying and mitigating vulnerabilities across a heterogeneous set of systems.
  - **Adaptation**: Conduct regular, synchronized vulnerability assessments and penetration testing. Use automated patch management solutions to ensure timely updates across all systems.
- **6. Configuration Management**:
  - **Challenge**: Ensuring consistent and secure configurations across diverse systems.
  - **Adaptation**: Implement centralized configuration management tools and enforce baseline security configurations. Utilize Infrastructure as Code (IaC) practices to manage configurations programmatically.

Examples of System of Systems Environments

- **1. Smart City Infrastructure**:
  - **Components**: Traffic management systems, public transportation, emergency response, utility management.
  - **Security Controls**: Implement federated identity management for unified access, encrypt data exchanges between systems, and use SIEM for centralized monitoring.
- **2. Military Defense Systems**:

- **Components**: Command and control systems, intelligence gathering, logistics, and communication networks.
- **Security Controls**: Use secure communication protocols, employ advanced encryption for sensitive data, and integrate incident response plans across all systems.

3. Healthcare Networks:
- **Components**: Electronic health records (EHR) systems, diagnostic imaging systems, patient management systems.
- **Security Controls**: Ensure data privacy through encryption and access controls, use centralized logging and monitoring, and implement consistent vulnerability management practices.

In a system of systems environment, defining the system scope and determining security compliance requirements necessitates a holistic, integrated approach. Security controls must be adapted and enhanced to address the complexities and interdependencies inherent in such environments. By implementing robust, unified security measures, organizations can effectively manage risks and ensure compliance across all constituent systems.

Mapping information flows within a system is a detailed process that involves tracing the movement of data through various components, processes, and interfaces. This mapping provides a clear picture of how information is collected, processed, stored, and transmitted within the system. Understanding these flows is essential for defining the system's scope and identifying potential security vulnerabilities.

Process of Mapping Information Flows

1. Identify Data Sources and Destinations:
- Begin by identifying all sources of data entering the system and all destinations where data is output. This includes external entities, users, and other systems.

2. Catalog Data Types:
- Document the types of data involved, such as personal identifiable information (PII), financial data, intellectual property, and operational data. This helps in understanding the sensitivity and criticality of the data.

3. Diagram Data Movement:
- Create visual diagrams, such as Data Flow Diagrams (DFDs), to represent the flow of information. These diagrams should illustrate how data moves from one component to another, including data entry points, processing steps, storage locations, and output points.

4. Detail Data Processes:
- Document each process that handles data, including data collection, transformation, storage, and transmission. Specify the purpose of each process and the operations performed on the data.

5. Identify Data Storage Locations:
- Map where data is stored within the system, including databases, file servers, cloud storage, and other repositories. Note any temporary storage locations used during processing.

6. Map Data Transmission Paths:
- Trace the paths data takes as it is transmitted between components. Include details on communication channels, protocols used, and encryption mechanisms in place.

7. Document External Interactions:
- Identify and document interactions with external entities, such as third-party service providers, partners, and regulatory bodies. Note the data shared and the methods of transmission.

8. Validate and Review:
- Validate the information flow maps with stakeholders to ensure accuracy and completeness. Regularly review and update the maps to reflect changes in the system.

Contributions to Understanding System Scope and Identifying Potential Security Vulnerabilities

1. Comprehensive System Understanding:
- Information flow mapping provides a holistic view of the system, highlighting all components and their interactions. This comprehensive understanding is crucial for defining the system scope accurately.

2. Identification of Sensitive Data Paths:

- Mapping data flows helps identify where sensitive data travels within the system. This awareness allows for the implementation of appropriate security controls to protect critical data paths.

3. **Detection of Unprotected Data**:
    - By tracing data movements, it becomes easier to spot points where data is unprotected, such as unencrypted transmission channels or unsecured storage locations.

4. **Exposure of Redundant or Unnecessary Data Flows**:
    - Information flow maps can reveal redundant or unnecessary data flows that do not add value but increase the attack surface. Eliminating these flows reduces potential vulnerabilities.

5. **Compliance and Audit Readiness**:
    - Detailed information flow documentation helps in demonstrating compliance with regulatory requirements. It provides auditors with a clear understanding of data handling practices and controls in place.

6. **Enhanced Risk Assessment**:
    - Understanding how data flows through the system enables more accurate risk assessments. It helps identify critical points where data might be exposed to risks, guiding the implementation of targeted security measures.

Example of Information Flow Mapping Revealing Unexpected Data Exposures

Scenario: An e-commerce platform undergoes a security review to ensure compliance with PCI-DSS and protect customer payment information.

Mapping Insight:
- The information flow map reveals that customer payment data, including credit card details, is processed through multiple systems: the web application, the payment gateway, and the internal billing system.
- During mapping, it is discovered that the payment data is temporarily stored in a plaintext log file on the web server before being transmitted to the payment gateway. This storage was intended for debugging purposes but was not properly secured or encrypted.
- Additionally, the map shows that customer data is transmitted between the web application and the billing system over an unencrypted internal network, exposing it to potential interception.

Unexpected Data Exposures Revealed:
1. **Plaintext Storage**: The temporary storage of payment data in plaintext log files represents a significant security risk. If an attacker gains access to these log files, they could easily extract sensitive payment information.
2. **Unencrypted Transmission**: Transmitting customer data over an unencrypted internal network exposes it to interception and potential compromise, especially if an internal network segment is breached.

Actions Taken:
- **Encrypt Log Files**: The platform implements immediate measures to stop logging sensitive payment data in plaintext. Existing log files are securely deleted, and future logging practices are updated to exclude sensitive information or encrypt it if necessary.
- **Secure Transmission**: Encryption protocols, such as TLS, are implemented for all data transmissions between the web application and the billing system to ensure that data is protected from interception.

Mapping information flows within a system is essential for understanding the full scope of the system and identifying potential security vulnerabilities. This process involves detailed documentation of data sources, types, processes, storage locations, and transmission paths. By providing a clear visualization of how data moves through the system, information flow mapping helps detect unprotected data, redundant flows, and compliance gaps. The example of the e-commerce platform highlights how information flow mapping can reveal unexpected data exposures, guiding the implementation of targeted security measures to protect sensitive information and ensure regulatory compliance.

The concept of an "authorization boundary" is critical in the context of defining the system scope within information security. The authorization boundary delineates the limits within which an information system operates and within which the system owner has control and responsibility for implementing security measures. It essentially marks the perimeter that encompasses all components, resources, and information flows that the system's security authorization covers.

Authorization Boundary and System Scope Definition

1. Definition:
- The authorization boundary defines the exact limits of the system's responsibility, including all hardware, software, data, and communication channels that are part of the system and under its security oversight.

2. Purpose:
- It helps in identifying all components that need to be secured and ensures that there are no ambiguous areas where security responsibilities might be neglected. Clear boundaries are essential for effective risk management and compliance.

Relationship to System Interconnections and Data Flows

1. System Interconnections:
- Systems often interact with other systems outside their authorization boundary. These interactions must be well-defined to ensure that security responsibilities are clearly demarcated.
- Interconnections need to be managed with explicit agreements on security controls, data protection measures, and incident response procedures.

2. Data Flows:
- Data flowing across the authorization boundary needs to be protected both within the boundary and as it enters or exits the system.
- Encryption, access controls, and auditing are critical to safeguarding data at these points of intersection.

Examples of Unclear Authorization Boundaries and Resulting Security Gaps

1. Case of Shared Services:
- **Scenario**: Two departments within an organization share a data storage service. The boundary of this shared service is not clearly defined.
- **Potential Issue**: If neither department takes responsibility for securing the shared storage, it may lack necessary encryption, access controls, or monitoring, leading to vulnerabilities and potential data breaches.

2. Cloud Services Integration:
- **Scenario**: An organization uses a cloud service provider (CSP) to host some of its applications. The authorization boundary between the organization's on-premises systems and the CSP is not clearly established.
- **Potential Issue**: Ambiguity over who is responsible for securing data in transit and data at rest in the cloud can lead to gaps where sensitive data is exposed or inadequately protected, especially during data transfer phases.

3. Third-Party Vendor Interconnections:
- **Scenario**: An organization connects its internal customer management system with a third-party vendor's marketing platform. The authorization boundary concerning data exchange is poorly defined.
- **Potential Issue**: If it is unclear who is responsible for securing the data as it moves between systems, there may be insufficient encryption or logging, making it easier for attackers to intercept or manipulate the data.

Enhancing Clarity in Authorization Boundaries

1. Explicit Documentation:
- Clearly document the scope of the authorization boundary in system security plans, including all components, interconnections, and data flows.
- Ensure that roles and responsibilities for each component within the boundary are well defined.

2. Interconnection Security Agreements (ISAs):
- Establish ISAs with all interconnected systems, defining security requirements and responsibilities for protecting data at the boundaries.
- Include provisions for encryption, authentication, monitoring, and incident response.

3. Regular Audits and Reviews:
- Conduct regular security audits to verify that the authorization boundary is maintained and that all controls are effectively implemented.
- Review and update authorization boundaries periodically to reflect changes in the system environment or interconnections.

Practical Examples of Clear Authorization Boundaries
1. Financial Systems Integration:
- **Scenario**: A bank integrates its core banking system with an external payment gateway.
- **Control Measures**: Define clear boundaries where the bank's responsibility ends and the payment gateway's begins. Use ISAs to ensure data encryption during transmission and mutual authentication mechanisms.

2. Government Data Sharing:
- **Scenario**: A federal agency shares data with state governments through a central data repository.
- **Control Measures**: The federal agency's authorization boundary ends at the repository's interface. State agencies are responsible for securing data within their own systems. Clear agreements and documented controls ensure data protection and compliance with federal regulations.

3. Healthcare Information Exchange:
- **Scenario**: A hospital shares patient data with a health information exchange (HIE) platform.
- **Control Measures**: The hospital's authorization boundary includes all internal systems and extends to the point where data is transferred to the HIE. Security controls, such as data encryption and secure APIs, are defined at this boundary to ensure data integrity and confidentiality.

Clear and well-defined authorization boundaries are essential for effective security management in interconnected environments. They help ensure that all components within the boundary are adequately protected and that security responsibilities are clearly delineated, preventing gaps that could be exploited by malicious actors. Through explicit documentation, interconnection agreements, and regular reviews, organizations can maintain robust security postures even in complex, multi-system environments.

Threat modeling is a structured approach to identifying and prioritizing potential threats to a system, understanding their impact, and determining the necessary security controls to mitigate them. This process is crucial for determining security compliance requirements as it provides a detailed understanding of potential attack vectors and the specific controls needed to address them. Here's an analysis of the role of threat modeling in this context:

Role of Threat Modeling in Determining Security Compliance Requirements

1. Identifying Potential Attack Vectors:
- Threat modeling helps identify how an attacker might compromise a system. By understanding the various ways an attacker can exploit vulnerabilities, organizations can better anticipate and defend against potential threats.
- It involves looking at the system from an attacker's perspective, considering all possible entry points, the means of attack, and the potential impact.

2. Prioritizing Risks:
- Not all threats pose the same level of risk. Threat modeling helps prioritize these threats based on their likelihood and potential impact on the system.
- This prioritization is essential for focusing security resources on the most significant threats, ensuring that critical vulnerabilities are addressed first.

3. Defining Security Controls:
- By understanding the specific threats a system faces, threat modeling guides the selection and implementation of appropriate security controls.
- These controls are tailored to mitigate identified threats, ensuring that they effectively reduce the risk of a successful attack.

4. Enhancing Security Compliance:
- Threat modeling ensures that security controls align with regulatory and compliance requirements. By identifying specific threats and corresponding controls, organizations can demonstrate due diligence in protecting sensitive information.
- It provides a documented rationale for the chosen security measures, which is essential for compliance audits and assessments.

Contribution to Identifying Potential Attack Vectors and Necessary Security Controls

1. **Systematic Threat Identification**:
   - Threat modeling systematically identifies potential threats using various methodologies such as STRIDE (Spoofing, Tampering, Repudiation, Information Disclosure, Denial of Service, Elevation of Privilege), DREAD (Damage, Reproducibility, Exploitability, Affected Users, Discoverability), and attack trees.
   - These methodologies help uncover a comprehensive range of threats, ensuring that no significant attack vectors are overlooked.
2. **Contextual Risk Analysis**:
   - Threat modeling considers the specific context of the system, including its architecture, data flows, and user interactions. This contextual analysis is crucial for identifying realistic threats and appropriate controls.
   - It evaluates both internal and external threats, considering how different elements of the system can be targeted.
3. **Informing Security Control Implementation**:
   - By mapping identified threats to specific controls, threat modeling ensures that security measures are directly relevant to the risks faced by the system.
   - It provides a clear linkage between threats, vulnerabilities, and controls, ensuring that each control has a defined purpose and effectiveness.

Example of Threat Modeling Revealing Security Requirements

Scenario: Consider an online banking application.

Threat Modeling Insight:
- During the threat modeling process, several potential attack vectors are identified, including:
    - **Phishing Attacks**: Attackers may attempt to steal user credentials through phishing.
    - **SQL Injection**: The application might be vulnerable to SQL injection attacks on the login and transaction pages.
    - **Man-in-the-Middle (MitM) Attacks**: Data transmitted between the client and server could be intercepted if not properly encrypted.
    - **Cross-Site Scripting (XSS)**: The application may be susceptible to XSS attacks, allowing attackers to execute malicious scripts in the user's browser.

Revealed Security Requirements:
- **Multi-Factor Authentication (MFA)**: To mitigate phishing attacks, the threat modeling process recommends implementing MFA, which requires users to provide two or more verification factors to gain access.
- **Input Validation and Parameterized Queries**: To prevent SQL injection, it's identified that the application should implement strict input validation and use parameterized queries.
- **End-to-End Encryption**: For protecting against MitM attacks, the requirement for using TLS encryption for all data transmitted between the client and server is emphasized.
- **Content Security Policy (CSP) and Input Sanitization**: To defend against XSS attacks, the application should enforce a robust content security policy and sanitize user inputs.

Benefits of Threat Modeling

1. **Early Identification of Security Requirements**:
   - Threat modeling is typically performed during the design phase, allowing security requirements to be identified and integrated early in the development lifecycle. This proactive approach reduces the cost and effort of implementing security controls later.
2. **Comprehensive Risk Coverage**:
   - By considering a wide range of potential threats, threat modeling ensures that all relevant risks are addressed, providing comprehensive security coverage.
3. **Enhanced Communication and Understanding**:
   - The visual and structured nature of threat modeling aids in communicating risks and controls to stakeholders, enhancing their understanding and support for security initiatives.
4. **Continuous Improvement**:

- Threat modeling is not a one-time activity. It should be revisited periodically to address new threats and changes in the system. This continuous improvement approach ensures that the system remains secure over time.

Threat modeling is a critical process for determining security compliance requirements. It systematically identifies potential attack vectors and guides the implementation of necessary security controls, ensuring that they are directly relevant to the risks faced by the system. Through contextual risk analysis and the use of methodologies like STRIDE and attack trees, threat modeling provides a comprehensive understanding of threats and helps prioritize security efforts. An example of an online banking application demonstrates how threat modeling can reveal security requirements not apparent through other analysis methods, such as the need for MFA, input validation, encryption, and CSP. This process ensures robust protection against identified threats and supports compliance with regulatory requirements.

Selection and Approval of Framework, Security, and Privacy Controls

Identifying and documenting baseline controls for an information system involves a systematic approach to ensuring that fundamental security measures are in place to protect the system's confidentiality, integrity, and availability. This process is critical for establishing a minimum security posture that can be built upon based on the specific needs and risk profile of the organization.

Process of Identifying and Documenting Baseline Controls

1. **Understand Regulatory and Organizational Requirements**:
    - Begin by reviewing relevant regulatory requirements, industry standards, and organizational policies. Frameworks such as NIST SP 800-53, ISO/IEC 27001, and the CIS Controls provide comprehensive guidelines on baseline security measures.
    - Ensure alignment with any legal and compliance obligations that mandate specific security controls.
2. **Conduct a Risk Assessment**:
    - Perform a thorough risk assessment to identify potential threats, vulnerabilities, and the impact of security breaches on the organization. This helps prioritize the controls that address the most significant risks.
    - Use methodologies like qualitative risk assessments (e.g., risk matrices) or quantitative approaches (e.g., value-at-risk calculations) to evaluate risk levels.
3. **Select Baseline Controls**:
    - Based on the risk assessment and regulatory requirements, select baseline controls that provide foundational security. These controls should address common threats and vulnerabilities and ensure a basic level of protection.
    - Involve key stakeholders, including IT, security, compliance, and business units, to ensure that selected controls are practical and effective.
4. **Document Controls**:
    - Create detailed documentation for each baseline control, including the control objective, implementation procedures, responsible parties, and metrics for measuring effectiveness.
    - Ensure that documentation is clear, comprehensive, and accessible to relevant personnel.
5. **Implement and Monitor Controls**:
    - Implement the baseline controls across the organization. This may involve configuring systems, developing policies and procedures, and training employees.
    - Establish monitoring mechanisms to ensure that controls are functioning as intended and to detect any deviations or issues.
6. **Review and Update Baseline Controls**:
    - Periodically review and update the baseline controls to account for changes in the threat landscape, technological advancements, and evolving business needs.
    - Incorporate feedback from audits, security incidents, and continuous monitoring to improve the baseline security posture.

Determining Essential Baseline Controls

Organizations determine essential baseline controls through a combination of regulatory compliance, risk assessment, and industry best practices. Key factors include:

- **Regulatory Compliance**: Mandatory controls required by laws and regulations (e.g., GDPR, HIPAA, PCI-DSS).
- **Risk Assessment Findings**: Controls that mitigate identified high-risk threats and vulnerabilities.
- **Industry Standards**: Recommendations from industry-standard frameworks that reflect best practices for security.

Role of Risk Assessment

Risk assessment plays a crucial role in identifying baseline controls by providing a structured approach to evaluating potential threats and their impact. Through risk assessment, organizations can prioritize controls that address the most significant risks, ensuring that resources are allocated effectively. This process helps in:

- **Identifying High-Risk Areas**: Pinpointing critical assets and processes that require robust protection.
- **Evaluating Control Effectiveness**: Assessing how well existing controls mitigate identified risks and identifying gaps that need to be addressed.
- **Balancing Cost and Benefit**: Ensuring that the chosen controls provide sufficient protection without unnecessary expenditure.

Examples of Common Baseline Controls Across Frameworks

NIST SP 800-53:

- **Access Control (AC-1)**: Establish policies and procedures for granting and revoking access to information systems.
- **Audit and Accountability (AU-2)**: Implement audit logging to monitor and record system activities.
- **Configuration Management (CM-2)**: Maintain baseline configurations for information systems to ensure security settings are correctly applied.

ISO/IEC 27001:

- **A.9.2 User Access Management**: Ensure that user access to information and information processing facilities is controlled.
- **A.12.2 Protection from Malware**: Implement measures to detect and prevent malware infections.
- **A.13.1 Network Security Management**: Protect information in networks and supporting information processing facilities.

CIS Controls:

- **Inventory and Control of Hardware Assets**: Maintain an accurate inventory of all hardware devices within the organization.
- **Secure Configurations for Hardware and Software**: Establish and enforce secure configurations for hardware and software to reduce vulnerabilities.
- **Continuous Vulnerability Management**: Continuously acquire, assess, and take action on information regarding new vulnerabilities.

By systematically identifying, selecting, and documenting baseline controls, organizations can establish a solid foundation for their security posture. This foundation supports further enhancements tailored to specific threats and regulatory requirements, ensuring comprehensive protection for information systems.

Inherited controls refer to security measures implemented at a higher organizational level that are applicable and extended to lower-level systems or entities within a multi-tiered organizational structure. These controls are designed to provide a consistent security baseline across various layers of the organization, ensuring that subordinate systems benefit from standardized protective measures without the need to independently replicate them.

Impact of Inherited Controls on Overall Security Posture

Inherited controls significantly enhance the overall security posture of subordinate systems by ensuring uniformity in the application of security measures. This consistency helps in reducing the risk of vulnerabilities arising from uneven security practices across different tiers. Subordinate systems can leverage robust, centrally managed security controls such as access management, encryption protocols, and incident response plans, which are often more comprehensive and rigorously maintained at the higher organizational level.

By inheriting controls, subordinate systems save resources and effort that would otherwise be spent on developing and implementing similar controls independently. This approach not only fosters efficiency but also ensures that the subordinate systems adhere to the organization's security policies and compliance requirements.

Scenarios Where Inherited Controls Might Need Supplementation or Modification

1. Unique Operational Requirements:

- **Scenario**: A subordinate business unit operates in a regulated industry with specific security requirements that are not fully addressed by the inherited controls.

- **Solution**: The unit supplements the inherited controls with additional measures to meet industry-specific standards, such as implementing specialized encryption for financial transactions or enhanced logging for healthcare data.

2. **Advanced Threat Landscape**:
    - **Scenario**: A subsidiary located in a region with a high incidence of cyberattacks faces more sophisticated threats compared to the parent organization.
    - **Solution**: The subsidiary modifies the inherited controls by incorporating advanced threat detection and response mechanisms, such as deploying additional intrusion detection systems (IDS) and conducting more frequent security assessments.
3. **Integration with Third-Party Services**:
    - **Scenario**: A lower-tier department integrates with third-party vendors that handle sensitive data, requiring tailored security measures beyond the inherited controls.
    - **Solution**: The department supplements inherited controls by implementing vendor-specific security agreements, conducting third-party risk assessments, and applying stricter data sharing protocols.
4. **Specialized Data Handling Needs**:
    - **Scenario**: A division within the organization handles classified or proprietary information that demands higher levels of confidentiality and integrity than those covered by inherited controls.
    - **Solution**: This division modifies inherited controls to include additional data encryption standards, access control mechanisms, and physical security measures to protect sensitive information.
5. **Legacy Systems and Infrastructure**:
    - **Scenario**: A subordinate unit maintains legacy systems that are incompatible with some of the inherited security controls, posing a risk of non-compliance or security gaps.
    - **Solution**: The unit adapts the inherited controls to fit the legacy environment by implementing compensating controls, such as network segmentation, strict access controls, and enhanced monitoring to mitigate the associated risks.

Inherited controls provide a foundational layer of security across an organization's multi-tiered structure, ensuring a unified approach to risk management and compliance. However, specific operational needs, advanced threat environments, third-party integrations, specialized data handling requirements, and legacy systems may necessitate the supplementation or modification of these controls at lower tiers. By addressing these unique challenges, subordinate systems can maintain a robust security posture that aligns with both organizational standards and their specific operational contexts.

Tailoring security controls to meet specific organizational needs is a crucial process that ensures security measures are both effective and practical within the context of the organization's operations, risk environment, and regulatory requirements. This process involves adjusting baseline security controls to better align with the specific threats, vulnerabilities, and operational requirements of the organization.

Factors to Consider When Customizing Controls

1. **Risk Assessment Results**:
    - The findings from risk assessments should guide the customization of controls. Understanding the specific threats and vulnerabilities faced by the organization helps prioritize and adjust controls to address the most significant risks.
2. **Regulatory and Compliance Requirements**:
    - Different industries have varying regulatory requirements. Tailoring controls must ensure compliance with relevant regulations such as GDPR, HIPAA, PCI-DSS, and others.
3. **Business Objectives and Operations**:
    - Security controls should support, not hinder, business operations. It's essential to understand the organization's mission, objectives, and workflows to ensure that controls are practical and do not impede productivity.
4. **Resource Availability**:

- Tailoring controls should take into account the availability of resources, including budget, personnel, and technology. Controls must be feasible to implement and maintain with the available resources.
5. **Technical Environment**:
    - The existing IT infrastructure, including hardware, software, and network configurations, should be considered to ensure that tailored controls are compatible and effectively integrated.
6. **User Behavior and Culture**:
    - Understanding the behavior and culture of the organization's workforce is important. Controls should be user-friendly and should encourage compliance rather than resistance.
7. **Scalability and Flexibility**:
    - Controls should be scalable to accommodate organizational growth and flexible enough to adapt to changes in the threat landscape and business environment.

Potential Risks and Benefits of Control Tailoring

Benefits:
1. **Enhanced Relevance and Effectiveness**:
    - Tailored controls are more likely to address specific threats and vulnerabilities effectively, improving overall security posture.
    - Example: A financial institution might implement advanced encryption protocols tailored to protect sensitive financial transactions, significantly reducing the risk of data breaches.
2. **Improved Compliance**:
    - Customized controls ensure that regulatory requirements specific to the organization's industry are met, reducing the risk of non-compliance penalties.
    - Example: A healthcare provider tailors access controls to comply with HIPAA by implementing strict patient data access policies, ensuring sensitive health information is protected.
3. **Operational Efficiency**:
    - Tailoring controls can help maintain or even enhance operational efficiency by aligning security measures with business processes.
    - Example: An e-commerce company implements tailored authentication mechanisms that balance security with customer convenience, maintaining a seamless shopping experience.
4. **Resource Optimization**:
    - By tailoring controls, organizations can allocate resources more efficiently, focusing on critical areas and avoiding unnecessary expenditures.
    - Example: A small business customizes its endpoint protection strategy to focus on high-risk devices, optimizing its limited IT budget.

Risks:
1. **Inadequate Protection**:
    - If controls are overly customized or incorrectly tailored, they may fail to provide adequate protection, leaving the organization vulnerable.
    - Example: A company might downsize its incident response team to save costs, leading to delayed responses and increased damage during a security incident.
2. **Increased Complexity**:
    - Customizing controls can lead to increased complexity in security management, potentially introducing new vulnerabilities if not managed properly.
    - Example: A multinational corporation implements highly customized controls across different regions, leading to inconsistent security practices and gaps that could be exploited.
3. **Non-Compliance**:
    - Poorly tailored controls may fail to meet regulatory requirements, resulting in legal penalties and reputational damage.
    - Example: A firm tailors its data retention policies but overlooks a specific regulatory mandate, leading to non-compliance with data protection laws.
4. **Overreliance on Customization**:

- Excessive reliance on tailored controls might lead to neglect of baseline security measures, weakening the overall security framework.
- Example: An organization focuses heavily on customizing its application security controls but neglects basic network security, leading to network-based attacks.

Examples of Tailoring Scenarios
Successful Tailoring:
- **Example**: A large retail chain tailors its network security controls by segmenting its network to isolate point-of-sale (POS) systems from other corporate systems. This customization effectively reduces the risk of attackers gaining access to payment data through compromised corporate systems.

Problematic Tailoring:
- **Example**: A startup customizes its access controls to be extremely lax in order to foster a more open and collaborative environment. This decision leads to multiple security breaches as unauthorized individuals gain access to sensitive corporate data, resulting in significant financial and reputational damage.

Tailoring security controls is a nuanced process that requires balancing the specific needs and constraints of the organization with the need for robust security. By considering factors such as risk assessment results, regulatory requirements, business objectives, and resource availability, organizations can effectively customize controls to enhance their security posture while maintaining operational efficiency. However, it's crucial to manage the risks associated with customization to avoid creating vulnerabilities and ensure compliance.

Selecting appropriate control enhancements beyond baseline controls involves a structured methodology that ensures the additional controls effectively mitigate risks without imposing unnecessary costs. Organizations use a risk-based approach to determine which enhancements are necessary and cost-effective, focusing on the unique requirements of their information systems and operational environment.

Methodology for Selecting Appropriate Control Enhancements
1. Risk Assessment:
- Conduct a comprehensive risk assessment to identify threats, vulnerabilities, and the potential impact of security incidents on the organization's assets.
- Use the risk assessment results to prioritize risks based on their likelihood and potential impact.

2. Baseline Control Evaluation:
- Review the baseline security controls (e.g., those recommended by NIST SP 800-53) to determine their adequacy in addressing identified risks.
- Identify any gaps or areas where baseline controls may be insufficient to mitigate specific threats or vulnerabilities.

3. Determine Control Enhancements:
- Identify potential control enhancements that address the gaps identified during the risk assessment. Enhancements may include additional security measures, stricter implementation of existing controls, or new technologies.
- Consider the specific security requirements of the system, including regulatory and compliance obligations, industry best practices, and organizational policies.

4. Cost-Benefit Analysis:
- Evaluate the cost of implementing each control enhancement, including initial setup, ongoing maintenance, and potential operational impacts.
- Assess the benefits in terms of risk reduction, compliance, and overall security posture improvement.
- Use cost-benefit analysis to determine the most cost-effective enhancements that provide significant security improvements relative to their cost.

5. Implementation and Integration:
- Develop an implementation plan for selected control enhancements, ensuring they integrate seamlessly with existing controls and processes.
- Prioritize enhancements based on risk criticality and resource availability.

6. Continuous Monitoring and Review:

- Regularly monitor the effectiveness of implemented control enhancements through security assessments, audits, and real-time monitoring.
- Update the risk assessment and control strategy as the threat landscape evolves and new vulnerabilities emerge.

Examples of Common Control Enhancements and Their Impact

1. Multi-Factor Authentication (MFA):
- **Description**: Requires users to provide two or more verification factors to gain access to a system.
- **Impact**: Significantly enhances access control by reducing the risk of unauthorized access due to compromised credentials. It provides an additional layer of security beyond password protection.

2. Advanced Encryption Standards (AES):
- **Description**: Utilizes stronger encryption algorithms (e.g., AES-256) for data at rest and in transit.
- **Impact**: Enhances data confidentiality and integrity by making it more difficult for attackers to decrypt sensitive information without the correct key.

3. Intrusion Detection and Prevention Systems (IDPS):
- **Description**: Monitors network and system activities for malicious activities or policy violations and can take action to block or mitigate threats.
- **Impact**: Improves the organization's ability to detect and respond to threats in real-time, reducing the potential impact of security incidents.

4. Security Information and Event Management (SIEM):
- **Description**: Aggregates and analyzes log data from multiple sources to detect and respond to security events.
- **Impact**: Provides comprehensive visibility into security events across the organization, enabling quicker detection and response to incidents.

5. Data Loss Prevention (DLP):
- **Description**: Monitors and controls data transfers to prevent unauthorized data exfiltration.
- **Impact**: Protects sensitive information from being leaked or stolen, ensuring compliance with data protection regulations and protecting intellectual property.

6. Network Segmentation:
- **Description**: Divides the network into segments to limit the spread of threats and restrict access to sensitive resources.
- **Impact**: Contains potential breaches within a segment, reducing the risk of widespread impact and providing better control over access to critical systems.

7. Regular Security Training and Awareness Programs:
- **Description**: Provides ongoing education for employees on security best practices, emerging threats, and organizational policies.
- **Impact**: Enhances the overall security culture within the organization, reducing the likelihood of human error and increasing vigilance against social engineering attacks.

By following a structured methodology for selecting control enhancements, organizations can ensure they implement effective and cost-efficient measures to bolster their security posture. These enhancements, tailored to address specific risks and requirements, provide significant improvements in protecting information systems against evolving threats.

Data classification is a fundamental process in information security management, playing a crucial role in determining specific data handling requirements. By categorizing data based on its sensitivity and criticality, organizations can tailor security controls to protect data appropriately throughout its lifecycle. Here's an analysis of how data sensitivity influences the selection of security controls and how handling requirements vary across different classification levels.

Role of Data Classification in Determining Data Handling Requirements

1. **Identifying Sensitivity and Value**:
    - Data classification involves categorizing data based on its sensitivity, value, and regulatory requirements. Common classification levels include public, internal, confidential, and restricted.

- This categorization helps in understanding the potential impact of data breaches and guides the selection of appropriate security measures.
2. **Tailoring Security Controls**:
    - Based on the classification, specific security controls are implemented to ensure data is protected according to its sensitivity. More sensitive data requires stronger and more comprehensive controls.
    - Controls are selected to address risks specific to each classification level, ensuring that data confidentiality, integrity, and availability are maintained.
3. **Compliance with Regulations**:
    - Many regulatory frameworks mandate specific handling requirements for different types of data. Data classification ensures that data handling practices comply with relevant regulations such as GDPR, HIPAA, and PCI-DSS.

Influence of Data Sensitivity on Security Controls

1. Confidentiality:
- Highly sensitive data requires stringent confidentiality controls to prevent unauthorized access and disclosure.
- Example: Implementing encryption for restricted data ensures that even if data is intercepted, it cannot be read without the decryption key.

2. Integrity:
- Ensuring the integrity of sensitive data is critical to prevent unauthorized modifications that could compromise its accuracy and reliability.
- Example: Using cryptographic hash functions and digital signatures for confidential data helps detect and prevent unauthorized changes.

3. Availability:
- Availability controls ensure that data is accessible to authorized users when needed, which is especially important for critical business operations.
- Example: Implementing redundancy and backup solutions for internal and confidential data ensures that it can be restored quickly in case of system failures.

Examples of Data Handling Requirements for Various Classification Levels

1. Public Data:
- **Characteristics**: Information intended for public disclosure with no significant risk if accessed by anyone.
- **Security Controls**:
    - Minimal access controls.
    - Regular backups to ensure availability.
- **Handling Requirements**:
    - Can be stored on public websites and shared openly.
    - Basic integrity checks to ensure data is not corrupted.

2. Internal Data:
- **Characteristics**: Information intended for use within the organization, not for public release.
- **Security Controls**:
    - Access controls to limit access to employees only.
    - Regular backups and disaster recovery plans.
- **Handling Requirements**:
    - Stored on internal servers with restricted access.
    - Shared within the organization through secure channels.

3. Confidential Data:
- **Characteristics**: Sensitive information that could cause harm if disclosed or altered.
- **Security Controls**:
    - Strong access controls with role-based access.
    - Encryption at rest and in transit.

- o Regular integrity checks and audits.
- **Handling Requirements**:
    - o Stored in encrypted databases.
    - o Access restricted to authorized personnel only.
    - o Secure deletion methods to ensure data is completely removed when no longer needed.

4. **Restricted Data**:
    - **Characteristics**: Highly sensitive information with the highest impact if disclosed or altered, such as trade secrets or classified government data.
    - **Security Controls**:
        - o Multi-factor authentication for access.
        - o Advanced encryption techniques.
        - o Detailed logging and monitoring of access and changes.
    - **Handling Requirements**:
        - o Stored in highly secure, access-controlled environments.
        - o Regular security audits and compliance checks.
        - o Data masking or tokenization when used in less secure environments.

Examples of Specific Handling Requirements

Example 1: Financial Services:
- **Public Data**: Marketing materials and financial reports available on the company's website. Handling requirements include ensuring the data is up-to-date and backed up regularly.
- **Confidential Data**: Customer account information, which requires encryption, strict access controls, and regular audits to comply with regulations like PCI-DSS.

Example 2: Healthcare Provider:
- **Internal Data**: Staff schedules and internal communications, requiring access controls and regular backups.
- **Restricted Data**: Patient health records, necessitating compliance with HIPAA, including encryption, access controls, and regular integrity checks to protect sensitive health information.

Example 3: Technology Company:
- **Internal Data**: Employee contact information, requiring restricted access and secure storage.
- **Confidential Data**: Proprietary source code, which must be encrypted, access-controlled, and regularly reviewed to prevent unauthorized access or alterations.

Data classification is essential for tailoring security controls to the sensitivity and criticality of information. By categorizing data into different levels, organizations can implement appropriate security measures to protect it throughout its lifecycle, ensuring compliance with regulations and safeguarding against potential breaches. Proper handling requirements for each classification level help maintain data confidentiality, integrity, and availability, supporting overall organizational security.

Documenting control selection decisions is a critical part of an organization's risk management and compliance processes. It ensures transparency, accountability, and consistency in the implementation of security controls. Proper documentation supports the organization's efforts in demonstrating compliance with regulatory requirements and facilitates audits and reviews.

Process of Documenting Control Selection Decisions

1. Identify and Assess Risks:
- Conduct a comprehensive risk assessment to identify potential threats and vulnerabilities, and evaluate the potential impact on the organization's assets.
- Use the results of this assessment to prioritize risks based on their likelihood and potential impact.

2. Select Appropriate Controls:
- Review baseline controls (e.g., those from frameworks like NIST SP 800-53) and determine their adequacy in addressing identified risks.
- Identify additional control enhancements needed to mitigate any remaining risks effectively.
- Conduct a cost-benefit analysis to ensure the selected controls are both effective and cost-efficient.

3. Document Control Decisions:
- Clearly document each control selected, including both baseline controls and enhancements.
- Include the rationale for selecting each control, linking it directly to the identified risks and the results of the risk assessment.
- Outline how each control addresses specific risks and complies with relevant regulatory or industry standards.

Key Information to Include in Control Selection Documentation

1. Risk Assessment Summary:
- Description of the identified risks, including potential threats and vulnerabilities.
- Assessment of the impact and likelihood of each risk.
- Prioritization of risks based on their severity.

2. Selected Controls:
- List of all selected controls, categorized by baseline controls and enhancements.
- Detailed description of each control, including its purpose and implementation specifics.

3. Rationale for Control Selection:
- Explanation of why each control was chosen, including how it addresses specific risks identified in the risk assessment.
- Linkage between each control and the corresponding risk or compliance requirement it mitigates.

4. Cost-Benefit Analysis:
- Summary of the cost-benefit analysis performed for each control, demonstrating its cost-effectiveness.
- Consideration of resource allocation, including any trade-offs made during the selection process.

5. Implementation Plan:
- Timeline and steps for implementing each control.
- Identification of responsible parties and any required resources or dependencies.

6. Review and Approval:
- Record of reviews and approvals by relevant stakeholders, including security officers, IT managers, and compliance officers.
- Documentation of any feedback or modifications made during the review process.

Importance of Maintaining a Clear Audit Trail

Maintaining a clear audit trail for control selection is essential for several reasons:
- **Accountability**: Provides a record of decisions made and the individuals responsible for those decisions, promoting accountability within the organization.
- **Transparency**: Ensures that the control selection process is transparent and can be reviewed or audited by internal and external parties.
- **Compliance**: Demonstrates compliance with regulatory requirements and industry standards, facilitating audits and inspections by regulatory bodies.
- **Continuous Improvement**: Enables the organization to review past decisions, learn from them, and make informed adjustments to improve the security posture over time.

Examples of Effective Documentation Practices

1. Comprehensive Control Selection Reports:
- Create detailed reports for each risk assessment and control selection process. These reports should include all key information, such as risk summaries, selected controls, rationales, and cost-benefit analyses.
- Use standardized templates to ensure consistency and completeness in documentation.

2. Version Control and Updates:
- Implement version control for all documentation to track changes and updates over time. This practice ensures that the most current information is always available and historical changes are recorded.
- Regularly update documentation to reflect changes in the threat landscape, business processes, or regulatory requirements.

3. Centralized Documentation Repositories:

- Use a centralized documentation repository, such as a secure document management system, to store all control selection documentation. This repository should be accessible to authorized personnel and support efficient retrieval and review processes.
- Ensure the repository includes search and indexing features to facilitate quick access to specific documents or information.

4. Stakeholder Review and Sign-Off:
- Incorporate a formal review and sign-off process for control selection documentation. Key stakeholders, such as security officers, IT managers, and compliance officers, should review and approve documentation to ensure accuracy and completeness.
- Record all reviews and approvals, including the date and names of the individuals involved, to maintain a clear audit trail.

Documenting control selection decisions is vital for maintaining a robust security posture and demonstrating compliance with regulatory requirements. By including comprehensive information, maintaining a clear audit trail, and implementing effective documentation practices, organizations can ensure transparency, accountability, and continuous improvement in their security and risk management processes.

Compensating controls are alternative security measures implemented to satisfy a requirement when the primary controls are not feasible or practical. These controls provide an equivalent level of security and are essential in maintaining compliance and safeguarding information systems under various constraints. Here's an evaluation of the concept, including when and how to implement compensating controls, along with examples and potential challenges.

When to Implement Compensating Controls
1. **Technical Limitations**:
    - When the existing technology does not support the required control or the control cannot be integrated with the current system architecture.
2. **Operational Constraints**:
    - When implementing the primary control would disrupt critical business operations or processes.
3. **Cost Considerations**:
    - When the cost of implementing the primary control is prohibitive, but the risk still needs to be mitigated.
4. **Legacy Systems**:
    - When dealing with legacy systems that cannot support modern security controls but still need to be protected.
5. **Regulatory Compliance**:
    - When meeting regulatory requirements through primary controls is not possible, and an alternative measure must be used to demonstrate compliance.

How to Implement Compensating Controls
1. **Risk Assessment**:
    - Conduct a thorough risk assessment to understand the risks associated with not implementing the primary control and identify potential compensating controls that can mitigate these risks.
2. **Effectiveness Evaluation**:
    - Ensure that the compensating control provides an equivalent level of security. It should be evaluated for its effectiveness in mitigating the identified risks.
3. **Documentation**:
    - Document the justification for using compensating controls, including the reasons why the primary control is not feasible, how the compensating control meets the security requirements, and any residual risks.
4. **Approval**:
    - Obtain approval from relevant stakeholders, including security, compliance, and management, to ensure that the compensating control is acceptable.
5. **Implementation and Monitoring**:

- Implement the compensating control and establish monitoring mechanisms to ensure it remains effective over time. Regularly review and update the control as necessary.

Examples of Compensating Controls

Example 1: Financial Institution
- **Scenario**: A financial institution needs to encrypt data at rest to comply with regulatory requirements, but the legacy systems in use do not support encryption.
- **Compensating Control**: Implement strict physical security controls, such as secure access to data centers, robust access control policies, and enhanced monitoring of physical access to the data storage facilities. Additionally, implement file integrity monitoring to detect unauthorized changes.

Example 2: Healthcare Provider
- **Scenario**: A healthcare provider must ensure multi-factor authentication (MFA) for accessing electronic health records (EHR), but the EHR system does not support MFA integration.
- **Compensating Control**: Use strong, complex passwords combined with regular password changes and enhanced user training on security practices. Implement contextual authentication methods, such as monitoring user behavior and device health, to detect anomalies.

Example 3: Retail Company
- **Scenario**: A retail company needs to segment its network to isolate payment card data (PCI-DSS requirement), but the existing network infrastructure cannot be easily reconfigured.
- **Compensating Control**: Implement comprehensive endpoint security measures, such as host-based intrusion prevention systems (HIPS), advanced malware protection, and strict access controls on systems handling payment card data. Additionally, use data tokenization to protect cardholder data in transit and at rest.

Potential Challenges in Implementing Compensating Controls

1. **Equivalence in Security**:
   - Ensuring that the compensating control provides an equivalent level of security as the primary control can be challenging. It requires careful assessment and validation.
2. **Documentation and Justification**:
   - Thoroughly documenting and justifying the use of compensating controls can be time-consuming and requires a clear understanding of both the risks and the alternative controls.
3. **Approval and Acceptance**:
   - Obtaining approval from stakeholders can be difficult, especially if there is resistance to deviating from standard controls or if the compensating control is perceived as less effective.
4. **Ongoing Management and Monitoring**:
   - Compensating controls often require additional monitoring and management efforts to ensure they remain effective over time. This can increase the operational burden on security teams.
5. **Regulatory Scrutiny**:
   - Regulatory bodies may scrutinize compensating controls more closely, requiring detailed evidence that the controls are adequate and effective in meeting compliance requirements.

Compensating controls are a vital component of a flexible and adaptive security strategy. They allow organizations to maintain a robust security posture and compliance in the face of technical, operational, and financial constraints. While implementing these controls presents certain challenges, careful planning, documentation, and validation can ensure that compensating controls effectively mitigate risks and meet security objectives.

Developing a continuous compliance strategy is essential for organizations to maintain ongoing adherence to selected security controls and regulatory requirements. This approach ensures that compliance is not a one-time effort but a continuous process integrated into the organization's operations and culture. Here's how organizations can ensure ongoing adherence to selected controls and the role of automated compliance monitoring tools in this process.

Ensuring Ongoing Adherence to Selected Controls
1. Establish a Compliance Framework:

- Develop a comprehensive compliance framework that aligns with regulatory requirements, industry standards, and organizational policies. This framework should detail the specific controls and processes needed to maintain compliance.
- Regularly update the framework to reflect changes in regulations, emerging threats, and organizational changes.

2. Assign Responsibilities and Governance:
- Clearly define roles and responsibilities for compliance within the organization. This includes appointing compliance officers, security managers, and other key personnel who oversee adherence to controls.
- Establish a governance structure that includes a compliance committee or board to provide oversight and ensure accountability.

3. Regular Training and Awareness Programs:
- Implement ongoing training and awareness programs to educate employees about compliance requirements, security policies, and best practices. Ensure that all staff members understand their role in maintaining compliance.
- Use training sessions, workshops, and online modules to keep employees informed about updates and changes in compliance requirements.

4. Conduct Regular Audits and Assessments:
- Schedule regular internal and external audits to assess the effectiveness of implemented controls and identify any gaps or areas for improvement.
- Use the findings from these audits to update and enhance the compliance strategy, ensuring continuous improvement.

5. Develop Policies and Procedures:
- Create detailed policies and procedures that guide the implementation and maintenance of security controls. These documents should provide clear instructions for employees to follow and help standardize compliance efforts across the organization.
- Ensure that policies and procedures are easily accessible to all relevant personnel and are regularly reviewed and updated.

Role of Automated Compliance Monitoring Tools

Automated compliance monitoring tools play a crucial role in continuous compliance strategies by providing real-time insights, reducing manual effort, and ensuring consistent application of controls. These tools help organizations maintain compliance efficiently and effectively.

1. Continuous Monitoring and Real-Time Alerts:
- Automated tools continuously monitor systems, networks, and applications for compliance with predefined controls and policies. They can detect anomalies, unauthorized changes, and potential compliance violations in real-time.
- Example: A Security Information and Event Management (SIEM) system aggregates and analyzes log data from multiple sources, generating alerts for suspicious activities or policy breaches.

2. Automated Reporting and Documentation:
- These tools generate comprehensive compliance reports, providing detailed insights into the organization's compliance status. Automated documentation ensures that compliance records are accurate, up-to-date, and readily available for audits.
- Example: A compliance management tool that automatically generates audit reports, tracks control implementation, and maintains an evidence repository for regulatory inspections.

3. Policy Enforcement and Configuration Management:
- Automated tools can enforce compliance policies by managing configurations, applying security patches, and ensuring that systems adhere to baseline security standards. They help maintain a consistent security posture across the organization.
- Example: A configuration management tool that automatically checks system configurations against security baselines and applies necessary updates to maintain compliance.

Examples of Effective Continuous Compliance Practices

1. Continuous Vulnerability Management:
- Regularly scan systems for vulnerabilities using automated tools. Prioritize and remediate identified vulnerabilities promptly to reduce the risk of exploitation.
- Example: Implementing a vulnerability management solution that conducts weekly scans, prioritizes vulnerabilities based on risk, and integrates with ticketing systems for remediation tracking.

2. Automated Access Control Reviews:
- Use automated tools to regularly review and update user access controls, ensuring that access permissions are aligned with the principle of least privilege.
- Example: Deploying an Identity and Access Management (IAM) solution that periodically reviews user roles and permissions, flags anomalies, and automates the process of adjusting access levels.

3. Patch Management:
- Implement an automated patch management system that identifies, tests, and deploys security patches across all systems and applications.
- Example: Using a patch management tool that integrates with the organization's IT infrastructure to automatically apply patches during scheduled maintenance windows, reducing the risk of vulnerabilities.

4. Incident Response Automation:
- Develop automated incident response workflows that detect, analyze, and respond to security incidents promptly. Automation reduces response times and minimizes the impact of incidents.
- Example: Implementing an automated incident response platform that uses predefined playbooks to investigate alerts, isolate affected systems, and remediate threats.

Developing a continuous compliance strategy involves establishing a robust framework, assigning clear responsibilities, conducting regular audits, and leveraging automated tools for monitoring and enforcement. Automated compliance monitoring tools enhance the efficiency and effectiveness of compliance efforts by providing real-time insights, ensuring consistent policy enforcement, and facilitating continuous improvement. By integrating these practices, organizations can maintain a strong compliance posture and effectively mitigate risks.

Control allocation in a complex organizational structure involves distributing the responsibilities for implementing and maintaining security controls across various departments or teams. This ensures that all aspects of the organization's security posture are addressed and maintained consistently. Here's an in-depth look at the process, challenges, and strategies for effective coordination in control allocation.

Process of Control Allocation
1. **Identify Controls and Objectives**:
    - Determine the specific security controls required based on risk assessments, regulatory requirements, and organizational policies. Define clear objectives for each control, outlining what it aims to achieve.
2. **Map Controls to Organizational Units**:
    - Identify which departments or teams are best suited to implement and maintain each control. This mapping should consider each unit's expertise, role, and operational capabilities.
3. **Define Responsibilities and Roles**:
    - Clearly define the responsibilities for each control, including implementation, maintenance, monitoring, and reporting. Assign specific roles to individuals or teams within the relevant departments.
4. **Develop Implementation Plans**:
    - Create detailed plans for implementing each control, including timelines, resource allocation, and specific tasks. Ensure that all involved parties understand their roles and the overall plan.
5. **Coordinate and Communicate**:
    - Establish communication channels and coordination mechanisms to ensure that all departments and teams work together effectively. Regular meetings, status reports, and collaboration tools can facilitate this coordination.
6. **Monitor and Review**:

- Implement monitoring and review processes to ensure that controls are functioning as intended. Regular audits, assessments, and feedback loops help maintain control effectiveness and identify areas for improvement.

Distribution of Responsibilities

1. IT and Security Teams:
- **Implementation**: Responsible for the technical implementation of controls, such as firewalls, intrusion detection systems, encryption, and access controls.
- **Maintenance**: Ongoing management and updating of technical controls, ensuring they remain effective against evolving threats.
- **Monitoring**: Continuous monitoring of network traffic, system logs, and security alerts to detect and respond to incidents.

2. Compliance and Risk Management:
- **Implementation**: Ensure that controls align with regulatory requirements and organizational risk management policies.
- **Monitoring**: Conduct regular compliance audits and risk assessments to verify that controls are in place and effective.
- **Reporting**: Provide reports on compliance status and risk exposure to senior management and regulatory bodies.

3. Human Resources (HR):
- **Implementation**: Develop and enforce policies related to employee behavior, such as acceptable use policies, security awareness training, and incident response protocols.
- **Monitoring**: Monitor compliance with HR-related controls through performance reviews and training records.
- **Reporting**: Report on employee compliance and incidents to the security and risk management teams.

4. Business Units:
- **Implementation**: Apply relevant controls to protect business-specific processes and data, such as securing customer information or financial records.
- **Maintenance**: Ensure that business processes adhere to security policies and update practices as necessary.
- **Monitoring**: Track and report any deviations from security practices or potential risks identified within the business unit.

Potential Challenges in Control Allocation

1. **Coordination Across Departments**:
   - Ensuring that all departments work together effectively can be challenging, especially in large organizations with diverse functions and priorities.
2. **Resource Constraints**:
   - Different departments may have varying levels of resources, which can impact their ability to implement and maintain controls effectively.
3. **Communication Gaps**:
   - Lack of clear communication channels and protocols can lead to misunderstandings and gaps in control implementation and monitoring.
4. **Resistance to Change**:
   - Departments may resist changes to their processes or additional responsibilities, hindering the implementation of new controls.
5. **Consistency and Standardization**:
   - Ensuring that controls are implemented consistently across all departments can be difficult, particularly when dealing with different systems and processes.

Strategies for Effective Coordination

1. **Establish Clear Governance Structures**:

            - ○ Create a governance framework that defines the roles, responsibilities, and reporting lines for all departments involved in control allocation. This should include a central oversight body or committee to ensure coordination and accountability.
    2. **Develop Standardized Procedures**:
        - ○ Implement standardized procedures for control implementation, monitoring, and reporting. This ensures consistency and makes it easier to coordinate efforts across different departments.
    3. **Enhance Communication and Collaboration**:
        - ○ Use collaboration tools and regular meetings to facilitate communication between departments. Establish clear communication protocols and ensure that all relevant parties are kept informed of progress and issues.
    4. **Provide Training and Support**:
        - ○ Offer training and resources to help departments understand their roles and responsibilities. Providing ongoing support and guidance can help overcome resistance and ensure effective implementation of controls.
    5. **Monitor and Adjust**:
        - ○ Continuously monitor the effectiveness of control allocation and make adjustments as necessary. Regular reviews and feedback loops can help identify and address any issues that arise.
    6. **Foster a Security Culture**:
        - ○ Promote a culture of security awareness and responsibility across the organization. Encourage all employees to take ownership of security practices and understand the importance of their role in protecting the organization.

Effective control allocation in a complex organizational structure requires careful planning, clear communication, and ongoing coordination. By mapping controls to the appropriate departments, defining roles and responsibilities, and implementing standardized procedures, organizations can ensure that security measures are applied consistently and effectively. Addressing potential challenges through governance structures, training, and continuous monitoring helps maintain a robust security posture and supports the organization's overall security goals.

Stakeholder agreement in the control selection process is crucial for ensuring that security measures align with the organization's overall goals, comply with regulatory requirements, and address the specific needs of different departments or business units. Engaging stakeholders early and continuously helps build consensus, facilitates the adoption of security controls, and enhances the overall security posture.

Importance of Stakeholder Agreement

1. Alignment with Organizational Goals:
- Stakeholders from different departments (e.g., IT, finance, legal, HR) bring diverse perspectives and expertise, ensuring that selected controls support the organization's strategic objectives.
- Agreement ensures that security measures are not only technically sound but also practical and aligned with business processes.

2. Compliance and Risk Management:
- Engaging stakeholders helps ensure that all regulatory and compliance requirements are considered and met.
- Stakeholders can identify unique risks associated with their functions, leading to a more comprehensive risk management strategy.

3. Resource Allocation:
- Consensus on control selection helps in prioritizing resources effectively, ensuring that critical areas receive the necessary funding and support.
- Avoids conflicts and redundancy, optimizing the use of resources across the organization.

Balancing Potentially Conflicting Stakeholder Requirements

1. Understanding Stakeholder Needs:
- Conduct thorough consultations with stakeholders to understand their specific needs, concerns, and priorities.
- Use tools like surveys, interviews, and workshops to gather detailed input from each stakeholder group.

2. Prioritization and Trade-offs:
- Assess and prioritize requirements based on risk assessments, business impact, and regulatory obligations.
- Make informed trade-offs by balancing the importance of security controls against their impact on business operations and resources.

3. Transparency and Communication:
- Maintain open and transparent communication throughout the process. Clearly explain the rationale behind control selection decisions.
- Use regular meetings, status updates, and detailed documentation to keep stakeholders informed and engaged.

Examples of Successful Stakeholder Engagement Strategies

1. Stakeholder Steering Committees:
- Establish a steering committee comprising representatives from key departments to oversee the control selection process.
- Example: A financial services company forms a steering committee with members from IT, legal, compliance, and business operations to guide the implementation of new data protection controls.

2. Workshops and Collaborative Sessions:
- Organize workshops to facilitate collaborative discussions and brainstorming sessions. This approach helps stakeholders understand each other's perspectives and jointly develop solutions.
- Example: An e-commerce company conducts workshops with marketing, IT, and customer service teams to align on security measures for protecting customer data while ensuring a seamless user experience.

3. Pilot Programs and Proof of Concepts:
- Implement pilot programs to test selected controls in a controlled environment. Gather feedback from stakeholders to refine and optimize controls before full-scale deployment.
- Example: A healthcare provider runs a pilot program for a new access control system in one department, collects feedback, and makes necessary adjustments before rolling it out across the entire organization.

Methods for Resolving Disagreements

1. Facilitated Discussions:
- Use neutral facilitators to guide discussions and mediate conflicts. Facilitators help ensure that all voices are heard and that discussions remain focused on finding solutions.
- Example: An external consultant facilitates discussions between IT and HR departments to resolve differences over employee monitoring controls, ensuring a balance between security and privacy.

2. Decision Matrices and Weighted Scoring:
- Develop decision matrices that use weighted scoring to evaluate and prioritize control options based on various criteria such as risk reduction, cost, impact on operations, and compliance.
- Example: A manufacturing company uses a weighted scoring matrix to evaluate different cybersecurity tools, considering factors like effectiveness, ease of use, and budget constraints.

3. Executive Arbitration:
- In cases where consensus cannot be reached, escalate the decision to senior executives or a designated decision-making body. Executives can provide a strategic perspective and make final decisions.
- Example: A retail chain's CISO escalates a disagreement over cloud security controls to the executive board, which makes a final decision based on the company's risk tolerance and strategic goals.

4. Compromise and Iterative Solutions:
- Encourage stakeholders to compromise and adopt iterative solutions. Implement controls incrementally, allowing for adjustments based on feedback and changing requirements.
- Example: A technology firm agrees to implement basic encryption controls immediately and plans to enhance them in subsequent phases, addressing both immediate security needs and long-term goals.

Stakeholder agreement in the control selection process is vital for aligning security measures with organizational goals, ensuring compliance, and managing risks effectively. Organizations can balance conflicting requirements through thorough consultations, prioritization, transparent communication, and collaborative engagement strategies.

When disagreements arise, facilitated discussions, decision matrices, executive arbitration, and iterative solutions can help resolve conflicts and achieve consensus. By fostering a collaborative environment, organizations can ensure that their security controls are effective, efficient, and broadly supported.

The concept of "defense-in-depth" is a strategic approach in information security that employs multiple layers of controls to protect information systems. This principle is based on the idea that if one control fails, additional layers of security will provide backup protection, reducing the overall risk of compromise. By implementing overlapping security measures, organizations can create a more resilient security posture that is harder for attackers to penetrate. Here's an evaluation of how defense-in-depth influences control selection and implementation, along with examples of its application across different layers of an information system.

Influence of Defense-in-Depth on Control Selection and Implementation
1. **Layered Security Approach**:
    - Defense-in-depth encourages the use of multiple, diverse security controls at different layers of the information system. This includes physical, technical, and administrative controls that work together to provide comprehensive protection.
2. **Redundancy and Backup**:
    - By deploying overlapping controls, organizations ensure that the failure or bypass of one control does not lead to a complete security breakdown. Each layer acts as a backup to the others.
3. **Diverse Control Types**:
    - Defense-in-depth promotes the use of a variety of control types (preventive, detective, corrective) to address different aspects of security and create a holistic defense mechanism.
4. **Contextual Adaptation**:
    - The principle requires security controls to be adapted to the specific context and risks associated with each layer of the system. This ensures that controls are relevant and effective in addressing the unique threats at each level.
5. **Increased Complexity for Attackers**:
    - Multiple layers of security increase the complexity and effort required for attackers to breach the system. This can deter attackers and increase the likelihood of detection before significant damage occurs.

Examples of Defense-in-Depth Across Different Layers
1. Physical Layer:
- **Controls**: Physical security measures include locked doors, security guards, surveillance cameras, and access control systems.
- **Application**: In a data center, access might be restricted to authorized personnel using biometric authentication, monitored by security cameras, and reinforced by physical barriers such as locked server racks.

2. Network Layer:
- **Controls**: Network security controls include firewalls, intrusion detection/prevention systems (IDS/IPS), virtual private networks (VPNs), and network segmentation.
- **Application**: A corporate network might use a perimeter firewall to block unauthorized traffic, IDS/IPS to monitor and block suspicious activities, VPNs to secure remote access, and segmentation to isolate sensitive network segments from the rest of the network.

3. Endpoint Layer:
- **Controls**: Endpoint security controls encompass antivirus software, endpoint detection and response (EDR) tools, and device encryption.
- **Application**: Employee laptops could be equipped with antivirus software to detect and block malware, EDR tools to monitor and respond to suspicious activities, and full-disk encryption to protect data in case the device is lost or stolen.

4. Application Layer:
- **Controls**: Application security measures include secure coding practices, application firewalls, input validation, and regular security testing.

- **Application**: A web application might use input validation to prevent SQL injection attacks, an application firewall to block malicious traffic, and undergo regular penetration testing to identify and fix vulnerabilities.

5. **Data Layer**:
    - **Controls**: Data security controls involve encryption, access controls, data masking, and backup solutions.
    - **Application**: Sensitive customer data might be encrypted both at rest and in transit, with access restricted to authorized users only. Data masking could be used to obscure sensitive information in non-production environments, and regular backups ensure data can be restored in case of corruption or loss.

6. **User Layer**:
    - **Controls**: User-focused controls include strong authentication mechanisms, user training and awareness programs, and role-based access controls (RBAC).
    - **Application**: Employees might use multi-factor authentication (MFA) to access critical systems, participate in regular security awareness training to recognize phishing attempts, and have their access rights restricted based on their job roles and responsibilities.

Challenges and Considerations

1. **Complexity and Management**:
    - Implementing multiple layers of security controls can increase the complexity of the security architecture, making it more challenging to manage and maintain. Organizations need robust processes and tools to ensure that all controls are functioning as intended.
2. **Cost**:
    - Defense-in-depth can be resource-intensive, both in terms of financial cost and manpower. Organizations need to balance the benefits of additional security layers with the associated costs.
3. **Integration and Compatibility**:
    - Ensuring that different security controls work seamlessly together is crucial. Poor integration can lead to gaps in security coverage or conflicts between controls.
4. **User Experience**:
    - Security measures should be designed to minimize disruption to users while maintaining effectiveness. Overly stringent controls can lead to user frustration and potential circumvention of security measures.

Defense-in-depth is a comprehensive security strategy that involves deploying multiple layers of controls across different aspects of an information system. By considering the unique risks and requirements of each layer, organizations can implement diverse and overlapping controls that provide robust protection against various threats. This approach not only increases the complexity for attackers but also ensures that the failure of one control does not compromise the entire system. Effective implementation of defense-in-depth requires careful planning, coordination, and ongoing management to address the challenges associated with this multi-layered security approach.

Threat intelligence plays a crucial role in the control selection process by providing organizations with timely, relevant, and actionable information about current and emerging threats. By leveraging threat intelligence, organizations can make informed decisions about which security controls to implement, prioritize, or enhance to better protect their assets and data against potential attacks.

Role of Threat Intelligence in Control Selection

1. Informed Risk Assessment:
- Threat intelligence enhances the risk assessment process by providing detailed insights into the latest threats, attack vectors, and tactics used by adversaries. This information helps organizations accurately assess the risks they face.
- By understanding the threat landscape, organizations can identify which assets are most likely to be targeted and which vulnerabilities are being actively exploited.

2. Prioritization of Controls:
- Threat intelligence helps prioritize security controls based on the likelihood and impact of threats. Organizations can focus their resources on implementing controls that address the most significant risks.
- For example, if threat intelligence indicates a surge in ransomware attacks, organizations might prioritize controls related to data backup, network segmentation, and endpoint protection.

3. Adaptation to Emerging Threats:
- Threat intelligence allows organizations to stay ahead of emerging threats by continuously adapting their security controls. This proactive approach ensures that controls remain effective against the evolving threat landscape.
- Regular updates to threat intelligence enable organizations to identify new vulnerabilities and attack patterns, prompting timely adjustments to their security posture.

4. Enhanced Incident Response:
- Integrating threat intelligence into incident response plans ensures that organizations are prepared to respond to specific types of attacks. Knowing the characteristics and indicators of compromise (IOCs) of particular threats helps in quicker detection and response.
- Incident response teams can use threat intelligence to develop playbooks and response strategies tailored to the most relevant threats.

Leveraging Threat Intelligence to Inform Control Choices

1. Source and Analyze Threat Intelligence:
- Collect threat intelligence from various sources, including threat feeds, security vendors, industry reports, and information-sharing platforms such as ISACs (Information Sharing and Analysis Centers).
- Analyze the gathered intelligence to identify patterns, trends, and specific threats that could impact the organization.

2. Integrate with Risk Management Frameworks:
- Incorporate threat intelligence into existing risk management frameworks (e.g., NIST RMF) to ensure that control selection is based on the latest threat data.
- Use threat modeling techniques to map identified threats to potential vulnerabilities and assess their impact on the organization.

3. Update Control Baselines:
- Regularly update the organization's control baseline based on the latest threat intelligence. Ensure that baseline controls address newly identified threats and vulnerabilities.
- For example, if threat intelligence reveals a new type of malware targeting specific software, update the baseline controls to include measures such as patch management and malware detection specific to that software.

4. Communicate and Educate:
- Share threat intelligence findings with relevant stakeholders, including security teams, management, and employees. Ensure that everyone understands the importance of the selected controls and the threats they mitigate.
- Conduct training sessions and awareness programs to keep staff informed about emerging threats and the controls in place to address them.

Examples of Emerging Threats Necessitating Changes to Control Baseline

1. Ransomware Attacks:
- **Emerging Threat**: Increasingly sophisticated ransomware attacks targeting critical infrastructure and sensitive data.
- **Control Changes**: Enhance data backup procedures, implement network segmentation to limit the spread of ransomware, deploy advanced endpoint detection and response (EDR) solutions, and conduct regular phishing training for employees to prevent initial infection vectors.

2. Supply Chain Attacks:
- **Emerging Threat**: Attacks targeting third-party vendors and software supply chains to compromise the organization indirectly.
- **Control Changes**: Implement stricter vendor management practices, conduct thorough security assessments of third-party vendors, enforce the use of software bills of materials (SBOMs) to track software components, and deploy monitoring tools to detect anomalies in software behavior.

3. Zero-Day Vulnerabilities:
- **Emerging Threat**: Exploitation of previously unknown vulnerabilities in widely used software and hardware.

- **Control Changes**: Adopt a more aggressive patch management strategy to quickly apply updates and patches, use threat intelligence feeds to stay informed about zero-day vulnerabilities, and deploy application whitelisting to limit the execution of unauthorized applications.

4. Advanced Persistent Threats (APTs):
- **Emerging Threat**: Sophisticated, long-term attacks aimed at stealing sensitive data or disrupting operations.
- **Control Changes**: Implement advanced network monitoring and anomaly detection tools, deploy deception technologies (e.g., honeypots) to detect and analyze APT activities, enhance user access controls, and conduct regular security audits and penetration testing to identify and mitigate vulnerabilities.

By leveraging threat intelligence, organizations can make more informed decisions about control selection, ensuring that their security measures are aligned with the current threat landscape. This approach helps maintain a robust security posture, effectively mitigating risks and protecting critical assets against both known and emerging threats.

Conducting a gap analysis between existing controls and required controls is an essential process in ensuring that an organization's security posture meets its objectives and compliance requirements. This process involves comparing the current state of controls against the desired state to identify deficiencies, prioritize remediation efforts, and strengthen overall security.

Process of Conducting a Gap Analysis
1. **Define Objectives and Scope**:
   - Establish the goals of the gap analysis, such as compliance with specific regulations (e.g., GDPR, HIPAA), alignment with security frameworks (e.g., NIST, ISO/IEC 27001), or improving overall security posture.
   - Determine the scope of the analysis, including systems, processes, and control areas to be reviewed.
2. **Inventory Existing Controls**:
   - Document all current security controls, including technical, administrative, and physical controls. Use tools like control frameworks, control catalogs, and security policies to gather this information.
   - Ensure that the inventory is comprehensive and accurately reflects the current state of controls.
3. **Identify Required Controls**:
   - Define the desired state of controls based on regulatory requirements, industry standards, and organizational policies.
   - Utilize established frameworks like NIST SP 800-53, ISO/IEC 27001, or CIS Controls to determine required controls.
4. **Compare Existing and Required Controls**:
   - Conduct a detailed comparison of existing controls against the required controls to identify gaps. This involves mapping each required control to the corresponding existing control and noting any deficiencies or absences.
   - Use tools like control matrices or gap analysis templates to organize and visualize the comparison.
5. **Document Findings**:
   - Create a comprehensive report that outlines identified gaps, including descriptions of each gap, its potential impact, and the associated risks.
   - Include supporting documentation and evidence to provide a clear understanding of the current control environment and the gaps.

Methodologies for Identifying Control Gaps
1. **Control Framework Mapping**:
   - Use a control framework (e.g., NIST SP 800-53, ISO/IEC 27001) to map existing controls to required controls. This structured approach ensures that all necessary controls are considered and gaps are systematically identified.
2. **Interviews and Workshops**:
   - Conduct interviews and workshops with key stakeholders, including IT, security, compliance, and business units, to gather insights into the current control environment and identify areas where controls may be lacking.

3. **Self-Assessments and Audits**:
    - Perform self-assessments or internal audits to evaluate the effectiveness of existing controls. Use standardized checklists and questionnaires to ensure consistency and thoroughness.
4. **Automated Tools**:
    - Utilize automated tools and platforms that support control gap analysis. These tools can streamline the process by automatically mapping controls, identifying gaps, and generating reports.

Strategies for Prioritizing and Addressing Identified Gaps

1. **Risk Assessment and Prioritization**:
    - Assess the risk associated with each identified gap based on its potential impact and likelihood of exploitation. Use risk assessment methodologies such as qualitative (e.g., risk matrices) or quantitative (e.g., probabilistic risk assessment) approaches.
    - Prioritize gaps based on the assessed risk, focusing on those that pose the greatest threat to the organization's security and compliance.
2. **Develop a Remediation Plan**:
    - Create a detailed remediation plan that outlines the steps needed to address each gap. Include timelines, resource requirements, and responsible parties for implementing the necessary controls.
    - Ensure that the plan is realistic and achievable within the organization's resource constraints.
3. **Implement Quick Wins**:
    - Identify and implement "quick wins"—gaps that can be addressed with minimal effort and resources but provide significant security improvements. This can help build momentum and demonstrate progress.
4. **Leverage Existing Resources**:
    - Utilize existing tools, technologies, and processes to address gaps wherever possible. This can reduce the time and cost associated with implementing new controls.
5. **Continuous Monitoring and Review**:
    - Establish continuous monitoring and review processes to track the implementation of remediation efforts and ensure that gaps are effectively closed. Regularly update the gap analysis to reflect changes in the control environment and emerging threats.

Examples of Prioritizing and Addressing Gaps

Example 1: Financial Institution Compliance with PCI-DSS:
- **Identified Gap**: Lack of encryption for cardholder data at rest.
- **Risk Assessment**: High risk due to the potential for data breaches and non-compliance with PCI-DSS requirements.
- **Remediation Plan**: Implement encryption solutions for databases and storage systems that handle cardholder data. Allocate budget for encryption software and hardware, and assign IT and security teams to deploy and manage the encryption.

Example 2: Healthcare Provider Compliance with HIPAA:
- **Identified Gap**: Insufficient access controls for electronic health records (EHRs).
- **Risk Assessment**: Medium risk due to potential unauthorized access to sensitive patient information.
- **Remediation Plan**: Implement role-based access controls (RBAC) to ensure that only authorized personnel can access EHRs. Conduct training sessions for staff on the new access control policies and update existing systems to support RBAC.

Example 3: Manufacturing Company Alignment with NIST SP 800-53:
- **Identified Gap**: Lack of incident response procedures.
- **Risk Assessment**: High risk due to the potential for delayed or ineffective response to security incidents.
- **Remediation Plan**: Develop and document comprehensive incident response procedures, including identification, containment, eradication, and recovery steps. Conduct incident response drills and training for the IT and security teams to ensure preparedness.

Conducting a gap analysis is a systematic process that involves comparing existing controls against required controls to identify deficiencies. By using methodologies such as control framework mapping, interviews, self-assessments, and automated tools, organizations can effectively identify control gaps. Prioritizing and addressing these gaps through risk assessment, remediation planning, quick wins, leveraging existing resources, and continuous monitoring ensures that the organization maintains a robust security posture and meets its compliance requirements.

The concept of "least functionality" in control selection refers to the principle of configuring systems to operate with only the necessary features, services, and capabilities required to perform their intended functions. By minimizing the functionalities available within a system, organizations can reduce potential attack vectors and enhance their overall security posture.

Impact on Choice of System Components and Features
1. Minimization of Attack Surface:
- By disabling unnecessary features and services, the number of potential entry points for attackers is reduced. Each additional feature or service can introduce vulnerabilities that could be exploited.
- Limiting system functionality to essential components means there are fewer aspects of the system to secure, making it easier to manage and protect.

2. Simplified Configuration Management:
- Systems with minimal functionality are simpler to configure, monitor, and maintain. This simplicity reduces the risk of misconfigurations, which are common sources of security breaches.
- Simplified systems are also easier to audit, ensuring that all components comply with security policies and standards.

3. Enhanced Performance and Stability:
- Removing extraneous features can improve system performance and stability by reducing the load on resources. This can lead to faster, more reliable systems that are easier to troubleshoot and maintain.

Examples of Implementing Least Functionality
1. Operating Systems:
- **Example**: On a server, unnecessary services such as FTP, telnet, or web services that are not needed for the server's primary function are disabled.
- **Impact**: This reduces the number of services that could potentially be exploited by attackers. By disabling unused ports and services, the server becomes less susceptible to network-based attacks.

2. Application Software:
- **Example**: In a corporate environment, user workstations are configured to include only essential software applications. Advanced features of productivity software that are not required for most users' daily tasks are disabled.
- **Impact**: Reducing the number of applications and features decreases the likelihood of software vulnerabilities being exploited. It also limits the potential impact of malware or other malicious software that often leverages unnecessary functionalities.

3. Network Devices:
- **Example**: On a network router, administrative interfaces that are not needed (e.g., SNMP if not used for network management) are disabled. Additionally, features such as UPnP, which are not necessary for enterprise environments, are turned off.
- **Impact**: Disabling unnecessary network services and interfaces reduces the risk of unauthorized access and mitigates potential vulnerabilities that could be exploited remotely.

4. Database Systems:
- **Example**: A database management system is configured to disable features not required for the application, such as certain database engines, stored procedures, or unused extensions.
- **Impact**: This reduces the attack surface by limiting the ways in which the database can be interacted with and helps prevent SQL injection attacks or other database-specific exploits.

5. User Accounts and Permissions:

- **Example**: User accounts are granted only the permissions necessary to perform their job functions. Administrative privileges are restricted to those who absolutely need them.
- **Impact**: Limiting user privileges helps prevent the exploitation of elevated permissions, which could lead to broader system compromises. It also minimizes the risk of insider threats.

6. Web Applications:
- **Example**: A web application is designed with only the necessary modules and plugins. Optional features that are not essential for the core functionality, such as social media integration or advanced analytics, are not included in the deployed version.
- **Impact**: By reducing the number of external integrations and plugins, the application has fewer dependencies and potential vulnerabilities, making it more secure against attacks like cross-site scripting (XSS) or SQL injection.

Implementing the principle of least functionality involves carefully evaluating the necessity of each component, feature, and service within a system. By minimizing functionalities to what is essential, organizations can significantly reduce their attack surface, leading to improved security and manageability. This principle is a key aspect of a robust security strategy, contributing to more resilient and secure information systems.

Quantitative risk analysis plays a crucial role in control selection by providing a data-driven approach to evaluate the potential impact of risks and the effectiveness of various control options. This method involves the use of numerical data and statistical techniques to estimate the likelihood and impact of different risks, helping organizations make informed decisions about where to invest in security controls.

Using Quantitative Methods to Assess Cost-Effectiveness of Controls

1. **Risk Quantification**:
    - **Annualized Loss Expectancy (ALE)**: Calculate the expected monetary loss for each risk per year by multiplying the single loss expectancy (SLE) by the annual rate of occurrence (ARO). ALE helps quantify the financial impact of risks.
    - **Expected Monetary Value (EMV)**: Use EMV to evaluate potential costs and benefits of different control options by assigning probabilities to various outcomes and calculating their expected values.
2. **Cost-Benefit Analysis (CBA)**:
    - Compare the costs of implementing a control against the quantified reduction in risk. This involves calculating the Return on Security Investment (ROSI) by dividing the risk reduction (savings from reduced ALE) by the cost of the control.
    - Prioritize controls that offer the highest ROSI, ensuring that resources are allocated to the most cost-effective security measures.
3. **Sensitivity Analysis**:
    - Assess how changes in key variables (e.g., likelihood of occurrence, impact severity) affect the overall risk and control effectiveness. This helps identify which controls remain effective under varying conditions and which are most sensitive to changes.
4. **Monte Carlo Simulation**:
    - Use Monte Carlo simulations to model the probability distributions of risks and control outcomes. By running numerous simulations, organizations can gain insights into the range of possible impacts and the likelihood of different scenarios, providing a more robust basis for decision-making.

Limitations of Quantitative Approaches

1. **Data Quality and Availability**:
    - Quantitative methods rely on accurate and comprehensive data, which may not always be available. Incomplete or inaccurate data can lead to unreliable results.
2. **Complexity**:
    - Quantitative risk analysis can be complex and require specialized knowledge and tools. Smaller organizations may lack the resources or expertise to perform detailed quantitative analysis effectively.

3. **Uncertainty and Assumptions**:
    - Quantitative analysis often involves assumptions about probabilities and impacts, which can introduce uncertainty. If these assumptions are flawed, the analysis may not accurately reflect the real-world situation.
4. **Focus on Financial Metrics**:
    - Quantitative methods primarily focus on financial impacts, potentially overlooking qualitative factors such as reputational damage, legal implications, and customer trust.

Combining Quantitative and Qualitative Assessments

To address the limitations of quantitative methods and enhance decision-making, organizations can combine quantitative and qualitative assessments.

1. **Qualitative Risk Assessment**:
    - Use qualitative methods such as risk matrices, expert judgment, and scenario analysis to evaluate risks that are difficult to quantify. This can provide context and insights into non-financial impacts and the broader organizational implications of risks.
2. **Risk Matrices**:
    - Employ risk matrices to categorize risks based on their likelihood and impact using qualitative descriptions (e.g., low, medium, high). This helps prioritize risks and identify areas where quantitative analysis should be focused.
3. **Expert Judgment and Workshops**:
    - Conduct workshops and interviews with subject matter experts to gather qualitative insights on risks and controls. Experts can provide context, identify potential blind spots, and validate quantitative findings.
4. **Hybrid Approaches**:
    - Integrate quantitative and qualitative data in a hybrid approach to provide a more comprehensive view of risks and controls. For example, use quantitative methods to calculate ALE and ROSI, while incorporating qualitative assessments to evaluate reputational impacts and compliance considerations.

Examples of Combined Assessments

Example 1: Financial Institution:
- **Quantitative Assessment**: The institution calculates ALE for risks associated with data breaches and uses ROSI to evaluate the cost-effectiveness of encryption solutions.
- **Qualitative Assessment**: Workshops with legal and compliance experts highlight potential regulatory fines and reputational damage, influencing the final decision to implement more robust encryption measures.

Example 2: Healthcare Provider:
- **Quantitative Assessment**: The provider uses Monte Carlo simulations to model the impact of ransomware attacks on patient data and service availability, estimating potential financial losses.
- **Qualitative Assessment**: Interviews with clinical staff and IT teams identify critical systems and patient safety concerns, leading to the adoption of additional controls such as network segmentation and enhanced incident response protocols.

Example 3: Manufacturing Company:
- **Quantitative Assessment**: The company performs CBA to compare the costs of implementing intrusion detection systems (IDS) versus firewalls, based on expected reductions in ALE.
- **Qualitative Assessment**: Risk matrices and expert judgment reveal that the IDS provides better visibility into potential threats and faster response times, leading to a decision to implement both controls in a layered security strategy.

Quantitative risk analysis is a valuable tool for assessing the cost-effectiveness of security controls, providing a clear financial rationale for investment decisions. However, its limitations necessitate the integration of qualitative assessments to capture a complete picture of risks and their impacts. By combining quantitative and qualitative methods, organizations can make more informed, balanced decisions that address both financial and non-financial aspects of risk management. This holistic approach ensures that security controls are not only cost-effective but also aligned with broader organizational goals and values.

Implementation of Security and Privacy Controls

Developing a comprehensive implementation strategy for security and privacy controls is essential for ensuring that an organization's information assets are adequately protected. This process involves several key steps, including prioritizing control implementation based on risk assessment results, balancing resource allocation, funding considerations, and carefully planning timelines. Here's an analysis of this process:

Steps to Develop a Comprehensive Implementation Strategy

1. **Conduct a Risk Assessment**:
   - Perform a thorough risk assessment to identify and evaluate potential threats and vulnerabilities. Determine the likelihood and impact of each risk to prioritize which security and privacy controls are most critical.
2. **Identify Required Controls**:
   - Based on the risk assessment, identify the necessary security and privacy controls. Utilize relevant frameworks (e.g., NIST SP 800-53, ISO/IEC 27001) and regulatory requirements to guide the selection of controls.
3. **Prioritize Control Implementation**:
   - Rank the identified controls by their importance and urgency. High-priority controls should address the most significant risks, especially those with high impact and high likelihood.
4. **Develop a Detailed Implementation Plan**:
   - Create a comprehensive plan that outlines the steps for implementing each control. Include detailed descriptions, responsibilities, timelines, and milestones.
5. **Resource Allocation and Funding Considerations**:
   - Assess the resources (e.g., personnel, technology, budget) available for implementing the controls. Secure necessary funding and allocate resources efficiently to ensure that high-priority controls are addressed first.
6. **Timeline Planning**:
   - Develop a realistic timeline for implementing the controls. Consider dependencies between tasks, resource availability, and potential bottlenecks. Ensure that critical controls are implemented as soon as possible while balancing the workload to avoid burnout.
7. **Monitor and Adjust**:
   - Continuously monitor the implementation process to ensure progress and address any issues that arise. Be prepared to adjust the plan as needed based on new information or changes in the risk environment.

Prioritizing Control Implementation Based on Risk Assessment

1. **High-Risk Areas**:
   - Focus on implementing controls that mitigate the highest risks first. Risks with high impact and high likelihood should be prioritized to prevent significant harm to the organization.
2. **Compliance Requirements**:
   - Ensure that controls required for regulatory compliance are implemented promptly to avoid legal penalties and reputational damage.
3. **Critical Assets**:
   - Protect critical assets that are essential to the organization's operations. Controls that secure these assets should be implemented early in the process.
4. **Quick Wins**:
   - Identify and implement controls that can be quickly deployed and provide immediate benefits. Quick wins help build momentum and demonstrate progress.

Resource Allocation, Funding Considerations, and Timeline Planning

1. Resource Allocation:
   - **Personnel**: Assign dedicated teams or individuals responsible for implementing specific controls. Ensure that they have the necessary skills and knowledge.

- **Technology**: Leverage existing technologies and tools where possible to maximize efficiency. Invest in new technologies only when necessary.
- **Collaboration**: Foster collaboration between departments to share resources and expertise. This can enhance the effectiveness of control implementation.

2. **Funding Considerations**:
   - **Budgeting**: Develop a budget that covers all aspects of control implementation, including technology, training, and ongoing maintenance. Secure funding approval from senior management.
   - **Cost-Benefit Analysis**: Perform cost-benefit analyses to justify expenditures on security and privacy controls. Demonstrate how investments will reduce risk and provide long-term benefits.

3. **Timeline Planning**:
   - **Phased Approach**: Implement controls in phases, starting with the most critical ones. This allows for gradual improvement and manageable workloads.
   - **Dependencies**: Identify dependencies between tasks and plan accordingly. Ensure that prerequisite tasks are completed before subsequent tasks begin.
   - **Milestones**: Set clear milestones to track progress and maintain momentum. Regularly review milestones to ensure the project stays on track.
   - **Flexibility**: Build flexibility into the timeline to accommodate unexpected delays or changes in priorities.

Example of an Effective Implementation Strategy

Scenario: A mid-sized healthcare provider needs to enhance its security and privacy controls to comply with HIPAA and protect patient data.

1. **Risk Assessment Results**:
   - High-risk areas identified include unencrypted patient data at rest, insufficient access controls, and lack of an incident response plan.
2. **Prioritized Controls**:
   - **Encryption**: Implement encryption for all patient data at rest.
   - **Access Controls**: Deploy role-based access controls (RBAC) to ensure only authorized personnel can access patient data.
   - **Incident Response Plan**: Develop and test an incident response plan to handle data breaches effectively.
3. **Resource Allocation and Funding**:
   - **Personnel**: Assign a dedicated team to handle encryption implementation, another for access control, and a third for incident response planning.
   - **Technology**: Invest in encryption software and RBAC tools. Use existing infrastructure where possible to reduce costs.
   - **Budget**: Allocate a budget for new technology, training, and incident response drills. Justify the budget based on the potential costs of data breaches and non-compliance penalties.
4. **Timeline Planning**:
   - **Phase 1**: Implement encryption for patient data within the first three months.
   - **Phase 2**: Deploy RBAC within the next two months.
   - **Phase 3**: Develop and test the incident response plan over the following three months.
   - **Milestones**: Set monthly milestones to review progress and make necessary adjustments.

By following this comprehensive approach, organizations can ensure that their security and privacy controls are effectively implemented and maintained. Prioritizing controls based on risk assessment results, efficiently allocating resources, securing necessary funding, and planning realistic timelines are critical components of a successful implementation strategy. This holistic approach helps mitigate risks, achieve compliance, and protect valuable information assets.

Resource allocation is a critical aspect of control implementation in any organization's information security strategy. Effectively deploying security controls requires a balanced mix of personnel, technology, and financial resources to ensure robust protection while optimizing costs and efficiency. Here's how organizations determine the appropriate mix and manage challenges in resource allocation.

Determining the Appropriate Mix of Resources
1. Risk Assessment and Prioritization:
- Conduct a comprehensive risk assessment to identify and prioritize risks based on their potential impact and likelihood. This helps in determining where to allocate resources for maximum risk reduction.
- Prioritize controls that address the highest risks and are critical to regulatory compliance and business continuity.

2. Budget Planning:
- Align the security budget with the organization's overall financial planning. This involves forecasting the costs associated with implementing and maintaining security controls.
- Allocate financial resources based on the prioritization of risks and the cost-effectiveness of controls.

3. Personnel and Expertise:
- Assess the existing skill sets and expertise within the organization to determine the need for additional training or hiring specialized personnel.
- Ensure that there are enough qualified staff to manage, monitor, and maintain the deployed controls effectively.

4. Technology and Tools:
- Evaluate the technological requirements for implementing the selected controls, including hardware, software, and support infrastructure.
- Choose technologies that are scalable, integrate well with existing systems, and provide the necessary capabilities to mitigate identified risks.

5. Strategic Planning:
- Develop a strategic plan that outlines the goals, timelines, and milestones for control implementation. This plan should align with the organization's overall security strategy and business objectives.

Examples of Resource Allocation Challenges and Strategies
1. Limited Budget:
- **Challenge**: Organizations often face budget constraints that limit their ability to implement all necessary controls.
- **Strategy**: Prioritize controls that address the most critical risks and provide the highest return on investment (ROI). Consider phased implementation to spread costs over time and focus on high-impact areas first.

2. Skill Gaps:
- **Challenge**: A lack of skilled personnel can hinder the effective deployment and management of security controls.
- **Strategy**: Invest in training and professional development to upskill existing staff. Alternatively, hire external experts or consultants for specialized tasks and leverage managed security services to fill gaps.

3. Technology Integration:
- **Challenge**: Integrating new security technologies with existing systems can be complex and resource-intensive.
- **Strategy**: Choose technologies that are compatible with current infrastructure and have strong vendor support. Use pilot projects to test integration and address issues before full-scale deployment.

4. Operational Disruptions:
- **Challenge**: Implementing security controls can disrupt normal business operations, especially in resource-constrained environments.
- **Strategy**: Plan implementations during low-activity periods or maintenance windows. Ensure thorough testing in a staging environment before deployment to minimize operational impact.

5. Balancing Day-to-Day Operations with Security Projects:
- **Challenge**: Security projects can compete with other operational priorities for resources and attention.

- **Strategy**: Use project management techniques to balance workloads and allocate resources efficiently. Establish a dedicated security team to focus on implementation while allowing operational teams to maintain business functions.

6. Vendor and Third-Party Management:
- **Challenge**: Coordinating with vendors and third-party providers can complicate resource allocation, particularly if their timelines and capabilities do not align with internal plans.
- **Strategy**: Develop clear contracts and service-level agreements (SLAs) that define expectations and timelines. Maintain regular communication and collaboration with vendors to ensure alignment.

Strategies for Optimizing Resource Utilization

1. Automation:
- Use automated tools for routine tasks such as monitoring, reporting, and patch management to free up personnel for more strategic activities.
- Example: Implement a Security Information and Event Management (SIEM) system to automate log analysis and alerting.

2. Outsourcing and Managed Services:
- Outsource non-core security functions to managed service providers to leverage external expertise and reduce the burden on internal resources.
- Example: Use a managed security service provider (MSSP) for continuous monitoring and incident response.

3. Cross-Training and Multi-Skilling:
- Cross-train employees to handle multiple roles and responsibilities, ensuring flexibility and resilience in the security team.
- Example: Train IT staff in basic security functions to support security initiatives without needing additional hires.

4. Resource Sharing and Collaboration:
- Collaborate with other organizations, industry groups, or government agencies to share resources, threat intelligence, and best practices.
- Example: Participate in Information Sharing and Analysis Centers (ISACs) to gain insights and share resources with peers.

5. Regular Reviews and Adjustments:
- Conduct regular reviews of resource allocation and control effectiveness to identify areas for improvement and reallocation.
- Example: Perform quarterly audits to assess the performance of security controls and adjust resource distribution as needed.

Resource allocation in control implementation requires a careful balance of personnel, technology, and financial resources. By conducting thorough risk assessments, prioritizing controls, and employing strategic planning, organizations can effectively deploy security measures within their resource constraints. Addressing challenges through automation, outsourcing, cross-training, and collaboration ensures optimal utilization of resources and strengthens the overall security posture.

The concept of Total Cost of Ownership (TCO) in the context of security control implementation encompasses all costs associated with the deployment, maintenance, and operation of security measures over their entire lifecycle. TCO provides a comprehensive view of the financial commitment required to sustain security controls, beyond just the initial purchase price, helping organizations make informed decisions about investments in security.

Components of TCO for Security Controls

1. **Initial Costs**:
    - **Purchase Price**: Cost of acquiring hardware, software, and licenses.
    - **Implementation Costs**: Expenses related to deploying and configuring the controls, including consulting fees, installation, and initial setup.
2. **Operational Costs**:

- o **Maintenance and Support**: Ongoing costs for software updates, hardware maintenance, and vendor support contracts.
- o **Personnel**: Salaries and training costs for staff required to operate, monitor, and maintain the controls.
- o **Utilities and Facilities**: Costs related to the physical space and utilities required to house and operate security infrastructure.

3. **Indirect Costs**:
    - o **Downtime and Productivity Losses**: Potential impact on productivity due to system downtime during implementation or maintenance.
    - o **Integration Costs**: Expenses related to integrating new controls with existing systems and processes.
4. **Opportunity Costs**:
    - o **Alternative Investments**: Potential benefits or returns lost by investing resources in security controls rather than other projects or initiatives.

Calculating TCO
1. **Identify All Relevant Costs**:
    - o Gather detailed information on all costs associated with the security controls, both direct and indirect. This includes initial acquisition, implementation, ongoing operation, and any potential indirect costs.
2. **Quantify Each Cost Element**:
    - o Estimate the monetary value for each cost component over the expected lifecycle of the control. This often involves projections based on historical data, vendor quotes, and industry benchmarks.
3. **Aggregate Costs Over Time**:
    - o Sum all the identified costs to get the total cost over the control's lifecycle. This requires considering the time value of money, often using methods like Net Present Value (NPV) to discount future costs to their present value.
4. **Compare TCO Against Alternatives**:
    - o Evaluate the TCO of different security controls and compare them to determine the most cost-effective solution. This comparison should consider not only the financial costs but also the security benefits and risk reductions offered by each option.

Importance of Considering TCO in Funding Decisions
1. **Comprehensive Financial Planning**:
    - o TCO provides a holistic view of the financial commitment required, ensuring that all potential costs are considered in the decision-making process. This helps prevent budget overruns and financial surprises.
2. **Long-Term Sustainability**:
    - o By factoring in long-term costs, organizations can ensure they have the resources necessary to maintain security controls over time, preventing lapses in security due to underfunded maintenance or support.
3. **Better Risk Management**:
    - o Understanding TCO helps in aligning security investments with the organization's risk management strategy, ensuring that resources are allocated effectively to mitigate the most significant risks.

Pitfalls of Focusing Solely on Initial Implementation Costs
1. **Underestimating Long-Term Expenses**:
    - o Focusing only on initial costs can lead to underestimating the true financial burden of maintaining and operating security controls. This may result in inadequate budgeting for ongoing support, leading to degraded security over time.
2. **Inadequate Maintenance and Support**:
    - o Without accounting for maintenance and support costs, organizations may find themselves unable to keep security controls up to date, making them vulnerable to emerging threats and compliance issues.

3. **Short-Lived Solutions**:
   - Solutions chosen based solely on lower initial costs may be less robust or have shorter lifespans, requiring more frequent replacements and potentially higher overall costs in the long run.
4. **Hidden Costs**:
   - Initial cost-focused decisions may overlook hidden costs such as training, integration, and productivity losses, which can significantly impact the total expenditure.

Examples of TCO Considerations

Example 1: Endpoint Protection Solution:
- **Initial Costs**: Purchasing endpoint protection software licenses.
- **Operational Costs**: Annual renewal fees, regular updates, and technical support.
- **Personnel Costs**: Hiring and training IT staff to manage the solution.
- **Indirect Costs**: Downtime during initial deployment and periodic updates.

Example 2: Network Firewall:
- **Initial Costs**: Buying firewall hardware and initial configuration.
- **Operational Costs**: Ongoing maintenance contracts, software updates, and support.
- **Personnel Costs**: Network administrators to monitor and manage firewall rules.
- **Integration Costs**: Ensuring the firewall works seamlessly with existing network infrastructure.

Example 3: Data Encryption:
- **Initial Costs**: Purchasing encryption software and implementation services.
- **Operational Costs**: Annual licensing fees, support, and compliance auditing.
- **Personnel Costs**: Security team members to manage encryption keys and processes.
- **Indirect Costs**: Potential performance impacts on systems using encryption.

Balancing TCO and Security

To effectively balance TCO and security, organizations should:

- **Perform Comprehensive Assessments**: Include both quantitative and qualitative evaluations to capture the full scope of costs and benefits.
- **Prioritize Based on Risk**: Allocate resources to address the most significant risks first, ensuring that critical assets are adequately protected.
- **Plan for the Long Term**: Develop long-term budget plans that account for the ongoing costs of maintaining and upgrading security controls.
- **Evaluate Vendor Contracts Carefully**: Ensure that vendor contracts include clear terms for ongoing support, updates, and maintenance to avoid unexpected costs.

Considering TCO in security control implementation helps organizations make informed, sustainable decisions that align with their risk management and financial planning strategies. By looking beyond initial costs and factoring in long-term expenses, organizations can avoid common pitfalls and ensure that their security investments provide lasting value and protection.

Creating a realistic timeline for control implementation is essential to ensure that security measures are deployed effectively and efficiently without disrupting business operations. A well-planned timeline includes clearly defined milestones and considers various factors such as resource availability, project scope, and potential risks.

Factors to Consider When Developing Implementation Milestones

1. Project Scope and Complexity:
- Understand the full scope of the control implementation project, including the specific controls to be deployed, their complexity, and the systems they will affect.
- Break down the project into smaller, manageable tasks and phases, each with its own set of milestones.

2. Resource Availability:
- Assess the availability of personnel, technology, and financial resources required for implementation.
- Ensure that the necessary skills and expertise are available, either within the organization or through external partners.

3. Risk Assessment and Prioritization:
- Conduct a risk assessment to identify and prioritize the most critical controls that need to be implemented first.
- Prioritize controls that address the highest risks and provide the greatest impact on security posture.

4. Regulatory and Compliance Deadlines:
- Identify any regulatory or compliance deadlines that must be met and incorporate these into the timeline.
- Ensure that the implementation schedule aligns with these deadlines to avoid non-compliance penalties.

5. Existing Infrastructure and Dependencies:
- Evaluate the current infrastructure and identify any dependencies between different systems and controls.
- Plan for the integration of new controls with existing systems, considering compatibility and potential conflicts.

6. Stakeholder Involvement and Communication:
- Engage stakeholders early in the planning process to gather input and ensure alignment with organizational goals.
- Maintain regular communication with stakeholders to provide updates on progress and address any concerns.

7. Contingency Planning:
- Develop contingency plans to address potential risks and delays.
- Allocate buffer time in the schedule to accommodate unexpected issues and ensure flexibility.

Strategies for Managing Dependencies Between Different Control Implementations

1. Sequential and Parallel Implementation:
- Identify which controls can be implemented sequentially and which can be deployed in parallel.
- Plan the timeline to maximize efficiency by implementing parallel tasks where possible, without overloading resources.

2. Critical Path Analysis:
- Use critical path analysis to identify the sequence of tasks that determine the project's overall duration.
- Focus on managing tasks on the critical path to ensure that delays in these tasks do not impact the overall timeline.

3. Dependency Mapping:
- Create a dependency map to visualize the relationships between different controls and tasks.
- Identify and manage interdependencies to prevent bottlenecks and ensure smooth progression from one task to the next.

4. Regular Progress Reviews:
- Conduct regular progress reviews to monitor the status of control implementations and address any issues promptly.
- Adjust the timeline as needed based on the outcomes of these reviews and any changes in project scope or resource availability.

5. Resource Allocation and Optimization:
- Allocate resources efficiently to manage dependencies and ensure that critical tasks have the necessary support.
- Optimize resource utilization by balancing workloads and avoiding overcommitment.

Examples of Handling Unexpected Delays

1. Delay in Vendor Deliverables:
- **Scenario**: A key technology component from a vendor is delayed, impacting the implementation of a critical control.
- **Strategy**: Communicate with the vendor to get a clear understanding of the delay and expected delivery timeline. Adjust the project timeline to focus on other tasks that can be completed in parallel. Explore temporary or alternative solutions to mitigate the impact of the delay.

2. Unanticipated Technical Challenges:

- **Scenario**: During implementation, technical challenges arise that were not anticipated, requiring additional time and resources to resolve.
- **Strategy**: Allocate additional resources to address the technical challenges. Reassess and adjust the project timeline, incorporating buffer time for similar unforeseen issues. Document the challenges and solutions to improve future planning and risk mitigation.

3. Resource Constraints:
- **Scenario**: Key personnel are unavailable due to unexpected leave or reassignment, slowing down the implementation process.
- **Strategy**: Identify backup resources or cross-train existing team members to cover critical roles. Adjust the timeline to reflect the new resource availability and consider extending deadlines where necessary. Maintain a resource contingency plan to quickly address similar issues in the future.

4. Regulatory Changes:
- **Scenario**: New regulatory requirements are introduced during the implementation process, necessitating additional controls or modifications to existing plans.
- **Strategy**: Conduct a rapid assessment of the new requirements and their impact on the project. Update the project scope and timeline to incorporate the necessary changes. Communicate the changes and revised timeline to stakeholders to ensure continued alignment and support.

Creating a realistic timeline for control implementation involves careful consideration of project scope, resource availability, risk prioritization, and dependencies. By employing strategies such as critical path analysis, dependency mapping, and regular progress reviews, organizations can effectively manage the complexities of control deployment. Handling unexpected delays requires flexibility, clear communication, and contingency planning to ensure that the project stays on track and achieves its security objectives.

Effectiveness measures are crucial for assessing the success of control implementation in an organization. These measures help determine whether the controls are performing as intended, mitigating risks, and contributing to overall security and compliance goals. Organizations develop meaningful metrics for different types of controls by considering both quantitative and qualitative measures. Here's an evaluation of various effectiveness measures, including examples and their strengths and weaknesses.

Developing Meaningful Metrics for Controls

1. Align with Objectives:
- Metrics should be aligned with the organization's security and business objectives. This ensures that they are relevant and provide meaningful insights into control performance.

2. Specificity and Relevance:
- Develop metrics that are specific to the controls being evaluated and relevant to the risks they address. This involves understanding the purpose of each control and the expected outcomes.

3. Measurability:
- Choose metrics that can be measured accurately and consistently. This may involve quantitative data collection or structured qualitative assessments.

4. Balance Between Quantitative and Qualitative:
- Use a mix of quantitative and qualitative measures to capture a comprehensive view of control effectiveness. Quantitative metrics provide hard data, while qualitative measures offer context and insights.

Examples of Quantitative Measures

1. **Incident Frequency**:
   - **Metric**: Number of security incidents reported within a specific period.
   - **Strengths**: Provides a clear, measurable indicator of how often controls are preventing or failing to prevent incidents.
   - **Weaknesses**: Does not indicate the severity or impact of incidents, and external factors can influence incident frequency.

2. **Mean Time to Detect (MTTD) and Mean Time to Respond (MTTR)**:
   - **Metric**: Average time taken to detect and respond to security incidents.

- **Strengths**: Helps measure the efficiency of detection and response controls, providing insights into the speed and effectiveness of the incident management process.
- **Weaknesses**: Requires accurate incident logging and can be influenced by the nature and complexity of incidents.
3. **Compliance Rates**:
    - **Metric**: Percentage of controls passing compliance audits or assessments.
    - **Strengths**: Provides a clear indicator of compliance with regulatory or internal standards.
    - **Weaknesses**: May not fully reflect the effectiveness of controls in mitigating actual risks.
4. **Vulnerability Remediation Time**:
    - **Metric**: Average time taken to remediate identified vulnerabilities.
    - **Strengths**: Measures the effectiveness of vulnerability management processes and the ability to address security weaknesses promptly.
    - **Weaknesses**: Does not account for the criticality or potential impact of vulnerabilities.
5. **False Positive/Negative Rates**:
    - **Metric**: Rate of false positives and false negatives in security monitoring and detection systems.
    - **Strengths**: Helps evaluate the accuracy and reliability of detection controls.
    - **Weaknesses**: High rates can indicate issues with tuning and configuring detection systems.

Examples of Qualitative Measures
1. **User Feedback**:
    - **Metric**: Qualitative feedback from users regarding the usability and impact of security controls.
    - **Strengths**: Provides insights into how controls affect user behavior and productivity, identifying areas for improvement.
    - **Weaknesses**: Subjective and can be influenced by user perceptions and biases.
2. **Control Maturity Assessments**:
    - **Metric**: Evaluations of control maturity based on established frameworks (e.g., CMMI).
    - **Strengths**: Provides a structured way to assess the development and sophistication of controls over time.
    - **Weaknesses**: Can be time-consuming and requires expertise to conduct assessments effectively.
3. **Audit Findings and Recommendations**:
    - **Metric**: Qualitative analysis of audit findings and the implementation of recommendations.
    - **Strengths**: Offers detailed insights into control effectiveness and areas for improvement.
    - **Weaknesses**: Relies on the thoroughness and objectivity of the audit process.
4. **Incident Post-Mortem Reviews**:
    - **Metric**: Lessons learned and improvements identified from post-mortem reviews of security incidents.
    - **Strengths**: Provides deep insights into control failures and successes, guiding future improvements.
    - **Weaknesses**: Requires thorough documentation and analysis, which can be resource-intensive.

Relative Strengths and Weaknesses
Quantitative Measures:
- **Strengths**:
    - Objective and measurable, providing clear and actionable data.
    - Easier to track over time and compare against benchmarks.
    - Can be automated, reducing the burden on personnel.
- **Weaknesses**:
    - May not capture the full context or nuances of control effectiveness.
    - Can be influenced by external factors and require accurate data collection processes.
    - Risk of focusing on easily measurable metrics while neglecting harder-to-measure but important aspects.

Qualitative Measures:
- **Strengths**:
    - Provides context and depth, offering insights that quantitative measures may miss.

- o Can capture user perceptions, experiences, and the practical impact of controls.
- o Useful for understanding the root causes of issues and identifying improvement opportunities.
- **Weaknesses**:
    - o Subjective and can be influenced by personal biases and perceptions.
    - o More challenging to measure consistently and systematically.
    - o Requires significant effort to collect and analyze effectively.

Combining Quantitative and Qualitative Measures

To develop a comprehensive view of control effectiveness, organizations should combine both quantitative and qualitative measures. This blended approach ensures that metrics provide not only hard data but also contextual insights, leading to more informed decision-making.

Example:
- **Control**: Multi-Factor Authentication (MFA)
    - o **Quantitative Measures**:
        - Number of unauthorized access attempts prevented.
        - User adoption rates and login success rates.
    - o **Qualitative Measures**:
        - User feedback on the ease of use and impact on productivity.
        - IT support feedback on the implementation process and any issues encountered.

Example:
- **Control**: Security Awareness Training
    - o **Quantitative Measures**:
        - Percentage of employees completing training.
        - Reduction in phishing incident rates over time.
    - o **Qualitative Measures**:
        - Employee feedback on the training content and delivery.
        - Observations from trainers on engagement levels and knowledge retention.

By leveraging both types of measures, organizations can more effectively assess the success of control implementation, ensuring robust security and compliance outcomes.

Control maturity models are frameworks used to assess the effectiveness and maturity of an organization's security controls over time. These models help organizations evaluate their current control implementations, identify areas for improvement, and develop a roadmap for enhancing their security posture. By using maturity models, organizations can systematically measure the progress and effectiveness of their controls, ensuring they are continuously improving and adapting to new threats and challenges.

Concept of Control Maturity Models

**1. Purpose:
- Control maturity models provide a structured approach to evaluate how well security controls are implemented and managed. They help organizations understand the current state of their controls, identify gaps, and prioritize improvements.
- Maturity models facilitate benchmarking against best practices and industry standards, enabling organizations to align their security programs with recognized frameworks.

**2. Components:
- **Levels of Maturity**: Maturity models typically define several levels of maturity, ranging from initial or ad hoc processes to optimized and fully integrated practices.
- **Assessment Criteria**: Specific criteria are used to evaluate the maturity of controls at each level. These criteria may include process documentation, implementation consistency, effectiveness, and continuous improvement.

Using Maturity Models to Assess and Improve Control Implementation

**1. Assessment:
- Conduct an initial assessment to determine the current maturity level of each control. This involves evaluating how well the controls are documented, implemented, monitored, and continuously improved.

- Use standardized assessment tools and questionnaires to ensure consistency and objectivity in the evaluation process.

2. Gap Analysis:
- Identify gaps between the current maturity level and the desired level. This helps prioritize areas that require improvement and allocate resources effectively.
- Develop a detailed action plan to address the identified gaps, including specific tasks, timelines, and responsible parties.

3. Continuous Improvement:
- Implement the action plan and track progress over time. Regularly reassess the maturity levels to ensure that improvements are being made and controls are becoming more effective.
- Use the maturity model as a continuous improvement tool, regularly updating the assessment criteria and benchmarks to reflect evolving best practices and emerging threats.

Examples of Common Maturity Models

1. Capability Maturity Model Integration (CMMI):
- **Levels**: CMMI defines five levels of maturity: Initial, Managed, Defined, Quantitatively Managed, and Optimizing.
- **Applicability**: CMMI is widely used in software development and IT process management but can also be applied to information security controls. It helps organizations move from ad hoc and reactive processes to proactive and optimized practices.

2. NIST Cybersecurity Framework (CSF):
- **Levels**: The NIST CSF includes a maturity model with levels ranging from Partial, Risk Informed, Repeatable, Adaptable, to Optimized.
- **Applicability**: NIST CSF is specifically designed for cybersecurity and is applicable to a wide range of controls, including access management, incident response, and risk assessment.

3. ISO/IEC 27001 Maturity Model:
- **Levels**: This model uses levels such as No Formal Process, Informal Process, Standardized Process, Managed and Measurable, and Optimized.
- **Applicability**: The ISO/IEC 27001 maturity model is suitable for assessing the implementation of information security management systems (ISMS) and related controls, ensuring alignment with the ISO/IEC 27001 standard.

4. COBIT (Control Objectives for Information and Related Technologies):
- **Levels**: COBIT defines maturity levels from Non-existent, Initial/Ad Hoc, Repeatable but Intuitive, Defined Process, Managed and Measurable, to Optimized.
- **Applicability**: COBIT is used for IT governance and management, providing a comprehensive framework for evaluating the maturity of IT-related controls, including security, risk management, and compliance.

Applicability to Different Types of Controls

1. Technical Controls:
- **Example**: For access control mechanisms, maturity models can assess how well access policies are defined, implemented, monitored, and reviewed. A higher maturity level would indicate that access controls are consistently enforced, monitored in real-time, and regularly updated based on risk assessments.

2. Administrative Controls:
- **Example**: For security awareness training programs, maturity models can evaluate the frequency, quality, and effectiveness of training sessions. Higher maturity levels would reflect comprehensive training that is regularly updated, measured for effectiveness, and integrated into the organizational culture.

3. Physical Controls:
- **Example**: For physical security measures such as surveillance and access control systems, maturity models can assess the extent of coverage, monitoring capabilities, and incident response procedures. Higher maturity levels would indicate advanced integration of physical and IT security, continuous monitoring, and swift response to incidents.

By using control maturity models, organizations can systematically evaluate and improve their control implementations. These models provide a clear framework for assessing current capabilities, identifying gaps, and driving continuous improvement. Whether applied to technical, administrative, or physical controls, maturity models help organizations enhance their security posture and ensure robust protection against evolving threats.

Aligning control implementation with organizational expectations is crucial for ensuring that security measures support and enhance broader business objectives rather than hinder them. This involves integrating security controls into business processes in a way that balances risk management with operational efficiency and strategic goals. Here's an analysis of the process, potential conflicts, and strategies for resolution.

Process of Aligning Control Implementation with Organizational Expectations
1. **Understand Business Objectives and Context**:
    - Engage with business leaders and stakeholders to understand the organization's strategic goals, operational priorities, and risk appetite.
    - Identify critical business processes and assets that need protection.
2. **Integrate Risk Management and Business Planning**:
    - Ensure that risk management processes are integrated into business planning activities. This helps in identifying potential security risks that could impact business objectives.
    - Use risk assessments to prioritize controls based on their relevance to business-critical operations.
3. **Develop a Security Governance Framework**:
    - Establish a security governance framework that aligns with the organization's structure and decision-making processes. This framework should define roles, responsibilities, and accountability for security across the organization.
    - Create a cross-functional security steering committee that includes representatives from key business units to ensure alignment and collaboration.
4. **Align Control Selection with Business Impact**:
    - Select security controls that not only address identified risks but also support business objectives. For example, implementing controls that enhance customer trust can directly support business growth.
    - Use frameworks like NIST, ISO/IEC 27001, and CIS Controls to guide control selection and ensure they are relevant to the organization's context.
5. **Ensure Executive Support and Communication**:
    - Secure executive support for security initiatives by demonstrating how controls contribute to achieving business objectives and managing risks.
    - Communicate the value and benefits of security controls to all stakeholders, emphasizing their role in protecting business operations and enabling growth.
6. **Monitor and Adjust**:
    - Continuously monitor the effectiveness of implemented controls and their alignment with business objectives. Use metrics and KPIs to assess performance and make adjustments as needed.
    - Regularly review and update security policies and procedures to reflect changes in business priorities and the threat landscape.

Potential Conflicts Between Security Requirements and Business Operations
1. **Operational Efficiency vs. Security Controls**:
    - **Conflict**: Security controls can sometimes slow down business processes or add complexity, leading to reduced efficiency.
    - **Resolution**: Implement user-friendly and streamlined controls that minimize disruption. For example, use single sign-on (SSO) solutions to simplify authentication while maintaining security.
2. **Cost vs. Security Investment**:
    - **Conflict**: Allocating budget for security controls can be challenging, especially when resources are limited and there are competing business priorities.

- **Resolution**: Perform cost-benefit analyses to demonstrate the value of security investments. Highlight the potential cost of security breaches compared to the investment in preventive measures.
3. **User Experience vs. Security Measures**:
    - **Conflict**: Security measures like multi-factor authentication (MFA) can sometimes be perceived as cumbersome by users, leading to resistance.
    - **Resolution**: Select security solutions that balance security and usability. Provide training and awareness programs to help users understand the importance of security measures and how to use them effectively.
4. **Innovation and Agility vs. Security Compliance**:
    - **Conflict**: Rapid innovation and agile development processes may conflict with the need for thorough security assessments and compliance checks.
    - **Resolution**: Integrate security into the development lifecycle (DevSecOps) to ensure that security is considered from the outset and does not hinder innovation. Use automated security testing tools to keep pace with agile development.

Strategies for Resolving Conflicts
1. **Adopt a Risk-Based Approach**:
    - Focus on implementing controls that address the highest risks and have the most significant impact on business objectives. This ensures that resources are used effectively and that critical areas are protected.
2. **Collaborate and Engage Stakeholders**:
    - Involve business units, IT, and security teams in the decision-making process to ensure that security controls are practical and aligned with business needs. Regular communication and collaboration help in identifying potential conflicts early and finding mutually acceptable solutions.
3. **Implement Flexible and Scalable Controls**:
    - Choose security controls that can be easily adapted and scaled to meet changing business needs. This flexibility allows the organization to maintain security without hindering growth and innovation.
4. **Develop Security Awareness and Training Programs**:
    - Educate employees about the importance of security and how it supports business objectives. Effective training can reduce resistance to security measures and encourage a culture of security awareness.
5. **Leverage Technology and Automation**:
    - Use advanced technologies and automation to streamline security processes and reduce the burden on business operations. For example, automated threat detection and response can enhance security without requiring extensive manual intervention.
6. **Continuous Improvement and Feedback Loops**:
    - Establish feedback mechanisms to continuously assess the impact of security controls on business operations. Use this feedback to make iterative improvements and ensure ongoing alignment with business goals.

Examples of Aligning Control Implementation with Business Objectives
Example 1: Financial Services:
- **Business Objective**: Enhance customer trust and protect sensitive financial data.
- **Control Implementation**: Implement strong encryption for data at rest and in transit, multi-factor authentication for customer access, and continuous monitoring for suspicious activities.
- **Resolution**: Balance security and user experience by using user-friendly authentication methods and providing clear communication about security measures to customers.

Example 2: Healthcare Provider:
- **Business Objective**: Ensure compliance with HIPAA while maintaining efficient patient care.

- **Control Implementation**: Deploy electronic health record (EHR) systems with built-in access controls, audit trails, and data encryption.
- **Resolution**: Work with healthcare professionals to integrate security controls seamlessly into their workflows, minimizing disruption to patient care.

Example 3: E-commerce Company:
- **Business Objective**: Protect customer data and support business growth through secure online transactions.
- **Control Implementation**: Implement secure payment processing systems, regular security audits, and customer data protection measures.
- **Resolution**: Use secure coding practices and regular security testing during development to ensure that security controls do not delay new feature releases.

Aligning control implementation with organizational expectations requires a strategic approach that balances security needs with business objectives. By understanding business goals, integrating risk management with business planning, and using a combination of technical and organizational strategies, organizations can effectively implement security controls that support and enhance their overall mission. Regular communication, stakeholder engagement, and continuous improvement are key to resolving conflicts and ensuring that security measures are both effective and aligned with business operations.

Meeting both national and international security requirements in control implementation presents several challenges for organizations, especially those operating in multiple jurisdictions. These challenges include navigating conflicting standards, ensuring compliance with various regulatory frameworks, and maintaining a consistent security posture across all operations. Here's how organizations can address these challenges and develop a unified approach to control implementation.

Challenges of Meeting National and International Security Requirements

1. Conflicting Standards:
- Different countries and regions have their own security regulations and standards, which may have conflicting requirements. For example, data residency laws may mandate that data be stored within specific geographical boundaries, while other regulations may have specific encryption standards that differ from local requirements.

2. Complex Regulatory Landscape:
- The global regulatory landscape is complex and constantly evolving. Organizations must keep abreast of changes in laws and regulations across all jurisdictions in which they operate, which can be resource-intensive and challenging.

3. Resource Allocation:
- Implementing and maintaining controls that meet diverse regulatory requirements require significant resources, including time, money, and personnel. Balancing these resources effectively while ensuring compliance can be difficult.

4. Operational Consistency:
- Maintaining a consistent security posture across all global operations is challenging, especially when dealing with local variations in technology infrastructure, business practices, and cultural attitudes toward security.

Navigating Potentially Conflicting Standards

1. Harmonization of Controls:
- Develop a set of harmonized security controls that meet the highest common requirements across all applicable regulations. This approach involves identifying overlapping requirements and creating a unified set of controls that can be applied globally.
- Example: An organization might align its security program with internationally recognized frameworks such as ISO/IEC 27001 or NIST CSF, which provide a comprehensive set of controls that can be mapped to various national requirements.

2. Risk-Based Approach:

- Use a risk-based approach to prioritize compliance efforts. Focus on high-risk areas and critical business processes that have the most significant regulatory impact. Tailor controls to address the most stringent requirements first.
- Example: Prioritize implementing GDPR compliance measures for European operations while ensuring that other global data protection standards are also met.

3. Centralized Compliance Management:
- Establish a centralized compliance management function that oversees global regulatory requirements and ensures that control implementations are consistent across all jurisdictions.
- Example: A global compliance team that monitors changes in regulations, updates control frameworks accordingly, and ensures local teams are aware of and adhere to these updates.

4. Local Adaptations and Exceptions:
- Allow for local adaptations and exceptions where necessary. While maintaining a global control framework, permit local modifications to address specific regulatory requirements or business needs.
- Example: Implementing additional encryption measures in countries with stricter data protection laws while maintaining baseline encryption standards globally.

Developing a Unified Approach to Control Implementation

1. Global Framework with Local Implementation:
- Develop a global security framework based on internationally recognized standards and best practices. Allow local teams to adapt and implement these controls to meet specific national requirements.
- Example: A multinational company might adopt the ISO/IEC 27001 framework globally but tailor specific controls to meet local regulations such as GDPR in Europe, CCPA in California, and PIPEDA in Canada.

2. Regular Audits and Assessments:
- Conduct regular internal and external audits to ensure compliance with both global and local regulations. Use the findings to continuously improve the control framework and address any compliance gaps.
- Example: Implementing a global audit schedule that includes assessments of local compliance efforts and integrates findings into a centralized compliance reporting system.

3. Cross-Functional Teams:
- Establish cross-functional teams that include representatives from different regions and functions (e.g., legal, IT, security, operations) to ensure a holistic approach to compliance and control implementation.
- Example: A cross-functional compliance committee that meets regularly to discuss regulatory changes, share best practices, and coordinate control implementations across regions.

4. Training and Awareness Programs:
- Develop comprehensive training and awareness programs that educate employees about global and local security requirements. Ensure that all staff understand their role in maintaining compliance.
- Example: Offering regular training sessions and e-learning modules that cover global security standards and specific local regulatory requirements.

5. Leverage Technology:
- Use technology solutions such as Governance, Risk, and Compliance (GRC) tools to manage compliance efforts across multiple jurisdictions. These tools can help track regulatory requirements, map them to controls, and provide real-time compliance monitoring.
- Example: Implementing a GRC platform that integrates with existing security tools to provide a centralized view of compliance status and automate compliance reporting.

Global organizations face significant challenges in meeting both national and international security requirements. By adopting a harmonized control framework, employing a risk-based approach, and allowing for local adaptations, organizations can navigate conflicting standards and maintain a consistent security posture. Regular audits, cross-functional teams, comprehensive training programs, and leveraging technology further support a unified approach to control implementation across different jurisdictions.

Concept of Compensating Controls

Compensating controls are alternative security measures implemented to fulfill the requirements of a primary control that cannot be fully implemented due to technical, financial, or operational constraints. These controls are designed to provide a similar level of protection and mitigate the same risks as the original control. They are not direct replacements but serve to address the specific security requirements in a different manner.

When and How to Implement Compensating Controls

When to Implement Compensating Controls:

1. **Technical Constraints**:
   - When the existing technology infrastructure does not support the required control.
   - Example: Legacy systems that cannot support modern encryption standards.
2. **Operational Constraints**:
   - When implementing the primary control would disrupt critical business operations.
   - Example: A real-time processing system that cannot afford the latency introduced by certain security controls.
3. **Financial Constraints**:
   - When the cost of implementing the primary control is prohibitive.
   - Example: Small businesses that cannot afford expensive multi-factor authentication solutions.
4. **Compliance and Regulatory Requirements**:
   - When compliance with regulatory requirements is mandatory but the prescribed controls are impractical.
   - Example: Specific industry regulations requiring certain controls that are not feasible for the organization.

How to Implement Compensating Controls:

1. **Risk Assessment**:
   - Conduct a thorough risk assessment to understand the specific risks associated with not implementing the primary control.
   - Identify the threats, vulnerabilities, and potential impacts.
2. **Identify Alternative Controls**:
   - Determine alternative controls that can mitigate the identified risks.
   - Ensure these controls provide equivalent protection and address the same objectives as the primary control.
3. **Evaluate Effectiveness**:
   - Assess the effectiveness of the compensating controls to ensure they provide the required level of security.
   - Use metrics and testing to validate their performance.
4. **Documentation**:
   - Document the justification for using compensating controls, including why the primary control is not feasible, how the compensating controls mitigate the risks, and any residual risks.
   - Provide detailed descriptions of the compensating controls, their implementation, and how they are monitored and maintained.
5. **Approval**:
   - Obtain approval from senior management, security governance bodies, and any relevant stakeholders.
   - Ensure there is a consensus on the adequacy and implementation of the compensating controls.
6. **Implementation and Monitoring**:
   - Implement the compensating controls and integrate them into the existing security framework.
   - Continuously monitor their effectiveness and make adjustments as necessary.

Examples of Scenarios Where Compensating Controls Might Be Necessary

Example 1: Legacy Systems and Encryption

- **Scenario**: A financial institution uses legacy systems that do not support modern encryption standards required by PCI-DSS.

- **Compensating Control**: Implement stringent physical security measures to protect the systems, such as secured data centers with restricted access, regular security audits, and enhanced network security measures to monitor and control data access.
- **Justification**: Document how these physical and network controls provide equivalent protection for the data, ensuring its confidentiality and integrity.

Example 2: Small Business and Multi-Factor Authentication (MFA)
- **Scenario**: A small business cannot afford the costs associated with implementing multi-factor authentication for all employees.
- **Compensating Control**: Use strong password policies combined with regular security awareness training, enforce account lockout after multiple failed login attempts, and monitor login activities for anomalies.
- **Justification**: Explain how these measures collectively reduce the risk of unauthorized access to a level comparable to MFA, detailing the effectiveness of each control.

Example 3: Real-Time Processing and Latency Issues
- **Scenario**: A manufacturing company's real-time processing system cannot tolerate the latency introduced by deep packet inspection (DPI) for network security.
- **Compensating Control**: Implement network segmentation to isolate critical systems, use host-based intrusion detection systems (HIDS) on the most sensitive systems, and enforce strict access controls and monitoring.
- **Justification**: Describe how network segmentation and host-based controls mitigate the risks that DPI would address, ensuring real-time operations remain unaffected.

Justifying the Use of Compensating Controls to Auditors or Regulators

1. **Detailed Documentation**:
   - Provide comprehensive documentation that explains why the primary control cannot be implemented.
   - Detail the compensating controls, their objectives, and how they mitigate the same risks as the primary control.
2. **Risk Assessment Results**:
   - Present the results of the risk assessment that identifies the risks associated with not implementing the primary control.
   - Show how the compensating controls address these risks effectively.
3. **Effectiveness Evidence**:
   - Provide evidence of the effectiveness of the compensating controls, including test results, performance metrics, and monitoring data.
   - Demonstrate through empirical data that the compensating controls offer equivalent protection.
4. **Compliance Mapping**:
   - Map the compensating controls to the relevant regulatory or compliance requirements, showing how they fulfill the intended security objectives.
   - Use industry standards and guidelines to support the equivalency of the compensating controls.
5. **Approval and Endorsement**:
   - Include documentation of approval from senior management and security governance bodies.
   - Ensure that the decision to implement compensating controls is backed by internal stakeholders and, if possible, by third-party assessments.
6. **Continuous Improvement**:
   - Highlight the organization's commitment to continuous monitoring and improvement of the compensating controls.
   - Show plans for regular reviews, audits, and updates to ensure the controls remain effective in the evolving threat landscape.

Example Justification:
- **Scenario**: A healthcare provider cannot implement end-to-end encryption for all data transmissions due to interoperability issues with third-party systems.

- **Compensating Control**: Implement rigorous network security measures, including VPNs for external connections, strict firewall rules, regular vulnerability scanning, and enhanced monitoring of data flows.
- **Justification Document**:
    - **Introduction**: State the regulatory requirement and the primary control.
    - **Constraint Explanation**: Detail why end-to-end encryption is not feasible.
    - **Risk Assessment Summary**: Present the identified risks and potential impacts.
    - **Compensating Controls Description**: Describe the compensating controls in detail.
    - **Effectiveness Evidence**: Provide data and analysis demonstrating the effectiveness of the compensating controls.
    - **Compliance Mapping**: Show how the compensating controls meet the regulatory objectives.
    - **Approval Documentation**: Include endorsements from senior management and relevant committees.
    - **Conclusion**: Reaffirm the commitment to maintaining and improving the compensating controls.

Compensating controls are critical for addressing security requirements when primary controls are impractical. By carefully assessing risks, selecting appropriate alternatives, and providing thorough documentation and justification, organizations can ensure that these controls are accepted by auditors and regulators, maintaining compliance and security effectiveness.

Automation plays a critical role in the implementation of security controls, helping organizations enhance efficiency, reduce human error, and ensure consistent application of security measures. By leveraging automated tools and processes, organizations can streamline their security operations, respond faster to threats, and maintain a robust security posture. However, while automation offers many benefits, it also introduces certain risks that need to be managed carefully.

Leveraging Automation in Control Implementation

1. Automated Monitoring and Alerting:
- Automated tools continuously monitor systems and networks for suspicious activity and potential threats. These tools can generate alerts in real-time, enabling rapid response.
- Example: Security Information and Event Management (SIEM) systems aggregate and analyze log data from various sources, identifying anomalies and generating alerts for security teams to investigate.

2. Automated Patch Management:
- Automated patch management tools scan for vulnerabilities and apply patches across systems without manual intervention, ensuring timely updates and reducing the risk of exploitation.
- Example: Tools like Microsoft WSUS or third-party solutions like SolarWinds Patch Manager automate the deployment of patches for operating systems and applications.

3. Identity and Access Management (IAM):
- Automation in IAM can enforce access control policies, manage user credentials, and provision/deprovision access based on predefined rules.
- Example: Identity governance tools like Okta or SailPoint automatically manage user roles and permissions, ensuring that access rights are consistent with organizational policies.

4. Incident Response Automation:
- Automated incident response tools can execute predefined playbooks to contain and mitigate security incidents quickly.
- Example: Security Orchestration, Automation, and Response (SOAR) platforms like Palo Alto Networks' Cortex XSOAR automate incident response tasks such as isolating compromised devices and blocking malicious IP addresses.

5. Compliance and Audit Automation:
- Automated compliance tools can continuously check systems against regulatory requirements and organizational policies, generating audit reports and highlighting non-compliance issues.
- Example: Tools like Qualys Compliance Monitoring automate the assessment of compliance with standards like PCI-DSS, HIPAA, and GDPR, providing continuous compliance status.

Potential Benefits of Automation in Control Implementation
1. Increased Efficiency:
- Automation reduces the manual effort required to implement and maintain controls, freeing up resources for more strategic tasks.
- Example: Automated vulnerability scanning tools continuously identify and report on vulnerabilities, allowing security teams to focus on remediation rather than manual scanning.

2. Consistency and Accuracy:
- Automated processes ensure that controls are applied consistently across the organization, reducing the risk of human error.
- Example: Automated configuration management tools enforce consistent security configurations across all devices, ensuring compliance with security policies.

3. Rapid Response to Threats:
- Automation enables faster detection and response to security incidents, minimizing the potential impact of attacks.
- Example: Automated threat detection systems can instantly identify and block malicious activity, reducing the window of opportunity for attackers.

4. Scalability:
- Automated tools can scale to handle large volumes of data and complex environments, ensuring that security controls are effective even as the organization grows.
- Example: Cloud security automation tools can manage security controls across thousands of cloud instances, providing comprehensive protection for large-scale deployments.

Potential Risks of Automation in Control Implementation
1. Over-Reliance on Automation:
- Over-reliance on automated systems can lead to complacency, with organizations potentially neglecting the need for human oversight and manual verification.
- Example: Relying solely on automated threat detection without regular review and tuning can result in missed threats or false positives being ignored.

2. Automation Failures:
- Automation systems can fail or be misconfigured, leading to gaps in security coverage or unintended consequences.
- Example: A misconfigured automated patch management tool could apply patches indiscriminately, potentially disrupting critical systems or services.

3. Complexity and Integration Challenges:
- Implementing and managing automated tools can add complexity, especially when integrating with existing systems and processes.
- Example: Integrating a new SOAR platform with legacy systems may require significant customization and testing, increasing the complexity of the security environment.

4. Security of Automation Tools:
- Automation tools themselves can become targets for attackers, who may seek to exploit vulnerabilities in these tools to compromise the organization's security.
- Example: If an attacker gains control over an automated configuration management tool, they could deploy malicious configurations across the entire network.

Examples of Automation in Control Implementation
1. Automated Endpoint Protection:
- Endpoint Detection and Response (EDR) tools like CrowdStrike Falcon automate the detection and remediation of threats on endpoint devices, reducing the time to respond to and neutralize threats.

2. Automated Network Security:
- Network Access Control (NAC) solutions like Cisco Identity Services Engine (ISE) automatically enforce network security policies, controlling device access based on predefined rules.

3. Automated Data Loss Prevention (DLP):
- DLP tools like Symantec DLP automatically monitor, detect, and prevent the unauthorized transfer of sensitive data, ensuring data protection compliance.

By leveraging automation, organizations can significantly enhance the efficiency and effectiveness of control implementation. Automation provides numerous benefits, including increased efficiency, consistency, rapid threat response, and scalability. However, organizations must also be mindful of the potential risks, such as over-reliance on automation, automation failures, complexity, and the security of the automation tools themselves. Balancing automation with human oversight and regular review can help organizations achieve robust and resilient security control implementations.

Evaluating the Process of Documenting Residual Security Risks

Residual security risks are the remaining risks that persist after security controls have been implemented. Documenting these risks is crucial for ongoing risk management and ensuring transparency and accountability within the organization. Here's how organizations effectively document residual security risks and use Plan of Action and Milestones (POA&M) documents to manage ongoing risk mitigation efforts:

Steps to Document Residual Security Risks

1. **Conduct a Post-Implementation Review**:
   - After implementing security controls, conduct a thorough review to assess their effectiveness.
   - Identify any remaining vulnerabilities or risks that have not been fully mitigated by the controls.
2. **Risk Assessment**:
   - Reassess the identified risks considering the implemented controls.
   - Determine the residual risk level, considering factors like likelihood, impact, and exposure.
3. **Documentation**:
   - Document the residual risks in detail, including their nature, potential impact, likelihood of occurrence, and any relevant metrics.
   - Clearly specify which controls have been implemented and their effectiveness in mitigating the risk.
4. **Approval and Reporting**:
   - Present the documented residual risks to relevant stakeholders, including senior management and risk management committees.
   - Ensure that there is a clear understanding and acceptance of the residual risks at the appropriate management level.

Using Plan of Action and Milestones (POA&M) Documents

POA&M documents are essential tools for managing and tracking the mitigation of identified risks. They provide a structured approach to plan, execute, and monitor risk mitigation efforts.

Key Components of a Well-Structured POA&M

1. **Identification Information**:
   - **Unique Identifier**: A unique ID for each POA&M entry to track and reference specific actions.
   - **Risk Description**: Detailed description of the residual risk or vulnerability, including the context and its potential impact on the organization.
2. **Action Plan**:
   - **Mitigation Strategy**: Detailed steps and measures planned to address the residual risk. This may include additional controls, process improvements, or other risk mitigation actions.
   - **Assigned Responsibilities**: Identification of the individuals or teams responsible for implementing each action item.
   - **Resource Requirements**: Resources needed, such as budget, personnel, technology, and time.
3. **Milestones and Deadlines**:
   - **Milestones**: Key milestones with specific dates to track progress. These milestones should represent significant steps towards mitigating the risk.
   - **Deadlines**: Target completion dates for each action item and milestone to ensure timely execution.
4. **Status Tracking**:

- o **Current Status**: Ongoing status updates, such as "Not Started," "In Progress," "Completed," or "Delayed."
- o **Progress Metrics**: Quantitative or qualitative metrics to assess progress towards risk mitigation.
5. **Risk Reassessment**:
    - o **Residual Risk Evaluation**: Reassessment of the risk level after implementing mitigation actions, determining if the residual risk has been adequately addressed.
    - o **Effectiveness Review**: Evaluation of the effectiveness of the implemented controls and measures.

Examples of Using POA&M to Manage Ongoing Risk Mitigation
Example 1: Addressing Network Vulnerabilities
- **Identification Information**:
    - o **Unique Identifier**: POAM-001
    - o **Risk Description**: Multiple critical vulnerabilities identified in the network infrastructure, potentially allowing unauthorized access.
- **Action Plan**:
    - o **Mitigation Strategy**: Upgrade network devices, apply security patches, and enhance network monitoring.
    - o **Assigned Responsibilities**: IT Security Team.
    - o **Resource Requirements**: $50,000 for new hardware and software, 200 man-hours.
- **Milestones and Deadlines**:
    - o **Milestone 1**: Complete vulnerability assessment – Deadline: March 31.
    - o **Milestone 2**: Procure new network devices – Deadline: April 30.
    - o **Milestone 3**: Deploy patches and upgrades – Deadline: May 15.
- **Status Tracking**:
    - o **Current Status**: In Progress (Milestone 1 complete, Milestone 2 in procurement phase).
    - o **Progress Metrics**: Percentage of network devices upgraded, number of vulnerabilities patched.
- **Risk Reassessment**:
    - o **Residual Risk Evaluation**: Post-upgrade risk assessment shows a significant reduction in vulnerabilities.
    - o **Effectiveness Review**: Review indicates improved network security posture and reduced unauthorized access attempts.

Example 2: Enhancing Data Encryption
- **Identification Information**:
    - o **Unique Identifier**: POAM-002
    - o **Risk Description**: Sensitive data at rest is not encrypted, posing a risk of data breach.
- **Action Plan**:
    - o **Mitigation Strategy**: Implement encryption for all sensitive data at rest.
    - o **Assigned Responsibilities**: Data Management Team, IT Department.
    - o **Resource Requirements**: $20,000 for encryption software, 100 man-hours.
- **Milestones and Deadlines**:
    - o **Milestone 1**: Select and procure encryption software – Deadline: April 15.
    - o **Milestone 2**: Encrypt all sensitive data at rest – Deadline: May 31.
- **Status Tracking**:
    - o **Current Status**: Not Started (Vendor selection in progress).
    - o **Progress Metrics**: Percentage of sensitive data encrypted, encryption software deployment progress.
- **Risk Reassessment**:
    - o **Residual Risk Evaluation**: Risk assessment post-encryption shows data is protected against unauthorized access.
    - o **Effectiveness Review**: Encryption implementation validated through security testing, showing no data breaches.

Benefits of POA&M in Managing Risk Mitigation

- **Structured Approach**: Provides a clear and organized method for planning and tracking risk mitigation efforts.
- **Accountability**: Assigns specific responsibilities and deadlines, ensuring accountability and timely action.
- **Progress Monitoring**: Allows for continuous tracking of progress and adjustments as needed, ensuring that mitigation efforts stay on track.
- **Transparency**: Offers transparency to stakeholders and regulators, demonstrating the organization's commitment to addressing risks and enhancing security.
- **Effectiveness Review**: Facilitates regular reassessment of risks and the effectiveness of controls, promoting continuous improvement in the security posture.

By documenting residual security risks and using well-structured POA&M documents, organizations can effectively manage ongoing risk mitigation efforts. This approach ensures that risks are addressed systematically, responsibilities are clearly defined, and progress is monitored, ultimately enhancing the organization's overall security and compliance.

A risk register is a crucial tool in the context of control implementation, serving as a comprehensive document that records identified risks, their assessments, and the corresponding mitigation measures. It is used to track the status of risks over time, ensuring that they are managed effectively and that control implementations are aligned with the organization's risk management strategy.

Concept of a Risk Register

1. Definition:
- A risk register is a centralized repository that lists all identified risks related to an organization's assets, operations, and projects. It includes detailed information about each risk, such as its likelihood, impact, priority, and the mitigation actions taken to address it.

2. Components:
- **Risk Description**: A detailed description of the risk, including its source and potential impact.
- **Risk Owner**: The individual or team responsible for managing the risk.
- **Risk Assessment**: The evaluation of the risk's likelihood and impact, often represented as a risk score.
- **Mitigation Measures**: Actions taken to reduce the likelihood or impact of the risk.
- **Status**: The current status of the risk (e.g., identified, assessed, mitigated, or closed).
- **Review Date**: The date when the risk was last reviewed and updated.

Maintaining an Up-to-Date Risk Register

1. Continuous Monitoring:
- Regularly monitor the organization's environment to identify new risks and changes to existing risks. This involves staying informed about emerging threats, regulatory changes, and internal developments.
- Use automated monitoring tools and threat intelligence feeds to detect and assess risks in real-time.

2. Regular Updates:
- Schedule periodic reviews of the risk register to ensure it remains current. This can be done quarterly, biannually, or in response to significant changes in the organization's risk landscape.
- Involve relevant stakeholders in these reviews, including risk owners, security teams, and business unit leaders, to provide comprehensive updates and validations.

3. Integration with Other Processes:
- Integrate the risk register with other organizational processes, such as change management, incident response, and project management, to ensure that it reflects the latest information and actions taken.
- Example: When a new system is deployed, update the risk register to include any new risks associated with that system and document the mitigation measures implemented.

4. Documentation and Reporting:
- Maintain thorough documentation of all updates to the risk register, including the rationale for any changes and the outcomes of risk assessments.

- Generate regular reports for senior management and other stakeholders to keep them informed about the current risk landscape and the effectiveness of mitigation measures.

Relationship Between the Risk Register and Other Security Documentation

1. Control Implementation Plans:
- The risk register informs control implementation plans by highlighting the most significant risks that need to be addressed. It helps prioritize control implementations based on risk severity.
- Example: If the risk register identifies a high likelihood of phishing attacks, the control implementation plan might prioritize deploying email filtering and employee training programs.

2. Security Policies and Procedures:
- The risk register influences the development and updating of security policies and procedures by identifying areas where additional controls or changes in practices are necessary.
- Example: A risk identified in the register related to data leakage may lead to the creation or revision of data handling and classification policies.

3. Incident Response Plans:
- The risk register provides valuable insights into potential threats and vulnerabilities, informing the development of incident response plans and playbooks.
- Example: An identified risk of ransomware attacks would lead to specific incident response procedures focused on rapid isolation and recovery from such incidents.

4. Audit and Compliance Reports:
- The risk register supports audit and compliance activities by providing evidence of risk management practices and the effectiveness of control implementations.
- Example: During an audit, the risk register can demonstrate to auditors that the organization has a structured approach to identifying and mitigating risks, aiding in compliance with standards such as ISO/IEC 27001.

5. Strategic Decision-Making:
- The risk register informs strategic decision-making by providing a clear view of the organization's risk landscape and the effectiveness of current controls. This helps in resource allocation, budgeting, and planning for future security initiatives.
- Example: A trend of increasing cyber threats identified in the risk register might lead to strategic decisions to increase investment in advanced threat detection technologies.

Examples of How the Risk Register Informs Decision-Making

1. Prioritizing Security Investments:
- By identifying the most significant risks, the risk register helps prioritize investments in security technologies and initiatives that address those risks effectively.
- Example: If the risk register highlights a high risk of insider threats, the organization might invest in user behavior analytics and data loss prevention solutions.

2. Adjusting Control Measures:
- The risk register provides insights into which controls are effective and which are not, allowing for adjustments to be made to improve overall security posture.
- Example: If a control designed to mitigate phishing risks is found to be ineffective, the organization might enhance it by adding multi-factor authentication and more robust employee training.

3. Resource Allocation:
- The risk register aids in the efficient allocation of resources by identifying where the greatest needs are and ensuring that critical risks are addressed promptly.
- Example: During budget planning, the risk register can guide the allocation of funds to areas with the highest risk scores, ensuring that limited resources are used where they are most needed.

A risk register is a vital tool for managing risks and ensuring effective control implementation. By maintaining an up-to-date risk register, organizations can continuously monitor and assess risks, prioritize control measures, and make informed decisions. Integrating the risk register with other security documentation and processes enhances its value and ensures a cohesive approach to risk management and security control implementation.

Developing comprehensive security policies and procedures is critical for supporting control implementation and ensuring the effective management of security risks within an organization. These documents serve as the foundation for establishing security expectations, guiding behavior, and defining the responsibilities of all stakeholders. Here's an analysis of the process, key elements to include, strategies for ensuring adherence, and examples of how well-crafted policies can enhance the overall security posture.

Process of Developing Security Policies and Procedures

1. **Conduct a Risk Assessment**:
    - Identify and evaluate the specific security risks facing the organization.
    - Use the results to prioritize areas that require formal policies and procedures.
2. **Engage Stakeholders**:
    - Involve key stakeholders from various departments (IT, HR, legal, compliance, and business units) to ensure that policies address diverse perspectives and requirements.
    - Establish a governance structure for policy development and review.
3. **Define Objectives and Scope**:
    - Clearly articulate the objectives of each policy, ensuring alignment with organizational goals and regulatory requirements.
    - Determine the scope of each policy, specifying what is covered and any exclusions.
4. **Draft Policies and Procedures**:
    - Develop detailed, clear, and actionable policies that define expected behavior, roles, and responsibilities.
    - Create corresponding procedures that provide step-by-step instructions for implementing the policies.
5. **Review and Validate**:
    - Circulate draft policies and procedures for review and feedback from stakeholders.
    - Validate that the policies are practical, enforceable, and aligned with industry standards and regulatory requirements.
6. **Approve and Publish**:
    - Obtain formal approval from senior management or a governing body.
    - Publish the policies and procedures in an accessible format and location for all employees.
7. **Communicate and Train**:
    - Communicate the new policies and procedures to all relevant parties.
    - Provide training and resources to ensure employees understand their roles and responsibilities.
8. **Monitor and Review**:
    - Regularly review and update policies and procedures to reflect changes in the threat landscape, business operations, and regulatory requirements.
    - Monitor adherence and effectiveness through audits, assessments, and feedback mechanisms.

Key Elements of Security Policies and Procedures

1. **Purpose**:
    - Explain the rationale behind the policy, its importance, and how it supports the organization's security objectives.
2. **Scope**:
    - Define the boundaries of the policy, including which systems, processes, and personnel it applies to.
3. **Policy Statement**:
    - Clearly state the specific requirements, rules, and expectations that must be followed.
4. **Roles and Responsibilities**:
    - Outline the responsibilities of individuals and teams involved in implementing and adhering to the policy.
5. **Procedures**:
    - Provide detailed, step-by-step instructions for carrying out the policy requirements. Include flowcharts, checklists, or other tools to facilitate understanding.

6. **Compliance and Enforcement**:
   - Describe how compliance will be monitored, measured, and enforced. Include consequences for non-compliance.
7. **Review and Revision**:
   - Specify the process for regular review and updates to the policy, including who is responsible for this task.
8. **References**:
   - Include references to relevant laws, regulations, standards, and other policies that support or relate to the policy.

Strategies for Ensuring Policy Adherence

1. **Leadership Commitment**:
   - Ensure that senior management visibly supports and enforces the policies, demonstrating their importance to the organization.
2. **Regular Training and Awareness**:
   - Provide ongoing training and awareness programs to educate employees about policies, procedures, and their importance in maintaining security.
3. **Clear Communication**:
   - Use multiple communication channels to disseminate policies and ensure that all employees are aware of their existence and relevance.
4. **Incentives and Penalties**:
   - Implement a system of incentives for compliance and penalties for violations to reinforce the importance of adherence.
5. **Integration with Business Processes**:
   - Embed policies and procedures into daily business operations, making compliance a natural part of employees' workflows.
6. **Continuous Monitoring and Feedback**:
   - Monitor compliance through regular audits, assessments, and automated tools. Use feedback from these activities to make necessary adjustments.
7. **Accessible Documentation**:
   - Ensure that policies and procedures are easily accessible and written in clear, understandable language.

Examples of How Well-Crafted Policies Enhance Security Posture

Example 1: Data Protection Policy

- **Elements**:
  - **Purpose**: Protect sensitive data from unauthorized access, disclosure, alteration, and destruction.
  - **Policy Statement**: All sensitive data must be encrypted at rest and in transit. Access to sensitive data is restricted to authorized personnel only.
  - **Procedures**: Instructions for data encryption, access control mechanisms, and regular audits to ensure compliance.
- **Impact**:
  - **Enhanced Security Posture**: By enforcing encryption and access controls, the organization significantly reduces the risk of data breaches.
  - **Compliance**: Meets regulatory requirements such as GDPR, HIPAA, and PCI-DSS.

Example 2: Incident Response Policy

- **Elements**:
  - **Purpose**: Provide a structured approach to identifying, managing, and responding to security incidents.
  - **Policy Statement**: All security incidents must be reported within one hour of detection. An incident response team will be activated to assess and mitigate the incident.
  - **Procedures**: Steps for incident identification, reporting, assessment, containment, eradication, recovery, and post-incident analysis.

- Impact:
    - **Enhanced Security Posture**: Rapid detection and response minimize the impact of security incidents and reduce recovery time.
    - **Preparedness**: Clearly defined roles and procedures ensure that the organization is well-prepared to handle incidents effectively.

Example 3: Access Control Policy
- Elements:
    - **Purpose**: Ensure that access to systems and data is granted based on the principle of least privilege.
    - **Policy Statement**: Access to systems and data must be granted based on job roles and responsibilities. Regular reviews of access permissions are required.
    - **Procedures**: Instructions for granting, modifying, and revoking access, along with periodic access reviews.
- Impact:
    - **Enhanced Security Posture**: Reduces the risk of unauthorized access and potential data breaches.
    - **Operational Efficiency**: Clearly defined access controls streamline the process of granting and revoking access, ensuring that employees have the access they need without unnecessary privileges.

Well-crafted security policies and procedures are essential for supporting control implementation and enhancing an organization's security posture. By including key elements such as purpose, scope, roles, responsibilities, procedures, and compliance measures, organizations can create effective and actionable policies. Ensuring adherence through leadership commitment, training, clear communication, and continuous monitoring further strengthens the organization's ability to manage security risks effectively.

Change management is a crucial aspect of control implementation, particularly when introducing new security measures that impact existing processes and systems. Effective change management ensures that new controls are integrated smoothly, minimizing disruption to operations and ensuring user acceptance. Here's an evaluation of the role of change management in control implementation, strategies for managing the impact, and methods to ensure user acceptance.

Role of Change Management in Control Implementation

1. Facilitating Smooth Transitions:
- Change management provides a structured approach to transitioning from old processes and systems to new ones. It ensures that all aspects of the change are considered and addressed, reducing the risk of operational disruptions.

2. Ensuring Compliance and Consistency:
- By managing changes systematically, organizations can ensure that new controls comply with regulatory requirements and align with existing security policies and frameworks.

3. Managing Risks and Mitigating Negative Impacts:
- Change management involves identifying potential risks associated with implementing new controls and developing strategies to mitigate these risks. This helps in maintaining the integrity and availability of systems during transitions.

4. Enhancing Communication and Collaboration:
- Effective change management promotes clear communication and collaboration among stakeholders, ensuring that everyone understands the changes, their purpose, and their impact.

Managing the Impact of New Controls on Existing Processes and Systems

1. Comprehensive Planning:
- **Assess Current State**: Evaluate the current processes and systems to understand how new controls will interact with existing elements.
- **Define Objectives**: Clearly outline the objectives of the new controls and how they will enhance security.
- **Develop a Roadmap**: Create a detailed implementation plan that includes timelines, milestones, and responsible parties.

2. Stakeholder Engagement:
- **Identify Stakeholders**: Identify all stakeholders affected by the new controls, including IT staff, business units, and end-users.
- **Engage Early**: Involve stakeholders early in the planning process to gather input, address concerns, and build support.

3. Risk Assessment and Mitigation:
- **Conduct Risk Analysis**: Identify potential risks and impacts of implementing new controls.
- **Develop Mitigation Strategies**: Create plans to mitigate identified risks, such as backup procedures, failover systems, and communication plans.

4. Testing and Validation:
- **Pilot Programs**: Implement new controls in a controlled environment or pilot program to test their effectiveness and identify any issues.
- **User Acceptance Testing**: Conduct thorough testing with end-users to ensure the controls work as intended and are user-friendly.

5. Training and Education:
- **Develop Training Programs**: Create training materials and sessions to educate users about the new controls and how to use them effectively.
- **Provide Ongoing Support**: Offer continuous support and resources to help users adapt to the new controls.

Strategies for Minimizing Disruption

1. Gradual Implementation:
- **Phased Rollout**: Implement controls in phases to allow time for adjustment and reduce the risk of widespread disruption.
- **Priority-Based Deployment**: Start with critical systems and high-risk areas before expanding to other parts of the organization.

2. Clear Communication:
- **Communicate Changes**: Clearly communicate the changes, their benefits, and the implementation timeline to all stakeholders.
- **Feedback Channels**: Establish channels for users to provide feedback and report issues during the implementation process.

3. Backup and Recovery Plans:
- **Data Backups**: Ensure that data is backed up before implementing new controls to prevent data loss in case of issues.
- **Recovery Procedures**: Develop and test recovery procedures to quickly restore systems if problems arise.

Ensuring User Acceptance of New Security Measures

1. User Involvement:
- **Include Users in Planning**: Involve end-users in the planning and decision-making process to ensure their needs and concerns are addressed.
- **User Representatives**: Appoint user representatives to provide input and feedback on behalf of their peers.

2. Effective Training Programs:
- **Tailored Training**: Provide training tailored to different user groups, focusing on how the new controls impact their specific roles.
- **Hands-On Workshops**: Conduct hands-on workshops and practical sessions to help users understand and practice using the new controls.

3. Demonstrating Value:
- **Highlight Benefits**: Clearly communicate the benefits of the new controls, such as improved security, reduced risk, and compliance with regulations.
- **Showcase Successes**: Share success stories and examples of how the new controls have positively impacted the organization.

4. Ongoing Support and Resources:

- **Help Desks and Hotlines**: Set up help desks or hotlines to provide immediate support to users encountering issues.
- **Online Resources**: Create online resources, such as FAQs, guides, and video tutorials, for users to access at their convenience.

Example: Implementing Multi-Factor Authentication (MFA)

1. Planning and Assessment:
- Evaluate current authentication methods and identify systems and applications that will be affected by MFA.
- Develop a roadmap for rolling out MFA, starting with high-risk systems.

2. Stakeholder Engagement:
- Engage IT staff, security teams, and end-users to gather input and address concerns.
- Communicate the benefits of MFA, such as enhanced security and reduced risk of unauthorized access.

3. Risk Mitigation:
- Conduct a pilot program with a small group of users to test MFA implementation and gather feedback.
- Develop backup authentication methods in case users encounter issues with MFA.

4. Training and Communication:
- Provide training sessions and materials to educate users on how to set up and use MFA.
- Communicate the rollout plan and provide support channels for users to report issues and ask questions.

5. Implementation and Support:
- Implement MFA in phases, starting with critical systems and expanding to other areas.
- Offer ongoing support through help desks, online resources, and user feedback channels.

Effective change management is essential for successful control implementation. By involving stakeholders, conducting thorough planning and risk assessment, providing comprehensive training, and maintaining clear communication, organizations can minimize disruption and ensure user acceptance of new security measures. This approach not only enhances security but also fosters a positive attitude toward continuous improvement and innovation.

Concept of Control Testing and Validation

Control testing and validation are critical components of the security control implementation process. These activities ensure that controls are not only properly implemented but also functioning as intended to mitigate identified risks. Control testing involves evaluating the effectiveness and efficiency of security controls, while validation confirms that the controls meet the defined security requirements and objectives.

Methodologies for Verifying Implemented Controls

1. **Control Self-Assessments (CSA)**:
    - **Description**: Internal reviews conducted by control owners or management to assess the effectiveness of their own controls.
    - **Method**: Use checklists and questionnaires based on control objectives and criteria. Review documentation, processes, and records to ensure controls are in place and functioning.
2. **Internal Audits**:
    - **Description**: Independent evaluations conducted by an internal audit team within the organization.
    - **Method**: Audit teams review control design and operating effectiveness through documentation review, interviews, and testing procedures. They provide an unbiased assessment of control performance.
3. **External Audits and Assessments**:
    - **Description**: Evaluations conducted by third-party auditors to provide an independent perspective on control effectiveness.
    - **Method**: External auditors follow established frameworks and standards (e.g., ISO/IEC 27001, SOC 2) to assess control implementation and effectiveness.
4. **Penetration Testing (Pen Testing)**:

- **Description**: Simulated cyberattacks performed to identify vulnerabilities and test the effectiveness of security controls.
    - **Method**: Ethical hackers attempt to exploit weaknesses in the system to evaluate the robustness of controls. Pen testing includes network, application, and physical security testing.
5. **Vulnerability Scanning**:
    - **Description**: Automated tools used to identify vulnerabilities in systems, networks, and applications.
    - **Method**: Regular scans using tools like Nessus, Qualys, or OpenVAS to detect security weaknesses that need to be addressed.
6. **Continuous Monitoring**:
    - **Description**: Ongoing surveillance of security controls and systems to ensure they operate as intended.
    - **Method**: Use security information and event management (SIEM) systems, intrusion detection systems (IDS), and automated monitoring tools to detect anomalies and incidents in real-time.
7. **Control Testing (Design and Operating Effectiveness Tests)**:
    - **Description**: Specific tests to evaluate the design (whether controls are appropriately designed to mitigate risks) and operating effectiveness (whether controls are functioning as intended).
    - **Method**: Test the control's design through documentation review and effectiveness through observation, re-performance, and sample testing.

Importance of Independent Testing

Independent testing is crucial because it provides an unbiased evaluation of controls. Internal stakeholders may have conflicts of interest or lack the objectivity needed to identify deficiencies. Independent testing ensures:

- **Objectivity**: Provides an impartial assessment of control effectiveness.
- **Credibility**: Enhances trust and confidence among stakeholders, including regulators and customers.
- **Compliance**: Meets regulatory requirements for independent verification of controls.
- **Improvement**: Identifies areas for improvement that internal reviews might overlook.

Examples of Common Testing Approaches

1. Access Control Testing:
- **Approach**: Verify user access rights and permissions through reviews and re-performance of access provisioning processes. Test role-based access controls (RBAC) and least privilege principles.
- **Example**: Conduct periodic user access reviews to ensure only authorized personnel have access to critical systems and data.

2. Encryption and Data Protection:
- **Approach**: Test encryption mechanisms by verifying that data at rest and in transit are encrypted using approved algorithms. Validate encryption keys management processes.
- **Example**: Perform a review of database encryption settings and intercept network traffic to ensure data is encrypted.

3. Incident Response Testing:
- **Approach**: Conduct tabletop exercises and simulations to test the incident response plan. Evaluate the effectiveness of detection, response, and recovery procedures.
- **Example**: Simulate a ransomware attack to test the organization's ability to detect, contain, and recover from the incident.

4. Network Security Testing:
- **Approach**: Use penetration testing and vulnerability scanning to assess network security controls. Test firewall configurations, intrusion detection/prevention systems (IDS/IPS), and network segmentation.
- **Example**: Perform a pen test to attempt bypassing the firewall and accessing sensitive network segments.

5. Software Development Lifecycle (SDLC) Security:
- **Approach**: Integrate security testing throughout the SDLC, including static and dynamic application security testing (SAST/DAST). Conduct code reviews and security testing during development.

- **Example**: Use SAST tools to identify vulnerabilities in source code and DAST tools to test running applications for security issues.

Control testing and validation are essential to ensure that security controls are effectively mitigating risks as intended. Organizations use various methodologies, including self-assessments, internal and external audits, penetration testing, vulnerability scanning, continuous monitoring, and specific control tests. Independent testing is particularly important for providing objective and credible assessments. By employing a combination of these approaches, organizations can maintain a robust security posture, ensure compliance, and continuously improve their security controls.

Assessment/Audit of Security and Privacy Controls

Establishing stakeholder roles and responsibilities is a critical step in preparing for a security and privacy control assessment. This process ensures that all relevant parties are identified, engaged, and their responsibilities clearly defined to facilitate a thorough and effective assessment. Here's an analysis of this process, along with strategies for maintaining objectivity and managing potential conflicts of interest.

Process of Establishing Stakeholder Roles and Responsibilities

1. **Identify Relevant Stakeholders**:
   - **Internal Stakeholders**: Include individuals and teams directly involved in or affected by the security and privacy controls. This typically involves IT, security, compliance, legal, HR, and business unit leaders.
   - **External Stakeholders**: Consider external auditors, consultants, vendors, and regulatory bodies that may have a role in the assessment.

2. **Define Roles and Responsibilities**:
   - **Assessment Leader**: Responsible for overseeing the entire assessment process, ensuring it is carried out according to plan, and addressing any issues that arise.
   - **Control Owners**: Individuals or teams responsible for the implementation and operation of specific controls. They provide detailed information and evidence of control performance.
   - **Assessment Team**: A group of internal or external assessors who conduct the evaluation, testing, and validation of controls.
   - **Support Staff**: Includes administrative support, IT staff, and others who facilitate the logistics and execution of the assessment.

3. **Engage Stakeholders**:
   - **Communication Plan**: Develop a comprehensive communication plan to ensure all stakeholders are informed about the assessment's objectives, scope, timelines, and their specific roles.
   - **Kick-Off Meeting**: Conduct a kick-off meeting to align expectations, clarify roles and responsibilities, and address any initial questions or concerns.
   - **Regular Updates**: Provide regular updates throughout the assessment process to keep all parties informed of progress, findings, and any adjustments to the plan.

4. **Documentation**:
   - **Role Matrix**: Create a role matrix that outlines each stakeholder's responsibilities, deliverables, and deadlines. This helps ensure accountability and clarity.
   - **Assessment Plan**: Document the assessment plan, including the scope, methodology, schedule, and resources required. Ensure it is reviewed and approved by key stakeholders.

Ensuring All Relevant Parties are Identified and Engaged

1. **Comprehensive Stakeholder Analysis**:
   - Conduct a stakeholder analysis to identify all individuals and groups that have a stake in the assessment. Consider both direct and indirect impacts on various departments and functions.

2. **Consultation and Collaboration**:
   - Engage with department heads and key personnel to identify stakeholders who might not be immediately obvious. Collaborative discussions help uncover additional relevant parties.

3. **Role Clarification**:
   - Clearly define the roles and responsibilities of each stakeholder to avoid overlaps and ensure all critical areas are covered.

4. **Use of Stakeholder Registers**:
   - Maintain a stakeholder register that lists all identified stakeholders, their roles, contact information, and their interest or influence in the assessment.

Managing Potential Conflicts of Interest

Potential Conflicts of Interest:

- **Self-Assessment Bias**: Control owners might be biased in assessing their controls, leading to overly positive evaluations.

- **Internal Politics**: Organizational dynamics and politics can influence the objectivity of the assessment.
- **Resource Allocation**: Conflicts can arise over resource allocation and prioritization of assessment tasks.

Strategies for Maintaining Objectivity:
1. **Independent Assessment Teams**:
    - Use independent assessment teams, either from an internal audit function that operates independently of management or external consultants, to conduct the assessment.
2. **Segregation of Duties**:
    - Ensure that those responsible for implementing controls are not the same individuals assessing their effectiveness. This separation helps maintain objectivity.
3. **Clear Assessment Criteria**:
    - Develop clear, objective assessment criteria based on established frameworks and standards. This reduces subjective judgments and biases.
4. **Regular Oversight and Review**:
    - Establish a review committee or oversight board to monitor the assessment process, review findings, and ensure adherence to assessment methodologies.
5. **Anonymous Feedback Mechanisms**:
    - Implement anonymous feedback mechanisms to allow stakeholders to report concerns or provide input without fear of retribution or bias.
6. **Conflict of Interest Declarations**:
    - Require all assessment team members to declare any potential conflicts of interest. Address any identified conflicts through reassignments or additional oversight.

Examples of Roles and Responsibilities in a Control Assessment

Example 1: Financial Institution's Data Privacy Assessment
- **Assessment Leader**: Chief Information Security Officer (CISO)
    - Oversees the entire assessment process, ensures alignment with regulatory requirements (e.g., GDPR, CCPA), and addresses high-level issues.
- **Control Owners**: Data Protection Officers (DPO) and IT Security Managers
    - Provide evidence of implemented data protection controls, such as encryption and access controls. Respond to queries and facilitate evidence collection.
- **Assessment Team**: Internal Audit Team
    - Conducts detailed evaluations of data protection controls, including testing encryption mechanisms, reviewing access logs, and interviewing relevant staff.
- **Support Staff**: IT Support Team
    - Assists with technical aspects of the assessment, such as providing system access, extracting data logs, and configuring test environments.

Example 2: Healthcare Provider's Security Controls Assessment
- **Assessment Leader**: Director of Compliance
    - Ensures the assessment covers all relevant regulatory requirements (e.g., HIPAA) and coordinates with external auditors if necessary.
- **Control Owners**: Health Information Managers and IT Security Team
    - Present evidence of HIPAA compliance controls, such as audit trails, user access reviews, and secure communication protocols.
- **Assessment Team**: External Security Consultants
    - Conduct independent assessments of the security controls, including penetration testing, vulnerability assessments, and policy reviews.
- **Support Staff**: Administrative Staff
    - Manages scheduling, documentation, and communication logistics for the assessment process.

By clearly defining and documenting roles and responsibilities, engaging all relevant stakeholders, and implementing strategies to manage conflicts of interest, organizations can ensure a thorough and objective security and privacy control assessment. This structured approach enhances the reliability of the assessment findings and supports continuous improvement in the organization's security posture.

Clearly defined objectives and scope are fundamental to the success of security audits. They ensure that the audit process is focused, comprehensive, and aligned with organizational goals. Without clear objectives and a well-defined scope, audits can become unfocused, miss critical areas, or generate results that do not accurately reflect the organization's security posture.

Importance of Clearly Defined Objectives and Scope

1. Focus and Relevance:
- Clearly defined objectives help auditors concentrate on the most critical aspects of the security environment, ensuring that the audit addresses the most significant risks and compliance requirements.
- A well-defined scope delineates the boundaries of the audit, specifying which systems, processes, and controls are to be examined. This prevents scope creep and ensures that the audit remains manageable and relevant.

2. Resource Allocation:
- Defining the scope allows for effective allocation of resources, including time, personnel, and tools. This ensures that the audit can be conducted efficiently without overstretching available resources.
- Objectives help prioritize areas that need more attention, ensuring that critical systems and high-risk areas are thoroughly examined.

3. Consistency and Comparability:
- Clear objectives and scope provide a consistent framework for conducting audits, making it easier to compare results over time or across different parts of the organization.
- This consistency is essential for tracking improvements, identifying trends, and benchmarking against industry standards or regulatory requirements.

4. Audit Credibility and Buy-In:
- Audits with well-defined objectives and scope are more likely to be seen as credible and valuable by stakeholders. This can lead to greater acceptance of audit findings and recommendations.
- Clear parameters help manage expectations and reduce misunderstandings about the audit's purpose and coverage.

Determining the Appropriate Breadth and Depth of an Assessment

1. Risk Assessment:
- Conduct a preliminary risk assessment to identify the most significant threats, vulnerabilities, and potential impacts on the organization. This helps determine which areas need the most focus.
- Prioritize high-risk areas, critical assets, and systems that process sensitive information or are subject to regulatory requirements.

2. Regulatory and Compliance Requirements:
- Review relevant regulations, standards, and compliance requirements to ensure that the audit addresses all mandatory areas.
- Incorporate industry best practices and frameworks, such as ISO/IEC 27001, NIST CSF, or PCI-DSS, to guide the scope and depth of the audit.

3. Business Objectives and Goals:
- Align the audit objectives with the organization's strategic goals and business objectives. Ensure that the audit helps the organization achieve its broader security and operational goals.
- Consider the perspectives and concerns of key stakeholders, including senior management, IT staff, and business unit leaders.

4. Historical Audit Results:
- Review findings from previous audits to identify recurring issues, areas of concern, or gaps that need further examination.
- Use past audit results to refine the scope and focus on areas that have shown weaknesses or require ongoing monitoring.

Examples of Poorly Defined Scope Leading to Ineffective or Misleading Audit Results

1. Overly Broad Scope:

- **Example**: An audit aims to cover all IT systems, applications, and networks within a large organization without prioritizing specific areas.
- **Issue**: The audit becomes too extensive to manage effectively, leading to superficial assessments that miss critical details and vulnerabilities in high-risk areas.
- **Result**: The audit report may lack actionable insights and fail to provide a clear picture of the organization's security posture.

2. Overly Narrow Scope:
- **Example**: An audit focuses exclusively on the organization's firewall configurations, ignoring other critical areas such as user access controls, data encryption, and incident response procedures.
- **Issue**: Key vulnerabilities and security gaps outside the scope of the audit remain unaddressed, leading to a false sense of security.
- **Result**: The organization may overlook significant risks that could be exploited by attackers, leading to potential security breaches.

3. Misaligned Objectives:
- **Example**: An audit is conducted with the primary objective of meeting a regulatory compliance requirement, without considering the organization's specific risk landscape and business objectives.
- **Issue**: The audit focuses on checking compliance boxes rather than addressing actual security risks and enhancing the organization's security posture.
- **Result**: The audit fails to identify and mitigate real threats, leaving the organization vulnerable despite being technically compliant with regulations.

4. Ambiguous Scope Definitions:
- **Example**: An audit scope is vaguely defined, stating that "security controls" will be reviewed without specifying which controls, systems, or processes are included.
- **Issue**: Auditors and stakeholders may have different interpretations of the scope, leading to inconsistent assessments and gaps in coverage.
- **Result**: The audit results may be incomplete or misleading, as critical areas might be overlooked or assessed inconsistently.

Strategies for Effective Scope Definition

1. Clear and Specific Objectives:
- Define clear and specific audit objectives that align with the organization's risk management strategy, compliance requirements, and business goals.
- Example: "Assess the effectiveness of access controls for the organization's financial systems to ensure compliance with SOX requirements and mitigate unauthorized access risks."

2. Detailed Scope Statement:
- Develop a detailed scope statement that outlines the boundaries of the audit, including specific systems, processes, and controls to be examined.
- Example: "The audit will cover all user access controls, data encryption mechanisms, and incident response procedures for the organization's cloud infrastructure."

3. Stakeholder Involvement:
- Involve key stakeholders in defining the audit scope to ensure that their concerns and priorities are addressed.
- Example: Conduct workshops or meetings with IT, compliance, and business unit leaders to gather input on the most critical areas to be included in the audit.

4. Flexible Scope Adjustments:
- Allow for flexibility in the audit scope to accommodate emerging risks or changes in the organization's environment.
- Example: If a new regulatory requirement is introduced during the audit process, adjust the scope to include an assessment of compliance with the new regulation.

Clearly defined objectives and scope are essential for conducting effective security audits. They ensure that the audit is focused, relevant, and aligned with organizational goals, leading to actionable insights and meaningful improvements in the organization's security posture. By considering risk assessments, regulatory requirements, business objectives, and historical audit results, organizations can determine the appropriate breadth and depth of an assessment and avoid the pitfalls of poorly defined scope.

Scoping assets, methods, and the level of effort in a security assessment involves a systematic approach to ensure that the assessment is thorough yet feasible within given resource constraints. Organizations must identify the assets to be evaluated, determine the methods for assessment, and estimate the level of effort required. Balancing comprehensiveness with resource constraints is crucial to maximizing the effectiveness of the security assessment while ensuring it is manageable.

Methodology for Scoping Assets, Methods, and Level of Effort

1. Identify and Categorize Assets:
- Start by listing all assets within the organization that require assessment. This includes hardware, software, data, networks, and personnel.
- Categorize assets based on their criticality and sensitivity. High-value assets that impact business operations or contain sensitive information should be prioritized.

2. Define Assessment Methods:
- Choose appropriate methods for assessing each category of assets. Methods may include vulnerability scanning, penetration testing, configuration reviews, and security audits.
- Determine the tools and techniques necessary for each method, considering factors such as the asset type, the nature of potential threats, and compliance requirements.

3. Estimate Level of Effort:
- Assess the time, personnel, and financial resources required for each assessment method. This includes planning, execution, analysis, and reporting phases.
- Develop a timeline that aligns with organizational priorities and resource availability. Consider seasonal business cycles and resource constraints to minimize disruption.

Balancing Comprehensiveness with Resource Constraints

Organizations often face the challenge of conducting comprehensive assessments without overstretching resources. The following strategies can help balance these needs:

1. Risk-Based Approach:
- Focus on high-risk areas first. Conduct thorough assessments on critical assets and processes that pose the greatest risk to the organization.
- Use risk assessments to prioritize efforts, ensuring that the most significant vulnerabilities are addressed promptly.

2. Phased Assessments:
- Implement a phased approach where the assessment is spread over multiple stages or cycles. This allows for periodic reviews and adjustments based on findings from earlier phases.
- Phase assessments can also help manage workload and resource allocation more effectively.

3. Automation:
- Leverage automated tools for routine tasks such as vulnerability scanning and compliance checks. Automation reduces manual effort and allows resources to focus on more complex assessment activities.
- Automated tools can provide continuous monitoring, offering real-time insights into the security posture.

Concept of Sampling in Large-Scale Audits

In large-scale audits, assessing every single asset and control may be impractical. Sampling is a technique used to evaluate a subset of assets or transactions to draw conclusions about the entire population. Effective sampling strategies ensure that the sample is representative and the findings are reliable.

1. Random Sampling:
- Select a random subset of assets or transactions for assessment. Random sampling helps eliminate bias and ensures that each item has an equal chance of being selected.

- Example: In an organization with hundreds of servers, a random sample of 20% of servers might be selected for a detailed configuration review.

2. **Stratified Sampling**:
   - Divide the population into distinct strata or groups based on specific characteristics such as asset type, criticality, or geographic location. Select samples from each stratum proportionally.
   - Example: In a multinational company, stratified sampling might involve selecting samples from different regions to ensure geographical diversity in the assessment.

3. **Judgmental Sampling**:
   - Use expert judgment to select samples based on knowledge of the organization, known risk areas, or past incidents. This method relies on the assessor's expertise to target high-risk areas.
   - Example: If previous audits identified significant issues in a particular department, judgmental sampling might focus on assets within that department for the current assessment.

4. **Systematic Sampling**:
   - Select samples at regular intervals from an ordered list. Systematic sampling provides a structured approach and is easy to implement.
   - Example: In a list of 1,000 network devices, every 10th device might be selected for assessment.

By carefully scoping assets, methods, and the level of effort, organizations can conduct security assessments that are both comprehensive and resource-efficient. Effective sampling strategies further enhance the feasibility of large-scale audits, allowing organizations to maintain robust security postures without overburdening their resources.

Reviewing existing evidence and documentation prior to an assessment is a critical step in developing a comprehensive and effective audit strategy. This pre-assessment review helps auditors understand the organization's current security posture, identify potential gaps, and focus their efforts on the most relevant areas.

Types of Documents to Be Examined

1. Policies and Procedures:
- Security policies outline the organization's approach to managing security risks and provide a framework for the implementation of controls. Procedures detail specific actions required to comply with these policies.
- Examining these documents helps auditors assess whether they are up-to-date, comprehensive, and aligned with best practices and regulatory requirements.

2. Risk Assessments and Risk Registers:
- Risk assessments identify and evaluate risks to the organization's information assets. Risk registers document these risks, their severity, and the mitigation measures in place.
- Reviewing risk assessments and registers provides insights into the organization's risk management processes and highlights areas of potential concern.

3. Previous Audit Reports:
- Previous audit reports provide valuable information about past findings, recommendations, and corrective actions taken.
- Analyzing these reports helps auditors identify recurring issues, assess the effectiveness of implemented controls, and determine if past recommendations have been addressed.

4. Incident Reports and Response Plans:
- Incident reports document security incidents, their impact, and the actions taken to resolve them. Incident response plans outline procedures for detecting, responding to, and recovering from security incidents.
- Reviewing these documents helps auditors evaluate the organization's incident response capabilities and identify any gaps or areas for improvement.

5. System and Network Diagrams:
- Diagrams of the organization's IT infrastructure, including network architecture, data flows, and system interconnections, provide a visual representation of the environment.
- These diagrams help auditors understand the scope of the assessment, identify critical assets, and pinpoint potential vulnerabilities.

6. Access Control Logs and User Access Reviews:

- Access control logs track user access to systems and data, while user access reviews assess the appropriateness of access rights.
- Reviewing these documents helps auditors identify potential issues with access controls, such as unauthorized access or excessive privileges.

7. Configuration Management Records:
- Configuration management records document the settings and configurations of systems and applications.
- Analyzing these records helps auditors assess whether systems are configured securely and consistently with organizational policies.

8. Compliance Reports:
- Compliance reports document the organization's adherence to regulatory requirements and industry standards.
- Reviewing these reports helps auditors understand the regulatory landscape and identify any compliance gaps.

How Pre-Assessment Review Informs the Audit Strategy

1. Risk Identification and Prioritization:
- The pre-assessment review helps auditors identify and prioritize risks based on the organization's documented risk assessments and incident reports.
- This ensures that the audit strategy focuses on high-risk areas that require the most attention.

2. Scope Definition:
- By reviewing system and network diagrams, auditors can define the scope of the assessment, ensuring that all critical assets and interconnections are covered.
- This helps in developing a targeted audit plan that addresses key components of the IT environment.

3. Control Validation:
- Examining policies, procedures, and configuration records provides a baseline for evaluating the effectiveness of existing controls.
- Auditors can use this information to develop test plans that validate the implementation and effectiveness of these controls.

4. Audit Trail Establishment:
- Reviewing access control logs and user access reviews helps establish an audit trail, allowing auditors to trace actions and events back to their sources.
- This aids in identifying any anomalies or irregularities that may require further investigation.

5. Benchmarking and Best Practices:
- Previous audit reports and compliance reports provide benchmarks for assessing the organization's current security posture against industry best practices.
- This information helps auditors identify areas where the organization may need to improve or align with established standards.

Potential Red Flags Identified During the Review

1. Outdated Policies and Procedures:
- Policies and procedures that have not been updated regularly may indicate a lack of attention to evolving security threats and regulatory changes.
- This could suggest potential vulnerabilities in the organization's security framework.

2. Unresolved Past Findings:
- Recurring issues or unaddressed recommendations from previous audits may indicate ineffective remediation processes or a lack of commitment to improving security.
- This can highlight areas that require immediate attention and corrective action.

3. Inconsistent Risk Assessments:
- Discrepancies or inconsistencies in risk assessments and risk registers may suggest that the organization does not have a robust risk management process.
- This could result in overlooked risks or inadequate mitigation measures.

4. Frequent Security Incidents:
- A high number of security incidents or repeated incidents of the same type may indicate weaknesses in the organization's security controls or incident response capabilities.
- This underscores the need for a thorough evaluation of the organization's incident response plan and controls.

5. Excessive User Privileges:
- Access control logs that show excessive or inappropriate user privileges may indicate poor access management practices.
- This could lead to unauthorized access to sensitive data or systems, posing a significant security risk.

6. Non-Compliance with Regulations:
- Compliance reports that highlight gaps or non-compliance with regulatory requirements indicate potential legal and financial risks.
- This necessitates immediate corrective actions to align with regulatory standards.

Reviewing existing evidence and documentation prior to an assessment is essential for developing an effective audit strategy. It helps auditors identify and prioritize risks, define the scope, validate controls, establish an audit trail, and benchmark against best practices. Identifying potential red flags during this review can highlight areas that require focused attention, ensuring that the audit is thorough and provides valuable insights into the organization's security posture.

Verification methods in security audits are crucial for ensuring that controls are functioning as intended. The primary methods include interviews, examinations, and testing. Each has its own strengths and weaknesses, and organizations must determine the appropriate mix based on the audit objectives, the nature of the controls, and the specific context of the organization.

Interviews

Strengths:
- **Qualitative Insights**: Provide in-depth understanding and context that might not be evident through other methods.
- **Human Element**: Capture the perspectives, attitudes, and awareness of employees, which can highlight cultural and procedural issues.
- **Flexibility**: Allow auditors to explore responses in detail and ask follow-up questions.

Weaknesses:
- **Subjectivity**: Responses may be biased or inaccurate due to personal opinions, fear of repercussions, or misunderstanding.
- **Time-Consuming**: Conducting and analyzing interviews can be resource-intensive.
- **Limited Scope**: May not cover all aspects of technical controls effectively.

Effective Scenarios:
- **Policy Adherence**: Interviews are effective for assessing understanding and adherence to security policies among staff.
- **Incident Response Readiness**: Useful for gauging the preparedness and awareness of incident response teams.
- **Cultural Assessments**: Ideal for evaluating the security culture within the organization.

Examinations

Strengths:
- **Document Review**: Provides evidence of processes and control implementation through documentation.
- **Historical Insight**: Allows auditors to review historical records and logs for patterns and trends.
- **Compliance Verification**: Effective for verifying compliance with regulations and internal policies.

Weaknesses:
- **Static Nature**: Focuses on documentation, which might not reflect real-time practices.

- **Potential for Misrepresentation**: Documentation can be incomplete, outdated, or misleading if not maintained properly.
- **Limited Technical Insight**: Does not directly assess the technical efficacy of controls.

Effective Scenarios:
- **Policy and Procedure Review**: Examination is useful for verifying the existence and adequacy of documented policies and procedures.
- **Access Control Reviews**: Effective for reviewing user access logs and permission records to ensure proper access control.
- **Regulatory Compliance**: Ideal for ensuring that required documentation is in place and aligns with regulatory standards.

Testing
Strengths:
- **Hands-On Validation**: Provides direct evidence of control effectiveness by actively probing the controls.
- **Technical Accuracy**: Effective for validating technical configurations and the operational state of controls.
- **Real-Time Assessment**: Offers a current view of control performance under actual conditions.

Weaknesses:
- **Resource Intensive**: Requires technical expertise and can be time-consuming.
- **Potential Disruption**: Testing, especially penetration testing, can impact system performance or availability.
- **Scope Limitations**: May not provide a complete picture if testing scope is too narrow.

Effective Scenarios:
- **Penetration Testing**: Useful for identifying vulnerabilities in network security, applications, and infrastructure.
- **Configuration Audits**: Effective for verifying that systems and devices are configured according to security standards.
- **Incident Response Testing**: Ideal for simulating attacks to test the effectiveness of incident response procedures.

Determining the Appropriate Mix
Organizations should consider the following factors to determine the appropriate mix of verification methods:
1. **Audit Objectives**:
   - Define what the audit aims to achieve. For technical validation, testing might be prioritized. For procedural and compliance checks, examinations and interviews may be more appropriate.
2. **Nature of Controls**:
   - Technical controls (e.g., firewalls, encryption) often require testing for effective evaluation.
   - Administrative controls (e.g., policies, training) can be effectively assessed through interviews and examinations.
3. **Resource Availability**:
   - Consider the availability of technical expertise and time. Testing requires skilled personnel and can be resource-intensive, while interviews and examinations may be less demanding in terms of technical skills but can be time-consuming.
4. **Risk Profile**:
   - Higher-risk areas might warrant a greater emphasis on testing to ensure robust validation. Lower-risk areas might be sufficiently covered by interviews and examinations.

Examples of Effective Scenarios for Each Method
Interviews:
- **User Access Management**: Assessing employees' understanding of access management policies and their adherence to procedures.
- **Security Awareness**: Evaluating the effectiveness of security awareness programs by interviewing staff about their knowledge and practices.

Examinations:

- **Compliance Audits**: Verifying that all necessary documentation, such as data protection policies and incident response plans, is in place and up to date.
- **Change Management**: Reviewing change logs and approval records to ensure changes are managed and documented properly.

Testing:
- **Network Security**: Conducting penetration tests to identify vulnerabilities and assess the effectiveness of network security controls.
- **Patch Management**: Testing the deployment of security patches to ensure that systems are up to date and protected against known vulnerabilities.

By carefully selecting and balancing these methods based on the audit's specific needs, organizations can ensure a comprehensive and effective security assessment. This approach helps in identifying gaps, validating control effectiveness, and ultimately enhancing the organization's security posture.

Evidence validation is a critical component of security assessments, ensuring that the information collected during an audit is accurate, reliable, and can be trusted to inform decision-making. Validating evidence involves verifying its authenticity and integrity to confirm that it has not been tampered with and genuinely represents the state of the systems and controls under review.

Techniques for Ensuring Authenticity and Integrity of Collected Evidence

1. Checksum and Hashing:
- **Technique**: Generate checksums or hash values (e.g., MD5, SHA-256) for digital files and compare them to known values to verify that the files have not been altered.
- **Application**: Use hashing to validate log files, configuration files, and software binaries to ensure they are authentic and unchanged.

2. Digital Signatures:
- **Technique**: Apply digital signatures to documents and files to confirm their origin and integrity. Digital signatures use public key cryptography to create a unique signature that can be verified.
- **Application**: Validate signed documents, such as policies, reports, and emails, to ensure they have not been modified and originate from a trusted source.

3. Chain of Custody Documentation:
- **Technique**: Maintain a detailed chain of custody log that records the handling and transfer of evidence from collection to analysis. This log should include timestamps, individuals involved, and actions taken.
- **Application**: Ensure all collected evidence, such as physical devices or digital data, is tracked meticulously to prevent tampering and establish accountability.

4. Time Stamping:
- **Technique**: Use trusted time-stamping services to apply secure timestamps to digital records, ensuring they reflect the accurate time of creation or modification.
- **Application**: Validate the creation and modification times of logs, transactions, and audit trails to ensure they align with reported events.

5. Cross-Verification:
- **Technique**: Cross-verify evidence by collecting and comparing it from multiple independent sources. Consistency across sources enhances the credibility of the evidence.
- **Application**: Use multiple log sources (e.g., system logs, application logs, network logs) to verify the accuracy of reported incidents or system activities.

6. Forensic Tools:
- **Technique**: Employ digital forensic tools to analyze and verify evidence, ensuring it has not been altered and accurately reflects the system state.
- **Application**: Use forensic software to examine disk images, memory dumps, and network captures for authenticity and integrity.

Challenges of Evidence Validation in Complex IT Environments

1. Volume and Diversity of Data:

- **Challenge**: Complex IT environments generate vast amounts of diverse data, including logs, configurations, and transactions, making it difficult to validate all evidence comprehensively.
- **Strategy**: Implement automated tools and techniques, such as machine learning algorithms and data analytics, to filter and prioritize critical evidence for validation.

2. Dynamic and Distributed Systems:
- **Challenge**: In dynamic environments with cloud computing, microservices, and distributed architectures, evidence can be spread across multiple locations and systems, complicating validation.
- **Strategy**: Use centralized logging and monitoring solutions, such as SIEM systems, to aggregate and correlate data from distributed sources, simplifying validation.

3. Third-Party Dependencies:
- **Challenge**: Reliance on third-party services and providers can introduce challenges in accessing and validating evidence, especially if providers do not offer transparency.
- **Strategy**: Establish clear agreements and SLAs with third-party providers that include provisions for access to logs and evidence. Use independent verification methods where possible.

4. Encryption and Data Protection:
- **Challenge**: Encrypted data can be difficult to validate without appropriate keys and access controls, potentially hindering the validation process.
- **Strategy**: Ensure proper key management practices are in place and that auditors have the necessary permissions to decrypt and validate data. Document encryption and decryption processes thoroughly.

5. Evolving Threat Landscape:
- **Challenge**: The rapidly changing threat landscape can introduce new types of evidence and attack vectors that may not be accounted for in existing validation processes.
- **Strategy**: Stay updated with the latest threat intelligence and continuously update validation techniques and tools to address new types of evidence and attack methods.

Strategies for Overcoming Challenges in Evidence Validation

1. Standardized Procedures:
- Develop and implement standardized procedures for evidence collection, handling, and validation to ensure consistency and reliability across the organization.

2. Training and Awareness:
- Train auditors and relevant personnel on the importance of evidence validation and the specific techniques used to ensure authenticity and integrity. Promote a culture of diligence and accuracy in evidence handling.

3. Use of Advanced Tools:
- Leverage advanced tools and technologies, such as AI-driven analytics, automated forensic tools, and blockchain-based time-stamping, to enhance the efficiency and effectiveness of evidence validation.

4. Regular Audits and Reviews:
- Conduct regular internal and external audits to assess the effectiveness of evidence validation processes. Use audit findings to improve procedures and address any identified gaps.

5. Documentation and Reporting:
- Maintain thorough documentation of all evidence validation activities, including methodologies used, tools employed, and results obtained. Ensure that reports are clear, detailed, and accessible for future reference.

By employing robust techniques such as checksums, digital signatures, chain of custody documentation, time stamping, cross-verification, and forensic tools, organizations can ensure the authenticity and integrity of collected evidence. Overcoming challenges in complex IT environments requires standardized procedures, advanced tools, training, regular audits, and comprehensive documentation to maintain a reliable and effective evidence validation process.

Developing an initial assessment report is a critical step in the security and privacy control assessment process. It provides a detailed account of the findings, identifies areas of concern, and offers recommendations for improvement. The report must be clear, actionable, and structured to ensure that stakeholders can understand and act upon the findings. Here's an analysis of the process, key elements, and effective reporting techniques.

Key Elements of an Initial Assessment Report
1. **Executive Summary**:
    - **Purpose**: Provide a high-level overview of the assessment, including its objectives, scope, and key findings.
    - **Content**: Summarize the most critical issues, significant strengths, and overall security posture. Highlight urgent areas requiring immediate attention.
2. **Introduction**:
    - **Purpose**: Set the context for the assessment.
    - **Content**: Include the purpose, scope, and methodology of the assessment. Explain the assessment timeline and the teams involved.
3. **Methodology**:
    - **Purpose**: Describe the approach and techniques used during the assessment.
    - **Content**: Detail the assessment methods, such as interviews, document reviews, and technical testing. Explain the rationale behind the chosen methods.
4. **Findings**:
    - **Purpose**: Present the results of the assessment.
    - **Content**: Organize findings by categories or control areas. For each finding, include:
        - **Description**: Clear explanation of the issue or vulnerability.
        - **Evidence**: Supporting data, observations, or test results.
        - **Impact**: Potential risks or consequences if the issue is not addressed.
        - **Severity**: Classification of the issue's severity (e.g., high, medium, low).
5. **Recommendations**:
    - **Purpose**: Provide actionable steps to address the identified issues.
    - **Content**: For each finding, offer specific recommendations. Prioritize recommendations based on severity and potential impact. Include suggested timelines for remediation.
6. **Conclusion**:
    - **Purpose**: Summarize the overall assessment outcomes.
    - **Content**: Recap the key findings and recommendations. Emphasize the next steps and any follow-up actions.
7. **Appendices**:
    - **Purpose**: Provide additional details and supporting information.
    - **Content**: Include technical details, raw data, logs, and any supplementary materials that support the findings.

Presenting Findings Effectively
Clear, Actionable Language:
- Use straightforward, unambiguous language to ensure that findings and recommendations are easily understood.
- Avoid technical jargon when communicating with non-technical stakeholders. If technical terms are necessary, provide clear explanations.
- Actionable language helps stakeholders know precisely what actions to take, reducing the likelihood of misinterpretation or inaction.

Examples of Effective Reporting Techniques:
1. **Use of Visuals**:
    - **Charts and Graphs**: Visualize data to highlight trends, patterns, and the severity of issues. For example, use pie charts to show the distribution of findings by severity.
    - **Heatmaps**: Display risk levels across different areas of the organization, making it easy to identify high-risk zones.
2. **Prioritization and Categorization**:
    - **Severity Ratings**: Clearly indicate the severity of each finding (e.g., critical, high, medium, low). This helps prioritize remediation efforts.

- o **Categorization**: Group findings into categories (e.g., network security, access controls, data protection) to streamline the review process and assign responsibility.
3. **Action Plans**:
   - o **Table Format**: Present recommendations in a table format, including columns for the finding, recommended action, responsible party, and target completion date. This structure facilitates tracking and accountability.
   - o **SMART Goals**: Ensure recommendations are Specific, Measurable, Achievable, Relevant, and Time-bound to provide clear guidance and measurable objectives.
4. **Narrative Summaries**:
   - o **Case Studies**: Use narrative summaries or case studies to illustrate significant findings and their potential impact. This storytelling approach can make technical issues more relatable and understandable.
   - o **Executive Insights**: Include executive insights or quotes to provide context and emphasize the importance of findings.

Example of an Effective Reporting Technique
Finding:
- **Description**: The firewall ruleset allows unrestricted outbound traffic from the internal network.
- **Evidence**: During the network review, it was observed that outbound traffic was not filtered, posing a risk of data exfiltration.
- **Impact**: Unrestricted outbound traffic increases the risk of data breaches, as sensitive data can be transferred out without detection.
- **Severity**: High

Recommendation:
- **Action**: Implement and enforce outbound traffic filtering on the firewall. Only allow necessary traffic based on business needs.
- **Responsible Party**: Network Security Team
- **Timeline**: Within 30 days
- **SMART Goal**: By the end of Q1, restrict outbound traffic to essential services and implement monitoring to detect unauthorized data transfers.

Visualization:
- **Heatmap**: Display a heatmap highlighting the firewall issue as a critical risk area, emphasizing its urgency compared to other findings.

Incorporating these elements and techniques ensures that the initial assessment report is comprehensive, clear, and actionable. This approach not only communicates the findings effectively but also facilitates prompt and effective remediation, ultimately enhancing the organization's security posture.

Risk identification and mitigation summaries are essential components of audit reports. They help stakeholders understand the potential impacts of identified vulnerabilities and provide actionable recommendations for reducing risks. Effective communication of these risks involves balancing detailed technical information with executive-level summaries to ensure that both technical teams and senior management can understand and act upon the findings.

Role of Risk Identification and Mitigation Summaries
1. Clarity and Transparency:
- These summaries provide a clear and transparent overview of the vulnerabilities identified during the audit. They help stakeholders understand the nature and scope of the risks.

2. Prioritization of Risks:
- Summaries highlight the most critical risks, allowing the organization to prioritize its mitigation efforts. This ensures that resources are allocated efficiently to address the most significant threats first.

3. Actionable Recommendations:
- Mitigation summaries offer specific, actionable recommendations for reducing identified risks. This helps the organization implement effective controls and improve its security posture.

4. Informed Decision-Making:
- By providing comprehensive risk identification and mitigation information, these summaries support informed decision-making at all levels of the organization.

Communicating the Potential Impact of Identified Vulnerabilities

1. Quantitative and Qualitative Analysis:
- **Quantitative Analysis**: Use metrics and numerical data to quantify the potential impact of vulnerabilities. This can include the probability of occurrence, the potential financial loss, or the number of affected systems.
- **Qualitative Analysis**: Describe the nature of the vulnerabilities and their potential effects on the organization's operations, reputation, and compliance status. This provides context for the quantitative data.

2. Use of Impact Ratings:
- Assign impact ratings (e.g., high, medium, low) to each identified vulnerability based on its potential severity. This helps stakeholders quickly grasp the seriousness of the risks.
- Example: A high-impact rating might indicate a vulnerability that could lead to significant data breaches or operational disruptions.

3. Scenario-Based Descriptions:
- Provide scenarios that illustrate how vulnerabilities could be exploited and the potential consequences. This makes the risks more tangible and easier to understand.
- Example: Describe how a specific vulnerability in a web application could be used to steal customer data, leading to financial loss and reputational damage.

4. Visual Aids and Summaries:
- Use visual aids such as charts, graphs, and heat maps to represent the risks and their potential impacts. Visual representations can make complex information more accessible.
- Include executive summaries that distill the key findings and recommendations into concise, easily digestible formats.

Balancing Technical Detail and Executive-Level Summary

1. Executive Summary:
- **Purpose**: Provide a high-level overview of the audit findings, focusing on the most critical risks and recommended actions. This section should be brief and to the point, designed for senior management and board members.
- **Content**: Summarize the most significant vulnerabilities, their potential impacts, and the top priority mitigation steps. Highlight any trends or recurring issues that require strategic attention.

2. Detailed Technical Sections:
- **Purpose**: Offer in-depth technical analysis for IT and security teams who will be responsible for implementing the recommended controls. This section should provide comprehensive details about each identified vulnerability.
- **Content**: Include technical descriptions of vulnerabilities, affected systems, detailed mitigation steps, and any relevant logs or evidence. Provide clear instructions and references to technical documentation or best practices.

3. Integrated Approach:
- **Structure**: Organize the report so that the executive summary precedes the detailed technical sections. This allows senior management to get an overview before diving into the specifics.
- **Cross-Referencing**: Use cross-referencing between the executive summary and the detailed sections to ensure that readers can easily find additional information on specific points of interest.

4. Communication Strategy:
- **Tailored Presentations**: Present the findings and recommendations differently to various audiences within the organization. Use high-level presentations for executives and detailed briefings for technical teams.
- **Stakeholder Involvement**: Engage stakeholders throughout the audit process to ensure that the final report addresses their needs and concerns effectively.

Examples of Effective Risk Reporting
**1. Executive Summary Example:
- "During our recent audit, we identified 15 critical vulnerabilities in our network infrastructure. These vulnerabilities, if exploited, could lead to significant data breaches and operational disruptions. We recommend immediate patching of the identified systems, implementation of enhanced monitoring controls, and a review of our incident response plan. Addressing these vulnerabilities will significantly reduce our risk exposure and enhance our overall security posture."

**2. Technical Detail Example:
- "Vulnerability ID: 001
    - **Description**: A buffer overflow vulnerability was identified in the XYZ application, which could allow an attacker to execute arbitrary code.
    - **Impact**: High – Exploitation could lead to complete system compromise.
    - **Affected Systems**: Servers running XYZ version 1.2.3.
    - **Mitigation**: Apply patch XYZ-1.2.4 from the vendor, implement input validation controls, and monitor for signs of exploitation using IDS signatures."

Risk identification and mitigation summaries in audit reports play a vital role in communicating the potential impact of identified vulnerabilities. Effective communication requires a balance between detailed technical analysis and executive-level summaries. By using quantitative and qualitative analysis, impact ratings, scenario-based descriptions, and visual aids, auditors can ensure that their findings are understood and acted upon by both technical teams and senior management. This integrated approach supports informed decision-making and helps improve the organization's security posture.

Reviewing and planning risk response actions based on audit findings is a critical process that ensures identified risks are systematically addressed to enhance an organization's security posture. This process involves evaluating the significance of each risk, determining appropriate responses, and prioritizing actions based on the organization's risk tolerance and resource constraints.

Process of Reviewing and Planning Risk Response Actions
1. **Evaluate Audit Findings**:
    - **Gather Findings**: Compile all audit findings and categorize them based on severity, impact, and likelihood of occurrence.
    - **Analyze Impact**: Assess the potential impact of each finding on the organization's operations, reputation, and compliance status. Use qualitative and quantitative methods to estimate impact.
2. **Prioritize Risks**:
    - **Risk Rating**: Assign a risk rating (e.g., critical, high, medium, low) based on the combined assessment of impact and likelihood. This helps in identifying which risks need immediate attention.
    - **Business Context**: Consider the business context and strategic objectives when prioritizing risks. Focus on risks that could significantly disrupt business operations or lead to substantial financial losses.
3. **Determine Risk Response Actions**:
    - **Avoidance**: Eliminate the risk by discontinuing the activities that contribute to the risk.
    - **Mitigation**: Implement controls or measures to reduce the likelihood or impact of the risk.
    - **Transfer**: Shift the risk to a third party (e.g., through insurance or outsourcing).
    - **Acceptance**: Acknowledge the risk and decide to accept it without additional controls, usually because the cost of mitigation outweighs the benefit.
4. **Develop an Action Plan**:
    - **Action Steps**: For each risk, outline specific actions required to address the risk. This could include implementing new controls, enhancing existing ones, or taking corrective measures.
    - **Responsible Parties**: Assign responsibility for each action to specific individuals or teams.
    - **Timelines**: Set clear deadlines for the completion of each action item. Include short-term and long-term milestones.
5. **Monitor and Review**:

- **Regular Monitoring**: Continuously monitor the progress of risk response actions. Use dashboards, reports, and regular meetings to track progress.
- **Periodic Reviews**: Regularly review the effectiveness of risk responses and make adjustments as necessary. This includes reassessing risks and updating response strategies based on new information or changes in the risk landscape.

Prioritizing and Addressing Identified Risks

Organizations prioritize and address risks by considering factors such as the risk's potential impact, the likelihood of occurrence, available resources, and the organization's risk appetite. Here are some key steps in this process:

1. **Impact Assessment**:
   - Evaluate how each risk could affect key business processes, financial stability, regulatory compliance, and reputation.
   - Consider both direct and indirect impacts, including potential cascading effects on other parts of the organization.
2. **Likelihood Assessment**:
   - Assess the probability of each risk materializing. Use historical data, industry trends, and expert judgment to inform this assessment.
3. **Resource Allocation**:
   - Determine the resources required to address each risk, including financial costs, personnel, and time.
   - Allocate resources to address high-priority risks first, ensuring that the most significant threats are mitigated effectively.
4. **Cost-Benefit Analysis**:
   - Perform a cost-benefit analysis to evaluate the effectiveness of proposed risk responses. Compare the cost of implementing controls against the potential benefits of reduced risk exposure.
5. **Risk Response Strategies**:
   - Develop tailored strategies for each risk, considering the most effective and efficient methods to mitigate or transfer the risk.

Risk Acceptance

Risk acceptance is the decision to acknowledge a risk and not take any immediate action to mitigate it. This decision is based on a thorough evaluation of the risk's potential impact and likelihood, as well as the cost and feasibility of mitigation measures. Risk acceptance is appropriate under specific conditions:

1. **Cost of Mitigation Exceeds Benefits**:
   - When the cost of mitigating the risk is higher than the potential impact of the risk itself, it may be more practical to accept the risk.
   - Example: A small retail company may accept the risk of minor shoplifting incidents because the cost of implementing extensive security measures outweighs the financial impact of the occasional theft.
2. **Low Likelihood and Impact**:
   - When the risk has a low likelihood of occurring and a minimal impact, it may be acceptable to acknowledge the risk without further action.
   - Example: An organization may accept the risk of a rare natural disaster (e.g., a flood in a historically dry area) if the potential damage is minimal and the likelihood is extremely low.
3. **Strategic or Operational Necessity**:
   - In some cases, accepting a risk might be necessary for strategic or operational reasons. The organization might tolerate certain risks to pursue business opportunities or maintain competitive advantages.
   - Example: A tech startup might accept the risk of potential data breaches while rapidly developing its product to gain market share, focusing on addressing security in later stages of growth.
4. **Regulatory Compliance and Insurance Coverage**:
   - If regulatory requirements are met and adequate insurance coverage is in place, an organization might accept certain residual risks.

- Example: A manufacturing company might accept the risk of machinery breakdowns if it complies with safety regulations and holds comprehensive insurance to cover potential losses.

Examples of Risk Response Actions
1. **Avoidance**:
   - **Risk**: The risk of data breaches from using an unsecured cloud service.
   - **Action**: Discontinue the use of the unsecured cloud service and migrate data to a secure, compliant cloud provider.
2. **Mitigation**:
   - **Risk**: Vulnerabilities in the internal network.
   - **Action**: Implement network segmentation, enhance firewall rules, and conduct regular vulnerability assessments and patching.
3. **Transfer**:
   - **Risk**: Financial losses from cyber-attacks.
   - **Action**: Purchase cybersecurity insurance to transfer the financial impact of potential cyber incidents to the insurance provider.
4. **Acceptance**:
   - **Risk**: Minor disruptions from routine software updates.
   - **Action**: Accept the risk as the impact is minimal and the cost of implementing extensive change management controls is not justified.

By systematically reviewing and planning risk response actions based on audit findings, organizations can effectively manage their risk exposure. Prioritizing risks based on impact and likelihood, allocating resources efficiently, and adopting appropriate risk response strategies, including acceptance when justified, ensures a balanced approach to risk management. This proactive approach enhances the organization's ability to protect its assets, maintain compliance, and achieve its strategic objectives.

A comprehensive final audit report is essential for effectively communicating the findings of a security assessment. It should include all relevant information while maintaining clarity and focus, making it accessible and actionable for both technical and non-technical stakeholders. Here's an analysis of the components of such a report, along with strategies for presenting complex technical findings to non-technical stakeholders.

Components of a Comprehensive Final Audit Report

1. Executive Summary:
- **Purpose**: Provide a high-level overview of the audit's objectives, scope, key findings, and recommendations.
- **Content**: Summarize the most critical vulnerabilities, their potential impacts, and the top priority actions required to mitigate risks. Highlight any trends or patterns observed.

2. Introduction:
- **Purpose**: Set the context for the audit, explaining its purpose and significance.
- **Content**: Include the audit's objectives, scope, methodology, and any relevant background information. This section should also outline the audit timeline and key stakeholders involved.

3. Scope and Methodology:
- **Purpose**: Detail the boundaries of the audit and the methods used to conduct it.
- **Content**: Describe the systems, processes, and controls that were assessed, along with the tools and techniques used for testing. Mention any limitations or constraints encountered during the audit.

4. Findings:
- **Purpose**: Present the vulnerabilities and issues identified during the audit.
- **Content**: For each finding, include a detailed description, the severity rating, the affected systems or processes, the potential impact, and evidence supporting the finding. Use a consistent format to ensure clarity and ease of understanding.

5. Risk Assessment:
- **Purpose**: Provide an analysis of the risks associated with the identified findings.
- **Content**: Include a risk matrix or heat map to visually represent the risk levels. Discuss the likelihood and potential impact of each risk, prioritizing them based on their severity.

6. Recommendations:
- **Purpose**: Offer actionable steps to mitigate the identified risks.
- **Content**: Provide specific, practical recommendations for addressing each finding. Include short-term and long-term actions, as well as any quick wins. Ensure recommendations are feasible and aligned with the organization's resources and capabilities.

7. Conclusion:
- **Purpose**: Summarize the overall findings and emphasize the importance of addressing the identified risks.
- **Content**: Reinforce the key messages from the executive summary and recommendations sections. Highlight the benefits of implementing the recommended actions.

8. Appendices:
- **Purpose**: Provide additional details and supporting documentation.
- **Content**: Include technical details, raw data, screenshots, logs, and any other relevant evidence that supports the findings. Appendices should also contain references to industry standards and best practices.

Ensuring Relevance, Clarity, and Focus

1. Use a Clear and Consistent Structure:
- Follow a standardized format for presenting information, ensuring that each section flows logically and builds upon the previous one. Use headings, subheadings, and bullet points to organize content and improve readability.

2. Tailor Content to the Audience:
- Consider the needs and expertise of the report's intended audience. Provide sufficient detail for technical readers while summarizing key points for non-technical stakeholders. Use jargon-free language where possible and explain technical terms when necessary.

3. Highlight Key Findings and Recommendations:
- Use executive summaries, highlights, and callout boxes to draw attention to the most critical information. Ensure that key findings and recommendations are easy to locate and understand.

4. Visual Aids and Summaries:
- Use charts, graphs, heat maps, and other visual aids to present complex information clearly and concisely. Visual representations can help convey the severity of risks and the impact of findings more effectively than text alone.

Presenting Complex Technical Findings to Non-Technical Stakeholders

1. Simplify Technical Language:
- Translate technical terms and concepts into plain language that non-technical stakeholders can understand. Focus on the implications and impact of the findings rather than the technical details.

2. Use Analogies and Examples:
- Relate technical findings to everyday experiences or use analogies to make complex concepts more relatable. For example, compare a firewall to a security guard that controls access to a building.

3. Focus on Business Impact:
- Emphasize how the findings affect the organization's operations, financial health, and reputation. Discuss the potential consequences of not addressing the identified risks in terms of business continuity, regulatory compliance, and customer trust.

4. Provide Clear, Actionable Recommendations:
- Offer specific steps that can be taken to mitigate the risks, and explain the benefits of implementing these measures. Ensure that recommendations are practical and aligned with the organization's goals and resources.

5. Engage in Interactive Discussions:
- Present findings and recommendations in meetings or workshops where non-technical stakeholders can ask questions and seek clarification. Use these opportunities to provide additional context and ensure understanding.

6. Executive Summaries and Visuals:

- Include executive summaries that distill the key points into a concise format, and use visuals to highlight important information. This helps non-technical stakeholders quickly grasp the critical aspects of the report.

A comprehensive final audit report should include an executive summary, introduction, scope and methodology, findings, risk assessment, recommendations, conclusion, and appendices. Ensuring that all relevant information is included while maintaining clarity and focus involves using a clear structure, tailoring content to the audience, and highlighting key findings. Presenting complex technical findings to non-technical stakeholders requires simplifying language, using analogies, focusing on business impact, providing actionable recommendations, engaging in discussions, and leveraging executive summaries and visuals.

Developing a risk response plan based on audit results is a systematic process that involves identifying and categorizing residual risks and deficiencies, and then defining appropriate responses to manage those risks. This plan is essential for mitigating risks that remain after initial controls have been implemented and aligns with the organization's overall risk management strategy to ensure a comprehensive approach to risk mitigation.

Process of Developing a Risk Response Plan

1. Identify Residual Risks and Deficiencies:
- **Compile Audit Findings**: Gather all findings from the audit, focusing on areas where controls were found to be ineffective, insufficient, or absent.
- **Assess Residual Risks**: Evaluate the remaining risks after considering the existing controls. These are risks that have not been fully mitigated and still pose a threat to the organization.
- **Categorize Deficiencies**: Classify the deficiencies based on their nature, such as technical vulnerabilities, process weaknesses, compliance gaps, or human factors.

2. Categorize Risks:
- **Severity**: Determine the potential impact of each risk on the organization. This includes financial, reputational, operational, and legal impacts.
- **Likelihood**: Assess the probability of each risk materializing, based on historical data, expert judgment, and current threat landscape.
- **Risk Rating**: Combine severity and likelihood to assign a risk rating (e.g., critical, high, medium, low). This helps in prioritizing which risks to address first.

3. Develop Risk Response Strategies:
- **Avoidance**: Eliminate activities that introduce the risk.
- **Mitigation**: Implement additional controls to reduce the likelihood or impact of the risk.
- **Transfer**: Shift the risk to a third party, such as through insurance or outsourcing.
- **Acceptance**: Recognize the risk and decide to accept it without further action, usually because the cost of mitigation outweighs the benefits.

4. Define Specific Actions:
- For each identified risk, define specific actions required to address it. This could include implementing new technologies, revising processes, enhancing training programs, or updating policies.
- Assign responsibilities for each action to relevant individuals or teams.
- Establish timelines for completing each action, ensuring that critical risks are addressed promptly.

5. Integrate with Overall Risk Management Strategy:
- Ensure that the risk response plan aligns with the organization's broader risk management framework. This involves integrating the plan into ongoing risk management activities and ensuring consistency with the organization's risk appetite and tolerance levels.
- Use the risk response plan to update the organization's risk register, ensuring that all identified risks and their responses are documented and tracked over time.

6. Monitor and Review:
- Regularly monitor the implementation of the risk response actions to ensure they are completed as planned.

- Review the effectiveness of the risk responses periodically and make adjustments as needed. This includes reassessing the residual risks and updating the response strategies based on new information or changes in the risk environment.

Relationship Between the Risk Response Plan and the Organization's Overall Risk Management Strategy

1. Alignment with Risk Management Goals:
- The risk response plan should support the overall goals of the organization's risk management strategy. This includes protecting assets, ensuring compliance, maintaining operational continuity, and safeguarding the organization's reputation.

2. Consistency with Risk Appetite and Tolerance:
- The plan should reflect the organization's risk appetite (the level of risk the organization is willing to accept) and risk tolerance (the acceptable variation in performance relative to objectives). This ensures that the responses are appropriate and aligned with the organization's strategic direction.

3. Comprehensive Risk Coverage:
- The risk response plan should ensure that all significant risks are addressed, providing a comprehensive approach to risk mitigation. This includes both existing risks identified in the audit and emerging risks that may arise.

4. Integration with Risk Management Processes:
- The plan should be integrated into the organization's broader risk management processes, including risk identification, assessment, monitoring, and reporting. This ensures that risk management is an ongoing and dynamic process.

5. Facilitating Continuous Improvement:
- The risk response plan should facilitate continuous improvement in the organization's risk management practices. This involves regularly updating the plan based on audit results, changes in the risk landscape, and lessons learned from past incidents.

Examples of Risk Response Actions

1. Technical Vulnerabilities:
- **Risk**: Unpatched software vulnerabilities.
- **Response**: Implement a patch management process to ensure timely updates. Assign responsibility to the IT team and establish a timeline for regular patching cycles.

2. Process Weaknesses:
- **Risk**: Inadequate incident response procedures.
- **Response**: Develop and implement a comprehensive incident response plan, including regular training and simulation exercises. Assign responsibility to the security team and set milestones for plan development and testing.

3. Compliance Gaps:
- **Risk**: Non-compliance with data protection regulations.
- **Response**: Conduct a gap analysis to identify compliance deficiencies and implement corrective actions. Assign responsibility to the compliance officer and establish deadlines for achieving compliance.

4. Human Factors:
- **Risk**: Lack of employee awareness about phishing attacks.
- **Response**: Launch a security awareness training program focusing on phishing and social engineering. Assign responsibility to the HR and security teams and schedule regular training sessions.

Developing a risk response plan based on audit results involves systematically identifying and categorizing residual risks, defining appropriate responses, and ensuring alignment with the organization's overall risk management strategy. By integrating the plan into broader risk management processes and continuously monitoring and adjusting responses, organizations can effectively mitigate risks and enhance their security posture.

Prioritizing risks in a risk response plan is essential for effectively managing and mitigating potential threats. The methodology involves assessing and ranking risks based on various factors to determine which ones require immediate attention and resources. Here's a detailed explanation of the methodology, key factors to consider, different prioritization frameworks, and examples of their application.

Methodology for Prioritizing Risks

1. Identify Risks:
- Begin by identifying all potential risks that could impact the organization. This involves gathering information from risk assessments, audits, and other sources.

2. Assess Risks:
- Evaluate the likelihood and impact of each identified risk. This assessment can be qualitative, quantitative, or a combination of both.

3. Prioritize Risks:
- Rank the risks based on their assessed likelihood and impact. This helps determine which risks pose the greatest threat to the organization and should be addressed first.

Factors to Consider When Determining Risk Priority

1. Likelihood (Probability):
- The probability of a risk occurring. A higher likelihood means the risk is more likely to materialize and therefore might need higher prioritization.

2. Impact (Severity):
- The potential consequences or severity of the risk if it occurs. This includes financial loss, reputational damage, operational disruption, and compliance penalties.

3. Vulnerability:
- The extent to which the organization is susceptible to the risk. This includes the current state of controls and the organization's ability to detect and respond to the risk.

4. Risk Tolerance:
- The organization's willingness to accept or tolerate a certain level of risk. This varies based on the organization's objectives, industry, and regulatory environment.

5. Cost of Mitigation:
- The resources required to mitigate the risk. This includes financial costs, time, and manpower.

6. Regulatory and Compliance Requirements:
- The need to comply with laws, regulations, and standards. Non-compliance can lead to legal penalties and reputational damage.

7. Business Objectives:
- The alignment of the risk with the organization's strategic goals. Risks that threaten critical business objectives may be prioritized higher.

Prioritization Frameworks

1. Risk Matrix:
- A risk matrix is a visual tool that plots risks based on their likelihood and impact. Risks are typically categorized into low, medium, and high priority based on their position in the matrix.
- **Application Example:** In an IT security context, a risk matrix can help prioritize vulnerabilities in a network. A vulnerability that is highly exploitable and could lead to significant data breaches would be plotted in the high-risk quadrant and addressed first.

2. Risk Scoring:
- This method assigns numerical scores to risks based on likelihood and impact. The scores are then summed to give an overall risk score, which is used to prioritize the risks.
- **Application Example:** In a manufacturing environment, risks related to equipment failure can be scored based on the likelihood of failure and the potential impact on production. Equipment with the highest risk scores would be scheduled for maintenance or replacement first.

3. Heat Maps:
- Heat maps are similar to risk matrices but use color-coding to represent different levels of risk. This provides a quick visual representation of risk priorities.

- **Application Example**: A financial institution might use a heat map to prioritize risks related to fraudulent activities. High-likelihood, high-impact risks are highlighted in red, indicating the need for immediate action.

4. Bow-Tie Analysis:
- This method visualizes risk by showing the pathways from causes to consequences and identifying preventive and mitigative controls. It helps in understanding the full context of a risk.
- **Application Example**: In healthcare, bow-tie analysis can be used to prioritize risks associated with patient safety. By visualizing the causes and potential impacts of medical errors, healthcare providers can implement targeted controls to prevent these errors.

Examples of Prioritization in Various Scenarios

1. Cybersecurity:
- **Scenario**: A company identifies multiple cybersecurity risks, including phishing attacks, ransomware, and insider threats.
- **Framework**: Using a risk matrix, the company assesses the likelihood and impact of each risk. Phishing attacks are frequent but have a moderate impact, while ransomware is less frequent but has a high impact. Insider threats are rare but can have a severe impact. The company prioritizes ransomware and insider threats for immediate action due to their higher impact.

2. Supply Chain Management:
- **Scenario**: A retailer faces risks such as supplier failure, transportation delays, and quality issues.
- **Framework**: The retailer uses risk scoring to evaluate these risks. Supplier failure scores high on both likelihood and impact, transportation delays score high on likelihood but moderate on impact, and quality issues score moderate on both. The retailer prioritizes securing alternative suppliers and enhancing quality control measures.

3. Healthcare:
- **Scenario**: A hospital identifies risks related to patient data privacy, medication errors, and equipment malfunction.
- **Framework**: The hospital employs bow-tie analysis to understand the causes and impacts of each risk. Medication errors are identified as having a high impact on patient safety. Preventive controls are implemented, such as double-checking procedures and electronic prescribing systems, to mitigate this risk first.

Prioritizing risks in a risk response plan involves assessing the likelihood, impact, vulnerability, and other relevant factors. Using frameworks like risk matrices, risk scoring, heat maps, and bow-tie analysis helps organizations systematically rank risks and focus their resources on the most critical areas. This structured approach ensures that the organization addresses the most significant threats effectively, enhancing its overall security posture and resilience.

Resource allocation for risk mitigation is a critical process that ensures that an organization effectively addresses identified risks while optimizing the use of available resources. Organizations must balance the need to mitigate risks with the cost and feasibility of implementing controls. Here's an analysis of how organizations determine the appropriate level of investment for addressing identified risks, the concept of Return on Security Investment (ROSI), and examples of how it can be calculated.

Process of Resource Allocation for Risk Mitigation Efforts

1. Identify and Prioritize Risks:
- **Risk Assessment:** Conduct a comprehensive risk assessment to identify and evaluate risks. This involves analyzing the likelihood and impact of each risk.
- **Risk Rating:** Assign risk ratings (e.g., high, medium, low) to prioritize risks based on their potential impact on the organization's operations, reputation, and compliance.

2. Determine Risk Mitigation Strategies:
- **Control Selection:** Identify appropriate risk mitigation strategies for each risk. This could involve implementing new controls, enhancing existing controls, or transferring risks through insurance.

- **Cost-Benefit Analysis:** Evaluate the cost and benefits of each mitigation strategy. Consider factors such as implementation costs, ongoing maintenance, and the expected reduction in risk.

3. Estimate Costs and Resources:
   - **Direct Costs:** Calculate direct costs associated with each mitigation strategy, including hardware, software, personnel, and training.
   - **Indirect Costs:** Consider indirect costs such as potential downtime, productivity impacts, and opportunity costs.
   - **Resource Requirements:** Assess the personnel and time required to implement and maintain the mitigation strategies.

4. Allocate Resources Based on Priorities:
   - **Budget Allocation:** Allocate budget and resources based on the prioritization of risks and the cost-benefit analysis of mitigation strategies. High-priority risks with significant impact and reasonable mitigation costs should receive more resources.
   - **Strategic Alignment:** Ensure that resource allocation aligns with the organization's strategic objectives and risk appetite.

5. Monitor and Adjust:
   - **Continuous Monitoring:** Regularly monitor the effectiveness of risk mitigation efforts and adjust resource allocation as needed. This involves tracking progress, evaluating the performance of controls, and reassessing risks.

Return on Security Investment (ROSI)

Concept of ROSI: ROSI is a financial metric used to evaluate the effectiveness and efficiency of investments in security controls. It measures the financial return obtained from security investments relative to their costs. ROSI helps organizations justify security expenditures by demonstrating the value of risk mitigation efforts in financial terms.

Calculating ROSI:

1. **Estimate Annual Loss Expectancy (ALE):**
   - **Single Loss Expectancy (SLE):** Calculate the expected monetary loss from a single occurrence of the risk.
   - **Annual Rate of Occurrence (ARO):** Estimate the frequency with which the risk is expected to occur in a year.
   - **ALE Formula:** ALE = SLE * ARO
2. **Calculate the Cost of Security Investment:**
   - Include all costs associated with implementing and maintaining the security control, such as purchase costs, implementation costs, training, and ongoing maintenance.
3. **Determine the Expected Savings:**
   - **Reduced ALE:** Estimate the reduction in ALE due to the implementation of the security control. This represents the expected savings from avoiding potential losses.
   - **Cost Savings Formula:** Savings = Original ALE - Reduced ALE
4. **Calculate ROSI:**
   - **ROSI Formula:** ROSI = (Savings - Cost of Security Investment) / Cost of Security Investment * 100%

Example of ROSI Calculation:

Scenario: An organization is considering investing in an intrusion detection system (IDS) to mitigate the risk of data breaches.

1. **Estimate ALE:**
   - **SLE:** If a data breach occurs, the expected loss is $500,000.
   - **ARO:** The organization estimates that a data breach could occur once every two years (0.5 times per year).
   - **ALE:** $500,000 * 0.5 = $250,000
2. **Cost of Security Investment:**
   - The total cost of implementing and maintaining the IDS is $100,000 per year.
3. **Expected Savings:**

- **Reduced ALE:** With the IDS in place, the likelihood of a data breach is reduced, lowering the ARO to 0.1 times per year.
- **New ALE:** $500,000 * 0.1 = $50,000
- **Savings:** $250,000 - $50,000 = $200,000
4. **Calculate ROSI:**
    - ROSI = ($200,000 - $100,000) / $100,000 * 100% = 100%

By demonstrating a 100% return on security investment, the organization can justify the expenditure on the IDS, showing that the savings from risk reduction outweigh the costs.

Resource allocation for risk mitigation involves a systematic approach to identifying, prioritizing, and addressing risks based on their potential impact and the cost-effectiveness of mitigation strategies. Using ROSI helps organizations quantify the financial benefits of security investments, ensuring that resources are allocated efficiently and effectively to enhance overall security.

Continuous monitoring plays a crucial role in the context of security assessments and audits, providing organizations with real-time visibility into their security posture and enabling prompt identification and response to potential threats. Integrating continuous monitoring with periodic assessments creates a comprehensive security strategy that combines the depth of thorough audits with the agility of ongoing oversight.

Role of Continuous Monitoring

1. Real-Time Risk Management:
- Continuous monitoring involves the real-time collection, analysis, and reporting of security data. This approach allows organizations to detect and respond to security incidents as they occur, rather than waiting for the next scheduled audit.

2. Ongoing Compliance:
- By continuously monitoring security controls and compliance requirements, organizations can ensure they remain compliant with regulatory standards at all times. This reduces the risk of compliance violations and associated penalties.

3. Proactive Threat Detection:
- Continuous monitoring helps identify emerging threats and vulnerabilities quickly. This proactive stance enables organizations to address potential issues before they escalate into significant security incidents.

Integration of Continuous Monitoring with Periodic Assessments

1. Complementary Approaches:
- **Periodic Assessments**: These provide a comprehensive, in-depth review of the organization's security posture at a specific point in time. They involve detailed audits, risk assessments, and control evaluations.
- **Continuous Monitoring**: This involves real-time or near-real-time tracking of security metrics and events. It offers ongoing insights and enables immediate action.

2. Feedback Loop:
- Findings from periodic assessments can inform the configuration and focus of continuous monitoring tools. For example, if an audit identifies specific vulnerabilities or weak points, continuous monitoring can be adjusted to pay closer attention to these areas.
- Continuous monitoring can provide ongoing feedback to the periodic assessment process, highlighting areas that need more thorough examination during the next audit cycle.

3. Unified Reporting:
- Integrate data from continuous monitoring and periodic assessments into a unified reporting framework. This approach ensures that all stakeholders have a comprehensive view of the organization's security posture.

4. Automated Controls and Alerts:
- Use continuous monitoring to automate the enforcement of security controls and generate alerts for any deviations. These automated controls can be validated and adjusted during periodic assessments.

Benefits of Implementing Continuous Monitoring

1. Enhanced Visibility:

- Continuous monitoring provides ongoing visibility into the organization's security environment, allowing for timely detection and remediation of issues.

2. Improved Incident Response:
- By identifying threats and vulnerabilities in real-time, organizations can respond more swiftly to security incidents, reducing the potential damage and recovery time.

3. Dynamic Risk Management:
- Continuous monitoring enables organizations to adapt to the evolving threat landscape, ensuring that security controls remain effective against new and emerging threats.

4. Regulatory Compliance:
- Maintaining continuous compliance with regulatory requirements is easier with continuous monitoring, as it ensures that controls are always active and effective.

Challenges of Implementing Continuous Monitoring

1. Resource Intensive:
- Continuous monitoring requires significant resources, including advanced tools, skilled personnel, and constant attention to alerts and data. This can be costly and demanding for organizations.

2. Alert Fatigue:
- The sheer volume of alerts generated by continuous monitoring can lead to alert fatigue, where security teams become overwhelmed and may miss critical alerts.

3. Integration Complexity:
- Integrating continuous monitoring tools with existing systems and processes can be complex. Ensuring seamless data flow and consistent reporting requires careful planning and execution.

4. Data Management:
- Continuous monitoring generates vast amounts of data that must be stored, analyzed, and managed effectively. This requires robust data management strategies and infrastructure.

Strategies for Effective Continuous Monitoring

1. Prioritize Critical Assets:
- Focus continuous monitoring efforts on the most critical assets and systems. This ensures that resources are used efficiently and that the most important areas receive the most attention.

2. Automate Where Possible:
- Automate routine monitoring tasks and responses to common issues. This reduces the burden on security teams and ensures consistent action.

3. Use Advanced Analytics:
- Employ advanced analytics and machine learning to identify patterns and anomalies in the monitored data. This enhances threat detection capabilities and reduces false positives.

4. Regular Reviews and Updates:
- Continuously review and update monitoring tools and processes based on the latest threat intelligence and findings from periodic assessments. This ensures that the monitoring strategy remains relevant and effective.

5. Effective Training and Awareness:
- Train security personnel on the use of monitoring tools and the interpretation of alerts. Awareness and preparedness are key to leveraging continuous monitoring effectively.

Examples of Continuous Monitoring Integration

1. Financial Sector:
- Financial institutions often integrate continuous monitoring with periodic assessments to protect against fraud and cyber-attacks. Real-time transaction monitoring systems detect suspicious activities, while periodic audits review overall system security and compliance.

2. Healthcare:
- Healthcare organizations use continuous monitoring to ensure the protection of patient data and compliance with regulations like HIPAA. Continuous monitoring tools track access to electronic health records, and periodic assessments ensure that security controls are effective and up-to-date.

3. Manufacturing:
- In manufacturing, continuous monitoring of operational technology (OT) systems helps detect anomalies that could indicate cyber threats or operational failures. Periodic assessments evaluate the overall security posture of the OT environment and recommend improvements.

Continuous monitoring is essential for maintaining a robust and adaptive security posture. It complements periodic assessments by providing real-time insights and enabling swift responses to emerging threats. While it presents challenges such as resource demands and integration complexities, the benefits of enhanced visibility, improved incident response, and dynamic risk management make it a critical component of modern security strategies. Effective continuous monitoring requires prioritization of critical assets, automation, advanced analytics, regular reviews, and robust training for security personnel.

Audit trails are detailed records of activities and transactions within an information system, capturing who did what, when, and where. These records are crucial for maintaining security, ensuring compliance, and facilitating forensic investigations. They provide a chronological log of events that can be used to monitor, review, and verify the integrity of data and processes within an organization.

Concept of Audit Trails in Security Assessments

Definition: Audit trails are systematic records that document the sequence of activities within an IT system. These logs capture data on user actions, system changes, access to sensitive information, and other significant events.

Purpose:
- **Accountability**: Ensure that all actions can be traced back to the responsible individual or system.
- **Monitoring and Detection**: Facilitate real-time monitoring and detection of unauthorized activities or anomalies.
- **Compliance**: Meet regulatory and industry standards that require detailed logging of activities.
- **Forensic Analysis**: Provide detailed information necessary for investigating security incidents and breaches.

Ensuring the Integrity and Completeness of Audit Records

1. Implementing Robust Logging Mechanisms:
- **Comprehensive Coverage**: Ensure that all critical systems, applications, and network components are configured to generate detailed logs. This includes user activities, system changes, access to sensitive data, and security events.
- **Consistent Logging**: Standardize logging practices across the organization to ensure consistency in the types of data captured and the formats used.

2. Secure Storage:
- **Tamper-Proof Repositories**: Store logs in secure, tamper-proof repositories to prevent unauthorized access or alteration. Use techniques such as write-once-read-many (WORM) storage or blockchain-based solutions for immutability.
- **Access Controls**: Implement strict access controls to restrict who can view, modify, or delete audit logs. Ensure that only authorized personnel have access to these records.

3. Regular Backups:
- **Automated Backups**: Schedule regular automated backups of audit logs to secure locations to prevent data loss.
- **Offsite Storage**: Store backup copies in offsite or cloud locations to ensure availability in case of physical disasters.

4. Integrity Verification:
- **Checksums and Hashing**: Use cryptographic checksums or hashing techniques to verify the integrity of audit logs. Any alteration in the log data can be detected by comparing the current checksum with the original.
- **Regular Audits**: Conduct regular audits of the audit trails to ensure their integrity and completeness. Verify that logging mechanisms are functioning correctly and capturing all necessary events.

5. Retention Policies:
- **Defined Retention Periods**: Establish and enforce retention policies that specify how long audit logs should be kept. Ensure compliance with legal, regulatory, and business requirements.

- **Archival Processes**: Implement archival processes for logs that need to be retained for extended periods but are not frequently accessed. This helps manage storage costs and efficiency.

Importance of Audit Trails in Forensic Investigations

1. Incident Response:
- **Root Cause Analysis**: Audit trails provide detailed information that helps investigators understand the root cause of a security incident. They can trace the sequence of events leading up to the breach.
- **Evidence Collection**: Logs serve as crucial evidence in forensic investigations, providing a documented trail of activities that can be used to support legal actions or disciplinary measures.

2. Detection and Prevention:
- **Anomaly Detection**: Regular monitoring of audit trails can help detect anomalies and suspicious activities early, enabling proactive measures to prevent security incidents.
- **Policy Enforcement**: Audit trails help ensure that security policies and procedures are being followed. They provide the data needed to verify compliance with internal and external requirements.

3. Accountability:
- **User Accountability**: By tracking user activities, audit trails ensure that individuals are held accountable for their actions. This can deter malicious behavior and promote a culture of responsibility.
- **System Accountability**: Logs also track system changes and access, ensuring that system administrators and automated processes are performing as expected.

Examples of Effective Audit Trail Management Practices

1. Centralized Logging:
- Implement a centralized logging system where all logs from various sources are aggregated and stored in a single repository. This simplifies log management, monitoring, and analysis.

2. Real-Time Monitoring and Alerts:
- Use Security Information and Event Management (SIEM) systems to monitor logs in real time. Configure alerts for specific events or anomalies to ensure rapid detection and response to potential security incidents.

3. Regular Log Reviews:
- Schedule regular reviews of audit logs by security analysts to identify patterns, trends, and anomalies. This can be done manually or through automated log analysis tools that flag unusual activities.

4. Incident-Specific Logging:
- For critical systems or high-risk activities, implement detailed logging that captures additional context and data points. For example, logging every keystroke during sensitive transactions.

5. Compliance with Standards:
- Ensure that logging practices comply with relevant standards and regulations, such as ISO/IEC 27001, HIPAA, GDPR, or PCI-DSS. This includes maintaining logs for specified periods and ensuring their integrity and confidentiality.

Example:
A financial institution might use a centralized logging system to aggregate logs from all its servers, applications, and network devices. They implement SIEM for real-time monitoring, set up alerts for unauthorized access attempts, and conduct daily reviews of critical system logs. The logs are stored in a tamper-proof repository with regular backups and integrity checks. They also ensure compliance with financial regulations by retaining logs for a minimum of seven years and performing regular audits.

Audit trails are indispensable for security assessments, providing a detailed record of activities and transactions. Ensuring the integrity and completeness of audit records through robust logging mechanisms, secure storage, regular backups, and integrity verification is essential. These practices not only support forensic investigations and accountability but also enhance overall security by enabling effective monitoring and detection of suspicious activities.

System Compliance

Reviewing and submitting security and privacy documents for system compliance is a critical step in ensuring that an organization's systems meet regulatory and policy requirements. Accurate and complete documentation not only helps in maintaining compliance but also provides a clear record of the security measures in place, facilitating audits and assessments.

Process of Reviewing and Submitting Security and Privacy Documents

1. Document Collection and Organization:
- **Identify Required Documents**: Compile a list of all necessary security and privacy documents required for compliance. This may include policies, procedures, risk assessments, incident response plans, and audit logs.
- **Organize Documents**: Ensure that all documents are organized systematically. Use a standardized format and naming convention for ease of reference and review.

2. Document Review:
- **Content Review**: Verify that the content of each document is accurate and up-to-date. Ensure that it reflects current practices and policies.
- **Compliance Check**: Cross-check each document against relevant regulatory requirements and industry standards (e.g., ISO/IEC 27001, GDPR, HIPAA, PCI-DSS).
- **Technical Review**: Have subject matter experts review technical documents to ensure accuracy and relevance. This includes configuration settings, network diagrams, and technical controls.

3. Verification and Validation:
- **Internal Audits**: Conduct internal audits to validate the accuracy and completeness of the documents. Identify and address any discrepancies or gaps.
- **Peer Review**: Use peer review processes to ensure that multiple perspectives are considered and that documents are reviewed thoroughly.

4. Approval Process:
- **Management Approval**: Obtain approval from relevant management and governance bodies. Ensure that there is documented evidence of this approval.
- **Stakeholder Sign-Off**: Ensure that all key stakeholders, including legal, compliance, IT, and security teams, have reviewed and signed off on the documents.

5. Submission:
- **Compile Submission Package**: Gather all reviewed and approved documents into a submission package. Include a cover letter or summary that outlines the contents and highlights key points.
- **Submit to Regulatory Body**: Follow the submission guidelines provided by the regulatory body or audit organization. Ensure that the submission is made within the specified deadlines.
- **Acknowledge Receipt**: Confirm receipt of the submission by the regulatory body and keep a record of the submission details for future reference.

Key Elements to Include in Security and Privacy Documents

1. Policies and Procedures:
- Clearly defined security and privacy policies that outline the organization's approach to managing and protecting data.
- Detailed procedures that describe the steps to be followed to implement these policies.

2. Risk Assessments:
- Comprehensive risk assessments that identify potential threats and vulnerabilities, along with their likelihood and impact.
- Mitigation strategies and controls implemented to address identified risks.

3. Incident Response Plans:
- Detailed incident response plans that outline the steps to be taken in the event of a security or privacy incident.

- Roles and responsibilities of the incident response team, along with contact information and communication protocols.

4. Audit Logs and Monitoring Reports:
- Logs that capture significant events and activities within the system, including access logs, change logs, and security events.
- Regular monitoring reports that provide insights into the system's security posture and highlight any anomalies or incidents.

5. Compliance Checklists:
- Checklists that map the organization's controls and practices to the specific requirements of relevant regulations and standards.
- Evidence of compliance, such as screenshots, configurations, and audit results.

Importance of Accuracy and Completeness in Documentation

1. Regulatory Compliance:
- Accurate and complete documentation is essential for demonstrating compliance with regulatory requirements. Inaccurate or incomplete documents can lead to non-compliance, resulting in fines, penalties, and reputational damage.

2. Audit Readiness:
- Well-prepared documentation ensures that the organization is ready for audits and assessments. It provides auditors with clear evidence of the security measures in place, facilitating a smoother audit process.

3. Risk Management:
- Comprehensive documentation helps in identifying and managing risks effectively. It ensures that all potential threats and vulnerabilities are accounted for and addressed.

4. Accountability and Transparency:
- Clear and detailed documentation promotes accountability and transparency within the organization. It ensures that all stakeholders understand the security and privacy measures in place and their roles in maintaining them.

Common Pitfalls in Document Preparation

1. Outdated Information:
- **Pitfall**: Using outdated information that does not reflect current practices or system configurations.
- **Solution**: Regularly review and update documents to ensure they are current and accurate.

2. Inconsistent Formats:
- **Pitfall**: Inconsistencies in document formats, terminology, and structure can lead to confusion and make it difficult to review documents.
- **Solution**: Use standardized templates and guidelines for document preparation to ensure consistency.

3. Lack of Detail:
- **Pitfall**: Documents that lack sufficient detail to provide a clear understanding of the security measures in place.
- **Solution**: Ensure that documents are detailed and comprehensive, providing clear descriptions and evidence of controls.

4. Poor Documentation of Processes:
- **Pitfall**: Failing to document processes adequately, which can lead to gaps in understanding and implementation.
- **Solution**: Clearly document all processes, including step-by-step procedures and roles and responsibilities.

5. Missing Approvals and Sign-Offs:
- **Pitfall**: Submitting documents without the necessary approvals and sign-offs from key stakeholders.
- **Solution**: Implement a formal approval process and ensure that all required approvals are obtained and documented.

Example:
In preparing for a HIPAA compliance audit, a healthcare provider might:

1. **Compile Required Documents**: Gather all relevant policies, procedures, risk assessments, incident response plans, and audit logs.
2. **Review for Accuracy**: Ensure that each document reflects current practices and complies with HIPAA requirements.
3. **Conduct Internal Audits**: Perform internal audits to validate the accuracy and completeness of the documents.
4. **Obtain Approvals**: Get the necessary approvals from the compliance officer, IT director, and other relevant stakeholders.
5. **Submit to Auditors**: Compile the documents into a submission package and submit them to the auditors within the specified deadline.

By ensuring accuracy and completeness in documentation and following a structured review and submission process, organizations can effectively demonstrate compliance, manage risks, and facilitate successful audits and assessments.

The System Security Plan (SSP) is a critical document in demonstrating compliance with security requirements and standards. It provides a comprehensive overview of the security controls implemented for an information system, outlining how these controls meet specific regulatory and organizational requirements. The SSP serves as a foundational document in an organization's security documentation framework, ensuring that security measures are well-documented, understood, and maintained.

Role of the System Security Plan (SSP) in Demonstrating Compliance

1. Documentation of Security Controls:
- The SSP documents the specific security controls in place for an information system, detailing how these controls are implemented, managed, and maintained. This documentation is essential for demonstrating compliance with various security standards and regulations.

2. Evidence of Due Diligence:
- By detailing the security measures and processes in place, the SSP demonstrates that the organization is exercising due diligence in protecting its information assets. This is crucial for regulatory compliance and for building trust with stakeholders.

3. Support for Audits and Assessments:
- The SSP provides auditors and assessors with a clear understanding of the security posture of the information system. It serves as a key reference during audits and assessments, facilitating the review process and helping to verify compliance.

Relation of the SSP to Other Security Documentation

1. Risk Assessment Reports:
- The SSP is closely related to risk assessment reports, which identify potential threats, vulnerabilities, and the impact of security incidents. The SSP uses the findings from risk assessments to outline the controls implemented to mitigate identified risks.

2. Security Policies and Procedures:
- The SSP references and aligns with the organization's security policies and procedures. These documents provide the overarching framework for the security controls described in the SSP.

3. Incident Response Plans:
- Incident response plans are often detailed in the SSP, describing the procedures for detecting, responding to, and recovering from security incidents. The SSP ensures that these plans are integrated into the overall security strategy.

4. Compliance and Audit Reports:
- Compliance and audit reports use the SSP as a basis for verifying that the organization's security controls meet regulatory requirements. The SSP provides the necessary evidence to support these reports.

5. Configuration Management Plans:
- The SSP often includes or references configuration management plans that detail the baseline configurations of systems and applications. This ensures that systems are securely configured and maintained according to best practices.

Key Components of an Effective SSP

1. System Description:
- Provides a detailed description of the information system, including its purpose, functionality, and criticality to the organization. This section should also outline the system boundaries and interconnections with other systems.

2. Security Controls:
- Details the specific security controls implemented for the system. This includes technical, administrative, and physical controls, categorized by control families such as access control, audit and accountability, and system and communications protection.

3. Roles and Responsibilities:
- Defines the roles and responsibilities of individuals involved in the system's security. This includes system owners, security officers, administrators, and users.

4. Risk Assessment:
- Summarizes the results of risk assessments, including identified threats and vulnerabilities, and the impact and likelihood of potential security incidents. This section explains how the selected controls mitigate these risks.

5. Control Implementation:
- Describes how each security control is implemented, including the specific technologies, processes, and procedures used. This section should also outline how the effectiveness of these controls is monitored and maintained.

6. Incident Response and Recovery:
- Details the procedures for detecting, responding to, and recovering from security incidents. This includes incident reporting, response coordination, and post-incident analysis.

7. Continuous Monitoring:
- Outlines the continuous monitoring strategy for the system, including the tools and processes used to detect and respond to security events in real-time. This section also describes how monitoring results are used to improve security controls.

8. Compliance and Audit:
- Explains how the system meets specific regulatory and compliance requirements. This section should reference relevant standards and regulations and detail how compliance is verified and maintained.

Examples of How the SSP Supports Compliance Decision-Making

1. Facilitating Regulatory Audits:
- During regulatory audits, the SSP provides auditors with detailed information about the security controls and their implementation. For example, an auditor reviewing compliance with HIPAA requirements can use the SSP to verify that controls for protecting patient data are in place and functioning as intended.

2. Guiding Security Improvements:
- The SSP helps identify gaps in the current security posture and guides the implementation of improvements. For instance, if a risk assessment highlights vulnerabilities in access control, the SSP can be updated to include new controls and processes to address these weaknesses.

3. Supporting Risk Management:
- By documenting the risk assessment results and corresponding controls, the SSP supports ongoing risk management efforts. This ensures that the organization remains proactive in identifying and mitigating risks, aligning with frameworks such as NIST SP 800-37.

4. Enhancing Communication with Stakeholders:
- The SSP serves as a communication tool, providing stakeholders with a clear understanding of the system's security posture. This transparency builds trust and ensures that all parties are aware of their roles and responsibilities in maintaining security.

The System Security Plan (SSP) is integral to demonstrating compliance by documenting security controls, supporting audits, and providing evidence of due diligence. It is interrelated with other security documentation, including risk assessments, policies, and incident response plans. Key components of an effective SSP include a detailed system description, security controls, roles and responsibilities, risk assessment, control implementation, incident response, continuous monitoring, and compliance verification. By providing a comprehensive and clear overview of the system's security measures, the SSP supports informed decision-making and ensures continuous compliance with regulatory and organizational requirements.

The concept of risk acceptance criteria in determining system risk posture involves defining the level of risk an organization is willing to accept without implementing additional controls. Establishing appropriate risk thresholds is crucial for balancing security efforts with operational efficiency and cost-effectiveness. Organizations must consider various factors, such as regulatory requirements, industry standards, and their own risk tolerance, to make informed risk acceptance decisions.

Establishing Risk Acceptance Criteria

1. Define Risk Tolerance and Appetite:
- **Risk Tolerance:** The acceptable level of variation in performance relative to the achievement of objectives. It determines how much risk an organization is willing to take on.
- **Risk Appetite:** The overall amount and type of risk an organization is willing to pursue or retain in order to achieve its goals.

2. Identify and Categorize Risks:
- **Risk Identification:** Identify potential risks that could impact the organization's operations, reputation, compliance, and financial standing.
- **Risk Categorization**: Classify risks based on their nature (e.g., operational, financial, strategic, compliance) and the likelihood and impact of occurrence.

3. Quantitative and Qualitative Analysis:
- **Quantitative Analysis**: Use numerical data and metrics to assess the probability and impact of risks. Methods include risk matrices, scoring systems, and financial modeling.
- **Qualitative Analysis**: Use expert judgment, scenarios, and descriptive methods to evaluate risks that are difficult to quantify.

4. Determine Risk Thresholds:
- **Thresholds**: Establish thresholds for risk levels that are deemed acceptable, tolerable, or unacceptable. These thresholds can be numerical (e.g., financial loss limits) or qualitative (e.g., reputational damage criteria).
- **Documentation**: Clearly document the criteria and rationale for risk thresholds to ensure consistency and transparency in decision-making.

5. Stakeholder Involvement:
- **Consultation**: Engage key stakeholders, including senior management, risk management committees, and relevant departments, to gain consensus on risk acceptance criteria.
- **Approval:** Ensure that the established risk thresholds are formally approved by the appropriate governance bodies.

Factors Influencing Risk Acceptance Decisions

1. Regulatory Requirements:
- Organizations must comply with industry-specific regulations and standards that often dictate minimum acceptable levels of risk. Non-compliance can result in legal penalties and reputational damage.

2. Industry Standards:
- Industry standards and best practices provide benchmarks for risk management. Organizations often align their risk acceptance criteria with these standards to ensure competitiveness and compliance.

3. Organizational Goals and Strategy:
- The organization's strategic objectives and business goals influence its risk appetite. For example, a company pursuing aggressive growth may have a higher risk appetite compared to one focused on stability.

4. Financial Considerations:
- The potential financial impact of risks and the cost of mitigation measures play a significant role in risk acceptance decisions. Organizations balance the cost of controls against the potential benefits of risk reduction.

5. Risk Culture and Perception:
- The overall risk culture and perception within the organization affect how risks are viewed and managed. A risk-averse culture may set lower risk thresholds, while a more risk-tolerant culture may accept higher levels of risk.

6. Historical Data and Experience:
- Past incidents and historical data on risk occurrences and impacts inform future risk acceptance decisions. Organizations use this information to predict potential future risks and their likely effects.

Examples of Risk Acceptance Criteria Across Industries

1. Financial Services:
- **Regulatory Compliance**: Stringent regulatory requirements, such as those imposed by the Basel III framework or Sarbanes-Oxley Act, influence risk acceptance criteria. Financial institutions often have low tolerance for operational and compliance risks.
- **Risk Thresholds**: Acceptable financial loss might be defined as a small percentage of capital reserves. Cybersecurity risks may have strict thresholds due to the potential for significant financial and reputational damage.

2. Healthcare:
- **Patient Safety and Privacy**: Regulations like HIPAA mandate strict controls over patient data. Healthcare organizations typically have low risk tolerance for data breaches and patient safety risks.
- **Risk Thresholds**: Acceptable risk levels might be tied to the potential impact on patient health outcomes and data privacy. Even minor risks may be deemed unacceptable if they compromise patient safety.

3. Manufacturing:
- **Operational Continuity**: The manufacturing sector prioritizes operational continuity and equipment reliability. Risks that could disrupt production lines are closely monitored.
- **Risk Thresholds**: Risk acceptance criteria might include minimal acceptable downtime and tolerance for minor defects, provided they do not affect product safety or regulatory compliance.

4. Information Technology:
- **Innovation and Agility**: Tech companies often balance innovation with security risks. While there is a higher tolerance for risks associated with new technologies, critical infrastructure and data integrity are tightly controlled.
- **Risk Thresholds**: Acceptable risks might include a certain level of downtime for non-critical services, but stringent controls are in place for protecting sensitive data and ensuring service availability.

5. Government and Defense:
- **National Security and Public Safety**: Government agencies and defense organizations have very low risk tolerance for threats to national security and public safety.
- **Risk Thresholds**: Acceptable risk might be near zero for threats related to national security. Rigorous risk assessments and mitigation measures are mandated by regulations and internal policies.

Examples of Risk Acceptance Criteria

Example 1: Financial Services:
- **Regulatory Compliance**: An investment bank might set risk thresholds based on regulatory capital requirements, ensuring that operational losses do not exceed a specified percentage of their capital.
- **Cybersecurity**: Acceptable risk might include minor phishing attempts that are mitigated through employee training, but not allowing any unencrypted customer data to be stored.

Example 2: Healthcare:
- **Patient Data**: A hospital might have a risk acceptance criterion that no patient data breaches are acceptable, leading to investments in advanced encryption and access controls.
- **Medical Device Failure**: Acceptable risk might include very low failure rates for non-critical devices, but zero tolerance for failures in life-support equipment.

Example 3: Manufacturing:
- **Equipment Downtime**: A car manufacturer might accept up to 1% downtime for maintenance but require immediate action for any risk that could lead to production halts.

- **Product Defects**: Acceptable risk could include minor aesthetic defects in parts that do not impact safety or functionality, but no tolerance for safety-critical components.

Establishing risk acceptance criteria is a nuanced process that requires careful consideration of various factors, including regulatory requirements, industry standards, organizational goals, financial impact, and historical data. By setting clear and appropriate risk thresholds, organizations can effectively manage risks, align their risk posture with strategic objectives, and ensure compliance with relevant standards and regulations.

Residual risk determination is a crucial step in the risk management process, conducted after the implementation of security controls. It involves evaluating the remaining risk that persists despite the applied controls. This analysis ensures that the implemented controls are effective and that any remaining risks are within acceptable levels. Here's an in-depth look at the process, methodologies, challenges, and strategies for accurately measuring residual risk.

Process of Residual Risk Determination

1. Identify Implemented Controls:
- Document all the security controls that have been implemented to mitigate identified risks. This includes technical, administrative, and physical controls.

2. Assess Control Effectiveness:
- Evaluate how effectively the controls mitigate the identified risks. This involves testing, monitoring, and reviewing control performance.

3. Identify Residual Risks:
- Determine which risks remain after the implementation of controls. These are the risks that controls could not completely eliminate.

4. Evaluate Impact and Likelihood:
- Assess the potential impact and likelihood of the residual risks. This step quantifies the remaining risk in terms of its possible effects on the organization.

5. Document and Review:
- Document the findings of the residual risk assessment. Review the residual risks to ensure they are within acceptable thresholds defined by the organization's risk tolerance.

Methodologies to Assess and Quantify Residual Risk

1. Qualitative Risk Assessment:
- **Method**: Use descriptive categories (e.g., high, medium, low) to assess the likelihood and impact of residual risks.
- **Application**: This method is useful when precise data is not available, and it relies on expert judgment and experience to evaluate risks.
- **Example**: Assigning a "high" residual risk to a vulnerability that could lead to significant data breaches if exploited, despite the presence of strong firewalls.

2. Quantitative Risk Assessment:
- **Method**: Use numerical values to estimate the probability and impact of residual risks. This involves statistical models and historical data analysis.
- **Application**: This method provides a more precise measurement of risk, useful for making data-driven decisions.
- **Example**: Calculating the annual loss expectancy (ALE) by multiplying the single loss expectancy (SLE) with the annual rate of occurrence (ARO) for a particular risk.

3. Semi-Quantitative Risk Assessment:
- **Method**: Combine elements of both qualitative and quantitative assessments, using a scoring system to rate risks.
- **Application**: This method provides a balance between the simplicity of qualitative and the precision of quantitative assessments.
- **Example**: Using a risk matrix with scores from 1 to 5 for both likelihood and impact, and multiplying these scores to prioritize residual risks.

4. Scenario Analysis:

- **Method**: Develop hypothetical scenarios to evaluate the potential consequences of residual risks. This involves creating detailed narratives of how risks might manifest.
- **Application**: This method helps in understanding complex risks and their potential cascading effects.
- **Example**: Analyzing the impact of a potential insider threat scenario on critical business operations and customer trust.

Challenges of Accurately Measuring Residual Risk

1. Data Limitations:
- **Challenge**: Limited or incomplete data can hinder accurate risk assessment. This is particularly challenging for new threats or emerging technologies.
- **Strategy**: Use a combination of internal data, industry benchmarks, and threat intelligence to supplement gaps. Continuously update data sources to improve accuracy.

2. Evolving Threat Landscape:
- **Challenge**: The rapidly changing nature of cybersecurity threats makes it difficult to maintain up-to-date risk assessments.
- **Strategy**: Implement continuous monitoring and regular risk assessment updates to adapt to new threats. Leverage threat intelligence platforms to stay informed about emerging risks.

3. Subjectivity in Assessments:
- **Challenge**: Qualitative assessments can be subjective, relying heavily on the judgment of assessors.
- **Strategy**: Standardize assessment criteria and use a diverse team of experts to provide multiple perspectives. Document the rationale behind risk ratings to ensure transparency.

4. Complex Interdependencies:
- **Challenge**: Interdependencies between systems and processes can complicate the assessment of residual risk.
- **Strategy**: Use systems thinking and modeling techniques to map out interdependencies and their potential impacts. Conduct scenario analysis to explore different risk interactions.

5. Resource Constraints:
- **Challenge**: Limited resources (time, personnel, budget) can restrict the depth and frequency of risk assessments.
- **Strategy**: Prioritize critical assets and high-risk areas for detailed assessment. Automate parts of the risk assessment process to improve efficiency.

Strategies for Overcoming Challenges

1. Leveraging Automation and Tools:
- Use automated risk assessment tools and platforms to streamline data collection, analysis, and reporting. Tools like GRC (Governance, Risk, and Compliance) software can integrate various data sources and provide real-time insights.

2. Regular Training and Updates:
- Provide ongoing training for risk assessment teams to ensure they are equipped with the latest knowledge and skills. Regularly update assessment methodologies and frameworks to reflect current best practices.

3. Engaging Stakeholders:
- Involve stakeholders from different parts of the organization in the risk assessment process. This ensures a comprehensive understanding of risks and their impacts across the organization.

4. Scenario Planning and Simulation:
- Conduct regular scenario planning and simulation exercises to test the effectiveness of controls and understand the potential impacts of residual risks. This helps in refining risk assessment methodologies and improving response strategies.

5. Risk Communication and Reporting:
- Develop clear and effective communication channels for reporting residual risks to senior management and other stakeholders. Use visual aids like risk heat maps and dashboards to present findings clearly and concisely.

Determining residual risk after control implementation is a complex but vital process that ensures ongoing risk management and security posture. Using methodologies like qualitative, quantitative, and semi-quantitative assessments, as well as scenario analysis, helps in accurately identifying and quantifying residual risks. Despite challenges like data limitations, evolving threats, and resource constraints, organizations can employ strategies such as leveraging automation, regular training, stakeholder engagement, scenario planning, and effective communication to overcome these hurdles and maintain a robust risk management framework.

Stakeholder concurrence is crucial in risk acceptance decisions as it ensures that all perspectives and concerns are considered, leading to more comprehensive and balanced risk management strategies. When stakeholders agree on the level of risk acceptable to the organization, it fosters collective responsibility and supports the effective implementation of risk management plans. The following methods help organizations ensure that all relevant stakeholders are involved in the risk acceptance process:

1. **Stakeholder Identification and Analysis**: The first step is to identify all relevant stakeholders, including internal groups like executives, IT departments, and compliance teams, as well as external entities like customers, suppliers, and regulatory bodies. Analyzing their interests, influence, and impact on the organization helps in understanding their perspectives and prioritizing their involvement.
2. **Clear Communication Channels**: Establishing open and transparent communication channels is essential. Regular meetings, detailed reports, and collaborative platforms ensure stakeholders are kept informed and can provide input throughout the risk acceptance process.
3. **Structured Risk Assessment Workshops**: Conducting workshops that bring stakeholders together to discuss potential risks, their impacts, and mitigation strategies promotes active participation. These workshops should facilitate open discussions and encourage stakeholders to voice their concerns and suggestions.
4. **Documenting and Sharing Risk Criteria**: Clearly defining and documenting the criteria for risk acceptance ensures that all stakeholders understand the basis for decisions. Sharing these criteria helps in aligning expectations and reducing misunderstandings.
5. **Iterative Feedback Loops**: Implementing a process where stakeholder feedback is continuously gathered, reviewed, and integrated into risk management decisions allows for dynamic adjustments and enhances stakeholder buy-in.

Potential conflicts between different stakeholder groups are inevitable due to varying priorities, perspectives, and levels of risk tolerance. For instance, IT departments might prioritize security and advocate for stringent controls, while business units may focus on operational efficiency and profitability, preferring more lenient risk acceptance criteria.

To achieve consensus, consider these strategies:

1. **Mediation and Facilitation**: Appointing neutral facilitators or mediators can help navigate conflicts by fostering constructive dialogue, identifying common ground, and guiding stakeholders towards mutually acceptable solutions.
2. **Prioritization Frameworks**: Using frameworks like risk matrices or impact assessments helps quantify and compare risks objectively. This can assist stakeholders in understanding the trade-offs and prioritizing risks based on their potential impact and likelihood.
3. **Scenario Analysis and Simulation**: Running simulations or scenario analyses can demonstrate the potential outcomes of different risk acceptance decisions. This empirical approach helps stakeholders visualize the implications and make informed choices.
4. **Building Alliances and Coalitions**: Identifying and leveraging alliances among stakeholders with similar perspectives can strengthen the position during negotiations. Building coalitions can help in presenting a unified stance, making it easier to reach a consensus.
5. **Consensus-Building Workshops**: Organizing workshops focused specifically on consensus-building can help address conflicts. These workshops should be designed to encourage empathy, where stakeholders understand and appreciate each other's concerns and constraints.
6. **Risk Acceptance Policies**: Developing and enforcing risk acceptance policies that outline the roles, responsibilities, and decision-making processes for stakeholders can provide a structured approach to managing conflicts. These policies should emphasize the importance of collaboration and shared responsibility.

Ensuring stakeholder concurrence in risk acceptance decisions is fundamental to effective risk management. By involving all relevant parties, facilitating open communication, and employing strategies to resolve conflicts, organizations can achieve a balanced approach to risk that aligns with their strategic objectives and operational realities.

Risk appetite in the context of system compliance refers to the level of risk an organization is willing to accept in pursuit of its objectives before action is deemed necessary to reduce the risk. It sets the boundaries for acceptable risk and helps guide decision-making processes across the organization.

An organization's risk appetite significantly influences its compliance approach by determining the extent and rigor of controls and procedures it implements. For instance, an organization with a low risk appetite will likely adopt stringent compliance measures, investing heavily in security technologies, detailed monitoring systems, and comprehensive audits to mitigate risks as much as possible. Conversely, an organization with a higher risk appetite may opt for more flexible and cost-effective measures, accepting that some level of risk is inevitable.

The relationship between risk appetite and risk tolerance is crucial for understanding how an organization manages its risks. While risk appetite is the broad, strategic level of risk the organization is willing to embrace, risk tolerance refers to the acceptable variation in outcomes that the organization is prepared to deal with on a more operational level. Essentially, risk tolerance is the degree to which an organization can withstand deviations from its risk appetite.

For example, consider a financial institution that has a low risk appetite due to the sensitive nature of its operations and the high regulatory requirements. Its risk tolerance would involve specific metrics such as maximum allowable loss in a quarter or the acceptable number of security incidents per year. If the number of incidents exceeds this tolerance, it triggers corrective actions, like tightening security controls or revising policies.

In practice, these concepts are applied through risk assessments and continuous monitoring. Suppose a healthcare organization identifies a potential threat to patient data confidentiality. If its risk appetite is low, it might implement advanced encryption methods and conduct regular employee training sessions. Its risk tolerance might be defined by the number of minor security breaches it can accept annually. If breaches surpass this threshold, it indicates a need to reassess and enhance existing security measures.

Understanding and defining risk appetite and tolerance are essential for aligning compliance efforts with organizational objectives. It ensures that resources are appropriately allocated to manage risks within acceptable limits, fostering a balanced approach to achieving both compliance and business goals.

Documenting system compliance decisions is a critical process that ensures transparency, accountability, and adherence to legal and regulatory requirements. It involves creating detailed records of how compliance decisions were made, who was involved, and the rationale behind those decisions. Proper documentation supports ongoing compliance efforts, facilitates audits, and demonstrates the organization's commitment to regulatory standards.

Key Information in Formal Compliance Notifications
1. **Decision Summary**: A concise overview of the compliance decision, including what specific compliance requirements or standards are being addressed.
2. **Rationale**: The reasons behind the compliance decision, detailing the risk assessments, threat analyses, and business impacts considered.
3. **Stakeholders Involved**: Names and roles of all individuals and departments involved in the decision-making process. This includes risk managers, IT security personnel, compliance officers, and any relevant external consultants.
4. **Date and Time**: Precise timestamps of when the decision was made and when it is effective. This aids in tracking the timeline of compliance activities.
5. **Supporting Documentation**: References to any assessments, audits, or other documentation that informed the decision. This could include risk assessment reports, compliance checklists, or third-party audit findings.

6. **Compliance Standards and Regulations Referenced**: Specific laws, regulations, and industry standards that the compliance decision pertains to, such as GDPR, HIPAA, or ISO/IEC 27001.
7. **Implementation Plan**: Detailed steps for how the compliance decision will be implemented, including timelines, resource allocation, and responsible parties.
8. **Monitoring and Review Plan**: How the compliance decision will be monitored and reviewed over time to ensure ongoing adherence. This includes scheduled audits, regular reviews, and mechanisms for reporting non-compliance.
9. **Approval and Sign-off**: Signatures of the decision-makers, indicating their approval of the compliance decision. This usually includes senior management or designated compliance officers.

Legal and Regulatory Implications of Compliance Documentation

Proper compliance documentation is not just a best practice; it is often a legal requirement. Failure to maintain adequate records can lead to several legal and regulatory consequences:

1. **Audits and Inspections**: Regulatory bodies may require detailed records during audits and inspections. Inadequate documentation can result in penalties, fines, or other sanctions.
2. **Legal Defense**: In the event of legal action, thorough compliance documentation can serve as evidence that the organization took reasonable steps to meet regulatory requirements, potentially mitigating liability.
3. **Accountability**: Detailed records ensure that individuals and departments are accountable for their compliance responsibilities, which is crucial for maintaining organizational integrity and trust.

Best Practices in Record-Keeping

1. **Centralized Documentation**: Maintain a centralized repository for all compliance-related documents. This ensures easy access and retrieval during audits or reviews.
2. **Consistent Format**: Use standardized templates and formats for documenting compliance decisions. This promotes consistency and makes it easier to review and understand the records.
3. **Regular Updates**: Ensure that compliance documentation is regularly updated to reflect any changes in regulations, business processes, or compliance status.
4. **Access Controls**: Implement strict access controls to ensure that only authorized personnel can view or modify compliance records. This protects the integrity and confidentiality of the documentation.
5. **Retention Policies**: Establish and enforce document retention policies that comply with regulatory requirements. This includes specifying how long records should be kept and the process for securely disposing of outdated documents.
6. **Audit Trails**: Maintain detailed audit trails that record all changes made to compliance documentation, including who made the changes and when. This enhances transparency and accountability.

Examples of Best Practices in Record-Keeping

1. **Financial Institutions**: Banks and other financial institutions often use GRC (Governance, Risk, and Compliance) software to manage compliance documentation. These systems automate record-keeping, ensure compliance with regulations like the Sarbanes-Oxley Act, and provide audit-ready documentation.
2. **Healthcare Providers**: Hospitals and clinics maintain meticulous records to comply with HIPAA regulations. This includes detailed logs of patient data access and strict protocols for documenting any data breaches.
3. **Tech Companies**: Firms in the technology sector often follow frameworks like ISO/IEC 27001 for information security management. This involves maintaining comprehensive documentation of all security controls, risk assessments, and compliance audits.

By adhering to these best practices, organizations can ensure robust compliance documentation that not only meets regulatory requirements but also supports effective risk management and operational excellence.

The Authorizing Official (AO) plays a pivotal role in the system compliance process, acting as the senior official responsible for making critical decisions about whether a system can operate within an organization's risk environment. The AO's primary responsibility is to ensure that the system's risk posture aligns with the organization's risk appetite and tolerances, thereby safeguarding the organization's assets, operations, and reputation.

When making a compliance decision, the AO considers several factors:

1. **Risk Assessments**: Evaluates the results of comprehensive risk assessments to understand the potential impact and likelihood of identified threats and vulnerabilities.

2. **Security Controls:** Reviews the effectiveness of implemented security controls to determine if they adequately mitigate risks to an acceptable level.
3. **Compliance Requirements:** Ensures that the system complies with relevant laws, regulations, policies, and standards, such as the Federal Information Security Management Act (FISMA) or industry-specific guidelines.
4. **Residual Risk:** Considers the residual risk, which is the risk remaining after all security controls have been applied. The AO must decide if this residual risk is acceptable within the organization's risk appetite.
5. **System Impact:** Takes into account the potential impact of the system on the organization's mission, operations, and assets, particularly if the system processes sensitive or critical information.
6. **Continuous Monitoring:** Evaluates the plan for continuous monitoring to ensure that risks will be continually assessed and managed over the system's lifecycle.

Conditional Authorization

Conditional authorization is a temporary approval granted for a system to operate under specific conditions and constraints. This concept is employed when a system has not fully met all compliance requirements but is deemed necessary to operate due to operational needs or time constraints. The AO uses conditional authorization to balance the need for system functionality with the imperative of managing security risks effectively.

Examples of scenarios where conditional authorization might be appropriate include:

- **Critical Mission Needs:** If a system is essential for a critical mission and delaying its deployment would severely impact operations, the AO might grant conditional authorization while requiring immediate action on outstanding issues.
- **In-Progress Remediation:** When a system has several minor security issues that are currently being addressed, and the completion of these tasks is expected shortly. The AO might allow the system to operate with strict monitoring until full compliance is achieved.
- **External Dependencies:** If a system relies on external components or services that have yet to achieve full compliance but are crucial for its functionality, conditional authorization can be used. For example, a third-party service critical to the system's operations might still be under review.

Conditional authorization includes specific terms and conditions, such as additional monitoring requirements, periodic reporting of progress on remediation actions, and a defined timeline for achieving full compliance. The AO ensures that these conditions are strictly adhered to and reevaluates the system's status regularly to determine if continued operation is justified or if further actions, including potential suspension of authorization, are necessary.

Clear and effective stakeholder communication in system compliance is essential for ensuring that all parties understand their roles, responsibilities, and the importance of adhering to compliance standards. Effective communication fosters a culture of compliance, mitigates risks, and enhances the overall security posture of an organization. It ensures that everyone from top management to operational staff is aligned and aware of compliance requirements and procedures.

Importance of Clear and Effective Stakeholder Communication

1. **Alignment and Awareness**: Ensuring that all stakeholders are aware of compliance requirements and the organization's policies helps maintain alignment with regulatory standards and organizational goals. This collective understanding is crucial for cohesive compliance efforts.
2. **Risk Mitigation**: Clear communication helps in identifying and addressing potential compliance risks promptly. When stakeholders understand the implications of non-compliance, they are more likely to adhere to protocols and report any issues proactively.
3. **Accountability and Responsibility**: Effective communication delineates roles and responsibilities, ensuring that each stakeholder knows their part in maintaining compliance. This accountability reduces the likelihood of oversights and errors.
4. **Audit Readiness**: Well-documented and communicated compliance procedures and decisions make it easier to demonstrate compliance during audits. It shows regulators that the organization is diligent in maintaining compliance standards.

Strategies for Effective Compliance Communication

1. **Tailored Communication Plans**: Develop communication plans that are tailored to different stakeholder groups. This includes creating specific messages for executives, IT staff, and non-technical employees, ensuring that each group receives relevant information in a comprehensible format.
2. **Regular Training and Awareness Programs**: Implement regular training sessions and awareness programs to keep stakeholders informed about compliance requirements and updates. These sessions should be interactive and include real-world scenarios to enhance understanding.
3. **Clear and Concise Documentation**: Ensure that all compliance documentation is clear, concise, and easily accessible. Use plain language for non-technical stakeholders and detailed technical documentation for IT staff.
4. **Use of Visual Aids**: Incorporate visual aids such as infographics, flowcharts, and diagrams to explain complex compliance information. Visual representations can make technical details more digestible for non-technical audiences.
5. **Feedback Mechanisms**: Establish mechanisms for stakeholders to provide feedback and ask questions about compliance issues. This could include suggestion boxes, regular meetings, or dedicated communication channels.
6. **Compliance Champions**: Designate compliance champions within different departments who can act as points of contact for compliance-related queries and facilitate communication between the compliance team and their respective departments.

Challenges in Communicating Technical Compliance Information to Non-Technical Stakeholders

1. **Complexity of Technical Information**: Technical compliance information can be intricate and challenging for non-technical stakeholders to understand. This complexity can lead to misunderstandings and misinterpretations.
2. **Varying Levels of Knowledge**: Stakeholders have diverse backgrounds and levels of knowledge. Tailoring communication to address these varying levels without oversimplifying or overcomplicating the information is a significant challenge.
3. **Resistance to Change**: Non-technical stakeholders may resist compliance measures if they perceive them as cumbersome or unnecessary. Overcoming this resistance requires clear explanations of the benefits and importance of compliance.
4. **Language Barriers**: Technical jargon and acronyms can create language barriers. Non-technical stakeholders may find it difficult to follow communications filled with specialized terminology.

Strategies to Overcome These Challenges

1. **Simplify and Contextualize**: Simplify technical information and provide context by relating it to stakeholders' roles and responsibilities. Use analogies and real-world examples to make the information more relatable.
2. **Engage in Dialogue**: Foster an environment where stakeholders feel comfortable asking questions and seeking clarification. Encourage open dialogue to address any confusion and ensure understanding.
3. **Leverage Communication Tools**: Use diverse communication tools and platforms, such as intranet portals, newsletters, webinars, and workshops, to disseminate information. This variety ensures that stakeholders receive messages in formats they are comfortable with.
4. **Ongoing Support and Resources**: Provide ongoing support and resources, such as FAQs, glossaries, and helplines, to assist non-technical stakeholders in understanding compliance information. Ensure that these resources are readily available and user-friendly.
5. **Regular Updates and Reinforcement**: Regularly update stakeholders on compliance matters and reinforce key messages through multiple channels. Repetition and consistency help in embedding compliance awareness into the organizational culture.

Effective stakeholder communication in system compliance is vital for maintaining regulatory adherence and mitigating risks. By employing tailored communication strategies and addressing the challenges of conveying technical information to non-technical audiences, organizations can foster a robust compliance culture that supports their strategic and operational goals.

Continuous monitoring is a critical component in maintaining system compliance, involving the ongoing observation and assessment of a system's security posture to identify and mitigate risks in real-time. It ensures that security controls remain effective and that the system remains compliant with relevant policies, standards, and regulations over its operational life.

Implementing Effective Continuous Monitoring Programs

Organizations implement effective continuous monitoring programs through a series of structured steps:

1. **Defining Metrics and Indicators:** Organizations establish key security metrics and indicators to monitor. These might include system performance data, security incidents, vulnerabilities, and compliance status.
2. **Automation:** Utilizing automated tools and technologies is crucial for efficient continuous monitoring. These tools can include Security Information and Event Management (SIEM) systems, intrusion detection systems (IDS), and vulnerability scanners.
3. **Regular Data Collection:** Continuous monitoring involves the systematic collection of data from various sources, such as network devices, servers, applications, and databases. This data is then analyzed to detect anomalies or signs of potential security breaches.
4. **Risk Assessment and Analysis:** Organizations continuously assess and analyze the collected data to understand the risk landscape. This involves correlating security events, identifying trends, and prioritizing risks based on their potential impact.
5. **Incident Response:** Effective continuous monitoring programs include robust incident response mechanisms. When anomalies or security incidents are detected, organizations must have predefined procedures to respond swiftly and mitigate risks.
6. **Reporting and Documentation:** Continuous monitoring involves regular reporting to stakeholders about the security posture and compliance status. Detailed documentation is necessary to track the effectiveness of security controls and to provide evidence of compliance.

Relationship Between Continuous Monitoring and Periodic Compliance Assessments

Continuous monitoring and periodic compliance assessments complement each other by providing a comprehensive approach to managing and maintaining system compliance.

- **Continuous Monitoring:** Focuses on real-time or near-real-time detection and response to security threats and vulnerabilities. It provides ongoing assurance that security controls are functioning as intended and that the system remains within the acceptable risk threshold.
- **Periodic Compliance Assessments:** These are scheduled evaluations, typically conducted annually or semi-annually, to review the overall security posture of the system. They involve in-depth audits and assessments to verify compliance with established standards, policies, and regulations.

Complementing Each Other

1. **Dynamic Risk Management:** Continuous monitoring offers a dynamic approach to risk management by providing immediate insights into the system's security status. Periodic assessments provide a more thorough and comprehensive review of the system's compliance status, validating the findings from continuous monitoring efforts.
2. **Validation and Verification:** Periodic assessments serve to validate and verify the effectiveness of the continuous monitoring program. They can identify gaps or weaknesses in the monitoring process and recommend improvements.
3. **Regulatory Compliance:** While continuous monitoring ensures day-to-day compliance, periodic assessments provide the documentation and formal review required by regulatory bodies. Together, they ensure that the organization not only meets compliance requirements but also maintains a strong security posture continuously.

Examples

- **Financial Institutions:** A bank might use continuous monitoring to track transactions and detect fraudulent activities in real-time. Periodic assessments would then evaluate the overall effectiveness of these monitoring tools and processes, ensuring they comply with financial regulations like the Sarbanes-Oxley Act (SOX).
- **Healthcare Organizations:** Continuous monitoring in a healthcare setting might involve real-time logging and analysis of access to patient records to ensure compliance with HIPAA regulations. Periodic assessments would then thoroughly review these logs, access controls, and incident response mechanisms to ensure full regulatory compliance and address any gaps identified.

Continuous monitoring provides immediate feedback and a proactive approach to security, while periodic compliance assessments offer a detailed and retrospective evaluation, ensuring comprehensive compliance management. This dual approach helps organizations maintain a robust security posture and adapt to evolving threats and regulatory requirements.

Security metrics play a pivotal role in demonstrating ongoing system compliance by providing quantitative data that can be used to measure, track, and report on various aspects of an organization's security posture. These metrics offer objective evidence that security controls are effective and that the organization is adhering to regulatory and compliance requirements.

Role of Security Metrics in Demonstrating Ongoing System Compliance
1. **Monitoring and Reporting**: Security metrics allow organizations to continuously monitor their systems and processes to ensure compliance with established standards. They provide regular reporting that can be reviewed by management, auditors, and regulators.
2. **Risk Management**: By identifying trends and anomalies, security metrics help in assessing and managing risks. They enable organizations to proactively address vulnerabilities and mitigate potential threats before they result in non-compliance.
3. **Performance Measurement**: Metrics offer a way to measure the performance of security controls and processes over time. This helps in evaluating the effectiveness of implemented controls and identifying areas for improvement.
4. **Decision Support**: Security metrics provide critical data that supports informed decision-making regarding security investments, policy adjustments, and strategic planning.

Effective Types of Metrics for Different Compliance Requirements
1. **Quantitative Metrics**:
    - **Vulnerability Metrics**: Number of vulnerabilities detected, severity levels, and time to remediate. These metrics are crucial for standards like PCI DSS and HIPAA, where timely vulnerability management is essential.
    - **Incident Metrics**: Number of security incidents, types of incidents, and time to resolve. Relevant for frameworks like ISO/IEC 27001, which emphasize incident management and response.
    - **Access Control Metrics**: Number of access control violations, unauthorized access attempts, and successful logins. Important for compliance with regulations like SOX and GDPR.
2. **Qualitative Metrics**:
    - **Compliance Audit Results**: Results from internal and external audits, including findings and recommendations. Used for demonstrating compliance with various regulatory requirements.
    - **Employee Training and Awareness**: Percentage of employees who have completed security training and results from training assessments. Relevant for ensuring compliance with organizational security policies and standards.
3. **Operational Metrics**:
    - **Patch Management Metrics**: Percentage of systems patched within a specified timeframe, and compliance with patch management policies. Crucial for maintaining compliance with security standards like NIST SP 800-53.
    - **Backup and Recovery Metrics**: Frequency of backups, success rates, and time to recover. Important for demonstrating compliance with business continuity and disaster recovery requirements.

Challenges in Developing Meaningful Security Metrics
1. **Relevance and Alignment**: Ensuring that metrics are relevant and aligned with specific compliance requirements and organizational goals can be challenging. Metrics must be carefully selected to reflect the critical aspects of security and compliance.
2. **Data Collection and Accuracy**: Collecting accurate and comprehensive data can be difficult, especially in complex IT environments. Inaccurate or incomplete data can lead to misleading metrics and poor decision-making.
3. **Context and Interpretation**: Metrics need to be contextualized and interpreted correctly. Without proper context, raw metrics can be misinterpreted, leading to incorrect conclusions about the state of compliance.

4. **Integration with Business Processes**: Security metrics must be integrated with broader business processes and goals. This requires collaboration between IT, security teams, and business units to ensure metrics support overall organizational objectives.

Examples of How Metrics Can Support Compliance Decisions
1. **Trend Analysis**: Analyzing trends in vulnerability metrics can help an organization understand whether its security posture is improving or deteriorating over time. For instance, a decrease in the number of critical vulnerabilities detected might indicate that recent security measures are effective.
2. **Resource Allocation**: Incident metrics showing a high number of incidents related to phishing attacks can justify the need for additional resources to enhance email security and employee training programs.
3. **Audit Preparation**: Compliance audit results can be used to prepare for external audits by identifying and addressing areas of non-compliance beforehand. Regular internal audits can also provide assurance that controls are functioning as intended.
4. **Policy Adjustments**: Access control metrics indicating frequent unauthorized access attempts might prompt a review and tightening of access control policies and procedures.
5. **Performance Improvement**: Backup and recovery metrics demonstrating long recovery times could lead to investments in better backup solutions and more efficient recovery processes to ensure compliance with recovery time objectives (RTOs).

Security metrics are indispensable in demonstrating and maintaining ongoing system compliance. By providing objective, quantifiable data, they enable organizations to monitor their security posture, manage risks, and make informed decisions. Developing meaningful metrics requires careful selection, accurate data collection, and proper contextualization to ensure they effectively support compliance efforts and organizational goals.

A Business Impact Analysis (BIA) is a systematic process that helps organizations identify and evaluate the potential effects of disruptions to their critical business operations. In the context of system compliance, conducting a BIA is essential for understanding the consequences of system failures or security breaches and for informing risk management and compliance strategies.

Conducting a Business Impact Analysis (BIA)
1. **Preparation and Planning**:
    - Define the scope of the BIA, including the systems, processes, and functions to be analyzed.
    - Assemble a BIA team with representatives from various departments such as IT, operations, finance, and compliance.
    - Develop a project plan outlining the objectives, methodology, and timeline.
2. **Data Collection**:
    - Gather information through surveys, interviews, and questionnaires from stakeholders to identify critical business functions and processes.
    - Collect data on dependencies, resources, and assets required for each business function, including IT systems, personnel, and facilities.
3. **Impact Assessment**:
    - Evaluate the potential impact of disruptions on business operations, considering factors such as financial loss, regulatory penalties, reputational damage, and operational downtime.
    - Classify the impacts based on severity and duration, identifying the maximum tolerable downtime (MTD) for each critical function.
4. **Risk Identification**:
    - Identify potential threats and vulnerabilities that could cause disruptions to critical business functions. This may include natural disasters, cyberattacks, system failures, and human errors.
    - Assess the likelihood of these threats occurring and their potential impact on the organization.
5. **Analysis and Documentation**:
    - Analyze the collected data to prioritize business functions based on their criticality and the severity of potential impacts.
    - Document the findings, including detailed impact scenarios, recovery requirements, and dependencies for each critical function.

Informing Risk Acceptance Decisions

The BIA informs risk acceptance decisions by providing a clear understanding of the potential impacts of disruptions on critical business functions. This information helps organizations:
- **Prioritize Risks:** Identify and prioritize risks that pose the greatest threat to business operations, ensuring that resources are allocated to mitigate the most critical risks first.
- **Set Risk Tolerances:** Define acceptable levels of risk (risk appetite) based on the potential impact of disruptions and the organization's ability to recover within acceptable timeframes.
- **Develop Mitigation Strategies:** Design and implement controls and procedures to reduce the likelihood and impact of identified risks, aligning with the organization's risk appetite and compliance requirements.

Key Components of a Comprehensive BIA
1. **Executive Summary:** Provides an overview of the BIA objectives, scope, methodology, and key findings.
2. **Business Function Analysis:** Detailed analysis of critical business functions, including their dependencies, resources, and recovery requirements.
3. **Impact Scenarios:** Descriptions of potential disruption scenarios and their impact on business operations, categorized by severity and duration.
4. **Risk Assessment:** Identification and evaluation of threats and vulnerabilities that could impact critical business functions.
5. **Recovery Strategies:** Recommendations for mitigating risks and improving resilience, including business continuity and disaster recovery plans.
6. **Appendices:** Supporting documentation, such as data collection tools, interview notes, and detailed impact assessments.

Examples of How BIA Supports Compliance
- **Healthcare Sector:** A BIA in a healthcare organization might identify the criticality of electronic health records (EHR) systems. By understanding the impact of EHR system downtime on patient care and regulatory compliance (e.g., HIPAA), the organization can prioritize investments in robust security measures and backup systems to ensure data availability and integrity.
- **Financial Services:** In a financial institution, a BIA might reveal the significant impact of disruptions to payment processing systems. This analysis informs risk acceptance decisions by highlighting the need for redundant systems, enhanced security controls, and rapid recovery capabilities to meet compliance with regulations such as the Payment Card Industry Data Security Standard (PCI DSS).
- **Manufacturing Industry:** A BIA for a manufacturing company could uncover the critical dependencies between production systems and supply chain management. Understanding these dependencies helps the organization develop comprehensive compliance strategies that include supply chain risk management, ensuring continuity of operations and adherence to industry standards.

Conducting a BIA is integral to an organization's overall compliance process. It provides valuable insights into the potential impacts of disruptions, informs risk management and compliance strategies, and helps ensure that critical business functions can continue operating within acceptable risk levels.

Compensating controls are alternative security measures implemented when an organization cannot meet a specific compliance requirement through traditional means. These controls are designed to achieve the same or similar level of security as the original requirement. Understanding when and how to implement compensating controls is critical for maintaining compliance without compromising security.

When and How to Implement Compensating Controls
1. **When Traditional Controls Are Impractical**: Compensating controls are often implemented when standard controls are impractical due to technical limitations, cost constraints, or operational issues. For instance, if an organization cannot install a specific type of firewall due to legacy system constraints, it might implement network segmentation and enhanced monitoring as compensating controls.
2. **During Transitional Periods**: Organizations may use compensating controls during transitional periods when they are upgrading systems or implementing new technologies. This ensures continued compliance while new systems are being put in place.

3. **Resource Constraints**: When resources (budget, personnel, or time) are limited, compensating controls can provide a temporary solution that maintains compliance until more permanent measures can be implemented.

Implementing Compensating Controls
1. **Risk Assessment**: Conduct a thorough risk assessment to understand the risks associated with not implementing the standard control. This helps in identifying appropriate compensating controls that address those specific risks.
2. **Control Selection**: Choose compensating controls that provide equivalent or greater protection. These controls should mitigate the identified risks effectively and align with the overall security strategy.
3. **Documentation**: Document the rationale for using compensating controls, including why the standard control is impractical and how the compensating control provides equivalent protection. This documentation should include details of the risk assessment, the selected controls, and their expected effectiveness.
4. **Implementation and Monitoring**: Implement the compensating controls and establish monitoring mechanisms to ensure they are functioning as intended. Regularly review these controls to ensure they continue to provide adequate protection.

Justifying Compensating Controls to Auditors or Regulators
1. **Clear Documentation**: Present comprehensive documentation that includes the risk assessment, the rationale for choosing compensating controls, and evidence that these controls provide equivalent security. This documentation should be clear, detailed, and well-organized.
2. **Evidence of Effectiveness**: Provide data and metrics that demonstrate the effectiveness of the compensating controls. This can include logs, reports from monitoring tools, and results from security tests or audits.
3. **Compliance Mapping**: Map the compensating controls to the specific compliance requirements they address. Show how these controls achieve the same objectives as the original requirements, ensuring that auditors understand their relevance and effectiveness.
4. **Regular Reviews and Updates**: Demonstrate that the compensating controls are regularly reviewed and updated to address any changes in the threat landscape or organizational environment. This shows a commitment to ongoing compliance and security.

Examples of Compensating Controls
1. **Encryption of Data in Transit**:
    - **Scenario**: An organization cannot implement TLS for all data transmissions due to compatibility issues with legacy systems.
    - **Compensating Controls**: Implement IPsec for securing data transmissions and use robust network monitoring to detect and respond to any suspicious activity.
2. **Two-Factor Authentication (2FA)**:
    - **Scenario**: An organization cannot deploy 2FA for remote access due to limitations in the existing infrastructure.
    - **Compensating Controls**: Enhance password policies (e.g., requiring complex passwords and frequent changes), implement IP whitelisting, and increase logging and monitoring of remote access sessions.
3. **Physical Security**:
    - **Scenario**: An organization cannot secure all data centers with biometric access controls due to high costs.
    - **Compensating Controls**: Use a combination of traditional access controls (key cards, PINs), CCTV monitoring, and frequent security patrols to maintain a high level of physical security.
4. **Patch Management**:
    - **Scenario**: An organization cannot apply patches immediately due to critical operational requirements.
    - **Compensating Controls**: Implement virtual patching using intrusion prevention systems (IPS) and enhance network segmentation to contain potential exploits.

Compensating controls are vital for maintaining compliance when traditional controls are not feasible. They must be carefully selected based on thorough risk assessments and must provide equivalent protection to the original controls. Clear documentation, evidence of effectiveness, and regular reviews are essential for justifying these controls to auditors and regulators. By following these best practices, organizations can ensure that they remain compliant and secure even in challenging circumstances.

Supply chain risk management is crucial in system compliance because third-party vendors and service providers often have access to sensitive data, systems, and infrastructure. Any vulnerabilities within the supply chain can introduce significant risks to the organization, potentially leading to breaches, disruptions, or compliance violations.

Assessing and Mitigating Risks with Third-Party Vendors
1. **Risk Assessment:**
    - **Initial Due Diligence:** Organizations begin by conducting thorough due diligence on potential vendors. This includes reviewing their security policies, compliance certifications, financial stability, and past performance.
    - **Vendor Risk Profiling:** Categorize vendors based on the level of risk they present. Critical vendors, who have access to sensitive data or systems, are subject to more stringent evaluations than non-critical vendors.
    - **Security Audits:** Conduct security audits and assessments to identify vulnerabilities in the vendor's systems and processes. This can involve reviewing their network security, data protection measures, and incident response plans.
    - **Compliance Check:** Ensure that vendors comply with relevant laws, regulations, and standards (e.g., GDPR, HIPAA, PCI DSS) and that they maintain necessary certifications.
2. **Contractual Controls:**
    - **Service Level Agreements (SLAs):** Establish clear SLAs that define the vendor's responsibilities, security requirements, and performance metrics.
    - **Compliance Clauses:** Include specific compliance clauses in contracts that require vendors to adhere to applicable regulations and standards.
    - **Right to Audit:** Incorporate provisions that grant the organization the right to audit the vendor's compliance and security practices periodically.
3. **Ongoing Monitoring:**
    - **Continuous Monitoring:** Implement continuous monitoring mechanisms to keep track of the vendor's security posture and compliance status. This can include regular reporting, security reviews, and automated monitoring tools.
    - **Performance Reviews:** Conduct regular performance reviews and risk assessments to ensure that vendors meet their contractual obligations and maintain compliance.

Challenges of Maintaining Compliance Across Complex Supply Chains
1. **Lack of Transparency:** It can be difficult to gain full visibility into a vendor's operations and security practices, especially when dealing with large or geographically dispersed supply chains.
2. **Third-Party Risks:** The risk extends beyond direct vendors to their subcontractors and partners, who may not have the same level of security controls.
3. **Dynamic Risk Environment:** The risk landscape is constantly evolving, with new threats emerging regularly, making it challenging to keep compliance measures up-to-date.
4. **Regulatory Variability:** Different regions and industries have varying regulatory requirements, complicating the compliance efforts for global supply chains.

Strategies for Effective Vendor Management
1. **Centralized Vendor Management:**
    - Establish a centralized vendor management office (VMO) to oversee the vendor selection, assessment, and monitoring processes. This ensures consistency and efficiency in managing vendor risks.
2. **Risk-Based Approach:**
    - Prioritize vendor management efforts based on the risk profile of each vendor. Critical vendors should receive more focus and resources than those deemed low-risk.

3. **Vendor Education and Collaboration:**
   - Educate vendors about your organization's security and compliance requirements. Foster a collaborative relationship to ensure they understand and implement necessary controls.
4. **Automation and Tools:**
   - Utilize automated tools and platforms for continuous monitoring and risk assessment. These tools can provide real-time insights into vendor security postures and help identify potential issues early.
5. **Regular Audits and Assessments:**
   - Perform regular audits and assessments to verify vendor compliance. This includes both scheduled reviews and surprise audits to ensure ongoing adherence to security and compliance standards.
6. **Incident Response Planning:**
   - Develop and test incident response plans that include vendors. Ensure that there are clear communication channels and protocols for managing security incidents that involve third-party vendors.
7. **Third-Party Risk Management Framework:**
   - Implement a comprehensive third-party risk management framework that covers the entire lifecycle of vendor relationships, from selection and onboarding to continuous monitoring and offboarding.

Example

Consider a financial institution that relies on multiple vendors for various services, including cloud storage, payment processing, and IT support. To manage the associated risks, the institution might implement the following strategies:

- Conduct thorough due diligence on all potential vendors, focusing on their security measures, compliance certifications, and financial health.
- Include robust security requirements and compliance clauses in all vendor contracts, along with the right to audit their operations.
- Utilize automated tools to continuously monitor vendor activities and security postures, receiving alerts on any suspicious activities.
- Conduct regular performance reviews and risk assessments, prioritizing critical vendors that handle sensitive financial data.
- Educate vendors on the institution's security expectations and collaborate with them to address any identified vulnerabilities.

Supply chain risk management is an integral part of system compliance, ensuring that third-party vendors and service providers do not introduce vulnerabilities or compliance risks. By implementing comprehensive assessment and monitoring processes, establishing strong contractual controls, and fostering collaborative relationships, organizations can effectively manage and mitigate supply chain risks.

An Authorization to Operate (ATO) is a formal declaration that a government system has been reviewed and approved to operate within an acceptable level of risk. It is a critical component of the risk management framework (RMF) and is essential for ensuring that systems meet security and compliance requirements before they are deployed. The ATO process ensures that government systems are secure, reliable, and capable of protecting sensitive information.

Process for Obtaining an ATO
1. **Initiation**: The process begins with the initiation phase, where the need for the system is identified, and initial security categorization is conducted based on the system's confidentiality, integrity, and availability requirements.
2. **Security Planning**: A comprehensive security plan is developed, outlining the security controls that will be implemented to mitigate identified risks. This includes selecting the appropriate security controls from frameworks such as NIST SP 800-53.

3. **Implementation**: Security controls are implemented, and the system is configured according to the security plan. This phase involves installing and configuring hardware and software, as well as developing operational procedures.
4. **Assessment**: A thorough security assessment is conducted to evaluate the effectiveness of the implemented controls. This involves vulnerability scanning, penetration testing, and other evaluation methods to identify potential security weaknesses.
5. **Authorization**: Based on the assessment results, the system owner prepares an authorization package that includes the security plan, assessment report, and a plan of action and milestones (POA&M) for addressing any identified issues. This package is reviewed by an Authorizing Official (AO), who decides whether to grant the ATO.
6. **Continuous Monitoring**: Once the ATO is granted, continuous monitoring of the system is required to ensure ongoing compliance and to identify and mitigate new risks as they arise. This involves regular security assessments, updating the security plan, and maintaining an accurate inventory of system components.

Types of ATOs
1. **Full ATO**: A full ATO is granted when a system has undergone a complete security assessment and has met all security requirements. It indicates that the system operates at an acceptable level of risk with no significant security deficiencies. For example, a full ATO might be appropriate for a new system that has been developed with stringent security measures and has passed all security evaluations without any critical issues.
2. **Conditional ATO**: A conditional ATO, also known as a temporary ATO, is granted when a system has not fully met all security requirements but is allowed to operate under certain conditions and for a limited time. This type of ATO includes specific conditions that must be met and a timeline for resolving outstanding issues. For instance, a system may receive a conditional ATO if it has minor security deficiencies that do not pose a significant immediate risk but require remediation within a specified period.
3. **Interim ATO (IATO)**: An interim ATO is granted for a limited duration to allow a system to operate while significant security issues are being addressed. This is often used in situations where immediate operation is critical, but the system has not yet completed the full assessment process. For example, an IATO might be issued for a system supporting a critical mission where immediate deployment is necessary, and there is a clear plan and timeline for addressing outstanding security concerns.

Relation to Overall System Compliance

The ATO process is integral to overall system compliance as it ensures that systems are evaluated against security and regulatory requirements before they are operational. Obtaining an ATO demonstrates that a system has undergone rigorous review and is deemed secure enough to handle government data and operations. This process enforces accountability and ensures that security risks are managed effectively.

The Authorization to Operate (ATO) is a vital component of the government's risk management framework, ensuring that systems meet security and compliance standards. The process for obtaining an ATO involves rigorous planning, implementation, assessment, and continuous monitoring. Understanding the differences between full, conditional, and interim ATOs is essential for managing system risk and ensuring that systems can operate securely and effectively within the government framework.

Compliance Maintenance

System change management is crucial for maintaining compliance, ensuring that any modifications to a system do not inadvertently introduce security vulnerabilities or lead to non-compliance with regulatory standards. The process involves assessing, approving, implementing, and monitoring changes in a controlled and systematic manner to mitigate risks and maintain the integrity and security of the system.

Assessing the Impact of Changes on Compliance

Organizations must evaluate the potential impact of proposed changes on their compliance posture through a detailed risk assessment process. This involves:

1. **Identifying the Scope of Changes**: Clearly defining the changes to be made, whether they involve hardware, software, configurations, or processes.
2. **Assessing Compliance Requirements**: Reviewing the relevant compliance requirements that might be affected by the proposed changes. This includes regulatory frameworks such as GDPR, HIPAA, or industry standards like ISO/IEC 27001.
3. **Conducting Risk Assessments**: Performing a thorough risk assessment to identify potential security vulnerabilities and compliance issues that could arise from the changes. This involves evaluating the likelihood and impact of risks and determining the necessary controls to mitigate them.
4. **Testing and Validation**: Implementing changes in a test environment to validate that they do not negatively impact compliance controls. This includes conducting security testing, vulnerability assessments, and compliance checks.
5. **Documenting Findings**: Recording the assessment results, including identified risks, proposed mitigation measures, and the expected impact on compliance. Detailed documentation helps in decision-making and provides an audit trail.

Change Control Boards and Their Role in Compliance

Change control boards (CCBs) play a pivotal role in maintaining compliance during the system change management process. A CCB is a group of stakeholders responsible for reviewing and approving proposed changes to ensure they meet compliance and security requirements. The board typically includes representatives from IT, security, compliance, operations, and other relevant departments.

1. **Review and Approval**: The CCB reviews proposed changes to assess their potential impact on the system's compliance posture. They evaluate the risk assessment findings, ensure that necessary controls are in place, and decide whether to approve, reject, or request modifications to the proposed changes.
2. **Stakeholder Representation**: Having a diverse group of stakeholders ensures that multiple perspectives are considered, and all relevant compliance and security concerns are addressed. This collaborative approach helps in making informed decisions that balance operational needs with compliance requirements.
3. **Enforcing Policies and Procedures**: The CCB ensures that changes comply with established policies and procedures. They enforce adherence to change management processes, including documentation, testing, and validation steps.
4. **Continuous Monitoring and Feedback**: After changes are implemented, the CCB oversees the monitoring and review process to ensure the changes do not adversely affect compliance. They gather feedback, review incident reports, and make recommendations for further improvements.

Practical Examples

For instance, if an organization plans to upgrade its database management system, the CCB would:

- **Assess the impact** on data integrity, access controls, and encryption requirements as per relevant regulations (e.g., GDPR for data protection).
- **Review** the upgrade plan to ensure it includes adequate testing procedures and rollback strategies.
- **Approve** the change if the proposed measures adequately address potential compliance risks, or request modifications if necessary.
- **Monitor** the system post-implementation to verify that the changes have not introduced new vulnerabilities or compliance issues.

Effective system change management, facilitated by a robust change control board, ensures that organizations can adapt to evolving technology and business needs without compromising their compliance posture. This structured approach helps in maintaining continuous compliance, protecting sensitive information, and mitigating risks associated with system changes.

Comprehensive change documentation and approval processes are vital for ensuring that any modifications to systems or processes are thoroughly vetted, controlled, and aligned with organizational objectives and compliance requirements. They provide a clear record of what changes were made, why they were necessary, and who approved them, thereby reducing the risk of unauthorized or harmful changes.

Key Elements of Change Requests and Approval Documents
1. **Description of Change:** Detailed explanation of the proposed change, including its nature, scope, and objectives. This should provide a clear understanding of what is being altered and why it is necessary.
2. **Justification and Impact Analysis:** A rationale for the change, supported by an impact analysis that assesses the potential effects on the system, operations, and security. This includes identifying any risks, benefits, and how the change aligns with business goals.
3. **Risk Assessment:** Evaluation of the potential risks associated with the change, including security, compliance, and operational risks. This section should outline the likelihood and impact of these risks and propose mitigation strategies.
4. **Implementation Plan:** Step-by-step plan for implementing the change, including timelines, resource allocation, and roles and responsibilities. This ensures that everyone involved understands their part in the process.
5. **Testing and Validation:** Outline of the testing procedures to validate the change before full deployment. This includes details on the testing environment, test cases, and expected outcomes.
6. **Rollback Plan:** Contingency plan for reverting to the previous state if the change fails or causes unforeseen issues. This plan should be clear and actionable to minimize downtime and disruption.
7. **Approval Signatures:** Documentation of approvals from all necessary stakeholders, including IT, security, compliance, and business unit leaders. This ensures that all relevant parties have reviewed and agreed to the change.
8. **Post-Implementation Review:** Plan for reviewing the change after implementation to assess its effectiveness and identify any issues. This helps in learning from each change and improving future processes.

Balancing Thorough Documentation with Rapid Technological Change
1. **Automated Documentation Tools:** Use tools that automate parts of the documentation process, such as change management software that can track changes, collect necessary information, and generate reports. This reduces manual effort and speeds up the documentation process.
2. **Agile Change Management:** Incorporate agile methodologies that allow for iterative and incremental changes. This approach enables rapid adaptation while maintaining control through frequent reviews and adjustments.
3. **Risk-Based Approach:** Prioritize thorough documentation for high-risk changes, while using streamlined processes for low-risk modifications. This ensures that critical changes receive the necessary scrutiny without slowing down less impactful updates.
4. **Standardized Templates:** Develop standardized templates for change requests and approval documents. These templates ensure that all necessary information is captured consistently, making the process faster and more efficient.
5. **Clear Communication Channels:** Establish clear communication channels and protocols for submitting, reviewing, and approving changes. Effective communication can expedite the approval process without compromising thoroughness.
6. **Continuous Training:** Provide ongoing training for staff on change management processes and tools. Well-trained employees can navigate the documentation and approval processes more efficiently, reducing delays.
7. **Regular Audits and Reviews:** Conduct regular audits and reviews of the change management process to identify bottlenecks and areas for improvement. Continuous improvement efforts can help streamline the process over time.

For instance, in a healthcare setting where rapid technological changes are common, adopting an agile change management approach can ensure that updates to electronic health record systems are implemented swiftly while maintaining patient data security and compliance with HIPAA. Using automated tools to track and document changes can further enhance efficiency, allowing healthcare providers to adapt quickly to new regulations or emerging threats without sacrificing thoroughness.

Balancing comprehensive documentation with the need for agility requires strategic use of tools, methodologies, and processes that support both thorough oversight and rapid adaptation. By focusing on critical elements, leveraging technology, and continuously improving processes, organizations can manage changes effectively and maintain compliance in a dynamic technological landscape.

Deployment strategies in system change management refer to the methods used to implement changes in a controlled and systematic way. The choice of strategy depends on the type of change, its complexity, potential impact, and the organization's risk tolerance. Proper deployment strategies help minimize disruptions, ensure smooth transitions, and maintain system stability and compliance.

Determining the Most Appropriate Deployment Approach

Organizations assess several factors to determine the most suitable deployment strategy:

1. **Change Complexity and Scope**: The complexity and extent of the change influence the deployment approach. Minor changes may be rolled out quickly, while major updates might require more careful planning and phased implementation.
2. **Risk Assessment**: Evaluating the potential risks associated with the change is crucial. Higher-risk changes might benefit from more conservative strategies like pilot testing or phased rollouts to mitigate impact.
3. **User Impact**: Understanding how the change will affect end-users can guide the choice of strategy. Changes that significantly impact user experience may require gradual implementation to allow for user adaptation and feedback.
4. **Resource Availability**: The availability of resources, including personnel, budget, and time, affects the choice of deployment strategy. More complex strategies may require additional resources and time.
5. **System Environment**: The stability and architecture of the current system can dictate the deployment method. For example, critical systems might necessitate more cautious approaches like blue-green deployments to ensure continuous availability.

Pros and Cons of Various Deployment Strategies

Phased Rollouts

Pros:

- **Risk Mitigation**: Changes are introduced gradually, reducing the risk of widespread system failures or disruptions.
- **User Feedback**: Allows for user feedback and incremental improvements, enhancing the final implementation.
- **Scalability**: Easier to manage and scale the deployment, particularly in large organizations with multiple locations.

Cons:

- **Extended Implementation Time**: The rollout process takes longer, which might delay the full realization of benefits.
- **Complexity**: Managing different versions of the system simultaneously can be complex and resource-intensive.
- **Inconsistent User Experience**: Users may experience inconsistencies during the phased rollout period.

Pilot Testing

Pros:

- **Controlled Environment**: Limits the impact of changes by testing in a small, controlled environment before full deployment.
- **Early Issue Detection**: Identifies potential problems and allows for adjustments before broader implementation.
- **User Feedback**: Provides valuable insights and feedback from a subset of users, informing final adjustments.

Cons:
- **Limited Scope**: May not fully replicate the entire system environment, potentially missing broader issues.
- **Resource Intensive**: Requires dedicated resources to manage and monitor the pilot, which may be challenging for smaller organizations.
- **Delay in Benefits**: Full benefits of the change are delayed until after the pilot phase and subsequent adjustments.

Big Bang Deployment
Pros:
- **Immediate Change**: Entire system is updated at once, ensuring that all users have the same experience simultaneously.
- **Simplicity**: Easier to manage as there are no multiple versions of the system running at the same time.
- **Quick Realization of Benefits**: Full benefits of the change are realized immediately after deployment.

Cons:
- **High Risk**: If issues arise, they affect the entire system and all users, potentially causing significant disruptions.
- **Recovery Challenges**: Rollback or recovery can be complex and difficult if major problems occur.
- **User Resistance**: Users may struggle with abrupt changes, leading to resistance and a steep learning curve.

Blue-Green Deployment
Pros:
- **Minimal Downtime**: Reduces downtime by running two identical environments (blue and green) and switching traffic between them.
- **Easy Rollback**: Simplifies rollback in case of issues, as traffic can be reverted to the previous environment.
- **Testing in Production**: Allows for testing in a production-like environment without impacting users.

Cons:
- **Resource Intensive**: Requires maintaining two separate environments, which can be costly and resource-heavy.
- **Complex Management**: Managing and synchronizing two environments adds complexity to the deployment process.
- **Compatibility Issues**: Potential for compatibility issues between the two environments if not managed carefully.

Choosing the Right Strategy

Organizations typically select the most appropriate deployment strategy based on the specific context of the change. For instance:
- **Phased Rollouts** are ideal for large, complex changes that need to be tested incrementally and for organizations that need to mitigate risks gradually.
- **Pilot Testing** is suitable for experimental changes where user feedback is crucial before wider implementation.
- **Big Bang Deployments** might be used for less critical systems where the risks of a full-scale change are manageable, or when an immediate, organization-wide update is required.
- **Blue-Green Deployments** are beneficial for critical systems that require minimal downtime and easy rollback capabilities.

Each deployment strategy has its own strengths and weaknesses, and the choice should align with the organization's goals, risk tolerance, and resource availability.

Rollback planning is an essential component of change management, providing a safety net when changes do not go as planned. It involves creating a detailed plan to revert systems to their previous state if a new change fails or introduces issues. Effective rollback plans minimize downtime, reduce disruptions, and protect the integrity of systems and data.

Developing Effective Rollback Plans

1. **Pre-Change Assessment:**
   - **Baseline Documentation:** Document the current state of the system, including configurations, data, and dependencies. This serves as a reference point for rolling back changes.
   - **Impact Analysis:** Conduct an analysis to understand the potential effects of the change and the consequences of a rollback.
2. **Clear Rollback Procedures:**
   - **Step-by-Step Instructions:** Develop detailed, step-by-step instructions for reversing the change. This should include commands, scripts, and processes needed to restore the system.
   - **Testing:** Test the rollback plan in a controlled environment to ensure it works as expected and to identify any potential issues.
3. **Resource Allocation:**
   - **Roles and Responsibilities:** Assign clear roles and responsibilities for executing the rollback. Ensure that team members are trained and familiar with their tasks.
   - **Tools and Resources:** Ensure that the necessary tools, backups, and resources are readily available to facilitate the rollback process.
4. **Communication Plan:**
   - **Notification Procedures:** Establish communication protocols to inform stakeholders about the rollback process, including triggers for initiating the rollback and status updates during execution.

When to Implement Rollback Plans

- **Failed Implementations:** If a change fails during or after implementation, and it cannot be corrected promptly, initiating the rollback plan is necessary to restore normal operations.
- **Unexpected Issues:** If a change causes unanticipated problems that significantly impact system performance, security, or compliance, rolling back can be the best option.
- **Performance Degradation:** If a change leads to a noticeable decline in system performance or user experience, rolling back might be required to maintain service quality.
- **Security Breaches:** If a change inadvertently exposes security vulnerabilities, rolling back can be critical to protecting sensitive data and systems.

Challenges of Rolling Back Complex System Changes

1. **Interdependencies:** Complex systems often have numerous interdependencies. A change in one component can affect multiple other components, making rollback more complicated.
2. **Data Integrity:** Ensuring data consistency and integrity during a rollback can be challenging, particularly if changes have affected databases or data structures.
3. **Downtime:** Rolling back changes can result in system downtime, which can be costly and disruptive, especially for mission-critical systems.
4. **Configuration Drift:** Differences between the documented baseline and the actual system state can cause issues during rollback.

Strategies for Mitigating Risks

1. **Incremental Changes:**
   - Implement changes incrementally rather than all at once. This makes it easier to identify and address issues, reducing the scope of potential rollbacks.
2. **Snapshots and Backups:**
   - Use system snapshots and backups before implementing changes. This allows for a quick restoration to a known good state if a rollback is necessary.
3. **Parallel Environments:**
   - Use parallel environments (e.g., staging, development) to test changes thoroughly before applying them to production systems. This reduces the risk of encountering issues that necessitate a rollback.
4. **Change Freezes:**
   - Implement change freezes during critical periods (e.g., end-of-quarter financial processing) to minimize the risk of disruptions and the need for rollbacks.
5. **Comprehensive Testing:**

- Conduct extensive testing, including regression and stress testing, to identify potential issues before changes are applied to production.
6. **Documentation and Training:**
    - Ensure that rollback procedures are well-documented and that team members are trained to execute them efficiently. Regular drills can help prepare the team for real-world scenarios.

Example

Consider a large e-commerce platform that plans to update its payment processing system. The rollback plan would include:

- **Pre-Change Baseline:** Documenting the current system configuration and taking a full backup of the database.
- **Step-by-Step Rollback Instructions:** Clear instructions to revert code changes, restore database backups, and reconfigure network settings if necessary.
- **Testing in Staging:** Implementing and testing the change and rollback process in a staging environment to ensure no unforeseen issues arise.
- **Dedicated Rollback Team:** Assigning a team responsible for monitoring the change implementation and executing the rollback if needed.

Rolling back complex system changes requires meticulous planning, thorough testing, and effective communication. By anticipating potential issues and preparing comprehensive rollback procedures, organizations can minimize the risks and disruptions associated with changes, ensuring system stability and reliability.

Establishing review frequencies for ongoing compliance activities is a critical aspect of maintaining a robust compliance program. The goal is to ensure that compliance controls remain effective and that the organization can quickly adapt to any changes in regulatory requirements or the operating environment. Review frequencies should be carefully determined based on a variety of factors to balance thoroughness with practicality.

Factors to Consider When Determining Review Intervals

1. **Regulatory Requirements**: Specific laws and regulations often prescribe minimum review frequencies. For example, some standards may require annual audits, while others might necessitate more frequent checks.
2. **Risk Level**: The inherent risk associated with the activity or control. Higher-risk areas typically require more frequent reviews to ensure ongoing compliance and address potential issues promptly.
3. **Change Frequency**: How often the system or process changes. Systems undergoing frequent updates or modifications should be reviewed more regularly to ensure each change maintains compliance.
4. **Historical Performance**: The past performance of compliance controls. If an area has historically been problematic or has shown frequent non-compliance issues, it may warrant more frequent reviews.
5. **Criticality of the System**: The importance of the system or process to the organization's operations. Critical systems, particularly those handling sensitive data or supporting essential services, usually need more frequent reviews.
6. **Resource Availability**: The availability of resources (personnel, budget, and time) to conduct reviews. While it's important to maintain compliance, the frequency of reviews must be sustainable given the organization's resources.
7. **Industry Best Practices**: Established best practices within the industry can provide guidance on appropriate review frequencies. Benchmarking against similar organizations can offer insights into effective review intervals.

Risk-Based Monitoring

Risk-based monitoring focuses on allocating resources and setting review frequencies based on the risk profile of different compliance areas. This approach ensures that the most critical and high-risk areas receive the most attention, optimizing the use of resources and enhancing overall compliance effectiveness.

Application of Risk-Based Monitoring

1. **Data Privacy Compliance (e.g., GDPR)**:
    - **High-Risk Area**: Data processing activities involving sensitive personal data. These areas should have frequent reviews, such as quarterly assessments, to ensure that data protection measures are robust and up-to-date.

- o **Medium-Risk Area**: General data handling processes might be reviewed semi-annually to confirm that data minimization and other less critical GDPR principles are being followed.
- o **Low-Risk Area**: Routine administrative data that does not involve personal or sensitive information might only require annual reviews.
2. **Financial Compliance (e.g., SOX)**:
   - o **High-Risk Area**: Financial reporting and controls over financial data. Given the critical nature and regulatory scrutiny, these controls might be reviewed monthly or quarterly.
   - o **Medium-Risk Area**: Internal audit processes might be reviewed semi-annually to ensure they effectively support financial reporting accuracy.
   - o **Low-Risk Area**: Non-critical financial systems might undergo annual reviews to ensure they continue to support overall financial compliance.
3. **IT Security Compliance (e.g., ISO/IEC 27001)**:
   - o **High-Risk Area**: Network security and access controls, especially those protecting critical systems and sensitive information, should be reviewed frequently, such as monthly or quarterly.
   - o **Medium-Risk Area**: Regular IT maintenance processes, like patch management, might be reviewed quarterly to confirm compliance with security policies.
   - o **Low-Risk Area**: Peripheral systems that do not directly handle sensitive data might be reviewed annually.
4. **Environmental Compliance (e.g., EPA regulations)**:
   - o **High-Risk Area**: Emission controls and waste management systems that directly impact regulatory compliance and environmental safety should be reviewed frequently, perhaps monthly.
   - o **Medium-Risk Area**: Regular environmental audits and reporting processes might be reviewed semi-annually to ensure ongoing adherence to standards.
   - o **Low-Risk Area**: Routine monitoring of less critical environmental aspects might only need annual reviews.

Establishing review frequencies for ongoing compliance activities requires a careful consideration of various factors, including regulatory requirements, risk levels, and resource availability. By adopting a risk-based monitoring approach, organizations can prioritize high-risk areas for more frequent reviews, ensuring that critical compliance controls remain effective while optimizing resource use. This strategic approach helps maintain a robust compliance posture and enhances the organization's ability to adapt to changing regulatory and operational landscapes.

Continuous system and asset monitoring is crucial for maintaining security, compliance, and operational efficiency. Organizations employ a variety of methodologies and tools to monitor their systems and assets, balancing automated monitoring with manual oversight to ensure comprehensive coverage and quick response to potential issues.

Methodologies and Tools for Continuous Monitoring
1. **Security Information and Event Management (SIEM)**:
   - o SIEM systems collect, analyze, and correlate data from various sources to detect security threats and compliance violations in real-time. Tools like Splunk, IBM QRadar, and ArcSight are popular SIEM solutions.
2. **Network Monitoring**:
   - o Tools like SolarWinds, Nagios, and PRTG Network Monitor continuously observe network traffic, performance, and availability, identifying anomalies and potential security threats.
3. **Endpoint Detection and Response (EDR)**:
   - o EDR tools such as CrowdStrike, Carbon Black, and SentinelOne monitor endpoint devices to detect and respond to security threats at the device level.
4. **Vulnerability Management**:
   - o Tools like Nessus, Qualys, and OpenVAS scan systems and networks for vulnerabilities, providing reports and recommendations for remediation.
5. **Configuration Management**:
   - o Configuration management tools such as Ansible, Puppet, and Chef ensure that systems adhere to predefined configurations, automatically detecting and correcting deviations.
6. **Log Management**:

- Centralized log management solutions like LogRhythm and Graylog collect and analyze log data from various systems, helping detect patterns indicative of security issues or compliance breaches.

7. **Cloud Monitoring:**
   - For cloud environments, tools like AWS CloudWatch, Microsoft Azure Monitor, and Google Cloud Operations Suite provide visibility into cloud infrastructure, services, and applications.

Balancing Automated Monitoring with Manual Oversight

1. **Automation for Efficiency:**
   - Automated tools handle the bulk of data collection and initial analysis, identifying patterns and anomalies that require further investigation. Automation increases efficiency, reduces human error, and allows for real-time monitoring.

2. **Manual Oversight for Expertise:**
   - Manual oversight is essential for interpreting complex data, making judgment calls, and handling nuanced situations that automated tools might not fully understand. Security analysts and IT professionals review automated alerts, investigate suspicious activities, and determine appropriate responses.

3. **Regular Reviews:**
   - Conduct regular reviews of automated monitoring results to ensure the accuracy and relevance of alerts. Periodic audits and assessments help validate the effectiveness of automated tools and identify areas for improvement.

Challenges of Monitoring in Complex, Distributed Environments

1. **Data Overload:**
   - Large volumes of data from numerous sources can overwhelm monitoring systems, making it difficult to identify relevant information and detect genuine threats.

2. **Integration Issues:**
   - Integrating disparate monitoring tools and systems can be challenging, particularly in hybrid and multi-cloud environments where different platforms may have unique monitoring requirements.

3. **Latency and Real-Time Processing:**
   - Ensuring low latency and real-time processing of monitoring data is critical, particularly for detecting and responding to security incidents promptly.

4. **Resource Constraints:**
   - Monitoring complex environments requires significant computational and human resources, which can strain an organization's capabilities.

Strategies for Effective Real-Time Compliance Tracking

1. **Unified Monitoring Platforms:**
   - Utilize unified monitoring platforms that integrate data from various sources, providing a consolidated view of system health and security. Platforms like Splunk and ELK (Elasticsearch, Logstash, Kibana) stack can centralize monitoring efforts.

2. **Contextual Analysis:**
   - Implement contextual analysis to differentiate between false positives and genuine threats. Machine learning and AI can enhance this by learning from historical data to improve accuracy over time.

3. **Scalable Infrastructure:**
   - Ensure monitoring infrastructure is scalable to handle the increased data and processing demands of a growing or complex environment. Cloud-based monitoring solutions can offer scalability and flexibility.

4. **Granular Access Controls:**
   - Implement granular access controls to ensure only authorized personnel can access sensitive monitoring data and tools, reducing the risk of insider threats and data breaches.

5. **Incident Response Plans:**
   - Develop and regularly update incident response plans to ensure quick and effective action when monitoring systems detect potential issues. Conduct regular drills to keep teams prepared.

6. **Regular Training:**
   - Continuously train staff on the latest monitoring tools, threat detection techniques, and compliance requirements to maintain a high level of readiness and expertise.
7. **Automated Remediation:**
   - Integrate automated remediation processes where feasible. For example, tools like Ansible and Puppet can automatically correct configuration deviations, while EDR tools can isolate infected endpoints.

Example

In a large financial institution, continuous monitoring involves using a SIEM tool like Splunk to collect and analyze logs from various sources, including firewalls, servers, and applications. Network monitoring tools like SolarWinds keep track of network traffic and performance. Automated vulnerability scanners like Nessus regularly check for security weaknesses, while configuration management tools like Ansible ensure systems remain compliant with security policies.

The institution balances this with manual oversight by having a dedicated security operations center (SOC) where analysts review SIEM alerts, investigate anomalies, and respond to incidents. Regular training and drills keep the team prepared for real-world scenarios. By integrating automated tools with expert oversight, the institution can effectively manage compliance and security across its complex, distributed environment.

Incident response planning and compliance maintenance are closely intertwined, as effective incident response procedures are essential for meeting regulatory requirements and protecting sensitive information. Organizations must ensure that their incident response plans align with compliance mandates to minimize the impact of security incidents and demonstrate due diligence in safeguarding data.

Aligning Incident Response Procedures with Compliance Requirements

1. **Understanding Regulatory Requirements**: Organizations must thoroughly understand the specific incident response requirements outlined by relevant regulations and standards, such as GDPR, HIPAA, PCI DSS, and ISO/IEC 27001. These requirements often dictate the steps for incident detection, response, reporting, and documentation.
2. **Policy Development**: Develop incident response policies that incorporate regulatory requirements. These policies should outline roles, responsibilities, and procedures for identifying, containing, eradicating, and recovering from incidents.
3. **Integration with Risk Management**: Integrate incident response planning with the organization's overall risk management framework. This ensures that incident response is aligned with identified risks and that appropriate controls are in place to mitigate those risks.
4. **Regular Training and Awareness**: Ensure that all employees are trained on incident response procedures and understand their roles during an incident. Regular training sessions help maintain readiness and ensure that the response is swift and effective.
5. **Continuous Improvement**: Regularly review and update incident response plans to reflect changes in regulatory requirements, emerging threats, and lessons learned from past incidents. This ongoing process ensures that the organization remains compliant and prepared for new challenges.

Tabletop Exercises and Incident Response Readiness

Tabletop exercises are simulated incident response activities that involve key stakeholders discussing their roles and actions during a hypothetical incident. These exercises are crucial for maintaining incident response readiness and ensuring compliance with regulatory requirements.

Role of Tabletop Exercises

1. **Testing Plans and Procedures**: Tabletop exercises allow organizations to test their incident response plans and procedures in a controlled environment. This helps identify gaps, weaknesses, and areas for improvement.
2. **Enhancing Coordination and Communication**: These exercises involve multiple stakeholders, including IT, security, legal, compliance, and business units. By simulating an incident, organizations can improve coordination and communication among these groups, ensuring a more cohesive response during a real incident.

3. **Validating Roles and Responsibilities**: Tabletop exercises help clarify the roles and responsibilities of each team member during an incident. This ensures that everyone knows what is expected of them and can act promptly and effectively.
4. **Improving Decision-Making**: By simulating the decision-making process during an incident, tabletop exercises help participants practice making critical decisions under pressure. This enhances their ability to make informed and timely decisions during an actual incident.
5. **Demonstrating Compliance**: Conducting regular tabletop exercises can demonstrate to regulators and auditors that the organization is actively maintaining incident response readiness. This proactive approach can help meet compliance requirements and avoid penalties.

Implementing Tabletop Exercises
1. **Scenario Development**: Develop realistic and relevant scenarios that reflect potential incidents the organization might face. Scenarios should cover a range of incident types, such as data breaches, ransomware attacks, and insider threats.
2. **Stakeholder Involvement**: Involve all relevant stakeholders in the exercise, including IT, security, compliance, legal, and business units. This ensures a comprehensive approach and enhances collaboration.
3. **Facilitation and Moderation**: Use experienced facilitators to guide the exercise and ensure that discussions remain focused and productive. Facilitators can help keep the scenario realistic and ensure that all participants are engaged.
4. **Evaluation and Feedback**: After the exercise, conduct a thorough evaluation to identify strengths and areas for improvement. Gather feedback from participants and use this information to refine incident response plans and procedures.
5. **Documentation and Reporting**: Document the exercise, including the scenario, participant actions, and outcomes. This documentation can be used to demonstrate compliance and support continuous improvement efforts.

Incident response planning and compliance maintenance are fundamentally connected, as robust incident response procedures are essential for meeting regulatory requirements and protecting sensitive information. By aligning incident response plans with compliance mandates and conducting regular tabletop exercises, organizations can enhance their readiness to handle incidents, ensure regulatory compliance, and continuously improve their security posture.

Developing and maintaining effective contingency plans is crucial for organizations to ensure business continuity and resilience in the face of unexpected disruptions. These plans outline procedures and actions to be taken in the event of various emergencies, such as natural disasters, cyber-attacks, or system failures.

Key Elements of a Comprehensive Contingency Plan
1. **Risk Assessment and Business Impact Analysis (BIA):**
    - **Risk Assessment:** Identify potential threats and vulnerabilities that could impact the organization. Evaluate the likelihood and potential impact of these risks.
    - **Business Impact Analysis:** Determine the criticality of various business functions and processes. Assess the potential impact of disruptions on operations, finances, and reputation.
2. **Clear Objectives and Scope:**
    - Define the objectives of the contingency plan, such as minimizing downtime and ensuring the continuity of critical operations.
    - Clearly outline the scope, specifying which systems, processes, and locations are covered by the plan.
3. **Roles and Responsibilities:**
    - Assign roles and responsibilities to specific individuals or teams for executing the contingency plan. Ensure that everyone understands their duties and has the necessary training.
    - Designate a crisis management team to coordinate response efforts.
4. **Communication Plan:**
    - Develop a communication strategy to keep stakeholders informed during an incident. Include contact lists, communication channels, and message templates.

- Establish protocols for internal and external communication to ensure accurate and timely information dissemination.
5. **Detailed Response Procedures:**
   - Outline step-by-step procedures for responding to various types of incidents. Include instructions for initial response, containment, eradication, recovery, and restoration of normal operations.
   - Provide checklists and flowcharts to guide decision-making during a crisis.
6. **Resource Allocation:**
   - Identify and allocate the resources needed to implement the contingency plan, such as personnel, equipment, and financial resources.
   - Ensure that backup systems, data, and alternative work locations are available.
7. **Testing and Training:**
   - Regularly test the contingency plan through drills, simulations, and tabletop exercises to identify gaps and areas for improvement.
   - Provide ongoing training to employees on their roles in the contingency plan and ensure they are familiar with the procedures.
8. **Plan Review and Maintenance:**
   - Establish a schedule for regularly reviewing and updating the contingency plan to reflect changes in the organization, technology, and threat landscape.
   - Document lessons learned from tests and real incidents to continuously improve the plan.

Challenges of Keeping Contingency Plans Up-to-Date
1. **Rapid Technological Changes:**
   - Technology evolves quickly, introducing new systems, applications, and vulnerabilities. Keeping the contingency plan current with these changes can be challenging.
   - Solution: Implement a continuous monitoring process to track technological changes and assess their impact on the contingency plan. Regularly update the plan to incorporate new technologies and address emerging threats.
2. **Organizational Changes:**
   - Mergers, acquisitions, restructuring, and personnel changes can impact the effectiveness of a contingency plan.
   - Solution: Ensure that the plan includes provisions for integrating changes in organizational structure and personnel. Assign responsibility for updating the plan to a dedicated team or individual.
3. **Regulatory and Compliance Requirements:**
   - Regulatory requirements can change, necessitating updates to contingency plans to maintain compliance.
   - Solution: Stay informed about relevant regulatory changes and incorporate them into the plan promptly. Engage with legal and compliance teams to ensure adherence to current standards.
4. **Resource Constraints:**
   - Limited resources can hinder the ability to develop, test, and maintain comprehensive contingency plans.
   - Solution: Prioritize critical functions and allocate resources accordingly. Leverage technology and automation to streamline plan maintenance and testing.
5. **Coordination and Communication:**
   - Ensuring effective coordination and communication across departments and with external stakeholders can be complex.
   - Solution: Establish clear communication protocols and regularly train employees on their roles in the contingency plan. Use centralized communication platforms to facilitate coordination.

Example
Consider a healthcare organization that relies on electronic health records (EHR) systems. A comprehensive contingency plan for such an organization would include:
- **Risk Assessment and BIA:** Identifying risks such as cyber-attacks, natural disasters, and system failures. Assessing the impact of EHR system downtime on patient care and compliance with regulations like HIPAA.

- **Roles and Responsibilities:** Designating IT staff, healthcare providers, and administrative personnel with specific roles in executing the plan. Forming a crisis management team.
- **Communication Plan:** Creating a communication strategy to notify staff, patients, and regulatory bodies during an incident. Including contact lists and message templates.
- **Response Procedures:** Outlining steps to take in the event of an EHR system outage, including switching to manual record-keeping, restoring data from backups, and notifying affected parties.
- **Resource Allocation:** Ensuring availability of backup servers, data storage solutions, and alternative workspaces.
- **Testing and Training:** Conducting regular drills and simulations to test the plan. Providing training sessions for all staff members on their roles.
- **Plan Review and Maintenance:** Setting a schedule for quarterly reviews and updates of the plan. Incorporating lessons learned from past incidents and tests.

Maintaining effective contingency plans involves staying vigilant and proactive in the face of changing technologies and organizational dynamics. By implementing robust processes and leveraging appropriate tools, organizations can ensure their contingency plans remain relevant and effective.

Timely security updates and risk remediation are critical for maintaining compliance and safeguarding an organization's systems and data. These practices help prevent security breaches, protect sensitive information, and ensure adherence to regulatory requirements. Failure to apply timely updates and remediate risks can lead to vulnerabilities being exploited, resulting in data breaches, financial losses, and non-compliance penalties.

Importance of Timely Security Updates and Risk Remediation
1. **Protecting Against Exploits**: Applying security updates and patches promptly helps protect systems from known vulnerabilities that attackers could exploit. This reduces the risk of breaches and data loss.
2. **Compliance Requirements**: Many regulations and standards, such as PCI DSS, HIPAA, and GDPR, mandate regular updates and timely remediation of vulnerabilities to ensure that systems remain secure.
3. **Maintaining System Integrity**: Regular updates and patches help maintain the integrity and reliability of systems by addressing bugs, improving performance, and enhancing security features.
4. **Risk Reduction**: Timely remediation of identified risks helps to mitigate potential threats and reduces the overall risk profile of the organization. This proactive approach ensures a robust security posture.

Prioritizing and Implementing Security Patches and Updates
1. **Risk Assessment**: Conduct a thorough risk assessment to evaluate the severity and potential impact of identified vulnerabilities. This helps in prioritizing patches and updates based on the level of risk they pose to the organization.
2. **Classification and Categorization**: Classify vulnerabilities based on their criticality. Critical vulnerabilities that could lead to significant security breaches should be addressed immediately, while lower-risk vulnerabilities can be scheduled for regular updates.
3. **Patch Management Policies**: Develop and enforce patch management policies that outline the process for identifying, prioritizing, testing, and deploying patches. These policies should include timelines for applying different types of patches based on their severity.
4. **Testing and Validation**: Before deploying patches, test them in a controlled environment to ensure they do not disrupt system functionality or cause compatibility issues. Validation helps prevent new problems from being introduced.
5. **Automated Tools**: Use automated tools and systems for vulnerability scanning and patch management. These tools can help identify vulnerabilities, prioritize patches, and streamline the deployment process.
6. **Change Management**: Integrate patch management with the organization's change management processes to ensure that updates are implemented in a controlled and documented manner. This includes obtaining necessary approvals and notifying stakeholders of planned changes.
7. **Regular Monitoring and Reporting**: Continuously monitor systems for new vulnerabilities and track the status of applied patches. Generate regular reports to keep stakeholders informed of the patch management process and compliance status.

Vulnerability Management and Its Role in Ongoing Compliance Efforts

Vulnerability management is the ongoing process of identifying, evaluating, treating, and reporting on security vulnerabilities in systems and applications. It is a critical component of maintaining compliance and ensuring the security of an organization's IT infrastructure.

1. **Identification**: Regularly scan systems and applications to identify known vulnerabilities using automated vulnerability assessment tools. Keeping up-to-date with vulnerability databases and threat intelligence feeds is essential.
2. **Evaluation**: Assess the identified vulnerabilities to determine their severity and potential impact on the organization. This involves understanding the context of each vulnerability and how it might be exploited.
3. **Treatment**: Develop and implement a remediation plan for addressing identified vulnerabilities. This can include applying patches, reconfiguring systems, implementing additional security controls, or other mitigating actions.
4. **Reporting and Documentation**: Document the entire vulnerability management process, including identified vulnerabilities, risk assessments, remediation actions, and final outcomes. This documentation is crucial for demonstrating compliance during audits.
5. **Continuous Improvement**: Use the insights gained from vulnerability management activities to improve security policies, procedures, and controls continuously. This proactive approach helps to anticipate and mitigate future risks.

Practical Examples

- **Critical System Patches**: For a financial institution, a critical vulnerability in the core banking system would be prioritized for immediate patching. The risk assessment would highlight the potential for significant financial and reputational damage, leading to expedited testing and deployment of the patch.
- **Regular Software Updates**: A healthcare organization may follow a quarterly update schedule for its electronic health record (EHR) system, incorporating patches and updates that address less critical vulnerabilities identified in the interim scans.
- **Automated Patch Management**: An e-commerce company might use automated patch management tools to scan for and apply updates across its web servers and databases, ensuring minimal downtime and reducing the risk of exploitation.

Timely security updates and risk remediation are essential for maintaining compliance and ensuring the security and integrity of organizational systems. By prioritizing and systematically implementing patches and updates, organizations can effectively manage vulnerabilities and mitigate risks. A robust vulnerability management process supports ongoing compliance efforts, enhances security posture, and helps protect against emerging threats.

The process of evidence collection and documentation updates is critical for compliance maintenance, ensuring that organizations can demonstrate adherence to regulatory requirements and internal policies. Effective evidence collection and documentation provide a clear, verifiable trail of actions and decisions, facilitating audits and minimizing risks associated with non-compliance.

Types of Evidence to Collect

1. **System Logs:**
    - **Security Logs:** Include records of security events such as access attempts, login failures, and changes to system configurations.
    - **Audit Logs:** Capture detailed records of user activities, including file access, modifications, and administrative actions.
    - **Network Logs:** Document network traffic, including firewall logs, intrusion detection system (IDS) alerts, and VPN connections.
2. **Configuration Files:**
    - **System Configurations:** Store snapshots of system configurations, including software versions, settings, and applied patches.
    - **Policy Documents:** Maintain current versions of security policies, access control policies, and operational procedures.
3. **Access Records:**
    - **User Access Reports:** Document user access levels, permissions, and any changes to access rights.

- **Authentication Records:** Keep records of user authentication events, including successful and failed login attempts.
4. **Incident Reports:**
    - **Security Incidents:** Detailed documentation of security incidents, including incident response actions and outcomes.
    - **Operational Incidents:** Records of operational disruptions, root cause analyses, and remediation actions.
5. **Compliance Reports:**
    - **Audit Reports:** Results of internal and external audits, including findings and corrective action plans.
    - **Compliance Checklists:** Regularly updated checklists demonstrating adherence to specific regulatory requirements.
6. **Training Records:**
    - **Employee Training:** Documentation of training sessions attended by employees, including dates, content, and attendance.

Storage of Evidence

1. **Centralized Storage:**
    - Utilize centralized storage solutions such as a secure document management system (DMS) or a dedicated compliance management platform to store evidence. This ensures that all evidence is easily accessible, organized, and protected.
2. **Access Controls:**
    - Implement strict access controls to ensure that only authorized personnel can view, modify, or delete evidence. Use role-based access controls (RBAC) to enforce permissions.
3. **Redundancy and Backup:**
    - Ensure that evidence is regularly backed up and stored redundantly to prevent data loss. Utilize cloud storage solutions with versioning capabilities to maintain historical records.
4. **Encryption:**
    - Encrypt stored evidence to protect it from unauthorized access and ensure data integrity.

Challenges of Maintaining an Audit Trail in Dynamic IT Environments

1. **Volume and Complexity:**
    - The sheer volume and complexity of data generated in dynamic IT environments can make it challenging to maintain a comprehensive audit trail.
2. **Frequent Changes:**
    - Frequent changes in configurations, software updates, and system upgrades can complicate the tracking and documentation of evidence.
3. **Integration Issues:**
    - Integrating evidence collection across diverse systems and platforms can be difficult, leading to gaps in the audit trail.

Strategies for Ensuring Evidence Integrity

1. **Automated Collection:**
    - Implement automated tools for evidence collection and documentation. SIEM systems, log management tools, and configuration management databases (CMDB) can automate the capture and organization of relevant data.
2. **Regular Audits:**
    - Conduct regular internal audits to verify the completeness and accuracy of the audit trail. Use these audits to identify and address gaps or discrepancies.
3. **Immutable Storage:**
    - Store critical evidence in immutable storage solutions, such as write-once-read-many (WORM) storage, to prevent tampering and ensure data integrity.
4. **Timestamping and Hashing:**

- Use timestamping and hashing techniques to validate the integrity of evidence. Timestamping ensures that records are captured at the correct time, while hashing provides a means to detect any unauthorized modifications.
5. **Continuous Monitoring:**
    - Implement continuous monitoring solutions to detect and respond to anomalies in real-time. This helps ensure that evidence is collected consistently and accurately.

Example
In a healthcare organization, maintaining compliance with HIPAA requires meticulous evidence collection and documentation. The organization should collect and store:
- **System Logs:** Detailed logs of access to electronic health records (EHRs), including timestamps and user IDs.
- **Configuration Files:** Snapshots of system configurations, especially those related to data encryption and access controls.
- **Access Records:** Documentation of user access rights and authentication events, ensuring that only authorized personnel access sensitive patient data.
- **Incident Reports:** Comprehensive reports of any data breaches or security incidents, including steps taken to mitigate and prevent future occurrences.
- **Compliance Reports:** Regularly updated compliance checklists and audit reports demonstrating adherence to HIPAA requirements.

To address challenges in this dynamic environment, the healthcare organization could use automated SIEM tools to collect and analyze security logs, employ centralized and encrypted storage for all evidence, and implement regular audits to ensure the integrity and completeness of their audit trail. This ensures they maintain a robust compliance posture while efficiently managing the complexities of their IT environment.

Awareness and training programs are essential for maintaining compliance as they ensure that employees understand security policies, recognize potential threats, and know how to respond appropriately. These programs help foster a culture of security within the organization and minimize the risk of human error, which is often a significant factor in security incidents.

Developing Effective Security Awareness Training
1. **Identify Objectives**: Clearly define the goals of the security awareness training program. Objectives may include increasing employee understanding of security policies, compliance requirements, recognizing phishing attempts, and reporting suspicious activities.
2. **Understand the Audience**: Tailor the content to the knowledge level and roles of the participants. Employees across different departments and positions will have varying levels of technical understanding and different responsibilities.
3. **Engage Stakeholders**: Involve key stakeholders from different departments (e.g., IT, HR, legal, compliance) in the development of the training program to ensure comprehensive coverage and relevance.
4. **Use Varied Training Methods**: Employ a mix of training methods such as online modules, in-person workshops, interactive simulations, videos, and quizzes to keep the training engaging and effective.
5. **Incorporate Real-World Examples**: Use case studies and real-world examples to illustrate the importance of security practices and the consequences of non-compliance. This helps make the training relatable and memorable.
6. **Regular Updates and Refreshers**: Ensure the training program is continuously updated to reflect new threats, technological advancements, and changes in compliance requirements. Regular refresher courses help reinforce key concepts.
7. **Measure Effectiveness**: Use assessments and feedback to measure the effectiveness of the training. This can include pre- and post-training quizzes, employee surveys, and monitoring compliance incident reports to identify areas needing improvement.

Role-Based Training
Role-based training is a targeted approach to security awareness that tailors content to the specific responsibilities and risks associated with different roles within the organization. This ensures that employees receive relevant information that is directly applicable to their job functions.

Examples of Role-Based Training
1. **Executive Management**:
    - **Focus Areas**: Strategic risk management, regulatory compliance, and data protection laws.
    - **Content**: Briefings on recent security trends, legal obligations, and the impact of security breaches on business operations.
    - **Example**: A workshop on the implications of GDPR for business strategy, with case studies of high-profile data breaches.
2. **IT and Security Staff**:
    - **Focus Areas**: Technical security controls, incident response, and threat detection.
    - **Content**: Detailed technical training on advanced threat detection, system hardening, and secure coding practices.
    - **Example**: Hands-on labs for practicing incident response techniques and configuring security tools.
3. **Human Resources**:
    - **Focus Areas**: Data privacy, secure handling of employee information, and recognizing social engineering tactics.
    - **Content**: Training on secure onboarding and offboarding processes, and recognizing and reporting phishing attempts.
    - **Example**: Interactive sessions on identifying social engineering tactics and safeguarding personal data.
4. **Finance and Accounting**:
    - **Focus Areas**: Fraud prevention, secure financial transactions, and compliance with financial regulations.
    - **Content**: Guidelines for detecting fraudulent activities, securing payment systems, and ensuring compliance with SOX.
    - **Example**: Case studies on financial fraud and exercises on implementing secure financial practices.
5. **General Staff**:
    - **Focus Areas**: Basic cybersecurity hygiene, recognizing phishing emails, and proper data handling.
    - **Content**: Training on creating strong passwords, avoiding suspicious links, and the importance of regular software updates.
    - **Example**: E-learning modules on recognizing phishing attempts and reporting suspicious activities.

Benefits of Role-Based Training
- **Relevance**: Provides employees with information that is directly applicable to their roles, increasing engagement and retention of knowledge.
- **Efficiency**: Focuses training efforts where they are most needed, optimizing resource use and minimizing time away from primary job functions.
- **Risk Mitigation**: Addresses specific risks associated with different roles, enhancing overall security posture and reducing the likelihood of role-specific vulnerabilities being exploited.
- **Compliance**: Ensures that all employees are aware of and adhere to compliance requirements relevant to their roles, supporting the organization's overall compliance efforts.

Implementing Role-Based Training
1. **Role Analysis**: Conduct a thorough analysis of the roles within the organization to identify the specific security training needs for each.
2. **Custom Content Development**: Develop customized training materials tailored to the identified needs of each role.
3. **Scheduling and Delivery**: Schedule and deliver training sessions in a manner that accommodates the availability and workload of different employee groups.
4. **Assessment and Feedback**: Continuously assess the effectiveness of the training through quizzes, surveys, and monitoring compliance incidents. Use feedback to refine and improve the training program.

By incorporating comprehensive and role-based training programs, organizations can significantly enhance their security posture and ensure ongoing compliance with regulatory requirements. These efforts help build a culture of security awareness, reducing the risk of human error and improving overall organizational resilience against cyber threats.

Engaging in compliance-based audits is a critical process for organizations to ensure adherence to regulatory requirements, industry standards, and internal policies. These audits help identify areas of non-compliance, mitigate risks, and improve overall security and operational practices.

Process of Engaging in Compliance-Based Audits
Preparation:

Understanding Requirements: Review relevant regulations, standards, and guidelines to understand the scope and criteria of the audit.
Audit Team Formation: Assemble a team with the necessary expertise in compliance, legal, IT, and operations to oversee the audit process.
Documentation Review: Gather and organize all relevant documentation, such as policies, procedures, logs, configurations, and previous audit reports.
Self-Assessment: Conduct an internal self-assessment to identify and address potential issues before the external audit begins.
Engagement:

Auditor Selection: Choose a reputable external auditor with expertise in the relevant regulatory or industry standards.
Audit Planning: Collaborate with the auditor to define the audit scope, objectives, timelines, and key areas of focus.
Kickoff Meeting: Hold a kickoff meeting to align on expectations, provide background information, and establish communication channels.
Execution:

Evidence Collection: Provide auditors with access to necessary documents, systems, and personnel. Ensure that evidence is well-organized and readily available.
Interviews and Observations: Facilitate interviews with key personnel and allow auditors to observe operations to verify compliance practices.
Continuous Communication: Maintain open lines of communication with auditors to address questions, provide clarifications, and resolve any issues that arise during the audit.
Audit Report:

Draft Report Review: Review the draft audit report for accuracy and completeness. Provide feedback or corrections if necessary.
Final Report: Receive the final audit report, which includes findings, recommendations, and any identified non-compliance issues.
Response and Remediation:

Action Plan Development: Develop a detailed action plan to address audit findings and implement recommended improvements.
Follow-Up: Schedule follow-up audits or reviews to ensure that corrective actions have been effectively implemented.
Differences Between Internal and External Audits
Purpose:

Internal Audits: Conducted by the organization's own staff to assess compliance with internal policies, procedures, and controls. They aim to identify internal weaknesses and prepare for external audits.
External Audits: Performed by independent third-party auditors to verify compliance with external regulations, standards, and contractual obligations. They provide an objective assessment of the organization's compliance status.
Frequency:

Internal Audits: Typically conducted more frequently, often on a quarterly or semi-annual basis, to ensure continuous compliance.
External Audits: Usually conducted annually or as required by regulatory bodies, customers, or certification authorities.
Scope:

Internal Audits: Focus on specific areas of interest or concern within the organization, allowing for in-depth examination of particular processes or controls.
External Audits: Broader in scope, covering all relevant aspects of regulatory or standards compliance.
Strategies for Maximizing the Value of Audit Findings
Proactive Preparation:

Conduct regular internal audits and self-assessments to identify and address potential issues before external audits. This helps ensure that systems and processes are always audit-ready.
Collaboration and Communication:

Foster a collaborative relationship with auditors. Open and transparent communication can lead to more accurate findings and useful recommendations.
Comprehensive Action Plans:

Develop detailed action plans to address audit findings. Include specific tasks, responsible parties, timelines, and measurable outcomes to ensure effective remediation.
Continuous Improvement:

Treat audit findings as opportunities for continuous improvement rather than just compliance checkmarks. Implement systemic changes to enhance overall security, efficiency, and compliance.
Training and Awareness:

Regularly train employees on compliance requirements and best practices. Awareness and understanding across the organization can prevent compliance issues and streamline audit processes.
Leverage Technology:

Utilize compliance management software and automated tools to track compliance status, manage documentation, and monitor remediation efforts. This can increase efficiency and accuracy.
Example
Consider a financial institution preparing for an external audit to comply with the Sarbanes-Oxley Act (SOX). The institution would start by reviewing SOX requirements and conducting an internal audit to identify any gaps. The audit team would gather financial records, access logs, and internal control documentation.

During the audit engagement, the institution would select an external auditor and collaborate to define the audit scope, focusing on financial reporting and internal controls. The audit would involve providing access to systems, conducting interviews with finance and IT staff, and facilitating observations of control processes.

Upon receiving the audit report, the institution would review findings, develop an action plan to address any non-compliance issues, and schedule follow-up audits to verify remediation efforts. By treating audit findings as opportunities for improvement, the institution not only ensures compliance but also strengthens its financial integrity and operational resilience.

Effective engagement in compliance-based audits involves thorough preparation, clear communication, and a commitment to continuous improvement. By leveraging both internal and external audits, organizations can maintain a robust compliance posture and enhance overall performance.

System decommissioning is a critical process that involves retiring systems or components while ensuring compliance with regulatory and organizational policies. Properly managing this process is essential to prevent data breaches, ensure data integrity, and maintain compliance. Here are the key considerations and challenges, along with strategies for managing associated risks.

Key Considerations for System Decommissioning
1. **Data Retention and Disposal**:
    - **Compliance with Regulations**: Ensure that data retention and disposal practices comply with relevant regulations, such as GDPR, HIPAA, and SOX, which may mandate specific retention periods and secure disposal methods.
    - **Data Inventory**: Maintain an inventory of all data stored on the system to identify sensitive or regulated data that requires special handling.
    - **Secure Data Deletion**: Implement secure data deletion methods, such as data wiping or physical destruction of storage media, to prevent unauthorized access to residual data.
2. **Documentation and Audit Trails**:
    - **Decommissioning Plan**: Develop a comprehensive decommissioning plan that outlines the steps, responsible parties, and timelines for the process.
    - **Audit Trails**: Maintain detailed audit trails documenting the decommissioning process, including data transfer, deletion, and system shutdown activities. This documentation is crucial for demonstrating compliance during audits.
3. **Transfer of Data and Services**:
    - **Data Migration**: Ensure secure and compliant migration of data to new systems, maintaining data integrity and confidentiality throughout the transition.
    - **Service Continuity**: Plan for the continuity of services and functions performed by the retiring system, ensuring that there is no disruption to business operations.
4. **Access Control and Security**:
    - **Access Termination**: Revoke all access permissions to the retiring system to prevent unauthorized access.
    - **Security Controls**: Assess and maintain security controls during the decommissioning process to protect against vulnerabilities that could be exploited during the transition.
5. **Regulatory Reporting**:
    - **Notification Requirements**: Some regulations may require notification of system decommissioning, particularly if the system handled sensitive or regulated data.
    - **Compliance Reporting**: Provide necessary reports to regulatory bodies, ensuring that all compliance obligations are met.

Challenges of Maintaining Compliance During System Transitions
1. **Data Integrity and Security**: Ensuring the integrity and security of data during migration can be challenging, particularly if the data involves sensitive or regulated information.
2. **Complexity of Legacy Systems**: Legacy systems may have outdated technologies and insufficient documentation, complicating the decommissioning process.
3. **Resource Allocation**: Decommissioning projects require significant resources, including personnel, time, and budget, which can strain organizational capacity.
4. **Coordination Across Departments**: Effective decommissioning often requires coordination across multiple departments, including IT, legal, compliance, and operations, which can be difficult to manage.

Strategies for Managing Associated Risks
1. **Comprehensive Decommissioning Plan**:
    - **Project Planning**: Develop a detailed project plan that includes risk assessments, timelines, responsibilities, and contingencies for potential issues.
    - **Stakeholder Involvement**: Engage all relevant stakeholders early in the planning process to ensure comprehensive coverage of all compliance and operational considerations.
2. **Data Protection and Migration**:
    - **Encryption and Security Measures**: Use encryption and other security measures to protect data during transfer. Ensure that new systems have robust security controls in place.

- o **Validation and Verification**: Validate and verify the integrity of data before and after migration to ensure no data loss or corruption occurs.
3. **Training and Awareness:**
    - o **Staff Training**: Provide training for staff involved in the decommissioning process to ensure they understand compliance requirements and best practices.
    - o **Communication**: Maintain open communication channels to keep all stakeholders informed of progress and any issues that arise.
4. **Audit and Documentation**:
    - o **Detailed Documentation**: Keep thorough records of all actions taken during the decommissioning process, including data deletion methods, access revocations, and system shutdown procedures.
    - o **Audit Readiness**: Prepare for potential audits by ensuring that all documentation is organized and readily accessible.
5. **Third-Party Assistance:**
    - o **Consulting Services**: Consider engaging third-party experts or consultants who specialize in system decommissioning and compliance to provide guidance and support.
    - o **Vendor Coordination**: If third-party vendors are involved in the system or data management, coordinate closely with them to ensure compliance throughout the decommissioning process.

By addressing these key considerations and challenges, and implementing effective strategies, organizations can ensure a smooth and compliant system decommissioning process. This not only protects sensitive data but also helps maintain regulatory compliance and minimizes operational disruptions.

Requirements review is a critical step in the system decommissioning process, ensuring that all relevant compliance obligations are met and that no residual risks are left unmanaged. This process involves carefully evaluating regulatory, contractual, and internal policy requirements to ensure that the decommissioning is conducted in a manner that maintains security, data integrity, and legal compliance.

Importance of Requirements Review in System Decommissioning
1. **Compliance Assurance:**
    - o Reviewing requirements ensures that the decommissioning process adheres to all applicable laws, regulations, and standards. This is particularly important in regulated industries such as healthcare, finance, and telecommunications.
2. **Data Security and Integrity:**
    - o Ensuring that all data is securely handled, transferred, archived, or destroyed is crucial to prevent unauthorized access and data breaches. Requirements review helps identify specific actions needed to protect sensitive information.
3. **Operational Continuity:**
    - o By thoroughly reviewing requirements, organizations can plan and execute decommissioning without disrupting other systems and operations that might depend on the retiring system.
4. **Risk Mitigation:**
    - o Identifying and addressing potential risks associated with the decommissioning process helps prevent issues such as data loss, legal penalties, and reputational damage.

Ensuring Compliance During Decommissioning
1. **Comprehensive Requirements Gathering:**
    - o Compile all relevant compliance requirements from regulatory bodies, industry standards, contractual obligations, and internal policies. This should involve stakeholders from legal, compliance, IT, and business units.
2. **Decommissioning Plan Development:**
    - o Develop a detailed decommissioning plan that incorporates compliance requirements. This plan should outline the steps for data handling, system disconnection, hardware disposal, and verification of task completion.
3. **Data Handling Procedures:**
    - o Establish clear procedures for data migration, archiving, and destruction. Ensure that these procedures comply with data protection regulations such as GDPR, HIPAA, and CCPA.

4. **Stakeholder Involvement:**
   - Engage all relevant stakeholders in the decommissioning process. Regular communication ensures that everyone understands their roles and responsibilities and that compliance requirements are consistently met.
5. **Audit and Documentation:**
   - Maintain thorough documentation of the decommissioning process, including evidence of compliance actions taken. Conduct internal audits to verify that all steps were completed according to plan and compliance requirements.

Potential Consequences of Overlooking Compliance Obligations
1. **Data Breaches and Security Incidents:**
   - Failure to properly secure or destroy data can lead to data breaches, exposing sensitive information and leading to financial loss, legal penalties, and reputational damage.
2. **Regulatory Penalties:**
   - Non-compliance with regulations can result in significant fines and penalties from regulatory bodies. For instance, violations of GDPR can lead to fines of up to €20 million or 4% of annual global turnover, whichever is higher.
3. **Legal Liabilities:**
   - Overlooking contractual obligations or internal policies can expose the organization to legal liabilities, including lawsuits from affected parties or contractual partners.
4. **Operational Disruptions:**
   - Improper decommissioning can cause disruptions to other systems or processes that depend on the retiring system, leading to operational inefficiencies and potential downtime.
5. **Reputational Damage:**
   - Publicly disclosed compliance failures or data breaches can severely damage an organization's reputation, leading to loss of customer trust and negative impacts on business relationships.

Strategies for Effective Compliance in Decommissioning
1. **Regular Training and Awareness:**
   - Ensure that all personnel involved in the decommissioning process are aware of compliance requirements and best practices. Regular training sessions can help maintain a high level of awareness and preparedness.
2. **Automated Compliance Tools:**
   - Utilize automated tools and solutions to track and manage compliance requirements. These tools can help ensure that all necessary steps are taken and documented correctly.
3. **Continuous Monitoring and Review:**
   - Implement continuous monitoring and review mechanisms to track the progress of the decommissioning process. This helps identify and address any issues in real-time.
4. **Third-Party Verification:**
   - Consider engaging third-party auditors or consultants to review the decommissioning plan and process. External verification can provide an additional layer of assurance that compliance requirements are being met.

Example

In a healthcare organization decommissioning an outdated electronic health records (EHR) system, a comprehensive requirements review would involve:

- **Data Migration:** Securely transferring patient records to a new system, ensuring that the migration process adheres to HIPAA regulations.
- **Data Destruction:** Safely destroying any remaining data on the old system's storage devices to prevent unauthorized access.
- **System Disconnection:** Properly disconnecting the old system from the network, ensuring that no residual access points are left vulnerable.
- **Documentation:** Keeping detailed records of all actions taken during the decommissioning process, including data transfer logs, destruction certificates, and stakeholder communications.

By conducting a thorough requirements review and following a detailed decommissioning plan, the organization can mitigate risks, ensure compliance, and protect sensitive patient information throughout the process.
Overall, the requirements review in the system decommissioning process is essential for ensuring compliance, security, and operational continuity. By taking a proactive and structured approach, organizations can effectively manage the complexities of decommissioning and avoid the significant consequences of non-compliance.

Removing systems from operations while maintaining compliance involves a structured and well-documented process to ensure data integrity and security. This process minimizes risks associated with data breaches, loss of data integrity, and non-compliance with regulatory requirements. Here's a detailed breakdown of the steps organizations should take:

Steps for Ensuring Data Integrity and Security During System Shutdown

1. **Planning and Preparation**:
    - **Decommissioning Plan**: Develop a comprehensive decommissioning plan that outlines the scope, steps, roles, responsibilities, timelines, and compliance requirements.
    - **Risk Assessment**: Conduct a risk assessment to identify potential risks associated with shutting down the system and determine mitigation strategies.
    - **Stakeholder Involvement**: Engage key stakeholders, including IT, compliance, legal, and business units, to ensure all perspectives and requirements are considered.
2. **Data Inventory and Classification**:
    - **Data Inventory**: Create an inventory of all data stored on the system, categorizing it based on sensitivity and regulatory requirements.
    - **Data Classification**: Classify data to determine which data needs to be retained, migrated, or securely deleted.
3. **Data Backup and Migration**:
    - **Data Backup**: Perform a complete backup of all data to ensure that no information is lost during the shutdown process. Verify the integrity of the backup.
    - **Data Migration**: Plan and execute the migration of data to new systems or storage solutions. Ensure that the new environment complies with security and regulatory requirements.
    - **Migration Testing**: Test the migrated data in the new environment to verify integrity and functionality before fully decommissioning the old system.
4. **Data Security and Deletion**:
    - **Secure Data Deletion**: Use secure data deletion methods, such as data wiping or physical destruction of storage media, to ensure that residual data cannot be recovered.
    - **Encryption**: Encrypt data during transit and at rest during the migration process to protect it from unauthorized access.
    - **Access Revocation**: Revoke all access permissions to the system being decommissioned to prevent unauthorized access during and after the shutdown process.
5. **System Shutdown and Documentation**:
    - **Shutdown Procedures**: Follow a step-by-step shutdown procedure to ensure the system is properly and securely decommissioned.
    - **Documentation**: Maintain detailed documentation of the entire decommissioning process, including data migration, secure deletion methods, and shutdown steps. This documentation is essential for compliance audits and future reference.
6. **Compliance Verification and Reporting**:
    - **Compliance Check**: Verify that all decommissioning activities comply with relevant regulations and standards, such as GDPR, HIPAA, and PCI DSS.
    - **Reporting**: Prepare and submit any required compliance reports to regulatory bodies, documenting the decommissioning process and how compliance was maintained.

Data Migration and Its Implications for Compliance Maintenance

Data migration is a critical component of system decommissioning, involving the transfer of data from the old system to a new environment. This process has significant implications for compliance maintenance, as mishandling data during migration can lead to data breaches, loss of data integrity, and non-compliance.

Key Considerations for Data Migration
1. **Data Integrity**:
    - **Validation**: Validate the integrity of data before, during, and after migration to ensure that data is not corrupted or lost. Use checksums, hashes, or other validation techniques.
    - **Consistency**: Ensure that data remains consistent across the source and destination systems, especially for transactional data.
2. **Data Security**:
    - **Encryption**: Use encryption to protect data during transit and at rest in the new environment.
    - **Access Controls**: Implement strict access controls to limit who can access data during the migration process. Ensure that only authorized personnel are involved.
3. **Regulatory Compliance**:
    - **Retention Requirements**: Ensure that data retention policies comply with regulatory requirements, retaining data for the mandated period and securely deleting data that is no longer needed.
    - **Audit Trails**: Maintain audit trails documenting the data migration process, including who accessed the data, changes made, and how data integrity and security were ensured.
4. **Testing and Validation**:
    - **Pre-Migration Testing**: Test the migration process in a staging environment to identify and address potential issues before executing the actual migration.
    - **Post-Migration Testing**: Verify that the migrated data is complete, accurate, and functional in the new environment. Conduct user acceptance testing to ensure the new system meets business and compliance needs.

Examples of Data Migration in Compliance Contexts
- **Healthcare Sector (HIPAA Compliance)**: When migrating patient health records to a new electronic health record (EHR) system, ensure that all patient data is encrypted during transit and that access controls are in place to protect sensitive information. Validate that all records are accurately transferred and that the new system complies with HIPAA requirements for data storage and access.
- **Financial Services (PCI DSS Compliance)**: During the migration of payment processing data to a new system, ensure that cardholder data is encrypted and that the new system meets PCI DSS standards. Perform thorough testing to confirm that data integrity is maintained and that security controls are effective in the new environment.
- **General Data Protection Regulation (GDPR)**: For any organization handling EU citizens' data, ensure that personal data is migrated in compliance with GDPR. This includes ensuring data portability, implementing robust security measures, and maintaining records of processing activities.

By carefully planning and executing system decommissioning and data migration processes, organizations can ensure data integrity and security, maintain compliance with regulatory requirements, and minimize risks associated with system transitions. This structured approach helps protect sensitive information, supports business continuity, and upholds the organization's compliance posture.

Requirements for Documentation Retention Following System Decommissioning
Documentation retention following system decommissioning is crucial for regulatory compliance, legal protection, and operational continuity. The specific requirements for how long different types of documents should be retained vary based on regulatory standards, industry practices, and organizational policies. Here's a general overview of the retention requirements for common compliance-related documents:
1. **Regulatory Requirements**:
    - **Financial Records:** Generally required to be retained for 7-10 years, depending on the jurisdiction and regulatory body (e.g., SEC, IRS).
    - **Healthcare Records:** HIPAA mandates that healthcare-related records be retained for at least 6 years from the date of creation or the last effective date, whichever is later.
    - **Employment Records:** Records such as payroll and employee tax documents are often required to be retained for 7 years.

- **Environmental Compliance:** Records related to environmental compliance, such as hazardous waste disposal, may need to be kept for up to 10 years.
2. **Contractual Obligations:**
    - Retention periods for documents may also be dictated by contractual obligations with customers, partners, or vendors. These periods should be clearly defined in contracts and service level agreements (SLAs).
3. **Internal Policies:**
    - Organizations often have internal policies that define retention periods based on best practices and risk management strategies. These policies may extend beyond regulatory requirements to ensure comprehensive coverage.

Challenges of Long-Term Electronic Document Storage
1. **Data Integrity:**
    - Ensuring that electronic documents remain unaltered and authentic over time is critical. Risks include data corruption, unauthorized modifications, and hardware failures.
2. **Technological Obsolescence:**
    - As technology evolves, older storage formats and media can become obsolete, making it challenging to access or read stored documents.
3. **Security:**
    - Protecting long-term stored data from unauthorized access, breaches, and cyber-attacks is a constant challenge.
4. **Storage Costs:**
    - Maintaining large volumes of electronic documents over extended periods can be costly, particularly if high levels of redundancy and security are required.

Strategies for Ensuring Document Accessibility and Integrity Over Time
1. **Regular Audits and Integrity Checks:**
    - Implement periodic audits and integrity checks to ensure that stored documents have not been altered or corrupted. Use checksums, hash functions, and digital signatures to verify document integrity.
2. **Redundancy and Backup:**
    - Store multiple copies of critical documents in different locations using redundant storage solutions. Regularly back up data to protect against hardware failures and data loss.
3. **Use of Standardized Formats:**
    - Store documents in standardized and widely adopted formats such as PDF/A for long-term preservation. This reduces the risk of obsolescence and ensures compatibility with future systems.
4. **Access Controls and Encryption:**
    - Implement strict access controls to ensure that only authorized personnel can access or modify stored documents. Use encryption to protect data from unauthorized access both in transit and at rest.
5. **Migration Planning:**
    - Develop a migration plan to regularly update storage media and formats as technology evolves. This ensures that documents remain accessible and readable over time.
6. **Cloud Storage Solutions:**
    - Leverage cloud storage solutions that offer scalability, redundancy, and security. Cloud providers often have the resources to manage data integrity and accessibility over the long term, although it's essential to ensure compliance with data protection regulations.

Example
A financial institution decommissioning an old transaction processing system would need to retain various compliance-related documents, such as:
- **Audit Logs:** Retained for at least 7 years to comply with financial regulations.
- **Customer Transaction Records:** Retained for 7-10 years as per regulatory requirements.
- **System Configuration Files:** Retained for a defined period, typically 3-5 years, to support forensic investigations if needed.

To manage these documents:
- **Integrity Checks:** Regularly verify the integrity of stored files using hashing techniques.
- **Redundant Storage:** Store copies in both on-premises secure servers and a compliant cloud storage solution.
- **Standard Formats:** Convert files to standardized formats (e.g., PDF/A) to ensure long-term readability.
- **Access Control:** Use role-based access controls and encryption to protect sensitive data.
- **Migration Plan:** Plan for periodic updates to storage technology to prevent obsolescence.

By following these strategies, the financial institution can ensure that its compliance-related documents remain secure, accessible, and intact over the required retention periods.

Documentation retention is a critical aspect of compliance and risk management. Organizations must carefully balance regulatory requirements, technological challenges, and cost considerations to develop robust strategies for long-term electronic document storage, ensuring that critical information remains secure and accessible for as long as needed.

Configuration management plays a crucial role in compliance maintenance by ensuring that system settings and configurations align with regulatory requirements and organizational policies. Proper configuration management helps maintain system security, operational stability, and compliance by establishing and maintaining consistent configuration baselines. Here's how organizations ensure that system configurations remain compliant over time and address the challenges of configuration drift.

Ensuring Ongoing Compliance of System Configurations
1. **Configuration Baselines**: Establish and document configuration baselines that define the approved settings and configurations for systems and applications. These baselines serve as a reference point for compliance and security.
2. **Automated Configuration Management Tools**: Utilize automated tools for configuration management that can monitor, enforce, and report on configuration settings. Tools like Chef, Puppet, Ansible, and SCCM help ensure that configurations remain consistent and compliant.
3. **Regular Audits and Assessments**: Conduct regular configuration audits and assessments to verify that systems are configured according to the established baselines and compliance requirements. These audits help identify any deviations or unauthorized changes.
4. **Change Control Processes**: Implement robust change control processes to manage and approve configuration changes. This ensures that any modifications are reviewed, authorized, and documented before being applied.
5. **Continuous Monitoring**: Employ continuous monitoring solutions to track configuration changes in real-time. This allows organizations to quickly detect and respond to any unauthorized or non-compliant changes.

Configuration Drift

Configuration drift occurs when systems or applications deviate from their approved configuration baselines over time. This can happen due to unauthorized changes, manual interventions, software updates, or system patches. Configuration drift can lead to security vulnerabilities, operational issues, and non-compliance with regulatory requirements.

Strategies for Detecting and Addressing Configuration Drift
1. **Baseline Configuration Enforcement**: Use configuration management tools to enforce baseline configurations automatically. These tools can apply the correct settings and revert unauthorized changes to maintain compliance.
2. **Configuration Monitoring and Alerting**: Implement continuous monitoring and alerting systems that notify administrators of any changes to the configuration settings. Real-time alerts help quickly identify and address deviations from the baseline.
3. **Regular Compliance Scans**: Schedule regular compliance scans using automated tools to detect configuration drift. These scans compare current system settings against the approved baselines and generate reports highlighting any discrepancies.

4. **Incident Response Procedures**: Develop and implement incident response procedures for handling configuration drift. This includes identifying the root cause of the drift, assessing the impact, and taking corrective actions to restore compliance.
5. **Version Control and Documentation**: Maintain detailed documentation and version control for configuration changes. This includes keeping track of what changes were made, who authorized them, and when they were implemented. This documentation is vital for audits and troubleshooting.
6. **Training and Awareness**: Educate staff about the importance of adhering to configuration management practices and the potential risks of unauthorized changes. Regular training and awareness programs help prevent accidental or intentional deviations from the baseline.

Practical Examples
1. **Financial Services (SOX Compliance)**:
    - **Scenario**: A financial institution must ensure that its systems comply with the Sarbanes-Oxley Act (SOX), which requires strict controls over financial data and reporting.
    - **Strategy**: The institution uses configuration management tools to enforce baseline configurations for all financial systems. Regular audits and continuous monitoring help detect and address any configuration drift, ensuring ongoing SOX compliance.
2. **Healthcare Sector (HIPAA Compliance)**:
    - **Scenario**: A healthcare provider needs to maintain compliance with HIPAA, which mandates the protection of patient health information.
    - **Strategy**: The provider implements automated configuration management and continuous monitoring to ensure that all systems handling patient data are configured securely. Any detected configuration drift is promptly addressed to maintain HIPAA compliance.
3. **Retail Industry (PCI DSS Compliance)**:
    - **Scenario**: A retail company must comply with PCI DSS requirements to protect cardholder data.
    - **Strategy**: The company employs configuration management tools to enforce security settings on systems processing payment information. Continuous monitoring and regular compliance scans help detect configuration drift, ensuring that the systems remain PCI DSS compliant.

Configuration management is essential for maintaining compliance by ensuring that system configurations align with regulatory and organizational requirements. By implementing strategies to detect and address configuration drift, organizations can maintain secure and compliant systems, reducing the risk of security breaches and regulatory penalties.

Conducting compliance impact assessments for proposed system changes is a critical process that helps organizations ensure that any modifications to their systems do not lead to compliance violations. This process involves systematically evaluating the potential implications of changes on regulatory, contractual, and internal policy requirements.

Process of Conducting Compliance Impact Assessments
1. **Identify the Change:**
    - Clearly define the proposed change, including its scope, objectives, and components. This could involve software updates, hardware modifications, process alterations, or integrations with new systems.
2. **Assemble the Assessment Team:**
    - Form a cross-functional team comprising compliance officers, legal experts, IT professionals, and business stakeholders. This ensures a comprehensive evaluation from multiple perspectives.
3. **Review Relevant Regulations and Standards:**
    - Identify and review all applicable regulations, standards, and internal policies that might be impacted by the proposed change. This could include GDPR, HIPAA, SOX, PCI DSS, and industry-specific guidelines.
4. **Conduct Risk Assessment:**
    - Perform a risk assessment to identify potential compliance risks associated with the change. Evaluate the likelihood and impact of these risks on the organization's compliance posture.
5. **Impact Analysis:**

- Assess how the proposed change will affect existing compliance controls and processes. Determine if any current controls will be weakened or if new controls are required.
- Evaluate the impact on data security, privacy, audit trails, and record-keeping.

6. **Documentation and Reporting:**
    - Document the findings of the compliance impact assessment, including identified risks, required control changes, and recommended actions.
    - Prepare a detailed report for decision-makers to review before approving the proposed change.
7. **Mitigation Planning:**
    - Develop a mitigation plan to address identified compliance risks. This could involve implementing additional controls, revising policies, or providing additional training.
8. **Review and Approval:**
    - Submit the assessment report and mitigation plan to senior management or the appropriate governance body for review and approval.
    - Ensure that all relevant stakeholders are informed and agree on the proposed actions.
9. **Implementation and Monitoring:**
    - Implement the approved changes along with the mitigation measures. Continuously monitor the impact of the changes on compliance to ensure ongoing adherence to regulations and standards.

Factors to Consider in Evaluating Compliance Implications

1. **Regulatory Requirements:**
    - Ensure that the proposed change does not violate any existing laws, regulations, or industry standards. Consider both local and international regulations.
2. **Data Privacy and Security:**
    - Assess how the change will impact the security and privacy of sensitive data. Ensure that data protection measures remain robust and compliant with relevant regulations.
3. **Operational Impact:**
    - Evaluate how the change will affect operational processes and whether it introduces new risks or vulnerabilities that could lead to compliance issues.
4. **Control Effectiveness:**
    - Determine if existing controls are adequate to manage the new risks introduced by the change. Identify any gaps that need to be addressed.
5. **Audit and Reporting Requirements:**
    - Consider how the change will affect the organization's ability to generate accurate and timely compliance reports and maintain an auditable trail of activities.
6. **Third-Party Implications:**
    - Evaluate the impact on third-party vendors or partners, especially if they play a role in the affected systems or processes. Ensure that their compliance obligations are also considered.

Challenges of Predicting Compliance Impacts in Complex Systems

1. **Interdependencies:**
    - In complex, interconnected systems, changes in one component can have unforeseen effects on other components, making it difficult to predict compliance impacts accurately.
2. **Dynamic Environments:**
    - Rapid technological advancements and evolving regulatory landscapes can create moving targets for compliance, complicating the assessment process.
3. **Data Silos:**
    - Data stored in disparate systems or silos can hinder a comprehensive view of compliance impacts, leading to incomplete assessments.
4. **Resource Constraints:**
    - Limited resources, including time, personnel, and budget, can restrict the depth and thoroughness of compliance impact assessments.

Strategies for Ensuring Effective Assessments

1. **Holistic View:**

- o   Adopt a holistic approach to impact assessments by considering all aspects of the system and its interactions. Use system diagrams and data flow maps to visualize dependencies.
2. **Automated Tools:**
   - o   Utilize automated compliance management and risk assessment tools to streamline the assessment process, identify risks, and track regulatory changes.
3. **Continuous Monitoring:**
   - o   Implement continuous monitoring to detect and address compliance issues in real-time. This helps in adjusting controls promptly in response to dynamic environments.
4. **Stakeholder Collaboration:**
   - o   Foster collaboration among stakeholders from different departments to gather diverse insights and ensure that all potential compliance impacts are considered.
5. **Regular Training:**
   - o   Provide regular training to employees on compliance requirements and impact assessment procedures to ensure they are equipped to identify and mitigate risks effectively.

Example

Consider a financial institution planning to integrate a new cloud-based service for processing transactions. The compliance impact assessment would involve:

1. **Reviewing financial regulations like SOX and PCI DSS to ensure that data handling and security practices of the cloud service meet compliance standards.
2. **Assessing data privacy implications under GDPR to ensure that personal data of EU customers is adequately protected.
3. **Evaluating operational changes to identify potential vulnerabilities introduced by the new service.
4. **Ensuring existing security controls are sufficient or determining if additional controls are needed to safeguard transaction data.
5. **Preparing detailed documentation of findings, risk assessments, and mitigation plans, and submitting them for approval before proceeding with the integration.

By systematically evaluating the compliance implications of proposed system changes, organizations can mitigate risks, ensure regulatory adherence, and maintain robust security and operational standards in complex, interconnected environments.

Compliance automation in ongoing maintenance activities involves using technology to streamline and manage compliance tasks, reducing the manual effort required and enhancing accuracy and efficiency. Automation can significantly improve the consistency of compliance efforts, ensure timely updates, and minimize human error. However, it also comes with limitations and risks that need to be carefully managed.

Aspects of Compliance That Can Be Effectively Automated

1. **Policy Enforcement**: Automated tools can enforce compliance policies by ensuring that configurations, access controls, and other security measures adhere to predefined standards. Tools like Chef, Puppet, and Ansible can automatically apply and maintain these configurations across systems.
2. **Monitoring and Reporting**: Continuous monitoring tools can automatically track compliance with security policies and generate reports. These tools can identify deviations from compliance standards in real-time and alert administrators. Examples include Splunk, SolarWinds, and ELK Stack.
3. **Vulnerability Management**: Automated vulnerability scanners can regularly scan systems for known vulnerabilities and provide reports on their findings. Tools like Nessus, Qualys, and OpenVAS can automate this process, ensuring that vulnerabilities are identified and addressed promptly.
4. **Access Management**: Identity and access management (IAM) systems can automate the enforcement of access policies, ensuring that only authorized users have access to sensitive data and systems. Tools like Okta, Azure AD, and AWS IAM help automate user provisioning, de-provisioning, and access reviews.
5. **Audit Trails and Documentation**: Automated logging and documentation tools can create detailed audit trails of compliance activities, ensuring that all actions are recorded and can be reviewed during audits. Tools like AuditBoard and ServiceNow can automate documentation and compliance workflows.

Limitations of Compliance Automation

1. **Complexity of Regulations**: Not all aspects of compliance can be easily automated, especially those involving nuanced judgment or interpretation of complex regulations. Human oversight is often required to understand and apply these regulations correctly.
2. **Context-Specific Requirements**: Some compliance requirements may be specific to particular contexts or scenarios, requiring tailored approaches that automated tools might not handle effectively.
3. **Initial Setup and Maintenance**: Implementing compliance automation tools requires significant initial setup and ongoing maintenance. Misconfigurations or outdated automation scripts can lead to compliance failures.
4. **Over-reliance on Tools**: Relying too heavily on automation can create a false sense of security. It is essential to combine automation with regular manual reviews and audits to ensure comprehensive compliance.

Benefits of Relying on Automated Compliance Tools
1. **Consistency and Accuracy**: Automated tools can consistently apply compliance policies across all systems, reducing the risk of human error and ensuring that all systems adhere to the same standards.
2. **Efficiency**: Automation significantly reduces the time and effort required to perform routine compliance tasks, allowing staff to focus on more strategic activities.
3. **Timeliness**: Automated tools can perform compliance checks and updates in real-time, ensuring that compliance issues are identified and addressed promptly.
4. **Scalability**: Automation can easily scale to accommodate growing and complex IT environments, ensuring that compliance is maintained as the organization expands.

Risks of Relying on Automated Compliance Tools
1. **False Sense of Security**: Automation can lead to complacency, with organizations assuming that compliance is guaranteed by the tools. Regular manual oversight is necessary to validate automated processes.
2. **Configuration Errors**: Automated tools are only as effective as their configuration. Errors in setup or scripts can lead to compliance failures, potentially exposing the organization to risks.
3. **Dependency on Vendors**: Relying on third-party tools introduces dependency on vendors for updates, support, and continued service availability. Disruptions in these services can impact compliance efforts.

Examples of Successful Automation Implementations
1. **Financial Services (SOX Compliance)**:
    - **Scenario**: A large financial institution implemented automated compliance tools to ensure adherence to Sarbanes-Oxley (SOX) requirements.
    - **Implementation**: The organization used automated policy enforcement and continuous monitoring tools to maintain financial data integrity and access controls. These tools generated real-time compliance reports and alerts for any deviations.
    - **Outcome**: The automation significantly reduced the time required for compliance audits and improved the accuracy of financial reporting, ensuring ongoing SOX compliance.
2. **Healthcare Sector (HIPAA Compliance)**:
    - **Scenario**: A healthcare provider needed to maintain HIPAA compliance across its electronic health record (EHR) systems.
    - **Implementation**: The provider used automated vulnerability scanners, access management tools, and continuous monitoring solutions to protect patient data and ensure compliance with HIPAA requirements.
    - **Outcome**: Automation improved the provider's ability to detect and address security vulnerabilities quickly, ensuring that patient data remained secure and HIPAA compliant.
3. **Retail Industry (PCI DSS Compliance)**:
    - **Scenario**: A retail company sought to automate compliance with PCI DSS standards to protect payment card information.
    - **Implementation**: The company deployed automated configuration management and monitoring tools to enforce security policies across its payment processing systems. Regular automated scans identified vulnerabilities and compliance gaps.
    - **Outcome**: The automation streamlined the company's compliance efforts, reducing the risk of data breaches and ensuring adherence to PCI DSS requirements.

Compliance automation can greatly enhance an organization's ability to maintain compliance efficiently and effectively. However, it is crucial to balance automation with manual oversight and continuous improvement to address its limitations and risks. By doing so, organizations can achieve a robust compliance posture and mitigate potential compliance challenges.

Third-party vendor management is essential for maintaining compliance because vendors and service providers often have access to sensitive data, systems, and processes. A failure by a vendor to meet compliance standards can result in significant risks, including data breaches, regulatory penalties, and reputational damage. Therefore, organizations must ensure that their vendors adhere to the same compliance standards they themselves must follow.

Ensuring Vendor Compliance
1. **Vendor Selection and Due Diligence:**
    - **Pre-Qualification:** Conduct thorough due diligence during the vendor selection process to assess the potential vendor's compliance posture. This includes reviewing their security policies, compliance certifications, financial stability, and past performance.
    - **Risk Assessment:** Categorize vendors based on the level of risk they present, focusing more resources on assessing and monitoring high-risk vendors.
2. **Contractual Agreements:**
    - **Compliance Clauses:** Include specific compliance requirements in contracts, such as adherence to GDPR, HIPAA, PCI DSS, or other relevant regulations.
    - **Right to Audit:** Ensure contracts include the right to audit vendors to verify compliance with stipulated standards.
    - **SLAs and Penalties:** Establish clear Service Level Agreements (SLAs) and define penalties for non-compliance or breaches of contractual terms.
3. **Ongoing Assessment and Monitoring:**
    - **Regular Audits:** Conduct periodic audits and assessments of vendors to ensure ongoing compliance. This can include both scheduled reviews and surprise audits.
    - **Continuous Monitoring:** Use automated tools and technologies to continuously monitor vendor activities and compliance status.
    - **Performance Reviews:** Regularly review vendor performance and compliance reports to identify any potential issues early.

Strategies for Ongoing Vendor Assessment
1. **Regular Compliance Audits:**
    - Conduct audits to evaluate the vendor's compliance with contractual obligations and regulatory requirements. This can involve reviewing security practices, data protection measures, and incident response protocols.
2. **Risk-Based Approach:**
    - Focus more frequent and detailed assessments on high-risk vendors. This allows organizations to allocate resources efficiently and address the most critical risks.
3. **Vendor Self-Assessments:**
    - Require vendors to perform regular self-assessments and report their compliance status. These self-assessments can be supplemented with independent verification.
4. **Third-Party Certifications:**
    - Encourage or require vendors to obtain relevant third-party certifications, such as ISO 27001 or SOC 2, which provide assurance of their compliance with industry standards.
5. **Training and Awareness:**
    - Provide training and resources to vendors to help them understand and meet compliance requirements. This can include webinars, workshops, and regular communication on compliance updates.

Examples of Effective Vendor Compliance Monitoring Practices
1. **Automated Monitoring Tools:**

- Use tools such as Security Information and Event Management (SIEM) systems to monitor vendor activities in real-time. These tools can alert organizations to suspicious activities or potential compliance violations.
2. **Vendor Scorecards:**
    - Develop scorecards to track and rate vendor performance across various compliance metrics. This provides a clear overview of each vendor's compliance status and helps identify areas needing improvement.
3. **Incident Reporting and Response:**
    - Establish clear protocols for incident reporting and response. Require vendors to report security incidents promptly and work collaboratively to address and remediate issues.
4. **Regular Meetings and Reviews:**
    - Hold regular meetings with key vendors to discuss compliance status, review performance, and address any concerns. This fosters open communication and continuous improvement.
5. **Contractual Audits:**
    - Execute the right-to-audit clauses in vendor contracts by performing regular and ad-hoc audits. These audits can be conducted by internal teams or third-party auditors to ensure impartiality.

Example

Consider a healthcare organization working with a third-party vendor that provides cloud storage services. To ensure vendor compliance with HIPAA:

1. **Due Diligence:** The organization conducts a thorough review of the vendor's security policies, HIPAA compliance certifications, and past incident records before entering into a contract.
2. **Contractual Agreements:** The contract includes specific clauses requiring adherence to HIPAA regulations, the right to conduct audits, and clear SLAs related to data security and breach notification.
3. **Regular Audits:** The organization performs semi-annual audits of the vendor's data protection practices, reviewing access controls, encryption methods, and incident response plans.
4. **Continuous Monitoring:** Automated tools are used to monitor access to stored healthcare data, providing real-time alerts on any unauthorized access or suspicious activities.
5. **Incident Response:** Clear procedures are in place for the vendor to report any data breaches immediately, with a collaborative approach to incident investigation and resolution.

By implementing these strategies, the healthcare organization can ensure that its vendor maintains the required compliance standards, thereby protecting sensitive patient data and avoiding regulatory penalties.

Effective third-party vendor management involves a combination of due diligence, contractual safeguards, ongoing assessment, and continuous monitoring. By adopting a comprehensive approach, organizations can mitigate the risks associated with vendor non-compliance and maintain robust compliance across their supply chain.

Practice Section

Welcome to the practice exam section of the CGRC Exam Prep Study Guide. This section is designed to test your knowledge and understanding of key concepts related to the Certified in Governance, Risk, and Compliance (CGRC) certification. The questions cover a wide range of topics you will need to master to succeed on the exam.

Why Answers and Explanations are Provided Immediately

Instant Feedback: By having the answer and explanation readily available, you can quickly assess your understanding of each concept. If you answered correctly, the explanation will reinforce your knowledge. If you answered incorrectly, you can immediately learn from your mistake and clarify any misunderstandings.

Efficient Learning: Providing answers and explanations directly after each question eliminates the need to flip back and forth between the questions and an answer key. This streamlined approach allows you to focus on the content and maintain your momentum as you progress through the practice test.

Enhanced Retention: Research has shown that receiving immediate feedback on your responses can significantly improve learning and retention. By reviewing the answer and explanation right after answering a question, you'll be more likely to remember the information and apply it effectively in the future.

To maximize your practice exam experience, we recommend using a piece of paper or something similar to cover the answer and explanation while you attempt each question. This will simulate a real exam environment and help you gauge your preparedness more accurately.

Remember, some important topics may be covered several times to reinforce critical concepts and ensure you are well-prepared for the exam. Take your time with each question, review the provided explanations carefully, and use this opportunity to solidify your understanding of the material.

Good luck, and let's get started!

1. Which of the following frameworks focuses specifically on integrating IT with business strategy and goals?
a. NIST
b. ISO/IEC 27001
c. COBIT
d. PCI-DSS

Answer: c. COBIT. Explanation: COBIT (Control Objectives for Information and Related Technology) is specifically designed to align IT with business strategy and goals, providing a framework for IT management and governance.

2. Which of the following best describes the purpose of a Data Protection Impact Assessment (DPIA) under GDPR?
a. To identify and mitigate privacy risks before processing personal data
b. To document compliance with data retention policies
c. To assess the effectiveness of encryption methods
d. To determine the appropriate data classification levels

Answer: a. To identify and mitigate privacy risks before processing personal data. Explanation: A DPIA is a process mandated by GDPR for operations that are likely to result in high risk to individuals' rights and freedoms. It involves systematically analyzing, identifying, and minimizing the data protection risks of a project or plan. This proactive approach helps organizations comply with GDPR requirements and protect individual privacy. Options b, c, and d are important aspects of data protection, but they don't specifically describe the primary purpose of a DPIA as outlined in GDPR Article 35.

3. In the context of the NIST Cybersecurity Framework, which of the following activities would fall under the "Detect" function?
a. Implementing multi-factor authentication
b. Conducting a tabletop exercise for incident response
c. Establishing anomaly detection systems
d. Creating an asset inventory

Answer: c. Establishing anomaly detection systems. Explanation: The NIST Cybersecurity Framework's "Detect" function focuses on developing and implementing appropriate activities to identify the occurrence of a cybersecurity event. Anomaly detection systems are designed to identify unusual patterns that may indicate a security incident, aligning directly with this function. Option a (multi-factor authentication) falls under the "Protect" function. Option b (tabletop exercise) is part of the "Respond" function. Option d (asset inventory) is typically associated with the "Identify" function.

4. In the context of the GDPR, which of the following is a key requirement for the lawful processing of personal data under the principle of accountability?
a. Data encryption at rest
b. Maintenance of a data protection impact assessment (DPIA)
c. Implementation of multi-factor authentication
d. Regular employee cybersecurity training

Answer: b. Maintenance of a data protection impact assessment (DPIA). Explanation: The GDPR requires organizations to maintain a DPIA to identify and minimize data protection risks, demonstrating accountability in processing personal data.

5. Which of the following best describes the role of the FedRAMP program in cloud computing security?
a. Establishing industry-specific cybersecurity regulations
b. Providing a standardized approach to security assessment, authorization, and continuous monitoring for cloud products and services
c. Certifying individual cybersecurity professionals
d. Requiring encryption for all cloud data transmissions

Answer: b. Providing a standardized approach to security assessment, authorization, and continuous monitoring for cloud products and services. Explanation: FedRAMP (Federal Risk and Authorization Management Program) standardizes security assessments for cloud products used by U.S. federal agencies.

6. In a risk management context, what is the primary purpose of conducting a Business Impact Analysis (BIA)?
a. To identify potential threats to business continuity
b. To determine the financial implications of compliance failures
c. To evaluate the effectiveness of security controls
d. To prioritize critical business functions and the impact of their disruption

Answer: d. To prioritize critical business functions and the impact of their disruption. Explanation: A BIA helps identify and prioritize critical business functions, assessing the impact of their disruption to guide recovery planning.

7. Which control type focuses on policies and procedures to manage operational risk?
a. Technical controls
b. Management controls
c. Physical controls
d. Environmental controls

Answer: b. Management controls. Explanation: Management controls include policies and procedures designed to manage and reduce operational risk within an organization.

8. Under the NIST Cybersecurity Framework, which function involves activities like continuous monitoring and anomaly detection?
a. Identify
b. Protect
c. Detect
d. Respond

Answer: c. Detect. Explanation: The "Detect" function in the NIST Cybersecurity Framework focuses on developing and implementing activities to identify the occurrence of cybersecurity events through continuous monitoring and anomaly detection.

9. Which of the following is a characteristic of an effective governance framework within an organization?
a. Maximizing operational efficiency
b. Delegating decision-making to external consultants
c. Establishing clear roles, responsibilities, and accountability structures
d. Focusing exclusively on short-term financial goals

Answer: c. Establishing clear roles, responsibilities, and accountability structures. Explanation: An effective governance framework establishes clear roles and responsibilities to ensure accountability and alignment with the organization's strategic objectives.

10. In the context of ISO/IEC 27001, which document outlines the organization's approach to managing information security risks?
a. Business Continuity Plan
b. Statement of Applicability (SoA)
c. Risk Treatment Plan (RTP)
d. Incident Response Plan

Answer: b. Statement of Applicability (SoA). Explanation: The SoA in ISO/IEC 27001 outlines the organization's approach to managing information security risks, detailing the controls selected to address those risks.

11. Which type of control is primarily designed to restore normal operations after a security incident?
a. Preventive control
b. Detective control
c. Corrective control
d. Directive control

Answer: c. Corrective control. Explanation: Corrective controls are implemented to restore systems and processes to normal operations after a security incident has occurred.

12. Which international standard provides guidelines for implementing an effective risk management framework?
a. ISO/IEC 27002
b. ISO 31000
c. PCI-DSS
d. COBIT

Answer: b. ISO 31000. Explanation: ISO 31000 provides guidelines for implementing an effective risk management framework applicable to any organization.

13. When conducting a privacy impact assessment (PIA), what is the primary objective?
a. To encrypt all sensitive data
b. To determine the privacy risks associated with processing personal data
c. To train employees on privacy policies
d. To develop a disaster recovery plan

Answer: b. To determine the privacy risks associated with processing personal data. Explanation: A PIA aims to identify and mitigate privacy risks associated with the processing of personal data, ensuring compliance with privacy regulations.

14. An organization has implemented several security controls to protect its data. During an audit, the auditor requests evidence of the effectiveness of these controls. What type of document would best provide this evidence?
a. Security policy documents
b. Incident response plans
c. Security control test results
d. User access reviews

Answer: c. Security control test results. Explanation: Security control test results provide direct evidence of the effectiveness of implemented controls, showing how well they perform in protecting data and mitigating risks.

15. During a security audit, a discrepancy is found between the organization's documented policies and the actual practices being followed. Which of the following steps should be taken first to address this issue?
a. Update the documentation to reflect actual practices.
b. Train employees on the documented policies.
c. Perform a root cause analysis to understand the discrepancy.
d. Escalate the issue to senior management.

Answer: c. Perform a root cause analysis to understand the discrepancy. Explanation: Understanding the root cause of the discrepancy is essential to determine whether the policies need to be updated or if there is a compliance issue with current practices.

16. Which of the following frameworks focuses specifically on the alignment of IT strategy with business goals and the creation of value through IT?
a. NIST Cybersecurity Framework
b. ISO/IEC 27001
c. COBIT
d. PCI-DSS

Answer: c. COBIT. Explanation: COBIT (Control Objectives for Information and Related Technology) is a framework for developing, implementing, monitoring, and improving IT governance and management practices, ensuring alignment with business goals.

17. A healthcare organization is assessing its compliance with HIPAA regulations. Which of the following is a key requirement for maintaining compliance?
a. Annual penetration testing
b. Implementing a risk management program
c. Encrypting all patient data
d. Quarterly user access reviews

Answer: b. Implementing a risk management program. Explanation: HIPAA requires healthcare organizations to implement a comprehensive risk management program to identify, assess, and mitigate risks to patient data. While encryption and access reviews are important, risk management is a broader requirement.

18. An organization is preparing for a GDPR compliance audit. Which of the following documents is essential to demonstrate compliance with data subject access requests (DSARs)?
a. Data breach response plan
b. Record of processing activities (ROPA)
c. Data subject access request log

d. Privacy policy

Answer: c. Data subject access request log. Explanation: The DSAR log documents the organization's responses to data subject access requests, demonstrating compliance with GDPR requirements regarding individuals' rights to access their personal data.

19. A financial institution is developing its incident response plan. Which of the following is the most critical component to include to ensure the plan's effectiveness?
a. Contact information for all employees
b. A detailed incident classification scheme
c. A list of all IT assets
d. Regularly scheduled incident response training sessions

Answer: b. A detailed incident classification scheme. Explanation: An incident classification scheme helps in quickly identifying the type and severity of incidents, ensuring appropriate and timely response actions.

20. An organization must comply with multiple regulatory frameworks, including SOX and GDPR. What is the best approach to managing compliance requirements efficiently?
a. Develop separate compliance programs for each regulation.
b. Focus on the most stringent requirements of each regulation.
c. Implement an integrated compliance management system.
d. Conduct quarterly audits for all compliance requirements.

Answer: c. Implement an integrated compliance management system. Explanation: An integrated compliance management system allows the organization to manage multiple regulatory requirements efficiently by consolidating efforts and resources, reducing redundancy, and ensuring comprehensive compliance.

21. A company is planning to migrate its IT infrastructure to the cloud. Which of the following should be the primary focus of its risk assessment before migration?
a. The cost of cloud services
b. The cloud service provider's market reputation
c. Data security and privacy risks
d. The ease of use of the cloud platform

Answer: c. Data security and privacy risks. Explanation: Data security and privacy risks are critical considerations in cloud migration, as the company must ensure that sensitive data remains protected and compliant with relevant regulations in the new environment.

22. An audit reveals that an organization lacks formal procedures for the disposal of obsolete IT equipment. Which of the following risks is most likely associated with this gap?

a. Increased operational costs
b. Non-compliance with environmental regulations
c. Data breaches from improperly disposed equipment
d. Loss of physical assets

Answer: c. Data breaches from improperly disposed equipment. Explanation: Without formal disposal procedures, obsolete IT equipment may still contain sensitive data that could be accessed and misused, leading to data breaches.

23. A multinational company is developing a global compliance program. What is the first step in this process to ensure effectiveness across different regions?
a. Standardize compliance requirements globally.
b. Conduct a compliance risk assessment for each region.
c. Train employees on global compliance policies.
d. Hire local compliance officers in each region.

Answer: b. Conduct a compliance risk assessment for each region. Explanation: A compliance risk assessment for each region helps identify unique risks and regulatory requirements, enabling the company to tailor its compliance program to address specific regional needs effectively.

24. A multinational corporation is restructuring its GRC program and wants to implement the Three Lines of Defense model. Which of the following arrangements most accurately represents this model?
a. Legal, compliance, and internal audit
b. Management, risk management, and external audit
c. Operational management, risk and compliance functions, and internal audit
d. Board of directors, executive management, and risk committee

Answer: c. Operational management, risk and compliance functions, and internal audit. Explanation: The Three Lines of Defense model consists of operational management (first line), risk and compliance functions (second line), and internal audit (third line). This structure provides a clear delineation of responsibilities for risk management and control. The first line owns and manages risks, the second line oversees risks and ensures compliance, while the third line provides independent assurance. Options a, b, and d mix elements from different lines or include external entities not part of the model.

25. In developing a RACI matrix for a new enterprise-wide risk management initiative, which role would typically be assigned as "Responsible" for implementing risk mitigation strategies at the departmental level?
a. Chief Risk Officer
b. Department Manager
c. Internal Auditor
d. Board of Directors

Answer: b. Department Manager. Explanation: In a RACI matrix, "Responsible" refers to the role that performs the work. Department Managers are typically responsible for implementing risk mitigation strategies within their departments, as they have direct operational control. The Chief Risk Officer (a) would likely be "Accountable" for the overall initiative. Internal Auditors (c) are usually "Consulted" or provide independent assurance. The Board of Directors (d) would be "Informed" about significant risks and mitigation efforts but wouldn't directly implement strategies.

26. A company's risk appetite statement declares, "We have no tolerance for actions that could result in significant harm to our reputation." However, the company decides to enter a new market with known corruption issues, implementing strict anti-bribery measures. This scenario best illustrates the difference between:
a. Inherent risk and residual risk
b. Risk appetite and risk tolerance
c. Risk avoidance and risk mitigation
d. Strategic risk and operational risk

Answer: b. Risk appetite and risk tolerance. Explanation: This scenario demonstrates the difference between risk appetite (the broad level of risk the organization is willing to accept) and risk tolerance (the specific level of risk acceptable in pursuit of objectives). The company's overall risk appetite for reputational damage is low, but it shows a higher risk tolerance for a specific strategic initiative, balanced by implementing control measures. Options a, c, and d are relevant risk management concepts but don't directly explain the apparent contradiction in the scenario.

27. In assessing an organization's GRC maturity using the Capability Maturity Model Integration (CMMI) for GRC, which of the following observations would indicate a "Defined" level of maturity?
a. GRC processes are ad hoc and largely undocumented
b. Standard GRC processes are established and used consistently across the organization
c. GRC processes are quantitatively managed using statistical techniques
d. Continuous improvement of GRC processes is embedded in organizational culture

Answer: b. Standard GRC processes are established and used consistently across the organization. Explanation: In the CMMI for GRC, the "Defined" level (Level 3) is characterized by standard processes that are well documented and consistently applied across the organization. This level represents a significant improvement over ad hoc processes (Level 1 - Initial) or processes that are repeatable but not standardized (Level 2 - Managed). Option c describes Level 4 (Quantitatively Managed), while option d aligns with Level 5 (Optimizing). Option a describes Level 1 (Initial).

28. A newly appointed Chief Compliance Officer is tasked with enhancing the organization's GRC program. Which of the following actions would be most effective in improving the integration of governance, risk management, and compliance activities?
a. Implementing a centralized GRC technology platform
b. Increasing the frequency of compliance training for all employees
c. Outsourcing risk assessment activities to third-party consultants
d. Expanding the internal audit team's size and budget

Answer: a. Implementing a centralized GRC technology platform. Explanation: A centralized GRC technology platform can significantly enhance the integration of governance, risk management, and compliance activities by providing a unified view of risks, controls, and compliance requirements across the organization. This approach facilitates better data sharing, consistent reporting, and more efficient coordination among different GRC functions. While options b, c, and d may have benefits, they don't directly address the integration challenge as effectively as a centralized platform.

29. An organization's risk appetite statement includes the following: "We accept moderate financial risks in pursuit of our strategic objectives, but have low tolerance for compliance violations." In the context of this statement, which of the following scenarios would likely require immediate management attention?
a. A 5% decrease in quarterly profits due to market fluctuations
b. A minor data breach affecting 100 customer records
c. A potential regulatory fine for non-compliance with environmental regulations
d. A 15% increase in operational costs due to a new strategic initiative

Answer: c. A potential regulatory fine for non-compliance with environmental regulations. Explanation: The risk appetite statement indicates a low tolerance for compliance violations. A potential regulatory fine for non-compliance directly conflicts with this stated low tolerance and would require immediate attention. The 5% decrease in profits (a) and 15% increase in costs (d) likely fall within the "moderate financial risks" the organization is willing to accept. The minor data breach (b), while concerning, may not immediately violate the stated risk appetite without more context on its compliance implications.

30. In implementing a Three Lines of Defense model, an organization discovers significant overlap and confusion between the roles of the second line (risk management and compliance functions) and the third line (internal audit). Which of the following approaches would be most effective in addressing this issue?
a. Merging the second and third lines into a single risk and assurance function
b. Outsourcing the internal audit function to ensure independence
c. Clearly defining and communicating the distinct responsibilities of each line
d. Rotating staff between the second and third lines to improve understanding

Answer: c. Clearly defining and communicating the distinct responsibilities of each line. Explanation: The most effective approach to address role confusion in the Three Lines of Defense model is to clearly define and communicate the distinct responsibilities of each line. This ensures that each line understands its specific role and how it complements the others, maintaining the model's integrity. Merging the lines (a) would undermine the model's purpose of segregating duties. Outsourcing internal audit (b) doesn't address the root cause of confusion. Staff rotation (d) might improve understanding but could exacerbate confusion if roles aren't clearly defined.

31. A global financial services firm is developing a new RACI matrix for its enterprise risk management (ERM) program. Which of the following assignments would be most appropriate for the Board of Directors in this matrix?
a. Responsible for identifying operational risks
b. Accountable for implementing risk mitigation strategies
c. Consulted on the development of risk assessment methodologies
d. Informed about the overall risk profile and effectiveness of the ERM program

Answer: d. Informed about the overall risk profile and effectiveness of the ERM program. Explanation: In a RACI matrix for an ERM program, the Board of Directors is typically "Informed" about the overall risk profile and ERM program effectiveness. This aligns with the Board's oversight role and responsibility for setting risk appetite. The Board isn't directly responsible for identifying operational risks (a) or implementing strategies (b), which are management functions. While the Board might be consulted on some high-level aspects, they typically wouldn't be directly involved in developing risk assessment methodologies (c).

32. An organization is struggling to balance its strategic objectives with its stated risk appetite. Which of the following approaches would be most effective in addressing this challenge?
a. Revising the risk appetite statement to align with current strategic objectives
b. Implementing more stringent risk controls across all business units
c. Conducting a comprehensive review of the alignment between risk appetite and strategic planning processes
d. Increasing the risk management department's budget and resources

Answer: c. Conducting a comprehensive review of the alignment between risk appetite and strategic planning processes. Explanation: The most effective approach is to conduct a comprehensive review of how risk appetite aligns with strategic planning. This allows the organization to identify misalignments and adjust either the risk appetite or strategic objectives accordingly, ensuring consistency. Simply revising the risk appetite statement (a) without this review might lead to inappropriate risk-taking. Implementing more stringent controls (b) doesn't address the root cause of misalignment. Increasing resources (d) might help but doesn't directly address the strategic alignment issue.

33. In assessing an organization's GRC maturity using the CMMI for GRC, which of the following scenarios would most clearly indicate a transition from "Managed" (Level 2) to "Defined" (Level 3)?
a. Implementation of a enterprise-wide risk management software
b. Establishment of standardized GRC processes used consistently across all business units
c. Introduction of statistical process control for measuring GRC effectiveness
d. Creation of a dedicated GRC department reporting directly to the CEO

Answer: b. Establishment of standardized GRC processes used consistently across all business units. Explanation: The key differentiator between CMMI Level 2 (Managed) and Level 3 (Defined) is the establishment of standardized processes used consistently across the organization. This indicates a shift from processes that may be repeatable but specific to individual projects or units (Level 2) to organization-wide standardization (Level 3). Implementing software (a) doesn't necessarily indicate process standardization. Statistical process control (c) is more characteristic of Level 4 (Quantitatively Managed). Creating a dedicated department (d) might support maturity but doesn't specifically indicate Level 3 characteristics.

34. An organization is implementing the NIST Cybersecurity Framework and wants to prioritize its cybersecurity activities. Which of the following core functions should be addressed first to create a solid foundation for the rest of the framework?
a. Protect
b. Detect
c. Identify
d. Respond

Answer: c. Identify. Explanation: The Identify function is foundational as it helps the organization understand its environment, including assets, risks, and resources. This understanding is crucial for prioritizing and implementing subsequent protective, detective, and responsive measures.

35. A healthcare company is mapping NIST CSF to ISO/IEC 27001. Which aspect of the NIST CSF aligns most closely with ISO/IEC 27001's requirement for establishing an information security management system (ISMS)?
a. Protect
b. Detect
c. Respond
d. Identify

Answer: d. Identify. Explanation: The Identify function of NIST CSF aligns with ISO/IEC 27001's requirement to establish an ISMS because it involves understanding the organizational context, identifying risks, and defining the scope of the security management system.

36. During a cybersecurity incident, an organization follows the NIST CSF Respond function. Which of the following activities is most aligned with this function?
a. Asset management
b. Continuous monitoring
c. Incident analysis
d. Data encryption

Answer: c. Incident analysis. Explanation: Incident analysis is a key activity within the Respond function of the NIST CSF, as it involves understanding and mitigating the impact of cybersecurity incidents through effective response measures.

37. An organization is evaluating its cybersecurity maturity using the NIST CSF Implementation Tiers. Which of the following best describes a Tier 2 (Risk Informed) organization?
a. Risk management practices are not formalized and lack regular updates.
b. Risk management practices are approved by management but not consistently applied.
c. Risk management practices are formalized and regularly updated across the organization.
d. Risk management practices are adaptive and continuously improving.

Answer: b. Risk management practices are approved by management but not consistently applied. Explanation: Tier 2 (Risk Informed) organizations have risk management practices approved by management, but these practices are not consistently implemented across the entire organization.

38. A financial institution is enhancing its cybersecurity posture by focusing on the Detect function of the NIST CSF. Which activity is most critical for this function?
a. Access control implementation
b. Security incident detection and analysis

c. Risk assessment and management
d. Employee security training

Answer: b. Security incident detection and analysis. Explanation: The Detect function of the NIST CSF emphasizes timely discovery of cybersecurity events through monitoring, analysis, and detection processes.

39. In preparing for potential cybersecurity incidents, an organization develops a recovery plan. Under which NIST CSF core function does this activity fall?
a. Identify
b. Protect
c. Detect
d. Recover

Answer: d. Recover. Explanation: Developing and implementing a recovery plan is a key component of the Recover function, which focuses on restoring services and capabilities after a cybersecurity incident.

40. An organization uses NIST CSF Profiles to align its cybersecurity posture with business requirements. Which of the following best describes the use of profiles in this context?
a. Identifying critical assets and their vulnerabilities
b. Tailoring the framework to meet specific organizational needs
c. Monitoring the network for potential threats
d. Implementing baseline security controls

Answer: b. Tailoring the framework to meet specific organizational needs. Explanation: NIST CSF Profiles allow organizations to customize the framework's core functions and categories to align with their specific business objectives and risk management priorities.

41. Mapping NIST CSF to ISO/IEC 27001 can help streamline compliance efforts. Which core function of NIST CSF primarily correlates with ISO/IEC 27001's requirement for implementing and maintaining security controls?
a. Identify
b. Protect
c. Detect
d. Recover

Answer: b. Protect. Explanation: The Protect function of NIST CSF focuses on implementing and maintaining security measures, which closely aligns with ISO/IEC 27001's requirement for putting in place security controls to protect information assets.

42. A manufacturing firm wants to evaluate its cybersecurity practices against the highest NIST CSF Implementation Tier. Which of the following characteristics is most indicative of a Tier 4 (Adaptive) organization?

a. Risk management processes are informal and ad hoc.
b. Risk management practices are managed but not standardized.
c. Risk management practices are regularly reviewed and improved.
d. Risk management practices are integrated and continually improving.

Answer: d. Risk management practices are integrated and continually improving. Explanation: Tier 4 (Adaptive) organizations have risk management practices that are fully integrated into the organizational culture and continuously improved based on lessons learned and predictive indicators.

43. An organization seeks to improve its response capabilities by aligning with the NIST CSF Respond function. Which of the following activities should be prioritized to enhance this function?
a. Conducting regular security awareness training
b. Establishing incident response policies and procedures
c. Implementing data encryption mechanisms
d. Performing asset inventory and classification

Answer: b. Establishing incident response policies and procedures. Explanation: The Respond function of the NIST CSF focuses on developing and implementing appropriate policies and procedures for responding to cybersecurity incidents, ensuring the organization is prepared to manage and mitigate incidents effectively.

44. A company aims to align its IT strategy with business goals using the COBIT 5 framework. Which COBIT 5 principle directly focuses on creating optimal value from IT by balancing resource use, risk, and benefits?
a. Enabling a holistic approach
b. Meeting stakeholder needs
c. Separating governance from management
d. Applying a single integrated framework

Answer: b. Meeting stakeholder needs. Explanation: This principle focuses on achieving the best possible alignment between IT and business goals by balancing resource use, risk, and benefits to meet stakeholder expectations.

45. In the context of COBIT 5, which of the following processes is responsible for ensuring that the enterprise's IT supports and enables the achievement of business objectives through the use of appropriate governance and management practices?
a. APO13 Manage Security
b. EDM01 Ensure Governance Framework Setting and Maintenance
c. DSS05 Manage Security Services
d. MEA03 Monitor, Evaluate and Assess Compliance with External Requirements

Answer: b. EDM01 Ensure Governance Framework Setting and Maintenance. Explanation: EDM01 is responsible for setting and maintaining the governance framework, ensuring that IT aligns with business objectives through effective governance and management practices.

46. A multinational corporation is designing its IT governance system using COBIT 2019. Which design factor should they consider to ensure the governance system is customized to the enterprise's unique characteristics?
a. Enterprise goals
b. Regulatory compliance requirements
c. Organizational structure
d. Risk profile

Answer: c. Organizational structure. Explanation: COBIT 2019 emphasizes customizing the governance system based on various design factors, including the enterprise's organizational structure, to ensure it meets specific needs and characteristics.

47. When implementing COBIT 5 to enhance IT-Business alignment, which process focuses on defining the overall organizational IT strategy and its alignment with the enterprise strategy?
a. BAI02 Manage Requirements Definition
b. APO02 Manage Strategy
c. DSS01 Manage Operations
d. MEA02 Monitor, Evaluate and Assess the System of Internal Control

Answer: b. APO02 Manage Strategy. Explanation: APO02 is crucial for defining the IT strategy and ensuring its alignment with the enterprise's overall strategy, facilitating effective IT-Business alignment.

48. In COBIT 2019, how does the concept of "Focus Areas" enhance the framework's applicability to specific situations or issues within an organization?
a. By providing generic guidelines for all types of enterprises
b. By offering detailed, situation-specific guidance for addressing unique governance and management challenges
c. By standardizing processes across all business units
d. By eliminating the need for customization in governance practices

Answer: b. By offering detailed, situation-specific guidance for addressing unique governance and management challenges. Explanation: "Focus Areas" in COBIT 2019 provide tailored guidance for specific issues or situations, enhancing the framework's relevance and effectiveness in addressing unique organizational challenges.

49. A financial services firm is using COBIT 5 to manage IT-related risk. Which process should they emphasize to ensure continuous risk assessment and management aligned with enterprise objectives?
a. APO12 Manage Risk
b. BAI06 Manage Changes
c. DSS04 Manage Continuity
d. MEA01 Monitor, Evaluate and Assess Performance and Conformance

Answer: a. APO12 Manage Risk. Explanation: APO12 is focused on the continuous assessment and management of IT-related risks, ensuring they are aligned with and support the enterprise's overall risk management objectives.

50. During the implementation of COBIT 2019, which design factor specifically helps determine the balance between governance and management activities?
a. IT implementation methods
b. Threat landscape
c. Enterprise size
d. Technology adoption strategy

Answer: d. Technology adoption strategy. Explanation: The technology adoption strategy influences the balance between governance and management activities by determining how new technologies are integrated and managed within the enterprise, ensuring alignment with strategic goals.

51. In COBIT 5, which governance process aims to evaluate, direct, and monitor IT-related organizational changes to ensure they deliver the intended value and benefits?
a. APO08 Manage Relationships
b. BAI05 Manage Organizational Change Enablement
c. EDM04 Ensure Resource Optimization
d. DSS03 Manage Problems

Answer: b. BAI05 Manage Organizational Change Enablement. Explanation: BAI05 focuses on managing organizational changes related to IT, ensuring they deliver value and benefits in line with enterprise objectives.

52. A healthcare organization is tailoring COBIT 2019 to meet its regulatory compliance requirements. Which design factor will most influence the customization of their governance system?
a. Future enterprise size
b. Service delivery methods
c. Compliance requirements
d. Resource constraints

Answer: c. Compliance requirements. Explanation: Compliance requirements significantly influence the customization of the governance system to ensure that all regulatory mandates specific to the healthcare industry are adequately addressed.

53. In the context of COBIT 5, which process is essential for ensuring that IT-related incidents and problems are resolved efficiently, minimizing disruption to business operations?
a. DSS01 Manage Operations
b. DSS02 Manage Service Requests and Incidents
c. BAI04 Manage Availability and Capacity
d. APO10 Manage Suppliers

Answer: b. DSS02 Manage Service Requests and Incidents. Explanation: DSS02 is critical for managing and resolving IT-related incidents and problems efficiently, thereby minimizing disruptions and maintaining business operations.

54. An organization is adopting an Agile methodology for its software development projects. How does Agile address security considerations differently than the traditional Waterfall model?
a. Agile incorporates security testing only at the end of the development cycle.
b. Agile embeds security practices continuously throughout the development process.
c. Agile assumes security testing is the responsibility of a dedicated team at the end.
d. Agile does not prioritize security compared to Waterfall.

Answer: b. Agile embeds security practices continuously throughout the development process. Explanation: Agile methodology integrates security practices throughout the development lifecycle, allowing for continuous security testing and feedback, unlike Waterfall which often addresses security towards the end.

55. During the requirements gathering phase of the SDLC, which security consideration is most crucial?
a. Identifying potential security incidents and response plans.
b. Implementing encryption for data storage.
c. Establishing user access controls and permissions.
d. Conducting threat modeling and risk assessments.

Answer: d. Conducting threat modeling and risk assessments. Explanation: During the requirements gathering phase, it is crucial to identify potential threats and assess risks to ensure security requirements are integrated from the beginning.

56. In the context of DevSecOps, which of the following best describes the integration of security into the CI/CD pipeline?
a. Security is only applied during the deployment phase.
b. Security checks are automated and integrated into every stage of the CI/CD pipeline.
c. Security is manually reviewed at the end of the development cycle.
d. Security is considered only during the initial design phase.

Answer: b. Security checks are automated and integrated into every stage of the CI/CD pipeline. Explanation: DevSecOps promotes the automation of security checks within the Continuous Integration/Continuous Deployment (CI/CD) pipeline, ensuring security is a part of every stage of the development process.

57. Which security practice is essential during the design phase of the SDLC to ensure the development of secure software?
a. Regular code reviews and static analysis.
b. Conducting design reviews and threat modeling.
c. Implementing runtime application self-protection (RASP).

d. Performing regular security audits and compliance checks.

Answer: b. Conducting design reviews and threat modeling. Explanation: During the design phase, conducting design reviews and threat modeling helps identify potential security issues early, enabling the development of a secure architecture.

58. A development team using the Waterfall model is preparing for the testing phase. What is a significant drawback of addressing security primarily during this phase?
a. It ensures that all security vulnerabilities are identified.
b. It allows for comprehensive integration of security controls.
c. It may lead to high costs and delays if significant vulnerabilities are found.
d. It improves the accuracy of security testing outcomes.

Answer: c. It may lead to high costs and delays if significant vulnerabilities are found. Explanation: Addressing security primarily during the testing phase can result in high costs and delays if major vulnerabilities are identified, as fixing them late in the SDLC is more challenging and expensive.

59. In a DevSecOps environment, which tool or practice is most commonly used to ensure code security before deployment?
a. Penetration testing
b. Static Application Security Testing (SAST)
c. Security Information and Event Management (SIEM)
d. Network intrusion detection systems

Answer: b. Static Application Security Testing (SAST). Explanation: SAST tools are used in DevSecOps to analyze source code for security vulnerabilities early in the development cycle, ensuring code security before deployment.

60. Which of the following security practices should be implemented during the development phase of the SDLC to enhance software security?
a. Regular penetration testing by external teams.
b. Dynamic Application Security Testing (DAST).
c. Secure coding standards and practices.
d. Comprehensive user training on security policies.

Answer: c. Secure coding standards and practices. Explanation: During the development phase, implementing secure coding standards and practices is essential to prevent introducing security vulnerabilities into the software.

61. What is the primary benefit of integrating DevSecOps into the SDLC?
a. It reduces the need for security testing.
b. It shifts security responsibilities solely to the development team.

c. It ensures continuous security integration and faster remediation of vulnerabilities.
d. It eliminates the need for security audits.

Answer: c. It ensures continuous security integration and faster remediation of vulnerabilities. Explanation: DevSecOps integrates security continuously throughout the SDLC, facilitating quicker identification and remediation of vulnerabilities, thereby enhancing overall security.

62. A project team is transitioning from a Waterfall to an Agile SDLC model. Which of the following security practices should be adopted to align with Agile principles?
a. Periodic security assessments at major project milestones.
b. Comprehensive security review at the project's conclusion.
c. Continuous security testing and integration into daily builds.
d. Exclusive reliance on third-party security audits.

Answer: c. Continuous security testing and integration into daily builds. Explanation: To align with Agile principles, security practices should involve continuous testing and integration into daily builds, ensuring ongoing security assessment and remediation throughout the development lifecycle.

63. In the context of the SDLC, what is a primary advantage of performing security reviews during the planning phase?
a. It ensures that security is the sole responsibility of the security team.
b. It allows for the early identification and mitigation of potential security risks.
c. It delays the development process, allowing for more thorough testing.
d. It guarantees that all security vulnerabilities will be eliminated.

Answer: b. It allows for the early identification and mitigation of potential security risks. Explanation: Performing security reviews during the planning phase enables early identification and mitigation of potential security risks, facilitating the development of secure software from the outset.

64. A healthcare organization must implement a data classification scheme to protect patient records. Which of the following frameworks provides a method for categorizing information based on the impact of its unauthorized disclosure, modification, or destruction?
a. NIST SP 800-53
b. FIPS 199
c. ISO/IEC 27002
d. HIPAA

Answer: b. FIPS 199. Explanation: FIPS 199 provides a standardized method for categorizing information and information systems based on the potential impact on an organization should certain events occur, such as unauthorized disclosure, modification, or destruction.

65. An organization is developing its data retention policy. Which of the following is the most critical factor to consider when determining the retention period for different types of data?
a. The storage capacity of the organization's servers
b. The potential business value of the data
c. Compliance with applicable legal and regulatory requirements
d. The frequency of data access

Answer: c. Compliance with applicable legal and regulatory requirements. Explanation: Compliance with legal and regulatory requirements is the most critical factor in determining data retention periods to ensure the organization meets all mandated obligations.

66. A financial services company is preparing for a legal hold due to upcoming litigation. What is the first step the company should take to ensure data preservation?
a. Encrypt all sensitive data
b. Implement a comprehensive backup plan
c. Notify relevant personnel and stakeholders about the legal hold
d. Shred all non-essential documents

Answer: c. Notify relevant personnel and stakeholders about the legal hold. Explanation: The first step in preparing for a legal hold is to notify all relevant personnel and stakeholders to ensure they preserve all potentially relevant information and prevent any data destruction.

67. An organization needs to securely dispose of outdated hardware that contains sensitive information. Which method provides the highest level of data security?
a. Overwriting the data multiple times
b. Degaussing the storage media
c. Physically destroying the hardware
d. Reformatting the storage devices

Answer: c. Physically destroying the hardware. Explanation: Physically destroying the hardware ensures that the data cannot be recovered, providing the highest level of data security compared to other methods like overwriting or degaussing.

68. In the context of Information Lifecycle Management, what is the primary purpose of implementing a data classification scheme?
a. To reduce storage costs
b. To prioritize data recovery efforts
c. To ensure that data is handled appropriately based on its sensitivity and value
d. To streamline data migration processes

Answer: c. To ensure that data is handled appropriately based on its sensitivity and value. Explanation: Implementing a data classification scheme helps ensure that data is managed and protected according to its sensitivity and business value, guiding handling, access, and protection measures.

69. A global enterprise is developing a data retention policy for its subsidiaries across multiple jurisdictions. Which of the following challenges is most likely to complicate this process?
a. Variations in data encryption standards
b. Differences in international data retention laws and regulations
c. Inconsistent data classification schemes
d. Divergent data backup technologies

Answer: b. Differences in international data retention laws and regulations. Explanation: Variations in data retention laws and regulations across different jurisdictions complicate the development of a unified data retention policy, requiring careful consideration of each jurisdiction's requirements.

70. An organization opts for crypto-shredding to securely dispose of data. Which of the following best describes this method?
a. Overwriting data on the storage media multiple times with random data
b. Physically destroying the storage media to prevent data recovery
c. Encrypting the data and then deleting the encryption keys
d. Using electromagnetic fields to erase data on the storage media

Answer: c. Encrypting the data and then deleting the encryption keys. Explanation: Crypto-shredding involves encrypting the data and subsequently deleting the encryption keys, rendering the encrypted data inaccessible and effectively destroyed.

71. When implementing a data retention policy, what is the primary risk associated with retaining data for longer than necessary?
a. Increased storage costs
b. Enhanced data availability
c. Higher risk of data breaches and legal exposure
d. Improved data accuracy and integrity

Answer: c. Higher risk of data breaches and legal exposure. Explanation: Retaining data longer than necessary increases the risk of data breaches and legal exposure, as outdated or unnecessary data may be improperly secured or become subject to legal discovery.

72. Which of the following best practices should be followed to ensure secure data disposal in compliance with regulatory requirements?
a. Reformatting the storage device before disposal
b. Performing a factory reset on the device
c. Using certified data destruction services to physically destroy the storage media

d. Archiving the data for future reference

Answer: c. Using certified data destruction services to physically destroy the storage media. Explanation: Using certified data destruction services ensures compliance with regulatory requirements by securely and permanently destroying the storage media, preventing any possibility of data recovery.

73. In the context of FIPS 199, which impact level should be assigned to data where unauthorized disclosure could result in significant harm to individuals or the organization?
a. Low
b. Moderate
c. High
d. Critical

Answer: b. Moderate. Explanation: According to FIPS 199, a "moderate" impact level is assigned to data where unauthorized disclosure could result in significant harm to individuals or the organization, but not catastrophic consequences.

74. A multinational corporation is implementing ISO 27001 and has completed its Statement of Applicability (SoA). During the certification audit, the auditor notes that several controls listed in Annex A of ISO 27001 are marked as "not applicable" without sufficient justification. What is the most appropriate course of action for the organization?
a. Implement all controls in Annex A to ensure compliance
b. Provide a detailed risk assessment justifying each exclusion
c. Remove the excluded controls from the SoA entirely
d. Seek an exemption from the certification body for the excluded controls

Answer: b. Provide a detailed risk assessment justifying each exclusion. Explanation: ISO 27001 requires organizations to justify any exclusions of Annex A controls in their Statement of Applicability. This justification should be based on a thorough risk assessment demonstrating why the control is not applicable or necessary given the organization's specific context and risk profile. Simply implementing all controls (a) may be excessive and not risk-based. Removing excluded controls from the SoA (c) or seeking exemptions (d) would not meet the standard's requirements for transparency and justification.

75. An organization has implemented ISO 27002 controls and is now focusing on continuous improvement. Which of the following metrics would be most effective in measuring the maturity and effectiveness of the implemented information security controls over time?
a. Number of security incidents reported monthly
b. Percentage of employees who completed security awareness training
c. Time taken to patch critical vulnerabilities
d. Key Performance Indicators (KPIs) aligned with each control objective, tracked and trended over multiple periods

Answer: d. Key Performance Indicators (KPIs) aligned with each control objective, tracked and trended over multiple periods. Explanation: While all options provide valuable information, KPIs aligned with each control objective and tracked over time offer the most comprehensive view of control maturity and effectiveness. This approach allows for targeted measurement of each control's performance, enables trend analysis, and supports continuous improvement efforts. Options a, b, and c are useful metrics but are more narrowly focused and don't provide a holistic view of the entire control framework's effectiveness as required by ISO 27002.

76. During a risk assessment conducted using ISO 31000 principles, a financial services company identifies a high likelihood of a cyber attack resulting in data breach. The risk owner proposes purchasing cyber insurance to transfer the risk. Which of the following considerations is most critical in evaluating this risk treatment option?
a. The cost of the insurance premium compared to the potential loss
b. The impact on the organization's risk appetite statement
c. Whether risk transfer aligns with the organization's strategic objectives and risk management principles
d. The insurance provider's credit rating and claim payout history

Answer: c. Whether risk transfer aligns with the organization's strategic objectives and risk management principles. Explanation: While all factors are important, ISO 31000 emphasizes that risk treatment options should be selected based on their alignment with organizational objectives and overall risk management principles. This holistic view ensures that risk treatment decisions support the organization's strategy and values, rather than being made in isolation. Cost considerations (a), impact on risk appetite (b), and insurer reliability (d) are all relevant, but secondary to strategic alignment in the ISO 31000 framework.

77. An organization is implementing an Information Security Management System (ISMS) based on ISO 27001. During the risk assessment phase, they struggle to define the scope of the ISMS. Which of the following approaches best aligns with ISO 27001 requirements for determining ISMS scope?
a. Include all organizational departments and processes to ensure comprehensive coverage
b. Focus solely on IT infrastructure and systems to manage complexity
c. Determine the scope based on the organization's context, interested parties, and interfaces with external entities
d. Limit the scope to critical business functions identified by senior management

Answer: c. Determine the scope based on the organization's context, interested parties, and interfaces with external entities. Explanation: ISO 27001 requires that the ISMS scope be determined considering the organization's context, the needs and expectations of interested parties, and interfaces and dependencies between activities performed by the organization and those performed by other organizations. This approach ensures a relevant and appropriate scope that addresses key risks without unnecessarily expanding or limiting coverage. Options a and b are too broad or narrow, respectively, while d doesn't fully consider all factors required by the standard.

78. A company has implemented ISO 27002 controls and is preparing for an ISO 27001 certification audit. The auditor requests evidence of management commitment to information security. Which of the following would provide the strongest evidence of top management involvement and leadership in the ISMS?
a. A signed information security policy document
b. Records of management participation in risk assessment and treatment decisions
c. An increased budget allocation for the information security department
d. Regular security awareness training attendance by executives

Answer: b. Records of management participation in risk assessment and treatment decisions. Explanation: While all options demonstrate aspects of management commitment, records of management's active participation in risk assessment and treatment decisions provide the strongest evidence of ongoing involvement and leadership in the ISMS. This aligns with ISO 27001's requirement for management to demonstrate leadership and commitment by ensuring the integration of ISMS requirements into the organization's processes and strategic direction. A signed policy (a) is necessary but passive. Budget increases (c) and training attendance (d) are positive but don't directly show strategic involvement in ISMS processes.

79. An organization is implementing ISO 31000 and wants to ensure its risk management framework is effective. Which of the following is the most crucial factor in achieving this goal according to ISO 31000 principles?
a. Establishing a comprehensive risk register covering all potential risks
b. Implementing advanced risk quantification methodologies
c. Integrating risk management into all organizational processes and decision-making
d. Conducting frequent third-party risk assessments

Answer: c. Integrating risk management into all organizational processes and decision-making. Explanation: ISO 31000 emphasizes that risk management should be an integral part of all organizational activities, not a stand-alone function. This integration ensures that risk considerations are embedded in governance, strategy-setting, planning, and all other organizational processes and decisions. While a risk register (a), quantification methods (b), and third-party assessments (d) can be valuable tools, they don't address the fundamental principle of integration that ISO 31000 prioritizes for effective risk management.

80. During an ISO 27001 implementation, an organization is struggling with the concept of "interested parties" as defined in the standard. Which of the following best describes the approach to identifying and addressing the needs of interested parties in the context of an ISMS?
a. Focus exclusively on regulatory bodies and customers to ensure compliance
b. Identify all possible stakeholders and treat their needs equally
c. Determine relevant interested parties based on their ability to affect ISMS outcomes, and prioritize their needs accordingly
d. Limit consideration to internal stakeholders to maintain control over the ISMS

Answer: c. Determine relevant interested parties based on their ability to affect ISMS outcomes, and prioritize their needs accordingly. Explanation: ISO 27001 requires organizations to determine interested parties relevant to the ISMS and their requirements. The key is to focus on parties that can significantly affect or be affected by the organization's information security. This approach allows for a targeted and effective consideration of external context without becoming overwhelmed. Options a and d are too limited, while b could lead to an unmanageable scope. The correct approach balances comprehensiveness with relevance and impact.

81. An organization has implemented ISO 27002 controls but is experiencing a high rate of security incidents despite compliance with the standard. Which of the following actions would be most effective in addressing this issue while maintaining alignment with ISO principles?
a. Implement additional technical controls beyond those specified in ISO 27002
b. Increase the frequency of compliance audits to identify control weaknesses

c. Conduct a thorough review of the risk assessment process and control selection criteria
d. Outsource security operations to a managed security service provider

Answer: c. Conduct a thorough review of the risk assessment process and control selection criteria. Explanation: ISO 27002 provides a comprehensive set of controls, but their effectiveness depends on proper risk assessment and selection based on the organization's specific context and risks. A high incident rate despite compliance suggests a misalignment between implemented controls and actual risks. Reviewing the risk assessment process and control selection criteria addresses the root cause by ensuring controls are appropriate and effective for the organization's specific risk landscape. Options a, b, and d may have benefits but don't address the fundamental issue of control-risk alignment emphasized in ISO standards.

82. A multinational corporation is implementing ISO 31000 and wants to ensure its risk management framework is adaptable to different cultural contexts across its global operations. Which of the following approaches best supports this goal while maintaining consistency with ISO 31000 principles?
a. Implement a standardized risk assessment methodology across all regions
b. Allow each regional office to develop its own risk management approach independently
c. Establish core risk management principles and customize processes for local contexts while maintaining alignment with those principles
d. Centralize all risk management activities at the corporate headquarters

Answer: c. Establish core risk management principles and customize processes for local contexts while maintaining alignment with those principles. Explanation: ISO 31000 emphasizes that risk management should be customized to the organization's context. For a multinational corporation, this means balancing global consistency with local adaptation. Establishing core principles ensures alignment across the organization, while allowing customization of processes accommodates different cultural and operational contexts. This approach maintains the integrity of the risk management framework while enhancing its effectiveness in diverse settings. Options a and d are too rigid, while b could lead to inconsistencies and inefficiencies.

83. During an ISO 27001 certification audit, the auditor identifies a nonconformity related to the organization's information classification scheme. The scheme doesn't adequately address the handling of personal data as required by applicable data protection regulations. Which of the following actions would best address this nonconformity while aligning with ISO 27001 principles?
a. Immediately implement a new classification level specifically for personal data
b. Conduct a gap analysis between current practices and regulatory requirements, then update the classification scheme and related controls accordingly
c. Exclude personal data handling from the ISMS scope to avoid the nonconformity
d. Implement additional technical controls to protect all data equally, regardless of classification

Answer: b. Conduct a gap analysis between current practices and regulatory requirements, then update the classification scheme and related controls accordingly. Explanation: This approach aligns with ISO 27001's emphasis on risk-based decision making and continuous improvement. It addresses the root cause of the nonconformity by ensuring that the classification scheme and related controls are updated to meet both regulatory requirements and the organization's risk profile. Option a is reactive and may not fully address the underlying issues. Option c contradicts ISO 27001's principle of addressing legal and regulatory requirements. Option d doesn't address the specific need for appropriate data classification and handling procedures.

84. An organization is implementing an asset inventory system as part of its asset management program. Which of the following best practices should be prioritized to ensure the accuracy and completeness of the asset inventory?
a. Perform annual asset audits
b. Implement automated asset discovery tools
c. Maintain a manual inventory system
d. Rely on employee self-reporting

Answer: b. Implement automated asset discovery tools. Explanation: Automated asset discovery tools help ensure the accuracy and completeness of the asset inventory by continuously identifying and cataloging assets, reducing the risk of human error and outdated information.

85. During the implementation of a Configuration Management Database (CMDB), which of the following steps is critical to ensure effective configuration management?
a. Documenting all software licenses
b. Establishing relationships between configuration items (CIs)
c. Performing regular backups of all CIs
d. Scheduling weekly CMDB updates

Answer: b. Establishing relationships between configuration items (CIs). Explanation: Establishing relationships between CIs is critical for effective configuration management, as it helps understand dependencies, impacts, and interactions within the IT environment, facilitating more accurate change management and incident response.

86. An IT manager is tasked with improving asset lifecycle management. Which activity should be the initial focus to enhance the overall management of IT assets?
a. Conducting end-of-life asset disposal
b. Tracking asset performance metrics
c. Implementing a standardized procurement process
d. Developing an asset tagging system

Answer: c. Implementing a standardized procurement process. Explanation: A standardized procurement process ensures that all assets are acquired through a controlled, consistent method, allowing for better tracking, inventory management, and lifecycle management from acquisition to disposal.

87. A company is reviewing its asset management policies to ensure compliance with industry standards. Which of the following frameworks is most relevant for guiding asset management practices?
a. NIST SP 800-37
b. ISO/IEC 27002
c. COBIT 2019
d. ITIL

Answer: d. ITIL. Explanation: ITIL (Information Technology Infrastructure Library) provides a comprehensive framework for IT service management, including detailed guidance on asset management practices, ensuring effective management and utilization of IT assets throughout their lifecycle.

88. Which of the following is a primary benefit of maintaining an accurate asset inventory?
a. Reduced need for security policies
b. Improved incident response and recovery
c. Decreased software licensing costs
d. Enhanced user experience

Answer: b. Improved incident response and recovery. Explanation: Maintaining an accurate asset inventory helps quickly identify affected assets during incidents, allowing for more efficient response and recovery efforts, minimizing downtime and impact.

89. A financial institution is implementing a CMDB to enhance its asset management capabilities. What is the primary purpose of a CMDB in this context?
a. To store backup data for all financial transactions
b. To document the configuration and relationships of IT assets
c. To manage customer account information
d. To monitor network traffic in real-time

Answer: b. To document the configuration and relationships of IT assets. Explanation: The primary purpose of a CMDB is to document the configuration and relationships of IT assets, providing a centralized repository that supports change management, incident response, and overall IT governance.

90. During an asset audit, discrepancies are found between the actual assets and the recorded inventory. What is the most effective action to address these discrepancies?
a. Update the inventory records to match the actual assets
b. Ignore minor discrepancies and focus on major ones
c. Conduct a root cause analysis to understand the discrepancies
d. Implement stricter access controls to prevent future discrepancies

Answer: c. Conduct a root cause analysis to understand the discrepancies. Explanation: Conducting a root cause analysis helps identify why discrepancies occurred, enabling the organization to address underlying issues and improve the accuracy and reliability of the asset inventory.

91. An organization wants to enhance its asset lifecycle management by integrating sustainability practices. Which of the following actions aligns with this goal?
a. Implementing a rapid deployment process

b. Establishing a recycling and disposal program for obsolete assets
c. Reducing the frequency of asset audits
d. Increasing the procurement of single-use assets

Answer: b. Establishing a recycling and disposal program for obsolete assets. Explanation: Integrating sustainability practices into asset lifecycle management includes establishing a recycling and disposal program, ensuring that obsolete assets are disposed of in an environmentally responsible manner.

92. A company's IT department is responsible for managing the lifecycle of all IT assets. Which phase of the asset lifecycle should focus on the decommissioning and secure disposal of assets?
a. Acquisition phase
b. Operation and maintenance phase
c. Disposal phase
d. Planning phase

Answer: c. Disposal phase. Explanation: The disposal phase focuses on the decommissioning and secure disposal of assets, ensuring that sensitive data is removed and the asset is disposed of according to environmental and regulatory requirements.

93. An organization is using a CMDB to manage its IT assets. Which of the following is a key feature that distinguishes a CMDB from a simple asset inventory?
a. Listing all hardware and software assets
b. Tracking asset purchase dates and costs
c. Documenting configuration details and relationships between assets
d. Maintaining a log of asset usage hours

Answer: c. Documenting configuration details and relationships between assets. Explanation: A CMDB not only lists assets but also documents their configuration details and relationships, providing a comprehensive view of the IT environment and supporting effective management and decision-making.

94. An organization is adopting cloud services and needs to understand the concept of control inheritance. Which of the following best describes control inheritance in a cloud environment?
a. The cloud service provider automatically inherits all security controls from the client
b. Security controls implemented by the cloud service provider that are inherited by the client
c. The client inherits the risk assessment processes of the cloud service provider
d. Security controls that are only applicable to the client's on-premises infrastructure

Answer: b. Security controls implemented by the cloud service provider that are inherited by the client. Explanation: In a cloud environment, control inheritance refers to the security controls that are implemented by the cloud service provider and are applicable to the client's environment, thus reducing the need for the client to implement these controls independently.

95. During a privacy impact assessment (PIA), which of the following privacy-enhancing technologies (PETs) would be most effective in minimizing the collection of personally identifiable information (PII)?
a. Encryption
b. Anonymization
c. Multi-factor authentication
d. Data backup

Answer: b. Anonymization. Explanation: Anonymization is a PET that minimizes the collection of PII by removing or masking identifiable information, thus protecting individuals' privacy and reducing the risk of unauthorized disclosure.

96. An organization is implementing NIST SP 800-53 controls for a new information system. Which control family focuses on establishing policies and procedures for managing information security within the organization?
a. Access Control (AC)
b. Security Assessment and Authorization (CA)
c. Planning (PL)
d. System and Services Acquisition (SA)

Answer: c. Planning (PL). Explanation: The Planning (PL) control family in NIST SP 800-53 focuses on establishing policies and procedures for managing information security within the organization, including the development of security plans and related documentation.

97. A healthcare provider needs to ensure compliance with security and privacy regulations. Which NIST SP 800-53 control family is most relevant for protecting the confidentiality, integrity, and availability of patient records?
a. Incident Response (IR)
b. Personnel Security (PS)
c. Media Protection (MP)
d. Access Control (AC)

Answer: d. Access Control (AC). Explanation: The Access Control (AC) control family is most relevant for protecting patient records by ensuring that only authorized individuals have access to sensitive information, thereby maintaining its confidentiality, integrity, and availability.

98. In the context of NIST SP 800-53, which control family addresses the need for contingency planning to ensure the continuity of operations during and after a disruption?
a. Risk Assessment (RA)
b. Contingency Planning (CP)
c. System and Communications Protection (SC)
d. Configuration Management (CM)

Answer: b. Contingency Planning (CP). Explanation: The Contingency Planning (CP) control family focuses on establishing plans and procedures to ensure the continuity of operations during and after a disruption, covering aspects such as disaster recovery and business continuity.

99. An organization plans to implement privacy-enhancing technologies (PETs) to comply with GDPR requirements. Which of the following PETs is specifically designed to ensure data minimization?
a. Homomorphic encryption
b. Differential privacy
c. Secure multiparty computation
d. Data masking

Answer: b. Differential privacy. Explanation: Differential privacy is a PET designed to ensure data minimization by allowing organizations to collect and share aggregate data while minimizing the risk of identifying individuals within the dataset.

100. When conducting a security assessment using NIST SP 800-53 controls, which control family focuses on establishing mechanisms for incident detection and response?
a. System and Information Integrity (SI)
b. Program Management (PM)
c. Maintenance (MA)
d. Incident Response (IR)

Answer: d. Incident Response (IR). Explanation: The Incident Response (IR) control family focuses on establishing mechanisms for detecting, reporting, and responding to security incidents to mitigate their impact and prevent future occurrences.

101. A company needs to implement controls for secure data disposal to comply with NIST SP 800-53 guidelines. Which control family addresses the procedures for media sanitization and disposal?
a. Media Protection (MP)
b. System and Information Integrity (SI)
c. Physical and Environmental Protection (PE)
d. System and Communications Protection (SC)

Answer: a. Media Protection (MP). Explanation: The Media Protection (MP) control family addresses procedures for media sanitization and disposal, ensuring that data is securely removed from storage media to prevent unauthorized access or disclosure.

102. In a cloud environment, which of the following is an example of a control that the cloud service provider is typically responsible for implementing and maintaining?
a. User access management
b. Data encryption at rest
c. Endpoint protection on client devices

d. Security awareness training for client employees

Answer: b. Data encryption at rest. Explanation: In a cloud environment, the cloud service provider is typically responsible for implementing and maintaining controls such as data encryption at rest, ensuring that stored data is protected from unauthorized access.

103. Which privacy-enhancing technology (PET) allows multiple parties to jointly compute a function over their inputs while keeping those inputs private?
a. Homomorphic encryption
b. Secure multiparty computation
c. Tokenization
d. Data anonymization

Answer: b. Secure multiparty computation. Explanation: Secure multiparty computation is a PET that allows multiple parties to jointly compute a function over their inputs while keeping those inputs private, ensuring data confidentiality and privacy.

104. A financial institution is implementing a new online transaction system and needs to ensure non-repudiation for all customer transactions. Which combination of technologies would best achieve this goal while also maintaining confidentiality?
a. SSL/TLS encryption and multi-factor authentication
b. Digital signatures with PKI and encrypted audit logs
c. Biometric authentication and blockchain ledger
d. One-time passwords and encrypted database backups

Answer: b. Digital signatures with PKI and encrypted audit logs. Explanation: Digital signatures using Public Key Infrastructure (PKI) provide strong non-repudiation by uniquely identifying the signer and ensuring the integrity of the signed data. Encrypted audit logs further enhance non-repudiation by securely recording transaction details. This combination addresses both non-repudiation and confidentiality requirements. SSL/TLS (a) provides confidentiality but not non-repudiation. Biometrics and blockchain (c) can support non-repudiation but may have privacy implications. One-time passwords and backups (d) don't directly address non-repudiation.

105. An organization is designing a high-availability system for its critical web application. Which of the following architectures would provide the highest level of availability while also considering potential points of failure?
a. Active-passive failover with a single load balancer
b. Active-active cluster with DNS round-robin
c. Active-active cluster with redundant load balancers and geographic distribution
d. Cloud-based auto-scaling with a single region deployment

Answer: c. Active-active cluster with redundant load balancers and geographic distribution. Explanation: This architecture offers the highest availability by eliminating single points of failure and providing geographic redundancy.

Active-active clusters ensure continuous operation, redundant load balancers prevent bottlenecks, and geographic distribution mitigates regional outages. Option (a) has a single point of failure in the load balancer. DNS round-robin (b) doesn't handle real-time failure as effectively. Single region deployment (d) is vulnerable to regional outages.

106. A company is implementing a data loss prevention (DLP) system to protect sensitive information. Which of the following techniques would be most effective in preserving confidentiality while allowing necessary business operations?
a. Full disk encryption on all endpoints
b. Content-aware DLP with policy-based encryption and access controls
c. Network segmentation with strict firewall rules
d. Mandatory access control (MAC) on all systems

Answer: b. Content-aware DLP with policy-based encryption and access controls. Explanation: Content-aware DLP can identify sensitive data and apply appropriate protections based on predefined policies, balancing security with operational needs. It can encrypt data in transit and at rest while allowing authorized access. Full disk encryption (a) protects data at rest but not in use or transit. Network segmentation (c) helps but doesn't address data handling directly. MAC (d) can be too restrictive for many business environments and doesn't address data in transit.

107. An organization wants to implement a robust integrity checking mechanism for its software distribution process. Which of the following approaches provides the strongest integrity assurance while also supporting non-repudiation?
a. MD5 hashing of software packages
b. SHA-256 hashing with a published hash value
c. Digital signatures using code signing certificates
d. Cyclic Redundancy Check (CRC) with encrypted transmission

Answer: c. Digital signatures using code signing certificates. Explanation: Digital signatures using code signing certificates provide both integrity checking and non-repudiation. They ensure the software hasn't been altered (integrity) and verify its origin (non-repudiation). MD5 (a) is considered cryptographically broken. SHA-256 (b) provides integrity but not non-repudiation. CRC (d) is for error detection, not cryptographic integrity, and encrypted transmission doesn't provide non-repudiation.

108. A critical system requires 99.999% availability ("five nines"). Which of the following strategies would be most effective in achieving this level of availability?
a. Implementing RAID 10 for all storage systems
b. Using active-active clustering with automatic failover
c. Employing a comprehensive approach including redundant hardware, multiple data centers, and continuous monitoring with automated recovery
d. Utilizing cloud-based services with a guaranteed SLA of 99.999%

Answer: c. Employing a comprehensive approach including redundant hardware, multiple data centers, and continuous monitoring with automated recovery. Explanation: Achieving "five nines" availability requires a multi-faceted approach addressing all potential points of failure. This includes hardware redundancy, geographic distribution to mitigate regional issues, and automated systems for quick recovery. RAID 10 (a) addresses only storage reliability. Active-active clustering (b) is important but insufficient alone. Cloud SLAs (d) typically have exclusions and don't guarantee this level of availability for the entire system.

109. An organization needs to implement a secure file transfer system that ensures confidentiality, integrity, and non-repudiation. Which of the following solutions best meets all these requirements?
a. SFTP with password authentication
b. HTTPS file upload with client certificates
c. PGP-encrypted email attachments
d. Secure FTP with digital signatures and recipient-specific encryption

Answer: d. Secure FTP with digital signatures and recipient-specific encryption. Explanation: This solution addresses all requirements: encryption ensures confidentiality, digital signatures provide integrity and non-repudiation, and recipient-specific encryption enhances confidentiality and access control. SFTP (a) lacks non-repudiation. HTTPS with client certificates (b) provides confidentiality and some non-repudiation but may not ensure end-to-end encryption. PGP email (c) is suitable for small transfers but less efficient for large files or frequent transfers.

110. A financial services company is implementing a blockchain-based system for inter-bank transactions. Which aspect of the CIA triad does blockchain technology inherently strengthen the most?
a. Confidentiality
b. Integrity
c. Availability
d. All aspects equally

Answer: b. Integrity. Explanation: Blockchain technology inherently strengthens integrity through its immutable ledger and consensus mechanisms. Once a transaction is recorded and confirmed, it cannot be altered without consensus from the network, ensuring data integrity. While blockchain can support confidentiality through encryption and availability through distributed networks, its primary strength lies in maintaining data integrity. The immutability and transparency of blockchain transactions don't automatically ensure confidentiality (a) or availability (c).

111. An organization is implementing a zero-trust architecture to enhance its security posture. Which of the following principles is most critical in preserving confidentiality within a zero-trust model?
a. Network segmentation
b. Multi-factor authentication
c. Continuous monitoring and logging
d. Least privilege access with just-in-time (JIT) provisioning

Answer: d. Least privilege access with just-in-time (JIT) provisioning. Explanation: In a zero-trust model, least privilege access combined with JIT provisioning is crucial for preserving confidentiality. This approach ensures users have only the minimum necessary access for the shortest required time, significantly reducing the risk of unauthorized data exposure. While network segmentation (a), multi-factor authentication (b), and continuous monitoring (c) are important in zero-trust, they don't directly address the principle of minimizing unnecessary access to confidential information.

112. A company is designing a disaster recovery plan for its mission-critical systems. Which of the following recovery time objective (RTO) and recovery point objective (RPO) combinations would provide the highest level of availability while being technically and economically feasible for most organizations?
a. RTO: 0 seconds, RPO: 0 seconds
b. RTO: 4 hours, RPO: 15 minutes
c. RTO: 24 hours, RPO: 1 hour
d. RTO: 1 hour, RPO: 0 seconds

Answer: b. RTO: 4 hours, RPO: 15 minutes. Explanation: This combination balances high availability with feasibility. An RTO of 4 hours allows for robust recovery procedures without requiring instant failover, which can be extremely costly. An RPO of 15 minutes ensures minimal data loss while being achievable with current replication technologies. Option (a) represents zero downtime and data loss, which is often prohibitively expensive. Option (c) has too long an RTO for mission-critical systems. Option (d) has a challenging RTO with a perfect RPO, which is often technically difficult to achieve.

113. An e-commerce platform needs to implement a system ensuring non-repudiation for customer orders while maintaining high performance during peak shopping periods. Which of the following approaches best addresses both requirements?
a. Synchronous digital signatures for each transaction
b. Blockchain-based ledger for all transactions
c. Asynchronous digital signatures with a centralized timestamping service
d. Multi-factor authentication with detailed server-side logging

Answer: c. Asynchronous digital signatures with a centralized timestamping service. Explanation: This approach balances non-repudiation with performance. Asynchronous signatures allow the main transaction processing to continue without waiting for signature verification, maintaining performance. The centralized timestamping service provides a trusted time reference, enhancing non-repudiation. Synchronous signatures (a) could impact performance during high loads. Blockchain (b) might introduce latency and scalability issues. Multi-factor authentication and logging (d) enhance security but don't provide strong non-repudiation for individual transactions.

114. An organization is establishing a compliance program and needs to develop a compliance charter. Which of the following elements is most critical to include in the compliance charter to ensure it is effective?
a. Detailed job descriptions for all compliance staff
b. The organization's mission and values
c. Specific procedures for handling compliance violations
d. The scope, authority, and responsibilities of the compliance program

Answer: d. The scope, authority, and responsibilities of the compliance program. Explanation: The compliance charter should clearly define the scope, authority, and responsibilities of the compliance program to ensure clarity and accountability, providing a solid foundation for the program's effectiveness.

115. Which of the following is a key performance indicator (KPI) that can effectively measure the success of a compliance training program?
a. The number of training sessions conducted
b. Employee satisfaction with the training program
c. The percentage of employees completing the training on time
d. The frequency of compliance violations before and after training

Answer: d. The frequency of compliance violations before and after training. Explanation: Measuring the frequency of compliance violations before and after training provides a direct indicator of the training program's effectiveness in improving compliance behavior.

116. A company is developing a compliance awareness strategy. Which approach is most likely to ensure continuous employee engagement and retention of compliance information?
a. Annual compliance training sessions
b. Interactive and gamified training modules
c. Detailed compliance manuals distributed to all employees
d. Monthly newsletters highlighting compliance policies

Answer: b. Interactive and gamified training modules. Explanation: Interactive and gamified training modules engage employees actively, making learning more enjoyable and memorable, thus improving retention of compliance information.

117. In the context of establishing a compliance program, what is the primary purpose of conducting a risk assessment?
a. To identify and prioritize compliance risks
b. To develop a compliance communication plan
c. To create a budget for compliance activities
d. To document compliance policies and procedures

Answer: a. To identify and prioritize compliance risks. Explanation: Conducting a risk assessment helps identify and prioritize compliance risks, ensuring that the compliance program focuses on the most significant areas of concern and allocates resources effectively.

118. When developing a compliance training program, which of the following methods is most effective in ensuring that employees understand and apply compliance policies?
a. Reading and signing off on compliance policy documents
b. Classroom-based training sessions with quizzes
c. Online training modules with interactive scenarios
d. Watching compliance-related videos

Answer: c. Online training modules with interactive scenarios. Explanation: Online training modules with interactive scenarios allow employees to engage with real-world situations, enhancing their understanding and ability to apply compliance policies effectively.

119. A financial institution needs to track the effectiveness of its compliance program. Which KPI would best indicate ongoing compliance adherence across the organization?
a. The total number of compliance audits conducted annually
b. The percentage of employees who receive compliance training
c. The rate of compliance issues identified during internal audits
d. The budget allocated to the compliance department

Answer: c. The rate of compliance issues identified during internal audits. Explanation: The rate of compliance issues identified during internal audits provides insight into how well compliance policies are being followed and where improvements may be needed.

120. During the development of a compliance charter, which stakeholder group is most critical to involve to ensure the charter is comprehensive and enforceable?
a. External auditors
b. Middle management
c. Legal and compliance teams
d. IT department

Answer: c. Legal and compliance teams. Explanation: Involving the legal and compliance teams is crucial as they have the expertise to ensure the charter is comprehensive, aligns with legal requirements, and is enforceable within the organization.

121. A multinational company is rolling out a compliance program across different regions. What is the most effective strategy to address varying regional regulations and ensure global compliance?
a. Implement a single global compliance policy
b. Tailor the compliance program to meet specific regional regulations
c. Focus only on the most stringent regulations globally
d. Centralize compliance management at the headquarters

Answer: b. Tailor the compliance program to meet specific regional regulations. Explanation: Tailoring the compliance program to meet regional regulations ensures that the program is relevant and effective in each region, addressing local legal and regulatory requirements.

122. Which of the following is a primary benefit of establishing a compliance program charter?
a. It reduces the need for external audits.
b. It outlines the penalties for non-compliance.
c. It formalizes the compliance program's purpose and framework.
d. It provides detailed instructions for compliance training.

Answer: c. It formalizes the compliance program's purpose and framework. Explanation: A compliance program charter formalizes the program's purpose, scope, and framework, providing a clear and authoritative guide for compliance activities and accountability.

123. An organization wants to measure the impact of its compliance program on overall corporate governance. Which metric would best provide this insight?
a. Employee participation rate in compliance training
b. The number of regulatory fines imposed annually
c. The effectiveness of internal control audits
d. The frequency of compliance-related internal reports

Answer: b. The number of regulatory fines imposed annually. Explanation: The number of regulatory fines imposed annually is a direct measure of how well the organization adheres to compliance requirements, reflecting the program's impact on corporate governance.

124. A cloud service provider (CSP) is seeking FedRAMP authorization to offer services to federal agencies. Which initial document must the CSP submit to begin the authorization process?
a. Security Assessment Plan (SAP)
b. System Security Plan (SSP)
c. Security Assessment Report (SAR)
d. Authorization to Operate (ATO) letter

Answer: b. System Security Plan (SSP). Explanation: The System Security Plan (SSP) is the initial document that a CSP must submit, detailing the system's security controls and how they meet FedRAMP requirements, forming the basis for further assessment and authorization.

125. An organization is reviewing its security controls to meet the FedRAMP Moderate baseline requirements. Which of the following controls is typically more stringent at the Moderate level compared to the Low baseline?
a. Account management controls
b. Physical access controls
c. Encryption standards for data at rest
d. Incident response planning

Answer: c. Encryption standards for data at rest. Explanation: FedRAMP Moderate baseline includes more stringent encryption requirements for data at rest compared to the Low baseline, ensuring higher protection for sensitive data.

126. During the FedRAMP authorization process, a Third-Party Assessment Organization (3PAO) plays a crucial role. What is the primary responsibility of a 3PAO?
a. Developing the CSP's System Security Plan (SSP)

b. Issuing the Authorization to Operate (ATO) letter
c. Conducting an independent security assessment of the CSP's system
d. Providing continuous monitoring services

Answer: c. Conducting an independent security assessment of the CSP's system. Explanation: A 3PAO is responsible for performing an independent security assessment to verify that the CSP's system meets FedRAMP requirements and operates as described in the SSP.

127. A federal agency is using a cloud service with FedRAMP High authorization. Which of the following security controls is likely to be implemented more rigorously in a High baseline compared to a Moderate baseline?
a. User training and awareness programs
b. Multi-factor authentication for privileged access
c. Backup and recovery procedures
d. Patch management policies

Answer: b. Multi-factor authentication for privileged access. Explanation: The High baseline requires more rigorous implementation of security controls, such as multi-factor authentication for privileged access, to protect highly sensitive information.

128. Continuous monitoring is a key component of FedRAMP compliance. Which activity is NOT typically part of a continuous monitoring program?
a. Regular vulnerability scanning
b. Real-time security event analysis
c. Quarterly reviews of the System Security Plan (SSP)
d. Annual reauthorization assessments

Answer: d. Annual reauthorization assessments. Explanation: Continuous monitoring involves ongoing activities such as vulnerability scanning and real-time event analysis. Annual reauthorization assessments are periodic reviews but not a part of continuous monitoring activities.

129. A cloud service provider is preparing for a FedRAMP audit. Which document would detail the results of security control assessments and any findings?
a. System Security Plan (SSP)
b. Security Assessment Report (SAR)
c. Plan of Action and Milestones (POA&M)
d. Incident Response Plan (IRP)

Answer: b. Security Assessment Report (SAR). Explanation: The Security Assessment Report (SAR) details the results of the security control assessments, including any findings and recommendations for addressing identified vulnerabilities.

130. In the context of FedRAMP continuous monitoring, what is the purpose of the Plan of Action and Milestones (POA&M)?
a. To document security incidents and response actions
b. To outline the system's security baseline requirements
c. To identify and manage risks associated with system vulnerabilities
d. To track the progress of security control implementation

Answer: c. To identify and manage risks associated with system vulnerabilities. Explanation: The POA&M is used to document identified security vulnerabilities and manage the associated risks by outlining corrective actions and tracking their progress.

131. A cloud service provider seeking FedRAMP Moderate authorization needs to demonstrate compliance with several control families. Which control family focuses on ensuring secure configuration settings for information systems?
a. Access Control (AC)
b. Configuration Management (CM)
c. Risk Assessment (RA)
d. Security Assessment and Authorization (CA)

Answer: b. Configuration Management (CM). Explanation: The Configuration Management (CM) control family focuses on ensuring that information systems are securely configured and maintained, addressing vulnerabilities related to system configurations.

132. What role does the Joint Authorization Board (JAB) play in the FedRAMP authorization process?
a. Performing independent security assessments
b. Issuing security assessment reports
c. Granting Provisional Authorizations to Operate (P-ATOs)
d. Conducting continuous monitoring of authorized systems

Answer: c. Granting Provisional Authorizations to Operate (P-ATOs). Explanation: The JAB reviews security documentation and assessment reports and grants Provisional Authorizations to Operate (P-ATOs) for cloud services, indicating that the services meet FedRAMP requirements.

133. In a FedRAMP continuous monitoring program, how often must a cloud service provider typically submit vulnerability scan results for review?
a. Monthly
b. Quarterly
c. Semi-annually
d. Annually

Answer: a. Monthly. Explanation: Cloud service providers must submit vulnerability scan results monthly as part of their continuous monitoring program to ensure ongoing compliance and security of the authorized system.

134. A large e-commerce company is preparing for its annual PCI DSS assessment. During the scoping process, they identify a legacy system that processes cardholder data but cannot be easily upgraded to meet PCI DSS requirements. Which of the following approaches would be most appropriate to address this situation while maintaining compliance?
a. Implement network segmentation to isolate the legacy system
b. Develop and document compensating controls for the legacy system
c. Exclude the legacy system from the CDE scope
d. Outsource the functionality of the legacy system to a compliant third-party provider

Answer: b. Develop and document compensating controls for the legacy system. Explanation: When a system cannot meet specific PCI DSS requirements due to legitimate technical or business constraints, developing compensating controls is an appropriate approach. These controls must meet the intent and rigor of the original requirement and provide a similar level of defense. Network segmentation (a) alone doesn't address the compliance gap. Excluding the system from scope (c) is not valid if it processes cardholder data. Outsourcing (d) may be a long-term solution but doesn't address immediate compliance needs.

135. An organization is implementing PCI DSS Requirement 3.4 for protecting stored cardholder data. Which of the following methods provides the strongest protection while still allowing the last four digits of the PAN to be displayed for business purposes?
a. One-way hash of the entire PAN
b. Strong cryptography with associated key management processes
c. Tokenization with the ability to detokenize when necessary
d. Index tokens and pads

Answer: c. Tokenization with the ability to detokenize when necessary. Explanation: Tokenization replaces the PAN with a token while securely storing the original data, allowing for strong protection and the ability to retrieve the full PAN when necessary. It also easily allows display of the last four digits. One-way hashing (a) doesn't allow for retrieval of the original PAN. Strong cryptography (b) is acceptable but may be more complex to manage. Index tokens and pads (d) are not a standard method in PCI DSS and may not provide sufficient security.

136. During a PCI DSS assessment, an auditor finds that a company's password policy allows for passwords with a minimum length of 7 characters, contradicting Requirement 8.2.3. The company argues that their implementation of multi-factor authentication (MFA) compensates for this. Which of the following is the most appropriate evaluation of this situation?
a. The use of MFA fully compensates for the password length discrepancy
b. The password policy must be changed to meet the requirement regardless of MFA
c. A formal compensating control worksheet must be completed and evaluated
d. The company can be considered compliant if they implement password complexity rules

Answer: c. A formal compensating control worksheet must be completed and evaluated. Explanation: When an entity cannot meet a PCI DSS requirement exactly as stated, a formal compensating control worksheet must be completed. This documents the constraint, the proposed compensating control, and how it addresses the intent of the original requirement. While MFA strengthens authentication, it doesn't automatically compensate for not meeting specific password requirements. The worksheet allows for a thorough evaluation of the proposed alternative. Options (a) and (b) are too absolute, while (d) doesn't address the specific issue of password length.

137. A retail company is implementing a new point-of-sale (POS) system and needs to ensure PCI DSS compliance. Which of the following configurations would best satisfy Requirement 3.2 regarding storage of sensitive authentication data after authorization?
a. Encrypt and store the full magnetic stripe data for 30 days for chargeback resolution
b. Store the CVV2 code in a separate, access-controlled database for recurring transactions
c. Hash and store the PIN blocks for fraud analysis purposes
d. Do not store any sensitive authentication data post-authorization

Answer: d. Do not store any sensitive authentication data post-authorization. Explanation: PCI DSS Requirement 3.2 explicitly prohibits storing sensitive authentication data after authorization, even if encrypted. This includes full track data, CVV2/CVC2 codes, and PIN blocks. The correct approach is to not store this data at all post-authorization. Options (a), (b), and (c) all violate this requirement, regardless of the security measures applied or the business justification provided.

138. An organization is scoping its Cardholder Data Environment (CDE) for PCI DSS compliance. Which of the following systems should be included in the CDE scope?
a. HR system containing employee social security numbers
b. Marketing database with customer email addresses
c. Network monitoring tool that can access systems processing cardholder data
d. Guest Wi-Fi network isolated from the corporate network

Answer: c. Network monitoring tool that can access systems processing cardholder data. Explanation: PCI DSS scoping requires inclusion of all systems that store, process, or transmit cardholder data, as well as systems that could impact the security of the CDE. A network monitoring tool with access to cardholder data processing systems could potentially impact CDE security and must be included in scope. The HR system (a) and marketing database (b) don't handle cardholder data. The isolated guest Wi-Fi (d) doesn't impact the CDE if truly segregated.

139. A company is implementing PCI DSS Requirement 6.6 for protecting public-facing web applications. They have limited resources and must choose between implementing a Web Application Firewall (WAF) or conducting application vulnerability security assessments. Which of the following factors is most critical in making this decision?
a. The cost difference between WAF implementation and vulnerability assessments
b. The company's current patch management capabilities
c. The complexity and change frequency of the web applications
d. The preference of the acquiring bank

Answer: c. The complexity and change frequency of the web applications. Explanation: The choice between a WAF and vulnerability assessments should primarily be based on the nature of the web applications. Highly complex or frequently changing applications may benefit more from a WAF, which can provide real-time protection against evolving threats. Vulnerability assessments are more suitable for stable applications with less frequent changes. While cost (a) is a factor, it shouldn't be the primary consideration for security decisions. Patch management (b) is important but not directly related to this choice. The acquiring bank's preference (d) may be considered but isn't the most critical factor in this technical decision.

140. An e-commerce platform is implementing tokenization to protect stored cardholder data. Which of the following approaches best satisfies PCI DSS requirements while minimizing the compliance scope?
a. Use reversible encryption to generate tokens, storing the encryption keys in a separate, secure location
b. Implement format-preserving tokenization, maintaining the original PAN format for all tokens
c. Generate non-reversible tokens for storage and processing, with the detokenization process occurring outside the e-commerce environment
d. Create tokens using a combination of one-way hashing and partial PAN data

Answer: c. Generate non-reversible tokens for storage and processing, with the detokenization process occurring outside the e-commerce environment. Explanation: This approach provides strong protection for cardholder data while significantly reducing the PCI DSS compliance scope of the e-commerce platform. By using non-reversible tokens and keeping the detokenization process separate, the platform itself doesn't store or process actual PANs, minimizing its compliance requirements. Option (a) introduces key management complexities. Format-preserving tokenization (b) may inadvertently expand the compliance scope. Combining hashing with partial PAN data (d) could potentially allow for PAN reconstruction, violating PCI DSS.

141. A company is implementing PCI DSS Requirement 10 for tracking and monitoring access to cardholder data. They are struggling to meet the requirement for daily log reviews due to the volume of log data. Which of the following solutions best addresses this challenge while maintaining compliance?
a. Review a random sample of 10% of logs daily
b. Implement automated log analysis tools with alert mechanisms for suspicious activities
c. Outsource log review to a managed security service provider
d. Reduce the types of events being logged to manageable levels

Answer: b. Implement automated log analysis tools with alert mechanisms for suspicious activities. Explanation: Automated log analysis tools with alerting capabilities can satisfy the daily log review requirement efficiently, even with large volumes of data. This approach allows for comprehensive monitoring while focusing human attention on suspicious or anomalous activities. Sampling logs (a) may miss critical events. Outsourcing (c) is acceptable but doesn't address the core issue of efficient review. Reducing logged event types (d) could result in missing important security information and violate PCI DSS requirements.

142. An organization is preparing for PCI DSS compliance and discovers that its legacy backup system cannot encrypt cardholder data backups as required by Requirement 3.4. Which of the following would be the most appropriate compensating control?
a. Store backup media in a secure, access-controlled facility
b. Implement strong access controls and logging on the backup system
c. Use full-disk encryption on the backup server

d. Encrypt the network path used to transfer backups

Answer: c. Use full-disk encryption on the backup server. Explanation: When the backup system itself cannot encrypt data, full-disk encryption on the backup server can serve as an effective compensating control. This ensures that all data stored on the server, including backups, is encrypted at rest, meeting the intent of Requirement 3.4. Secure storage (a) and access controls (b) are important but don't directly address the encryption requirement. Encrypting the network path (d) only protects data in transit, not at rest on the backup server.

143. A multinational corporation is implementing PCI DSS controls across its global operations. They find that a specific requirement conflicts with local laws in one country. How should they address this situation to maintain PCI DSS compliance?
a. Ignore the conflicting requirement in that country and document the legal conflict
b. Implement the PCI DSS requirement regardless of local laws
c. Develop compensating controls that meet the intent of the requirement without violating local laws
d. Exclude the operations in that country from PCI DSS scope

Answer: c. Develop compensating controls that meet the intent of the requirement without violating local laws. Explanation: When PCI DSS requirements conflict with local laws, the appropriate approach is to develop compensating controls that meet the security intent of the original requirement while complying with local regulations. This maintains the spirit of PCI DSS compliance without legal violations. Simply ignoring the requirement (a) or implementing it despite legal conflicts (b) are not acceptable approaches. Excluding operations from scope (d) is not viable if they handle cardholder data.

144. A company is aiming to achieve CMMC Level 3 certification. Which of the following practices is a key requirement at this level that is not present at Level 1?
a. Perform basic cybersecurity hygiene
b. Implement multifactor authentication
c. Conduct continuous monitoring
d. Documented cybersecurity policies and procedures

Answer: d. Documented cybersecurity policies and procedures. Explanation: CMMC Level 3 requires organizations to have documented cybersecurity policies and procedures, which is not required at Level 1. This ensures a more structured approach to managing cybersecurity practices.

145. During a CMMC assessment, which of the following is a primary focus for auditors when evaluating an organization's adherence to the framework?
a. The number of cybersecurity incidents in the past year
b. The presence of a certified cybersecurity professional on staff
c. The implementation and effectiveness of required practices and processes
d. The company's overall IT budget

Answer: c. The implementation and effectiveness of required practices and processes. Explanation: The CMMC assessment focuses on the implementation and effectiveness of cybersecurity practices and processes specified for the required level, ensuring that the organization meets the necessary standards.

146. Which CMMC level is specifically designed to protect Controlled Unclassified Information (CUI) and requires the implementation of security controls from NIST SP 800-171?
a. Level 1
b. Level 2
c. Level 3
d. Level 4

Answer: c. Level 3. Explanation: CMMC Level 3 is designed to protect CUI and requires organizations to implement security controls as specified in NIST SP 800-171, ensuring the confidentiality of sensitive information.

147. A defense contractor is preparing for a CMMC assessment. Which of the following steps should they prioritize to ensure compliance with CMMC Level 3?
a. Increase the cybersecurity budget significantly
b. Align existing security practices with NIST SP 800-171 controls
c. Hire an external cybersecurity firm to manage their security operations
d. Conduct an annual cybersecurity awareness training for all employees

Answer: b. Align existing security practices with NIST SP 800-171 controls. Explanation: For CMMC Level 3, organizations must align their security practices with the controls specified in NIST SP 800-171 to protect CUI and meet compliance requirements.

148. In comparing CMMC and NIST SP 800-171, which of the following is a key difference between the two frameworks?
a. NIST SP 800-171 includes more stringent physical security requirements
b. CMMC includes a certification requirement with third-party assessments
c. NIST SP 800-171 is applicable only to federal agencies
d. CMMC focuses solely on technical controls

Answer: b. CMMC includes a certification requirement with third-party assessments. Explanation: Unlike NIST SP 800-171, CMMC requires third-party assessments for certification, ensuring that organizations are independently verified for compliance.

149. A small business is seeking CMMC Level 1 certification. Which of the following practices must they implement to achieve this certification?
a. Advanced persistent threat (APT) detection mechanisms
b. Basic cybersecurity hygiene practices
c. Continuous security monitoring
d. Incident response plan and testing

Answer: b. Basic cybersecurity hygiene practices. Explanation: CMMC Level 1 focuses on basic cybersecurity hygiene practices to protect Federal Contract Information (FCI), which includes fundamental security measures.

150. During the CMMC assessment process, what is the primary role of the Certified Third-Party Assessor Organization (C3PAO)?
a. To provide cybersecurity training to the organization's staff
b. To independently verify and validate the organization's compliance with CMMC requirements
c. To develop the organization's cybersecurity policies and procedures
d. To manage the organization's day-to-day cybersecurity operations

Answer: b. To independently verify and validate the organization's compliance with CMMC requirements. Explanation: The C3PAO's primary role is to conduct independent assessments to verify and validate that organizations meet the specified CMMC requirements.

151. Which domain within the CMMC framework includes practices related to managing physical access to information systems and facilities?
a. Access Control (AC)
b. Physical Protection (PE)
c. Asset Management (AM)
d. Incident Response (IR)

Answer: b. Physical Protection (PE). Explanation: The Physical Protection (PE) domain within the CMMC framework includes practices for managing physical access to information systems and facilities, ensuring that only authorized personnel have access.

152. An organization is confused about the different CMMC levels. How does CMMC Level 5 differ fundamentally from the lower levels?
a. It focuses exclusively on compliance with existing cybersecurity laws.
b. It includes advanced and progressive practices to protect against Advanced Persistent Threats (APTs).
c. It requires no documentation of cybersecurity policies.
d. It eliminates the need for any basic cybersecurity hygiene practices.

Answer: b. It includes advanced and progressive practices to protect against Advanced Persistent Threats (APTs). Explanation: CMMC Level 5 requires organizations to implement advanced and progressive cybersecurity practices specifically designed to protect against APTs, making it more rigorous than lower levels.

153. A manufacturing firm wants to understand the benefits of achieving a higher CMMC level certification. Which of the following best describes a significant advantage of obtaining CMMC Level 4 or 5?
a. Reduced need for regular cybersecurity assessments

b. Ability to bid on more sensitive and critical DoD contracts
c. Complete exemption from all NIST SP 800-171 requirements
d. Lower overall costs for cybersecurity implementation

Answer: b. Ability to bid on more sensitive and critical DoD contracts. Explanation: Achieving higher CMMC levels, such as Level 4 or 5, allows organizations to bid on more sensitive and critical Department of Defense (DoD) contracts, expanding their business opportunities.

154. A federal agency is updating its information system to comply with FISMA. Which document provides the minimum security requirements that the agency must meet to protect federal information and information systems?
a. NIST SP 800-37
b. FIPS 200
c. NIST SP 800-53
d. FIPS 199

Answer: b. FIPS 200. Explanation: FIPS 200 provides the minimum security requirements for federal information and information systems, outlining the necessary security controls to ensure adequate protection.

155. An organization must report its FISMA compliance status to OMB. What key element must be included in this report to demonstrate compliance?
a. The list of security policies
b. The results of the annual security control assessment
c. The budget allocated for cybersecurity
d. The number of security incidents reported

Answer: b. The results of the annual security control assessment. Explanation: FISMA compliance reporting to OMB requires the results of the annual security control assessment to demonstrate the effectiveness of implemented security controls.

156. A federal agency is implementing FIPS 200 minimum security requirements. Which of the following areas must the agency address to comply with these requirements?
a. Incident response capabilities
b. Network performance optimization
c. Employee training programs
d. Software development methodologies

Answer: a. Incident response capabilities. Explanation: FIPS 200 outlines minimum security requirements across various areas, including incident response capabilities, to ensure comprehensive protection of federal information systems.

157. Under FISMA, continuous monitoring is critical for maintaining information security. Which activity is a core component of a continuous monitoring program?
a. Quarterly financial audits
b. Regular vulnerability scanning
c. Monthly user access reviews
d. Annual policy updates

Answer: b. Regular vulnerability scanning. Explanation: Continuous monitoring under FISMA includes regular vulnerability scanning to detect and mitigate potential security weaknesses in a timely manner.

158. A federal agency needs to categorize its information system according to FISMA requirements. Which standard provides the guidelines for categorizing information and information systems based on the impact level?
a. NIST SP 800-53
b. FIPS 199
c. NIST SP 800-37
d. FIPS 200

Answer: b. FIPS 199. Explanation: FIPS 199 provides guidelines for categorizing information and information systems based on the potential impact on the organization should certain events occur, such as unauthorized access or data breaches.

159. In the context of FISMA, what is the primary purpose of implementing a Risk Management Framework (RMF)?
a. To streamline budget allocations for IT projects
b. To manage and mitigate risks to federal information systems
c. To facilitate interagency collaboration on cybersecurity
d. To ensure compliance with international security standards

Answer: b. To manage and mitigate risks to federal information systems. Explanation: The RMF provides a structured approach for managing and mitigating risks to federal information systems, ensuring compliance with FISMA requirements.

160. A federal agency is conducting an annual security control assessment as required by FISMA. Which document outlines the specific security controls that must be assessed?
a. FIPS 200
b. NIST SP 800-37
c. NIST SP 800-53
d. FIPS 199

Answer: c. NIST SP 800-53. Explanation: NIST SP 800-53 outlines the specific security controls that must be assessed during the annual security control assessment to ensure compliance with FISMA requirements.

161. Which of the following is a key FISMA reporting requirement for federal agencies?
a. Submission of an annual financial report
b. Documentation of all software licenses
c. Development and maintenance of an information security program
d. Implementation of a bring-your-own-device (BYOD) policy

Answer: c. Development and maintenance of an information security program. Explanation: FISMA requires federal agencies to develop, document, and maintain an information security program to protect their information systems.

162. An agency's continuous monitoring strategy must align with FISMA. Which of the following activities is essential for continuous monitoring?
a. Annual performance reviews
b. Ongoing security control assessments
c. Quarterly employee satisfaction surveys
d. Semi-annual hardware inventory checks

Answer: b. Ongoing security control assessments. Explanation: Ongoing security control assessments are essential for continuous monitoring, enabling agencies to identify and address security issues promptly, in alignment with FISMA.

163. A federal information system is categorized as high-impact according to FIPS 199. Which of the following security controls is most critical to implement for such a system?
a. Basic user authentication
b. Enhanced encryption for data in transit and at rest
c. Regular software updates
d. Standard incident response procedures

Answer: b. Enhanced encryption for data in transit and at rest. Explanation: For high-impact systems, implementing enhanced encryption for data in transit and at rest is critical to protect sensitive information and ensure compliance with FISMA security requirements.

164. A healthcare provider is implementing a new telemedicine platform and needs to ensure HIPAA compliance. Which of the following technical safeguards is most critical for protecting electronic protected health information (ePHI) during video consultations?
a. Implement role-based access control for all users
b. Use end-to-end encryption for all video and audio transmissions
c. Enable automatic logoff after 15 minutes of inactivity
d. Implement multi-factor authentication for provider access

Answer: b. Use end-to-end encryption for all video and audio transmissions. Explanation: While all options are important security measures, end-to-end encryption is crucial for protecting ePHI during telemedicine consultations.

It ensures that the entire communication stream, including video and audio, is secured from unauthorized access or interception, which is essential given the sensitive nature of medical consultations. Role-based access (a), automatic logoff (c), and multi-factor authentication (d) are valuable but don't directly address the confidentiality of data in transit during a telemedicine session.

165. A hospital is conducting its annual HIPAA Security Rule risk analysis. Which of the following approaches would be most comprehensive in identifying potential risks and vulnerabilities to ePHI?
a. Review of access logs and incident reports from the past year
b. Penetration testing of all internet-facing systems
c. Survey of all employees about their security awareness and practices
d. Systematic evaluation of all systems, applications, and processes that interact with ePHI, considering technical, physical, and administrative safeguards

Answer: d. Systematic evaluation of all systems, applications, and processes that interact with ePHI, considering technical, physical, and administrative safeguards. Explanation: A comprehensive HIPAA Security Rule risk analysis requires a holistic approach that examines all aspects of ePHI handling. This includes evaluating technical systems, physical security measures, and administrative procedures. While log reviews (a), penetration testing (b), and employee surveys (c) are valuable components, they individually don't provide the comprehensive view required by the Security Rule. The systematic evaluation ensures all potential vulnerabilities are identified across all safeguard categories.

166. A healthcare organization is entering into a contract with a cloud service provider for storing patient records. Which of the following is most critical to include in the Business Associate Agreement (BAA) to ensure HIPAA compliance?
a. Detailed pricing structure for the cloud services
b. Specific technical security measures implemented by the provider
c. Clear delineation of responsibilities for breach notification and mitigation
d. Service level agreements for system uptime and performance

Answer: c. Clear delineation of responsibilities for breach notification and mitigation. Explanation: While all elements are important in a cloud service contract, the clear delineation of responsibilities for breach notification and mitigation is crucial in a BAA for HIPAA compliance. This ensures that both parties understand their obligations in the event of a data breach, which is critical for timely reporting and effective response as required by HIPAA. Pricing (a) is not directly related to HIPAA compliance. Specific technical measures (b) may change over time and are better addressed in separate documentation. Service level agreements (d) are important for operations but not specifically required in a BAA for HIPAA compliance.

167. A small medical practice is implementing HIPAA physical safeguards and has limited resources. Which of the following measures would provide the most effective protection for ePHI with the least financial impact?
a. Install biometric access controls on all doors
b. Implement a clear desk policy and provide locking storage for all workstations
c. Hire 24/7 security personnel to monitor the premises
d. Install a state-of-the-art video surveillance system

Answer: b. Implement a clear desk policy and provide locking storage for all workstations. Explanation: For a small practice with limited resources, implementing a clear desk policy and providing locking storage offers significant protection for ePHI at a relatively low cost. This addresses the physical safeguard requirements by ensuring that ePHI is not left unattended and is secured when not in use. Biometric access controls (a) and 24/7 security personnel (c) are likely too costly for a small practice. A state-of-the-art surveillance system (d) may be expensive and doesn't directly secure ePHI.

168. An employee at a covered entity accidentally emails a file containing ePHI to the wrong recipient. Which of the following actions should be taken first to comply with HIPAA requirements?
a. Immediately terminate the employee responsible for the breach
b. Conduct a risk assessment to determine if the incident constitutes a breach requiring notification
c. Notify all patients whose information was included in the file
d. Implement additional email security software to prevent future incidents

Answer: b. Conduct a risk assessment to determine if the incident constitutes a breach requiring notification. Explanation: The first step in responding to a potential breach under HIPAA is to conduct a risk assessment. This assessment determines whether the incident meets the definition of a breach requiring notification. Not all unauthorized disclosures necessarily constitute a breach if the risk of compromise is low. Terminating the employee (a) is premature and doesn't address the immediate issue. Notifying patients (c) should only occur if the risk assessment determines it's necessary. Implementing new software (d) is a preventive measure but doesn't address the immediate incident.

169. A healthcare organization is implementing administrative safeguards under the HIPAA Security Rule. Which of the following policies is most critical for ensuring ongoing compliance and effectiveness of security measures?
a. Annual security awareness training for all employees
b. Regular review and update of security policies and procedures
c. Background checks for all new hires
d. Strict password complexity requirements

Answer: b. Regular review and update of security policies and procedures. Explanation: While all options are important administrative safeguards, the regular review and update of security policies and procedures is crucial for maintaining ongoing HIPAA compliance. This process ensures that security measures remain current and effective in the face of evolving threats and technological changes. It also demonstrates the organization's commitment to continuous improvement in security practices. Annual training (a) is important but doesn't ensure policies remain current. Background checks (c) and password policies (d) are specific measures that, while valuable, don't encompass the broad scope of security management that regular policy reviews provide.

170. A hospital is implementing a new electronic health record (EHR) system. Which of the following technical safeguards is most essential for compliance with the HIPAA Security Rule's access control requirements?
a. Implement biometric authentication for all users
b. Use role-based access control with unique user identification
c. Encrypt all data within the EHR database
d. Implement automatic logoff after 10 minutes of inactivity

Answer: b. Use role-based access control with unique user identification. Explanation: Role-based access control with unique user identification is a fundamental requirement of the HIPAA Security Rule's access control standard. It ensures that each user has the appropriate level of access based on their role and that all access can be tracked to specific individuals. This addresses both the need for access control and audit capabilities. Biometric authentication (a) can enhance security but isn't specifically required. Database encryption (c) is important for data at rest but doesn't address access control. Automatic logoff (d) is valuable but doesn't provide the granular access control required by HIPAA.

171. A covered entity is considering using a third-party service for medical transcription. Which of the following is the most crucial step in ensuring HIPAA compliance when engaging this service?
a. Conduct a thorough background check on all transcriptionists
b. Require the service to use HIPAA-compliant software for transcription
c. Execute a comprehensive Business Associate Agreement (BAA) with the service provider
d. Implement end-to-end encryption for all data transfers to and from the service

Answer: c. Execute a comprehensive Business Associate Agreement (BAA) with the service provider. Explanation: Executing a BAA is a legal requirement under HIPAA when a covered entity engages a business associate that will have access to PHI. The BAA establishes the permitted uses and disclosures of PHI and requires the business associate to implement appropriate safeguards. While background checks (a), compliant software (b), and encryption (d) are important security measures, they don't fulfill the legal requirement of having a BAA in place, which is fundamental to establishing the business associate relationship and associated HIPAA obligations.

172. A healthcare provider is conducting a risk analysis and identifies that their current method of disposing of old hardware containing ePHI is inadequate. Which of the following methods would best address this vulnerability while complying with HIPAA requirements?
a. Physically destroy all hard drives before disposing of hardware
b. Use a certified e-waste recycling service for all hardware disposal
c. Implement a data wiping procedure using DOD 5220.22-M standard, followed by physical destruction for non-functional drives
d. Store all old hardware indefinitely in a secure location to avoid disposal risks

Answer: c. Implement a data wiping procedure using DOD 5220.22-M standard, followed by physical destruction for non-functional drives. Explanation: This approach provides a comprehensive solution that addresses both the security and practical aspects of hardware disposal. The DOD 5220.22-M standard is widely recognized as an effective method for securely erasing data, making it virtually unrecoverable. Physical destruction of non-functional drives ensures that data cannot be recovered from drives that can't be securely wiped. This method balances security with the potential for hardware reuse or recycling. Physical destruction of all drives (a) may be excessive and wasteful. A certified e-waste service (b) alone doesn't guarantee secure data removal. Indefinite storage (d) is impractical and doesn't address the need for eventual disposal.

173. A small dental practice is struggling to fully implement all recommended HIPAA technical safeguards due to budget constraints. Which of the following approaches would be most appropriate to address this situation while maintaining compliance?

a. Implement only the most critical technical safeguards and document the rationale for omitting others
b. Outsource all IT operations to a HIPAA-compliant managed service provider
c. Apply for a small business exemption from certain HIPAA requirements
d. Conduct a thorough risk analysis and implement a combination of compensating controls and technical safeguards based on identified risks

Answer: d. Conduct a thorough risk analysis and implement a combination of compensating controls and technical safeguards based on identified risks. Explanation: This approach aligns with HIPAA's flexibility provisions, which allow organizations to implement security measures appropriate to their size, complexity, and capabilities. By conducting a thorough risk analysis, the practice can identify its most significant vulnerabilities and allocate resources to address them effectively, potentially using a mix of technical and non-technical controls. Simply implementing select safeguards without analysis (a) may leave critical risks unaddressed. Outsourcing all IT (b) may be costly and doesn't absolve the practice of its compliance responsibilities. There is no small business exemption (c) for HIPAA compliance.

174. A defense contractor is preparing for a CMMC assessment and needs to ensure compliance with Level 3 requirements. They currently have basic access control measures in place. Which of the following additional practices should they implement to meet Level 3 requirements?
a. Develop an incident response plan
b. Perform regular security awareness training
c. Enforce multifactor authentication for network access
d. Implement basic encryption for data at rest

Answer: c. Enforce multifactor authentication for network access. Explanation: CMMC Level 3 requires more advanced security controls such as multifactor authentication for network access, which enhances the security of user authentication processes.

175. An organization undergoing a CMMC Level 2 assessment needs to demonstrate compliance with configuration management practices. Which activity is essential for meeting these requirements?
a. Conducting regular penetration tests
b. Maintaining an inventory of hardware assets
c. Establishing baseline configurations for IT systems
d. Implementing data encryption for all sensitive information

Answer: c. Establishing baseline configurations for IT systems. Explanation: Establishing and maintaining baseline configurations for IT systems is crucial for ensuring that systems are configured securely and consistently, which is a key requirement for CMMC Level 2.

176. A small business aiming for CMMC Level 1 certification needs to implement basic cybersecurity practices. Which of the following practices is mandatory at this level?
a. Conducting a comprehensive risk assessment
b. Performing multifactor authentication
c. Implementing access control measures
d. Developing a security awareness program

Answer: c. Implementing access control measures. Explanation: CMMC Level 1 focuses on basic cybersecurity hygiene, including implementing access control measures to restrict access to information systems and ensure only authorized users have access.

177. In comparing CMMC to NIST SP 800-171, which statement accurately reflects a key difference between the two frameworks?
a. CMMC does not require any documentation of security practices.
b. NIST SP 800-171 mandates third-party assessments for compliance.
c. CMMC includes multiple levels of certification with increasing security requirements.
d. NIST SP 800-171 is specifically designed for cloud service providers.

Answer: c. CMMC includes multiple levels of certification with increasing security requirements. Explanation: CMMC has a tiered certification system with five levels, each with progressively more stringent security requirements, whereas NIST SP 800-171 provides a single set of controls.

178. An organization needs to prepare for a CMMC Level 4 assessment, focusing on advanced threat detection and response. Which of the following practices is most critical to implement?
a. Basic cybersecurity hygiene practices
b. Continuous monitoring and analysis of network traffic
c. Annual security policy reviews
d. Basic user access control measures

Answer: b. Continuous monitoring and analysis of network traffic. Explanation: CMMC Level 4 requires advanced cybersecurity practices, including continuous monitoring and analysis of network traffic to detect and respond to sophisticated threats in real-time.

179. A manufacturing firm must align its cybersecurity practices with both CMMC and NIST SP 800-171 to protect Controlled Unclassified Information (CUI). Which CMMC level should they aim for to meet the NIST SP 800-171 requirements?
a. Level 1
b. Level 2
c. Level 3
d. Level 5

Answer: c. Level 3. Explanation: CMMC Level 3 is designed to align with the security controls outlined in NIST SP 800-171, ensuring protection for Controlled Unclassified Information (CUI).

180. A defense contractor must establish incident response capabilities to comply with CMMC Level 3. Which of the following actions should be taken first?

a. Develop and document an incident response plan
b. Train employees on basic cybersecurity principles
c. Encrypt all sensitive data at rest
d. Conduct regular vulnerability assessments

Answer: a. Develop and document an incident response plan. Explanation: Developing and documenting an incident response plan is the first step in establishing incident response capabilities, ensuring that there are clear procedures for identifying, managing, and mitigating security incidents.

181. To achieve CMMC Level 5 certification, an organization needs to implement advanced cybersecurity practices. Which of the following is a characteristic of Level 5?
a. Basic access control measures
b. Comprehensive risk assessments
c. Advanced persistent threat (APT) detection and response
d. Periodic security awareness training

Answer: c. Advanced persistent threat (APT) detection and response. Explanation: CMMC Level 5 focuses on protecting against advanced persistent threats (APTs) and requires sophisticated detection and response capabilities to address these high-level security threats.

182. An organization is mapping its security controls to both CMMC and ISO/IEC 27001. Which of the following best describes the relationship between CMMC and ISO/IEC 27001?
a. CMMC requires a higher level of encryption for all data
b. ISO/IEC 27001 provides specific controls for cloud security not covered by CMMC
c. CMMC includes a certification process, whereas ISO/IEC 27001 does not
d. Both frameworks emphasize risk management and continuous improvement

Answer: d. Both frameworks emphasize risk management and continuous improvement. Explanation: Both CMMC and ISO/IEC 27001 emphasize the importance of risk management and continuous improvement in cybersecurity practices, ensuring that organizations maintain a proactive approach to security.

183. A company preparing for a CMMC Level 3 assessment is unsure how to document its cybersecurity policies. Which of the following best practices should they follow to ensure compliance?
a. Keep policies informal to allow flexibility
b. Use standardized templates and regularly update the policies
c. Focus only on technical controls and exclude administrative policies
d. Document policies in a way that is difficult for auditors to understand

Answer: b. Use standardized templates and regularly update the policies. Explanation: Using standardized templates and regularly updating policies ensures consistency, clarity, and relevance, which are critical for demonstrating compliance with CMMC Level 3 requirements.

184. A federal agency is implementing a risk management framework (RMF) and needs to categorize its information system. Which NIST publication should the agency refer to for guidance on security categorization?
a. NIST SP 800-53
b. NIST SP 800-37
c. FIPS 199
d. FIPS 200

Answer: c. FIPS 199. Explanation: FIPS 199 provides the standards for security categorization of federal information and information systems based on the potential impact on the organization if certain events occur, such as unauthorized disclosure or data breaches.

185. A federal information system requires continuous monitoring under FISMA. Which of the following is NOT typically included in a continuous monitoring program?
a. Regular vulnerability scanning
b. Real-time security event analysis
c. Annual security control assessment
d. Monthly configuration audits

Answer: c. Annual security control assessment. Explanation: Continuous monitoring focuses on ongoing activities like vulnerability scanning, security event analysis, and configuration audits. Annual security control assessments are periodic evaluations but not part of continuous monitoring.

186. Which of the following FISMA reporting requirements directly demonstrates the effectiveness of an agency's information security program?
a. Submission of a budget allocation report for IT projects
b. Documentation of employee security training sessions
c. Results of the annual security control assessment
d. List of approved software and hardware assets

Answer: c. Results of the annual security control assessment. Explanation: The results of the annual security control assessment demonstrate the effectiveness of the agency's information security program by showing how well security controls are implemented and functioning.

187. A federal agency is required to implement minimum security requirements as per FIPS 200. Which of the following areas must be addressed to ensure compliance with these requirements?
a. Financial management
b. Network performance
c. Incident response
d. Employee productivity

Answer: c. Incident response. Explanation: FIPS 200 outlines minimum security requirements across various areas, including incident response, to ensure comprehensive protection of federal information systems.

188. During a privacy impact assessment (PIA), which privacy-enhancing technology (PET) would be most effective in ensuring the anonymization of personally identifiable information (PII)?
a. Encryption
b. Differential privacy
c. Tokenization
d. Homomorphic encryption

Answer: b. Differential privacy. Explanation: Differential privacy is a PET that ensures data anonymization by allowing organizations to collect and share aggregate data while minimizing the risk of identifying individuals within the dataset.

189. A federal agency is conducting a security control assessment as part of its FISMA compliance efforts. Which NIST publication provides the guidelines for assessing the security controls?
a. NIST SP 800-53
b. NIST SP 800-37
c. NIST SP 800-30
d. NIST SP 800-39

Answer: a. NIST SP 800-53. Explanation: NIST SP 800-53 provides comprehensive guidelines for assessing the security controls in federal information systems to ensure they meet FISMA requirements.

190. Which of the following is a primary objective of the FISMA Risk Management Framework (RMF)?
a. To ensure compliance with international cybersecurity standards
b. To manage and mitigate risks to federal information systems
c. To allocate financial resources for IT projects
d. To enhance interagency collaboration on cybersecurity

Answer: b. To manage and mitigate risks to federal information systems. Explanation: The RMF provides a structured approach for managing and mitigating risks to federal information systems, ensuring compliance with FISMA requirements and enhancing security posture.

191. A cloud service provider must comply with FISMA and demonstrate that its information system meets the required security standards. Which document is essential for detailing the system's security controls and their implementation?
a. Security Assessment Report (SAR)
b. Plan of Action and Milestones (POA&M)
c. System Security Plan (SSP)
d. Authorization to Operate (ATO) letter

Answer: c. System Security Plan (SSP). Explanation: The SSP details the security controls implemented in the system and how they meet the required standards, serving as a critical document in the FISMA compliance process.

192. In the context of FISMA continuous monitoring, what is the primary purpose of the Plan of Action and Milestones (POA&M)?
a. To document security incidents and response actions
b. To outline the system's security baseline requirements
c. To identify and manage risks associated with system vulnerabilities
d. To track the progress of security control implementation

Answer: c. To identify and manage risks associated with system vulnerabilities. Explanation: The POA&M is used to document identified security vulnerabilities and manage the associated risks by outlining corrective actions and tracking their progress.

193. An information system categorized as high-impact according to FIPS 199 requires stringent security measures. Which of the following controls is most critical to ensure the system's protection?
a. Basic user authentication
b. Enhanced encryption for data in transit and at rest
c. Regular software updates
d. Standard incident response procedures

Answer: b. Enhanced encryption for data in transit and at rest. Explanation: For high-impact systems, implementing enhanced encryption for data in transit and at rest is critical to protect sensitive information and ensure compliance with FISMA security requirements.

194. A multinational corporation is planning to implement a new AI-powered customer profiling system that will process personal data of EU residents. Which of the following is the most appropriate first step to ensure GDPR compliance?
a. Obtain explicit consent from all customers before implementing the system
b. Conduct a Data Protection Impact Assessment (DPIA)
c. Appoint a Data Protection Officer (DPO) specifically for this project
d. Implement state-of-the-art encryption for all data processed by the system

Answer: b. Conduct a Data Protection Impact Assessment (DPIA). Explanation: When implementing new technology that is likely to result in a high risk to the rights and freedoms of individuals, such as AI-powered profiling, conducting a DPIA is a mandatory first step under GDPR. The DPIA helps identify and minimize data protection risks early in the project. While consent (a) may be necessary, it's not the first step. Appointing a DPO (c) might be required but isn't specific to this project. Encryption (d) is important but doesn't address the broader compliance issues a DPIA would cover.

195. An EU-based company wants to transfer personal data to a service provider in the United States. Following the invalidation of the Privacy Shield, which of the following mechanisms would provide the most robust legal basis for this transfer under GDPR?
a. Binding Corporate Rules (BCRs)
b. Standard Contractual Clauses (SCCs) with supplementary measures
c. Explicit consent from all data subjects
d. Adequacy decision for the specific US state where the provider is located

Answer: b. Standard Contractual Clauses (SCCs) with supplementary measures. Explanation: In the absence of an adequacy decision for the US, SCCs with supplementary measures provide the most practical and robust mechanism for most companies to transfer data to the US under GDPR. The supplementary measures address the concerns raised in the Schrems II decision regarding US surveillance laws. BCRs (a) are complex and typically used within a corporate group. Explicit consent (c) is generally not considered a stable basis for systematic transfers. There are no state-specific adequacy decisions (d) for the US under GDPR.

196. A data subject requests the erasure of all their personal data under GDPR's "right to be forgotten." The company identifies valid grounds to reject the request. What is the most appropriate next step?
a. Immediately inform the data subject that their request has been denied
b. Partially erase the data to show good faith compliance
c. Ignore the request as it's not valid
d. Document the rationale for rejection, inform the data subject of the decision, reasons, and their right to lodge a complaint with a supervisory authority

Answer: d. Document the rationale for rejection, inform the data subject of the decision, reasons, and their right to lodge a complaint with a supervisory authority. Explanation: When rejecting a valid GDPR right request, it's crucial to document the decision-making process, clearly communicate the reasons to the data subject, and inform them of their right to appeal to a supervisory authority. This approach ensures transparency and compliance with GDPR's accountability principle. Simply informing of denial (a) or partially erasing (b) doesn't fulfill the obligation to explain. Ignoring the request (c) violates GDPR's requirement to respond to all requests.

197. During a DPIA for a new IoT product, a company identifies high risks to data subjects that cannot be sufficiently mitigated. What is the required next step under GDPR?
a. Abandon the project as it's too risky
b. Implement additional security measures and proceed with the project
c. Consult with the relevant supervisory authority before proceeding
d. Obtain explicit consent from potential users to accept the risks

Answer: c. Consult with the relevant supervisory authority before proceeding. Explanation: When a DPIA indicates high risks that cannot be sufficiently mitigated, GDPR requires consultation with the supervisory authority before proceeding with the processing. This allows for expert input on whether the processing can proceed and under what conditions. Abandoning the project (a) isn't necessarily required. Implementing additional measures (b) without consultation doesn't address the unmitigated high risks. Obtaining consent (d) doesn't override the need for supervisory consultation in this scenario.

198. A company offers a mobile app to EU residents that collects location data for personalized services. Which of the following approaches best satisfies GDPR's data minimization principle?
a. Collect location data only when the app is in use and allow users to opt-out
b. Store location data for 30 days to improve service quality
c. Collect precise location data but anonymize it before storage
d. Use coarse location (e.g., city-level) unless fine-grained location is necessary for a specific feature, with clear user control

Answer: d. Use coarse location (e.g., city-level) unless fine-grained location is necessary for a specific feature, with clear user control. Explanation: This approach best embodies GDPR's data minimization principle by collecting only the level of detail necessary for each feature and giving users control. It limits data collection while still allowing functionality. Option (a) might collect more data than necessary. Storing for 30 days (b) may violate storage limitation principles. Anonymization (c) is good but collecting precise data initially may be more than necessary.

199. An organization discovers a data breach affecting EU residents' personal data. The breach is unlikely to result in a risk to the rights and freedoms of natural persons. What is the correct course of action under GDPR?
a. Notify the supervisory authority within 72 hours
b. Notify affected individuals immediately
c. Document the breach internally but no external notification is required
d. Conduct a Data Protection Impact Assessment (DPIA) to reassess the risk

Answer: c. Document the breach internally but no external notification is required. Explanation: GDPR requires notification to the supervisory authority only when a breach is likely to result in a risk to the rights and freedoms of natural persons. If the organization has assessed that the breach is unlikely to result in such risk, they must document the breach internally but are not required to notify externally. This emphasizes the importance of proper risk assessment and documentation. Options (a) and (b) are required for higher-risk breaches. A DPIA (d) is not typically part of breach response procedures.

200. A company is implementing a new cross-border data transfer mechanism following the Schrems II decision. Which of the following is most crucial to ensure compliance with GDPR requirements?
a. Encrypt all data during transfer using AES-256
b. Conduct a transfer impact assessment evaluating the laws and practices of the recipient country
c. Obtain explicit consent from all data subjects for international transfers
d. Use only cloud providers with data centers within the EU

Answer: b. Conduct a transfer impact assessment evaluating the laws and practices of the recipient country. Explanation: Following Schrems II, organizations must assess whether the laws and practices of the recipient country ensure adequate protection for the transferred data, particularly regarding government access. This assessment is crucial for determining if supplementary measures are needed. Encryption (a) is important but doesn't address all Schrems II concerns. Consent (c) is generally not considered a stable basis for systematic transfers. Using EU-based data centers (d) doesn't necessarily prevent data access by non-EU authorities.

201. An individual exercises their right to data portability under GDPR, requesting their data in a specific format. The company finds providing data in this format would create a significant burden. What's the most appropriate response?
a. Refuse the request as it's too burdensome
b. Provide the data in the company's standard format and explain why the requested format can't be accommodated
c. Offer to provide the data in the requested format for a reasonable fee
d. Extend the response deadline and allocate resources to fulfill the request as specified

Answer: b. Provide the data in the company's standard format and explain why the requested format can't be accommodated. Explanation: GDPR requires data to be provided in a structured, commonly used, and machine-readable format, but doesn't obligate companies to create new or maintain multiple formats. Providing data in a standard format while explaining why the specific request can't be accommodated balances the data subject's rights with the company's capabilities. Refusal (a) violates GDPR. Charging a fee (c) is generally not allowed for data subject rights. Extending the deadline (d) may be unnecessary if a standard format is available.

202. A company plans to use legitimate interests as the legal basis for processing personal data for direct marketing purposes. Which of the following steps is most critical to ensure compliance with GDPR?
a. Obtain opt-in consent from all individuals before processing
b. Conduct and document a legitimate interests assessment (LIA)
c. Limit processing to existing customers only
d. Encrypt all marketing databases to ensure data security

Answer: b. Conduct and document a legitimate interests assessment (LIA). Explanation: When relying on legitimate interests, especially for activities like direct marketing, conducting and documenting a legitimate interests assessment is crucial. This assessment balances the company's interests against the individual's rights and freedoms, demonstrating compliance with GDPR's accountability principle. Consent (a) isn't required if legitimate interests is the chosen basis, though an opt-out must be offered. Limiting to existing customers (c) may be part of the assessment but isn't always necessary. Encryption (d) is important for security but doesn't address the legal basis for processing.

203. A healthcare organization is documenting the scope of its electronic health record (EHR) system. Which of the following elements is most critical to include in the system scope documentation to ensure comprehensive security coverage?
a. The number of users accessing the system
b. Detailed descriptions of data flows within the system
c. The physical location of backup servers
d. The organization's financial budget for the system

Answer: b. Detailed descriptions of data flows within the system. Explanation: Including detailed descriptions of data flows helps identify how data moves within the system, enabling better identification of security controls needed to protect sensitive information and ensure compliance with regulations.

204. When defining the system boundary for a new financial application, which technique is most effective in ensuring all relevant components are included?
a. Interviewing key stakeholders about system usage
b. Mapping out all hardware and software components used
c. Documenting the organization's overall IT infrastructure
d. Listing all employees who will use the system

Answer: b. Mapping out all hardware and software components used. Explanation: Mapping out all hardware and software components ensures that the system boundary includes every element involved in the financial application's operation, providing a clear scope for security and compliance measures.

205. In accordance with FIPS 199, how should a system that processes sensitive but unclassified data impacting national security be categorized?
a. Low
b. Moderate
c. High
d. Confidential

Answer: c. High. Explanation: FIPS 199 categorizes systems based on the impact of a security breach. A system processing sensitive but unclassified data impacting national security would be categorized as High due to the potential severe impact on national security.

206. A company needs to document the interconnections between its customer database system and third-party applications. What is the primary purpose of this documentation?
a. To reduce the cost of IT support
b. To improve the user interface design
c. To identify potential security risks and control requirements
d. To increase system performance and speed

Answer: c. To identify potential security risks and control requirements. Explanation: Documenting system interconnections helps identify potential security risks and necessary controls to protect data as it moves between systems, ensuring secure and compliant operations.

207. During a security review, a discrepancy is found between the documented system boundary and the actual implementation. What is the most appropriate next step to address this issue?
a. Update the documentation to reflect the actual implementation
b. Ignore the discrepancy if it does not affect performance
c. Revise the system architecture to match the documentation
d. Conduct a risk assessment to understand the impact

Answer: d. Conduct a risk assessment to understand the impact. Explanation: Conducting a risk assessment helps determine the potential security implications of the discrepancy, allowing for informed decisions on whether to update documentation or revise the system architecture.

208. In the context of system interconnections, what should be included in an interconnection security agreement (ISA)?
a. Budget details for the connected systems
b. Contact information for system users
c. Security requirements and responsibilities for each party
d. Historical performance data of interconnected systems

Answer: c. Security requirements and responsibilities for each party. Explanation: An ISA outlines the security requirements and responsibilities for each party involved in the interconnection, ensuring that both sides understand and agree on the necessary security measures to protect data.

209. An organization is categorizing its systems according to FIPS 199. Which impact level would be assigned to a system where a breach could result in minor financial loss and minimal impact on operations?
a. Low
b. Moderate
c. High
d. Critical

Answer: a. Low. Explanation: A system that would result in minor financial loss and minimal impact on operations is categorized as Low impact under FIPS 199, indicating limited adverse effects on organizational operations and assets.

210. To ensure comprehensive documentation of system boundaries, what key element should be included in the documentation process?
a. Employee training schedules
b. Data classification guidelines
c. Network topology diagrams
d. User satisfaction surveys

Answer: c. Network topology diagrams. Explanation: Network topology diagrams provide a visual representation of the system's architecture, helping to define and understand system boundaries and identify all components and connections involved.

211. A security team needs to document the interconnections of an email system with other corporate applications. Which factor is most critical to consider during this documentation process?
a. The physical location of the email servers
b. The types of data exchanged between systems
c. The total number of emails sent daily
d. The email client software versions

Answer: b. The types of data exchanged between systems. Explanation: Understanding the types of data exchanged between systems is critical to identifying security requirements and ensuring that data is appropriately protected during transmission.

212. In preparing for an audit, a company must document the scope of its network monitoring system. What is the primary reason for clearly defining the system's scope?
a. To allocate sufficient financial resources
b. To comply with privacy regulations
c. To identify and mitigate security risks effectively
d. To streamline network traffic

Answer: c. To identify and mitigate security risks effectively. Explanation: Clearly defining the system's scope helps identify and mitigate security risks, ensuring that all relevant components and data flows are considered in security planning and compliance efforts.

213. An organization is categorizing its information system under FIPS 199. If unauthorized disclosure of certain data could cause severe financial loss and damage the organization's reputation, which impact level should be assigned to this information type?
a. Low
b. Moderate
c. High
d. Critical

Answer: c. High. Explanation: FIPS 199 defines the high impact level as one where the loss of confidentiality, integrity, or availability could cause severe harm to the organization, including significant financial loss and damage to reputation.

214. A financial institution must map its information types to appropriate security objectives. Which information type is most likely to require a high level of integrity?
a. Marketing materials
b. Customer account data
c. Public financial reports
d. Internal training documents

Answer: b. Customer account data. Explanation: Customer account data requires a high level of integrity to ensure that the financial information is accurate and reliable, preventing errors or fraudulent activities.

215. A federal agency is assessing the security objectives for a system that processes personally identifiable information (PII). Which security objective should be prioritized for this information type?

a. Confidentiality
b. Integrity
c. Availability
d. Authenticity

Answer: a. Confidentiality. Explanation: For personally identifiable information (PII), confidentiality is a primary security objective to protect sensitive personal data from unauthorized access and breaches.

216. During a risk assessment, an organization determines that the availability of its online services is crucial for customer satisfaction. What impact level should be assigned to the availability objective for these services?
a. Low
b. Moderate
c. High
d. Critical

Answer: c. High. Explanation: If the availability of online services is crucial for customer satisfaction, a high impact level should be assigned, as downtime could significantly disrupt operations and harm the organization's reputation and customer trust.

217. In the context of FIPS 199, which security objective addresses the need to protect information from unauthorized modification or destruction?
a. Confidentiality
b. Integrity
c. Availability
d. Authenticity

Answer: b. Integrity. Explanation: Integrity ensures that information is protected from unauthorized modification or destruction, maintaining its accuracy and trustworthiness.

218. A healthcare provider is mapping information types to security objectives. Which of the following information types is most likely to require a high level of availability?
a. Patient medical records
b. Internal audit reports
c. Marketing brochures
d. Employee training schedules

Answer: a. Patient medical records. Explanation: Patient medical records require a high level of availability to ensure that healthcare providers have timely access to critical medical information, enabling effective patient care.

219. An organization is tailoring its security objectives based on the context of its information system. Which factor is least likely to influence the tailoring process?
a. Regulatory requirements
b. The organization's mission
c. The system's hardware specifications
d. Potential impact of security breaches

Answer: c. The system's hardware specifications. Explanation: While hardware specifications are important, they are less likely to influence the tailoring of security objectives compared to regulatory requirements, the organization's mission, and the potential impact of security breaches.

220. A government agency is categorizing its information system according to FIPS 199. Which of the following best describes a moderate impact level for the confidentiality objective?
a. Unauthorized disclosure could cause a limited adverse effect on organizational operations.
b. Unauthorized disclosure could cause a serious adverse effect on organizational operations.
c. Unauthorized disclosure could cause a severe or catastrophic adverse effect on organizational operations.
d. Unauthorized disclosure is unlikely to have any adverse effect on organizational operations.

Answer: b. Unauthorized disclosure could cause a serious adverse effect on organizational operations. Explanation: The moderate impact level for confidentiality indicates that unauthorized disclosure could cause serious harm, such as significant financial loss or damage to the organization's reputation.

221. An organization must ensure the integrity of its transaction data. Which security measure is most effective in achieving this objective?
a. Data encryption
b. Multi-factor authentication
c. Digital signatures
d. Firewalls

Answer: c. Digital signatures. Explanation: Digital signatures provide a means to verify the integrity and authenticity of transaction data, ensuring it has not been altered or tampered with during transmission.

222. In tailoring security objectives based on system context, which scenario would most likely result in assigning a high impact level to the availability objective?
a. An online retail platform's transaction processing system
b. A public library's digital catalog
c. A social media platform's messaging service
d. A corporate intranet used for employee communications

Answer: a. An online retail platform's transaction processing system. Explanation: An online retail platform's transaction processing system would likely be assigned a high impact level for availability, as downtime could result in significant financial loss and customer dissatisfaction.

223. A government contractor is required to implement additional security measures to protect classified information. Which of the following control enhancements would best address the need for enhanced access control?
a. Implementing multifactor authentication for all users
b. Enforcing periodic password changes every 90 days
c. Increasing the length of user passwords to 12 characters
d. Conducting annual security awareness training

Answer: a. Implementing multifactor authentication for all users. Explanation: Multifactor authentication significantly enhances access control by requiring multiple forms of verification, reducing the risk of unauthorized access to classified information.

224. In a high-risk environment, an organization must protect sensitive data from advanced persistent threats (APTs). Which control enhancement should be prioritized to mitigate this risk effectively?
a. Enforcing complex password policies
b. Implementing continuous monitoring and anomaly detection
c. Scheduling regular data backups
d. Conducting quarterly phishing simulations

Answer: b. Implementing continuous monitoring and anomaly detection. Explanation: Continuous monitoring and anomaly detection are critical for identifying and responding to advanced persistent threats in real-time, providing enhanced protection for sensitive data.

225. A financial institution is deploying an overlay to address the specific risk of insider threats. Which of the following control enhancements is most appropriate for this scenario?
a. Restricting administrative privileges to a minimal number of users
b. Encrypting all data in transit
c. Implementing a robust firewall configuration
d. Scheduling monthly external security audits

Answer: a. Restricting administrative privileges to a minimal number of users. Explanation: Limiting administrative privileges helps mitigate insider threats by reducing the number of users with access to critical systems and data, thereby decreasing the potential for malicious activity from within.

226. An organization needs to justify the selection of control enhancements to its board of directors. Which approach provides the strongest justification?
a. Highlighting the industry best practices that support the enhancements
b. Demonstrating the cost-effectiveness of the selected enhancements
c. Presenting the potential risks mitigated by the enhancements

d. Comparing the selected enhancements with those of competitors

Answer: c. Presenting the potential risks mitigated by the enhancements. Explanation: Demonstrating how the selected control enhancements mitigate specific risks provides a clear, risk-based rationale for their implementation, aligning with the board's interest in protecting the organization from threats.

227. A healthcare provider must ensure the integrity of patient data during transmission. Which control enhancement is most suitable for this requirement?
a. Implementing encryption for data at rest
b. Using digital signatures to verify data integrity
c. Conducting regular vulnerability scans
d. Enforcing strict password policies

Answer: b. Using digital signatures to verify data integrity. Explanation: Digital signatures provide a mechanism to verify the integrity and authenticity of data during transmission, ensuring that patient data has not been altered or tampered with.

228. When selecting control enhancements for a cloud-based application, which factor is most critical to consider?
a. The geographical location of the cloud service provider's data centers
b. The scalability of the control enhancements with the application
c. The reputation of the cloud service provider
d. The physical security measures at the cloud service provider's facilities

Answer: b. The scalability of the control enhancements with the application. Explanation: Ensuring that control enhancements can scale with the cloud-based application is crucial for maintaining security as the application grows and evolves, preventing potential gaps in protection.

229. A retail company is implementing an overlay to enhance the security of its payment processing system. Which control enhancement should be prioritized to protect against cardholder data breaches?
a. Implementing end-to-end encryption for payment transactions
b. Conducting semi-annual penetration tests
c. Enforcing multi-layered firewall defenses
d. Requiring employees to undergo annual security training

Answer: a. Implementing end-to-end encryption for payment transactions. Explanation: End-to-end encryption for payment transactions protects cardholder data throughout the entire transaction process, significantly reducing the risk of data breaches.

230. An organization has decided to enhance its incident response capabilities. Which control enhancement is most appropriate to achieve this objective?

a. Establishing a dedicated incident response team
b. Enforcing regular password updates
c. Implementing a web application firewall
d. Conducting daily data backups

Answer: a. Establishing a dedicated incident response team. Explanation: Having a dedicated incident response team ensures that the organization can quickly and effectively respond to security incidents, minimizing potential damage and recovery time.

231. In a scenario where compliance with stringent data privacy regulations is required, which control enhancement should an organization implement to ensure compliance?
a. Encrypting data both at rest and in transit
b. Enforcing password changes every 60 days
c. Conducting annual compliance audits
d. Restricting physical access to data centers

Answer: a. Encrypting data both at rest and in transit. Explanation: Encrypting data both at rest and in transit ensures that sensitive data is protected from unauthorized access at all times, meeting stringent data privacy regulation requirements.

232. A multinational corporation is implementing control enhancements to address the risk of data leakage. Which of the following should be prioritized?
a. Deploying data loss prevention (DLP) solutions
b. Increasing the frequency of employee security training sessions
c. Implementing single sign-on (SSO) for all corporate applications
d. Conducting regular physical security assessments

Answer: a. Deploying data loss prevention (DLP) solutions. Explanation: Data loss prevention (DLP) solutions are designed to detect and prevent the unauthorized transmission of sensitive data, effectively addressing the risk of data leakage across the organization.

233. An organization is developing a data handling matrix to ensure proper data management. Which of the following should be the first step in creating this matrix?
a. Assigning data handling responsibilities to employees
b. Conducting a data classification exercise
c. Implementing data encryption techniques
d. Performing a risk assessment

Answer: b. Conducting a data classification exercise. Explanation: The first step in creating a data handling matrix is to classify the data based on its sensitivity and criticality. This classification helps determine the appropriate handling procedures for different types of data.

234. A healthcare provider is required to implement data labeling and marking procedures. Which of the following labels would be most appropriate for patient medical records?
a. Public
b. Internal Use Only
c. Confidential
d. Restricted

Answer: c. Confidential. Explanation: Patient medical records contain sensitive information and should be labeled as "Confidential" to ensure they are handled with a higher level of security and privacy protection.

235. During a data flow mapping exercise, which of the following steps is crucial for ensuring the accuracy of the data flow diagram?
a. Identifying and documenting all data storage locations
b. Implementing access controls on the data flow diagrams
c. Training employees on data flow mapping techniques
d. Encrypting all data in transit

Answer: a. Identifying and documenting all data storage locations. Explanation: Identifying and documenting all data storage locations is crucial for creating an accurate data flow diagram, as it ensures that all points where data is stored, processed, or transmitted are accounted for.

236. An organization is implementing data handling requirements for sensitive data. Which of the following is the best practice for handling such data during transmission?
a. Compressing the data before transmission
b. Using public Wi-Fi networks for transmission
c. Encrypting the data in transit
d. Sending the data in multiple smaller packets

Answer: c. Encrypting the data in transit. Explanation: Encrypting the data in transit ensures that sensitive information is protected from unauthorized access during transmission, maintaining its confidentiality and integrity.

237. A financial institution is required to maintain strict data handling procedures. What is the primary purpose of data labeling and marking within the organization?
a. To categorize data based on its size
b. To identify the owner of the data
c. To define the appropriate handling and protection measures
d. To track the data's access history

Answer: c. To define the appropriate handling and protection measures. Explanation: Data labeling and marking are used to define and communicate the appropriate handling and protection measures for different types of data, based on their classification and sensitivity.

238. In the context of data flow mapping, which of the following techniques is most effective for visualizing the movement of data within an organization?
a. Flowcharts
b. Gantt charts
c. Histograms
d. Pie charts

Answer: a. Flowcharts. Explanation: Flowcharts are effective for visualizing the movement of data within an organization, as they can clearly represent the flow of data between different processes, systems, and storage locations.

239. An organization needs to ensure that data handling procedures are followed consistently. Which of the following tools can help enforce these procedures?
a. Data Loss Prevention (DLP) systems
b. Content Management Systems (CMS)
c. Project Management Software
d. Customer Relationship Management (CRM) systems

Answer: a. Data Loss Prevention (DLP) systems. Explanation: DLP systems can help enforce data handling procedures by monitoring and controlling the movement of sensitive data, preventing unauthorized access and data breaches.

240. A company is mapping the data flow for a new application. Which of the following should be included in the data flow mapping to ensure comprehensive coverage?
a. Only internal data flows
b. Data entry points, data processing stages, and data exit points
c. Historical data storage locations
d. User access levels

Answer: b. Data entry points, data processing stages, and data exit points. Explanation: A comprehensive data flow mapping should include data entry points, data processing stages, and data exit points to ensure that all stages of data handling are accounted for.

241. In a highly regulated industry, data handling matrices must be developed. What is the primary benefit of using a data handling matrix?
a. Reducing data storage costs
b. Streamlining data processing workflows
c. Ensuring consistent data handling practices across the organization
d. Increasing employee productivity

Answer: c. Ensuring consistent data handling practices across the organization. Explanation: A data handling matrix helps ensure that data handling practices are consistent across the organization, providing clear guidelines for managing different types of data based on their classification.

242. An organization is revising its data handling procedures. Which of the following actions should be prioritized to enhance data security during handling and processing?
a. Increasing the speed of data processing
b. Implementing strong access controls and encryption
c. Reducing the number of employees handling the data
d. Outsourcing data handling to third-party vendors

Answer: b. Implementing strong access controls and encryption. Explanation: Implementing strong access controls and encryption enhances data security by restricting access to authorized personnel and protecting data from unauthorized access and breaches during handling and processing.

243. A federal agency is implementing a new information system classified as moderate impact according to FIPS 199. Which of the following best describes the initial set of security controls that should be considered for this system?
a. The low baseline from NIST SP 800-53
b. The moderate baseline from NIST SP 800-53
c. The high baseline from NIST SP 800-53
d. A custom set of controls based on the system's specific requirements

Answer: b. The moderate baseline from NIST SP 800-53. Explanation: NIST SP 800-53 provides security control baselines aligned with the FIPS 199 impact levels. For a system classified as moderate impact, the initial set of controls to consider is the moderate baseline from NIST SP 800-53. This baseline provides a starting point for security control selection, which can then be tailored based on the system's specific requirements and risk factors. The low baseline (a) would be insufficient for a moderate impact system. The high baseline (c) might be excessive. While customization (d) is part of the process, it starts with the appropriate baseline.

244. During the tailoring process for a moderate-impact system, the organization decides to implement a control from the high baseline instead of the corresponding moderate baseline control. What is the most appropriate way to document this decision?
a. No documentation is necessary as long as the control provides greater security
b. Note the change in the system security plan without further justification
c. Document the rationale for selecting the high baseline control, including the risk-based justification, in the system security plan
d. Obtain a waiver from the authorizing official to deviate from the moderate baseline

Answer: c. Document the rationale for selecting the high baseline control, including the risk-based justification, in the system security plan. Explanation: When tailoring controls, especially when implementing controls from a higher baseline, it's crucial to document the rationale and risk-based justification in the system security plan. This documentation demonstrates due diligence, supports the risk management process, and provides transparency for assessors and authorizing officials. Simply implementing the control without documentation (a) or with minimal notation (b) doesn't provide sufficient justification. A waiver (d) is not typically required for enhancing security through higher baseline controls.

245. An organization is tailoring the access control (AC) family of controls for a new system. They determine that AC-17 (Remote Access) is not applicable due to the system's isolated nature. What is the correct approach to handling this control?
a. Remove AC-17 from the security control baseline entirely
b. Implement AC-17 anyway to ensure comprehensive security
c. Replace AC-17 with a compensating control that addresses similar risks
d. Document the rationale for why AC-17 is not applicable in the system security plan

Answer: d. Document the rationale for why AC-17 is not applicable in the system security plan. Explanation: When a control is deemed not applicable during the tailoring process, the correct approach is to document the rationale for this decision in the system security plan. This provides transparency and justification for why the control is not implemented. Removing the control without documentation (a) lacks accountability. Implementing an unnecessary control (b) wastes resources. Replacing with a compensating control (c) is not appropriate if the original control is truly not applicable due to the system's nature.

246. During the security control selection process for a low-impact system, the organization identifies a unique threat not adequately addressed by the low baseline controls. Which of the following approaches is most appropriate?
a. Upgrade the entire system to the moderate baseline to address the threat
b. Ignore the threat as it's beyond the scope of a low-impact system
c. Select and implement additional controls or control enhancements that specifically address the identified threat
d. Accept the risk without additional controls as it's a low-impact system

Answer: c. Select and implement additional controls or control enhancements that specifically address the identified threat. Explanation: The tailoring process allows for the addition of controls or control enhancements beyond the baseline to address specific threats or risks. This approach provides targeted risk mitigation without unnecessarily increasing the overall control burden. Upgrading to the moderate baseline (a) may be excessive. Ignoring the threat (b) or accepting the risk without consideration (d) could leave the system vulnerable, even if it's low-impact.

247. A government contractor is implementing NIST SP 800-53 controls for a system that will process Controlled Unclassified Information (CUI). They find that certain moderate baseline controls conflict with operational requirements. What is the most appropriate way to address this situation?
a. Implement all moderate baseline controls without exception to ensure compliance
b. Downgrade to the low baseline to avoid operational conflicts
c. Document the operational constraints and implement alternative security measures that meet the intent of the conflicting controls
d. Seek a formal exemption from NIST for the conflicting controls

Answer: c. Document the operational constraints and implement alternative security measures that meet the intent of the conflicting controls. Explanation: When baseline controls conflict with operational requirements, the appropriate approach is to document the constraints and implement alternative security measures that meet the intent of the original controls. This aligns with the flexibility built into NIST guidelines, allowing organizations to adapt controls to their specific environments while maintaining security objectives. Implementing all controls without consideration of operational impact (a) may hinder system functionality. Downgrading to a lower baseline (b) would likely be insufficient for CUI protection. Seeking a NIST exemption (d) is not a standard process for control tailoring.

248. An organization is selecting security controls for a new cloud-based system. They identify that several controls in the baseline are already implemented by the cloud service provider. What is the best approach to handling these controls in the system's security plan?
a. Exclude the controls from the system's security plan as they're the provider's responsibility
b. Implement the controls again within the organization to ensure redundancy
c. Document the controls as inherited, specifying the implementation details and any organizational responsibilities
d. Replace the inherited controls with organization-specific controls

Answer: c. Document the controls as inherited, specifying the implementation details and any organizational responsibilities. Explanation: When controls are provided by a cloud service provider, they should be documented as inherited in the system's security plan. This documentation should include details on how the control is implemented by the provider and any residual responsibilities of the organization. This approach ensures clarity on control implementation and accountability. Excluding the controls (a) loses important information about the system's security posture. Redundant implementation (b) is usually unnecessary and inefficient. Replacing inherited controls (d) may leave gaps in security coverage.

249. During the tailoring process for a moderate-impact system, the organization decides to scoping a control to apply only to a specific subset of the system. Which of the following is the most critical element to include in the documentation of this decision?
a. A cost-benefit analysis of the scoping decision
b. Approval signatures from all system stakeholders
c. A clear definition of the scoping parameters and the rationale behind the decision
d. A comparison to how peer organizations have scoped similar controls

Answer: c. A clear definition of the scoping parameters and the rationale behind the decision. Explanation: When scoping a control to apply to only part of a system, it's crucial to clearly define the scoping parameters and provide a rationale for the decision. This documentation ensures transparency, supports risk management decisions, and provides context for future assessments or system changes. While cost-benefit analysis (a) can be useful, it's not the most critical element. Stakeholder signatures (b) may be part of the process but don't provide the necessary context. Peer comparisons (d) can inform decisions but aren't as important as system-specific rationale.

250. An organization is implementing a new system and finds that certain high baseline controls are necessary, even though the system is categorized as moderate impact. What is the most appropriate way to incorporate these controls?
a. Recategorize the entire system as high impact
b. Implement the high baseline controls as supplemental to the moderate baseline, documenting the justification
c. Create a hybrid baseline mixing moderate and high controls without formal documentation

d. Seek approval from NIST to modify the standard moderate baseline

Answer: b. Implement the high baseline controls as supplemental to the moderate baseline, documenting the justification. Explanation: NIST SP 800-53 allows for the implementation of controls from higher baselines when necessary to address specific risks or requirements. The appropriate approach is to implement these as supplemental to the moderate baseline, clearly documenting the justification for each addition. This maintains the integrity of the baseline selection process while allowing for necessary enhancements. Recategorizing the entire system (a) may be excessive. Creating an undocumented hybrid (c) lacks transparency and justification. Seeking NIST approval (d) is not necessary for tailoring decisions.

251. A federal agency is tailoring controls for a system that processes sensitive but unclassified information. They determine that a control enhancement from NIST SP 800-53 is necessary but will require significant resources to implement. What is the most appropriate next step?
a. Exclude the control enhancement due to resource constraints
b. Implement a compensating control that partially addresses the security objective
c. Conduct a cost-benefit analysis and risk assessment to justify the allocation of resources
d. Seek a waiver from the agency head to avoid implementing the control enhancement

Answer: c. Conduct a cost-benefit analysis and risk assessment to justify the allocation of resources. Explanation: When a necessary control or enhancement requires significant resources, the appropriate step is to conduct a thorough cost-benefit analysis and risk assessment. This process helps justify the allocation of resources and ensures that the security benefit outweighs the cost. It also provides documentation to support the decision-making process. Excluding the enhancement (a) without proper analysis could leave the system vulnerable. Implementing a partial solution (b) may not fully address the security objective. Seeking a waiver (d) should only be considered after a thorough analysis determines the control is truly not feasible or beneficial.

252. During an assessment of security control implementation, it's discovered that several tailored controls deviate significantly from their original NIST SP 800-53 descriptions. What action should be taken to ensure compliance and transparency?
a. Revert all modified controls to their original NIST SP 800-53 descriptions
b. Document the deviations, including rationale and risk acceptance, in the system security plan
c. Implement compensating controls for each modified control
d. Seek retroactive approval from the authorizing official for all modifications

Answer: b. Document the deviations, including rationale and risk acceptance, in the system security plan. Explanation: When controls are tailored to the point of significant deviation from their original descriptions, it's crucial to document these changes, including the rationale and any associated risk acceptance, in the system security plan. This documentation ensures transparency, supports risk management decisions, and provides context for assessors and authorizing officials. Reverting to original descriptions (a) may not meet the system's specific needs. Implementing compensating controls (c) isn't necessary if the modifications are justified. Seeking retroactive approval (d) may be part of the process but doesn't replace the need for thorough documentation.

253. An organization is selecting security controls for a new project and needs to ensure all relevant stakeholders are involved. Which of the following is the first step in stakeholder identification and analysis?
a. Conducting a risk assessment to identify key areas of concern
b. Creating a list of all employees in the organization
c. Identifying individuals and groups with a vested interest in the project
d. Scheduling regular meetings to discuss project progress

Answer: c. Identifying individuals and groups with a vested interest in the project. Explanation: Identifying individuals and groups with a vested interest in the project is the first step in stakeholder identification and analysis, ensuring that all relevant parties are considered and involved in the control selection process.

254. During a control selection workshop, differing opinions among stakeholders arise about the priority of implementing certain security controls. What is the best approach to reach a consensus?
a. Proceed with the majority decision and disregard minority opinions
b. Defer the decision to the highest-ranking stakeholder
c. Facilitate a discussion to address concerns and find common ground
d. Implement all proposed controls regardless of cost

Answer: c. Facilitate a discussion to address concerns and find common ground. Explanation: Facilitating a discussion to address concerns and find common ground ensures that all stakeholder viewpoints are considered, leading to a more balanced and accepted decision on security control implementation.

255. A compliance manager is preparing documentation for stakeholder sign-off on selected security controls. Which element is most critical to include in the documentation to ensure clarity and accountability?
a. The cost of each security control
b. The names and roles of all stakeholders involved
c. The technical specifications of each control
d. The potential risks mitigated by each control

Answer: b. The names and roles of all stakeholders involved. Explanation: Including the names and roles of all stakeholders involved in the documentation ensures clarity and accountability, making it clear who is responsible for approving and implementing the selected security controls.

256. An organization must ensure that its selected controls align with regulatory requirements. Which stakeholder group is most critical to involve in this process to ensure compliance?
a. IT department
b. Legal and compliance team
c. Human resources department
d. Marketing team

Answer: b. Legal and compliance team. Explanation: Involving the legal and compliance team is critical to ensure that selected controls align with regulatory requirements, providing expertise on legal obligations and compliance standards.

257. In a project meeting, stakeholders disagree on the necessity of a particular control due to its high implementation cost. What is the best way to justify the selection of this control?
a. Highlighting industry trends and peer practices
b. Emphasizing the potential legal consequences of not implementing the control
c. Stressing the technical complexity of the control
d. Pointing out the ease of integration with existing systems

Answer: b. Emphasizing the potential legal consequences of not implementing the control. Explanation: Emphasizing the potential legal consequences of not implementing the control provides a strong justification by demonstrating the risk of non-compliance and potential penalties, which can outweigh the implementation cost.

258. During the control selection process, a key stakeholder raises concerns about the potential impact on system performance. What approach should be taken to address these concerns?
a. Ignore the concerns and proceed with the control implementation
b. Replace the control with a less impactful alternative
c. Conduct a performance impact assessment and present the findings
d. Delay the control implementation until the concerns subside

Answer: c. Conduct a performance impact assessment and present the findings. Explanation: Conducting a performance impact assessment and presenting the findings addresses the stakeholder's concerns by providing data-driven insights into the actual impact, allowing for informed decision-making.

259. To document stakeholder sign-off on selected controls effectively, what key information should be included in the sign-off sheet?
a. The implementation timeline for each control
b. The budget allocation for the control implementation
c. The date and signature of each stakeholder
d. A summary of alternative controls considered

Answer: c. The date and signature of each stakeholder. Explanation: Including the date and signature of each stakeholder on the sign-off sheet ensures formal agreement and accountability, confirming that all stakeholders have reviewed and approved the selected controls.

260. An organization is conducting a control selection workshop. Which method is most effective for ensuring active participation and input from all stakeholders?
a. Providing stakeholders with the control list prior to the meeting
b. Conducting the workshop through a series of email exchanges
c. Using an anonymous voting system during the workshop

d. Allowing only senior management to make final decisions

Answer: a. Providing stakeholders with the control list prior to the meeting. Explanation: Providing stakeholders with the control list prior to the meeting ensures that they have time to review and consider the options, leading to more informed and active participation during the workshop.

261. A project manager needs to ensure that selected controls are aligned with organizational objectives. Which stakeholder should be consulted to verify this alignment?
a. Financial officer
b. Human resources manager
c. Chief Information Officer (CIO)
d. Marketing director

Answer: c. Chief Information Officer (CIO). Explanation: Consulting the Chief Information Officer (CIO) is crucial as they are responsible for ensuring that IT strategies and selected controls align with overall organizational objectives and strategic goals.

262. To ensure long-term commitment and support for the selected controls, what is the most effective strategy for engaging stakeholders?
a. Involving them only during the initial selection phase
b. Providing periodic updates on control effectiveness and adjustments
c. Offering financial incentives for their participation
d. Limiting their involvement to avoid decision-making conflicts

Answer: b. Providing periodic updates on control effectiveness and adjustments. Explanation: Providing periodic updates on control effectiveness and adjustments keeps stakeholders informed and engaged, ensuring ongoing support and commitment to the selected controls.

263. A company is developing an implementation strategy for a new security control framework. Which of the following is the most critical first step in this process?
a. Allocating budget for the project
b. Identifying and prioritizing security risks
c. Hiring additional IT staff
d. Purchasing necessary software and hardware

Answer: b. Identifying and prioritizing security risks. Explanation: The first step in developing an implementation strategy is to identify and prioritize security risks to ensure that the most critical vulnerabilities are addressed first and resources are allocated effectively.

264. When allocating resources for implementing security controls, which methodology ensures that resources are prioritized based on the risk and potential impact of threats?
a. Waterfall methodology
b. Agile methodology
c. Risk-based approach
d. Timeboxing

Answer: c. Risk-based approach. Explanation: A risk-based approach ensures that resources are prioritized and allocated based on the risk and potential impact of threats, allowing the organization to focus on the most critical areas.

265. A federal agency is planning to implement a new security control using a specific funding model. Which funding model involves obtaining financial resources from multiple departments that benefit from the control implementation?
a. Capital budgeting
b. Chargeback model
c. Centralized funding
d. Crowdfunding

Answer: b. Chargeback model. Explanation: The chargeback model involves obtaining financial resources from multiple departments that benefit from the control implementation, ensuring that costs are shared proportionally.

266. An organization needs to manage a complex security control implementation project. Which project management approach is best suited for handling changes and adapting to new security requirements as they arise?
a. Waterfall approach
b. Agile approach
c. Critical path method
d. Six Sigma

Answer: b. Agile approach. Explanation: The Agile approach is best suited for handling changes and adapting to new security requirements due to its iterative and flexible nature, allowing for continuous improvement throughout the project lifecycle.

267. During the development of an implementation strategy, which of the following is a key factor in determining the timeline for control implementation?
a. The availability of technical staff
b. The cost of control implementation
c. The criticality of the control to overall security posture
d. The number of controls to be implemented

Answer: c. The criticality of the control to overall security posture. Explanation: The timeline for control implementation should prioritize controls that are most critical to the overall security posture, ensuring that the most important vulnerabilities are addressed first.

268. In securing funding for security initiatives, which funding model allows for the distribution of costs over the useful life of the security control?
a. Capital budgeting
b. Operational expenditure (OPEX)
c. Leasing
d. Depreciation

Answer: a. Capital budgeting. Explanation: Capital budgeting allows for the distribution of costs over the useful life of the security control, providing a long-term funding approach for significant investments in security infrastructure.

269. An organization decides to use the critical path method (CPM) for a security control implementation project. What is the primary benefit of using CPM in this context?
a. Maximizing resource utilization
b. Reducing project costs
c. Identifying the longest sequence of critical tasks
d. Ensuring flexibility in project scheduling

Answer: c. Identifying the longest sequence of critical tasks. Explanation: The primary benefit of using the critical path method (CPM) is identifying the longest sequence of critical tasks that determine the project's duration, allowing the organization to focus on tasks that directly impact the project's completion time.

270. When planning the implementation of multiple security controls, what is the advantage of using a phased approach?
a. Immediate cost savings
b. Simplified project documentation
c. Reduced risk of implementation failure
d. Accelerated overall implementation timeline

Answer: c. Reduced risk of implementation failure. Explanation: A phased approach reduces the risk of implementation failure by allowing the organization to implement and test controls incrementally, making adjustments as needed before proceeding to the next phase.

271. In a project management context, which of the following tools is most effective for tracking progress and ensuring that security control implementation stays on schedule?
a. SWOT analysis
b. Gantt chart
c. Root cause analysis
d. Balanced scorecard

Answer: b. Gantt chart. Explanation: A Gantt chart is most effective for tracking progress and ensuring that security control implementation stays on schedule by visually representing the project timeline and the dependencies between tasks.

272. An organization is evaluating different funding models for its security initiatives. Which model is characterized by funding that is directly allocated from the central budget of the organization?
a. Chargeback model
b. Project-based funding
c. Centralized funding
d. Crowdfunding

Answer: c. Centralized funding. Explanation: Centralized funding is characterized by financial resources that are directly allocated from the central budget of the organization, ensuring a consistent and coordinated approach to funding security initiatives.

273. An organization is implementing a continuous monitoring program based on NIST SP 800-137. Which of the following metrics would be most effective in measuring the overall security posture of the organization's information systems?
a. Number of security incidents reported monthly
b. Percentage of systems with current patch levels
c. Time taken to detect and respond to security events
d. A composite score derived from multiple security metrics across various control families

Answer: d. A composite score derived from multiple security metrics across various control families. Explanation: NIST SP 800-137 emphasizes a holistic approach to continuous monitoring. A composite score derived from multiple metrics provides a comprehensive view of the organization's security posture, incorporating various aspects such as vulnerability management, incident response, and control effectiveness. While individual metrics like incident counts (a), patch levels (b), and response times (c) are valuable, they don't provide the broad perspective needed for overall security posture assessment in a continuous monitoring context.

274. A large enterprise is implementing a Security Information and Event Management (SIEM) system as part of its continuous monitoring strategy. Which of the following approaches would be most effective in reducing false positives while ensuring critical security events are not missed?
a. Implement machine learning algorithms to adapt alert thresholds automatically
b. Increase the sensitivity of all detection rules to capture more potential threats
c. Manually review and tune each alert rule based on historical data
d. Implement a tiered alert system with correlation rules and contextual analysis

Answer: d. Implement a tiered alert system with correlation rules and contextual analysis. Explanation: A tiered alert system with correlation rules and contextual analysis provides a balanced approach to SIEM implementation. This method allows for the detection of complex attack patterns by correlating multiple events and considering context, reducing false positives while still catching sophisticated threats. Machine learning (a) can be effective but may require significant historical data and ongoing tuning. Increasing sensitivity (b) would likely increase false positives. Manual review (c) is time-consuming and may not scale well in a large enterprise.

275. In the context of the Continuous Diagnostics and Mitigation (CDM) program, which of the following best describes the primary purpose of the "Manage What Is Happening on Your Network" phase?
a. Asset management and software inventory
b. Vulnerability management and patch deployment
c. Network access control and authentication
d. Ongoing assessment of security events and anomalies

Answer: d. Ongoing assessment of security events and anomalies. Explanation: The "Manage What Is Happening on Your Network" phase of the CDM program focuses on ongoing assessment and analysis of security-relevant events and anomalies on the network. This phase involves monitoring network activity, detecting unusual behavior, and identifying potential security incidents in real-time. Asset management (a) is part of the "What is on the Network" phase. Vulnerability management (b) aligns more with the "How is the Network Protected" phase. Network access control (c) is part of the "Who is on the Network" phase.

276. An organization is struggling to prioritize remediation efforts based on the volume of data generated by its continuous monitoring tools. Which of the following approaches would be most effective in addressing this challenge?
a. Implement automated patching for all identified vulnerabilities
b. Focus exclusively on vulnerabilities with available exploits
c. Develop a risk-based scoring system that considers vulnerability severity, asset criticality, and threat intelligence
d. Outsource all remediation activities to a managed security service provider

Answer: c. Develop a risk-based scoring system that considers vulnerability severity, asset criticality, and threat intelligence. Explanation: A risk-based scoring system that incorporates multiple factors provides a nuanced approach to prioritizing remediation efforts. This method allows the organization to focus on the most critical vulnerabilities that pose the greatest risk, considering both the technical severity and the business context. Automated patching (a) may introduce operational risks. Focusing only on known exploits (b) may overlook potentially critical vulnerabilities. Outsourcing remediation (d) doesn't address the prioritization challenge and may not align with the organization's specific risk profile.

277. Which of the following metrics would be most valuable in assessing the effectiveness of an organization's continuous monitoring program as outlined in NIST SP 800-137?
a. Number of assets scanned for vulnerabilities weekly
b. Percentage of high-risk vulnerabilities remediated within defined timeframes
c. Frequency of security status reports generated for senior management
d. Number of security tools integrated into the continuous monitoring platform

Answer: b. Percentage of high-risk vulnerabilities remediated within defined timeframes. Explanation: This metric directly measures the organization's ability to identify and address significant security risks in a timely manner, which is a key objective of continuous monitoring. It demonstrates the practical effectiveness of the program in improving security posture. The number of assets scanned (a) doesn't indicate whether issues are being addressed. Report frequency (c) is important but doesn't measure actual security improvement. The number of integrated tools (d) is a capability metric but doesn't necessarily reflect program effectiveness.

278. An organization implementing a SIEM system discovers that certain critical security events are not being logged by some legacy systems. Which of the following approaches would be most appropriate to address this gap in monitoring coverage?
a. Replace all legacy systems with modern equivalents that support comprehensive logging
b. Implement network-based monitoring and log collection to capture relevant events
c. Exclude the legacy systems from the scope of continuous monitoring
d. Apply a higher risk rating to the legacy systems in all security assessments

Answer: b. Implement network-based monitoring and log collection to capture relevant events. Explanation: When legacy systems can't provide necessary log data, network-based monitoring and log collection offer a practical solution to capture relevant security events without requiring immediate system replacement. This approach allows for comprehensive monitoring while working within existing infrastructure constraints. Replacing all legacy systems (a) may be costly and disruptive. Excluding systems from monitoring (c) creates security blind spots. Applying a higher risk rating (d) acknowledges the issue but doesn't address the monitoring gap.

279. In the context of the CDM program, what is the primary purpose of the "Ongoing Authorization" concept?
a. To eliminate the need for periodic security assessments
b. To provide real-time risk updates to system owners and authorizing officials
c. To automate the deployment of security patches across the network
d. To centralize all authorization decisions at the agency level

Answer: b. To provide real-time risk updates to system owners and authorizing officials. Explanation: The "Ongoing Authorization" concept in CDM aims to transform the traditional point-in-time authorization process into a dynamic, data-driven approach. It provides near real-time risk updates to relevant stakeholders, enabling more timely and informed risk management decisions. This doesn't eliminate the need for assessments (a) but changes their nature. It's not primarily about patch automation (c), although that may be a component. While it may inform agency-level decisions, it doesn't necessarily centralize all authorizations (d).

280. An organization is enhancing its continuous monitoring capabilities and wants to implement automated configuration checking. Which of the following approaches would be most effective in ensuring ongoing compliance with security baselines?
a. Conduct monthly manual audits of system configurations
b. Implement agent-based tools that continuously compare configurations against approved baselines and report deviations
c. Rely on system administrators to self-report any configuration changes
d. Perform annual penetration tests to identify misconfigurations

Answer: b. Implement agent-based tools that continuously compare configurations against approved baselines and report deviations. Explanation: Agent-based tools that continuously monitor and compare system configurations against approved baselines provide real-time visibility into configuration compliance. This approach aligns with the principles of continuous monitoring by enabling rapid detection and response to unauthorized changes. Monthly audits (a) leave gaps in coverage. Self-reporting (c) is prone to errors and omissions. Annual penetration tests (d) are valuable but don't provide the ongoing visibility required for continuous monitoring.

281. A federal agency is implementing the CDM program and needs to prioritize its efforts across the different capability areas. Which of the following should be the first priority according to the CDM methodology?
a. Manage What Is Happening on Your Network
b. Manage Who Is on Your Network
c. Manage What Is on Your Network
d. Manage How Is Your Data Protected

Answer: c. Manage What Is on Your Network. Explanation: The CDM program follows a layered approach, with "Manage What Is on Your Network" as the first priority. This phase focuses on asset management, providing a foundation for all other security efforts by ensuring a complete and accurate inventory of all devices and software on the network. Without this baseline knowledge, effective management of users, events, and data protection (options a, b, and d) becomes significantly more challenging.

282. An organization has implemented a comprehensive continuous monitoring program but is struggling to derive actionable insights from the large volume of data generated. Which of the following approaches would be most effective in improving the utility of the monitoring data?
a. Increase the frequency of data collection across all systems
b. Implement data visualization tools with customizable dashboards for different stakeholder groups
c. Store all raw monitoring data indefinitely for future analysis
d. Outsource data analysis to a specialized third-party service

Answer: b. Implement data visualization tools with customizable dashboards for different stakeholder groups. Explanation: Data visualization tools with customizable dashboards can significantly improve the ability to derive actionable insights from large volumes of monitoring data. By presenting information in a clear, visually intuitive manner tailored to different stakeholder needs, these tools facilitate faster and more informed decision-making. Increasing data collection frequency (a) may exacerbate the data volume challenge. Indefinite storage of raw data (c) doesn't address the immediate need for insights. Outsourcing analysis (d) may not align with the organization's specific context and may introduce delays in decision-making.

283. A financial institution is implementing a new security policy and needs to select appropriate controls to enforce it. Which of the following best describes a management control?
a. Implementing a firewall to protect the network
b. Conducting regular security awareness training for employees
c. Installing antivirus software on all company devices
d. Performing continuous vulnerability scanning

Answer: b. Conducting regular security awareness training for employees. Explanation: Management controls involve policies, procedures, and guidelines that direct the management of the organization. Security awareness training is a management control because it involves educating employees on security policies and best practices.

284. An organization needs to identify common controls that can be applied across multiple systems. Which of the following is an example of a common control?
a. User authentication protocols specific to a single application
b. Encryption standards applied to all data transmissions
c. Network configuration settings unique to one server
d. Incident response procedures tailored to a particular department

Answer: b. Encryption standards applied to all data transmissions. Explanation: Common controls are security measures that are implemented uniformly across multiple systems within an organization. Encryption standards for data transmissions are a common control as they apply broadly to protect data integrity and confidentiality across the entire network.

285. A company is implementing a hybrid control strategy to enhance its security posture. What is a key characteristic of hybrid controls?
a. They are solely technical in nature.
b. They combine elements of management, operational, and technical controls.
c. They require no ongoing maintenance or review.
d. They are designed to address physical security threats only.

Answer: b. They combine elements of management, operational, and technical controls. Explanation: Hybrid controls integrate aspects of management, operational, and technical controls to provide a comprehensive approach to security. This combination helps ensure that all facets of security are addressed in a coordinated manner.

286. During a security review, the audit team recommends implementing technical controls. Which of the following is considered a technical control?
a. Establishing a data classification policy
b. Implementing an intrusion detection system (IDS)
c. Conducting physical security assessments
d. Developing an incident response plan

Answer: b. Implementing an intrusion detection system (IDS). Explanation: Technical controls involve hardware and software mechanisms used to protect systems and data. An intrusion detection system (IDS) is a technical control that monitors network traffic for suspicious activity and alerts administrators to potential threats.

287. An operational control is being evaluated for its effectiveness in a manufacturing environment. Which of the following is an example of an operational control?
a. Creating an access control policy

b. Using biometric authentication for facility access
c. Scheduling regular backups of critical data
d. Developing a business continuity plan

Answer: c. Scheduling regular backups of critical data. Explanation: Operational controls involve day-to-day activities and procedures that ensure security and business continuity. Regular backups of critical data are an operational control, as they involve routine processes to protect data integrity and availability.

288. A company is deploying a new system and wants to ensure it meets both technical and management control requirements. What would be a suitable hybrid control to implement?
a. Developing a security policy
b. Installing a firewall
c. Establishing a security operations center (SOC) with defined procedures
d. Conducting quarterly security awareness training

Answer: c. Establishing a security operations center (SOC) with defined procedures. Explanation: A SOC with defined procedures is a hybrid control because it combines technical aspects (e.g., monitoring tools and technologies) with management elements (e.g., policies and procedures), providing a comprehensive approach to managing security.

289. When designing a new security architecture, which of the following would be classified as a management control?
a. Installing antivirus software
b. Establishing a risk management framework
c. Configuring access control lists (ACLs)
d. Performing real-time network monitoring

Answer: b. Establishing a risk management framework. Explanation: Management controls are designed to manage and oversee the security program. A risk management framework is a management control that helps identify, assess, and mitigate risks, guiding the overall security strategy.

290. To enhance the security of a cloud-based application, the IT team is considering various controls. Which of the following represents a technical control suitable for this scenario?
a. Developing a cloud usage policy
b. Conducting regular security audits
c. Encrypting data stored in the cloud
d. Training employees on cloud security best practices

Answer: c. Encrypting data stored in the cloud. Explanation: Encrypting data stored in the cloud is a technical control that helps protect sensitive information from unauthorized access by using cryptographic techniques to secure data.

291. A company is implementing controls to secure its physical data center. Which of the following is an operational control that should be included?
a. Setting up surveillance cameras
b. Developing a data center access policy
c. Installing biometric access controls
d. Regularly reviewing access logs

Answer: d. Regularly reviewing access logs. Explanation: Regularly reviewing access logs is an operational control because it involves ongoing monitoring and analysis of access records to ensure that only authorized personnel are accessing the data center, helping to detect and respond to potential security incidents.

292. In a high-security environment, which combination of controls would best mitigate risks associated with unauthorized data access?
a. Implementing encryption and developing a security policy
b. Establishing user training programs and scheduling backups
c. Deploying multifactor authentication and conducting risk assessments
d. Configuring firewalls and creating incident response plans

Answer: c. Deploying multifactor authentication and conducting risk assessments. Explanation: Deploying multifactor authentication (technical control) and conducting risk assessments (management control) provides a robust combination of measures to mitigate risks associated with unauthorized data access, ensuring that access is secure and risks are continuously evaluated.

293. An organization needs to establish a review cycle for its compliance documentation to ensure it remains current. Which of the following review cycles is most appropriate for high-risk compliance areas?
a. Annually
b. Semi-annually
c. Quarterly
d. Monthly

Answer: c. Quarterly. Explanation: High-risk compliance areas require more frequent reviews to ensure that documentation remains current and responsive to any changes in the regulatory environment or business operations.

294. A compliance officer is tasked with managing version control for compliance documents. Which of the following practices is essential for effective version control?
a. Allowing multiple employees to edit documents simultaneously
b. Maintaining a single version of each document to avoid confusion
c. Using a centralized versioning system that tracks changes and authorizes updates
d. Allowing unrestricted access to compliance documents for all employees

Answer: c. Using a centralized versioning system that tracks changes and authorizes updates. Explanation: A centralized versioning system ensures that all changes are tracked, authorized, and documented, maintaining the integrity and accuracy of compliance documents.

295. An organization is developing a repository for compliance documents. Which feature is most critical for ensuring the security and accessibility of these documents?
a. High storage capacity
b. Advanced search capabilities
c. Role-based access control
d. Integration with social media platforms

Answer: c. Role-based access control. Explanation: Role-based access control is critical for ensuring that only authorized personnel can access, modify, or view compliance documents, thereby maintaining their security and integrity.

296. A compliance manager needs to ensure that all compliance documents are regularly updated. What is the best approach to achieve this?
a. Assigning document review tasks to a single individual
b. Implementing an automated reminder system for document review deadlines
c. Reviewing all documents only when a compliance audit is announced
d. Relying on employees to voluntarily update documents

Answer: b. Implementing an automated reminder system for document review deadlines. Explanation: An automated reminder system helps ensure that document review deadlines are met consistently, facilitating regular updates and maintaining compliance.

297. During an internal audit, the team discovers several outdated compliance documents. What immediate action should the compliance officer take?
a. Remove all outdated documents from the repository
b. Notify relevant stakeholders and initiate an urgent review and update process
c. Ignore the outdated documents until the next scheduled review
d. Archive the outdated documents without review

Answer: b. Notify relevant stakeholders and initiate an urgent review and update process. Explanation: Immediate notification and an urgent review process are necessary to update the outdated documents, ensuring that compliance requirements are met and reducing the risk of non-compliance.

298. Which of the following is the best practice for managing compliance documentation review cycles?
a. Reviewing documents only when regulatory changes occur
b. Setting review cycles based on the risk level associated with each document
c. Conducting reviews during annual performance evaluations
d. Delegating review responsibilities to junior staff members

Answer: b. Setting review cycles based on the risk level associated with each document. Explanation: Tailoring review cycles to the risk level of each document ensures that higher-risk documents are reviewed more frequently, maintaining compliance and mitigating potential risks.

299. A compliance officer is tasked with implementing version control for a large volume of documents. Which tool would be most effective for this purpose?
a. Email distribution lists
b. Spreadsheets
c. Document management system (DMS)
d. Manual filing system

Answer: c. Document management system (DMS). Explanation: A Document Management System (DMS) is designed to handle version control efficiently, track changes, and maintain an audit trail, making it the most effective tool for managing large volumes of compliance documents.

300. To ensure compliance documentation is easily accessible and secure, what is the best practice for repository management?
a. Storing documents on individual employee computers
b. Utilizing a centralized, cloud-based repository with encryption
c. Printing and filing documents in a physical storage room
d. Allowing unrestricted remote access to all employees

Answer: b. Utilizing a centralized, cloud-based repository with encryption. Explanation: A centralized, cloud-based repository with encryption ensures secure storage and easy access to compliance documents from authorized personnel, enhancing both security and accessibility.

301. An organization notices frequent discrepancies in their compliance documents. What practice should they implement to improve accuracy and consistency?
a. Limiting document access to top management only
b. Conducting regular training sessions on document management for all employees
c. Using a shared drive without version control
d. Reviewing and updating documents only once a year

Answer: b. Conducting regular training sessions on document management for all employees. Explanation: Regular training sessions help ensure that all employees understand proper document management practices, improving accuracy and consistency in compliance documentation.

302. A compliance officer needs to track changes in compliance documents over time. Which feature of a document management system is most useful for this purpose?

a. Full-text search
b. Workflow automation
c. Audit trail functionality
d. Customizable templates

Answer: c. Audit trail functionality. Explanation: Audit trail functionality tracks changes, providing a history of who made changes, what changes were made, and when, thereby ensuring transparency and accountability in compliance documentation management.

303. A financial institution is unable to implement multi-factor authentication for a legacy application critical to its operations. Which of the following would be the most appropriate compensating control in this scenario?
a. Implement strong password policies with regular forced changes
b. Restrict access to the application to a specific IP range and require VPN for remote access
c. Increase logging and implement real-time monitoring of all access attempts to the application
d. Require managerial approval for each login attempt

Answer: c. Increase logging and implement real-time monitoring of all access attempts to the application. Explanation: When multi-factor authentication cannot be implemented, enhanced monitoring and logging provide a strong compensating control by enabling rapid detection and response to suspicious access attempts. This aligns with the principle of detection and response when prevention (MFA) isn't possible. Strong passwords (a) don't provide the same level of security as MFA. IP restrictions (b) can be bypassed. Managerial approval for each login (d) is impractical and doesn't provide real-time security.

304. When documenting the rationale for a compensating control, which of the following elements is most critical to include?
a. The cost savings achieved by implementing the compensating control
b. A detailed technical description of how the control is implemented
c. An explanation of how the compensating control meets or exceeds the intent of the original control
d. A comparison to industry best practices for similar controls

Answer: c. An explanation of how the compensating control meets or exceeds the intent of the original control. Explanation: The most critical element in documenting compensating control rationale is explaining how it meets or exceeds the intent of the original control. This demonstrates that the security objective is still being achieved, even if through different means. Cost savings (a) may be relevant but aren't the primary concern for security effectiveness. Technical details (b) are important but secondary to the control's intent. Industry comparisons (d) can be useful but don't directly justify the control's effectiveness in the specific context.

305. An organization is assessing the effectiveness of a compensating control implemented in lieu of network segmentation. Which of the following metrics would be most valuable in this assessment?
a. The number of devices connected to the network
b. The frequency of network scans performed
c. The time taken to detect and contain unauthorized access attempts between different parts of the network
d. The cost savings compared to implementing full network segmentation

Answer: c. The time taken to detect and contain unauthorized access attempts between different parts of the network. Explanation: When assessing a compensating control for network segmentation, the key is to measure how effectively it mimics the security benefits of segmentation. The time to detect and contain unauthorized access attempts directly reflects the control's ability to limit lateral movement, which is a primary goal of network segmentation. The number of devices (a) doesn't indicate effectiveness. Scan frequency (b) is a process metric, not an effectiveness metric. Cost savings (d) don't measure security effectiveness.

306. A healthcare provider cannot encrypt a legacy medical device's data at rest due to performance issues. Which compensating control would best address the security objective while considering the operational constraints?
a. Implement strict physical access controls to the device
b. Increase the frequency of data backups
c. Apply enhanced access logging and alerting for all data access
d. Segment the device onto its own isolated network with strict access controls

Answer: d. Segment the device onto its own isolated network with strict access controls. Explanation: When encryption isn't possible, isolating the device on a separate network segment with strict access controls provides a strong compensating control. This approach limits potential access to the unencrypted data, addressing the security objective of protecting data at rest. Physical access controls (a) don't protect against network-based attacks. Frequent backups (b) don't protect the data at rest. Enhanced logging (c) is valuable but doesn't prevent unauthorized access as effectively as network segmentation.

307. When implementing a compensating control, which of the following criteria is most important in ensuring its acceptability?
a. The control must be less expensive to implement than the original control
b. The control must use more advanced technology than the original control
c. The control must address the same risk and provide an equivalent level of protection as the original control
d. The control must be easier to manage and maintain than the original control

Answer: c. The control must address the same risk and provide an equivalent level of protection as the original control. Explanation: The most critical criterion for an acceptable compensating control is that it addresses the same risk and provides an equivalent (or greater) level of protection as the original control. This ensures that the security objective is met, even if through different means. Cost (a), technological advancement (b), and ease of management (d) may be considerations but are secondary to the primary goal of maintaining or improving security.

308. An e-commerce company cannot implement end-to-end encryption for a critical transaction processing system due to integration issues with legacy components. Which combination of compensating controls would most effectively mitigate the associated risks?
a. Implement strong access controls and increase transaction monitoring
b. Require additional authentication steps for high-value transactions
c. Encrypt data at rest and implement robust network segmentation
d. All of the above

Answer: d. All of the above. Explanation: When end-to-end encryption isn't possible, a layered approach using multiple compensating controls often provides the most comprehensive risk mitigation. Strong access controls and increased monitoring (a) help detect and prevent unauthorized access. Additional authentication for high-value transactions (b) adds a layer of security at critical points. Encrypting data at rest and network segmentation (c) protect data and limit potential exposure. Combined, these controls address various aspects of the risk that end-to-end encryption would have mitigated.

309. In assessing the effectiveness of a compensating control implemented to address a specific compliance requirement, which of the following approaches would provide the most comprehensive evaluation?
a. Conduct a penetration test targeting the specific vulnerability the control addresses
b. Review logs and reports generated by the control over a 30-day period
c. Perform a tabletop exercise simulating various attack scenarios
d. Use a combination of technical testing, log review, and scenario-based evaluation

Answer: d. Use a combination of technical testing, log review, and scenario-based evaluation. Explanation: A comprehensive assessment of compensating control effectiveness should involve multiple evaluation methods. Technical testing (like penetration tests) verifies the control's technical efficacy. Log reviews provide insights into the control's ongoing operation and effectiveness. Scenario-based evaluations (such as tabletop exercises) help assess the control's effectiveness against various potential threats. This multi-faceted approach provides a more thorough evaluation than any single method alone.

310. An organization has implemented a compensating control for a regulatory requirement but finds that the control is causing significant operational inefficiencies. What is the most appropriate next step?
a. Remove the compensating control and accept the risk
b. Revert to the original control specified by the regulation
c. Conduct a cost-benefit analysis and explore alternative compensating controls
d. Seek an exemption from the regulatory requirement

Answer: c. Conduct a cost-benefit analysis and explore alternative compensating controls. Explanation: When a compensating control causes operational issues, the best approach is to reassess the situation considering both security and operational needs. Conducting a cost-benefit analysis helps quantify the impact, while exploring alternatives may identify a solution that better balances security and operational efficiency. Simply removing the control (a) or seeking exemption (d) may create unacceptable security risks. Reverting to the original control (b) may not be feasible if it wasn't implemented for valid reasons.

311. A government agency is documenting compensating controls for an audit. Which of the following should NOT be included in the documentation?
a. The specific compliance requirement that cannot be met
b. A detailed explanation of why the original control cannot be implemented
c. The names and personal information of individuals responsible for the control
d. An analysis of how the compensating control addresses the intent of the original requirement

Answer: c. The names and personal information of individuals responsible for the control. Explanation: While documenting compensating controls, it's important to focus on the control itself rather than specific individuals. Including personal information may create privacy concerns and is generally not necessary for explaining the control's effectiveness. The compliance requirement (a), reasons for not implementing the original control (b), and analysis of how the compensating control meets the intent (d) are all crucial elements that should be included in the documentation.

312. An organization has implemented a compensating control to address a vulnerability in a critical system that cannot be patched. Six months later, a new exploit targeting this vulnerability is discovered. What is the most appropriate immediate action?
a. Shut down the affected system until a patch is available
b. Reassess the effectiveness of the compensating control against the new exploit
c. Implement additional layers of security around the affected system
d. Conduct a full penetration test of the entire network

Answer: b. Reassess the effectiveness of the compensating control against the new exploit. Explanation: When new threats emerge that could potentially bypass existing compensating controls, the immediate priority should be to reassess the control's effectiveness against this specific new threat. This allows for quick identification of any gaps and informs decisions on whether additional measures are needed. Shutting down the system (a) may be an overreaction and disruptive to operations. Implementing additional security layers (c) or conducting a full penetration test (d) may be appropriate steps but should follow the reassessment of the existing control.

313. An organization identifies several security vulnerabilities during an internal audit. What is the first step in developing a Plan of Action and Milestones (POA&M) to address these vulnerabilities?
a. Assign responsibility for each identified vulnerability
b. Prioritize vulnerabilities based on risk impact
c. Document potential mitigation strategies for each vulnerability
d. Schedule follow-up audits to ensure mitigation effectiveness

Answer: b. Prioritize vulnerabilities based on risk impact. Explanation: The first step in developing a POA&M is to prioritize vulnerabilities based on their risk impact, ensuring that the most critical issues are addressed first to minimize potential harm to the organization.

314. In the context of POA&M tracking and reporting, which of the following metrics is most critical to monitor for effective management?
a. Number of identified vulnerabilities
b. Total cost of mitigation efforts
c. Percentage of mitigations completed on schedule
d. Number of personnel involved in mitigation

Answer: c. Percentage of mitigations completed on schedule. Explanation: Monitoring the percentage of mitigations completed on schedule is crucial for effective POA&M management, as it indicates whether the organization is adhering to its planned timeline for addressing vulnerabilities.

315. A compliance officer needs to integrate the POA&M with the organization's overall risk management process. Which activity best supports this integration?
a. Conducting regular training sessions on risk management
b. Aligning POA&M items with the organization's risk register
c. Increasing the frequency of internal audits
d. Expanding the scope of risk assessments to include operational risks

Answer: b. Aligning POA&M items with the organization's risk register. Explanation: Aligning POA&M items with the risk register ensures that identified vulnerabilities are consistently tracked and managed within the broader context of the organization's risk management framework.

316. During a quarterly review, the risk management team identifies a delay in mitigating several high-risk vulnerabilities. What is the best course of action to address this issue in the POA&M?
a. Reassess the priority of the delayed vulnerabilities
b. Increase the budget for mitigation efforts
c. Extend the deadlines for all mitigation activities
d. Assign additional resources to accelerate mitigation

Answer: d. Assign additional resources to accelerate mitigation. Explanation: Assigning additional resources to address high-risk vulnerabilities can help accelerate mitigation efforts and ensure that critical security issues are resolved promptly, maintaining the integrity of the POA&M schedule.

317. An organization must report on the progress of its POA&M to senior management. Which element is most important to include in the report to provide a clear overview?
a. Detailed technical descriptions of each vulnerability
b. The names of team members responsible for each mitigation
c. The current status and completion dates of each POA&M item
d. The total number of vulnerabilities identified during the audit

Answer: c. The current status and completion dates of each POA&M item. Explanation: Providing the current status and completion dates of each POA&M item gives senior management a clear overview of progress and helps them understand whether the organization is on track to address identified vulnerabilities.

318. A security team is developing mitigation strategies for several identified vulnerabilities. Which factor is most critical to consider when prioritizing these strategies in the POA&M?
a. The cost of implementation
b. The potential impact on business operations
c. The availability of mitigation tools

d. The level of technical expertise required

Answer: b. The potential impact on business operations. Explanation: Prioritizing mitigation strategies based on their potential impact on business operations ensures that the most critical vulnerabilities that could disrupt essential functions are addressed first.

319. An organization has integrated its POA&M with its risk management process. How can it ensure continuous improvement in managing vulnerabilities?
a. Conducting annual reviews of the POA&M
b. Soliciting feedback from external auditors
c. Regularly updating the risk register with new vulnerabilities
d. Implementing a continuous monitoring program

Answer: d. Implementing a continuous monitoring program. Explanation: A continuous monitoring program enables the organization to detect and respond to new vulnerabilities in real-time, ensuring that the POA&M and risk management processes are continuously updated and improved.

320. In a review meeting, it is found that some mitigation activities are consistently delayed. What action should be taken to improve adherence to the POA&M schedule?
a. Reduce the number of identified vulnerabilities
b. Implement stricter penalties for missed deadlines
c. Conduct root cause analysis to identify reasons for delays
d. Reassign responsibilities to different team members

Answer: c. Conduct root cause analysis to identify reasons for delays. Explanation: Conducting root cause analysis helps identify underlying issues causing delays, allowing the organization to address these problems and improve adherence to the POA&M schedule.

321. A cybersecurity manager is tasked with documenting the POA&M for an upcoming audit. Which information is essential to include for each identified vulnerability?
a. Estimated cost of mitigation
b. Detailed description of the vulnerability
c. Affected systems and potential impact
d. Names of external auditors involved in the audit

Answer: c. Affected systems and potential impact. Explanation: Including the affected systems and potential impact for each vulnerability is essential for understanding the scope and significance of the issue, helping prioritize and plan appropriate mitigation strategies.

322. An organization is integrating its POA&M with its incident response plan. Which step is critical to ensure effective coordination between the two?
a. Conducting joint training exercises for incident response and risk management teams
b. Merging the budgets for incident response and POA&M activities
c. Simplifying the documentation process for both plans
d. Reducing the frequency of incident response drills

Answer: a. Conducting joint training exercises for incident response and risk management teams. Explanation: Joint training exercises help ensure that incident response and risk management teams can work together effectively, coordinating their efforts to address vulnerabilities and incidents in a unified manner.

323. An organization is developing a risk register as part of its risk management strategy. Which component is essential for capturing the source or origin of each identified risk?
a. Risk owner
b. Risk category
c. Risk score
d. Risk treatment plan

Answer: b. Risk category. Explanation: The risk category component is essential for capturing the source or origin of each identified risk, helping to classify and manage risks based on their nature and origin.

324. A risk register needs to include a method for scoring and prioritizing risks. Which scoring method combines the likelihood of a risk occurring with the potential impact if it does occur?
a. Qualitative analysis
b. Heat mapping
c. Quantitative analysis
d. Risk matrix

Answer: d. Risk matrix. Explanation: A risk matrix combines the likelihood of a risk occurring with the potential impact, providing a visual representation that helps prioritize risks based on their severity and probability.

325. During the maintenance of a risk register, what is the most important activity to ensure that risk information remains current and relevant?
a. Conducting annual reviews
b. Updating risk scores based on new data
c. Archiving old risks
d. Implementing automated alerts for risk owners

Answer: b. Updating risk scores based on new data. Explanation: Regularly updating risk scores based on new data ensures that the risk register reflects the current risk environment and helps maintain its relevance for decision-making.

326. An organization uses a qualitative method for risk scoring. Which of the following is a key characteristic of this approach?
a. Numerical risk values
b. Detailed probability distributions
c. Descriptive risk levels (e.g., high, medium, low)
d. Monte Carlo simulations

Answer: c. Descriptive risk levels (e.g., high, medium, low). Explanation: The qualitative method for risk scoring uses descriptive risk levels such as high, medium, and low, providing a more subjective assessment of risks compared to quantitative methods.

327. A project manager is reviewing the risk register and notices that some risks have not been updated in over a year. What is the best action to take?
a. Remove the outdated risks from the register
b. Notify the risk owners to review and update their risks
c. Leave the risks as they are until the next scheduled review
d. Reassign the risks to a different project team

Answer: b. Notify the risk owners to review and update their risks. Explanation: The best action is to notify the risk owners to review and update their risks to ensure the risk register remains accurate and up to date.

328. When developing a risk register, what is the primary purpose of assigning a risk owner to each identified risk?
a. To document the origin of the risk
b. To ensure accountability for managing the risk
c. To prioritize the risk based on its impact
d. To provide a qualitative description of the risk

Answer: b. To ensure accountability for managing the risk. Explanation: Assigning a risk owner to each identified risk ensures accountability and responsibility for managing the risk, helping to ensure that appropriate actions are taken to mitigate or control the risk.

329. Which component of a risk register typically includes strategies for mitigating or addressing the risk?
a. Risk score
b. Risk category
c. Risk description
d. Risk treatment plan

Answer: d. Risk treatment plan. Explanation: The risk treatment plan component includes strategies for mitigating or addressing the risk, outlining the actions to be taken to manage the risk effectively.

330. A risk register is being used to manage ongoing risks in an organization. Which of the following is a best practice for ensuring its effectiveness?
a. Limiting access to the risk register to senior management only
b. Reviewing and updating the risk register on a regular basis
c. Using a static document that is only updated during audits
d. Keeping the risk register confidential from all employees

Answer: b. Reviewing and updating the risk register on a regular basis. Explanation: Regular review and updating of the risk register ensure that it remains an effective tool for managing ongoing risks, reflecting the current risk environment and facilitating informed decision-making.

331. In the context of risk prioritization, which of the following factors is typically used to determine the overall risk score in a risk register?
a. The number of risk owners
b. The financial cost of the risk
c. The likelihood of occurrence and the impact severity
d. The organizational department affected

Answer: c. The likelihood of occurrence and the impact severity. Explanation: The overall risk score is typically determined by combining the likelihood of the risk occurring with the severity of its impact, allowing for effective prioritization of risks.

332. An organization is implementing automated alerts for its risk register. What is the primary benefit of this feature?
a. Reducing the need for risk owners
b. Ensuring timely updates and reviews of risks
c. Simplifying the risk scoring process
d. Enhancing the confidentiality of risk information

Answer: b. Ensuring timely updates and reviews of risks. Explanation: Automated alerts help ensure that risks are reviewed and updated in a timely manner, maintaining the accuracy and relevance of the risk register.

333. A multinational corporation is preparing for a comprehensive governance, risk, and compliance (GRC) audit across its global operations. Which of the following approaches would be most effective in defining the audit scope?
a. Focus exclusively on high-risk areas identified in previous audits
b. Include all business units and processes to ensure complete coverage
c. Align the scope with regulatory requirements applicable to each region
d. Use a risk-based approach considering business objectives, regulatory landscape, and recent organizational changes

Answer: d. Use a risk-based approach considering business objectives, regulatory landscape, and recent organizational changes. Explanation: A risk-based approach to defining audit scope ensures that the audit focuses on areas of greatest impact and risk to the organization. This method considers multiple factors including business objectives, regulatory requirements, and recent changes, providing a comprehensive yet targeted scope. Focusing only on previously identified high-risk areas (a) may miss new risks. Including all units and processes (b) may be inefficient and impractical for a large multinational. Aligning solely with regulatory requirements (c) might overlook important business-specific risks.

334. During evidence collection for a security compliance audit, an auditor discovers that some critical log files have been overwritten due to insufficient storage capacity. Which of the following actions should the auditor take first?
a. Immediately report a major non-compliance to senior management
b. Exclude the affected systems from the audit scope
c. Document the issue and its potential impact on the audit findings
d. Attempt to reconstruct the lost data from backup sources

Answer: c. Document the issue and its potential impact on the audit findings. Explanation: The auditor's primary responsibility is to document the situation accurately and assess its impact on the audit objectives. This approach maintains audit integrity while providing context for the findings. Reporting immediately to management (a) may be premature without full assessment. Excluding systems from scope (b) could compromise the audit's completeness. Attempting to reconstruct data (d) might be a next step but isn't the auditor's immediate responsibility and could potentially compromise evidence integrity.

335. An organization is conducting a pre-audit readiness assessment for an upcoming ISO 27001 certification audit. Which of the following activities would be most crucial in this assessment?
a. Conduct a full penetration test of all IT systems
b. Review and update all documented information security policies and procedures
c. Perform a gap analysis against the ISO 27001 requirements and current organizational practices
d. Provide comprehensive security awareness training to all employees

Answer: c. Perform a gap analysis against the ISO 27001 requirements and current organizational practices. Explanation: A gap analysis is the most critical activity in a pre-audit readiness assessment for ISO 27001. It directly compares the organization's current state against the standard's requirements, identifying areas needing improvement before the audit. This focused approach ensures efficient preparation. While important, a penetration test (a) is too narrow in scope for overall ISO 27001 readiness. Reviewing policies (b) is valuable but doesn't provide a comprehensive view of compliance. Security awareness training (d) is important but not the most crucial pre-audit activity.

336. When preparing for a compliance audit in a highly regulated industry, which evidence collection strategy would be most effective in demonstrating continuous compliance?
a. Collect all available documentation from the past year, regardless of relevance
b. Focus on collecting evidence only for areas where non-compliance was previously identified
c. Implement automated, continuous monitoring tools and provide trend data and real-time compliance status
d. Prepare detailed narratives explaining compliance processes without supporting documentation

Answer: c. Implement automated, continuous monitoring tools and provide trend data and real-time compliance status. Explanation: Automated, continuous monitoring provides the strongest evidence of ongoing compliance, offering real-time data and historical trends. This approach demonstrates proactive compliance management and provides auditors with comprehensive, reliable data. Collecting all documentation (a) is inefficient and may overwhelm auditors with irrelevant information. Focusing only on previous non-compliance areas (b) may miss new issues. Narratives without supporting documentation (d) lack the necessary evidence for a thorough audit.

337. A global financial services firm is defining the scope for its annual IT governance audit. Which of the following factors should be given the highest priority when determining the audit scope?
a. The audit budget and available resources
b. Areas of concern raised by external stakeholders
c. Systems and processes handling critical financial data and customer information
d. Newly implemented technologies and solutions

Answer: c. Systems and processes handling critical financial data and customer information. Explanation: For a financial services firm, systems and processes handling critical financial data and customer information should be the highest priority in an IT governance audit. These areas represent the core of the business and pose the highest risk in terms of regulatory compliance and potential impact of failures. While budget constraints (a), stakeholder concerns (b), and new technologies (d) are important considerations, they are secondary to the core systems handling sensitive financial and customer data in this context.

338. During an audit evidence collection process, an auditor encounters conflicting information from different sources within the organization. What is the most appropriate course of action?
a. Accept the information that presents the organization in the best light
b. Disregard all conflicting information and seek new sources
c. Use professional judgment to determine which source is most reliable
d. Document the conflicting information, seek clarification, and perform additional testing if necessary

Answer: d. Document the conflicting information, seek clarification, and perform additional testing if necessary. Explanation: When faced with conflicting evidence, the most appropriate action is to document the discrepancies, seek clarification from relevant parties, and conduct additional testing if needed. This approach maintains audit integrity, ensures thorough investigation, and provides a clear audit trail. Accepting favorable information (a) or disregarding conflicting data (b) compromises audit objectivity. Relying solely on professional judgment (c) without further investigation may lead to incorrect conclusions.

339. An organization is preparing for a compliance audit and discovers that some required controls were not implemented due to resource constraints. Which of the following approaches would be most appropriate in this situation?
a. Delay the audit until all required controls can be fully implemented
b. Proceed with the audit but exclude the areas where controls are missing
c. Implement temporary controls quickly before the audit begins
d. Document the resource constraints, any compensating controls, and plans for full implementation

Answer: d. Document the resource constraints, any compensating controls, and plans for full implementation. Explanation: When facing incomplete control implementation, the best approach is transparency. Documenting the constraints, any compensating controls in place, and concrete plans for full implementation demonstrates awareness of the issues and a commitment to compliance. This approach allows for an accurate assessment of the current state and future plans. Delaying the audit (a) may not be feasible and doesn't address the core issue. Excluding areas (b) compromises the audit's integrity. Implementing temporary controls (c) may be superficial and doesn't address the root cause.

340. In preparing for a third-party security assessment, an organization is struggling to define the appropriate scope. Which of the following approaches would be most effective in ensuring a meaningful yet manageable assessment?
a. Include all IT systems and processes to ensure comprehensive coverage
b. Focus only on systems that have direct internet exposure
c. Limit the scope to areas where previous assessments found issues
d. Use a risk-based approach to identify critical assets and processes, considering both impact and likelihood of compromise

Answer: d. Use a risk-based approach to identify critical assets and processes, considering both impact and likelihood of compromise. Explanation: A risk-based approach to scoping ensures that the assessment focuses on the most critical areas while remaining manageable. This method considers both the potential impact of a compromise and the likelihood of it occurring, providing a balanced and prioritized scope. Including all systems (a) may be overly broad and resource-intensive. Focusing only on internet-exposed systems (b) may miss critical internal vulnerabilities. Limiting to previous problem areas (c) could overlook new or evolving risks.

341. During a pre-audit readiness assessment for a HIPAA compliance audit, which of the following findings would be most critical to address immediately?
a. Outdated antivirus software on non-clinical workstations
b. Lack of a formal process for regularly reviewing and updating access rights to electronic protected health information (ePHI)
c. Incomplete documentation of security awareness training for new employees
d. Absence of encryption for internal email communications

Answer: b. Lack of a formal process for regularly reviewing and updating access rights to electronic protected health information (ePHI). Explanation: In HIPAA compliance, managing access to ePHI is crucial. The lack of a formal process for reviewing and updating access rights poses a significant risk of unauthorized access to sensitive health information, which is a core focus of HIPAA. This issue directly impacts the confidentiality and integrity of ePHI and should be addressed immediately. While important, outdated antivirus (a) on non-clinical systems is less critical. Incomplete training documentation (c) is an administrative issue. Internal email encryption (d), while valuable, is not explicitly required by HIPAA if other safeguards are in place.

342. An auditor is assessing the effectiveness of an organization's risk management process. Which of the following pieces of evidence would provide the strongest indication of a mature risk management approach?
a. A comprehensive list of all identified risks across the organization
b. Detailed risk mitigation plans for high-impact risks

c. Regular risk committee meeting minutes showing ongoing risk discussions and decision-making
d. A state-of-the-art risk management software tool implemented across all departments

Answer: c. Regular risk committee meeting minutes showing ongoing risk discussions and decision-making. Explanation: Regular risk committee meeting minutes demonstrating ongoing discussions and decision-making provide strong evidence of an active, mature risk management process. This shows that risk management is integrated into organizational governance and decision-making, not just a periodic or compliance-driven activity. A risk list (a) is important but doesn't show how risks are managed. Mitigation plans (b) are valuable but don't indicate ongoing management. A software tool (d) can support risk management but doesn't necessarily indicate maturity in process or culture.

343. During a security assessment interview, the assessor notices that some interviewees are hesitant to provide detailed answers. Which technique should the assessor use to encourage more openness?
a. Ask leading questions to guide responses
b. Use open-ended questions to allow for expansive answers
c. Insist on yes/no answers to keep the interview concise
d. Record the interview to ensure accountability

Answer: b. Use open-ended questions to allow for expansive answers. Explanation: Open-ended questions encourage interviewees to provide more detailed and informative responses, promoting a more comprehensive understanding of the security posture.

344. A company is preparing for a document examination as part of a compliance audit. Which best practice should be followed to ensure the examination is thorough and effective?
a. Review only the most recent documents to save time
b. Verify the authenticity and integrity of all documents
c. Focus on documents provided by upper management
d. Examine documents without cross-referencing them

Answer: b. Verify the authenticity and integrity of all documents. Explanation: Ensuring the authenticity and integrity of documents is crucial for an accurate and reliable assessment, as it confirms that the documents are genuine and have not been tampered with.

345. When conducting a vulnerability scan, what is the primary objective?
a. To exploit system weaknesses
b. To identify and report security vulnerabilities
c. To test the organization's incident response capabilities
d. To assess user compliance with security policies

Answer: b. To identify and report security vulnerabilities. Explanation: The primary objective of a vulnerability scan is to identify and report potential security vulnerabilities in the system, enabling the organization to address and mitigate these risks.

346. A penetration test is scheduled to evaluate an organization's network security. Which phase is crucial to ensure the test's effectiveness?
a. Reporting findings to senior management
b. Scoping and planning the test objectives
c. Conducting employee training sessions
d. Reviewing past security incidents

Answer: b. Scoping and planning the test objectives. Explanation: Proper scoping and planning are crucial for defining the objectives and scope of the penetration test, ensuring that the test targets relevant areas and meets the organization's security needs.

347. During a security assessment, the assessor uses document examination to verify compliance with security policies. What should the assessor look for to ensure completeness?
a. The length and complexity of the documents
b. Evidence that documents are periodically reviewed and updated
c. The use of technical jargon to demonstrate expertise
d. A high volume of documents to show thoroughness

Answer: b. Evidence that documents are periodically reviewed and updated. Explanation: Assessors should look for evidence that documents are periodically reviewed and updated to ensure they remain relevant and compliant with current security policies and regulations.

348. An organization wants to use interviews to gather information about its security practices. Which type of questions should be avoided to ensure the accuracy of the information collected?
a. Open-ended questions
b. Closed-ended questions
c. Leading questions
d. Clarifying questions

Answer: c. Leading questions. Explanation: Leading questions can bias the responses and lead to inaccurate information. It is important to ask neutral questions that allow interviewees to provide honest and unbiased answers.

349. What is a key benefit of conducting technical testing such as penetration tests, in addition to regular vulnerability scans?
a. Reducing the overall cost of security assessments
b. Providing real-world attack scenarios to test defenses
c. Simplifying the process of compliance reporting
d. Minimizing the need for security training

Answer: b. Providing real-world attack scenarios to test defenses. Explanation: Penetration tests simulate real-world attack scenarios, providing a practical evaluation of the organization's defenses and identifying vulnerabilities that may not be detected through regular vulnerability scans.

350. An assessor is examining logs as part of a technical assessment. What should they focus on to identify potential security incidents?
a. The volume of log entries
b. Patterns of unusual activity
c. The timestamps of the log entries
d. The size of the log files

Answer: b. Patterns of unusual activity. Explanation: Identifying patterns of unusual activity in logs can help assessors detect potential security incidents and understand their nature and impact, aiding in timely and effective response.

351. During a security assessment, why is it important to corroborate information obtained through interviews with other data sources?
a. To streamline the assessment process
b. To ensure the information is comprehensive and accurate
c. To reduce the time needed for the assessment
d. To make the interviewees feel more comfortable

Answer: b. To ensure the information is comprehensive and accurate. Explanation: Corroborating interview information with other data sources helps ensure its accuracy and comprehensiveness, providing a more reliable assessment of the organization's security posture.

352. A company is conducting a technical assessment using both automated tools and manual techniques. What is a primary advantage of this combined approach?
a. It increases the cost-effectiveness of the assessment
b. It allows for a faster assessment process
c. It ensures a more thorough identification of vulnerabilities
d. It simplifies the reporting process

Answer: c. It ensures a more thorough identification of vulnerabilities. Explanation: Combining automated tools and manual techniques ensures a more thorough assessment, as automated tools can quickly identify known vulnerabilities while manual techniques can uncover complex and context-specific issues.

353. During an internal audit, an organization must ensure that the evidence collected is valid and reliable. Which method best ensures the integrity and authenticity of digital evidence?
a. Using unencrypted USB drives for storage

b. Conducting a forensic image of the original media
c. Copying files directly from the original source
d. Relying on witness testimony to verify the evidence

Answer: b. Conducting a forensic image of the original media. Explanation: Creating a forensic image of the original media ensures that the digital evidence is an exact copy, preserving the integrity and authenticity of the evidence without altering the original data.

354. A company is establishing procedures for the chain of custody for audit evidence. Which of the following is most critical to include in the chain of custody documentation?
a. The cost of collecting the evidence
b. The location where the evidence was found
c. The names of all individuals who handled the evidence
d. The date when the evidence will be disposed of

Answer: c. The names of all individuals who handled the evidence. Explanation: Documenting the names of all individuals who handled the evidence is crucial for maintaining the chain of custody, ensuring accountability and traceability of the evidence from collection to presentation.

355. An auditor needs to select a representative sample of transactions for testing. Which sampling methodology is best suited for ensuring that all types of transactions are adequately represented?
a. Judgmental sampling
b. Random sampling
c. Stratified sampling
d. Convenience sampling

Answer: c. Stratified sampling. Explanation: Stratified sampling divides the population into distinct subgroups (strata) and selects samples from each subgroup, ensuring that all types of transactions are adequately represented in the sample.

356. In a digital forensics investigation, what is the primary purpose of maintaining a hash value for each piece of evidence?
a. To determine the size of the evidence file
b. To verify the integrity of the evidence
c. To categorize the evidence by type
d. To simplify the evidence analysis process

Answer: b. To verify the integrity of the evidence. Explanation: Maintaining a hash value for each piece of evidence ensures its integrity by providing a unique digital fingerprint that can be used to detect any alterations to the evidence.

357. An organization is using evidence sampling methodologies to verify compliance with its policies. Which of the following sampling methods is least likely to introduce bias?
a. Random sampling
b. Systematic sampling
c. Convenience sampling
d. Judgmental sampling

Answer: a. Random sampling. Explanation: Random sampling is least likely to introduce bias because it gives all items in the population an equal chance of being selected, ensuring a representative and unbiased sample.

358. During an audit, the team needs to ensure that the digital evidence collected can be admitted in court. Which practice is essential for achieving this?
a. Collecting evidence from multiple sources
b. Ensuring the evidence is stored in a central location
c. Following established forensic procedures for evidence collection and preservation
d. Having multiple auditors review the evidence

Answer: c. Following established forensic procedures for evidence collection and preservation. Explanation: Adhering to established forensic procedures ensures that the digital evidence is collected, preserved, and documented in a manner that maintains its admissibility in court.

359. An auditor is conducting an evidence validation process. What is the primary goal of this process?
a. To determine the financial impact of the findings
b. To confirm the accuracy and reliability of the evidence
c. To categorize the types of evidence collected
d. To identify potential witnesses for interviews

Answer: b. To confirm the accuracy and reliability of the evidence. Explanation: The primary goal of evidence validation is to ensure that the evidence is accurate and reliable, providing a solid foundation for audit findings and conclusions.

360. In a case-based scenario, an auditor suspects fraudulent activities within the company's financial records. Which digital forensics tool would be most effective for identifying unauthorized transactions?
a. Data recovery software
b. Network monitoring tools
c. File integrity checkers
d. Transaction analysis software

Answer: d. Transaction analysis software. Explanation: Transaction analysis software is specifically designed to identify and analyze financial transactions, making it an effective tool for detecting unauthorized or fraudulent activities within financial records.

361. When collecting digital evidence, which factor is most important to consider to ensure the evidence is admissible in legal proceedings?
a. The ease of accessing the evidence
b. The format of the evidence
c. The chain of custody documentation
d. The cost of collecting the evidence

Answer: c. The chain of custody documentation. Explanation: Maintaining proper chain of custody documentation is crucial for ensuring that digital evidence is admissible in legal proceedings, as it provides a verifiable record of how the evidence was handled and preserved.

362. An organization is implementing a new procedure for evidence sampling during audits. Which aspect is essential for ensuring the procedure's effectiveness?
a. The speed of evidence collection
b. The representativeness of the sample
c. The familiarity of auditors with the procedure
d. The number of samples collected

Answer: b. The representativeness of the sample. Explanation: Ensuring the representativeness of the sample is essential for the effectiveness of the evidence sampling procedure, as it guarantees that the sample accurately reflects the entire population being audited.

363. A global financial institution is conducting a comprehensive IT audit. During the risk identification phase, which of the following approaches would be most effective in ensuring a thorough assessment of cyber risks?
a. Focus exclusively on technical vulnerabilities identified by automated scanning tools
b. Rely primarily on historical incident data to predict future risks
c. Combine threat intelligence, vulnerability assessments, and business impact analysis in a holistic risk model
d. Prioritize risks based solely on compliance requirements applicable to the financial sector

Answer: c. Combine threat intelligence, vulnerability assessments, and business impact analysis in a holistic risk model. Explanation: A comprehensive approach that combines threat intelligence, vulnerability assessments, and business impact analysis provides the most thorough assessment of cyber risks. This method considers external threats, internal vulnerabilities, and potential business impacts, offering a holistic view of the risk landscape. Focusing only on technical vulnerabilities (a) misses broader strategic risks. Relying solely on historical data (b) may overlook emerging threats. Prioritizing based only on compliance (d) may miss critical business-specific risks not covered by regulations.

364. During an audit of a healthcare provider's information systems, the auditor needs to categorize and score vulnerabilities. Which of the following scoring systems would be most appropriate for this context?
a. CVSS (Common Vulnerability Scoring System)
b. FMEA (Failure Mode and Effects Analysis)
c. DREAD (Damage, Reproducibility, Exploitability, Affected users, Discoverability)
d. PASTA (Process for Attack Simulation and Threat Analysis)

Answer: a. CVSS (Common Vulnerability Scoring System). Explanation: CVSS is the most appropriate scoring system for categorizing and scoring vulnerabilities in information systems. It provides a standardized method for assessing the severity of software vulnerabilities, considering factors like exploitability and impact. This makes it particularly suitable for healthcare information systems where understanding the potential impact of vulnerabilities is crucial. FMEA (b) is more suited to product design and manufacturing. DREAD (c) is a legacy system less commonly used now. PASTA (d) is a risk-centric threat modeling methodology, not a vulnerability scoring system.

365. An auditor is using the NIST Risk Management Framework during an assessment. At which step of the framework would the auditor most likely identify new, previously unknown risks to the organization?
a. Prepare
b. Categorize
c. Select
d. Assess

Answer: d. Assess. Explanation: In the NIST Risk Management Framework, the "Assess" step is where the auditor would most likely identify new, previously unknown risks. This step involves a comprehensive evaluation of the selected security and privacy controls to determine if they are implemented correctly, operating as intended, and producing the desired outcomes. During this assessment, auditors often uncover risks that weren't apparent in earlier stages. The "Prepare" (a) and "Categorize" (b) steps focus on contextual and system categorization activities. "Select" (c) involves choosing controls, not identifying new risks.

366. During a threat modeling exercise as part of an IT governance audit, which of the following techniques would be most effective in identifying potential attack vectors for a complex, interconnected system?
a. Brainstorming sessions with IT staff
b. STRIDE (Spoofing, Tampering, Repudiation, Information disclosure, Denial of service, Elevation of privilege) methodology
c. Reviewing past incident reports
d. Conducting a network vulnerability scan

Answer: b. STRIDE (Spoofing, Tampering, Repudiation, Information disclosure, Denial of service, Elevation of privilege) methodology. Explanation: The STRIDE methodology is particularly effective for threat modeling in complex, interconnected systems. It provides a structured approach to identifying a wide range of potential threats across different categories, making it comprehensive and systematic. Brainstorming (a) can be useful but may lack structure for complex systems. Reviewing past incidents (c) might miss new or evolving threats. Network vulnerability scans (d) focus on technical vulnerabilities rather than broader threat modeling.

367. An auditor is assessing the risk management process of a multinational corporation. Which of the following findings would most strongly indicate a mature risk assessment framework?
a. The organization maintains a comprehensive risk register updated quarterly
b. All identified risks have detailed mitigation plans
c. The organization uses quantitative risk analysis methods to prioritize risks and allocate resources
d. Risk assessments are conducted annually for all business units

Answer: c. The organization uses quantitative risk analysis methods to prioritize risks and allocate resources. Explanation: The use of quantitative risk analysis methods for prioritization and resource allocation indicates a highly mature risk assessment framework. This approach demonstrates a sophisticated understanding of risk, allowing for more objective comparisons between different types of risks and informed decision-making. While a comprehensive risk register (a), detailed mitigation plans (b), and regular assessments (d) are important, they don't necessarily indicate the same level of maturity in risk analysis and decision-making as quantitative methods.

368. During an audit of a cloud service provider, the auditor needs to assess the effectiveness of the provider's vulnerability management program. Which of the following metrics would be most indicative of a robust vulnerability management process?
a. Number of vulnerabilities patched within the last month
b. Percentage of critical vulnerabilities remediated within defined SLAs
c. Total number of vulnerabilities identified across all systems
d. Frequency of vulnerability scans performed

Answer: b. Percentage of critical vulnerabilities remediated within defined SLAs. Explanation: The percentage of critical vulnerabilities remediated within defined Service Level Agreements (SLAs) is the most indicative metric of a robust vulnerability management process. This metric combines the prioritization of critical issues with the timeliness of remediation, reflecting both the effectiveness and efficiency of the process. The number of patched vulnerabilities (a) doesn't indicate prioritization. The total number of vulnerabilities (c) doesn't reflect remediation effectiveness. Scan frequency (d) is important but doesn't directly indicate remediation performance.

369. An organization is implementing a new risk assessment framework for IT audits. Which of the following approaches would be most effective in ensuring consistent risk evaluations across different auditors and audits?
a. Provide extensive training to all auditors on risk assessment techniques
b. Implement a standardized risk assessment matrix with clearly defined impact and likelihood criteria
c. Require all risk assessments to be reviewed and approved by a senior auditor
d. Use automated risk assessment tools for all audits

Answer: b. Implement a standardized risk assessment matrix with clearly defined impact and likelihood criteria. Explanation: A standardized risk assessment matrix with clearly defined criteria for impact and likelihood provides the most effective means of ensuring consistency across different auditors and audits. This approach establishes a common framework and language for risk evaluation, reducing subjectivity. While training (a) is valuable, it may not ensure consistency without standardized criteria. Senior review (c) can help but may introduce its own biases. Automated tools (d) can aid consistency but may lack the nuanced judgment needed in complex scenarios.

370. During a risk identification phase of an audit, an auditor discovers a potential conflict between regulatory compliance requirements and the organization's operational needs. Which of the following actions should the auditor take first?
a. Immediately report the conflict as a high-risk finding
b. Ignore the conflict as it's outside the scope of the audit
c. Investigate further to understand the full context and potential implications of the conflict
d. Recommend that the organization prioritize compliance over operational needs

Answer: c. Investigate further to understand the full context and potential implications of the conflict. Explanation: The most appropriate first action is to investigate further to fully understand the context and implications of the apparent conflict. This allows the auditor to gather all relevant information before making any judgments or recommendations. Immediately reporting as high-risk (a) may be premature without full understanding. Ignoring the conflict (b) would be neglectful of the auditor's responsibilities. Recommending prioritization of compliance (d) without full investigation could lead to inappropriate or unnecessary operational disruptions.

371. An auditor is assessing the vulnerability management process of a large e-commerce platform. Which of the following scenarios would represent the highest risk in this context?
a. A critical vulnerability in the payment processing system that has been identified but not yet patched
b. Multiple low-severity vulnerabilities in the content management system
c. An unpatched moderate vulnerability in an internal HR system
d. A high-severity vulnerability in a third-party analytics tool used on the website

Answer: a. A critical vulnerability in the payment processing system that has been identified but not yet patched. Explanation: In an e-commerce context, a critical vulnerability in the payment processing system represents the highest risk. It directly threatens the core business function (processing payments) and could lead to significant financial losses and reputational damage if exploited. Multiple low-severity vulnerabilities (b) are concerning but less urgent. An unpatched moderate vulnerability in an internal system (c) is important but likely has less direct impact on core e-commerce operations. A high-severity vulnerability in a third-party tool (d) is serious but typically less critical than core payment systems.

372. During a threat modeling exercise for a new IoT product line, which of the following threat actors should be considered most critical in the risk assessment?
a. Script kiddies using readily available hacking tools
b. Insider threats from disgruntled employees
c. Nation-state actors conducting industrial espionage
d. Cybercriminals seeking to create large-scale botnets

Answer: d. Cybercriminals seeking to create large-scale botnets. Explanation: For IoT devices, the threat of cybercriminals creating large-scale botnets is often the most critical to consider. IoT devices are frequently targeted for botnet creation due to their often weak security measures and constant connectivity, posing risks not just to the devices themselves but to the broader internet ecosystem. While script kiddies (a) can cause disruption, their impact is usually limited. Insider threats (b) are important but may have less widespread impact in IoT contexts. Nation-state actors (c) are a serious threat but typically target more specific, high-value assets rather than consumer IoT devices en masse.

373. An organization identifies a critical security vulnerability in its online payment system that could lead to a data breach. Which risk response strategy should be prioritized to address this issue?
a. Accept the risk and monitor the system for breaches
b. Mitigate the risk by implementing additional security controls
c. Transfer the risk by purchasing cybersecurity insurance
d. Avoid the risk by discontinuing the online payment system

Answer: b. Mitigate the risk by implementing additional security controls. Explanation: Mitigating the risk by implementing additional security controls is the most appropriate strategy, as it directly addresses the vulnerability and reduces the likelihood of a data breach, maintaining the functionality of the online payment system.

374. A company decides to transfer the risk associated with a potential data breach by purchasing cybersecurity insurance. What should be the primary consideration when selecting an insurance policy?
a. The cost of the insurance premiums
b. The reputation of the insurance provider
c. The coverage limits and exclusions of the policy
d. The payment terms and conditions

Answer: c. The coverage limits and exclusions of the policy. Explanation: The coverage limits and exclusions of the policy are crucial to ensure that the insurance adequately covers the potential impact of a data breach, providing financial protection against specific risks.

375. During a risk assessment, a company identifies a low-probability, high-impact risk. After conducting a cost-benefit analysis, the decision is made to accept the risk. What is the most appropriate next step?
a. Develop a contingency plan to address potential impacts
b. Ignore the risk and focus on more probable threats
c. Implement additional controls to further reduce the risk
d. Transfer the risk to a third party

Answer: a. Develop a contingency plan to address potential impacts. Explanation: Developing a contingency plan ensures that the organization is prepared to respond effectively if the low-probability, high-impact risk materializes, minimizing potential damage.

376. An organization has identified multiple risks and needs to document its risk response plans. Which element is essential to include in the risk response documentation?
a. A detailed history of past risk assessments
b. The names of the team members who identified the risks
c. Specific actions to be taken to address each risk
d. The budget allocated for risk management activities

Answer: c. Specific actions to be taken to address each risk. Explanation: Including specific actions to address each risk in the documentation ensures clarity and accountability, providing a clear plan for mitigating or managing the identified risks.

377. In preparing a risk response plan, an organization decides to mitigate a risk by implementing a new security technology. What should be the primary factor in the cost-benefit analysis of this decision?
a. The initial cost of the technology
b. The potential reduction in risk exposure
c. The ease of implementation
d. The vendor's reputation

Answer: b. The potential reduction in risk exposure. Explanation: The primary factor in the cost-benefit analysis should be the potential reduction in risk exposure, as the goal is to determine whether the benefits of the new security technology justify its costs in terms of reducing the identified risk.

378. A company's risk response plan includes transferring a risk to a third-party vendor. What is a critical step in ensuring the effectiveness of this strategy?
a. Negotiating the lowest possible contract cost
b. Ensuring the vendor has adequate security measures in place
c. Limiting the vendor's access to company data
d. Reviewing the vendor's financial stability

Answer: b. Ensuring the vendor has adequate security measures in place. Explanation: Ensuring the vendor has adequate security measures in place is critical for effective risk transfer, as it ensures that the vendor can appropriately manage the risk on behalf of the company.

379. In documenting the risk response plan, the risk management team includes a tracking mechanism. What is the primary purpose of this mechanism?
a. To monitor the progress of risk response actions
b. To allocate budget for risk management
c. To evaluate the effectiveness of the risk response team
d. To document compliance with regulatory requirements

Answer: a. To monitor the progress of risk response actions. Explanation: The primary purpose of a tracking mechanism in the risk response plan is to monitor the progress of risk response actions, ensuring that they are implemented as planned and are effective in mitigating risks.

380. An organization decides to avoid a risk by discontinuing a particular business operation. What should be considered to ensure this decision aligns with the overall business strategy?
a. The impact on the company's revenue streams
b. The ease of discontinuing the operation

c. The availability of alternative business operations
d. The feedback from customers and stakeholders

Answer: a. The impact on the company's revenue streams. Explanation: Considering the impact on the company's revenue streams ensures that the decision to avoid the risk does not adversely affect the overall business strategy and financial health of the organization.

381. A risk response plan includes accepting a risk due to its low impact and probability. How should this decision be communicated within the organization?
a. Through a formal memo to the risk management team only
b. By updating the risk register and informing all relevant stakeholders
c. By conducting a company-wide meeting to discuss the decision
d. Through informal conversations with department heads

Answer: b. By updating the risk register and informing all relevant stakeholders. Explanation: Updating the risk register and informing all relevant stakeholders ensures transparency and that everyone involved is aware of the accepted risk and its rationale, promoting informed decision-making and accountability.

382. During a risk review meeting, it is discovered that a previously mitigated risk has re-emerged. What should be the immediate course of action?
a. Re-evaluate and update the risk response plan
b. Accept the risk and monitor its development
c. Transfer the risk to an external party
d. Ignore the risk if it is deemed non-critical

Answer: a. Re-evaluate and update the risk response plan. Explanation: Re-evaluating and updating the risk response plan ensures that the re-emerged risk is appropriately addressed based on current conditions, maintaining the organization's risk management effectiveness.

383. An internal audit team is finalizing the audit report for a recent compliance review. Which component is essential to include in the executive summary?
a. Detailed risk assessment methodology
b. Comprehensive audit plan
c. Key findings and recommendations
d. Complete list of audit participants

Answer: c. Key findings and recommendations. Explanation: The executive summary should provide a concise overview of the key findings and recommendations from the audit, giving stakeholders a quick understanding of the audit's results and suggested actions.

384. In the final audit report, how should critical findings be classified and presented?
a. Integrated into the general findings section
b. Highlighted separately with specific emphasis and detailed explanations
c. Mentioned briefly in the conclusion
d. Included as an appendix

Answer: b. Highlighted separately with specific emphasis and detailed explanations. Explanation: Critical findings should be clearly highlighted and presented with detailed explanations to ensure they receive the necessary attention and prompt action from management.

385. An auditor needs to ensure that management's response is included in the final audit report. What is the primary purpose of including management's response?
a. To provide additional audit findings
b. To document management's acceptance or rejection of audit recommendations
c. To extend the length of the audit report
d. To justify the audit's scope and objectives

Answer: b. To document management's acceptance or rejection of audit recommendations. Explanation: Including management's response in the audit report documents their acceptance or rejection of the recommendations and outlines their proposed actions to address the findings.

386. When developing an audit report, which section typically provides a detailed description of the scope and objectives of the audit?
a. Background section
b. Findings and recommendations section
c. Executive summary
d. Conclusion

Answer: a. Background section. Explanation: The background section of the audit report typically provides a detailed description of the scope and objectives, setting the context for the audit and explaining what was reviewed and why.

387. During the preparation of the final audit report, the team must classify findings based on their severity. Which of the following represents the correct order of severity from highest to lowest?
a. High, Medium, Low, Critical
b. Critical, High, Medium, Low
c. Low, Medium, High, Critical
d. Medium, High, Low, Critical

Answer: b. Critical, High, Medium, Low. Explanation: The correct order of severity from highest to lowest is Critical, High, Medium, and Low, ensuring that the most serious issues are prioritized for attention and remediation.

388. A significant portion of the final audit report is dedicated to the findings and recommendations section. What is the primary goal of this section?
a. To summarize the audit methodology
b. To highlight the auditor's credentials
c. To present the identified issues and suggest corrective actions
d. To detail the financial impact of the audit

Answer: c. To present the identified issues and suggest corrective actions. Explanation: The findings and recommendations section presents the issues identified during the audit and provides suggestions for corrective actions to address these issues.

389. In the final audit report, which element is most crucial for ensuring that the report is actionable for management?
a. Length of the report
b. Use of technical jargon
c. Clarity and specificity of recommendations
d. Inclusion of historical audit data

Answer: c. Clarity and specificity of recommendations. Explanation: Clear and specific recommendations are crucial for ensuring that the audit report is actionable, providing management with precise guidance on how to address the identified issues.

390. When presenting audit findings, what is the advantage of categorizing them by severity (e.g., critical, high, medium, low)?
a. It simplifies the audit report writing process
b. It allows management to prioritize their response efforts
c. It makes the report more aesthetically pleasing
d. It reduces the need for detailed explanations

Answer: b. It allows management to prioritize their response efforts. Explanation: Categorizing findings by severity helps management prioritize their response efforts, focusing first on the most critical issues that pose the greatest risk to the organization.

391. An auditor is drafting the conclusion of the final audit report. Which statement best describes the purpose of the conclusion section?
a. To introduce the audit team
b. To reiterate the audit scope and objectives
c. To summarize the overall results and effectiveness of the audit
d. To provide a detailed list of all findings

Answer: c. To summarize the overall results and effectiveness of the audit. Explanation: The conclusion section summarizes the overall results and effectiveness of the audit, providing a final assessment and any overarching comments or recommendations.

392. Which best practice should auditors follow to ensure that management responses are effectively integrated into the final audit report?
a. Write the management responses themselves
b. Collaborate with management to review and refine their responses
c. Include only positive feedback from management
d. Limit management responses to a single paragraph

Answer: b. Collaborate with management to review and refine their responses. Explanation: Collaborating with management to review and refine their responses ensures that the responses are clear, actionable, and adequately address the audit findings and recommendations.

393. An organization is developing a System Security Plan (SSP) for a new application. Which of the following elements is essential to include in the SSP to ensure it is comprehensive and effective?
a. A list of all users who will access the application
b. Detailed descriptions of the security controls implemented
c. The marketing strategy for the application
d. A summary of the application's user interface design

Answer: b. Detailed descriptions of the security controls implemented. Explanation: The SSP must include detailed descriptions of the security controls implemented to ensure that all security measures are documented, understood, and can be reviewed for effectiveness and compliance.

394. During the Privacy Impact Assessment (PIA) for a new customer database, what is the primary focus of the assessment?
a. Evaluating the technical performance of the database
b. Determining the potential impact on customer privacy
c. Assessing the financial cost of implementing the database
d. Identifying the key stakeholders involved in the project

Answer: b. Determining the potential impact on customer privacy. Explanation: The primary focus of a PIA is to evaluate the potential impact on privacy, ensuring that any risks to personal data are identified and mitigated before the system is implemented.

395. A Security Assessment Report (SAR) is being prepared following a security assessment. Which component is most critical to include to provide a clear understanding of the system's security posture?
a. The names of the assessment team members
b. Detailed findings of identified vulnerabilities
c. The budget allocated for the security assessment

d. A list of software licenses used in the system

Answer: b. Detailed findings of identified vulnerabilities. Explanation: The SAR should include detailed findings of identified vulnerabilities to provide a clear understanding of the system's security posture and the specific areas that need remediation.

396. In developing the SSP, an organization needs to ensure that all applicable security controls are documented. What methodology should be used to select and tailor these controls?
a. Cost-benefit analysis
b. Risk-based approach
c. Industry benchmarking
d. Stakeholder voting

Answer: b. Risk-based approach. Explanation: A risk-based approach ensures that security controls are selected and tailored based on the specific risks faced by the system, providing a targeted and effective security strategy.

397. When conducting a PIA, which of the following is a key consideration for identifying privacy risks?
a. The usability of the system interface
b. The type and sensitivity of the personal data collected
c. The physical location of the data center
d. The training level of system administrators

Answer: b. The type and sensitivity of the personal data collected. Explanation: Identifying the type and sensitivity of the personal data collected is crucial for assessing privacy risks and ensuring appropriate protections are in place to safeguard sensitive information.

398. A company is preparing a Security Assessment Report (SAR) and needs to include recommendations for addressing identified vulnerabilities. What should be the primary factor in prioritizing these recommendations?
a. The potential impact on system functionality
b. The cost of implementing the recommendations
c. The severity and likelihood of the vulnerabilities being exploited
d. The ease of implementing the recommendations

Answer: c. The severity and likelihood of the vulnerabilities being exploited. Explanation: Prioritizing recommendations based on the severity and likelihood of vulnerabilities being exploited ensures that the most critical issues are addressed first, enhancing the overall security posture of the system.

399. An organization is required to update its System Security Plan (SSP) regularly. What is the primary reason for this requirement?
a. To comply with financial reporting standards

b. To reflect changes in the system environment and security controls
c. To increase the complexity of the SSP
d. To improve the readability of the document

Answer: b. To reflect changes in the system environment and security controls. Explanation: Regular updates to the SSP ensure that it accurately reflects the current system environment and security controls, maintaining its relevance and effectiveness in managing security risks.

400. During the PIA process, stakeholders express concerns about data retention policies. What is the best approach to address these concerns?
a. Increase the data retention period to ensure availability
b. Shorten the data retention period to minimize risk
c. Align data retention policies with regulatory requirements and best practices
d. Exclude data retention policies from the PIA scope

Answer: c. Align data retention policies with regulatory requirements and best practices. Explanation: Aligning data retention policies with regulatory requirements and best practices addresses stakeholder concerns by ensuring compliance and minimizing privacy risks associated with data retention.

401. A Security Assessment Report (SAR) includes a section on the effectiveness of existing security controls. Which type of information is most relevant for this section?
a. The historical performance data of the security controls
b. The feedback from end-users about the controls
c. The results of recent security tests and audits
d. The opinions of the security team about the controls

Answer: c. The results of recent security tests and audits. Explanation: Including the results of recent security tests and audits provides objective evidence of the effectiveness of existing security controls, offering a reliable basis for evaluating the system's security posture.

402. An organization is developing its SSP and needs to ensure that it includes appropriate contingency planning controls. What should be the focus of these controls?
a. Preventing data breaches
b. Ensuring the system's availability and integrity during disruptions
c. Reducing the complexity of the system
d. Enhancing user experience

Answer: b. Ensuring the system's availability and integrity during disruptions. Explanation: Contingency planning controls focus on ensuring that the system remains available and its integrity is maintained during disruptions, providing resilience against incidents and minimizing downtime.

403. A cybersecurity manager is using the OCTAVE (Operationally Critical Threat, Asset, and Vulnerability Evaluation) methodology to assess system risk. What is the primary focus of the OCTAVE methodology?
a. Identifying and classifying threats
b. Evaluating the impact of external threats
c. Balancing operational risk and strategic goals
d. Managing and mitigating risks to critical assets

Answer: d. Managing and mitigating risks to critical assets. Explanation: The OCTAVE methodology focuses on managing and mitigating risks to an organization's critical assets by identifying vulnerabilities, threats, and the associated risks.

404. During a risk assessment, an organization uses the FAIR (Factor Analysis of Information Risk) methodology. Which aspect does FAIR primarily focus on to quantify risk?
a. Potential regulatory fines
b. Asset replacement costs
c. Frequency and magnitude of loss events
d. Employee training costs

Answer: c. Frequency and magnitude of loss events. Explanation: The FAIR methodology quantifies risk by focusing on the frequency and magnitude of potential loss events, providing a structured approach to analyzing and quantifying information risk.

405. A company is deciding between quantitative and qualitative risk analysis. Which of the following is a primary advantage of quantitative risk analysis?
a. Simplicity and ease of understanding
b. Ability to prioritize risks based on descriptive levels
c. Precision in estimating potential financial impacts
d. Flexibility in interpreting risk scenarios

Answer: c. Precision in estimating potential financial impacts. Explanation: Quantitative risk analysis provides precise estimates of potential financial impacts, allowing organizations to make data-driven decisions based on numerical values and statistical models.

406. An organization needs to aggregate system-level risks to determine its overall risk posture. Which approach best ensures a comprehensive aggregation of these risks?
a. Summarizing all risks without considering interdependencies
b. Focusing only on high-severity risks
c. Integrating risk data from all systems and considering interdependencies and cumulative effects
d. Relying on historical data to predict future risks

Answer: c. Integrating risk data from all systems and considering interdependencies and cumulative effects. Explanation: A comprehensive aggregation of risks involves integrating risk data from all systems and considering interdependencies and cumulative effects, providing a holistic view of the organization's overall risk posture.

407. A risk assessment reveals that a critical system has multiple high-impact vulnerabilities. What should be the immediate priority for the organization?
a. Documenting the vulnerabilities in the risk register
b. Conducting a cost-benefit analysis of remediation options
c. Implementing immediate mitigation measures to reduce the risk
d. Communicating the findings to all employees

Answer: c. Implementing immediate mitigation measures to reduce the risk. Explanation: The immediate priority should be to implement mitigation measures to reduce the risk associated with high-impact vulnerabilities, protecting the critical system from potential threats.

408. An auditor needs to validate the effectiveness of a risk assessment methodology used by an organization. Which element is most critical to review?
a. The number of risks identified
b. The alignment with industry best practices and standards
c. The cost of conducting the risk assessment
d. The ease of use of the risk assessment tools

Answer: b. The alignment with industry best practices and standards. Explanation: Reviewing the alignment with industry best practices and standards ensures that the risk assessment methodology is robust, comprehensive, and effective in identifying and mitigating risks.

409. When determining the risk posture of an information system, which factor is least likely to be considered?
a. The system's compliance with regulatory requirements
b. The technical specifications of the system hardware
c. The potential impact of data breaches on organizational operations
d. The effectiveness of implemented security controls

Answer: b. The technical specifications of the system hardware. Explanation: While important, the technical specifications of the system hardware are less likely to be considered when determining risk posture compared to factors like compliance, impact of data breaches, and effectiveness of security controls.

410. An organization performs a qualitative risk analysis and identifies several high-risk scenarios. What is a key benefit of using qualitative analysis in this context?
a. Providing precise financial estimates of risks
b. Enabling rapid identification and prioritization of risks
c. Allowing for detailed statistical analysis of risks
d. Ensuring consistent risk measurement across different systems

Answer: b. Enabling rapid identification and prioritization of risks. Explanation: Qualitative risk analysis allows for the rapid identification and prioritization of risks based on descriptive levels, enabling organizations to quickly focus on the most significant risks.

411. A system risk assessment indicates that the likelihood of a particular threat is low, but the impact would be catastrophic if it occurred. How should the organization address this risk?
a. Ignore the risk due to its low likelihood
b. Accept the risk as part of doing business
c. Implement robust mitigation strategies despite the low likelihood
d. Focus on more likely but less severe risks

Answer: c. Implement robust mitigation strategies despite the low likelihood. Explanation: Even though the likelihood is low, the catastrophic impact warrants implementing robust mitigation strategies to protect the organization from severe consequences.

412. In the context of risk posture determination, what is the primary purpose of integrating risk assessment results with strategic business objectives?
a. To ensure compliance with all regulatory requirements
b. To align risk management efforts with organizational goals
c. To minimize the costs of risk mitigation
d. To simplify the risk assessment process

Answer: b. To align risk management efforts with organizational goals. Explanation: Integrating risk assessment results with strategic business objectives ensures that risk management efforts support and enhance the organization's overall goals, providing a cohesive approach to managing risk.

413. A large financial institution has implemented a new fraud detection system. After applying several controls, the organization calculates a residual risk score of 6 out of 10. Which of the following actions would be most appropriate given this residual risk level?
a. Accept the risk and implement the system as-is
b. Delay implementation until the risk score can be reduced to 3 or lower
c. Implement additional controls to further reduce the risk score
d. Conduct a cost-benefit analysis to determine if the residual risk is acceptable given the system's benefits

Answer: d. Conduct a cost-benefit analysis to determine if the residual risk is acceptable given the system's benefits. Explanation: When faced with a moderate residual risk score, the most appropriate action is to conduct a cost-benefit analysis. This approach allows the organization to weigh the potential benefits of the fraud detection system against the remaining risks, ensuring an informed decision. Simply accepting the risk (a) without further analysis may be premature. Delaying implementation (b) or implementing additional controls (c) without considering the system's benefits could result in missed opportunities or unnecessary costs.

414. Which of the following methods is most effective for calculating residual risk in a complex IT environment with multiple, interconnected systems?
a. Subtracting the sum of control effectiveness from inherent risk
b. Using a risk matrix to plot likelihood and impact after control implementation
c. Applying Monte Carlo simulation to model various risk scenarios post-control implementation
d. Calculating the average risk score across all systems after controls are applied

Answer: c. Applying Monte Carlo simulation to model various risk scenarios post-control implementation. Explanation: In a complex, interconnected IT environment, Monte Carlo simulation provides the most comprehensive approach to calculating residual risk. This method allows for modeling multiple variables and their interactions, providing a more nuanced understanding of residual risk across various scenarios. Simple subtraction (a) or risk matrix plotting (b) may oversimplify complex relationships between risks and controls. Averaging risk scores (d) could obscure critical high-risk areas within the overall environment.

415. An organization has established a residual risk acceptance criterion of "no high risks" for its critical systems. During a risk assessment, a system is found to have a residual risk classified as "high" due to a newly discovered vulnerability. What should be the immediate next step?
a. Shut down the system until the risk can be mitigated
b. Escalate the issue to senior management for risk acceptance decision
c. Implement emergency controls to reduce the risk level
d. Reassess the risk classification criteria to see if the "high" classification is warranted

Answer: b. Escalate the issue to senior management for risk acceptance decision. Explanation: When a residual risk exceeds established acceptance criteria, the immediate next step should be to escalate the issue to senior management. This allows for a strategic decision on whether to accept the risk (potentially revising the acceptance criteria) or allocate resources for further mitigation. Shutting down the system (a) may be an overreaction without management input. Implementing emergency controls (c) or reassessing classification criteria (d) should not be done without management awareness and approval, given the violation of established risk criteria.

416. In the context of ongoing monitoring of residual risks, which of the following indicators would most strongly suggest that a previously accepted residual risk needs to be re-evaluated?
a. A 5% increase in the number of attempted security breaches
b. Introduction of new regulatory requirements in the industry
c. A change in the organization's senior leadership
d. A minor update to the system's operating system

Answer: b. Introduction of new regulatory requirements in the industry. Explanation: The introduction of new regulatory requirements is the strongest indicator that previously accepted residual risks need re-evaluation. New regulations can significantly change the risk landscape, potentially making previously acceptable residual risks no longer compliant or acceptable. A small increase in attempted breaches (a) may not necessarily change the risk profile significantly. Leadership changes (c) might affect risk appetite but don't directly impact existing residual risks. Minor system updates (d) typically don't warrant full risk re-evaluation unless they address specific vulnerabilities.

417. An organization uses a quantitative approach to residual risk calculation. After implementing controls, the Annual Loss Expectancy (ALE) for a particular risk is reduced from $100,000 to $20,000. The cost of controls is $15,000 annually. Which of the following best describes the residual risk in financial terms?
a. $20,000
b. $5,000
c. $80,000
d. $35,000

Answer: a. $20,000. Explanation: In quantitative risk analysis, the residual risk is typically expressed as the remaining ALE after controls are implemented. In this case, the residual risk is $20,000, which represents the expected annual loss that remains despite the implemented controls. The $5,000 (b) represents the net benefit of the controls (risk reduction minus control cost) but not the residual risk itself. $80,000 (c) is the risk reduction achieved. $35,000 (d) incorrectly adds the control cost to the residual ALE.

418. A healthcare organization is assessing residual risks related to patient data protection. Which of the following scenarios represents the most critical residual risk requiring immediate attention?
a. Potential for unauthorized physical access to a server room, mitigated by keycard access and security cameras
b. Risk of data interception during transmission, mitigated by encryption but without regular key rotation
c. Possibility of insider threat, partially mitigated by access controls and audit logs
d. Risk of data loss due to hardware failure, mitigated by regular backups but with untested restoration processes

Answer: d. Risk of data loss due to hardware failure, mitigated by regular backups but with untested restoration processes. Explanation: In a healthcare context, the risk of data loss with untested restoration processes represents the most critical residual risk. While backups mitigate the initial risk, the inability to ensure successful data restoration could lead to significant operational disruptions and potential violation of data protection regulations. The other scenarios (a, b, c) have more robust mitigation measures in place, even if not perfect. Untested restoration processes leave a critical gap in the overall data protection strategy.

419. An organization uses a 5x5 risk matrix for residual risk assessment, with likelihood and impact each rated from 1 (lowest) to 5 (highest). After implementing controls, a particular risk is assessed as having a likelihood of 2 and an impact of 4. What is the most appropriate next step in managing this residual risk?
a. Accept the risk as it falls within the moderate range
b. Implement additional controls to further reduce the likelihood
c. Transfer the risk through insurance or third-party contracts
d. Conduct a detailed analysis of the potential impact to determine if it can be reduced

Answer: d. Conduct a detailed analysis of the potential impact to determine if it can be reduced. Explanation: With a moderate likelihood (2) but high impact (4), the most appropriate next step is to analyze the potential impact in detail. This approach focuses on the aspect of the risk that remains significant despite controls. Understanding the impact more thoroughly can reveal opportunities for impact reduction strategies or inform better-prepared response plans. Simply accepting the risk (a) may overlook opportunities for further mitigation. Focusing on likelihood reduction (b) may not be the most effective approach given the already low likelihood. Risk transfer (c) might be considered but shouldn't be the first option without a more detailed understanding of the impact.

420. In establishing residual risk acceptance criteria, an organization is debating between using quantitative thresholds and qualitative descriptions. Which of the following approaches would likely provide the most consistent and defensible basis for residual risk acceptance decisions?
a. Use qualitative descriptions (e.g., "low," "medium," "high") based on industry best practices
b. Establish quantitative thresholds based on the organization's risk appetite and financial capacity
c. Adopt a hybrid approach using quantitative thresholds with qualitative descriptors
d. Allow each department to set its own acceptance criteria based on its specific context

Answer: c. Adopt a hybrid approach using quantitative thresholds with qualitative descriptors. Explanation: A hybrid approach combining quantitative thresholds with qualitative descriptors often provides the most robust basis for residual risk acceptance decisions. Quantitative thresholds offer objective, measurable criteria, while qualitative descriptors provide context and aid in communication. This combination supports consistent decision-making while allowing for nuanced interpretation. Purely qualitative descriptions (a) can be subjective and inconsistent. Solely quantitative thresholds (b) may miss important contextual factors. Allowing each department to set criteria (d) could lead to inconsistencies across the organization.

421. An IT audit reveals that the residual risks for several systems exceed the organization's defined acceptance criteria. However, immediate mitigation is not feasible due to budget constraints. Which of the following approaches would be most appropriate in this situation?
a. Ignore the excess risks until the next budget cycle when mitigation funds may be available
b. Revise the risk acceptance criteria to accommodate the current risk levels
c. Develop a phased mitigation plan prioritizing the most critical risks, and document formal risk acceptance for the interim period
d. Transfer all excess risks to a third-party service provider

Answer: c. Develop a phased mitigation plan prioritizing the most critical risks, and document formal risk acceptance for the interim period. Explanation: When immediate full mitigation isn't feasible, the most appropriate approach is to develop a phased plan that addresses the most critical risks first while formally accepting the remaining risks for a defined interim period. This balanced approach demonstrates due diligence in risk management within resource constraints. Ignoring the risks (a) is irresponsible and potentially non-compliant. Revising acceptance criteria (b) to fit current levels undermines the purpose of having criteria. Transferring all excess risks (d) may not be practical or cost-effective and doesn't address the root issues.

422. An organization implements a new control expected to reduce a particular risk by 70%. However, post-implementation monitoring shows only a 50% reduction. Which of the following is the most appropriate next step in managing this residual risk?
a. Accept the 50% reduction as sufficient and maintain current controls
b. Immediately implement additional controls to achieve the expected 70% reduction
c. Analyze the discrepancy between expected and actual risk reduction to understand the underlying factors
d. Revert to the previous control setup as the new control didn't meet expectations

Answer: c. Analyze the discrepancy between expected and actual risk reduction to understand the underlying factors. Explanation: When there's a significant difference between expected and actual risk reduction, the most appropriate step is to analyze this discrepancy. This analysis can reveal important insights about the nature of the risk, the effectiveness of the control, or changes in the risk environment. Understanding these factors is crucial for making informed decisions about further risk management actions. Accepting the reduction without analysis (a) misses an opportunity for improvement. Implementing additional controls (b) without understanding why the initial control underperformed may lead to inefficient or ineffective solutions. Reverting to the previous setup (d) discards the benefits achieved without understanding the full picture.

423. An organization has completed all necessary security assessments and is ready to apply for an Authority to Operate (ATO). What is the first step in the ATO issuance process?
a. Submit the final security assessment report to the Chief Information Officer (CIO)
b. Develop a Plan of Action and Milestones (POA&M) for unresolved vulnerabilities
c. Conduct a risk analysis to identify potential threats
d. Submit the System Security Plan (SSP) to the authorizing official for review

Answer: d. Submit the System Security Plan (SSP) to the authorizing official for review. Explanation: The first step in the ATO issuance process is to submit the SSP to the authorizing official, as it contains comprehensive information about the system's security controls and their effectiveness.

424. During the conditional ATO process, an organization is granted temporary authorization while certain conditions are met. What is typically required to maintain this conditional ATO?
a. Implementation of additional security controls within a specified timeframe
b. Immediate elimination of all identified vulnerabilities
c. Reduction of operational costs related to security
d. Ongoing security training for all employees

Answer: a. Implementation of additional security controls within a specified timeframe. Explanation: A conditional ATO often requires the organization to implement specific security controls within a given timeframe to address identified vulnerabilities or deficiencies.

425. A cybersecurity manager needs to communicate a compliance decision to all stakeholders. Which element is most critical to include in the communication plan to ensure clarity and transparency?
a. A detailed technical report of all security measures
b. The decision rationale and its impact on operations
c. A summary of the organization's financial status
d. A list of all team members involved in the compliance process

Answer: b. The decision rationale and its impact on operations. Explanation: Including the decision rationale and its impact on operations ensures that stakeholders understand the reasons behind the compliance decision and how it will affect the organization's activities.

426. An organization has received a conditional ATO with several requirements. Which of the following actions is most important to ensure compliance with the conditional ATO?
a. Documenting all security incidents that occur during the conditional period
b. Regularly updating the authorizing official on progress towards meeting the requirements
c. Reducing the number of users with system access
d. Increasing the budget for the security department

Answer: b. Regularly updating the authorizing official on progress towards meeting the requirements. Explanation: Regular updates to the authorizing official on progress demonstrate the organization's commitment to addressing the conditions and maintaining compliance.

427. In preparing for the ATO issuance process, an organization must compile documentation to support its request. Which document is most critical to include to demonstrate the system's security posture?
a. The budget allocation for the security program
b. The results of recent vulnerability assessments and mitigation actions
c. A list of all employees with access to the system
d. The marketing strategy for the organization

Answer: b. The results of recent vulnerability assessments and mitigation actions. Explanation: The results of vulnerability assessments and the corresponding mitigation actions provide concrete evidence of the system's security posture and the effectiveness of implemented controls.

428. What is the primary purpose of a communication plan in the context of compliance decisions?
a. To inform stakeholders about the technical specifications of the system
b. To ensure timely and clear dissemination of compliance decisions and their implications
c. To gather feedback on the compliance process
d. To allocate resources for future compliance efforts

Answer: b. To ensure timely and clear dissemination of compliance decisions and their implications. Explanation: The primary purpose of a communication plan is to ensure that all stakeholders are informed about compliance decisions and their implications in a timely and clear manner.

429. When an ATO is issued, what responsibility does the authorizing official (AO) retain throughout the system's operational life?
a. Conducting annual security awareness training for staff
b. Monitoring the system's compliance with security requirements
c. Managing the organization's overall IT budget
d. Reviewing user access logs on a daily basis

Answer: b. Monitoring the system's compliance with security requirements. Explanation: The AO retains the responsibility of monitoring the system's compliance with security requirements throughout its operational life to ensure continuous security and compliance.

430. An organization must address several high-risk vulnerabilities identified during the ATO assessment. What is the most effective way to prioritize these vulnerabilities?
a. By the potential impact on critical business functions
b. By the order in which they were discovered
c. By the ease of remediation
d. By the cost of mitigation

Answer: a. By the potential impact on critical business functions. Explanation: Prioritizing vulnerabilities based on their potential impact on critical business functions ensures that the most significant risks are addressed first, thereby protecting essential operations.

431. Which of the following is a key component of a formal compliance notification?
a. A detailed description of the organization's future strategic goals
b. The specific compliance status and any conditions that must be met
c. A list of all employees who participated in the compliance process
d. The organization's stock market performance over the past year

Answer: b. The specific compliance status and any conditions that must be met. Explanation: A formal compliance notification should clearly state the compliance status and any conditions that must be met, providing clear guidance on the requirements for maintaining compliance.

432. A conditional ATO requires the organization to implement a Plan of Action and Milestones (POA&M). What is the primary goal of the POA&M in this context?
a. To improve the organization's financial performance
b. To outline steps to address and mitigate identified vulnerabilities
c. To enhance the user experience of the system
d. To document the organization's marketing strategies

Answer: b. To outline steps to address and mitigate identified vulnerabilities. Explanation: The primary goal of the POA&M is to provide a detailed plan for addressing and mitigating identified vulnerabilities, ensuring that the organization meets the conditions of the conditional ATO.

433. An organization is implementing a new system change management process. Which role does the Change Advisory Board (CAB) primarily play in this process?
a. Developing change implementation plans
b. Approving or rejecting proposed changes
c. Conducting user training for new systems
d. Documenting the details of all changes

Answer: b. Approving or rejecting proposed changes. Explanation: The primary role of the Change Advisory Board (CAB) is to review, approve, or reject proposed changes based on their impact and alignment with business objectives and policies.

434. During a system upgrade, an emergency change is required to fix a critical security vulnerability. What is the first step that should be taken in this emergency change process?
a. Implement the change immediately
b. Document the change in the change log
c. Notify the Change Advisory Board (CAB)
d. Perform a quick impact analysis

Answer: d. Perform a quick impact analysis. Explanation: Before implementing an emergency change, it is crucial to perform a quick impact analysis to understand the potential effects on the system and ensure that the change will not cause additional issues.

435. An IT department is conducting a change impact analysis for a proposed system modification. Which technique is most effective for identifying all possible impacts of the change?
a. Root cause analysis
b. Fishbone diagram
c. Regression testing
d. Stakeholder interviews

Answer: c. Regression testing. Explanation: Regression testing is effective for identifying all possible impacts of a change by ensuring that existing functionalities still work correctly after the new changes are implemented.

436. A critical business system requires an urgent change that cannot wait for the next CAB meeting. What procedure should be followed for this emergency change?
a. Bypass the CAB and implement the change immediately
b. Obtain approval from a designated emergency change authority
c. Wait for the next scheduled CAB meeting
d. Document the change after implementation

Answer: b. Obtain approval from a designated emergency change authority. Explanation: For urgent changes that cannot wait for the next CAB meeting, it is essential to obtain approval from a designated emergency change authority to ensure proper authorization and oversight.

437. Which of the following is a key component of an effective change impact analysis?
a. Cost-benefit analysis
b. Business continuity planning

315

c. Identification of affected systems and processes
d. Development of a training plan

Answer: c. Identification of affected systems and processes. Explanation: Identifying the systems and processes affected by the proposed change is crucial for understanding the scope and potential impacts, enabling informed decision-making.

438. An organization has implemented a change management process but is experiencing frequent service disruptions after changes are made. What is the most likely cause of this issue?
a. Insufficient training for the change management team
b. Lack of stakeholder engagement
c. Inadequate impact analysis
d. Delays in the change approval process

Answer: c. Inadequate impact analysis. Explanation: Frequent service disruptions after changes often result from inadequate impact analysis, leading to unforeseen consequences and disruptions.

439. The Change Advisory Board (CAB) is reviewing a major system change. What is the primary factor the CAB should consider when making their decision?
a. The cost of implementing the change
b. The technical complexity of the change
c. The potential impact on business operations
d. The personal preferences of the CAB members

Answer: c. The potential impact on business operations. Explanation: The CAB should primarily consider the potential impact on business operations to ensure that the change aligns with organizational goals and minimizes disruption.

440. In the context of system change management, what is the purpose of a change freeze period?
a. To reduce costs associated with changes
b. To prevent any changes during critical business periods
c. To allow time for stakeholder feedback
d. To implement multiple changes simultaneously

Answer: b. To prevent any changes during critical business periods. Explanation: A change freeze period is implemented to prevent any changes during critical business periods, ensuring stability and reducing the risk of disruptions during these times.

441. When documenting a change request, which information is essential to include for the Change Advisory Board (CAB) review?
a. The names of the implementation team members

b. A detailed timeline of the proposed change
c. The expected benefits and potential risks
d. The personal opinions of the requester

Answer: c. The expected benefits and potential risks. Explanation: Including the expected benefits and potential risks of the proposed change provides the CAB with the necessary information to make an informed decision about whether to approve or reject the change.

442. After implementing a system change, what is the most important activity to ensure the change was successful and did not introduce new issues?
a. Conducting a post-implementation review
b. Celebrating the successful change with the team
c. Updating the change management documentation
d. Communicating the change to all employees

Answer: a. Conducting a post-implementation review. Explanation: A post-implementation review is critical for evaluating the success of the change, identifying any new issues introduced, and ensuring that the change met its objectives without causing unintended disruptions.

443. An organization plans to migrate its data center to a cloud service provider. What is the first step in assessing the proposed changes against compliance requirements?
a. Reviewing the cloud provider's marketing materials
b. Conducting a compliance impact analysis
c. Training staff on the new cloud platform
d. Signing a service level agreement (SLA) with the cloud provider

Answer: b. Conducting a compliance impact analysis. Explanation: The first step is to conduct a compliance impact analysis to determine how the migration will affect compliance with relevant regulations and standards, identifying any gaps or necessary adjustments.

444. During a compliance impact analysis for a proposed software upgrade, which factor is most critical to evaluate?
a. The cost of the upgrade
b. The potential downtime during the upgrade
c. The software's compliance with existing security policies
d. The user interface improvements in the new software

Answer: c. The software's compliance with existing security policies. Explanation: Evaluating the software's compliance with existing security policies is critical to ensure that the upgrade does not introduce vulnerabilities or violate regulatory requirements.

445. A company uses a compliance matrix to evaluate changes to its IT infrastructure. What is the primary purpose of a compliance matrix in this context?
a. To prioritize changes based on user preferences
b. To map each proposed change against relevant compliance requirements
c. To document the financial benefits of each change
d. To schedule the implementation of each change

Answer: b. To map each proposed change against relevant compliance requirements. Explanation: The primary purpose of a compliance matrix is to map each proposed change against relevant compliance requirements, ensuring that all changes are evaluated for their potential impact on compliance.

446. When documenting the compliance impacts of a system change, which information is most important to include?
a. The names of the project team members
b. The technical specifications of the change
c. The potential risks and mitigation strategies
d. The expected timeline for implementing the change

Answer: c. The potential risks and mitigation strategies. Explanation: Documenting the potential risks and mitigation strategies is crucial for understanding how the system change may affect compliance and what steps need to be taken to address any identified risks.

447. An organization is evaluating the impact of a new data retention policy. What is the most important compliance-related question to address during this evaluation?
a. How will the policy affect data storage costs?
b. Will the policy improve system performance?
c. Does the policy comply with relevant data protection regulations?
d. How will users react to the new policy?

Answer: c. Does the policy comply with relevant data protection regulations? Explanation: The most important compliance-related question is whether the new data retention policy complies with relevant data protection regulations, as non-compliance could result in legal and financial penalties.

448. Which of the following best describes the role of a compliance impact analysis in the change management process?
a. It identifies the most cost-effective changes.
b. It assesses the potential effects of proposed changes on regulatory compliance.
c. It prioritizes changes based on user feedback.
d. It ensures changes are implemented on time.

Answer: b. It assesses the potential effects of proposed changes on regulatory compliance. Explanation: A compliance impact analysis assesses how proposed changes might affect the organization's adherence to regulatory requirements, helping to ensure that changes do not compromise compliance.

449. A proposed change to an access control system involves adding multi-factor authentication (MFA). What should be the focus of the compliance impact analysis for this change?
a. The cost of implementing MFA
b. The potential reduction in user convenience
c. The compliance benefits of enhanced security
d. The training required for users

Answer: c. The compliance benefits of enhanced security. Explanation: The focus of the compliance impact analysis should be on the compliance benefits of enhanced security provided by MFA, as it strengthens access controls and helps meet regulatory requirements.

450. When creating a compliance matrix, which element is essential to ensure it effectively evaluates proposed changes?
a. A detailed budget for each proposed change
b. A list of stakeholders affected by the changes
c. The specific compliance requirements applicable to each change
d. The technical specifications of the current system

Answer: c. The specific compliance requirements applicable to each change. Explanation: Including the specific compliance requirements applicable to each change ensures that the compliance matrix effectively evaluates how each proposed change aligns with regulatory standards.

451. An organization must document the compliance impacts of integrating a new third-party application. What is the primary goal of this documentation?
a. To provide a technical overview of the new application
b. To demonstrate that the integration will not violate compliance requirements
c. To outline the cost-benefit analysis of the integration
d. To schedule training sessions for users

Answer: b. To demonstrate that the integration will not violate compliance requirements. Explanation: The primary goal of documenting the compliance impacts is to show that integrating the new third-party application will not lead to any compliance violations, ensuring regulatory adherence.

452. A compliance officer is preparing a report on the impact of a system upgrade. What key information should be included to address compliance concerns?
a. The user satisfaction ratings of the current system
b. The projected timeline for completing the upgrade
c. The analysis of how the upgrade aligns with regulatory requirements

d. The names of the vendors involved in the upgrade

Answer: c. The analysis of how the upgrade aligns with regulatory requirements. Explanation: Including an analysis of how the upgrade aligns with regulatory requirements addresses compliance concerns by ensuring that the system upgrade will not lead to non-compliance issues.

453. An organization is planning to implement a new software system using a phased deployment approach. What is a key advantage of using a phased deployment strategy?
a. Immediate availability of the entire system
b. Ability to deploy the system without any downtime
c. Gradual transition and reduced risk of widespread issues
d. Simplified rollback process for the entire deployment

Answer: c. Gradual transition and reduced risk of widespread issues. Explanation: Phased deployment allows the organization to implement the system gradually, which helps in identifying and addressing issues in smaller, more manageable segments, thereby reducing the risk of widespread issues.

454. A company is considering using blue-green deployment for a new application update. In the context of compliance, what is a primary benefit of this approach?
a. Simplified version control management
b. Continuous compliance monitoring with minimal disruption
c. Reduced cost of deployment
d. Faster development cycle

Answer: b. Continuous compliance monitoring with minimal disruption. Explanation: Blue-green deployment involves running two identical production environments (blue and green) and switching traffic between them. This approach allows continuous compliance monitoring and validation in the green environment before fully switching from the blue environment, minimizing disruption.

455. For a compliance-sensitive change, a company is planning to use canary releases. What is the primary purpose of using canary releases in this context?
a. To test new features in a non-production environment
b. To incrementally deploy changes to a small subset of users and monitor the impact
c. To reduce the overall cost of compliance audits
d. To ensure complete data migration before going live

Answer: b. To incrementally deploy changes to a small subset of users and monitor the impact. Explanation: Canary releases involve deploying changes to a small, selected group of users first, monitoring the impact, and ensuring that any issues are identified and addressed before a full-scale deployment, which is particularly useful for compliance-sensitive changes.

456. An organization is deploying a critical update using a phased approach. Which of the following should be the first step in this deployment strategy?
a. Deploying the update to all production servers simultaneously
b. Implementing the update in a controlled test environment
c. Conducting a full compliance audit post-deployment
d. Informing all end-users about the upcoming changes

Answer: b. Implementing the update in a controlled test environment. Explanation: The first step in a phased deployment strategy should be to implement the update in a controlled test environment to identify any issues and ensure the update works as expected before deploying it to production.

457. A company needs to ensure that their deployment strategy for a compliance-sensitive application meets regulatory requirements. Which deployment strategy offers the best rollback capability in case of compliance violations?
a. Phased deployment
b. Blue-green deployment
c. Canary releases
d. Big bang deployment

Answer: b. Blue-green deployment. Explanation: Blue-green deployment offers excellent rollback capabilities because it allows the organization to switch back to the previous (blue) environment instantly if any compliance violations or issues are detected in the new (green) environment.

458. During a phased deployment, what is the best way to ensure compliance requirements are continually met?
a. Deploying to all users at once and conducting post-deployment reviews
b. Gradually rolling out changes and conducting compliance checks at each phase
c. Waiting until the final phase to conduct a full compliance audit
d. Relying on user feedback to identify compliance issues

Answer: b. Gradually rolling out changes and conducting compliance checks at each phase. Explanation: By gradually rolling out changes and conducting compliance checks at each phase, the organization can ensure that compliance requirements are continually met and any issues are addressed promptly.

459. Which deployment strategy is most suitable for minimizing the risk of downtime while ensuring compliance for a mission-critical application?
a. Big bang deployment
b. Phased deployment
c. Blue-green deployment
d. Canary releases

Answer: c. Blue-green deployment. Explanation: Blue-green deployment minimizes the risk of downtime by allowing the organization to switch between two identical production environments, ensuring that compliance can be verified in the green environment before traffic is fully directed to it.

460. A company using canary releases discovers a compliance issue during the initial rollout phase. What is the best immediate action to take?
a. Halting the deployment and rolling back changes for the affected users
b. Continuing the deployment to gather more data
c. Ignoring the issue and proceeding with the deployment
d. Informing all users about the potential compliance issue

Answer: a. Halting the deployment and rolling back changes for the affected users. Explanation: The best immediate action is to halt the deployment and roll back changes for the affected users to prevent further compliance issues and address the identified problems before proceeding.

461. In a phased deployment, how should an organization handle user feedback to ensure compliance and security?
a. Collect feedback only after the final phase is complete
b. Ignore feedback to maintain deployment schedule
c. Gather and analyze feedback after each phase and adjust the deployment as necessary
d. Implement all feedback immediately without review

Answer: c. Gather and analyze feedback after each phase and adjust the deployment as necessary. Explanation: Gathering and analyzing feedback after each phase allows the organization to make necessary adjustments to ensure compliance and security before proceeding to the next phase.

462. Which deployment strategy allows for the highest level of monitoring and compliance verification during the rollout of a new application feature?
a. Big bang deployment
b. Blue-green deployment
c. Phased deployment
d. Canary releases

Answer: d. Canary releases. Explanation: Canary releases allow for the highest level of monitoring and compliance verification by deploying changes to a small group of users first, ensuring that any issues are detected and resolved before a wider rollout.

463. A multinational corporation is considering implementing a new cloud-based ERP system. The risk assessment identifies significant data privacy risks due to cross-border data transfers. Which risk treatment option would likely require the most extensive stakeholder concurrence?
a. Implement additional technical controls to enhance data encryption
b. Maintain the current on-premises system and forgo cloud migration
c. Proceed with implementation while accepting the identified risks

d. Adopt a hybrid model, keeping sensitive data on-premises

Answer: c. Proceed with implementation while accepting the identified risks. Explanation: Accepting significant risks, especially those related to data privacy in a multinational context, typically requires the most extensive stakeholder concurrence. This decision involves potential legal, reputational, and operational impacts that affect various organizational levels and functions. It would likely require approval from legal, compliance, IT, business units, and executive leadership. Implementing additional controls (a) or adopting a hybrid model (d) are mitigation strategies that generally require less extensive concurrence. Maintaining the current system (b) avoids new risks but might need justification for forgoing potential benefits.

464. An organization's risk committee is evaluating treatment options for a high-impact, low-likelihood risk. Which of the following factors should be given the highest priority in the decision-making process?
a. The cost of implementing risk mitigation measures
b. The potential impact on the organization's strategic objectives
c. The complexity of the proposed risk treatment options
d. The preferences of the risk owner

Answer: b. The potential impact on the organization's strategic objectives. Explanation: When evaluating risk treatment options, the potential impact on strategic objectives should be the highest priority. This approach ensures that risk management decisions align with and support the organization's overall goals. While cost (a), complexity (c), and risk owner preferences (d) are important considerations, they should be secondary to strategic alignment. This focus helps ensure that risk treatment decisions contribute to the organization's long-term success and don't inadvertently hinder key objectives.

465. A healthcare organization is implementing a new telemedicine platform. The CISO has identified several security risks but is struggling to gain support for proposed controls from clinical stakeholders. Which communication strategy would be most effective in achieving stakeholder concurrence?
a. Present detailed technical specifications of the proposed security controls
b. Emphasize potential regulatory fines and legal liabilities of non-compliance
c. Demonstrate how the proposed controls support patient care objectives while managing risks
d. Delegate the decision to a third-party security consultant

Answer: c. Demonstrate how the proposed controls support patient care objectives while managing risks. Explanation: In a healthcare setting, aligning security measures with patient care objectives is likely to be the most effective strategy for gaining clinical stakeholder support. This approach bridges the gap between security and clinical priorities, making the relevance of controls clear to non-technical stakeholders. Detailed technical specifications (a) may not resonate with clinical staff. Emphasizing fines and liabilities (b) might create resistance. Delegating to a consultant (d) doesn't address the need for internal stakeholder buy-in.

466. When documenting formal risk acceptance by leadership, which of the following elements is most critical to include?
a. A detailed technical description of the risk and controls
b. The names and titles of all individuals involved in the risk assessment process

c. The specific conditions under which the risk is being accepted and the review/expiration date
d. A comparison of the organization's risk posture to industry benchmarks

Answer: c. The specific conditions under which the risk is being accepted and the review/expiration date. Explanation: When documenting risk acceptance, it's crucial to clearly state the conditions of acceptance and when the decision will be reviewed. This ensures that risk acceptance is not open-ended and prompts regular reassessment as conditions change. While technical details (a) are important, they're less critical in the formal acceptance document. Names of all involved individuals (b) may be unnecessary and could change. Industry comparisons (d) can be useful context but are not as critical as the specific terms of acceptance.

467. A financial services company is considering outsourcing its data center operations. The CIO proposes transferring associated cybersecurity risks to the service provider. Which stakeholder would be most critical in challenging or validating this risk treatment decision?
a. Chief Financial Officer
b. Chief Compliance Officer
c. Board of Directors
d. Head of Internal Audit

Answer: b. Chief Compliance Officer. Explanation: The Chief Compliance Officer would be most critical in challenging or validating the decision to transfer cybersecurity risks in this scenario. In financial services, regulatory compliance often requires maintaining responsibility for data security, even when operations are outsourced. The CCO can provide insight into whether risk transfer is permissible and adequate under relevant regulations. While the CFO (a) would be concerned with costs, the Board (c) with overall strategy, and Internal Audit (d) with control effectiveness, the compliance perspective is particularly crucial in this regulated industry context.

468. An energy company is evaluating the risk of a potential cybersecurity breach in its industrial control systems. The risk assessment indicates a low likelihood but catastrophic impact. Which risk treatment approach would likely require the most comprehensive stakeholder communication strategy?
a. Implement all available technical controls regardless of cost
b. Transfer the risk through cyber insurance
c. Accept the risk with enhanced monitoring and incident response plans
d. Avoid the risk by air-gapping all critical systems

Answer: c. Accept the risk with enhanced monitoring and incident response plans. Explanation: Accepting a low-likelihood, high-impact risk in critical infrastructure would require the most comprehensive stakeholder communication. This decision needs to be understood and supported across various levels, including technical teams, executive leadership, and possibly regulatory bodies. It requires explaining the rationale for acceptance, the enhanced monitoring approach, and incident response capabilities. Implementing all controls (a) or air-gapping systems (d) might be easier to justify. Transferring risk through insurance (b) doesn't eliminate the need to manage the risk and might require less extensive communication.

469. A retail company is implementing a new customer loyalty program that involves collecting and analyzing extensive personal data. Which risk treatment option analysis technique would be most effective in gaining stakeholder concurrence?
a. Cost-benefit analysis of different data protection measures
b. Scenario-based risk analysis demonstrating potential privacy breaches and their impacts
c. Compliance checklist against relevant data protection regulations
d. Peer comparison of data handling practices in the retail industry

Answer: b. Scenario-based risk analysis demonstrating potential privacy breaches and their impacts. Explanation: Scenario-based risk analysis is particularly effective for privacy-related risks in a customer-facing program. It allows stakeholders to visualize potential incidents, their impacts on customers, brand reputation, and regulatory compliance. This approach can make abstract risks more concrete for non-technical stakeholders. While cost-benefit analysis (a) is important, it may not fully capture reputational risks. A compliance checklist (c) is necessary but may not engage stakeholders as effectively. Peer comparison (d) can provide context but doesn't directly address the organization's specific risks.

470. An organization's board of directors is reviewing the annual risk report, which includes several accepted risks. Which of the following would be the most appropriate method for documenting the board's concurrence with these risk acceptance decisions?
a. Individual signed statements from each board member
b. A general note in the board meeting minutes indicating the report was reviewed
c. A formal board resolution detailing reviewed risks and acceptance decisions
d. An email confirmation from the board chair to the Chief Risk Officer

Answer: c. A formal board resolution detailing reviewed risks and acceptance decisions. Explanation: A formal board resolution provides the most appropriate and robust documentation of the board's concurrence with risk acceptance decisions. It offers a clear, official record that specifies which risks were reviewed and accepted, demonstrating due diligence in governance. Individual signed statements (a) may be excessive and unwieldy. A general note in minutes (b) may lack necessary detail. An email confirmation (d) is too informal for board-level decisions on significant risks.

471. A technology company is launching a new AI-powered product with potential ethical implications. The risk assessment identifies several novel risks related to AI bias and decision transparency. Which stakeholder group should be prioritized in the risk treatment communication strategy?
a. Legal and compliance team
b. Product development team
c. Marketing and public relations team
d. Cross-functional ethics committee

Answer: d. Cross-functional ethics committee. Explanation: For novel risks related to AI ethics, a cross-functional ethics committee should be prioritized in the communication strategy. This group can provide a balanced perspective on the ethical implications, considering technical, legal, societal, and business aspects. Their insights are crucial for developing comprehensive risk treatment strategies that address the multifaceted nature of AI ethics risks. While legal/compliance (a), product development (b), and marketing (c) teams are important stakeholders, the ethics committee's holistic view is most critical for these emerging, ethically complex risks.

472. During a merger, the acquiring company discovers that the target company has accepted several high risks that don't align with the acquirer's risk appetite. Which approach would be most effective in reconciling these differences and gaining stakeholder concurrence on a unified risk treatment strategy?
a. Immediately implement the acquiring company's risk controls in the target company
b. Maintain separate risk management approaches for each entity post-merger
c. Conduct a joint risk reassessment workshop with key stakeholders from both companies
d. Adopt the target company's risk acceptance levels to avoid disruption

Answer: c. Conduct a joint risk reassessment workshop with key stakeholders from both companies. Explanation: A joint risk reassessment workshop allows for a collaborative approach to reconciling different risk perspectives. It provides an opportunity to understand the context of each company's risk decisions, reassess risks in light of the merged entity's objectives, and develop a unified strategy with buy-in from both sides. Immediately imposing the acquirer's controls (a) may overlook valid reasons for the target's risk decisions. Maintaining separate approaches (b) doesn't achieve integration. Adopting the target's risk levels (d) may expose the merged entity to unacceptable risks.

473. An organization is implementing continuous control monitoring tools to maintain ongoing compliance. Which feature is most critical for these tools to effectively detect non-compliance?
a. Automated alerts for control failures
b. User-friendly interface for administrators
c. Integration with marketing software
d. High storage capacity for logs

Answer: a. Automated alerts for control failures. Explanation: Automated alerts for control failures are crucial as they enable real-time detection and response to compliance issues, ensuring that any deviations are promptly addressed.

474. A compliance officer is setting up a compliance dashboard to monitor key metrics. Which metric should be prioritized to provide a clear view of compliance status?
a. Number of employees trained on compliance policies
b. Percentage of controls passing automated checks
c. Total cost of compliance initiatives
d. Number of new hires in the compliance department

Answer: b. Percentage of controls passing automated checks. Explanation: The percentage of controls passing automated checks provides a direct and quantifiable measure of the organization's compliance status, highlighting areas that need attention.

475. During a compliance review, it is noted that automated compliance checking techniques are underutilized. What is the primary benefit of increasing the use of automated compliance checking?
a. Reducing the need for human auditors
b. Increasing the speed and accuracy of compliance assessments
c. Enhancing the user experience of compliance software

d. Lowering the overall IT budget

Answer: b. Increasing the speed and accuracy of compliance assessments. Explanation: Automated compliance checking improves the speed and accuracy of compliance assessments by continuously monitoring controls and quickly identifying any non-compliance issues.

476. An organization uses compliance dashboards for real-time monitoring. What is a key characteristic that these dashboards should have to be most effective?
a. Detailed graphical representations of historical data
b. Customizable views for different stakeholders
c. Integration with social media platforms
d. High-resolution images of system diagrams

Answer: b. Customizable views for different stakeholders. Explanation: Customizable views for different stakeholders ensure that each user can access the specific compliance information relevant to their role, enhancing the effectiveness of the monitoring process.

477. A company is evaluating various continuous control monitoring tools. Which factor is most important when selecting a tool for ensuring ongoing compliance?
a. The ability to generate detailed financial reports
b. The frequency and depth of control assessments
c. The tool's popularity in the market
d. The availability of customer support services

Answer: b. The frequency and depth of control assessments. Explanation: The frequency and depth of control assessments are critical for ensuring that the continuous control monitoring tool can effectively detect and report compliance issues in a timely manner.

478. When configuring automated compliance checking techniques, what is the most critical aspect to ensure their effectiveness?
a. Comprehensive documentation of all compliance policies
b. Regular updates to reflect changes in regulations and internal policies
c. Inclusion of advanced graphical interfaces for user interaction
d. Availability of extensive training modules for staff

Answer: b. Regular updates to reflect changes in regulations and internal policies. Explanation: Regular updates to the automated compliance checking system ensure that it remains aligned with the latest regulations and internal policies, maintaining its relevance and effectiveness.

479. A compliance team is designing a dashboard to report on compliance metrics. What should be the primary focus to ensure the dashboard is actionable?
a. Including historical compliance trends over several years
b. Highlighting current compliance issues and their statuses
c. Showing detailed technical specifications of compliance tools
d. Displaying general information about compliance policies

Answer: b. Highlighting current compliance issues and their statuses. Explanation: Focusing on current compliance issues and their statuses makes the dashboard actionable, enabling the compliance team to prioritize and address immediate concerns.

480. An organization faces frequent changes in regulatory requirements. How should automated compliance checking tools be managed to adapt to these changes effectively?
a. Increase the number of manual audits
b. Implement regular updates and patches to the tools
c. Hire additional compliance staff to monitor changes
d. Decrease the frequency of automated checks to reduce workload

Answer: b. Implement regular updates and patches to the tools. Explanation: Regular updates and patches to automated compliance checking tools ensure that they remain current with the latest regulatory requirements, maintaining their effectiveness in monitoring compliance.

481. A company is setting up a continuous control monitoring system. Which element is essential for ensuring that the system provides accurate and timely compliance data?
a. High-speed network connections
b. Access to external compliance consultants
c. Real-time data integration with compliance databases
d. Large-scale data storage solutions

Answer: c. Real-time data integration with compliance databases. Explanation: Real-time data integration with compliance databases ensures that the continuous control monitoring system provides up-to-date and accurate compliance data, facilitating prompt detection and resolution of issues.

482. When implementing a new compliance dashboard, which feature is most beneficial for senior management to ensure they have a clear overview of compliance health?
a. Drill-down capabilities to view detailed data
b. Static monthly reports
c. Access to raw data logs
d. Simplified summary metrics with visual indicators

Answer: d. Simplified summary metrics with visual indicators. Explanation: Simplified summary metrics with visual indicators provide senior management with a clear and concise overview of the organization's compliance health, enabling them to quickly identify and respond to issues.

483. An organization is implementing an asset tagging and tracking system for its physical assets. Which of the following technologies is most effective for real-time tracking of these assets within a large facility?
a. Barcode scanning
b. RFID (Radio Frequency Identification)
c. Manual inventory logs
d. GPS tracking

Answer: b. RFID (Radio Frequency Identification). Explanation: RFID technology is most effective for real-time tracking of physical assets within a large facility due to its ability to automatically identify and track tags attached to objects, providing continuous and accurate location data.

484. A company wants to enhance network access control for its asset management system. Which method should be employed to ensure that only authorized devices can connect to the network?
a. Implementing strong password policies
b. Using MAC address filtering
c. Conducting regular employee training
d. Installing antivirus software

Answer: b. Using MAC address filtering. Explanation: MAC address filtering enhances network access control by allowing only devices with specific MAC addresses to connect to the network, thereby restricting unauthorized devices from accessing network resources.

485. An organization is concerned about the potential loss of sensitive data stored on its logical assets. Which Data Loss Prevention (DLP) strategy is most effective for protecting data in motion?
a. Endpoint encryption
b. Network DLP
c. Physical security controls
d. User access reviews

Answer: b. Network DLP. Explanation: Network DLP is most effective for protecting data in motion by monitoring and controlling data transfers over the network, preventing sensitive information from being transmitted outside the organization.

486. In the context of physical asset monitoring, what is the primary benefit of using asset tagging systems?
a. Reducing the need for physical security personnel
b. Enhancing the aesthetic appearance of assets
c. Improving inventory accuracy and asset visibility
d. Simplifying the asset disposal process

Answer: c. Improving inventory accuracy and asset visibility. Explanation: Asset tagging systems improve inventory accuracy and asset visibility by providing a systematic way to track and manage assets, ensuring that their location and status are always known.

487. Which of the following is a key consideration when implementing a Data Loss Prevention (DLP) solution for logical assets?
a. The physical location of data centers
b. The sensitivity and classification of data
c. The design of the company's logo
d. The color coding of asset tags

Answer: b. The sensitivity and classification of data. Explanation: The sensitivity and classification of data are key considerations when implementing a DLP solution, as they determine the specific policies and controls needed to protect different types of data.

488. An organization plans to implement network access control (NAC) to enhance the security of its logical assets. Which of the following best describes the primary function of NAC?
a. Restricting physical access to server rooms
b. Monitoring network traffic for anomalies
c. Enforcing security policies for devices attempting to connect to the network
d. Performing regular backups of critical data

Answer: c. Enforcing security policies for devices attempting to connect to the network. Explanation: Network access control (NAC) enforces security policies for devices attempting to connect to the network, ensuring that only compliant and authorized devices are granted access.

489. A company is using RFID tags for asset management. Which potential issue should be carefully managed to ensure effective tracking?
a. Difficulty in attaching tags to small assets
b. High cost of RFID tags compared to barcodes
c. Interference from metal objects and electronic devices
d. Limited range of RFID readers

Answer: c. Interference from metal objects and electronic devices. Explanation: Interference from metal objects and electronic devices can affect the performance of RFID systems, making it important to manage and mitigate this issue for effective asset tracking.

490. To monitor logical assets and prevent unauthorized access, an organization decides to use a Data Loss Prevention (DLP) solution. Which feature is critical for monitoring data usage and transfer on endpoint devices?

a. Full disk encryption
b. Content discovery and inspection
c. Physical access control systems
d. User training programs

Answer: b. Content discovery and inspection. Explanation: Content discovery and inspection is critical for monitoring data usage and transfer on endpoint devices, allowing the DLP solution to identify and control sensitive information being accessed or transmitted.

491. An organization wants to ensure the integrity and security of its physical assets. What is the primary role of asset tracking systems in achieving this goal?
a. Enhancing the appearance of asset storage areas
b. Providing real-time location and status updates of assets
c. Reducing the need for cybersecurity measures
d. Simplifying the hiring process for security personnel

Answer: b. Providing real-time location and status updates of assets. Explanation: Asset tracking systems provide real-time location and status updates of physical assets, helping to ensure their integrity and security by enabling timely monitoring and management.

492. Which network access control (NAC) method is most effective for ensuring that only compliant devices can access sensitive data within a corporate network?
a. Password-protected Wi-Fi
b. Endpoint security software
c. Role-based access control
d. Posture assessment and remediation

Answer: d. Posture assessment and remediation. Explanation: Posture assessment and remediation is most effective for ensuring that only compliant devices can access sensitive data, as it evaluates the security posture of devices and enforces remediation actions before granting network access.

493. A major financial institution is planning to upgrade its core banking system. Which of the following is the most critical factor to consider when establishing rollback triggers for this upgrade?
a. The time required to complete the rollback process
b. The impact on customer-facing services and transaction integrity
c. The cost associated with executing the rollback plan
d. The effect on internal administrative processes

Answer: b. The impact on customer-facing services and transaction integrity. Explanation: For a core banking system upgrade, the most critical factor in establishing rollback triggers is the impact on customer-facing services and transaction integrity. Any issues affecting customer transactions or account data could have severe consequences for the bank's operations, reputation, and regulatory compliance. While time (a), cost (c), and internal processes (d) are important considerations, they are secondary to maintaining the integrity of customer services and financial data in a banking context.

494. During the rollback of a failed software deployment, the operations team discovers inconsistencies between the current state and the pre-deployment backup. Which of the following approaches should be prioritized to resolve this issue?
a. Proceed with the rollback and address data discrepancies afterwards
b. Halt the rollback and attempt to reconcile the data differences in real-time
c. Revert to the last known good configuration and replay transaction logs
d. Create a new hybrid state merging the current and backup data

Answer: c. Revert to the last known good configuration and replay transaction logs. Explanation: When faced with data inconsistencies during a rollback, reverting to the last known good configuration and replaying transaction logs is often the safest approach. This method ensures data integrity by starting from a reliable baseline and incorporating all subsequent valid transactions. Proceeding with inconsistent data (a) risks data corruption. Attempting real-time reconciliation (b) during a critical rollback is risky and time-consuming. Creating a hybrid state (d) without a clear understanding of the discrepancies could introduce new errors.

495. A global e-commerce platform is implementing a new recommendation engine. Which rollback testing approach would provide the most comprehensive assurance of the ability to revert changes safely?
a. Conduct a full rollback test in the production environment during off-peak hours
b. Perform multiple partial rollbacks in a staging environment that closely mimics production
c. Simulate rollback scenarios using virtualized environments and synthetic data
d. Test the rollback process on a small subset of live users without their knowledge

Answer: b. Perform multiple partial rollbacks in a staging environment that closely mimics production. Explanation: Testing multiple partial rollbacks in a staging environment that closely mimics production offers the most comprehensive assurance without risking live operations. This approach allows for testing various rollback scenarios and identifying potential issues in a controlled environment that reflects real-world conditions. A full rollback test in production (a) is too risky for a global platform. Simulations with synthetic data (c) may not capture all real-world complexities. Testing on live users without consent (d) is unethical and potentially illegal.

496. In planning the rollback strategy for a major network infrastructure upgrade, which of the following should be the primary consideration in setting rollback thresholds?
a. The number of user complaints received after the upgrade
b. The percentage decrease in network performance metrics
c. The time elapsed since the start of the upgrade
d. The number of failed configuration changes

Answer: b. The percentage decrease in network performance metrics. Explanation: For a network infrastructure upgrade, the primary consideration for rollback thresholds should be quantifiable performance metrics. A percentage decrease in network performance provides an objective, measurable indicator of the upgrade's impact on critical operations. User complaints (a) can be subjective and may not reflect systemic issues. Time elapsed (c) alone doesn't indicate success or failure. The number of failed configuration changes (d) may not directly correlate with overall network performance impact.

497. A healthcare provider is implementing a new electronic health record (EHR) system. Which aspect of rollback planning is most crucial to ensure patient safety and data integrity?
a. Ability to quickly revert to paper-based records if necessary
b. Maintaining parallel operation of old and new systems during the transition
c. Ensuring all historical patient data is preserved and accurately mapped in the rollback process
d. Having a team of data entry specialists ready to manually update records post-rollback

Answer: c. Ensuring all historical patient data is preserved and accurately mapped in the rollback process. Explanation: In healthcare, preserving the integrity and accessibility of patient data is paramount for patient safety and continuity of care. The rollback plan must ensure that all historical data remains intact and correctly mapped, allowing for seamless reversion without loss or corruption of critical medical information. Reverting to paper records (a) is impractical and risky for data consistency. Parallel operation (b) is a transition strategy, not a rollback plan. Manual data entry post-rollback (d) introduces risks of errors and delays in accessing critical patient information.

498. A financial trading platform is upgrading its order matching engine. Which rollback trigger would be most appropriate to ensure market integrity and regulatory compliance?
a. A 10% increase in trade execution time
b. Any discrepancy in order matching results between the new and old systems
c. More than 50 user-reported issues within the first hour of operation
d. Failure to process more than 95% of the previous day's transaction volume

Answer: b. Any discrepancy in order matching results between the new and old systems. Explanation: For a financial trading platform, any discrepancy in order matching results is a critical issue that could impact market integrity, financial outcomes, and regulatory compliance. Even small discrepancies could have significant financial and legal implications. While increased execution time (a), user-reported issues (c), and reduced transaction volume (d) are important, they don't pose the same immediate risk to the core function and integrity of the trading platform as matching discrepancies.

499. During the rollback of a cloud migration project, the team encounters issues with data synchronization between on-premises and cloud environments. Which approach would be most effective in ensuring data consistency?
a. Prioritize cloud data and overwrite on-premises data
b. Implement a bi-directional synchronization process with conflict resolution rules
c. Freeze all data changes during the rollback process
d. Manually reconcile differences based on timestamps

Answer: b. Implement a bi-directional synchronization process with conflict resolution rules. Explanation: In a complex rollback scenario involving cloud and on-premises environments, a bi-directional synchronization process with defined conflict resolution rules offers the most effective approach to ensuring data consistency. This method allows for systematic handling of data discrepancies while minimizing data loss or corruption. Prioritizing one data source over another (a) risks losing valid changes. Freezing all changes (c) may not be feasible in a business context. Manual reconciliation (d) is time-consuming and error-prone for large datasets.

500. A telecommunications company is updating its billing system. Which of the following should be the primary focus of rollback procedure testing for this update?
a. The speed of reverting to the previous system version
b. The accuracy of customer account balances and transaction histories post-rollback
c. The ability to generate invoices immediately after rollback
d. The impact on the customer service representatives' workflow

Answer: b. The accuracy of customer account balances and transaction histories post-rollback. Explanation: For a billing system update, the primary focus of rollback testing should be ensuring the accuracy of customer account balances and transaction histories. Any discrepancies in financial data could lead to billing errors, customer disputes, and potential regulatory issues. While rollback speed (a), invoice generation (c), and workflow impacts (d) are important, they are secondary to maintaining the integrity and accuracy of core financial data in a billing system.

501. An e-commerce company is implementing a new inventory management system integrated with multiple suppliers. In developing the rollback plan, which of the following should be given the highest priority?
a. Ensuring all supplier connections can be quickly severed and restored
b. Maintaining accurate stock levels and order fulfillment capabilities during the rollback
c. Preserving customer order history and preferences
d. Minimizing the downtime of the company's website during the rollback process

Answer: b. Maintaining accurate stock levels and order fulfillment capabilities during the rollback. Explanation: In an e-commerce context, maintaining accurate stock levels and order fulfillment capabilities is crucial during a rollback of an inventory management system. This directly impacts the company's ability to conduct business, fulfill customer orders, and manage supplier relationships. While supplier connections (a), customer history (c), and website uptime (d) are important, they are less critical than ensuring the core function of inventory management and order fulfillment remains accurate and operational.

502. A global manufacturing company is rolling out a new Enterprise Resource Planning (ERP) system across multiple locations. Which approach to rollback planning would be most effective in managing the complexities of this multi-site deployment?
a. Implement a single, comprehensive rollback plan for all locations
b. Develop individual rollback plans for each location without central coordination
c. Create a modular rollback framework with site-specific adaptations and a central coordination mechanism
d. Outsource rollback planning to local IT teams at each site

Answer: c. Create a modular rollback framework with site-specific adaptations and a central coordination mechanism. Explanation: For a complex, multi-site ERP rollout, a modular rollback framework with site-specific adaptations and central coordination offers the best balance of consistency and flexibility. This approach allows for tailoring to local requirements while maintaining overall coherence and control. A single comprehensive plan (a) may not address site-specific needs. Individual, uncoordinated plans (b) risk inconsistencies and gaps. Outsourcing to local teams without central oversight (d) could lead to disparate approaches and difficulties in managing the rollback across the organization.

503. An organization experiences a data breach involving personal information. What is the first step in classifying this incident to align with compliance requirements?
a. Notifying affected individuals immediately
b. Conducting a preliminary assessment to determine the nature and scope of the breach
c. Shutting down all affected systems
d. Implementing additional security controls

Answer: b. Conducting a preliminary assessment to determine the nature and scope of the breach. Explanation: The first step is to conduct a preliminary assessment to understand the nature and scope of the breach. This helps determine the appropriate classification and subsequent response actions required to comply with regulatory requirements.

504. Following an incident, which regulatory reporting requirement is most critical for compliance when personal data is compromised?
a. Reporting the incident to law enforcement
b. Notifying the organization's board of directors
c. Informing the relevant data protection authority within the mandated timeframe
d. Posting a public notice on the company website

Answer: c. Informing the relevant data protection authority within the mandated timeframe. Explanation: Many data protection regulations, such as the GDPR, require organizations to notify the relevant data protection authority within a specified timeframe (e.g., 72 hours) when personal data is compromised. This step is crucial to ensure regulatory compliance.

505. After addressing a security incident, what is the primary purpose of conducting a post-incident compliance review?
a. To identify and penalize responsible individuals
b. To evaluate the effectiveness of the incident response plan and ensure compliance with regulatory requirements
c. To estimate the financial impact of the incident
d. To prepare a press release for public relations purposes

Answer: b. To evaluate the effectiveness of the incident response plan and ensure compliance with regulatory requirements. Explanation: A post-incident compliance review aims to assess how well the incident response plan was executed and to identify any compliance gaps or areas for improvement to prevent future incidents.

506. A company is updating its incident response plan to include compliance considerations. Which element is most important to ensure regulatory reporting requirements are met?
a. A list of all employees involved in the incident response team
b. Detailed procedures for documenting and reporting incidents to regulatory bodies

c. Contact information for all customers
d. A schedule for regular incident response training sessions

Answer: b. Detailed procedures for documenting and reporting incidents to regulatory bodies. Explanation: Including detailed procedures for documenting and reporting incidents ensures that the organization meets regulatory requirements promptly and accurately.

507. During an incident response, it is discovered that the organization's data breach notification policy is outdated. What should be the immediate action to address this issue?
a. Continue with the current policy and update it after the incident is resolved
b. Update the notification policy immediately to comply with current regulations
c. Ignore the outdated policy and focus on mitigating the breach
d. Delegate the update to a junior staff member

Answer: b. Update the notification policy immediately to comply with current regulations. Explanation: Updating the notification policy immediately ensures that the organization's response aligns with current regulatory requirements, minimizing the risk of non-compliance penalties.

508. An organization is preparing for potential cybersecurity incidents by establishing incident classification criteria. Which factor is most critical for aligning these criteria with compliance requirements?
a. The potential financial impact of the incident
b. The number of users affected by the incident
c. The type of data involved and the regulatory implications
d. The duration of the incident

Answer: c. The type of data involved and the regulatory implications. Explanation: The type of data involved and its regulatory implications are critical factors in incident classification, as different types of data (e.g., personal data, financial data) may have specific regulatory requirements for reporting and response.

509. A healthcare provider experiences a ransomware attack affecting patient records. Which compliance requirement must be considered in the incident response plan?
a. Reporting the incident to the Federal Trade Commission (FTC)
b. Notifying patients and the Department of Health and Human Services (HHS) within 60 days
c. Conducting quarterly security awareness training
d. Shutting down all systems immediately

Answer: b. Notifying patients and the Department of Health and Human Services (HHS) within 60 days. Explanation: Under the Health Insurance Portability and Accountability Act (HIPAA), covered entities must notify affected individuals and the HHS within 60 days of discovering a breach affecting protected health information (PHI).

510. After a data breach, what should be the focus of a post-incident compliance review to enhance future incident response efforts?
a. Increasing the IT department's budget
b. Reviewing the timelines of notifications to ensure regulatory compliance
c. Hiring additional cybersecurity staff
d. Implementing a new customer relationship management (CRM) system

Answer: b. Reviewing the timelines of notifications to ensure regulatory compliance. Explanation: Reviewing the timelines of notifications helps ensure that the organization complied with regulatory reporting requirements and identifies any delays or gaps to improve future incident response.

511. In the event of a security incident involving credit card information, which regulatory framework must the organization comply with when responding to the incident?
a. General Data Protection Regulation (GDPR)
b. Federal Information Security Modernization Act (FISMA)
c. Payment Card Industry Data Security Standard (PCI DSS)
d. Sarbanes-Oxley Act (SOX)

Answer: c. Payment Card Industry Data Security Standard (PCI DSS). Explanation: The PCI DSS is a regulatory framework specifically designed to protect credit card information. Organizations handling credit card data must comply with PCI DSS requirements when responding to security incidents involving such data.

512. Which action should be prioritized to align incident response efforts with compliance requirements during an active data breach?
a. Enhancing system performance to prevent further breaches
b. Communicating with public relations to manage the company's image
c. Documenting all actions taken and decisions made during the response
d. Allocating additional funds for IT infrastructure upgrades

Answer: c. Documenting all actions taken and decisions made during the response. Explanation: Documenting all actions and decisions during the incident response is crucial for compliance, as it provides a clear record of how the incident was managed and helps demonstrate adherence to regulatory requirements.

513. An organization is conducting a Business Impact Analysis (BIA) as part of its contingency planning. Which of the following is a primary objective of the BIA?
a. Identify and prioritize critical business functions and processes
b. Develop detailed incident response procedures
c. Create a communication plan for stakeholders
d. Document all IT assets and their configurations

Answer: a. Identify and prioritize critical business functions and processes. Explanation: The primary objective of a Business Impact Analysis (BIA) is to identify and prioritize critical business functions and processes to understand the impact of their disruption and to inform the development of appropriate recovery strategies.

514. During a Disaster Recovery Plan (DRP) test, which activity is crucial for evaluating the effectiveness of the plan?
a. Conducting a full-scale evacuation of the facility
b. Simulating a realistic disaster scenario and assessing the response
c. Holding a meeting to discuss potential threats
d. Reviewing the plan for grammatical errors

Answer: b. Simulating a realistic disaster scenario and assessing the response. Explanation: Conducting a simulation of a realistic disaster scenario and assessing the response is crucial for evaluating the effectiveness of the Disaster Recovery Plan (DRP), identifying weaknesses, and ensuring that the plan works as intended.

515. A company is developing a Continuity of Operations Plan (COOP). What is the main purpose of a COOP?
a. To ensure that critical business operations continue during and after a disruption
b. To outline the process for hiring new employees
c. To establish guidelines for employee conduct
d. To document daily operational procedures

Answer: a. To ensure that critical business operations continue during and after a disruption. Explanation: The main purpose of a Continuity of Operations Plan (COOP) is to ensure that critical business operations can continue during and after a disruption, minimizing the impact on the organization and its stakeholders.

516. Which of the following is a key component of an effective Business Impact Analysis (BIA)?
a. Defining the organization's mission and vision
b. Identifying the financial and operational impacts of disruptions
c. Creating a marketing strategy for the organization
d. Developing a comprehensive IT infrastructure plan

Answer: b. Identifying the financial and operational impacts of disruptions. Explanation: A key component of an effective BIA is identifying the financial and operational impacts of disruptions on critical business functions, which helps prioritize recovery efforts and allocate resources appropriately.

517. In the context of disaster recovery, what is the significance of the Recovery Time Objective (RTO)?
a. The maximum acceptable amount of data loss measured in time
b. The time it takes to detect a disaster
c. The maximum allowable downtime for a business function before significant impact occurs
d. The time it takes to restore normal operations after a disaster

Answer: c. The maximum allowable downtime for a business function before significant impact occurs. Explanation: The Recovery Time Objective (RTO) is the maximum allowable downtime for a business function before significant impact occurs, guiding the development of recovery strategies to ensure timely restoration of services.

518. When testing a Disaster Recovery Plan (DRP), which metric is most useful for assessing the speed of recovery?
a. Number of participants in the test
b. Recovery Point Objective (RPO)
c. Recovery Time Objective (RTO)
d. Duration of the planning phase

Answer: c. Recovery Time Objective (RTO). Explanation: The Recovery Time Objective (RTO) is most useful for assessing the speed of recovery during a DRP test, as it measures the maximum acceptable downtime for business functions and the effectiveness of the recovery efforts.

519. A Business Impact Analysis (BIA) identifies a critical business function that must be restored within 4 hours to avoid severe consequences. Which term best describes this time frame?
a. Maximum Tolerable Downtime (MTD)
b. Recovery Time Objective (RTO)
c. Recovery Point Objective (RPO)
d. Mean Time to Recovery (MTTR)

Answer: b. Recovery Time Objective (RTO). Explanation: The Recovery Time Objective (RTO) is the time frame within which a critical business function must be restored to avoid severe consequences, as identified in the BIA.

520. In the development of a Continuity of Operations Plan (COOP), which step is essential to ensure all critical functions are identified and addressed?
a. Conducting a threat assessment
b. Holding regular team meetings
c. Reviewing industry best practices
d. Implementing a new IT system

Answer: a. Conducting a threat assessment. Explanation: Conducting a threat assessment is essential in the development of a COOP to identify potential threats and ensure that all critical functions are identified and addressed, enabling the organization to prepare for and mitigate disruptions.

521. Which of the following best describes the purpose of regular testing and updates to a Disaster Recovery Plan (DRP)?
a. To ensure the plan is grammatically correct
b. To validate the effectiveness of the plan and incorporate changes
c. To increase the length of the document
d. To reduce the cost of disaster recovery

Answer: b. To validate the effectiveness of the plan and incorporate changes. Explanation: Regular testing and updates to a DRP are necessary to validate its effectiveness, identify any gaps or weaknesses, and incorporate changes to reflect new risks, technologies, and business processes.

522. In the context of contingency planning, what is the primary goal of a Business Impact Analysis (BIA)?
a. To create a detailed inventory of IT assets
b. To assess the potential impacts of disruptions on business operations
c. To establish a communication plan for stakeholders
d. To document daily operational procedures

Answer: b. To assess the potential impacts of disruptions on business operations. Explanation: The primary goal of a Business Impact Analysis (BIA) is to assess the potential impacts of disruptions on business operations, helping the organization prioritize critical functions and develop appropriate recovery strategies.

523. A large financial institution discovers a critical vulnerability in its core banking software. The vendor has released a patch, but it hasn't undergone the organization's standard testing process. Which of the following approaches best balances security and operational risk?
a. Deploy the patch immediately to all systems without testing
b. Wait for the next scheduled patch cycle to apply the update
c. Apply the patch to a subset of non-critical systems for accelerated testing
d. Implement compensating controls and defer patching until full testing is complete

Answer: c. Apply the patch to a subset of non-critical systems for accelerated testing. Explanation: This approach balances the urgency of addressing a critical vulnerability with the need to mitigate the risk of untested patches in a critical environment. By applying the patch to non-critical systems, the organization can quickly assess its impact and stability before deploying to core systems. Immediate deployment without testing (a) risks operational disruptions. Waiting for the next cycle (b) leaves the vulnerability exposed too long. Deferring patching entirely (d) may not adequately address the security risk, even with compensating controls.

524. Which of the following best describes the primary objective of a vulnerability management lifecycle?
a. To eliminate all vulnerabilities in the IT environment
b. To prioritize and address vulnerabilities based on their risk to the organization
c. To achieve compliance with industry regulations
d. To reduce the cost of IT operations

Answer: b. To prioritize and address vulnerabilities based on their risk to the organization. Explanation: The primary objective of a vulnerability management lifecycle is to systematically prioritize and address vulnerabilities based on their risk to the organization. This approach recognizes that it's often impractical to eliminate all vulnerabilities and instead focuses resources on the most critical issues. While compliance (c) and cost reduction (d) can be benefits, they are secondary to risk management. Eliminating all vulnerabilities (a) is an unrealistic goal in most complex IT environments.

525. An organization's patch management policy requires all critical patches to be applied within 30 days of release. However, the security team often struggles to meet this deadline. Which of the following is the most effective long-term solution to this challenge?
a. Extend the policy deadline to 60 days for all patches
b. Implement automated patch deployment tools with staged rollouts
c. Increase the size of the security team to handle patching workload
d. Outsource patch management to a managed security service provider

Answer: b. Implement automated patch deployment tools with staged rollouts. Explanation: Automated patch deployment tools with staged rollouts offer the most effective long-term solution to consistently meet patching deadlines. This approach improves efficiency, reduces manual errors, and allows for controlled, systematic patch application across the environment. Simply extending the deadline (a) doesn't address the root cause of the delays. Increasing team size (c) may not be cost-effective or solve process inefficiencies. Outsourcing (d) can be helpful but may not align with all organizations' security policies and doesn't necessarily improve internal processes.

526. During a routine vulnerability scan, a critical vulnerability is discovered in a production server that cannot be taken offline for patching. Which of the following approaches is most appropriate?
a. Ignore the vulnerability as the server cannot be patched immediately
b. Take the server offline immediately to apply the patch
c. Implement temporary compensating controls and schedule patching for the next maintenance window
d. Apply the patch without testing and hope for the best

Answer: c. Implement temporary compensating controls and schedule patching for the next maintenance window. Explanation: When immediate patching isn't feasible for a critical system, implementing temporary compensating controls while scheduling the patch for the next available window is the most balanced approach. This method addresses the immediate security risk while respecting operational constraints. Ignoring the vulnerability (a) is irresponsible. Taking a critical server offline unexpectedly (b) could cause significant business disruption. Applying an untested patch (d) to a production server is risky and could lead to system instability.

527. Which of the following metrics is most effective in measuring the efficiency of an organization's patch management process?
a. Number of patches applied per month
b. Percentage of systems patched within defined SLAs for different severity levels
c. Total time spent on patching activities
d. Number of successful hacks prevented by patching

Answer: b. Percentage of systems patched within defined SLAs for different severity levels. Explanation: Measuring the percentage of systems patched within defined Service Level Agreements (SLAs) for different severity levels provides the most comprehensive view of patch management efficiency. This metric combines timeliness with prioritization, reflecting how well the organization manages both critical and less urgent vulnerabilities. The number of patches applied (a) doesn't indicate effectiveness or prioritization. Time spent on patching (c) doesn't necessarily correlate with efficiency. Prevented hacks (d) are difficult to quantify accurately and may not be directly attributable to patching alone.

528. An organization is developing an emergency patching process. Which of the following elements is most critical to include in this process?
a. A requirement for CEO approval for all emergency patches
b. A defined test plan for verifying patch stability in a representative environment
c. A policy to always apply emergency patches during business hours
d. A mandate to inform all employees about every emergency patch

Answer: b. A defined test plan for verifying patch stability in a representative environment. Explanation: In an emergency patching process, having a defined test plan for verifying patch stability is crucial. Even in urgent situations, applying untested patches to critical systems can lead to significant disruptions. A quick but thorough testing process in a representative environment helps balance the need for rapid response with the need for operational stability. CEO approval (a) for all patches is impractical and may cause delays. Applying patches only during business hours (c) may unnecessarily extend vulnerability exposure. Informing all employees about every patch (d) is excessive and not always relevant to emergency patching.

529. A global organization with diverse IT infrastructure is struggling with inconsistent patch management across different regions. Which approach would be most effective in addressing this issue?
a. Implement a single, global patching schedule for all regions
b. Allow each region to develop its own independent patch management process
c. Centralize patch management decisions but allow for regional scheduling flexibility
d. Outsource patch management to different vendors in each region

Answer: c. Centralize patch management decisions but allow for regional scheduling flexibility. Explanation: Centralizing patch management decisions while allowing for regional scheduling flexibility offers the best balance between consistency and adaptability. This approach ensures a unified strategy and prioritization across the organization while accommodating regional operational needs and constraints. A single global schedule (a) may not account for regional differences in operations or regulations. Completely independent regional processes (b) can lead to inconsistencies and gaps in security. Outsourcing to different vendors in each region (d) may exacerbate consistency issues.

530. In the context of vulnerability management, what is the primary purpose of conducting regular threat intelligence analysis?
a. To identify all possible vulnerabilities in the IT environment
b. To determine which patches to apply first
c. To understand the evolving threat landscape and prioritize vulnerability remediation
d. To comply with regulatory requirements for vulnerability scanning

Answer: c. To understand the evolving threat landscape and prioritize vulnerability remediation. Explanation: The primary purpose of threat intelligence analysis in vulnerability management is to understand the current threat landscape and use this information to prioritize vulnerability remediation efforts. This approach ensures that resources are focused on addressing the most relevant and potentially impactful vulnerabilities first. While threat intelligence can inform patch prioritization (b), this is a subset of its broader purpose. Identifying all vulnerabilities (a) is more the role of vulnerability scanning. Regulatory compliance (d) may be a benefit but is not the primary purpose of threat intelligence in this context.

531. An organization has a policy of applying all vendor-released patches within 90 days. A security audit reveals that this blanket policy may not adequately address critical vulnerabilities. Which of the following recommendations would most effectively improve this policy?
a. Reduce the blanket policy to 30 days for all patches
b. Implement a risk-based approach with tiered timelines based on vulnerability severity and asset criticality
c. Apply all patches immediately upon release, regardless of criticality
d. Increase the security team's size to handle a faster patching schedule

Answer: b. Implement a risk-based approach with tiered timelines based on vulnerability severity and asset criticality. Explanation: A risk-based approach with tiered timelines offers the most effective improvement to the patch management policy. This method ensures that the most critical vulnerabilities on the most important assets are addressed quickly, while less urgent patches are handled in a timely but less pressing manner. A blanket 30-day policy (a) may be too aggressive for low-risk patches and too lax for critical ones. Immediate application of all patches (c) is impractical and risky. Increasing team size (d) doesn't address the fundamental issue with the policy's approach to prioritization.

532. A healthcare organization is implementing a new medical device that requires strict change control procedures. Which of the following patch management strategies would best balance security needs with operational and regulatory requirements?
a. Apply all patches as soon as they are released by the vendor
b. Implement a quarterly patching cycle for all medical devices
c. Develop a customized patch management process in collaboration with the device vendor and internal stakeholders
d. Defer all patching decisions to the medical staff using the device

Answer: c. Develop a customized patch management process in collaboration with the device vendor and internal stakeholders. Explanation: For medical devices with strict change control requirements, a customized patch management process developed collaboratively is the best approach. This ensures that security, operational, and regulatory needs are all considered, and that the process is tailored to the specific device and its use in the healthcare environment. Applying all patches immediately (a) may violate change control procedures and risk device malfunction. A fixed quarterly cycle (b) may not adequately address urgent security issues. Deferring to medical staff (d) overlooks important technical and security considerations.

533. During a compliance audit, an organization needs to collect evidence to demonstrate adherence to security policies. Which tool is most effective for gathering and organizing digital evidence?
a. Spreadsheet software
b. File integrity monitoring system
c. Email client
d. Instant messaging platform

Answer: b. File integrity monitoring system. Explanation: A file integrity monitoring system is designed to track and log changes to files and configurations, providing comprehensive and organized evidence of adherence to security policies.

534. To ensure the integrity of compliance evidence, which practice is essential when handling digital evidence?
a. Limiting access to the evidence to a single person
b. Creating multiple copies of the evidence for backup
c. Documenting the chain of custody from collection to presentation
d. Encrypting the evidence using a basic encryption algorithm

Answer: c. Documenting the chain of custody from collection to presentation. Explanation: Documenting the chain of custody ensures that the evidence is tracked and accounted for at every step, maintaining its integrity and admissibility.

535. An organization needs to store compliance evidence for a minimum of seven years. What is the most important consideration for long-term evidence storage?
a. The cost of storage solutions
b. The frequency of access to the stored evidence
c. The security and integrity of the storage method
d. The physical location of the storage facility

Answer: c. The security and integrity of the storage method. Explanation: Ensuring the security and integrity of the storage method is critical for maintaining the reliability and accessibility of compliance evidence over the long term.

536. In a scenario where compliance evidence must be retrieved quickly during an audit, which system feature is most beneficial?
a. A user-friendly interface
b. High-speed data processing capabilities
c. Robust search and indexing functions
d. Integration with other compliance tools

Answer: c. Robust search and indexing functions. Explanation: Robust search and indexing functions enable quick and efficient retrieval of specific pieces of evidence, which is crucial during audits or investigations.

537. When collecting evidence for compliance purposes, which technique is most effective in ensuring the evidence is tamper-proof?
a. Storing the evidence in a secure cloud storage
b. Using write-once, read-many (WORM) storage media
c. Encrypting the evidence with a strong algorithm
d. Creating multiple backups of the evidence

Answer: b. Using write-once, read-many (WORM) storage media. Explanation: WORM storage media ensure that data cannot be altered once written, providing a tamper-proof solution for storing compliance evidence.

538. What is the primary benefit of maintaining a detailed chain of custody for compliance evidence?
a. It simplifies the process of evidence collection
b. It ensures evidence is handled only by IT personnel
c. It provides a clear record of evidence handling and transfer
d. It reduces the cost of evidence storage

Answer: c. It provides a clear record of evidence handling and transfer. Explanation: Maintaining a detailed chain of custody provides a documented trail that shows who handled the evidence and when, ensuring its integrity and admissibility.

539. A compliance officer needs to verify that all collected evidence is authentic. Which tool is most appropriate for this task?
a. Data deduplication software
b. Digital signature verification tool
c. Network monitoring system
d. Data compression software

Answer: b. Digital signature verification tool. Explanation: A digital signature verification tool can authenticate the origin and integrity of digital evidence, ensuring that it has not been tampered with.

540. To ensure compliance evidence remains accessible over long periods, what practice should be implemented?
a. Regularly migrating data to updated storage formats
b. Reducing the amount of evidence stored
c. Limiting access to the evidence to compliance officers
d. Storing evidence on high-capacity hard drives

Answer: a. Regularly migrating data to updated storage formats. Explanation: Regularly migrating data to updated storage formats helps prevent obsolescence and ensures that evidence remains accessible and readable over long periods.

541. When preparing for a compliance audit, which evidence collection technique is most effective for demonstrating adherence to data retention policies?
a. Conducting employee interviews
b. Reviewing system access logs
c. Analyzing data retention schedules and logs
d. Monitoring network traffic

Answer: c. Analyzing data retention schedules and logs. Explanation: Analyzing data retention schedules and logs provides concrete evidence that data is being retained according to established policies, demonstrating compliance with data retention requirements.

542. Which practice is most important for ensuring the confidentiality of compliance evidence during collection and storage?
a. Using physical locks on storage devices
b. Encrypting evidence with strong encryption algorithms
c. Allowing access only to senior management
d. Storing evidence in multiple geographic locations

Answer: b. Encrypting evidence with strong encryption algorithms. Explanation: Encrypting evidence with strong encryption algorithms ensures that the data remains confidential and protected from unauthorized access during collection and storage.

543. An organization is conducting a vendor risk assessment. Which factor is most critical to evaluate when assessing the potential risk posed by a third-party vendor?
a. The vendor's market share
b. The vendor's security policies and procedures
c. The vendor's marketing strategies
d. The vendor's customer service ratings

Answer: b. The vendor's security policies and procedures. Explanation: Evaluating a vendor's security policies and procedures is critical in a vendor risk assessment, as it directly impacts the organization's data security and compliance posture.

544. A company requires third-party vendors to provide compliance attestations. Which report is most commonly used to verify a vendor's controls related to security, availability, processing integrity, confidentiality, and privacy?
a. ISO 27001 certification
b. SOC 2 report
c. PCI DSS compliance report
d. GDPR compliance statement

Answer: b. SOC 2 report. Explanation: SOC 2 reports are specifically designed to assess a vendor's controls related to security, availability, processing integrity, confidentiality, and privacy, making them a key tool for third-party compliance verification.

545. An organization is implementing continuous monitoring of third-party compliance. Which tool or technique is most effective for real-time assessment of a vendor's security posture?

a. Annual compliance audits
b. Real-time security information and event management (SIEM) systems
c. Quarterly self-assessment questionnaires
d. Bi-annual risk assessments

Answer: b. Real-time security information and event management (SIEM) systems. Explanation: SIEM systems provide real-time assessment and monitoring of a vendor's security posture, allowing organizations to detect and respond to security incidents promptly.

546. A vendor has provided an outdated SOC 2 report as evidence of compliance. What is the most appropriate action for the organization to take?
a. Accept the report as long as it covers the relevant controls
b. Request an updated SOC 2 report from the vendor
c. Conduct an independent audit of the vendor's controls
d. Ignore the outdated report and rely on past performance

Answer: b. Request an updated SOC 2 report from the vendor. Explanation: Requesting an updated SOC 2 report ensures that the assessment of the vendor's controls is current and reflects their present security posture and compliance.

547. An organization identifies a critical security vulnerability in a third-party vendor's system. What should be the immediate next step?
a. Terminate the vendor contract
b. Notify the vendor and require immediate remediation
c. Ignore the vulnerability and continue operations
d. Implement internal controls to compensate for the vendor's vulnerability

Answer: b. Notify the vendor and require immediate remediation. Explanation: The immediate next step should be to notify the vendor of the critical security vulnerability and require them to remediate it promptly to protect the organization's data and operations.

548. During a vendor risk assessment, what is the significance of evaluating the vendor's incident response capabilities?
a. It ensures the vendor can recover from marketing mishaps
b. It verifies the vendor's ability to handle security incidents effectively
c. It assesses the vendor's product development lifecycle
d. It measures the vendor's financial stability

Answer: b. It verifies the vendor's ability to handle security incidents effectively. Explanation: Evaluating the vendor's incident response capabilities ensures they can effectively manage and mitigate security incidents, which is crucial for maintaining the security and integrity of the organization's data.

549. A third-party vendor has access to sensitive customer data. Which contractual clause is essential to include in the vendor agreement to ensure data protection?
a. A clause requiring regular product updates
b. A clause mandating compliance with relevant data protection laws and standards
c. A clause detailing the vendor's marketing strategies
d. A clause specifying the vendor's office locations

Answer: b. A clause mandating compliance with relevant data protection laws and standards. Explanation: Including a clause that mandates compliance with relevant data protection laws and standards ensures the vendor is legally obligated to protect sensitive customer data.

550. In continuous monitoring of third-party compliance, which metric is most useful for assessing the effectiveness of a vendor's security controls?
a. Number of customer service inquiries
b. Frequency of security incidents and breaches
c. Volume of sales transactions
d. Number of employees at the vendor organization

Answer: b. Frequency of security incidents and breaches. Explanation: The frequency of security incidents and breaches is a key metric for assessing the effectiveness of a vendor's security controls and their ability to protect data and systems.

551. A company uses multiple third-party vendors for various services. What is the best approach for managing and ensuring compliance across all vendors?
a. Conducting annual audits of each vendor
b. Implementing a centralized vendor management system
c. Allowing each department to manage their own vendors
d. Using a standardized contract template for all vendors

Answer: b. Implementing a centralized vendor management system. Explanation: A centralized vendor management system streamlines the management and compliance oversight of multiple vendors, ensuring consistency and comprehensive monitoring across the organization.

552. A new regulation requires additional compliance measures for third-party vendors. What should the organization do to ensure vendor compliance with the new regulation?
a. Terminate contracts with all current vendors
b. Require vendors to provide updated compliance attestations
c. Assume vendors will comply without verification
d. Reduce reliance on third-party vendors

Answer: b. Require vendors to provide updated compliance attestations. Explanation: Requiring vendors to provide updated compliance attestations ensures that they meet the new regulatory requirements and continue to comply with the organization's standards.

553. A multinational corporation is designing a new compliance training program. Which of the following approaches would be most effective in ensuring comprehensive coverage while addressing specific job function needs?
a. Implement a single, standardized training course for all employees globally
b. Develop separate training programs for each country's regulatory requirements
c. Create a modular training system with core modules for all employees and role-specific modules
d. Outsource all compliance training to third-party providers specializing in each regulatory area

Answer: c. Create a modular training system with core modules for all employees and role-specific modules. Explanation: A modular training system with core and role-specific components offers the most effective approach for comprehensive yet targeted compliance training. This method ensures all employees receive essential compliance knowledge while also addressing the specific compliance needs of different roles and functions. A single standardized course (a) may be too general or overwhelming. Separate programs for each country (b) may lead to inconsistencies and redundancies. Outsourcing all training (d) may not adequately address company-specific policies and culture.

554. When measuring the effectiveness of a compliance training program, which of the following metrics provides the most meaningful insight into behavioral change?
a. Percentage of employees who completed the training
b. Average scores on post-training quizzes
c. Reduction in compliance-related incidents or violations over time
d. Number of employees who rated the training as "excellent" in feedback surveys

Answer: c. Reduction in compliance-related incidents or violations over time. Explanation: The reduction in compliance-related incidents or violations over time is the most meaningful metric for assessing behavioral change resulting from compliance training. This metric directly reflects the practical application of training content in real-world situations. While completion rates (a) and quiz scores (b) are important, they don't necessarily indicate changes in behavior. Employee satisfaction ratings (d) may reflect the quality of the training experience but not its effectiveness in changing behaviors.

555. A financial services company is launching a compliance awareness campaign focused on anti-money laundering (AML) practices. Which of the following strategies would be most effective in engaging employees and promoting long-term retention of key concepts?
a. Distribute a comprehensive AML policy document to all employees
b. Conduct a one-day intensive workshop on AML regulations and procedures
c. Implement a multi-channel campaign including interactive e-learning, short video clips, and periodic quizzes
d. Post AML compliance posters in common areas of the office

Answer: c. Implement a multi-channel campaign including interactive e-learning, short video clips, and periodic quizzes. Explanation: A multi-channel campaign using various engaging formats is most likely to be effective in promoting awareness and long-term retention of AML concepts. This approach caters to different learning styles, reinforces key messages through repetition, and allows for ongoing engagement. Simply distributing a policy document (a) is passive and may not be read thoroughly. A one-day workshop (b) may be overwhelming and lead to poor retention. Posters (d) alone are insufficient for complex topics like AML.

556. In developing role-based compliance training for a healthcare organization, which of the following should be the primary focus for training designed for clinical staff?
a. General overview of all healthcare regulations
b. Detailed coverage of HIPAA privacy and security rules relevant to patient care
c. In-depth exploration of billing and coding compliance
d. Comprehensive review of corporate governance principles

Answer: b. Detailed coverage of HIPAA privacy and security rules relevant to patient care. Explanation: For clinical staff in a healthcare setting, detailed training on HIPAA privacy and security rules as they relate to patient care should be the primary focus. This directly addresses the most relevant compliance issues these staff members face in their daily roles. While a general regulatory overview (a) is useful, it may not provide enough depth on crucial topics. Billing and coding compliance (c) is more relevant to administrative staff. Corporate governance principles (d) are typically more pertinent to management-level employees.

557. A global manufacturing company wants to ensure consistent compliance understanding across its diverse workforce. Which of the following methods would be most effective in overcoming language and cultural barriers in compliance training?
a. Translate all training materials into local languages and deliver in-person sessions
b. Use universally understood symbols and icons in all training materials
c. Develop region-specific training programs tailored to local cultural norms
d. Implement a blended learning approach with localized content, interactive scenarios, and translation options

Answer: d. Implement a blended learning approach with localized content, interactive scenarios, and translation options. Explanation: A blended learning approach combining localized content, interactive scenarios, and translation options offers the most comprehensive solution for overcoming language and cultural barriers. This method allows for cultural adaptation while maintaining consistency in core messages, and provides flexible learning options to accommodate diverse needs. Simply translating materials (a) may not address cultural nuances. Using only symbols (b) may oversimplify complex concepts. Developing entirely separate regional programs (c) may lead to inconsistencies in compliance understanding across the organization.

558. A technology company is struggling with low engagement in its annual compliance training. Which of the following strategies would be most effective in increasing employee participation and interest?
a. Make the training mandatory and tie it to performance reviews
b. Offer monetary incentives for completing the training early
c. Gamify the training process with leaderboards, badges, and real-world rewards
d. Reduce the frequency of training to once every two years

Answer: c. Gamify the training process with leaderboards, badges, and real-world rewards. Explanation: Gamification of the compliance training process can significantly increase engagement by making the experience more interactive and rewarding. This approach taps into motivational psychology, encouraging participation through competition and recognition. While making training mandatory (a) ensures completion, it doesn't necessarily improve engagement. Monetary incentives (b) may be costly and don't address the core engagement issue. Reducing frequency (d) could lead to knowledge gaps and doesn't solve the engagement problem.

559. In designing a compliance training program for a rapidly growing startup, which of the following approaches would be most effective in ensuring scalability and adaptability?
a. Create a comprehensive, detailed training manual covering all possible compliance scenarios
b. Implement a flexible, modular e-learning system with easily updatable content
c. Rely primarily on one-on-one mentoring for compliance training
d. Outsource all compliance training to external legal counsel

Answer: b. Implement a flexible, modular e-learning system with easily updatable content. Explanation: For a rapidly growing startup, a flexible, modular e-learning system with easily updatable content offers the best scalability and adaptability. This approach allows for quick updates as the company grows and regulations change, and can easily accommodate new employees and evolving roles. A comprehensive manual (a) may quickly become outdated and is less adaptable. One-on-one mentoring (c) is not scalable for a growing company. Outsourcing all training to legal counsel (d) may be expensive and less tailored to the company's specific needs.

560. A multinational corporation wants to assess the long-term impact of its ethics and compliance training program. Which of the following methods would provide the most comprehensive evaluation?
a. Conduct annual compliance audits and compare results year-over-year
b. Track the number of calls to the company's ethics hotline
c. Implement a multi-faceted approach including behavioral assessments, scenario-based testing, and analysis of compliance incident trends
d. Survey employees on their satisfaction with the training program

Answer: c. Implement a multi-faceted approach including behavioral assessments, scenario-based testing, and analysis of compliance incident trends. Explanation: A multi-faceted approach combining behavioral assessments, scenario-based testing, and analysis of compliance incident trends provides the most comprehensive evaluation of the long-term impact of ethics and compliance training. This method assesses not only knowledge retention but also practical application and real-world outcomes. Annual audits (a) may not capture behavioral changes. Hotline calls (b) are a limited indicator. Employee satisfaction surveys (d) don't necessarily reflect the effectiveness of the training in changing behavior or improving compliance.

561. In developing compliance training for a company's board of directors, which of the following topics should be given the highest priority?
a. Detailed operational compliance procedures
b. Corporate governance principles and fiduciary responsibilities
c. Employee code of conduct guidelines
d. Step-by-step guide to using the company's compliance reporting system

Answer: b. Corporate governance principles and fiduciary responsibilities. Explanation: For board members, training on corporate governance principles and fiduciary responsibilities should be the highest priority. This focuses on the strategic, oversight role of the board in ensuring overall organizational compliance and ethical behavior. Detailed operational procedures (a) are typically more relevant for management and staff. Employee code of conduct (c) is important but usually not the board's direct responsibility. Step-by-step system guides (d) are more appropriate for those directly using the reporting system.

562. A company has implemented a new compliance training program and wants to ensure continuous improvement. Which of the following approaches would be most effective in gathering actionable feedback for program enhancement?
a. Conduct an annual survey asking employees to rate their satisfaction with the training
b. Analyze completion rates and quiz scores from the training modules
c. Implement ongoing feedback mechanisms including post-training surveys, focus groups, and real-time user feedback options
d. Review the number of compliance violations before and after training implementation

Answer: c. Implement ongoing feedback mechanisms including post-training surveys, focus groups, and real-time user feedback options. Explanation: Implementing diverse, ongoing feedback mechanisms provides the most comprehensive and actionable input for continuous improvement of the training program. This approach allows for both immediate and long-term feedback, capturing a range of perspectives and identifying specific areas for enhancement. An annual satisfaction survey (a) may miss timely improvement opportunities. Completion rates and quiz scores (b) don't provide qualitative feedback on content or delivery. Reviewing violation numbers (d) is important but doesn't provide specific feedback on the training itself.

563. A financial institution recently updated its compliance monitoring strategy after identifying a significant regulatory change. What should be the immediate next step to ensure the strategy's effectiveness?
a. Conducting a comprehensive internal audit
b. Training employees on the updated strategy
c. Re-evaluating the organization's risk appetite
d. Increasing the budget for compliance activities

Answer: b. Training employees on the updated strategy. Explanation: Training employees ensures they understand and can effectively implement the updated compliance monitoring strategy, aligning their actions with new regulatory requirements.

564. A company identifies a new type of cybersecurity threat. What should trigger an update to its compliance monitoring strategy?
a. Completion of an annual compliance report
b. Discovery of the new cybersecurity threat
c. Change in the company's executive leadership
d. Expansion into a new geographic market

Answer: b. Discovery of the new cybersecurity threat. Explanation: Discovering a new cybersecurity threat should trigger an update to the compliance monitoring strategy to address and mitigate the new risk, ensuring ongoing protection and compliance.

565. When integrating new regulatory requirements into an existing compliance monitoring strategy, what is the primary consideration?
a. The cost of implementing new controls
b. The timeline for regulatory compliance
c. The compatibility of new requirements with existing controls
d. The potential impact on company reputation

Answer: c. The compatibility of new requirements with existing controls. Explanation: Ensuring new regulatory requirements are compatible with existing controls helps integrate them smoothly into the current strategy, avoiding conflicts and redundancy.

566. An organization aims to continuously improve its compliance monitoring. Which approach is most effective for achieving this goal?
a. Conducting quarterly reviews of monitoring processes and outcomes
b. Increasing the number of compliance staff
c. Outsourcing the monitoring function to a third party
d. Implementing a static set of monitoring controls

Answer: a. Conducting quarterly reviews of monitoring processes and outcomes. Explanation: Regular reviews allow the organization to assess the effectiveness of its monitoring processes, identify areas for improvement, and make necessary adjustments to enhance compliance efforts.

567. Which of the following scenarios should trigger an immediate review and update of the compliance monitoring strategy?
a. A minor, low-impact compliance violation
b. The introduction of new compliance software
c. A major regulatory change impacting the industry
d. A routine internal audit with no significant findings

Answer: c. A major regulatory change impacting the industry. Explanation: Major regulatory changes can significantly affect compliance requirements, necessitating an immediate review and update of the monitoring strategy to ensure continued compliance.

568. A healthcare provider updates its compliance monitoring strategy to include new HIPAA regulations. What is a key step to integrate these new requirements effectively?
a. Hiring additional compliance officers
b. Updating the compliance documentation and control framework
c. Reducing the frequency of compliance audits

353

d. Expanding the healthcare provider's services

Answer: b. Updating the compliance documentation and control framework. Explanation: Updating the compliance documentation and control framework ensures that new HIPAA regulations are clearly defined and integrated into the provider's existing compliance processes.

569. How should an organization address continuous improvement in its compliance monitoring strategy?
a. Implementing a once-a-year review cycle
b. Establishing a feedback loop with periodic assessments
c. Hiring a new compliance team every few years
d. Reducing the number of compliance checks

Answer: b. Establishing a feedback loop with periodic assessments. Explanation: A feedback loop with periodic assessments allows the organization to continuously evaluate and enhance its compliance monitoring strategy, ensuring it remains effective and up-to-date.

570. An organization faces repeated compliance issues despite having a monitoring strategy in place. What is the most appropriate action to address this problem?
a. Ignoring minor compliance issues
b. Conducting a root cause analysis to identify underlying issues
c. Increasing penalties for non-compliance
d. Reducing the scope of compliance monitoring

Answer: b. Conducting a root cause analysis to identify underlying issues. Explanation: A root cause analysis helps identify the underlying reasons for repeated compliance issues, allowing the organization to address these problems effectively and improve its monitoring strategy.

571. When updating a compliance monitoring strategy, what is a critical component to ensure alignment with industry best practices?
a. Consulting with regulatory bodies for guidance
b. Increasing the organization's marketing budget
c. Implementing the latest technology trends
d. Reducing compliance training for staff

Answer: a. Consulting with regulatory bodies for guidance. Explanation: Consulting with regulatory bodies helps ensure that the updated compliance monitoring strategy aligns with industry best practices and meets all regulatory requirements.

572. A multinational corporation needs to update its compliance monitoring strategy to reflect new global regulations. What is the first step in this process?

a. Training the global workforce on new regulations
b. Conducting a gap analysis to identify current compliance deficiencies
c. Hiring local compliance experts in each region
d. Developing a global marketing campaign

Answer: b. Conducting a gap analysis to identify current compliance deficiencies. Explanation: Conducting a gap analysis identifies areas where the current compliance strategy falls short of new global regulations, providing a clear basis for necessary updates and improvements.

573. An organization is conducting a vulnerability scan using a popular vulnerability scanning tool. Which of the following best describes the primary purpose of this scan?
a. To identify and exploit vulnerabilities in the system
b. To document and review compliance policies
c. To detect and report security vulnerabilities in the system
d. To perform routine maintenance on the network

Answer: c. To detect and report security vulnerabilities in the system. Explanation: The primary purpose of a vulnerability scan is to detect and report security vulnerabilities within the system, allowing the organization to identify and address potential weaknesses before they can be exploited.

574. During a vulnerability assessment, a security team must prioritize the vulnerabilities for remediation. Which methodology is most effective for this purpose?
a. First-In, First-Out (FIFO)
b. Risk-based prioritization
c. Alphabetical order
d. Random selection

Answer: b. Risk-based prioritization. Explanation: Risk-based prioritization is the most effective methodology for prioritizing vulnerabilities for remediation, as it considers both the potential impact and the likelihood of exploitation, ensuring that the most critical vulnerabilities are addressed first.

575. An organization discovers several high-risk vulnerabilities in its systems. What should be the immediate action taken by the security team?
a. Document the vulnerabilities and plan for future remediation
b. Implement immediate remediation measures for the high-risk vulnerabilities
c. Notify the employees about the vulnerabilities
d. Ignore the vulnerabilities until the next scheduled assessment

Answer: b. Implement immediate remediation measures for the high-risk vulnerabilities. Explanation: The immediate action should be to implement remediation measures for high-risk vulnerabilities to mitigate the threat and protect the system from potential exploitation.

576. A company uses a vulnerability management tool to track remediation efforts. Which feature is most critical for ensuring effective remediation tracking?
a. Integration with social media platforms
b. Automated reporting and alerting
c. Customizable user interface themes
d. Support for multiple languages

Answer: b. Automated reporting and alerting. Explanation: Automated reporting and alerting are critical features for effective remediation tracking, as they provide timely updates on remediation progress and notify relevant stakeholders of any issues or delays.

577. In the context of vulnerability management, what is the purpose of performing a verification scan after remediation efforts have been completed?
a. To test the network's speed and performance
b. To ensure that the vulnerabilities have been successfully mitigated
c. To update the system documentation
d. To train new employees on security practices

Answer: b. To ensure that the vulnerabilities have been successfully mitigated. Explanation: Performing a verification scan after remediation efforts ensures that the identified vulnerabilities have been successfully mitigated and that no new vulnerabilities were introduced during the remediation process.

578. An organization conducts regular vulnerability scans as part of its security protocol. How often should high-priority systems be scanned to maintain optimal security?
a. Annually
b. Semi-annually
c. Quarterly
d. Monthly

Answer: d. Monthly. Explanation: High-priority systems should be scanned monthly to maintain optimal security and ensure that any new vulnerabilities are quickly identified and addressed.

579. A security analyst finds a critical vulnerability during a scan that affects multiple systems. What is the best approach to address this issue?
a. Remediate the vulnerability on a single system as a test case
b. Schedule remediation for all affected systems over the next quarter
c. Implement a patch across all affected systems immediately
d. Defer remediation until the next major system update

Answer: c. Implement a patch across all affected systems immediately. Explanation: The best approach is to implement a patch across all affected systems immediately to address the critical vulnerability and prevent potential exploitation.

580. During the vulnerability prioritization process, which factor is least likely to influence the prioritization decision?
a. The exploitability of the vulnerability
b. The business impact of the vulnerability
c. The location of the system within the organizational network
d. The color scheme of the vulnerability management tool

Answer: d. The color scheme of the vulnerability management tool. Explanation: The color scheme of the vulnerability management tool is irrelevant to the prioritization decision. Factors like exploitability, business impact, and system location are crucial for effective prioritization.

581. An organization uses a vulnerability management tool that includes a risk scoring system. Which metric is most commonly used in these systems to prioritize vulnerabilities?
a. Mean Time to Repair (MTTR)
b. Common Vulnerability Scoring System (CVSS) score
c. Return on Investment (ROI)
d. Number of affected users

Answer: b. Common Vulnerability Scoring System (CVSS) score. Explanation: The CVSS score is a widely used metric in vulnerability management tools to prioritize vulnerabilities based on their severity, providing a standardized method for assessing and comparing vulnerabilities.

582. To ensure continuous improvement in their vulnerability management program, what is a best practice for organizations?
a. Limiting vulnerability scans to only critical systems
b. Regularly updating vulnerability management policies and procedures
c. Performing vulnerability scans only when a breach is suspected
d. Relying solely on external audits for vulnerability assessments

Answer: b. Regularly updating vulnerability management policies and procedures. Explanation: Regularly updating vulnerability management policies and procedures is a best practice for ensuring continuous improvement, keeping the program current with emerging threats and industry best practices.

583. A compliance auditor is preparing to interview key personnel about a potential conflict of interest issue. Which of the following interview techniques would be most effective in eliciting detailed, accurate information?
a. Begin with direct, closed-ended questions about the specific conflict
b. Use leading questions to guide the interviewee towards the desired response
c. Start with open-ended questions and gradually focus on specific details
d. Present hypothetical scenarios unrelated to the actual issue to gauge reactions

Answer: c. Start with open-ended questions and gradually focus on specific details. Explanation: Starting with open-ended questions and gradually focusing on specific details is the most effective technique for compliance interviews. This approach allows the interviewee to provide information freely, potentially revealing aspects the auditor hadn't considered, while still ensuring all necessary details are covered. Direct, closed-ended questions (a) may limit the information gathered. Leading questions (b) can introduce bias and compromise the integrity of the interview. Hypothetical scenarios (d) may not address the actual issue effectively.

584. During a compliance assessment interview, an employee provides information that contradicts documented policies. What should be the auditor's immediate next step?
a. Conclude the interview and report the discrepancy to management
b. Confront the employee about the contradiction
c. Ignore the discrepancy and continue with the planned questions
d. Note the discrepancy and ask for clarification or additional context

Answer: d. Note the discrepancy and ask for clarification or additional context. Explanation: The most appropriate immediate action is to note the discrepancy and seek clarification or additional context from the interviewee. This approach allows for a fuller understanding of the situation without prematurely judging or escalating the issue. Concluding the interview (a) or confronting the employee (b) may prevent gathering important information. Ignoring the discrepancy (c) would be a failure to properly investigate a potential compliance issue.

585. In documenting findings from a compliance interview, which of the following is most critical to include?
a. The interviewer's personal opinions about the interviewee's credibility
b. Verbatim transcripts of the entire interview
c. Specific, factual statements made by the interviewee, clearly distinguished from interviewer interpretations
d. Detailed descriptions of the interviewee's body language and tone

Answer: c. Specific, factual statements made by the interviewee, clearly distinguished from interviewer interpretations. Explanation: The most critical element in documenting interview findings is to record specific, factual statements made by the interviewee, clearly distinguished from the interviewer's interpretations. This approach provides an objective record of the information gathered, which is essential for accurate assessment and potential follow-up. Personal opinions about credibility (a) can introduce bias. Verbatim transcripts (b) may be unnecessarily detailed and time-consuming. While nonverbal cues (d) can be relevant, they are secondary to the actual statements made.

586. A compliance officer is designing a follow-up procedure for addressing discrepancies identified during personnel interviews. Which of the following approaches would be most effective?
a. Immediately escalate all discrepancies to senior management for resolution
b. Develop a tiered approach based on the severity and potential impact of the discrepancy
c. Conduct a second round of interviews with all participants to verify information
d. Address all discrepancies through written communication to avoid confrontation

Answer: b. Develop a tiered approach based on the severity and potential impact of the discrepancy. Explanation: A tiered approach based on the severity and potential impact of discrepancies is the most effective follow-up procedure. This method allows for proportionate responses, ensuring that serious issues receive prompt attention while minor discrepancies are handled efficiently. Escalating all discrepancies to senior management (a) may overwhelm leadership with minor issues. Conducting second interviews with all participants (c) is time-consuming and may not be necessary for all discrepancies. Relying solely on written communication (d) may not be sufficient for addressing complex or serious issues.

587. During a compliance assessment, an auditor notices significant variations in how different departments interpret a key policy. Which interview strategy would be most effective in understanding the root cause of these variations?
a. Interview only department heads to get an official stance on policy interpretation
b. Conduct a series of cross-departmental group interviews to discuss policy interpretation
c. Interview a representative sample from each department, including various levels of employees
d. Send out a company-wide survey about policy understanding

Answer: c. Interview a representative sample from each department, including various levels of employees. Explanation: Interviewing a representative sample from each department, including various levels of employees, provides the most comprehensive understanding of policy interpretation variations. This approach captures diverse perspectives and can reveal how interpretations might differ at various organizational levels. Interviewing only department heads (a) may miss how policies are actually implemented. Group interviews (b) might lead to groupthink or discourage honest responses. A company-wide survey (d) lacks the depth and flexibility of personal interviews for understanding nuanced interpretations.

588. An auditor conducting compliance interviews discovers that several employees are reluctant to discuss certain topics. Which of the following approaches would be most appropriate to encourage open communication?
a. Offer anonymity to all interviewees and conduct interviews off-site
b. Emphasize the potential consequences of non-compliance to motivate honesty
c. Clearly explain the purpose of the interview, confidentiality measures, and non-retaliation policies
d. Involve senior management in the interviews to demonstrate the importance of the process

Answer: c. Clearly explain the purpose of the interview, confidentiality measures, and non-retaliation policies. Explanation: Clearly explaining the purpose of the interview, confidentiality measures, and non-retaliation policies is the most appropriate approach to encourage open communication. This method addresses common concerns that may cause reluctance, fostering a safe environment for honest discussion. Offering complete anonymity (a) may not be practical or necessary in all cases. Emphasizing consequences (b) could be perceived as threatening and further discourage openness. Involving senior management (d) might intimidate employees and inhibit candid responses.

589. In preparing to document findings from a series of compliance interviews, an auditor realizes that some information provided contradicts previous audit results. What is the most appropriate way to handle this situation in the documentation?
a. Omit the contradictory information to maintain consistency with previous audits
b. Document only the information that aligns with previous findings
c. Record all information gathered, clearly noting the discrepancies and plans for follow-up investigation
d. Reinterpret the new information to force alignment with previous audit results

Answer: c. Record all information gathered, clearly noting the discrepancies and plans for follow-up investigation. Explanation: The most appropriate approach is to document all information gathered, clearly noting discrepancies and outlining plans for follow-up investigation. This ensures transparency, maintains the integrity of the audit process, and provides a basis for resolving contradictions. Omitting (a) or selectively documenting (b) information compromises the audit's accuracy and completeness. Reinterpreting information to force alignment (d) is unethical and defeats the purpose of conducting new interviews.

590. A compliance officer is developing a protocol for following up on discrepancies identified in employee interviews regarding expense reporting practices. Which of the following approaches would be most effective?
a. Immediately implement stricter expense reporting policies across the organization
b. Conduct a thorough review of expense reports, correlating findings with interview data
c. Dismiss the discrepancies as individual misunderstandings of the policy
d. Repeat the same interviews with the same employees to verify the information

Answer: b. Conduct a thorough review of expense reports, correlating findings with interview data. Explanation: Conducting a thorough review of expense reports and correlating the findings with interview data is the most effective approach. This method allows for verification of the discrepancies identified in interviews against actual practice, providing concrete evidence of any compliance issues. Implementing stricter policies (a) without fully understanding the issue may be premature. Dismissing discrepancies (c) ignores potential compliance risks. Repeating the same interviews (d) may not provide new information and doesn't address the need for factual verification.

591. During a compliance assessment interview, an employee discloses potential fraudulent activity by a colleague. What should be the interviewer's immediate response?
a. End the interview and report the allegation to law enforcement
b. Probe for more details about the alleged fraudulent activity
c. Advise the employee to report the issue through the company's whistleblower hotline
d. Document the disclosure, explain next steps to the employee, and escalate according to company protocol

Answer: d. Document the disclosure, explain next steps to the employee, and escalate according to company protocol. Explanation: The most appropriate immediate response is to document the disclosure, explain next steps to the employee, and escalate the issue according to company protocol. This approach ensures the information is properly recorded and handled, while also providing transparency to the reporting employee. Ending the interview and reporting to law enforcement (a) is premature without internal verification. Probing for more details (b) may compromise a potential investigation. Advising use of the whistleblower hotline (c) is unnecessary since the disclosure has already been made directly.

592. An organization is revising its compliance interview process to improve the accuracy and completeness of gathered information. Which of the following additions would most effectively enhance the process?
a. Require all interviews to be conducted by at least two auditors
b. Implement a standardized post-interview verification process where interviewees review and confirm their statements
c. Mandate that all interviews be recorded on video for later analysis

d. Require interviewees to sign a legal statement attesting to the truthfulness of their responses

Answer: b. Implement a standardized post-interview verification process where interviewees review and confirm their statements. Explanation: Implementing a standardized post-interview verification process where interviewees review and confirm their statements is the most effective addition to enhance accuracy and completeness. This approach allows for clarification of any misunderstandings and ensures that the documented information accurately reflects the interviewee's intended statements. While having two auditors (a) can be beneficial, it doesn't directly address accuracy of the information provided. Mandatory video recording (c) may inhibit open communication. Requiring signed legal statements (d) could create an adversarial atmosphere and discourage candid responses.

593. An organization is decommissioning an old server that stored sensitive customer data. Which data sanitization method is most appropriate to ensure that the data cannot be recovered?
a. Formatting the hard drives
b. Using a degausser to disrupt the magnetic fields of the drives
c. Deleting all files and folders manually
d. Backing up the data and storing it on a new server

Answer: b. Using a degausser to disrupt the magnetic fields of the drives. Explanation: Using a degausser is an effective data sanitization method for magnetic storage devices, as it destroys the data by disrupting the magnetic fields, ensuring the data cannot be recovered.

594. A company is retiring several outdated laptops. What is a key compliance consideration when disposing of these assets?
a. Ensuring the laptops are sold at the highest possible price
b. Verifying that all proprietary software licenses are transferred
c. Documenting the disposal process to maintain a clear audit trail
d. Donating the laptops to a local charity

Answer: c. Documenting the disposal process to maintain a clear audit trail. Explanation: Documenting the disposal process ensures compliance with regulations by providing a clear record of how the assets were disposed of, which is essential for audits and accountability.

595. After decommissioning a system, an IT manager needs to update the organization's system inventory. What information is most critical to include in the update?
a. The purchase date of the decommissioned system
b. The serial numbers of the decommissioned components
c. The reason for decommissioning the system
d. The names of the employees who used the system

Answer: b. The serial numbers of the decommissioned components. Explanation: Including the serial numbers of the decommissioned components ensures accurate tracking of assets and prevents discrepancies in the system inventory.

596. During the decommissioning process of an old database server, which step is crucial to ensure compliance with data protection regulations?
a. Transferring all data to a new server
b. Performing a complete backup of the server
c. Physically destroying the hard drives
d. Running a software update on the server

Answer: c. Physically destroying the hard drives. Explanation: Physically destroying the hard drives ensures that sensitive data cannot be recovered, which is critical for compliance with data protection regulations.

597. An organization must ensure that all decommissioned systems are removed from their active inventory list. What is the best practice for verifying that this has been done correctly?
a. Cross-referencing the decommissioning records with the active inventory list
b. Asking the IT team to confirm the removal verbally
c. Conducting a physical count of all systems in the organization
d. Performing a quarterly audit of the inventory system

Answer: a. Cross-referencing the decommissioning records with the active inventory list. Explanation: Cross-referencing the decommissioning records with the active inventory list ensures that all decommissioned systems are accurately removed from the inventory, preventing potential errors or omissions.

598. When retiring a system that contains encrypted data, what additional step must be taken to ensure the data is unrecoverable?
a. Deleting the encryption keys
b. Disabling the encryption software
c. Changing the encryption algorithm
d. Re-encrypting the data with a different key

Answer: a. Deleting the encryption keys. Explanation: Deleting the encryption keys ensures that the encrypted data cannot be decrypted and accessed, rendering the data permanently unrecoverable.

599. A company needs to comply with environmental regulations when disposing of electronic assets. Which disposal method is most compliant with these regulations?
a. Dumping the assets in a landfill
b. Recycling the assets through an e-waste certified recycler
c. Storing the assets in a warehouse
d. Selling the assets to a third-party vendor

Answer: b. Recycling the assets through an e-waste certified recycler. Explanation: Recycling through an e-waste certified recycler ensures that electronic assets are disposed of in an environmentally responsible manner, complying with environmental regulations.

600. What is the primary reason for performing a final inventory check after decommissioning a system?
a. To update the financial records of the organization
b. To ensure no system components are left behind
c. To verify that all data has been successfully migrated
d. To confirm compliance with asset management policies

Answer: d. To confirm compliance with asset management policies. Explanation: Performing a final inventory check ensures that the decommissioning process complies with asset management policies and that all records are accurately updated.

601. During system decommissioning, which process ensures that sensitive information is not left on peripheral devices such as printers and copiers?
a. Running a self-diagnostic test on the devices
b. Shutting down the devices for a prolonged period
c. Sanitizing the internal storage and memory of the devices
d. Performing a firmware update on the devices

Answer: c. Sanitizing the internal storage and memory of the devices. Explanation: Sanitizing the internal storage and memory ensures that any residual data on peripheral devices is securely erased, preventing unauthorized access to sensitive information.

602. What should be included in a decommissioning report to ensure comprehensive documentation?
a. The names of all users affected by the decommissioning
b. A detailed timeline of the decommissioning process
c. The projected cost savings from decommissioning the system
d. The results of a user satisfaction survey

Answer: b. A detailed timeline of the decommissioning process. Explanation: A detailed timeline provides a clear record of all activities and steps taken during the decommissioning process, ensuring comprehensive documentation for compliance and audit purposes.

603. A company is creating a decommissioning plan for an outdated system. Which component is essential to include in the decommissioning plan?
a. Marketing strategies for new systems
b. Inventory of hardware and software assets to be decommissioned
c. Financial projections for next fiscal year
d. Employee satisfaction surveys

Answer: b. Inventory of hardware and software assets to be decommissioned. Explanation: An inventory of hardware and software assets to be decommissioned is essential for ensuring all components of the outdated system are accounted for and properly managed during the decommissioning process.

604. Before decommissioning a system, what should be conducted to determine the final security posture?
a. Financial audit
b. Security posture assessment
c. Employee performance review
d. Marketing analysis

Answer: b. Security posture assessment. Explanation: A security posture assessment is conducted to evaluate the system's current security status and ensure that all vulnerabilities and security issues are identified and mitigated before decommissioning.

605. Which of the following is a key consideration for the long-term retention of decommissioning records?
a. The color scheme used in the documentation
b. Compliance with legal and regulatory requirements
c. The personal preferences of the IT staff
d. The availability of marketing materials

Answer: b. Compliance with legal and regulatory requirements. Explanation: Compliance with legal and regulatory requirements is crucial for the long-term retention of decommissioning records to ensure that the organization meets all mandated obligations and can provide documentation if needed.

606. An organization is decommissioning a legacy system and needs to ensure that all sensitive data is securely disposed of. Which method is most appropriate for securely deleting data?
a. Reformatting the hard drives
b. Overwriting data with random patterns multiple times
c. Storing the hard drives in a locked cabinet
d. Backing up the data to an external drive

Answer: b. Overwriting data with random patterns multiple times. Explanation: Overwriting data with random patterns multiple times is a secure method for deleting data, making it difficult to recover and ensuring that sensitive information is properly disposed of.

607. During the decommissioning process, which step is necessary to ensure that no residual data remains on the system?
a. Performing a factory reset
b. Conducting a data verification audit
c. Archiving all system logs

d. Implementing new security policies

Answer: b. Conducting a data verification audit. Explanation: Conducting a data verification audit ensures that no residual data remains on the system, confirming that all data has been securely deleted and that there are no remnants that could be recovered.

608. What should be the primary focus when creating documentation for a decommissioned system?
a. Aesthetic presentation of the document
b. Detailed recording of the decommissioning process and actions taken
c. Inclusion of company branding and logos
d. Summarizing employee feedback

Answer: b. Detailed recording of the decommissioning process and actions taken. Explanation: The primary focus of decommissioning documentation should be the detailed recording of the decommissioning process and actions taken, ensuring a comprehensive and accurate record is maintained.

609. In the context of decommissioning, what is the significance of a final security posture assessment?
a. To celebrate the successful completion of the project
b. To ensure that all security vulnerabilities have been addressed before decommissioning
c. To evaluate the performance of the IT team
d. To create a marketing campaign for the new system

Answer: b. To ensure that all security vulnerabilities have been addressed before decommissioning. Explanation: A final security posture assessment is significant because it ensures that all security vulnerabilities have been identified and addressed, preventing potential data breaches or security issues after the system is decommissioned.

610. Which decommissioning plan component is essential for managing the transition of services to a new system?
a. Training materials for end-users
b. A detailed transition plan outlining steps for migrating services
c. Financial incentives for stakeholders
d. A survey of customer preferences

Answer: b. A detailed transition plan outlining steps for migrating services. Explanation: A detailed transition plan is essential for managing the transition of services to a new system, providing a clear roadmap for migrating services and ensuring continuity of operations.

611. An organization is finalizing its decommissioning plan. How should it ensure that all legal and regulatory compliance requirements are met?
a. Consult with legal and compliance experts to review the plan
b. Conduct a public survey on decommissioning practices

c. Implement new marketing strategies
d. Focus on employee training programs

Answer: a. Consult with legal and compliance experts to review the plan. Explanation: Consulting with legal and compliance experts ensures that the decommissioning plan meets all legal and regulatory requirements, helping the organization avoid potential legal issues and fines.

612. What is the best practice for storing decommissioning records to ensure they are accessible for future audits?
a. Printing and filing in a physical storage room
b. Storing in a centralized, secure digital repository with access controls
c. Keeping records on individual employees' personal devices
d. Uploading to a public cloud storage service

Answer: b. Storing in a centralized, secure digital repository with access controls. Explanation: Storing decommissioning records in a centralized, secure digital repository with access controls ensures that the records are accessible for future audits while maintaining security and preventing unauthorized access.

613. A global financial institution is implementing the NIST Risk Management Framework (RMF). Which of the following steps should be completed first to ensure a comprehensive risk management approach?
a. Select security controls based on the organization's risk assessment
b. Implement the selected security controls within the information systems
c. Prepare the organization for the RMF by identifying key stakeholders and defining risk tolerance
d. Categorize the information system based on its criticality and sensitivity

Answer: c. Prepare the organization for the RMF by identifying key stakeholders and defining risk tolerance. Explanation: The "Prepare" step is the first and foundational step in the NIST RMF. It involves identifying key stakeholders, defining risk tolerance, and establishing the context for risk-based decisions. This step ensures that the organization has the necessary groundwork in place before proceeding with system categorization, control selection, and implementation. Selecting controls (a), implementing controls (b), and categorizing systems (d) are important steps but come after the preparation phase in the NIST RMF process.

614. In the context of ISO 31000, which of the following best describes the relationship between risk management principles, framework, and process?
a. The principles guide the framework, which in turn supports the process
b. The framework dictates the principles, which then inform the process
c. The process determines the principles, which shape the framework
d. The principles, framework, and process operate independently of each other

Answer: a. The principles guide the framework, which in turn supports the process. Explanation: In ISO 31000, the risk management principles provide the foundation for managing risk and should be considered when establishing the risk management framework and processes. The framework provides the organizational arrangements for designing, implementing, and continually improving risk management across the organization. The process is the systematic application of policies, procedures, and practices to the activities of communicating, consulting, establishing context, and identifying, analyzing, evaluating, treating, monitoring, and reviewing risk. This hierarchical relationship ensures a coherent and effective approach to risk management.

615. A large healthcare provider is integrating Enterprise Risk Management (ERM) with its cybersecurity program. Which of the following approaches would be most effective in achieving this integration?
a. Replace the existing cybersecurity framework with the organization's ERM framework
b. Maintain separate ERM and cybersecurity processes to ensure specialized focus
c. Align cybersecurity risk assessments and reporting with the organization's overall ERM methodology and risk appetite
d. Prioritize ERM processes over cybersecurity considerations in all decision-making

Answer: c. Align cybersecurity risk assessments and reporting with the organization's overall ERM methodology and risk appetite. Explanation: The most effective approach to integrating ERM with cybersecurity is to align cybersecurity risk assessments and reporting with the organization's overall ERM methodology and risk appetite. This ensures that cybersecurity risks are evaluated and managed within the context of the organization's broader risk landscape and strategic objectives. Replacing the cybersecurity framework (a) may lead to loss of crucial domain-specific practices. Maintaining entirely separate processes (b) misses the benefits of integration. Prioritizing ERM over cybersecurity (d) may undervalue the specific and critical nature of cybersecurity risks.

616. In the NIST Risk Management Framework, which step is most critical for ensuring ongoing security and compliance in a rapidly changing threat landscape?
a. Assess the security controls to determine their effectiveness
b. Implement the selected security controls within the information systems
c. Monitor the security controls on an ongoing basis and report the findings
d. Authorize the information system for operation based on risk determination

Answer: c. Monitor the security controls on an ongoing basis and report the findings. Explanation: The "Monitor" step is most critical for ensuring ongoing security and compliance in a dynamic threat environment. This step involves continuous monitoring of security controls and their effectiveness, allowing for timely detection of changes in the system that may impact its security posture. While assessment (a), implementation (b), and authorization (d) are crucial, they are more point-in-time activities. Continuous monitoring enables organizations to maintain awareness of vulnerabilities, threats, and risks to their systems in a rapidly evolving landscape.

617. When applying the ISO 31000 risk management process, at which stage is it most crucial to involve a diverse group of stakeholders?
a. Risk identification
b. Risk analysis
c. Risk evaluation
d. Risk treatment

Answer: a. Risk identification. Explanation: Involving a diverse group of stakeholders is most crucial during the risk identification stage of the ISO 31000 process. This stage aims to find, recognize, and describe risks that might affect the achievement of objectives. A diverse group of stakeholders brings varied perspectives, experiences, and knowledge, enabling a more comprehensive identification of potential risks across different areas of the organization. While stakeholder involvement is important throughout the process, their diverse insights are particularly valuable in ensuring no significant risks are overlooked during the identification phase.

618. In integrating ERM with cybersecurity, which of the following metrics would be most valuable for reporting to the board of directors?
a. Number of blocked attacks by the firewall in the last month
b. Percentage of employees who completed security awareness training
c. Quantified potential financial impact of identified cybersecurity risks in relation to the organization's risk appetite
d. Number of unpatched vulnerabilities in the organization's systems

Answer: c. Quantified potential financial impact of identified cybersecurity risks in relation to the organization's risk appetite. Explanation: For board-level reporting in an integrated ERM and cybersecurity context, the quantified potential financial impact of cybersecurity risks in relation to the organization's risk appetite is the most valuable metric. This information allows the board to understand cybersecurity risks in the context of overall business risks and make informed decisions about resource allocation and risk mitigation strategies. Technical metrics like blocked attacks (a) or unpatched vulnerabilities (d) may be too granular for board-level discussions. Training completion rates (b), while important, don't directly convey the potential impact of cybersecurity risks on the organization.

619. Which of the following best describes the primary purpose of the "Categorize" step in the NIST Risk Management Framework?
a. To classify employees based on their access levels
b. To determine the criticality and sensitivity of the system and its information
c. To categorize threats based on their likelihood and impact
d. To group security controls into related families

Answer: b. To determine the criticality and sensitivity of the system and its information. Explanation: The primary purpose of the "Categorize" step in the NIST RMF is to determine the criticality and sensitivity of the information system and the information processed, stored, and transmitted by that system. This categorization is based on an impact analysis and informs the selection of an appropriate set of security controls. It does not involve classifying employees (a), categorizing threats (c), or grouping security controls (d), which are addressed in other steps or processes within the framework.

620. A multinational corporation is implementing ISO 31000 and struggles with inconsistent risk assessment approaches across different regional offices. Which of the following solutions would best address this issue while maintaining alignment with ISO 31000 principles?
a. Mandate a single, detailed risk assessment methodology for all offices globally
b. Allow each regional office to develop its own risk assessment approach independently
c. Develop a flexible risk assessment framework with core principles and customizable elements for regional adaptation
d. Outsource all risk assessments to a third-party consultant to ensure consistency

Answer: c. Develop a flexible risk assessment framework with core principles and customizable elements for regional adaptation. Explanation: This solution best aligns with ISO 31000 principles, which emphasize that risk management should be tailored to the organization's context. A flexible framework with core principles and customizable elements allows for consistency in the overall approach while accommodating regional differences in regulatory environments, business practices, and cultural factors. Mandating a single methodology (a) may not account for regional variations. Allowing completely independent approaches (b) could lead to inconsistencies in risk management across the organization. Outsourcing all assessments (d) may not adequately capture the nuances of each region's business environment.

621. In the context of integrating ERM with cybersecurity, which of the following represents the most significant challenge?
a. Ensuring technical staff understand business risk concepts
b. Aligning the timing of cybersecurity assessments with financial reporting cycles
c. Translating technical cybersecurity metrics into business risk language that aligns with the organization's risk appetite and tolerance
d. Convincing the board of directors to prioritize cybersecurity investments

Answer: c. Translating technical cybersecurity metrics into business risk language that aligns with the organization's risk appetite and tolerance. Explanation: The most significant challenge in integrating ERM with cybersecurity is often translating technical cybersecurity metrics into business risk language that aligns with the organization's risk appetite and tolerance. This translation is crucial for effective communication and decision-making at the enterprise level. While educating technical staff on business concepts (a) is important, it's less challenging than the translation of metrics. Aligning assessment timing (b) is a logistical issue. Board prioritization (d) is typically easier once risks are effectively translated into business terms.

622. A government agency is implementing the NIST Risk Management Framework and has completed the initial risk assessment and security control selection. However, budget constraints prevent the immediate implementation of all selected controls. Which of the following approaches best aligns with RMF principles?
a. Delay the implementation of all controls until full funding is available
b. Implement only the lowest-cost controls regardless of their priority
c. Prioritize control implementation based on risk assessment results and document the rationale for deferred controls
d. Seek a waiver from NIST to bypass the control implementation step

Answer: c. Prioritize control implementation based on risk assessment results and document the rationale for deferred controls. Explanation: This approach best aligns with NIST RMF principles, which emphasize risk-based decision-making and the importance of documentation. By prioritizing controls based on risk assessment results, the agency addresses the most critical risks first within budget constraints. Documenting the rationale for deferred controls demonstrates due diligence and provides a basis for future implementation planning. Delaying all implementation (a) leaves the agency exposed to known risks. Implementing only based on cost (b) disregards the risk-based approach central to the RMF. Seeking a waiver (d) is not a standard practice and doesn't address the underlying resource allocation challenge.

623. An organization is designing a new customer relationship management (CRM) system. To align with the principle of "Proactive not Reactive; Preventative not Remedial" in Privacy by Design, what should the organization prioritize?
a. Implementing robust data breach response protocols
b. Ensuring regular audits of the CRM system after deployment
c. Embedding privacy controls during the initial design phase
d. Providing extensive user training post-deployment

Answer: c. Embedding privacy controls during the initial design phase. Explanation: Embedding privacy controls during the initial design phase ensures that privacy issues are anticipated and addressed proactively, rather than reacting to problems after they occur.

624. A healthcare provider plans to implement privacy-enhancing technologies (PETs) in its patient data management system. Which PET is most appropriate for ensuring data minimization?
a. Data anonymization techniques
b. Multi-factor authentication
c. Encrypted communication channels
d. User access logs

Answer: a. Data anonymization techniques. Explanation: Data anonymization techniques help achieve data minimization by removing or masking personal identifiers, ensuring that only the necessary data is retained and used.

625. During the system design process, which consideration is essential to adhere to the "End-to-End Security" principle of Privacy by Design?
a. Incorporating privacy policies in user agreements
b. Implementing encryption from data collection to storage
c. Training employees on privacy awareness
d. Conducting periodic privacy impact assessments

Answer: b. Implementing encryption from data collection to storage. Explanation: Ensuring end-to-end security involves protecting data throughout its entire lifecycle, from collection to storage and disposal, and encryption is a key technology for achieving this.

626. A company needs to ensure transparency in its data processing activities. Which of the following actions aligns with the "Visibility and Transparency" principle of Privacy by Design?
a. Keeping privacy policies internal and confidential
b. Providing users with clear and accessible privacy notices
c. Limiting the sharing of data with third parties
d. Encrypting all user data

Answer: b. Providing users with clear and accessible privacy notices. Explanation: Providing clear and accessible privacy notices ensures that users are informed about how their data is being processed, enhancing transparency.

627. In the context of Privacy by Design, what is the primary goal of "Privacy as the Default Setting"?
a. To ensure that users must manually opt-in to privacy settings
b. To configure systems to collect and use the minimal amount of personal data by default
c. To maximize data collection for business analytics
d. To make privacy features optional for advanced users

Answer: b. To configure systems to collect and use the minimal amount of personal data by default. Explanation: Privacy as the Default Setting means that systems should be designed to protect personal data automatically, without requiring users to take any action to opt into privacy protections.

628. A financial institution is redesigning its online banking platform. How can the institution implement the "Full Lifecycle Protection" principle of Privacy by Design?
a. By providing users with detailed data usage reports annually
b. By ensuring continuous monitoring and protection of data from collection to deletion
c. By conducting quarterly user satisfaction surveys
d. By employing a dedicated team to handle customer complaints

Answer: b. By ensuring continuous monitoring and protection of data from collection to deletion. Explanation: Full Lifecycle Protection involves securing data throughout its entire lifecycle, including collection, use, storage, and eventual deletion.

629. Which Privacy by Design principle emphasizes the need for privacy to be integrated into business practices and culture?
a. Privacy as the Default Setting
b. End-to-End Security
c. Visibility and Transparency
d. Privacy Embedded into Design

Answer: d. Privacy Embedded into Design. Explanation: Privacy Embedded into Design emphasizes integrating privacy considerations into all business practices and processes, ensuring that privacy is a core part of the organization's culture and operations.

630. An e-commerce company wants to enhance its system design by incorporating Privacy by Design principles. Which action reflects the principle of "Respect for User Privacy"?
a. Collecting user data without consent for targeted advertising
b. Offering clear and easily accessible options for users to manage their privacy settings
c. Sharing user data with third-party partners without informing users
d. Storing user data indefinitely for potential future use

Answer: b. Offering clear and easily accessible options for users to manage their privacy settings. Explanation: Respect for User Privacy involves giving users control over their personal data and ensuring they can easily manage their privacy preferences.

631. When considering Privacy by Design in system architecture, what is a key benefit of implementing differential privacy techniques?
a. Enhancing user experience by personalizing content
b. Protecting individual data while allowing for aggregate data analysis
c. Simplifying the data processing workflow
d. Reducing the cost of data storage

Answer: b. Protecting individual data while allowing for aggregate data analysis. Explanation: Differential privacy techniques allow organizations to analyze large datasets while protecting the privacy of individual data points, balancing data utility with privacy.

632. In the development of a new mobile application, how can an organization apply the "Proactive not Reactive; Preventative not Remedial" principle to mitigate privacy risks?
a. Conducting a privacy impact assessment after the app is released
b. Regularly updating the app to patch security vulnerabilities
c. Designing the app with built-in privacy features from the outset
d. Informing users of potential privacy risks after they occur

Answer: c. Designing the app with built-in privacy features from the outset. Explanation: Designing the app with built-in privacy features from the outset ensures that privacy risks are mitigated proactively, rather than reacting to issues after they arise.

633. An organization is developing a baseline configuration for its servers. Which of the following is the most critical aspect to include in the baseline configuration?
a. The aesthetic appearance of the server rack
b. The default administrator password
c. The approved security settings and software versions
d. The server's physical location

Answer: c. The approved security settings and software versions. Explanation: The most critical aspect of a baseline configuration is the approved security settings and software versions, ensuring that all servers are configured securely and consistently to protect against vulnerabilities.

634. During a routine audit, a configuration drift is detected in the database server settings. What is the best immediate course of action?
a. Ignore the drift if the system is still operational
b. Update the baseline configuration to match the drifted settings
c. Investigate and remediate the drift to restore the server to the baseline configuration

d. Document the drift and review it during the next annual audit

Answer: c. Investigate and remediate the drift to restore the server to the baseline configuration. Explanation: The best immediate action is to investigate and remediate the configuration drift to ensure the server settings align with the baseline configuration, maintaining security and compliance.

635. A company is considering the use of automated configuration management tools. Which feature is most beneficial for maintaining secure configurations?
a. Ability to generate marketing reports
b. Real-time monitoring and automatic remediation of configuration changes
c. Support for multiple operating systems
d. User-friendly interface for non-technical staff

Answer: b. Real-time monitoring and automatic remediation of configuration changes. Explanation: Real-time monitoring and automatic remediation of configuration changes are crucial features for maintaining secure configurations, ensuring that any unauthorized changes are quickly detected and corrected.

636. In a case-based scenario, a system administrator notices that several workstations have deviated from the established baseline configuration. What tool would best help in identifying and correcting these deviations?
a. Antivirus software
b. Automated configuration management tool
c. Spreadsheet for manual tracking
d. Network monitoring tool

Answer: b. Automated configuration management tool. Explanation: An automated configuration management tool is best suited for identifying and correcting deviations from the established baseline configuration, providing automated detection and remediation capabilities.

637. When developing a baseline configuration, which of the following should be included to ensure compliance with industry standards?
a. The organization's mission statement
b. Detailed configuration settings that adhere to industry security guidelines
c. Employee contact information
d. Future technology trends

Answer: b. Detailed configuration settings that adhere to industry security guidelines. Explanation: Including detailed configuration settings that adhere to industry security guidelines ensures that the baseline configuration is compliant with relevant standards and best practices.

638. A configuration drift detection tool identifies unauthorized changes in the firewall settings. What should be the next step in the configuration management process?
a. Ignore the changes if there are no immediate issues
b. Reconfigure the firewall settings manually
c. Use the automated tool to revert to the approved baseline configuration
d. Schedule a team meeting to discuss the changes

Answer: c. Use the automated tool to revert to the approved baseline configuration. Explanation: Using the automated tool to revert to the approved baseline configuration ensures that the firewall settings are quickly restored to a secure and compliant state, mitigating any potential risks.

639. An organization wants to ensure that its baseline configurations are up to date. What is the best practice for maintaining current baseline configurations?
a. Review and update the configurations annually
b. Update configurations only when a security breach occurs
c. Conduct regular reviews and updates based on emerging threats and new technologies
d. Change configurations frequently without reviews

Answer: c. Conduct regular reviews and updates based on emerging threats and new technologies. Explanation: Regular reviews and updates based on emerging threats and new technologies ensure that baseline configurations remain current and effective in protecting the organization's systems.

640. In a secure configuration management process, what is the primary purpose of version control for configuration files?
a. To track changes and maintain a history of configurations
b. To simplify the configuration process
c. To reduce the cost of configuration management
d. To enhance the visual appeal of configuration files

Answer: a. To track changes and maintain a history of configurations. Explanation: The primary purpose of version control for configuration files is to track changes and maintain a history of configurations, providing an audit trail and enabling rollback to previous versions if needed.

641. A security team is implementing an automated configuration management tool. Which benefit is most likely to improve the organization's security posture?
a. Reduced need for technical staff
b. Consistent enforcement of security policies across all systems
c. Enhanced employee satisfaction
d. Increased marketing capabilities

Answer: b. Consistent enforcement of security policies across all systems. Explanation: An automated configuration management tool improves the organization's security posture by ensuring consistent enforcement of security policies across all systems, reducing the risk of configuration-related vulnerabilities.

642. Which of the following is an essential step in the remediation of configuration drift?
a. Ignoring minor configuration changes
b. Conducting a root cause analysis to identify why the drift occurred
c. Delegating the task to the marketing department
d. Disabling all automated configuration management tools

Answer: b. Conducting a root cause analysis to identify why the drift occurred. Explanation: Conducting a root cause analysis is essential for understanding why the configuration drift occurred, enabling the organization to address underlying issues and prevent future occurrences.

643. A large multinational corporation is implementing a new identity and access management system. Which access control model would be most effective in managing complex, dynamic access rights across diverse business units and geographical locations?
a. Discretionary Access Control (DAC)
b. Mandatory Access Control (MAC)
c. Role-Based Access Control (RBAC)
d. Attribute-Based Access Control (ABAC)

Answer: d. Attribute-Based Access Control (ABAC). Explanation: ABAC is the most suitable model for managing complex, dynamic access rights in a diverse multinational environment. ABAC allows for fine-grained access control based on a combination of user attributes, resource attributes, and environmental conditions. This flexibility enables the organization to define and enforce access policies that can adapt to various business units, geographical locations, and changing circumstances. While RBAC (c) is powerful, it can become unwieldy with numerous roles in a complex organization. DAC (a) lacks centralized control, and MAC (b) is too rigid for a dynamic business environment.

644. In implementing Role-Based Access Control (RBAC), which of the following strategies is most crucial for ensuring effective access management over time?
a. Creating a role for every job title in the organization
b. Implementing a formal process for regular role review and recertification
c. Assigning the most permissive roles by default to ensure productivity
d. Centralizing all role management under the IT department

Answer: b. Implementing a formal process for regular role review and recertification. Explanation: Regular role review and recertification is crucial for maintaining the effectiveness of RBAC over time. This process ensures that roles remain aligned with business needs, prevents role creep, and helps identify and remove unnecessary or outdated access rights. Creating roles for every job title (a) can lead to role explosion and management complexity. Assigning permissive roles by default (c) violates the principle of least privilege. Centralizing all role management under IT (d) may not adequately reflect business needs and changes.

645. A healthcare organization is struggling with enforcing the principle of least privilege due to the complex nature of clinical roles and shifting responsibilities. Which access control approach would best address this challenge?
a. Implement strict Role-Based Access Control with granular role definitions
b. Adopt a hybrid model combining RBAC with Attribute-Based Access Control
c. Enforce Mandatory Access Control based on security clearance levels
d. Allow department heads to manage access rights using Discretionary Access Control

Answer: b. Adopt a hybrid model combining RBAC with Attribute-Based Access Control. Explanation: A hybrid model combining RBAC and ABAC provides the best solution for enforcing least privilege in a complex healthcare environment. RBAC can define broad role-based permissions, while ABAC allows for dynamic, context-aware access decisions based on attributes like patient relationship, time of day, or location. This combination offers the structure of roles with the flexibility to adapt to shifting responsibilities. Strict RBAC alone (a) may be too rigid. MAC (c) is too inflexible for healthcare's dynamic nature. DAC (d) lacks the centralized control necessary for ensuring least privilege.

646. When implementing Attribute-Based Access Control (ABAC), which of the following is the most significant challenge organizations typically face?
a. Defining and maintaining accurate attribute values across diverse systems
b. Training users to understand their attribute-based permissions
c. Integrating ABAC with legacy applications
d. Convincing management of the benefits of ABAC over simpler models

Answer: a. Defining and maintaining accurate attribute values across diverse systems. Explanation: The most significant challenge in ABAC implementation is often defining and maintaining accurate attribute values across diverse systems. ABAC relies on attributes from various sources (user, resource, environment) to make access decisions. Ensuring these attributes are consistently defined, accurately maintained, and promptly updated across different systems is crucial for ABAC's effectiveness but can be complex in large, diverse IT environments. While user training (b), legacy integration (c), and management buy-in (d) are important, they are generally less challenging than maintaining the attribute ecosystem.

647. In enforcing the principle of least privilege, which of the following approaches is most effective for handling temporary elevated access needs?
a. Create separate accounts with higher privileges for users to switch between
b. Implement time-bound privilege elevation with automated revocation
c. Require manager approval for each instance of elevated access use
d. Assign all potentially needed privileges permanently to avoid disruption

Answer: b. Implement time-bound privilege elevation with automated revocation. Explanation: Time-bound privilege elevation with automated revocation is the most effective approach for handling temporary elevated access needs while adhering to the principle of least privilege. This method allows users to obtain necessary elevated rights for a limited time, after which the access is automatically revoked, minimizing the window of potential misuse or risk. Creating separate accounts (a) can lead to account sprawl and potential misuse. Requiring approval for each use (c) can be inefficient and delay work. Assigning all privileges permanently (d) violates the principle of least privilege.

648. A financial services company is implementing Role-Based Access Control and needs to design roles for its trading department. Which of the following approaches best balances security with operational efficiency?
a. Create a single role with all possible permissions for the entire trading department
b. Design roles based on job titles, with each title having a unique set of permissions
c. Implement a hierarchical role structure with inheritance, based on job functions and seniority
d. Allow each trader to customize their own role based on their specific needs

Answer: c. Implement a hierarchical role structure with inheritance, based on job functions and seniority. Explanation: A hierarchical role structure with inheritance, based on job functions and seniority, provides the best balance between security and operational efficiency for a trading department. This approach allows for granular access control while minimizing the number of roles to manage. Junior roles can inherit basic permissions, with additional permissions added for more senior or specialized roles. A single role for all (a) violates least privilege. Roles based solely on job titles (b) may not reflect actual access needs. Allowing individual customization (d) can lead to access creep and management difficulties.

649. In implementing Attribute-Based Access Control, which type of attribute is typically the most challenging to manage effectively?
a. Subject (user) attributes
b. Object (resource) attributes
c. Environmental (context) attributes
d. Action attributes

Answer: c. Environmental (context) attributes. Explanation: Environmental or context attributes are often the most challenging to manage effectively in ABAC implementations. These attributes, which can include time, location, device type, or security posture, are dynamic and can change rapidly. Ensuring real-time accuracy and availability of these attributes for access decisions can be complex, especially in large, distributed environments. Subject attributes (a) are typically more stable and tied to identity management systems. Object attributes (b) are usually defined with the resource. Action attributes (d) are generally a finite set defined by the system.

650. A government agency is transitioning from a legacy Discretionary Access Control system to Role-Based Access Control. Which of the following should be the first step in this transition?
a. Map existing user permissions to a set of predefined roles
b. Conduct a comprehensive review of current access rights and business needs
c. Implement new RBAC software and migrate all users immediately
d. Create roles mirroring the organizational hierarchy

Answer: b. Conduct a comprehensive review of current access rights and business needs. Explanation: The first step in transitioning from DAC to RBAC should be a comprehensive review of current access rights and business needs. This review is crucial for understanding the actual access requirements across the organization, identifying any existing access control issues, and forming the basis for well-designed roles. Simply mapping existing permissions to roles (a) may perpetuate existing access control problems. Implementing new software immediately (c) without proper planning can lead to disruptions. Creating roles based solely on organizational hierarchy (d) may not accurately reflect functional access needs.

651. In enforcing the principle of least privilege through Role-Based Access Control, which of the following metrics is most indicative of effective implementation?
a. The total number of roles in the system
b. The percentage of users with administrator privileges
c. The frequency of access request approvals
d. The number of permission exceptions required for daily operations

Answer: d. The number of permission exceptions required for daily operations. Explanation: The number of permission exceptions required for daily operations is the most indicative metric of effective least privilege enforcement in RBAC. Frequent need for exceptions suggests that the defined roles do not adequately match actual work requirements, potentially indicating over-restriction or poorly designed roles. The total number of roles (a) doesn't necessarily reflect appropriate access levels. The percentage of admin users (b) is important but narrow in focus. Access request approval frequency (c) may indicate process efficiency but not necessarily appropriate privilege levels.

652. A healthcare provider is implementing Attribute-Based Access Control to manage access to patient records. Which combination of attributes would most effectively enforce privacy regulations while ensuring necessary access for patient care?
a. User role, patient ID, and time of day
b. User department, record type, and system load
c. User role, patient-provider relationship, and access location
d. User seniority, record sensitivity, and device type

Answer: c. User role, patient-provider relationship, and access location. Explanation: The combination of user role, patient-provider relationship, and access location provides the most effective attributes for enforcing privacy regulations while ensuring necessary access in a healthcare setting. User role defines the base level of access, patient-provider relationship ensures access is limited to relevant patients, and location can restrict access to appropriate physical or network locations. This combination allows for dynamic, context-aware access decisions that can adapt to various clinical scenarios while maintaining patient privacy. The other options either lack critical elements (like patient relationship) or include less relevant factors for patient record access.

653. A healthcare provider must ensure its cryptographic modules meet regulatory standards. Which certification should the provider seek for compliance with federal requirements?
a. ISO/IEC 27001
b. SOC 2 Type II
c. FIPS 140-2/3
d. GDPR

Answer: c. FIPS 140-2/3. Explanation: FIPS 140-2/3 is a U.S. government standard that specifies security requirements for cryptographic modules, ensuring that they provide adequate protection for sensitive data.

654. An organization is designing a key management system for its encrypted communications. Which principle is most critical to ensure secure key management?
a. Storing all encryption keys in a central database
b. Regularly rotating encryption keys and limiting access to them
c. Allowing users to share keys through email
d. Using the same key for all encryption purposes

Answer: b. Regularly rotating encryption keys and limiting access to them. Explanation: Regularly rotating keys and restricting access minimize the risk of key compromise, ensuring that encryption remains secure over time.

655. A company needs to encrypt sensitive customer data stored in its databases. Which encryption method is most suitable for data at rest?
a. SSL/TLS encryption
b. AES-256 encryption
c. WEP encryption
d. DES encryption

Answer: b. AES-256 encryption. Explanation: AES-256 encryption is a strong encryption standard suitable for protecting data at rest, offering robust security against unauthorized access.

656. An organization is implementing encryption for data transmitted over its network. What is the most appropriate protocol to use for ensuring data integrity and confidentiality in transit?
a. FTP
b. HTTP
c. TLS
d. Telnet

Answer: c. TLS. Explanation: TLS (Transport Layer Security) provides strong encryption for data in transit, ensuring both data integrity and confidentiality during transmission over networks.

657. During an audit, it was discovered that an organization's encryption keys are stored with the encrypted data. What is the primary risk associated with this practice?
a. Increased complexity in data retrieval
b. Higher costs for key management
c. Compromised encryption security if the storage location is breached
d. Difficulty in complying with GDPR regulations

Answer: c. Compromised encryption security if the storage location is breached. Explanation: Storing encryption keys with the encrypted data negates the security benefits of encryption, as a breach of the storage location would give attackers access to both the keys and the data.

658. An organization uses public-key infrastructure (PKI) for securing email communications. Which aspect of PKI ensures the authenticity of the sender's identity?
a. Encryption of the email content
b. Digital signatures
c. Use of symmetric keys
d. Hashing the email body

Answer: b. Digital signatures. Explanation: Digital signatures provide a way to verify the authenticity and integrity of the sender's identity in PKI by allowing the recipient to verify that the email was sent by the claimed sender and has not been altered.

659. A financial institution is required to validate its cryptographic modules for regulatory compliance. Which of the following is a necessary step in this validation process?
a. Implementing a custom encryption algorithm
b. Obtaining FIPS 140-2/3 certification from an accredited testing laboratory
c. Conducting an internal security review
d. Regularly updating the cryptographic software

Answer: b. Obtaining FIPS 140-2/3 certification from an accredited testing laboratory. Explanation: FIPS 140-2/3 certification from an accredited testing laboratory is necessary to validate that cryptographic modules meet the required security standards for regulatory compliance.

660. An organization needs to ensure that its data encryption practices comply with GDPR requirements. Which principle should be prioritized to protect personal data?
a. Storing encryption keys in plaintext for easy access
b. Encrypting personal data both at rest and in transit
c. Using the same encryption key for all users
d. Relying solely on physical security measures

Answer: b. Encrypting personal data both at rest and in transit. Explanation: GDPR mandates the protection of personal data, and encrypting data both at rest and in transit ensures comprehensive security and compliance with these requirements.

661. A company is considering the use of hardware security modules (HSMs) for key management. What is the primary benefit of using HSMs in a cryptographic system?
a. Enhanced processing speed for encryption operations
b. Simplified user access to cryptographic keys
c. Secure generation, storage, and management of cryptographic keys
d. Reduced costs associated with cryptographic implementations

Answer: c. Secure generation, storage, and management of cryptographic keys. Explanation: HSMs provide a highly secure environment for generating, storing, and managing cryptographic keys, reducing the risk of key compromise and enhancing the overall security of the cryptographic system.

662. An e-commerce company wants to protect customer payment information during transactions. Which encryption protocol is most appropriate for securing data in transit on their website?
a. SSL
b. SSH
c. PGP
d. IPsec

Answer: a. SSL (or its successor TLS). Explanation: SSL/TLS is the standard protocol for securing data in transit on websites, ensuring that customer payment information is encrypted and protected during online transactions.

663. A company is implementing NIST SP 800-161 supply chain risk management practices. What is the primary goal of these practices?
a. To reduce the cost of procurement
b. To enhance the security and resilience of the supply chain
c. To streamline vendor payment processes
d. To increase the speed of product delivery

Answer: b. To enhance the security and resilience of the supply chain. Explanation: NIST SP 800-161 focuses on enhancing the security and resilience of the supply chain by identifying, assessing, and mitigating risks associated with the supply chain components and processes.

664. During a vendor security assessment, which factor is most critical to evaluate?
a. The vendor's market share
b. The vendor's compliance with security standards and regulations
c. The vendor's customer satisfaction ratings
d. The vendor's marketing strategies

Answer: b. The vendor's compliance with security standards and regulations. Explanation: Evaluating the vendor's compliance with security standards and regulations is critical in a security assessment to ensure that the vendor adheres to best practices and legal requirements for information security.

665. An organization is analyzing third-party software components for security risks. Which tool or technique is most effective for this analysis?
a. SWOT analysis
b. Static application security testing (SAST)
c. Customer satisfaction surveys
d. Financial performance reviews

Answer: b. Static application security testing (SAST). Explanation: SAST is an effective technique for analyzing third-party software components for security risks, as it examines the source code for vulnerabilities before the software is executed.

666. A security team identifies a critical vulnerability in a third-party software component. What should be the immediate course of action?
a. Notify the vendor and request a patch
b. Continue using the software until the next scheduled update
c. Ignore the vulnerability if it hasn't been exploited yet
d. Switch to an alternative software immediately

Answer: a. Notify the vendor and request a patch. Explanation: The immediate course of action should be to notify the vendor and request a patch to address the critical vulnerability, ensuring the software remains secure.

667. Which of the following best describes the purpose of continuous monitoring in supply chain risk management?
a. To track the financial performance of vendors
b. To ensure ongoing compliance with security policies and identify new risks
c. To enhance the aesthetic presentation of products
d. To simplify the procurement process

Answer: b. To ensure ongoing compliance with security policies and identify new risks. Explanation: Continuous monitoring in supply chain risk management is essential for ensuring ongoing compliance with security policies and identifying new risks that may arise, allowing for timely mitigation.

668. In the context of NIST SP 800-161, what is a critical element to include in a supply chain risk management plan?
a. Detailed marketing strategies for vendors
b. Regular security assessments and audits of suppliers
c. Financial incentives for timely delivery
d. Customer feedback mechanisms

Answer: b. Regular security assessments and audits of suppliers. Explanation: A critical element of a supply chain risk management plan, according to NIST SP 800-161, is the regular security assessments and audits of suppliers to ensure that security risks are identified and managed effectively.

669. When assessing the security of a new vendor, which of the following is least relevant?
a. The vendor's incident response capabilities
b. The vendor's compliance with relevant security standards
c. The vendor's office decor
d. The vendor's history of security breaches

Answer: c. The vendor's office decor. Explanation: The vendor's office decor is irrelevant to the security assessment. The focus should be on their incident response capabilities, compliance with security standards, and history of security breaches.

670. What is the main advantage of performing a third-party software component analysis?
a. To reduce software development costs
b. To identify and mitigate security vulnerabilities in the software
c. To improve the software's user interface
d. To increase the software's marketability

Answer: b. To identify and mitigate security vulnerabilities in the software. Explanation: The main advantage of performing a third-party software component analysis is to identify and mitigate security vulnerabilities, ensuring the software is secure and reliable.

671. A company wants to ensure the integrity of its supply chain. Which strategy is most effective for achieving this goal?
a. Limiting the number of suppliers to reduce complexity
b. Implementing a robust vendor risk management program
c. Reducing the frequency of vendor assessments
d. Outsourcing all supply chain management activities

Answer: b. Implementing a robust vendor risk management program. Explanation: Implementing a robust vendor risk management program is most effective for ensuring the integrity of the supply chain by systematically identifying, assessing, and mitigating risks associated with vendors.

672. When developing a supply chain risk management policy, which element is essential for addressing third-party software risks?
a. Regularly scheduled product demos
b. Comprehensive contractual requirements for security
c. Detailed pricing negotiations
d. Monthly financial performance reviews

Answer: b. Comprehensive contractual requirements for security. Explanation: Comprehensive contractual requirements for security are essential in a supply chain risk management policy to ensure that third-party software vendors adhere to agreed-upon security standards and practices.

673. A multinational corporation is migrating its critical financial systems to a public cloud environment. Which aspect of compliance is most likely to be overlooked in this transition?
a. Encryption of data at rest
b. Multi-factor authentication for user access

c. Clear delineation of security responsibilities between the cloud provider and the corporation
d. Regular vulnerability scanning of cloud-hosted systems

Answer: c. Clear delineation of security responsibilities between the cloud provider and the corporation. Explanation: In cloud migrations, the most commonly overlooked aspect is often the clear delineation of security responsibilities between the cloud provider and the customer. This is crucial in the shared responsibility model of cloud security. While aspects like encryption (a), authentication (b), and vulnerability scanning (d) are important, they are typically well-understood. The shared responsibility model, however, requires a detailed understanding of which security controls are managed by the provider versus the customer, which can vary based on the service model (IaaS, PaaS, SaaS) and specific provider offerings.

674. In the context of the Cloud Security Alliance (CSA) STAR certification, which level provides the highest assurance of a cloud service provider's security posture?
a. Self-Assessment
b. CSA STAR Attestation
c. CSA STAR Certification
d. CSA STAR Continuous

Answer: d. CSA STAR Continuous. Explanation: CSA STAR Continuous provides the highest level of assurance in the STAR program. It builds upon the Certification level by adding continuous monitoring of the cloud provider's security posture. This ongoing assessment ensures that security controls remain effective over time, providing real-time visibility into the provider's compliance with CSA best practices. Self-Assessment (a) is the lowest level, relying on the provider's own evaluation. Attestation (b) and Certification (c) offer third-party validation but at specific points in time rather than continuously.

675. A global financial services firm is considering using a cloud-based CRM system. Which of the following is the most critical factor to consider regarding data residency and sovereignty?
a. The physical location of the cloud provider's headquarters
b. The jurisdictions where customer data will be stored and processed
c. The nationality of the cloud provider's employees
d. The location of the firm's primary data center

Answer: b. The jurisdictions where customer data will be stored and processed. Explanation: The jurisdictions where customer data will be stored and processed is the most critical factor for data residency and sovereignty considerations. Different countries have varying laws and regulations regarding data protection, privacy, and government access to data. The physical location of data storage and processing directly impacts compliance with these laws. The provider's headquarters location (a), employee nationalities (c), or the firm's own data center location (d) are less relevant to data sovereignty issues than the actual location of data storage and processing.

676. In implementing a cloud-based solution for healthcare data management, which compliance framework would be most relevant to address both general cloud security and healthcare-specific requirements?
a. ISO 27001 and HITRUST CSF
b. PCI DSS and NIST 800-53

c. GDPR and SOC 2
d. CSA STAR and HIPAA

Answer: d. CSA STAR and HIPAA. Explanation: The combination of CSA STAR and HIPAA provides the most comprehensive coverage for cloud-based healthcare data management. CSA STAR addresses cloud-specific security controls and best practices, while HIPAA covers the specific requirements for protecting health information. This combination ensures both general cloud security and healthcare-specific compliance are addressed. While ISO 27001 and HITRUST (a) are valuable, they don't specifically target cloud environments. PCI DSS and NIST 800-53 (b) are not healthcare-focused. GDPR and SOC 2 (c) don't provide healthcare-specific guidance.

677. A company is adopting a multi-cloud strategy and needs to ensure consistent security and compliance across different cloud providers. Which approach would be most effective in achieving this goal?
a. Rely solely on each cloud provider's native security tools
b. Implement a cloud-agnostic security and compliance management platform
c. Assign different security teams to manage each cloud environment independently
d. Apply on-premises security policies directly to cloud environments

Answer: b. Implement a cloud-agnostic security and compliance management platform. Explanation: Implementing a cloud-agnostic security and compliance management platform is the most effective approach for ensuring consistency across multiple cloud providers. This allows for centralized policy management, monitoring, and reporting across diverse cloud environments, enabling uniform security and compliance practices regardless of the underlying cloud infrastructure. Relying solely on provider-specific tools (a) can lead to inconsistencies and management complexities. Independent teams for each cloud (c) may result in disparate practices. Applying on-premises policies directly to cloud environments (d) often fails to address cloud-specific security considerations.

678. In the context of cloud compliance, which of the following best describes the concept of "data sovereignty"?
a. The ability to encrypt data in the cloud
b. The legal requirement to store data in specific geographic locations
c. The process of classifying data based on sensitivity
d. The right of cloud providers to access customer data

Answer: b. The legal requirement to store data in specific geographic locations. Explanation: Data sovereignty refers to the concept that data is subject to the laws and governance structures of the country in which it is physically located. In cloud compliance, this often translates to legal requirements to store certain types of data within specific geographic boundaries. This is distinct from data encryption (a), which is a security measure. Data classification (c) is a related but separate concept. The right of providers to access data (d) is not related to data sovereignty but rather to data ownership and privacy considerations.

679. A government agency is considering moving classified information to a cloud environment. Which of the following is the most appropriate approach to ensure compliance with government security standards?
a. Use any public cloud provider that offers encryption
b. Implement a private cloud within the agency's own data centers
c. Utilize a FedRAMP-authorized government cloud offering

d. Store encrypted data in a public cloud and keep encryption keys on-premises

Answer: c. Utilize a FedRAMP-authorized government cloud offering. Explanation: For a government agency handling classified information, utilizing a FedRAMP-authorized government cloud offering is the most appropriate approach. FedRAMP (Federal Risk and Authorization Management Program) provides a standardized approach to security assessment, authorization, and continuous monitoring for cloud products and services used by U.S. federal agencies. This ensures compliance with stringent government security standards. While encryption in public clouds (a) is important, it's insufficient for classified data. A private cloud (b) might be suitable but lacks the validated security controls of FedRAMP. Storing encrypted data in public clouds with on-premises keys (d) doesn't meet government standards for classified information.

680. In assessing a cloud service provider's compliance with data protection regulations, which of the following audit reports would provide the most comprehensive view of the provider's privacy and security controls?
a. SOC 2 Type II report
b. ISO 27001 certification
c. PCI DSS Attestation of Compliance
d. HIPAA compliance attestation

Answer: a. SOC 2 Type II report. Explanation: A SOC 2 Type II report provides the most comprehensive view of a cloud service provider's privacy and security controls. It assesses the provider's controls related to security, availability, processing integrity, confidentiality, and privacy over an extended period (typically 6-12 months). This report offers detailed insights into the operational effectiveness of these controls. While ISO 27001 certification (b) is valuable, it focuses more on the information security management system rather than specific control effectiveness. PCI DSS (c) is specific to payment card data. HIPAA compliance (d) is healthcare-specific and may not cover all aspects of general data protection.

681. A multinational corporation is implementing a cloud-based ERP system and needs to ensure compliance with various international data protection laws. Which of the following strategies would be most effective in addressing cross-border data transfer requirements?
a. Store all data in a single region and manage access controls strictly
b. Implement data localization for each country of operation
c. Use a distributed cloud architecture with regional data storage and processing capabilities
d. Encrypt all data and store encryption keys in the company's home country

Answer: c. Use a distributed cloud architecture with regional data storage and processing capabilities. Explanation: A distributed cloud architecture with regional data storage and processing capabilities offers the most effective strategy for complying with various international data protection laws. This approach allows the corporation to store and process data within specific geographic regions, addressing data residency requirements while maintaining the benefits of cloud computing. Storing all data in a single region (a) may violate data transfer restrictions. Implementing data localization for each country (b) can be overly complex and costly. Encrypting all data with keys stored in the home country (d) may not satisfy legal requirements for data localization in some jurisdictions.

682. In the context of cloud compliance, which of the following best describes the primary purpose of a Cloud Access Security Broker (CASB)?
a. To provide encryption for data stored in the cloud
b. To manage user authentication for cloud services
c. To monitor and control access to cloud services and enforce security policies
d. To perform vulnerability assessments of cloud infrastructure

Answer: c. To monitor and control access to cloud services and enforce security policies. Explanation: The primary purpose of a Cloud Access Security Broker (CASB) is to monitor and control access to cloud services and enforce security policies. CASBs act as intermediaries between users and cloud service providers, offering visibility into cloud usage, data protection, threat protection, and compliance management. While CASBs may facilitate encryption (a) and authentication (b), these are not their primary functions. Vulnerability assessments of cloud infrastructure (d) are typically performed by other specialized tools or services.

683. An organization is developing its Security and Privacy Governance framework. Which of the following principles is least relevant to this effort?
a. Establishing roles and responsibilities for security activities
b. Creating an incident response plan
c. Ensuring legal and regulatory compliance
d. Defining risk management processes

Answer: b. Creating an incident response plan. Explanation: While creating an incident response plan is critical, it is typically part of operational security rather than the governance framework, which focuses more on establishing roles, compliance, and risk management processes.

684. During a risk assessment, a company identifies that unauthorized access to a sensitive database could result in significant financial loss. What is the most appropriate risk response strategy?
a. Accept the risk
b. Transfer the risk
c. Mitigate the risk
d. Ignore the risk

Answer: c. Mitigate the risk. Explanation: Mitigating the risk by implementing controls to prevent unauthorized access is the most appropriate response to reduce the potential financial impact.

685. Which document provides the detailed description of security controls and their implementation in the context of CGRC?
a. System Security Plan (SSP)
b. Risk Assessment Report (RAR)
c. Incident Response Plan (IRP)
d. Business Continuity Plan (BCP)

Answer: a. System Security Plan (SSP). Explanation: The System Security Plan (SSP) provides a detailed description of the security controls implemented to protect an information system, outlining how these controls are applied and maintained.

686. An organization is required to comply with FISMA. Which document must be regularly updated to demonstrate compliance and manage ongoing risk?
a. Security Assessment Report (SAR)
b. Plan of Action and Milestones (POA&M)
c. Executive Summary
d. Annual Financial Report

Answer: b. Plan of Action and Milestones (POA&M). Explanation: The POA&M is a key document for FISMA compliance that tracks the progress of remediation efforts for identified security weaknesses, ensuring ongoing risk management.

687. Which aspect of the System Development Life Cycle (SDLC) is most critical for integrating security considerations into the development process?
a. Testing phase
b. Design phase
c. Deployment phase
d. Maintenance phase

Answer: b. Design phase. Explanation: The design phase is critical for integrating security considerations into the SDLC, as it sets the foundation for building security into the system architecture and ensuring that security requirements are addressed from the outset.

688. An organization has completed a privacy impact assessment (PIA). What is the primary purpose of conducting a PIA?
a. To evaluate the financial performance of the organization
b. To identify and mitigate privacy risks related to the handling of personal data
c. To assess the aesthetic design of user interfaces
d. To measure employee satisfaction with privacy policies

Answer: b. To identify and mitigate privacy risks related to the handling of personal data. Explanation: The primary purpose of a PIA is to identify and mitigate privacy risks associated with the collection, use, and storage of personal data, ensuring compliance with privacy regulations and protecting individual privacy rights.

689. In the context of continuous monitoring, what is the main objective of implementing a Security Information and Event Management (SIEM) system?
a. To track financial transactions
b. To improve user experience

c. To detect and respond to security incidents in real-time
d. To manage physical access to facilities

Answer: c. To detect and respond to security incidents in real-time. Explanation: A SIEM system is implemented to detect and respond to security incidents in real-time by collecting and analyzing security event data from various sources, enabling timely identification and mitigation of threats.

690. A CGRC professional is tasked with assessing the risk posture of a newly deployed information system. Which factor is least likely to be considered in this assessment?
a. The system's compliance with regulatory requirements
b. The potential impact of data breaches on organizational operations
c. The aesthetic design of the user interface
d. The effectiveness of implemented security controls

Answer: c. The aesthetic design of the user interface. Explanation: The aesthetic design of the user interface is irrelevant to the risk posture assessment, which focuses on compliance, potential impact, and the effectiveness of security controls.

691. An organization needs to document its ongoing compliance activities for a critical information system. Which document should be used to compile and review these activities?
a. Incident Response Plan (IRP)
b. Business Impact Analysis (BIA)
c. System Security Plan (SSP)
d. Continuous Monitoring Plan

Answer: d. Continuous Monitoring Plan. Explanation: The Continuous Monitoring Plan is used to document and review ongoing compliance activities, ensuring that security controls remain effective and that the organization stays compliant with regulatory requirements.

692. When performing a security assessment, a CGRC professional identifies a high likelihood of a security breach occurring with moderate impact. How should this risk be classified?
a. Low risk
b. Medium risk
c. High risk
d. Critical risk

Answer: c. High risk. Explanation: A high likelihood of occurrence combined with a moderate impact typically classifies the risk as high, requiring significant attention and mitigation efforts to reduce the potential threat.

693. An organization is developing a compliance program aligned with NIST SP 800-37 RMF. Which of the following steps should be performed first in the Risk Management Framework (RMF) process?
a. Select security controls
b. Implement security controls
c. Assess security controls
d. Categorize the information system

Answer: d. Categorize the information system. Explanation: The first step in the RMF process is to categorize the information system based on the impact of potential breaches of confidentiality, integrity, and availability, as this guides the selection and implementation of appropriate security controls.

694. A company is evaluating its risk management strategy. Which approach best describes the process of continuously monitoring the security state of an information system?
a. Conducting an annual risk assessment
b. Implementing a robust change management process
c. Regularly updating the System Security Plan (SSP)
d. Continuous monitoring and ongoing authorization

Answer: d. Continuous monitoring and ongoing authorization. Explanation: Continuous monitoring involves regularly assessing the security state of an information system to ensure that security controls are effective, and risks are managed continuously rather than only at discrete intervals.

695. During a security assessment, which type of control would be classified as a management control?
a. Firewalls and intrusion detection systems
b. Encryption protocols and algorithms
c. Risk assessment and security planning
d. User authentication and access control mechanisms

Answer: c. Risk assessment and security planning. Explanation: Management controls involve policies, procedures, and guidelines that help manage the organization's security program, including activities like risk assessment and security planning.

696. An organization must comply with both HIPAA and GDPR. How should the organization handle the differing data breach notification requirements?
a. Follow the more stringent requirement from either regulation
b. Notify affected individuals only if both regulations require it
c. Follow HIPAA requirements for U.S. citizens and GDPR for EU citizens
d. Choose one regulation to follow for all incidents

Answer: a. Follow the more stringent requirement from either regulation. Explanation: To ensure compliance with both regulations, the organization should follow the more stringent requirement, which will help avoid penalties and maintain adherence to both sets of laws.

697. An IT security team is updating their incident response plan. Which phase of incident response focuses on learning from past incidents and improving future responses?
a. Detection and analysis
b. Containment, eradication, and recovery
c. Post-incident activity
d. Preparation

Answer: c. Post-incident activity. Explanation: The post-incident activity phase involves reviewing and analyzing the incident to identify lessons learned, improve the incident response process, and enhance security measures to prevent future incidents.

698. In the context of the System Development Life Cycle (SDLC), when should security requirements be defined to ensure comprehensive protection?
a. During the development phase
b. During the implementation phase
c. During the design phase
d. During the maintenance phase

Answer: c. During the design phase. Explanation: Security requirements should be defined during the design phase of the SDLC to ensure that security considerations are integrated into the system architecture from the outset, rather than being retrofitted later.

699. An organization is conducting a Privacy Impact Assessment (PIA) for a new system. What is the primary purpose of a PIA?
a. To assess the system's performance
b. To evaluate the impact on user productivity
c. To determine the potential privacy risks and impacts of the system
d. To ensure compliance with financial regulations

Answer: c. To determine the potential privacy risks and impacts of the system. Explanation: A PIA is conducted to identify and mitigate potential privacy risks associated with a system, ensuring that personal data is protected and regulatory compliance is maintained.

700. A company needs to manage encryption keys securely. Which key management practice is essential for ensuring the integrity and confidentiality of cryptographic keys?
a. Storing all keys in plaintext in a secure physical location
b. Using a single key for all encryption purposes
c. Regularly rotating and updating encryption keys

d. Sharing encryption keys through email for convenience

Answer: c. Regularly rotating and updating encryption keys. Explanation: Regularly rotating and updating encryption keys helps prevent key compromise and ensures that the cryptographic system remains secure over time.

701. An organization is selecting security controls based on NIST SP 800-53. What is the key factor to consider when tailoring security controls to a specific information system?
a. The organization's budget constraints
b. The potential impact level of the system
c. The number of users accessing the system
d. The physical location of the system

Answer: b. The potential impact level of the system. Explanation: Tailoring security controls involves considering the potential impact level (low, moderate, high) of the information system, as this determines the baseline controls necessary to protect the system appropriately.

702. In the context of achieving an Authority to Operate (ATO), what role does the Authorizing Official (AO) play?
a. Implementing security controls for the system
b. Conducting vulnerability scans and penetration tests
c. Making the final decision on whether a system is authorized to operate
d. Managing the day-to-day operations of the information system

Answer: c. Making the final decision on whether a system is authorized to operate. Explanation: The AO is responsible for making the final decision on granting an ATO, based on the assessment of security controls, risk management, and compliance with relevant policies and regulations.

703. A healthcare organization is implementing a large-scale IoT solution for patient monitoring. Which of the following approaches would be most effective in establishing a security baseline for these devices?
a. Apply the same security controls used for standard IT equipment
b. Rely solely on the built-in security features provided by the IoT device manufacturers
c. Develop a custom security framework specific to IoT devices in healthcare
d. Implement a layered approach combining industry standards, healthcare regulations, and IoT-specific security measures

Answer: d. Implement a layered approach combining industry standards, healthcare regulations, and IoT-specific security measures. Explanation: A layered approach that combines industry standards, healthcare regulations, and IoT-specific security measures provides the most comprehensive security baseline for IoT devices in healthcare. This approach addresses the unique challenges of IoT security while ensuring compliance with healthcare-specific requirements like HIPAA. Standard IT controls (a) may not adequately address IoT-specific vulnerabilities. Relying solely on manufacturer security (b) is insufficient for a critical healthcare environment. While a custom framework (c) can be beneficial, it may lack the robustness of established standards and best practices.

704. In designing network segmentation for an industrial IoT environment, which of the following considerations is most critical for maintaining both security and operational efficiency?
a. Isolating all IoT devices on a single, separate network segment
b. Implementing microsegmentation based on device function and data sensitivity
c. Applying the same network segmentation rules used for corporate IT networks
d. Segmenting devices solely based on their physical location in the facility

Answer: b. Implementing microsegmentation based on device function and data sensitivity. Explanation: Implementing microsegmentation based on device function and data sensitivity is the most critical consideration for balancing security and operational efficiency in an industrial IoT environment. This approach allows for fine-grained control over device communications, minimizing the potential attack surface while ensuring necessary operational interactions. Isolating all IoT devices on a single segment (a) may impede necessary communications between devices. Applying standard IT network segmentation (c) may not address the unique requirements of industrial IoT. Segmenting solely based on physical location (d) doesn't account for varying security needs of different device types and functions.

705. A smart city project is collecting data from various IoT sensors for traffic management. Which privacy control would be most effective in addressing potential privacy concerns while maintaining the utility of the data?
a. Encrypting all data collected by the sensors
b. Implementing data minimization and anonymization techniques
c. Storing all collected data in a secure, off-site facility
d. Requiring user consent for all data collection

Answer: b. Implementing data minimization and anonymization techniques. Explanation: Implementing data minimization and anonymization techniques is the most effective privacy control for this scenario. This approach ensures that only necessary data is collected and that it cannot be linked to specific individuals, addressing privacy concerns while maintaining the data's utility for traffic management. Encryption (a) protects data confidentiality but doesn't address over-collection or identifiability issues. Secure off-site storage (c) doesn't solve privacy issues in data collection. Requiring user consent (d) is impractical for public space monitoring and doesn't inherently protect privacy.

706. In establishing security baselines for consumer IoT devices, which of the following should be the highest priority?
a. Implementing advanced AI-driven threat detection
b. Ensuring devices have unique, strong default credentials and easy update mechanisms
c. Requiring all devices to use blockchain for data integrity
d. Mandating physical tamper-proof casing for all devices

Answer: b. Ensuring devices have unique, strong default credentials and easy update mechanisms. Explanation: For consumer IoT devices, ensuring unique, strong default credentials and easy update mechanisms should be the highest priority in security baselines. This addresses two major vulnerabilities in consumer IoT: weak default passwords and difficulty in patching known vulnerabilities. Advanced AI-driven threat detection (a) may be excessive for most consumer devices. Blockchain (c) is often unnecessary and resource-intensive for consumer IoT. Physical tamper-proofing (d), while valuable, doesn't address the most common attack vectors in consumer IoT.

707. A multinational corporation is deploying IoT devices across its global supply chain. Which approach to data privacy compliance would be most effective in addressing varying international regulations?
a. Apply the strictest data privacy law globally to all collected data
b. Implement region-specific data handling practices based on local laws
c. Store all data in a single, highly secure central location
d. Avoid collecting any personally identifiable information from IoT devices

Answer: b. Implement region-specific data handling practices based on local laws. Explanation: Implementing region-specific data handling practices based on local laws is the most effective approach for a multinational corporation deploying IoT devices globally. This allows for compliance with varying international regulations while optimizing data usage within legal boundaries. Applying the strictest law globally (a) may be overly restrictive in some regions. Centralized storage (c) may violate data localization requirements in some countries. Avoiding all PII collection (d) may unnecessarily limit the utility of the IoT deployment in the supply chain.

708. In securing an IoT-based building management system, which network segmentation strategy would provide the best balance of security and functionality?
a. Place all IoT devices on a single, isolated VLAN
b. Segment devices based on their physical location within the building
c. Implement function-based microsegmentation with controlled inter-segment communication
d. Connect each IoT device directly to the corporate network with individual firewalls

Answer: c. Implement function-based microsegmentation with controlled inter-segment communication. Explanation: Function-based microsegmentation with controlled inter-segment communication provides the best balance of security and functionality for an IoT-based building management system. This approach allows for precise control over device interactions, minimizing the attack surface while enabling necessary communications between related systems (e.g., HVAC and occupancy sensors). A single isolated VLAN (a) may be too restrictive for inter-device communication. Physical location-based segmentation (b) doesn't account for functional relationships between devices. Individual firewalls for each device (d) would be complex to manage and may not adequately control inter-device communications.

709. A healthcare provider is implementing IoT devices for remote patient monitoring. Which of the following is the most critical consideration for ensuring HIPAA compliance?
a. Using military-grade encryption for all data transmissions
b. Storing all collected data indefinitely for potential future use
c. Implementing robust access controls and audit logging for all patient data
d. Requiring patients to sign a waiver for all data collected by IoT devices

Answer: c. Implementing robust access controls and audit logging for all patient data. Explanation: Implementing robust access controls and audit logging for all patient data is the most critical consideration for HIPAA compliance in IoT-based remote patient monitoring. This ensures that patient data is accessed only by authorized personnel and that all access is tracked, addressing key HIPAA requirements for data protection and accountability. While encryption (a) is important, it alone doesn't ensure HIPAA compliance. Indefinite data storage (b) may violate HIPAA's minimum necessary standard. Patient waivers (d) don't negate the healthcare provider's responsibility to protect patient data under HIPAA.

710. In developing a security baseline for industrial IoT devices, which of the following should be given the highest priority?
a. Implementing biometric authentication for all device access
b. Ensuring all devices support secure boot and firmware integrity checks
c. Requiring all devices to have a dedicated GPU for AI-based threat detection
d. Mandating quantum-resistant encryption for all data transmissions

Answer: b. Ensuring all devices support secure boot and firmware integrity checks. Explanation: For industrial IoT devices, ensuring support for secure boot and firmware integrity checks should be given the highest priority in security baselines. This protects against firmware tampering and ensures that only authorized code runs on the devices, which is crucial in industrial environments where device integrity is paramount. Biometric authentication (a) may be impractical for many industrial IoT devices. Dedicated GPUs for AI threat detection (c) are likely excessive for most industrial IoT applications. Quantum-resistant encryption (d), while forward-thinking, is not yet a standard requirement and may be resource-intensive for IoT devices.

711. A smart home device manufacturer is concerned about privacy implications of their products. Which of the following approaches would be most effective in addressing consumer privacy concerns?
a. Implement a privacy-by-design approach in product development
b. Offer a paid "privacy-enhanced" version of each product
c. Store all collected data in an encrypted cloud repository
d. Require users to opt-out of data collection for each feature

Answer: a. Implement a privacy-by-design approach in product development. Explanation: Implementing a privacy-by-design approach in product development is the most effective way to address consumer privacy concerns for smart home devices. This approach integrates privacy considerations into every stage of the product lifecycle, ensuring that privacy is a core feature rather than an afterthought. Offering a paid privacy version (b) implies that privacy is not a standard feature. Encrypted cloud storage (c) addresses data security but not necessarily data minimization or user control. Requiring opt-out for each feature (d) places the burden on users and may lead to over-collection of data by default.

712. In establishing compliance requirements for IoT devices in a regulated industry, which of the following approaches would be most effective?
a. Apply existing IT compliance frameworks directly to IoT devices
b. Rely on device manufacturers to ensure compliance with industry regulations
c. Develop a hybrid framework that adapts existing standards to IoT-specific challenges
d. Implement a separate, standalone compliance program for IoT devices

Answer: c. Develop a hybrid framework that adapts existing standards to IoT-specific challenges. Explanation: Developing a hybrid framework that adapts existing standards to IoT-specific challenges is the most effective approach for establishing compliance requirements in a regulated industry. This allows for leveraging established compliance principles while addressing the unique characteristics and risks of IoT devices. Applying existing IT frameworks directly (a) may not adequately cover IoT-specific issues. Relying solely on manufacturers (b) may result in inconsistent compliance across different devices. A separate, standalone program (d) might not align well with existing compliance efforts and could lead to gaps or redundancies.

As we bring this CGRC Exam Prep Study Guide to a close, it's important to remember the journey you've embarked on. You've delved deep into the realms of governance, risk, and compliance, arming yourself with knowledge that will not only help you pass the exam but also make a significant impact in your professional life.

You've explored the intricate processes of risk management, compliance audits, vendor management, system decommissioning, and more. Each section has been crafted to provide you with the tools and understanding needed to navigate the complex landscape of compliance.

Throughout this guide, we've included practice questions with immediate feedback to enhance your learning and retention. By engaging with these questions, you've had the opportunity to solidify your knowledge and identify areas that needed more attention. This immediate reinforcement is key to mastering the material and feeling confident on exam day.

Remember, preparation is more than just memorizing facts—it's about understanding concepts and being able to apply them in real-world scenarios. You've taken the time to understand the why behind each answer, which is a crucial step toward becoming a certified expert in governance, risk, and compliance.

As you prepare to take the CGRC exam, keep in mind the encouragement and support that have been woven throughout this guide. Believe in your abilities, trust the effort you've put in, and know that every step you've taken has brought you closer to your goal.

If doubts creep in, remember that it's okay to have fears and uncertainties—everyone does. What matters is how you face them. You've already shown dedication and perseverance, and those qualities will carry you through any challenge.

Stay confident, stay focused, and take a deep breath. You're ready for this. Your dreams of achieving the CGRC certification are within reach, and with the knowledge and skills you've gained, you're well-prepared to succeed.

Good luck on your exam, and remember that this is just one step in your ongoing journey of professional growth and excellence. You've got this!

Printed in Great Britain
by Amazon